1. ST. MARY'S
2. ST. PATRICK'S
3. SS. PETER & PAUL'S
4. ST. MICHAEL'S, BLACKROCK
5. OUR LADY OF LOURDES, BALLINLOUGH
6. ST. COLUMBA'S, DOUGLAS
7. CHRIST THE KING, TURNER'S CROSS
8. THE ASSUMPTION OF OUR LADY, Ballyphehane
9. ST. FINBARR'S SOUTH
10. ST. FINBARR'S WEST

MM
1969

✝ Cornelius Lucey.

EVELYN BOLSTER

A History of
the Diocese of Cork

From the Earliest Times
to the Reformation

IRISH UNIVERSITY PRESS

Shannon · Ireland

© 1972 Evelyn Bolster

SBN 7165 0995 4

All forms of micro-publishing
© Irish University Microforms Shannon Ireland

Irish University Press Shannon Ireland
T. M. MacGlinchey Publisher

FILMSET AND PRINTED IN THE REPUBLIC OF IRELAND
BY ROBERT HOGG PRINTER TO IRISH UNIVERSITY PRESS

To
Most Rev. Dr. Cornelius Lucey
Bishop of Cork and Ross

What I have learned without self-interest,
I pass on without reserve.
Wisdom, VII :13

CONTENTS

		page
Foreword	. . . .	xi
Acknowledgements	. . . . . .	xv
List of Abbreviations	. . . . .	xxv
Introduction .	. . . .	xxix
I	Saint Finbarr	1
II	A Church in Transition	34
III	The Origins of the Diocese . . .	61
IV	The Norman-Irish Church . . .	102
V	Early Post-Norman Religious Foundations .	131
VI	The Feudal Bishop of Cork . . .	153
VII	The Diocesan Episcopacy: Twelfth and Thirteenth Centuries	173
VIII	The Coming of the Friars	200
IX	The Cathedral Chapter	224
X	The Deaneries and Parishes . . .	253
XI	Catholic Cork in the Fourteenth Century .	288
XII	The Diocesan Economy	310
XIII	The Fourteenth-Century Gaelic Resurgence	343
XIV	The Diocesan Episcopacy, 1302–1393 . .	360
XV	The Diocese of Cork and the Great Western Schism	381
XVI	The United Dioceses of Cork and Cloyne .	401
XVII	The Observant Reform in the Diocese of Cork	429
XVIII	Blessed Thaddeus MacCarthy . . .	448
XIX	The Eve of the Reformation . . .	468
Appendix: Priests of Cork	. . . .	494
Bibliography .	. . . .	505
Index of Persons	. . . . . .	529
General Index	. . . .	538

CHAPTER APPENDICES

page

Chapter I
A   Alumni of the School of Loch Irce   .   .   .   27
B   Saints who Offered their Churches to Bairre .   .   28
C   Saints Associated with Bairre in the *Lives*   .   .   29
D   Succession-List of the Monastery of Cork   .   .   30

Chapter III
A   Dermot's Charter   95
B   Decretal Letter of Pope Innocent III, 1199   .   .   98
C   The Abbots of Gill Abbey (*de Antro*)   .   .   .   100

Chapter IV
A   Grants to the Church of Saint Nicholas, Exeter   .   121
B   Charters relating to Cork from the *Register of the
     Abbey of St. Thomas*   124

Chapter V
A   Saint John of Jerusalem   151
B   Saint John the Evangelist   151

Chapter IX
A   Dignitarial Members of the Medieval Chapter
     of Cork   248
B   Townlands of the Prebends   250

Chapter X
A   The Modern Deaneries   277
B   Canonical Erection of Kilmichael into a Parish
     Church   277
C   The Modern Parishes   280

Chapter XII
     Rental of Certain Places in County Cork:
     Sixteenth Century   337

ILLUSTRATIONS AND TABLES

Most Rev. Dr. Cornelius Lucey, Bishop of
Cork and Ross   *frontispiece*

Genealogical Table of the Ui Eachach   xxxii

Saint Finbarr's Journey to Cork

Gougane Barra   } *following* p. 12

Genealogical Table of the Ui Toirdealbhaigh   53

Decretal Letter, 1199

The Manor of Fayd   } *following* p. 98

Rental of the Diocese of Cork

Kilmichael Parish Document   } *following* p. 280

Diocese of Cork showing parishes   *endpapers*

FOREWORD

I welcome this timely—indeed I might almost say this long overdue—*History of the Diocese of Cork,* and, as Bishop, I am happy to be associated with the publication of it. It is a scholarly work, covering the whole field of our diocesan history and covering it in considerable detail; and so it will, I know, be welcomed by those anxious for an authoritative study of this particular field of ecclesiastical history. And because it is Cork history it is assured of a special welcome from Cork people at home and abroad, laity and clergy alike.

History as such is a factual account of the long ago. But in telling us about the past it inevitably tells us something too about the present through the insight it gives into the events and trends and personalities, the influence of which still persists. This is what makes the history of the institutions and places closest to us so fascinating and revealing for us. This is why Cork history must have special appeal for Cork people everywhere.

Gibson produced a secular history of Cork as long ago as 1860, followed a little later by Smith's more erudite *Ancient and Present State of the County and City of Cork.* Then in 1920, on the religious side, Chancellor Webster gave us the Church of Ireland history: *The Diocese of Cork.* Now at long last we are having the Catholic *History of the Diocese of Cork.* Not, of course, that difference of religion should make for all that difference of history till the time of the Reformation; but it must make for some difference, if only of selection and emphasis. In any case, since the Reformation, there being two separate Churches of Cork, two separate histories are an obvious necessity.

Incidentally, no attention is given in Webster's *History* to the relations of his church with the church of the majority, nor for that matter with the various other non-conforming churches that emerged here since the Reformation. This is an aspect of Cork's ecclesiastical history on which I expect the post-Reformation volumes of the present *History* will throw light.

A diocese is a complex organization. People are apt to think of it as so much territory with a bishop and priests of its own to look after religion in it. But it is far more than that, comprising as it does deaneries and parishes and a chapter; charitable institutions and establishments of all kinds, and an array of religious communities, some of which though in the diocese are largely not of it. Diocesan history, then, is as much the history of all these as it is of bishops, priests and the vicissitudes of religion among the population generally.

The first to undertake the writing of a Catholic history of Cork was Father Michael Murphy. Ordained in 1913, he was dogged by ill-health and died less than three years later. Then in the 1920s Father Patrick Cahalane took up where Father Murphy left off. For the next thirty years he worked assiduously collecting material from far and near, without, however, getting to the point of publication. Sister Angela describes her part in the present *History* as merely that of 'completing, arranging, organizing and adding to the work' done by him. In that she is far too modest. She did get all his manuscripts, it is true; but what is equally true is that she did not get all the present *History* from them.

I read through these manuscripts myself about the time Father Cahalane went to Enniskeane when I made suggestions to him about preparing them finally for publication. They were the materials of a comprehensive diocesan history, yes. But they were very much the raw materials, and they were very much in need of critical evaluation and background filling-in. Now I think it would be true to say that he did very little research or re-writing subsequent to his appointment to Enniskeane. Consequently, for a work as competent as the present volume, these notes of his, invaluable and scholarly though they were, can have been little more than a first-rate starting point. At the very least, then, the new diocesan *History* is as much Sister Angela's as it is Father Cahalane's.

The story to be told is a long one, too long to be told in the one volume. It begins in the sixth century, even before Finbarr became bishop and brought the diocese as such into being. Nor is it, of course, all straight history: there is so little historical material available before the twelfth century that place has to be given to conjecture and probability as well. And it is, as the author says, a mottled history of light and shade, of good times and bad: at which we must not be surprised and from which we can learn a lesson. The Church of Christ, wherever it is set among men, is a sign sure to be contradicted; nor can it expect always to be free of trouble from within, so easy is it for Church people to forget the grace that is in them. No wonder then that down the centuries the Church of Cork has had its ups and downs, its enemies from within and its enemies from without. And if today too the Church of Cork is under attack from within and from without—and it is—the lesson from history for us is that as long as we remain one, holy and Roman, we are being true to the Faith of our Fathers; and though we may seem to be losing out, Catholic Cork will survive and revive.

I warmly congratulate Sister Angela on work competently and quickly done. We are all in her debt: not just the priests and Catholics of Cork, but scholars everywhere with an interest in Irish ecclesiastical history. And may I add that I look forward to having us all more in her debt as the years go on and more and more volumes flow from her research and her pen. *Bail ó Dhia ar a saothar*.

✚ Cornelius Lucey
Bishop of Cork

ACKNOWLEDGEMENTS

Compilers of diocesan histories concur in stressing the difficulties of producing a text which will be at once scientific, accurate, scholarly and properly integrated. For me these ordinary difficulties were magnified by the fact that I have had to work, in part, from documents not of my own collecting, and while I have consulted original sources where possible I have relied in great measure on the work of copyists in London and Rome as well as on photostat and Xerox facsimiles of relevant documents. This *History of the Diocese of Cork* has been forty years in preparation and it was my privilege to have been entrusted with the task of completing, arranging, organizing and adding to the work to which the late Canon Patrick Cahalane devoted the greater part of his life.

Patrick Cahalane was born in Kilmichael in 1888 and was ordained to the priesthood in Saint Patrick's College, Maynooth, on 23 June 1912. In the following year he obtained the S.T.L. in the Dunboyne Institute and was awarded the degree of Master of Arts in University College, Dublin, on 14 October 1914. On his return to Cork he was appointed chaplain to the Presentation Monastery, Greenmount, 14 March 1915; he became chancellor of the curia in September 1926 and served in the church of the Immaculate Conception, Saint Finbarr's West, popularly known as the Lough Chapel. In the early nineteen-twenties he was commissioned by the late Bishop Daniel Cohalan to write a diocesan history; the research occupied him during the remaining years of his life and sent him delving wide and deep into local and distant archives. In January 1953 he became parish priest of Enniskeane, whence he was transferred to Bantry as parish priest and vicar forane of the diocese on 14 May 1955, and in the following month he became a canon of the cathedral chapter. His final appointment was to Kilmurry, and here on the spot hallowed by traditions of the early life of Saint Finbarr it was fitting that this disciple of the diocesan patron should find 'the place of his resurrection'. Canon Cahalane died on 4 June 1963: *Ar dheis Dé go raibh a anam.*

Sources for diocesan histories vary considerably in nature and extent. For the diocese of Cork difficulties abound for the period leading up to the twelfth century. Not the least of these is the confusing nature of the life and legend of Bairre of Cork which is one of the most obscure topics in early Irish monastic history, with anything but clear guidance or agreement from historians. In correlating the various texts of the *Lives* I have endeavoured to make the story of Saint Finbarr less obscure and somewhat more intelligible. I can offer no apology for drawing constantly on the standard *Lives*, most of which are twelfth-century compilations, as there are no other sources to hand and nothing of a contemporary nature. For all that, the stature of our diocesan saint continues to be that of a man who controlled the spiritual destinies of south Munster in his day.

Another initial handicap is the complete lack of diocesan records such as *The Black Book of Limerick, The Red Book of Ossory* and *The Pipe Roll of Cloyne.* Nor have we any surviving set of Irish annals from Cork even though the *Annals of Inisfallen* give invaluable information from some other Munster centre. The bulk of this text (it is a far more reliable commentary than the *Annals of the Four Masters*) was compiled in the last decade of the eleventh century by some unknown scribe. There are unbroken entries from 1092 until 1130, and except for two gaps (from 1130 to 1159 and from 1181 to 1189) we have here a highly important series of contemporary records for the twelfth century and on until 1215. Therefore, while fragmentary details of Cork history are found in *The Annals of Ulster, The Annals of Loch Cé, The Annals of Tigernach, The Annals of the Four Masters* and *The Miscellaneous Irish Annals*, our main source derives from *The Annals of Inisfallen.* The Dalcassian nature of the entries for the eleventh and twelfth centuries raise problems for the coarbial succession of that period in Cork. I have dealt with these difficulties in the body of the text.

For the twelfth century we also have two documents which Keating copied from the lost *Book of Clonenagh*: these again pose problems concerning the nature and extent of the diocese of Cork as envisaged at Rathbreasail in 1111 and at Kells in 1152. Finally, a few statements in *St. Bernard of Clairvaux's Life of St. Malachy of Armagh* exhaust our limited supply of early source materials for a diocesan history of Cork. It could be that this dearth of materials has deterred scholars from embarking before now on a work of such gigantic proportions and its corresponding difficulties.

Apart from a decretal letter issued to the reigning bishop of Cork in 1199 by Pope Innocent III our earliest diocesan record is contained in the taxation list of 1302–06 which is unfortunately incomplete and for that reason unsatisfactory. Papal records before the year 1250 have been calendared in two very useful volumes of *Pontificia Hibernica* by Maurice P. Sheehy, but for Cork history this source offers little beyond some confirmations of privileges, and it is not until the fourteenth century when papal records become more abundant that we are on surer ground. Complementary to the papal records are the annates which give us an insight into conditions obtaining in the Irish church on the eve of the Reformation. As the Cork annates were unpublished when I undertook this history I have worked from the original Costelloe transcript which I have since edited for *Archivium Hibernicum.* I wish to thank Reverend Dr. Patrick J. Corish of Maynooth for allowing me use the annates and to quote from them; and I wish to thank him more particularly for his helpful and constructive criticism of my first draft of this diocesan history. The book in its present form owes very much to him.

In addition to the sources already quoted I have given deep and serious study to all the printed records available for the period covered in this volume. These were the various calendars of patent and close rolls, statute rolls, justiciary rolls and charter rolls, full titles of which are given in the Bibliography. Though fragmentary and beginning only in the thirteenth century, these calendars give important data on English administration in Ireland, its impact on episcopal and abbatial elections and the consequent development of rival pockets of ecclesiastical juris- diction in areas officially designated *inter Hibernicos* and *inter Anglos*. While these points, together with the general political background of the period, will be encountered throughout the text, I have tried to keep foremost the idea of an *ecclesiastical* history and have introduced general political and local events merely as a backdrop against which the development of the church may be studied.

A folio volume edited by Edward Tresham and entitled *Rotul- orum Patentium et Clausorum Cancellariae Hiberniae Calendarium* ranging from the reign of Henry II to that of Henry VII more than repaid the time and trouble entailed in its perusal. The same is true of Sweetman's five-volume *Calendar of Documents relating to Ireland* for the years 1171–1307. Also of particular value was Berry's edition of *Statutes and Ordinances and Acts of the Parliament of Ireland, King John to Henry V.* Charles Smith's *Ancient and Present State of the County and City of Cork* (1893 edition) with its wealth of quotations from manuscripts no longer extant is a monumental contribution to Cork history, as are also the works of John Windele. The works of Cusack and Gibson (see Bibliography) fall very short of the mark by comparison with those of Smith and Windele, while the only diocesan history yet attempted is that by the Reverend Chancellor Charles A. Webster, who starts from the erroneous premise that Saint Finbarr was not in the Gregorian tradition. From this initial error so many other inaccuracies stem that Webster's *Diocese of Cork* cannot be seriously considered as even a basic text for a diocesan history in either Catholic or Protestant context.

For ecclesiastical history proper I have studied the fourteen volumes of the *Calendar of Papal Letters* (1198–1492) and the *Calendar of Petitions to the Pope* (1342–1419). Lynch's *De Praesulibus Hiberniae*, Theiner's *Vetera Monumenta Hibernorum et Scotorum* and Archdall's *Monasticon Hibernicum* made profitable if difficult reading, as did also *The Register of the Abbey of St. Thomas the Martyr*, *The Register of St. Nicholas's Priory, Exeter*, *The Chartularies of St. Mary's Abbey* and the volume entitled *Chartae, Privilegia et Immunitates*. Helpful diocesan histories were Canon William Carrigan's *History and Antiquities of the Diocese of Ossory*, Father Begley's *Diocese of Limerick, Ancient and Medieval*, Dr. McNamee's *History of the Diocese of Ardagh* and Dermot Gleeson's *History of the Diocese of Killaloe*. I found the revised edition of the *Handbook of British Chronology* (1961) of considerable help, more particularly the section on Irish episcopal succession contributed by Father Aubrey Gwynn, S.J., and prefaced by a lucid survey of the changing face of the Irish church over the medieval centuries. Kenney's *Sources for the Early History of Ireland*: Ecclesiastical, was another useful volume, while the works of William Maziere Brady, namely, *Episcopal Succession in England, Scotland and Ireland, A.D. 1400 to 1875*, and *Clerical and Parochial Records of Cork, Cloyne and Ross*, if slightly incorrect in places, are nevertheless good basic texts for any history of these three southern dioceses. I have gleaned a harvest of valuable information from early volumes of *Archivium Hibernicum* and *Analecta Hibernica*; from the *Proceedings of the Royal Irish Academy* and from the *Journal of the Royal Society of Antiquaries of Ireland*, while the *Proceedings of the Irish Catholic Historical Committee* have sign-posted new and profitable avenues of research and study for me. So much came to light as a result of independent research along these lines that I found it impossible to follow the scheme originally set out by Canon Cahalane.

On examination of his papers I discovered that he had envisaged a two-volume history—firstly, a general history from Saint Finbarr down to modern times; secondly, a parochial history. His work insofar as he had committed it to paper was mainly a chronicle of Cork affairs, incomplete and with little connection or correlation with general history or even with contemporary ecclesiastical history. For this reason a revision of lay-out was essential in order to make a composite whole of the Canon's and my own integrated efforts. There will still be two (and perhaps three) volumes to the *History of the Diocese of Cork*. The present volume deals with the medieval diocese and ends in 1536 with the death of John Benet, the last pre-Reformation bishop of Cork. Later volumes will bring the history down to modern times. I should like to stress, however, that even though the greater part of this volume was not catered for in the Cahalane Papers, this in no way derogates from the Canon's work, without which my own extensive studies would have been virtually unproductive.

I have overstepped the terminal date (1536) in several instances, mainly because material in later documents threw light on matters left untouched by medieval sources and I considered the information thus culled to be absolutely essential to a history of the medieval diocese of Cork. Post-Reformation documents quoted are mainly rent rolls and visitation records which go a long way towards complementing the defective taxation returns of 1302–06 and for this reason their inclusion is a *sine qua non* of a properly integrated history. As in the case of the standard *Lives* of Saint Finbarr I can offer no apology for constantly re-quoting these documents: after all, there is little else on which to work. For obvious reasons I have brought the story of Thaddeus MacCarthy to its logical conclusion, but in all other respects I have kept the idea of a medieval history in mind, and can only hope that the work and the worry it entailed will be ultimately productive of some good.

Historical exigencies, tribal warfare and countless other factors have created certain temporary unions between the diocese of Cork and those of Cloyne and Ross. In dealing with such unions I have adhered strictly to Cork diocesan affairs, leaving those of our ecclesiastical neighbours to their own historians. A new history of Ross is presently in preparation but so far no historian from Cloyne has undertaken any serious work in this line. It is my conviction that no single history of Cork, Cloyne or Ross can be complete unless it can be seen as part of a three-dimensional study involving each of the dioceses and portraying the complementary interplay of each upon the other. The publication of this first volume of the *History of the Diocese of Cork* and the promise of a new history of Ross make a Cloyne diocesan history not merely a desideratum but an absolute necessity.

And now it gives me great pleasure to record publicly my debt of gratitude to those whose suggestions, corrections and encouragement have made this diocesan history possible. In the first place I thank his lordship, Most Reverend Dr. Cornelius Lucey, bishop of Cork and Ross, for the confidence he has shown in permitting me to undertake a history of the diocese. I wish also to acknowledge my indebtedness to Father Thomas F. Kelleher whom I really tormented during the past few years and whose forbearance entitles him to my unstinted gratitude, knowing as I do the impositions which my requests laid upon him. Nothing was ever a trouble to Father Kelleher. His greatest gift to me was a large wall-map of the diocese without which I do not think I could ever have unravelled the intricacies of diocesan geography. Father Kelleher, who was bishop's secretary while this book was in preparation, is now on the mission in Peru. *Faoi choimirce chaoin Mhuire go raibh sé.*

Among our local historians none had a greater share in structuring the early chapters of this book than the late Liam Ó Buachalla. A keen student of history, Mr. Ó Buachalla was generous to the point of prodigality in imparting the vast store of knowledge he had accumulated through years of devoted study and research. His works are well known to readers of *Dinnseanchas* and the *Journal of the Cork Historical and Archaeological Society*, and his unexpected death on All Souls' Day 1966 left us the poorer for the passing of so great and unassuming a scholar. He more than anyone else was Canon Cahalane's confidant, and with the generosity which was his outstanding trait, Mr. Ó Buachalla spontaneously offered his services to me. I am sorry he did not live to see the book in print.

John T. Collins, our greatest authority on local history, is another whose direction and advice made the present volume possible, and to him I here record my very sincere thanks. I wish likewise to thank C. J. F. MacCarthy for his help and encouragement, for the use of several articles published by him and for some letters from his personal collection which were of considerable historical interest. Among these letters were several communications from Père Paul Grosjean, S.J., the great Bollandist scholar.

Words fail me when I try to convey my sense of gratitude to my good friend, Pádraig Ó Maidín, Cork county librarian, whom I can thank for keeping me relentlessly to the grind. With him I wish to associate Mr. Daniel O'Keeffe, M.A., librarian of University College, Cork, and his assistant Mr. William Cahill. All three were indefatigable in supplying me with books and most patient in face of my frequent and bothersome demands. I have happy memories of efficiency and co-operation in connection with the Royal Irish Academy, the National Library and Marsh's Library, Dublin, and wish hereby to thank all those concerned.

Mr. E. Fahy, University College, Cork, who plotted Saint Finbarr's journey from Gougane Barra into Cork has permitted me to use work originally done for Canon Cahalane. The diocesan map was drafted for me by Michael Mulcahy, B.E., to whom I here convey my very sincere thanks. The two Latin plates incorporated in the text are from the Vatican Library, and I am grateful to the trustees of the British Museum for permission to reproduce Add. MS 4787, f. 78v which will be found in Chapter 6.

Outside of Cork the greatest single influence directing my work was Father Aubrey Gwynn, S.J., who needs no introduction as an outstanding authority on early Irish monastic and medieval history. I have the privilege of personal acquaintance with Father Gwynn: correspondence and conversation with him have been major factors in helping me to resolve the many difficulties one encounters in monastic and early medieval Ireland. Personal contacts with Father Gwynn have given me a greater appreciation and grasp of the problems inherent in writing a diocesan history. Like Liam Ó Buachalla, Father Gwynn, despite advancing age and its accompanying ill-health, was unstinting in the help he offered and most generous in permitting me to quote from his works—even from an unpublished manuscript upon which he and Neville Hadcock had completed many years of research. The works of Father Gwynn relative to the period covered in the present study are listed in the Bibliography. I am deeply grateful to Father Gwynn for all his help.

A very pleasing aspect of the research which this diocesan history entailed was that connected with the Franciscan House of Studies at Killiney, county Dublin, where I found friendship and hospitality as well as history. My thanks goes mainly to Father Cathaldus Giblin, O.F.M., who gave me much assistance on details of Franciscan history which I could not otherwise have come by. Father Benignus Millett, O.F.M., is another to whom I wish to record my thanks; and indeed Irish scholars in general owe much to him and to Father Cathaldus, the results of whose dedicated research appear annually in the successive and highly valuable volumes of *Collectanea Hibernica*. I wish finally to include Father Fergall Grannell, O.F.M., in my expression of thanks to the Killiney community and to add my sense of indebtedness to the writings of the late Father Canice Mooney, O.F.M.

Dr. Michael D. McCarthy, president of University College, Cork, has shown a personal interest in having this diocesan history accepted and published, for which I thank him most sincerely. I am grateful also to his secretary, Miss Mary Manning, to Mrs. Mary F. Conroy, Secretary of Cork University Press and to all the personnel of the Press. Mr. Thomas Turley, editor-in-chief of Irish University Press, has been a sympathetic collaborator, and I am grateful to Mrs. Marilyn Norstedt, editor, who has given me generous direction and assistance.

I wish to express my deep gratitude to my superioress, Reverend Mother M. Bonaventure McKenna, for helps too numerous to mention: provision of time, facilities for work and above all for her sympathetic understanding and encouragement. All expenses entailed in my work over the past six years have been sustained by my headmistress, Sister M. Columba O'Leary, who has therefore contributed in a very practical way to this diocesan history. She knows I am grateful.

I should like to thank the superior of Saint Augustine's, Cork, for supplying me with books from his community library; my information on the Franciscans has been culled from various printed sources and I am fortunate in that the archives of my own convent of Saint Maries of the Isle contain interesting data on Cork's first Dominican abbey. My inquiries concerning the early Carmelite foundation at Kinsale were unproductive.

Father Patrick Cahalane has maintained a constant interest in this history over the years despite the fact that it has assumed a form other than that envisaged by his uncle. For that I am grateful to him and I can only hope that the book as it now appears will please him and perpetuate his uncle's memory. I should like to add that Father Cahalane has committed his uncle's papers to me until such time as the diocesan history is finally completed.

A word of gratitude now for the prayers, good wishes and sustained encouragement of my friends; and a special 'thank you' to Father Ernest Cronin, O.F.M., who has been with me through all the dark moments when the horizon seemed grey and the difficulties insurmountable, and who now rejoices with me in the publication of this first volume of Cork's diocesan history.

I derive great pleasure in presenting this book to the bishop and clergy, to the religious brotherhoods and sisterhoods and to all the people of the diocese; for I feel that the Lord who holds in His hands the lever of history has permitted me for a brief space to manipulate a fractional part of that lever and to contribute in a small way to the history of that part of His church on earth which is represented by the diocese of Cork.

My final word is a request that all who read this book will say a prayer for Canon Patrick Cahalane.

Evelyn Bolster
(Sister Mary Angela)

Saint Maries of the Isle, Cork.
Feast of Saint Finbarr 1971.

LIST OF ABBREVIATIONS

Based on the revised list compiled by T. W. Moody and printed in the Supplement to *Irish Historical Studies*, January 1968. Full details are given in the Bibliography.

A.F.M.	*Annála Ríoghachta Éireann: Annals of the Kingdom of Ireland by the Four Masters from the Earliest Period to the Year 1616*
A.L.C.	*The Annals of Loch Cé : A Chronicle of Irish Affairs, 1014–1690*
A.U.	*Annála Uladh, Annals of Ulster ; otherwise Annála Senait, Annals of Senat : A Chronicle of Irish Affairs, 431–1131, 1155–1541*
Anal. Hib.	*Analecta Hibernica*
Ann. Clon.	*The Annals of Clonmacnoise, being Annals of Ireland from the Earliest Period to A.D. 1408 . . .*
Ann. Inisf.	*The Annals of Inisfallen (MS Rawlinson B 503)*
Ann. Tig.	'The Annals of Tigernach'
Annats, Ulster	*De Annatis Hiberniae : A Calendar of the First-fruits' Fees Levied on Papal Appointments to Benefices in Ireland, A.D. 1400–1535 . . ., vol. i, Ulster*
Archiv. Hib.	*Archivium Hibernicum*
B.M.	British Museum
B.M., Add. MSS	British Museum, Additional MSS
Cal. Carew MSS, 1515–74 [etc.]	*Calendar of the Carew Manuscripts Preserved in the Archiepiscopal Library at Lambeth, 1515–74 [etc.]*

Cal. chart. rolls, *1226–57* [etc.]	*Calendar of the Charter Rolls,* *1226–57* [etc.]
Cal. close rolls, *1272–79* [etc.]	*Calendar of the Close Rolls, 1272–79* [etc.]
Cal. doc. Ire., *1171–1251* [etc.]	*Calendar of Documents Relating to Ireland, 1171–1251* [etc.]
Cal. justic. rolls Ire., *1295–1303* [etc.]	*Calendar of the Justiciary Rolls, or Proceedings in the Court of the Justiciar of Ireland . . . [1295–1303]* [etc.]
Cal. papal letters, *1198–1304* [etc.]	*Calendar of Entries in the Papal Registers Relating to Great Britain and Ireland : Papal Letters, 1198– 1304* [etc.]
Cal. papal petitions	*Calendar of Entries in the Papal Registers Relating to Great Britain and Ireland : Petitions to the Pope, 1342–1419*
Cal. pat. rolls, 1232–47 [etc.]	*Calendar of the Patent Rolls, 1232– 47* [etc.]
Cal. S.P. Ire., 1509–73 [etc.]	*Calendar of the State Papers Relating to Ireland, 1509–73* [etc.]
Chart. privil. immun.	*Chartae, Privilegia et Immunitates . . . 1171–1395*
Chron. Scot.	*Chronicon Scotorum : A Chronicle of Irish Affairs . . . to 1135 . . .*
Civil Survey	*The Civil Survey, A.D. 1654–56*
Colgan, *Acta SS Hib.*	John Colgan, *Acta sanctorum veteris et maioris Scotiae, seu Hiberniae sanctorum insulae . . .*
Collect. Hib.	*Collectanea Hibernica*
Corish, *Ir. catholicism*	Patrick J. Corish, ed., *A History of Irish Catholicism*
Cork Hist. Soc. Jn.	*Journal of the Cork Historical and Archaeological Society*
Curtis, *Med. Ire.*	Edmund Curtis, *A History of Medieval Ireland*
Extents Ir. mon. possessions	*Extents of Irish Monastic Possessions, 1540–1541, from Manuscripts in the Public Record Office, London*

Fitzmaurice and Little, *Franciscan province Ire.*	E. B. Fitzmaurice and A. G. Little, *Materials for the History of the Franciscan Province of Ireland*
Geneal. regum Hib.	*Genealogiae regum et sanctorum Hiberniae, by the Four Masters*
Hogan, *Onomasticon*	Edmund Hogan, *Onomasticon Goedelicum locorum et tribuum Hiberniae et Scotiae*
Hughes, *Ch. in early Ir. soc.*	Kathleen Hughes, *The Church in Early Irish Society*
I.E.R.	*Irish Ecclesiastical Record*
I.H.S.	*Irish Historical Studies*
Ir. Cath. Hist. Comm. Proc.	*Proceedings of the Irish Catholic Historical Committee*
Ir. Theol. Quart.	*Irish Theological Quarterly*
Kenney, *Sources*	J. F. Kenney, *The Sources for the Early History of Ireland : An Introduction and Guide*, vol. i: Ecclesiastical
Lynch, *De Praesulibus Hib.*	John Lynch, *De Praesulibus Hiberniae potissimis Catholicae Religionis in Hibernia, serendae, propagandae et conservandae authoribus*
Lynch, *Legal instit. Ire.*	William Lynch, *A View of the Legal Institutions, Honorary Hereditary Offices, and Feudal Baronies Established in Ireland during the Reign of Henry II*
Med. studies presented to A. Gwynn	*Medieval Studies Presented to Aubrey Gwynn, S.J.*
Orpen, *Normans*	G. H. Orpen, *Ireland under the Normans, 1169–1333*
O'Sullivan, *Econ. hist. Cork city*	William O'Sullivan, *The Economic History of Cork City, from the Earliest Times to the Act of Union*
Otway-Ruthven, *Med. Ire.*	A. J. Otway-Ruthven, *A History of Medieval Ireland*
P.R.I. rep. D.K. 1 [etc.]	*First* [etc.] *Report of the Deputy Keeper of the Public Records in Ireland*
P.R.O.	Public Record Office of England

P.R.O.I.	Public Record Office of Ireland
Plummer, *Bethada náem nÉrenn*	Charles Plummer, ed., *Bethada náem nÉrenn: Lives of Irish Saints* . . .
Plummer, *Vitae SS Hib.*	Charles Plummer, ed., *Vitae Sanctorum Hiberniae, partim hactenus ineditae* . . .
R.I.A. Proc.	*Proceedings of the Royal Irish Academy*
R.S.A.I. Jn.	*Journal of the Royal Society of Antiquaries of Ireland*
Reg. Kilmain.	*Registrum de Kilmainham, 1326–50*
Reg. St. Thomas, Dublin	*Register of the Abbey of St. Thomas the Martyr, Dublin*
Rot. pat. Hib.	*Rotulorum Patentium et Clausorum Cancellariae Hiberniae Calendarium*
Rymer, *Foedera*	Thomas Rymer, ed., *Foedera, Conventiones, Litterae et Cujuscunque Acta Publica* . . .
Sheehy, *Pontificia Hib.*	M. P. Sheehy, ed., *Pontificia Hibernica: Medieval Papal Chancery Documents concerning Ireland, 640-1261*
Stat. Ire. John-Hen. V	*Statutes and Ordinances, and Acts of the Parliament of Ireland, King John to Henry V*
Studia Hib.	*Studia Hibernica*
T.C.D.	Trinity College, Dublin
Theiner, *Vetera mon.*	A. Theiner, *Vetera Monumenta Hibernorum et Scotorum*
Y.B.L.	*The Yellow Book of Lecan* . . .

INTRODUCTION

The diocese of Cork sits astride a long serrated ridge of hilly ground extending from Cork city to Bantry Bay and is no different from other Irish dioceses in being the end-product of a multi-dimensional process involving factors tribal, political, social and economic as well as those which are categorized as essentially ecclesiastical. It is a diocese teeming with enigmas and geographical anomalies, having as its patron an elusive figure named Finbarr whose life still poses problems for the historian but who nevertheless dominated the spiritual life of south Munster in his day, and who was at once a saint, a teacher and a missionary. Again, it is a diocese which does not show any great geographical deviations from the limits laid down by the twelfth-century synods of Rathbreasail (1111) and Kells (1152), but for all that, it is a difficult diocese to assess, since in dealing with Cork the historian is seriously hampered by dearth of documents and is consequently compelled to theorize, to discuss whether events took this course or that, and whether certain statements of previous writers are tenable in the light of more modern research. There are many aspects of Cork diocesan history which can neither be definitely proved nor peremptorily dismissed, and for these no conclusion can be other than tentative in our present state of knowledge. Further complications arise as a result of ignorance of Irish toponymy or topography and/or insufficient acquaintance with the Irish language on the part of certain historians, some of whom may have had the advantage of being nearer in time than we are to the events they described, yet whose testimony must in many instances be rejected. It may well be that opinions formulated in the present study will be vitiated by the results of subsequent research; if so, then this book will have served at least one good purpose, namely, that of provoking a further appraisal of the limited sources presently at our disposal. Such as they are, these sources lead first to a short résumé of the early tribal migrations in Desmond as a prologue to the history of our diocese.

Fifth- and sixth-century records show a Munster ruled over by a dynasty named the Eoghanacht or Tribe of Eoghan. Eoghan, who was probably the tribal deity-ancestor, is represented as a great king who reigned over the province a century or two before the dawn of Christianity. Whatever its real origins, the dynasty of the Eoghanacht was to rule the greater part of Munster for many centuries and was to produce the families of MacCarthy, O'Sullivan, O'Donoghue, O'Mahony, O'Callaghan and O'Keeffe. But the Eoghanacht did not enjoy monopoly of rule in Munster. A sister-tribe, the Dairine, more familiarly known as the Corca Laighdhe, controlled extensive territories stretching from Ossory and county Kilkenny to the extremities of west Cork. Their chief seat was at Argatross or *Rath Bethaigh*, a great fort on the Nore some six miles north of Kilkenny city.[1] There were also in Munster the Ui Fidgheinte and the Ui Liathain, collateral branches of the Dairine, whose combined territories included the coastline from the Shannon estuary to east Cork, including the harbour of Cork but not that part of the west Cork coast where the Corca Laighdhe held sway. Other related septs were the Muscraighe (Muskerry), the Corca Baiscinn of west Clare and the Corca Dhuibhne of west Kerry. In earlier centuries before this tribal re-arrangement was structured the inhabitants of Munster were collectively designated *Iverni*, a name which was later transliterated into *Erainn, Eriu* and *Erna*. A map of Ireland which was drafted by Ptolemy, the second-century geographer, shows the dispersal of the *Iverni* in mid- and east Munster; and while Ptolemy's map has been submitted to contradictory interpretations, it is significant that 'all the authenticated names [in it] belong to the eastern and southern coasts'.[2]

From Corc, the first Eoghanacht king of Cashel, were descended the tribes of Mac Cais, Mac Iair (Mac Ciair) and Mac Broic, who peopled south Munster or Desmond (*Desmumha*). Mac Cais was ancestor of the powerful Eoghanacht of Raithleann; the tribeland of this people which at one time extended from Cork to Mizen Head became eventually the basis of the diocese of Cork. The Eoghanacht of Raithleann were also known as the Ui Eachach, and took this patronymic designation from Eachaidh or Eochaidh who was probably the first Christian chief of the tribe. In time the tribe divided into two main branches representa-

1   William Carrigan, *The History and Antiquities of the Diocese of Ossory*, iv, 24–7.

2   Eoin MacNeill, *Phases of Irish History*, pp. 136–7.

tive of Laeghaire and Aedh Uargarb, two great-grandsons of the
original settler, Mac Cais. Laeghaire's descendants, who were
known as the Cinel Laeghaire and the Clann Sealbaigh, held the
western part of the original tribeland from Murragh to Mizen
Head, and with the adoption of surnames in the eleventh century
they became known as the O'Donoghues. That part of the
Eoghanacht which claimed descent from Aedh Uargarb was
originally known as Cinel Aedh (Kinalea) and later as Cinel
mBeice (Kinalmeaky) from Bec who was fourth in descent from
Aedh Uargarb. They held the eastern sector of the tribeland between Bandon and Cork (this became the deanery of Kinalea
ultra in later times), and in the eleventh century they became
known as the O Mathghamhna or the O'Mahony clan. In course
of time the history of the Ui Eachach was primarily the history
of the O'Mahony clan. Thus, the diocese of Cork is the Ui
Eachach or O'Mahony diocese, even though no bishop of that
name ever governed the see of Finbarr.

The minor sept of the Ui Mic Ciair held some territory south
of the Lee at Cork where their name survived until at least 1199.
A decretal issued in that year by Pope Innocent III mentions
the bishop of Cork as holding, among other churches and lands,
all Umacciair: *totum Umacciair*. From a survey of this decretal
we may reasonably assume that the territory of Umacciair incorporated the parish of Saint Finbarr together with what were,
approximately, the old parishes of Carrigrohane, Kilnaglory
(Ballincollig) and Inishkenny (Waterfall) to the west. Notwithstanding that they were of royal stock, the Ui Mic Ciair
were apparently of little importance and their lands at Cork
would have been merely a subdivision or *baile biataigh* of the
larger Ui Eachach *tuath* or tribeland. Yet it was from Aedh of
the Mic Ciair that Saint Finbarr accepted a site on which to
build his great monastic school at Cork. It is not known where
the lands of the Ui Mic Broic lay, but the survival of this sept
until at least the ninth century is proved in the books of genealogies which contain pedigrees of the Ui Mic Broic chieftains
from about 450 to about 800. Of those whose pedigrees are thus
traced, Ruisine Mac Lapan[3] may possibly be identified with
Abbot Ruisine Mac Lappan of Saint Finbarr's monastery at
Cork, whose death is recorded for the year 683 in the *Chronicon
Scotorum* and for the year 687 in the *Annals of Inisfallen* and the
Annals of the Four Masters.

Excluding tribal histories and genealogies, the earliest
independent reference to members of the Ui Eachach sept is

---

3 *The Yellow Book of Lecan*, p. 411.

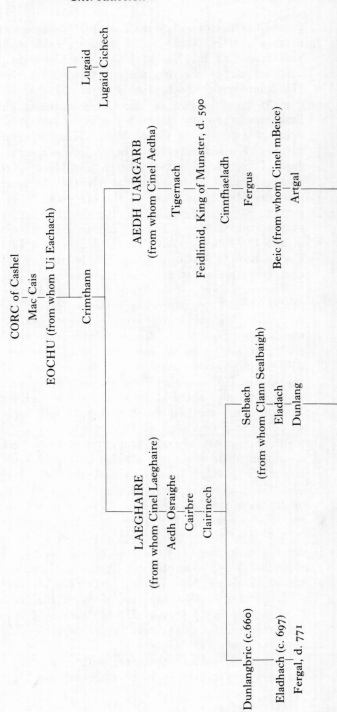

GENEALOGICAL TABLE OF UI EACHACH
(*Book of Lecan*, 410, 411; O'Clery, *Genealogies*, 156, 157)

Lugaid
Lugaid Cichech

CORC of Cashel
Mac Cais
EOCHU (from whom Ui Eachach)
Crimthann

AEDH UARGARB
(from whom Cinel Aedha)
Tigernach
Feidlimid, King of Munster, d. 590
Cinnfhaeladh
Fergus
Beic (from whom Cinel mBeice)
Artgal

LAEGHAIRE
(from whom Cinel Laeghaire)
Aedh Osraighe
Cairbre
Clairinech
Selbach
(from whom Clann Sealbaigh)
Eladach
Dunlang

Dunlangbric (c.660)
Eladhach (c. 697)
Fergal, d. 771

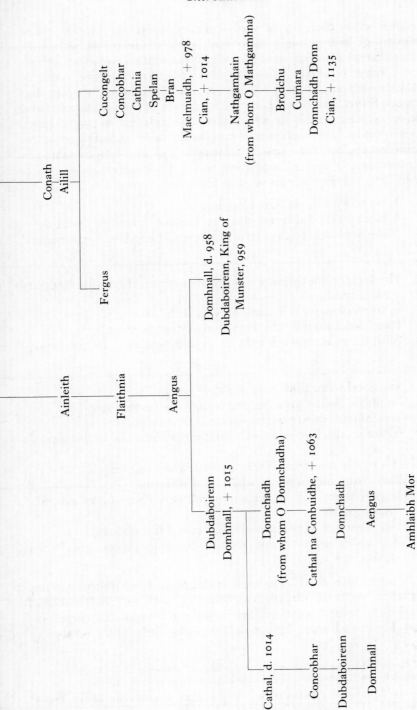

found embodied in a sixth-century metrical life of Saint Senan of Iniscathaigh who had close associations also with Inniscarra. This metrical life, which is ascribed to Saint Colman of Cloyne (d. 604) who was royal poet (*file*) at the court of Cairbre Crom, king of Cashel (d. 580), recounts a dispute between Saint Senan and Lughaidh,[4] prince of the Ui Eachach and king of Raithleann, to whom the saint refused to pay tribute; whereupon Lughaidh sent a race-horse to be maintained at the monastery, but the horse fell into the Lee and was drowned at Inniscarra. The verses relating to the Ui Eachach in the metrical life of Saint Senan read as follows:

A wonderful horse had Lugaidh,
A more beautiful horse than he was not found in Ireland:
'Take my horse to the cleric that it may be fed by him on corn.'

. . .

The king of Raithleann went to them from the south, haughty his onrush,
In front of every one until he was with hostful Senan.
Then did Lugaidh the Breasted say, as to the Cleric,
With fierce utterance, that he should be cast in to the water,

. . .

Not good what thou hast done, O Lugaidh,
To noble Senan give his desire, say his fosterlings,
Give his full desire to the Cleric as is very gladful
Without affliction of speech, that it may be a tale to the world's end.
The twain together, Aedh and radiant Loigure,
When they did Senan's will . . . of offering,
He gave them with peace and goodly children the kingdom of Raithleann,
Said the word of the apostle that ennobles labours,
That a realm not rude should be unto Aedh and heroic Loigure.[5]

Technically, the Ui Eachach or Eoghanacht of Raithleann had equal rights to the kingship of Munster with the Eoghanacht of Cashel, but the Cashel branch usually monopolized the office, and Feidlimid mac Tigernaigh was the only chief of the Ui

---

4 Lugaidh, brother of Criomthan, eldest son and successor of Eochaidh, acted as foster-father to Criomthan's children and succeeded him as Ri Raithleann.

5 John O'Mahony, *A History of the O'Mahony Septs*, p. 25, quoting Whitley Stokes' translation of Saint Colman's Irish verses.

Eachach to attain to the provincial kingship in the earlier centuries Feidlimid died in 589 or 590,[6] and from then until about 978 few historical records of the Cinel Aedh or O'Mahony sept are met with. From about the year 697, however, successive chiefs of the Ui Eachach bore the title of *Ri Desmuman*, king of Desmond, which at times was replaced by the less prestigious title of king of the Ui Eachach. The changes which seem to have sprung from inter-tribal conflict were no doubt responsible in great measure for the fluctuations in the distribution of diocesan territory about which we shall have more to say in the following chapters.

At this juncture it is impossible to evade the issue on two vital questions, namely, the incidence of pre-Patrician Christianity, and the extent to which the evangelization of Cork and its neighbourhood had progressed by the time of Finbarr's appearance in the valley of the Lee. As to the first problem, independent and multiform sources indicate that Ireland must have received Christianity from western Gaul and Britain in the fourth and early fifth centuries, and this in a variety of ways. Firstly, there were commercial relations between Ireland and western Gaul. Then came the wars and settlements of the Irish (*Scotti*) in Britain, their contacts as foes or auxiliaries with the Roman legions, the inevitable associations with Christians and the introduction of Christian captives into Ireland. Professor Heinrich Zimmer has drawn attention to the special veneration accorded to Saint Martin of Tours in the early Irish church, to which must be added the honour of a lesser nature which was given to Ninian, founder of *Candida Casa,* a monastic establishment among the Picts of Scotland. Traces in Ireland of fourth- and fifth-century European heresies of Arian, Priscillian and Pelagian vintage are another indication of pre-Patrician Christianity in this country. Pelagius, whose teaching revolved upon grace, free will and predestination, is depicted as 'stuffed with Irish porridge' (*Scotorum pultibus praegravatus*). The argument in favour of pre-Patrician Christianity is further strengthened by the testimony of an émigré movement from Gaul to Ireland in the fifth century and by linguistic evidence which, according to Kenney, is undoubtedly important if it can be correctly interpreted. The inference to be drawn from the incorporation in old Irish of modified words of Latin origin and of Christian significance is that the Irish learned these words

---

6   The Bodleian *Annals of Inisfallen* enter his death under the year 585 as follows: *Mors Fedlimthe meicc Tighernaig, Righ Caissil.*

from British Christians.[7] Finally the existence of Christianity in
Ireland is presupposed by an entry in *Prosper's Chronicle* concerning the appointment of Palladius in 431: 'To the Irish,
believing in Christ, Palladius, having been ordained by Pope
Celestine, is sent as first bishop.'[8] More important than any of
the foregoing considerations is the fact that the early labours of
Saint Patrick were confined to the eastern parts of Ireland, after
which he concentrated on the north and on certain areas in the
west. His missionary course as charted in the *Vita Tripartita*
did not cover either north or west Munster, nor did Patrick visit
any of the Desmond country. Here in Desmumha the work of
evangelization was a native effort which in a very real sense was
of pre-Patrician vintage.

<h3 style="text-align:center">SAINT CIARAN OF SAIGHIR</h3>

A claim not to be lightly dismissed is the claim of the people of
Kilmoe 'that Christianity was introduced into this parish long
before St. Patrick and may have come through commercial
contacts from Britain, France or Spain';[9] a claim which Professor
MacNeill endorses by maintaining that it was among them that
the cross was believed to have been first raised in Ireland.[10] The
pedigree of Ciaran of Cape Clear, better known as Ciaran of
Saighir in Ossory and 'senior of the saints of Ireland' is given in
the *Book of Genealogy of the Corca Laighdhe* which represents
him as the son of Lighin. Lighin or Laighin, his mother, was
born in Cashelean in the parish of Kilmoe and on her marriage
to Laighne, an Ossorian, went to live at Fintracht Cléire, now
Cape Clear Island, where her son Ciaran was born. Little is
known of Ciaran's early life except that he spent thirty years in
holiness and was fully grown in body and soul when he took
ship for the continent. Here he was baptized and ordained and
according to some sources consecrated bishop before his return
to Ireland sometime around the year 402. If this account is
correct, Ciaran preceded Saint Patrick by about thirty years
and presumably converted his native Cape Clear to the Christian faith. Saint Ciaran is more highly venerated at Saighir in
Ossory, his father's homeland, where he established a hermitage
which in time developed into an important monastery, the

7   J. F. Kenney, *The Sources for the Early History of Ireland: An Introduction and
Guide*, vol. i: Ecclesiastical, pp. 159–160.

8   Ibid., p. 165.

9   Expressed in a letter (dated 8 July 1945) to the late Canon P. Cahalane by Rev. J. V.
Hurley, parish priest of Goleen.

10   MacNeill, *Phases of Irish History*, p. 162.

paruchia of which forms the boundary of the modern diocese of Ossory.

Legend in the form of animal and voyage stories has become so interwoven in the life of Saint Ciaran (as of most of the Irish saints) that it is difficult to determine the boundary between history and hagiography. However, one would like to hazard the opinion that Ciaran's Odyssey was conceived against the wild and ruggedly beautiful panorama of Cape Clear and west Cork which, from being the area of his early formation, developed into the scene of his later ministry. Whether or not Ciaran was another Brendan the Navigator is a debatable point, but his voyaging is commemorated in an old litany of Irish voyager-saints which invokes 'the fifteen men who went with Ciaran of Saighir'.[11] What could be more natural than that some inlet of the west Cork coast should have been his port of call, his *statio bene*, if not indeed his nautical headquarters?

SAINT ABBAN

The first pre-Finbarrian, as distinct from pre-Patrician saint who is believed to have had connections with Cork is Abban or Gobban, in whose case biographers have so confused the lives of two holders of the name that it is virtually impossible to distinguish between them. The elder Abban, who belongs to the pre-Patrician group of Irish saints, is associated with the districts of Connacht and Kerry; the younger Abban with Meath, Leinster and Cork. Saint Abban is believed to have founded the nunnery of Boirneach or Ballyvourney on the borders of Mus-kerry for Saint Gobnait and her companions. A monastery at Cill Moyran or Killmurriheen in Kerrycurrihy, where traces of an ancient *cillín* or cemetery are still discernible, is similarly attributed to him. We also read in O'Clery's account of Abban's life that he blessed 'Cúl Cullainge and Brigoban and Cill Cruimthir and Cill na Marbh, and he left the office of the Holy Church in every church of them'. Cúl Cullainge may be identified with Kilcullen in Bantry; Brigowne and Cill na Marbh lay in the barony of Clangibbon in the diocese of Cloyne; Cill Cruimthir was part of the Ui Liathain territory in modern Barrymore. Abban's association with Saint Gobnait places him in the fifth century; and while it may be argued that Gobnait, whose dates of birth and death cannot be ascertained, is chronologically unreliable, there can be no doubt of the existence of a Saint Abban in Cork before the arrival of Saint Finbarr. It is unfortunate that Abban's identity becomes more complex when

11   D. D. C. Pochin Mould, *The Irish Saints*, p. 78.

he is considered side by side with the brothers Seadna, Eltin and Gobban of Kinsale who, like him, belong to the category of pre-Finbarrian diocesan saints.

Smith in his history states that Strawhall, formerly Kilbrenin, was an abbey which Colgan and Ussher claim to have been founded in the eighth century by Saint Aedus or Aedh Mac Bricc.[12] A footnote gives 10 November 789 as the date of the saint's death. On the other hand, the *Annals of Ulster* by placing the event in 589 and/or 595 would have us regard Aedh Mac Bricc as a pre-Finbarrian saint. His father, Brocc, was a member of the Uí Neill; his mother, whose name remains unknown, came from Munster, and Aedh Mac Bricc himself became renowned in the midlands where his principal foundation was at *Cell Áir* or Killare in Westmeath. He is also connected with *Sliabh Liac* or Slieve League, a promontory on the northern side of Donegal Bay. Tradition attributes many journeys to Aedh which make interesting reading but contribute little to authentic history. Aedh Mac Bricc's fame, according to Kenney, is more personal and general than monastic, while his reputation for sanctity and as a patron through whose supernatural intervention headaches might be cured, ensured him lasting fame. He is chronicled as *sui-liag*, the master-physician, in a fragmentary life of Brigit.[13] The length of Aedh's sojourn in Munster is not known. It is possible that the abbey of Kilbrennan was founded by him on one of his journeys and that it was entrusted to one of his disciples. Nothing has come to light concerning the subsequent history of this abbey, but some of its ruins were still visible when Smith was compiling his history in 1780. Kilbrennan, which was earlier known as *Enach mid Brenin* or *Brevin*,[14] was located in east Muskerry in the ancient parish of Moviddy near Bandon.

Saint Eltin, whose name in by-form is Multose, an anglicized diminutive of the Irish *Mo Eltín Óg*, flourished towards the middle of the sixth century. His brother Seadna is associated with county Clare; his second brother is commemorated in Kilgobban some miles north-east of Kinsale, and Eltin himself

---

12   Charles Smith, *The Ancient and Present State of the County and City of Cork*, i, 170; hereafter referred to as Smith, *History of Cork*.

13   Kenney, *Sources*, p. 393, quoting Rawlinson B 512, ff. 31–5v.

14   Smith, *History of Cork*, i, 170n.

is patron and putative founder of Kinsale. He has likewise left his distinctive stamp on Liselton in the parish of Clonfert, on Kilelton on the shores of Tralee Bay and possibly also on Terelton in the parish of Kilmichael, even though local tradition here pays tribute to Eltin Mac Cobtaigh. Whether or not Saint Multose pre-deceased Saint Finbarr is an open question; his non-inclusion in the list of local pioneer saints who 'offered their churches to God and to Bairre' is perhaps too tenuous to be regarded as an argument either for or against this supposition. The genealogy of these saints, Seadna, Gobban and Multose, contains a significant endorsement of the pre-Finbarrian evangelization of Cork. We read in the *Book of Leinster* of 'Magna, mother of Setna, son of Essen of the Arthraighe Cliach who dwell at Cluain Muccrais [Cluainbeg in the Glen of Aherlow] . . . and he and his two brothers Mogobban and Moeltioc are at Cend Sáile'.[15] From this district of Airthir Cliach on the Emly-Tipperary border came the holy man Mac Cuirp who baptized the young Finbarr and later became his tutor. Part of the Dal Modula sept to which Mac Cuirp belonged had emigrated to Muskerry, or more precisely, to a district called Corco Airchind Droma which has been tentatively identified as Dromorkan *alias* Clonherkin *alias* Kilmurry.[16] It is highly probable, therefore, that Mac Cuirp had established a Christian community in the Lee valley long before Saint Finbarr's arrival there. Mac Cuirp seems to have been attached to the great monastery of Emly and may have been 'one of the clerics from this and other large monasteries . . . who were engaged in extending Christianity to south and west Munster'.[17]

Existing records show evidence of many other isolated centres of Christianity in Cork and the surrounding district in the first half of the sixth century. At Inniscarra stood a monastery founded by Senan of Iniscathaigh who died in 544. Saint Brendan the Navigator, an elder contemporary of Saint Finbarr, was patron and probably founder of the churches of Cannaway and Kilmoe, where Saint Mochua, or Carthage, is also venerated. Also connected with Cork was Saint Brendan's brother Dosmangen who is referred to in the calendars of Irish saints as of Tuaim Muscraighe, which is probably Toames,

---

15 *The Book of Leinster*, p. 373.

16 Michael A. Murphy, 'The Royal Visitation of Cork, Cloyne, Ross and the College of Youghal', *Archiv. Hib.*, ii (1913) 187.

17 Liam Ó Buachalla, 'Commentary on the Life of St Finbarr'. *Cork Hist. Soc. Jn.*, lxx (1965), 2.

some miles south-west of Macroom.[18] In the city of Cork itself
a church dedicated to Saint Brendan was picturesquely situated
on the Glanmire heights overlooking the Lee. Next we find
that the *Martyrology of Tallaght* under 14 January commemorates *Fland Find i Cullind i fáil Chorcaigí*, that is, Flann Finn of
Cullen or Riverstick near Cork. The dates at which this saint
lived are unknown but it seems certain that he preceded
Finbarr. In further verification of his existence, a Latin register
transcribed in 1628 from an ancient roll and quoted by Smith
refers to 'the entire rect[ory] of Cullin, anciently called the
rect[ory] of St Flannan'.[19]

<h3 style="text-align:center">COLMAN OF CLOYNE: FACHTNA OF ROSS</h3>

Like Brendan the Navigator, Saint Colman of Cloyne (528–604)
was an elder contemporary of Saint Finbarr. The genealogies of
Irish saints refer to him as Colman Mittine, thus associating
him with the district of Muscraighe Mittine in mid-Cork. It is
probably in vindication of this association that the district of
Muskerry north of the Lee was included in the diocese of Cloyne
notwithstanding its great distance from the diocesan administrative centre at Cobh. Fachtna, patron saint of Ross, is rather
anomalously presented as a disciple of Saint Finbarr (see
below), but his death as registered in the *Annals of Inisfallen*
under date 600 leads to the conclusion that the foundation of
Ros Ailithir was at least as early as that of Cork; and it must be
borne in mind that the redactors of the lives of Irish saints had
no inhibitions about mutilating history. They rather specialized
in it. Ros Ailithir was the seat of an independent bishopric from
earliest times, and apart from various amalgamations of a
temporary nature it maintained its own separate existence until
1958 when the most recent amalgamation with Cork was effected by the bull *Qui arcana* of 18 April. Another Colman who
was an immediate contemporary of Saint Finbarr was Colman
of Kinneigh whose monastery dates from about the year 619.
There is likewise a Saint Coman connected with Bantry, the
ancient name of which was Kilmocomoge (*Mo Chomán Óg*),
and finally, tradition connects a Saint Ruadhan with Courceys
country. Lack of precise data renders incomplete any appraisal
of these saints Coman and Ruadhan.

18 *Genealogiae Regum et Sanctorum Hiberniae*, ed. Paul Walsh, p. 107.

19 Smith, *History of Cork*, i, 38.

RUISINE OF INIS PIC

Mention of Colman of Cloyne, Fachtna of Ross and Colman of Kinneigh opens up the real Finbarrian epoch in the history of the diocese of Cork. From these late sixth-century decades also come references to Saint Ruisine of Inis Pic or Spike Island and to Saint Gobban Corr of Fanlobbus or Dunmanway. The monastery of Spike Island points to an apostolate in south-east Cork conducted by Saint Mochua (Carthage) of Lismore whose missionary journeying brought him into the region of Kerry-currihy during the reign of Cathal Mac Aedha, king of Munster, who died in 616 (*A.U.*) or in 620 (*Ann. Inisf.*). In the course of one such visit and as a result of a grant of territory from King Cathal whom he cured of a grievous ailment, Mochua founded a monastery on Spike Island and another at Rosbeg near Ringaskiddy. On his departure he left behind him in the monastery of Spike Island, Bishop Goban, the priest Sraphan and Saint Laisren, together with two score more of his brethren. These foundations would coincide with the years of Finbarr's missionary apostolate in Cork; but for all that, the clerics here mentioned were not among those who later acknowledged Finbarr as spiritual head of all the churches in Cork. The *Martyrology of Tallaght* commemorates Ruissine of Insi Pich on 7 April. Little is known about Gobban Corn or Corr of Fanlobbus (*Fán Lópaist*) beyond that Dunmanway was the scene of his apostolate. Unlike the three saints on Spike Island, Gobban Corr 'offered his church to Bairre, and Bairre gave him an *offertorium* of silver and an altar chalice of gold'.[20]

The appendix to the first chapter of this history will show a still goodly number of lesser-known saints who had early associations with Cork. Taken all in all, these saints and their distribution present a viable overall impression of the extent to which Cork was Christianized before, during and after the Patrician age. Notwithstanding this galaxy of pioneer apostles, none had the charism granted to Finbarr, nor had any other the impact which he brought to bear on the great tribeland of the Ui Eachach with which his future diocese was to be coterminous. Before passing to an examination of the sources for the life of Saint Finbarr it is necessary to draw attention here to the fact that all early references show him to have been commonly called Bairre, Barre or Barra. The cathedral church of Cork was still designated *Ecclesia Sancti Barri* in 1199, and it is not until 1306 that the *Church of Saint Fynbarr* first appears in the records. No indication is given as to when the changeover took place.

20　Charles Plummer, ed., *Bethada náem nÉrenn ; Lives of Irish Saints*, i, 16.

SAINT FINBARR

In approaching the sources for a life of Bairre of Cork one is immediately confronted with a complete lack of contemporary documentation, a lack which evoked Kenney's unwarranted observation that 'The Lives of Bairre are of the late middle ages and quite fabulous'.[21] One cannot dismiss Finbarr on this thesis, any more than one can jettison other Irish saints whose lives are accretions of local legends and whose recorded *acta* contain as many contradictions and inconsistencies as do those of Finbarr. There is no gainsaying that miracles and anecdotes have made Irish hagiography a labyrinth of legend and wonder; and while it is difficult and at times impossible to sift the wheat of true history from the chaff of legend and fancy, it is nonetheless true that the very legend itself enhances the prestige of the individual around whom it has developed. The commonplace never becomes legendary and the person who becomes the centre of a legend must have possessed something more than the common run of his contemporaries. At the same time fancy can never be a substitute for fact, and legendary details must be treated with caution and with regard for that objectivity which is the criterion of true history. With this in view it is my purpose to show that, despite Kenney's arbitrary dogmatism, the patron saint of the diocese of Cork continues to stand out in point of time as an historical personality around whom a popular cult developed in the immediate aftermath of his death and whose school in Cork became the centre at which Munster learned.

Official *Lives* of Saint Finbarr derive mainly from two principal sources in Latin and in Irish. Six transcripts of an original Latin *vita* have survived. The oldest is that catalogued as Bodleian Rawlinson B 485 ff. 118ᵛ–21, which dates from about the year 1200. A complementary source is Bodleian B 505 ff. 137ᵛ–9ᵛ. Both are catalogued in the Franciscan Library at Killiney under A 24 pp. 124 sqq. Then comes the *Codex Kilkenniensis*, ff. 132ᵛ–4, which is catalogued in Marsh's Library as Z.3.1.5. and in Trinity College as TCD 175(E.3.11), f. 109 sqq. This dates from around 1400. These two compilations, which were published by Caulfield in 1864 under the title of *Life of St. Fin Barre*, are typical of the general run of Irish hagiography, are highly thaumaturgic and give only the barest biographical details. A third source is the *Codex Insulensis Collection*, dating from about 1627, which contains Bodleian Rawlinson B 485 s XIIIⁱ and Rawlinson B 505 s XIVⁱ. Kenney

21 Kenney, *Sources*, p. 402.

regards this collection as on the whole representing a later stage in the evolution of hagiography than the *Codex Salmanticensis* (which does not mention Finbarr) or even the *Codex Kilkenniensis*, but he does not consider this statement viable in the case of every individual life.[22] In addition to the foregoing the Bollandists had three *Lives* of Saint Finbarr. First, a copy *Ex MS. Hugonis Varaei* (? Vardaei, Hugh Ward) *Minoritae Hiberni*. The second was a *Life* copied from a Cork lectionary by Bernard Mede (Meade). The third was a copy found among the papers of Henry FitzSimon. The Bollandists attached no significance to any of these *Lives*.[23]

The oldest complete Irish version of the life of Saint Finbarr was copied locally in the early decades of the seventeenth century. Catalogued as volume nine of the Stowe MSS now in the Royal Irish Academy and numbered A.4.1., this version, of which pages 1–19 are damaged, was 'copied by Domnall O Duinnín . . . at Cork in September 1629 for Francis O Mathgamna . . . Provincial of the Friars Minor of Ireland'.[24] A second version which is a copy of O Duinnín's work is catalogued as MS 2324–40 ff. 122ᵛ–8 in the Bibliothèque Royale, Brussels. It too was executed at Cork in the house of the Friars Minor by Brother Michael O'Clery in or about the year 1629. Other Royal Irish Academy references to Saint Finbarr are RIA 23 B is XIX pp. 506–28; 23 M s o s XVIII, pp. 129–37 (imperfect); 23 A 44 s XLX pp. 110–16, and a fragment from the *Book of Fermoy* under catalogue number RIA Bk. Fer. s XV ff. 59ᵛ–60.[25] Another fragmentary note on Finbarr is found in *Lámhscríbhinní Gaeilge Choláiste Phádraig Má Nuad* in which an tAthair Pádraig Ó Fiannachta has catalogued the O'Renehan MSS. In volume sixty-four of this collection we find the following entry: *Beatha Bharra Naomtha*, 'i. céideasboig Chorcuighe.' *Barra an t-easbog naomhtha, do Chonachtaibh dhó, do shliocht Bhriain mic Eochaidh Mhuighe Mheadoin*.[26] The colophon, which gives Donchadh Ó Connaire of Cluain Umha as the scribe, quotes *Leabhar hÍ Chruimín Ó Eachadh Bolg* as his source. Ó Connaire wrote this extract in 1779; the original from which he worked is now lost.

Over and above the contents of the Latin and Irish *Lives*, details concerning Finbarr may be culled from the nocturn

---

22   Ibid., p. 307.

23   Charles Plummer, ed. *Vitae Sanctorum Hiberniae*, i, intro., p. xxxii.

24   Plummer, *Bethada náem nÉrenn*, i, intro., p. xii.

25   Kenney, *Sources*, p. 402.

26   Ó Fiannachta, Pádraig, *Lámhscríbhinní Gaeilge*, iv, 96.

lessons of matins for his feast day. Four extant versions of these lessons remain. First, there is the nine-lesson special office compiled for recitation in the cathedral of Cork on 25 September. Secondly, an early fourteenth-century manuscript which is preserved in Corpus Christi College, Cambridge, embodies certain texts relating to Saint Finbarr. These texts, which seem to have formed part of a special Irish supplement to the English breviary, were studied and published in *Analecta Bollandiana* by the late Père Paul Grosjean, S.J.[27] In the third place, six short lessons in the *Breviarum Aberdonense*, dating from about the fifteenth century, reflect the Scottish tradition concerning Finbarr, about which more will be told presently. Finally, an office of the late Middle Ages which was in use in the church of Lusk had nine lessons on Saint Finbarr, but popular sentiment was such that the *acta* of the Cork saint were taken over in their entirety and appropriated to a local patron named Bishop Mac-Cuillin.[28]

By comparison with its Latin counterpart, the Irish *Life* of Saint Finbarr is considerably longer, it contains valuable biographical data on the saint and on his contemporaries, it affords important topographical details on the area of Finbarr's life and apostolate and 'indicate[s] the existence of groups of federated churches under the headship of Cork'.[29] Granting such variations and allowing for the imbalance which gives twenty-seven chapters to the Irish and only fifteen to the Latin *Life*, both versions bear signs of being based on a common original and represent progressive stages in the evolution of Finbarr's biography. By re-arrangement the Latin version could be extended to eighteen chapters to accommodate an equal number of chapters in the Irish version where corresponding episodes are recounted. The longest and most important section in the Irish *Life* is the tenth chapter which is a miscellany dealing with Saint Finbarr, his disciples, their churches, the saints connected with the school at Loch Irce and the women saints who lived at Etargabail under the direction of Finbarr's sister Lasair. Other interpolated chapters deal with miracles and wonders attributed to Bairre during his formative years in Leinster; with his alleged foundation at Aghaboe (*Achad Bó*) in Ossory; with his final visit to Fiama, the hermit of Desertmore, in search of relics for his cemetery at Cork. Chapter twenty-two is a panegyric on the

---

27 *Analecta Bollandiana*, no. 69 (1951), 324–47.

28 Kenney, *Sources*, p. 299.

29 Plummer, *Bethada náem nÉrenn*, i, intro., p. xvi.

virtues of the saint which, as Plummer points out,[30] is almost identical with that found in the life of Saint Senan of Inis-cathaig.[31] The redactor of the Irish *Life*, then, fell into the common fault of endowing his subject with virtues and qualities which would enhance his prestige. This explains why the same miracle does service for saint after saint with inexorable regularity, the hagiographer in each case drawing from some common fund of accumulated anecdotal lore which was his for the taking. The final additional chapter of the Irish *Life* is highly and perhaps intentionally thaumaturgic; it relates that for twelve days after Bairre's death God did not allow the sun to set— *nír leicc Día gréin fo talmain . . . da la décc iarsin.*[32]

Taken as a whole, the Irish version with its wealth of supplementary data transforms the story of the diocesan patron into an epic of historical and topographical content. It is probable that the compiler had access to independent references to Bairre and his disciples other than those invoiced in the Latin *Life*. Such independent sources would be early calendars and martyrologies, as for instance the ninth-century *Martyrology of Tallaght* which refers to the 'seventeen holy bishops with seven hundred monks who with the blessed Bairre and Nessan were buried at Cork'. A somewhat similar entry in the twelfth-century *Book of Leinster* invokes 'the seven hundred and seventeen holy bishops of the grace of the Lord in Corcaig Mor'. This may or may not be a rationalization of the traditional lore, but it is worth noting that while the scribe of the *Book of Leinster* was at times careless and inaccurate in copying his documents, the book contains much material that is valuable.[33] In proof of this we have the testimony of Eugene O'Curry who discusses in his *Manuscript Materials* the inclusion of the earliest surviving text of the *Cogadh Gaedhel re Gallaibh* in the *Book of Leinster*, and says that its inclusion is proof that it 'must have been at that period recognised as an authentic and veritable narrative, and extensively known, else it could scarcely find a place in such a compilation'.[34] Robin Flower too adds his testimony to the worth of the *Book of Leinster* by drawing attention to the fact that it contains the only private letter in

30 Ibid., ii, 320 ff.

31 Whitley Stokes, *Lives of Irish Saints from the Book of Lismore*, pp. 73–4.

32 Plummer, *Bethada náen nÉrenn*, i, 21.

33 Kenney, *Sources*, p. 15.

34 Eugene O'Curry, *Lectures on the Manuscript Materials of Ancient Irish History*, p. 233.

Gaelic that has come down to us from the pre-Norman period.[35]

As already stated, the Irish version of Finbarr's *Life* was copied at Cork in 1629 by Michael O'Clery from an ancient vellum belonging to Domnall O Duinnín. The earlier account of Bairre, as found in the Latin versions of 1200 and 1400 (but not in *Codex Salmanticensis*), is believed to have been based on an original dating from the ninth or even the eighth century. Therefore, the Irish *Life*, as we now know it, was compiled between the years A.D. 800 and 1200, and the original version belongs in all probability to the period of cultural revival which followed the Irish victory of Clontarf in 1014.

The similarity between the panegyrics on Saint Senan and on Bairre of Cork urges to an appraisal of the extent to which the *acta* of the diocesan saint may have become confused with those of other saints; and conversely, the extent to which Bairre himself appropriated the *acta* of his predecessors and contemporaries. Appropriation is particularly exemplified in the case of those animal stories with which Irish hagiography abounds. The horse which reputedly carried Bairre over the sea was apparently his biographer's effort at emulating the whale legend of Brendan the Navigator, while the meeting of the two saints in the Irish Sea—Bairre on horseback and Brendan astride his whale—can only be seen as imaginative hagiography gone wild. Brendan of Clonfert died in 578, and Bairre's visit (if visit there was) to David of Minevia, during which this incident is said to have occurred, would have taken place early in the seventh century, probably in the year 606 or shortly afterwards. Another incident which tells of the milking of a wild doe to provide drink for the young Bairre is equally accredited to a female saint, Bearach of Ossory. Whether the incident was originally Bairre's or not is of little importance historically, but the blatant mutation of marvels and miracles and the extreme need for caution in their handling is once again brought clearly into focus.

Bairre's appropriation of the *acta* of other saints becomes more understandable, even inevitable, when it is remembered that apart from him, seven saints bearing the name Barrfind or Findbarr are commemorated in ancient calendars, martyrologies and genealogies. Quoting from the *Book of Ballymote* and the *Martyrology of Donegal* we have

Barfind of Inis Doimhle	Feast, 20 January
Bairfhionn, bishop	16 March
Barrfind of Drum Cuilin, bishop	21 May
Bairfhionn	1 July

35   Robin Flower, *The Irish Tradition*, p. 67.

Bairrfhionn, son of Ernin	22 September
Bairre, bishop of Cork	25 September
Barrfind of Achad Chaillten	8 November
Barrfind	13 November

Only two of these saints are in any way identifiable, namely, Barrfind of Achad Chaillten and Barfind of Inis Doimhle. As to the former, the *Félire of Oengus* and the *Martyrology of Donegal* agree on his pedigree and on the date of his commemoration. The *Félire* refers to him as Barrfind mac Aedha of Achad Cailden; this place, which has become obsolete, is said to have been 'west of the Barrow and south of Leighlin'. In other words, it lay in the Carlow barony of Idrone close to Kilmacahill where Bairre of Cork is believed to have been educated. Nothing further is recorded of Barrfind of Achad Chaillten, nor is there any indication that he was identical with Bairre of Cork. Difficulties abound in respect of Barfind of Inis Doimhle. Inis Doimhle is an elusive district which has been equated with Little Island on the Suir just below the city of Waterford, but for which Cork and Wexford have also been tentatively suggested. The *Félire of Oengus* accords Barfind of Inis Doimhle the same pedigree as his namesake of Achad Chaillten by calling him Findbarr mac Aedha Atha Cliath mac Dallain, thereby leading to the supposition that they were at least brothers, if not one and the same person. Another pedigree places Barfind of Inis Doimhle twelfth in descent from Feidhlimidh Rechtmor, king of Ireland, but it is left to the ingenuity of Michael O'Clery to produce the most baffling genealogy of the lot: '*Bairrfhionn Mittine m[eic] Muireadaigh, m. Domhnaill, m. Laoghaire, m. Eathach, a quo Ui Eathach Muman; m. Cais, m. Cuirc, m. Luighdeach, m. Oilealla flionn bicc, m. Fiacha Muillethain et cetera. Videtur esse qui colitur in Inis Doimhle 30 Januarii.*'[36] Here we are presented with a Leinster saint masquerading under an Ui Eachach pedigree, born in Muskerry Mittine and answering to the name of the diocesan patron of Cork.

On inspection, it could be maintained that while O'Clery's genealogy for Bairrfhionn runs counter to that given by Oengus the Culdee, the traditional Finbarr of Cork could indeed be called Bairrfhionn Mittine. As will be shown, Muskerry Mittine was the home of his parents; but the problem does not lend itself to so facile a solution. Finbarr's Connacht ancestry has persisted in tradition; the Leinster interlude of his life has not been sufficiently clarified, and many other passages referring

---

to him abound in ambiguities. In the final analysis however, the stature of Finbarr of Cork would not be minimized by deleting the Leinster interlude from his story. Much material of historical significance would still remain; and it is with this material, and with tradition and topography as its auxiliaries, that we now turn to a study of Finbarr, founder and first bishop of the diocese of Cork.

I

Saint Finbarr

Saint Finbarr is believed to have been descended from the stock of Ui Briuin Ratha of Connacht, a sept which once ruled over a vast area to the east and north-east of Galway and which traced its origins to Eochaidh Muigmedon. The saint's pedigree as given in the Irish *Life* calls him Bairre, son of Amairgen, son of Dubduibne, son of Art, son of Carthann, son of Fland, son of Ninnid, son of Brian, son of Eochaid Muigmedon.[1] The Latin *Life* represents his father Amairgen as the illegitimate son of Dubduibne (*in adulterio genuit filium nomine Amargenus*).[2] Amairgen was chief smith or artificer (*primh gobha*) under Tigernach, son of Aedh Uargarb, ruler of the *tuath* centre of Raithleann which in 1906 was identified as Garranes Fort in the barony of Kinalmeaky some six or seven miles north of Bandon. Most of the raths in this *tuath* centre have been destroyed, but the remains of the great rath of Lisnacaheragh are still to be seen in the present townland of Garranes in the civil parish of Templemartin, county Cork. This *tuath* or tribal city of the Ui Eachach Mumhan was established some time between 450 and 475 presumably by Eochaidh from whom the sept was named. The O'Mahonys as we have seen became the chief family of this sept, and though originally seated in Kinalmeaky they had by the eighth or ninth century encroached on the O'Driscoll sept of the Corca Laighdhe to the extent of becoming masters of the *Fonn Iartharach*, the western land which included most of the country from Bantry to Mizen Head. As Canon O'Mahony quotes in his *History of the O'Mahony Septs*, 'the Ui Eachach Mumhan or O'Mahonys had from the Corca Laidhe that portion of their territory called Fonn Iartharach, i.e. West Land, otherwise Ivagha, comprising the [later] parishes

---

1   Plummer, *Bethada náem nÉrenn*, i, 11.

2   Plummer, *Vitae SS Hib.*, i, 65.

of Kilmoe, Scoole [Schull], Kilcrohane, Durris, Kilmocomoge
[Bantry] and Caheragh.'[3]

The Irish *Life* next recounts that the townland of Achad
Durbcon in Muskerry Mitine (Mittine) was the property of
Amairgen; he apparently received it from Tigernach in lieu of
professional services rendered, and settled down there, *gur gabh
forba agus ferannus ind Achad Durbcon i ccrich Múscraighe Mitine.*[4]
Bairre's mother, whose name is not on record, seems to have been
a bondwoman (*cumhal*) in the house of Tigernach who ex-
pressly forbade any member of his household to take her to wife:
praecepit ut nemo assumerat eam in uxorem.[5] Amairgen trans-
gressed this prohibition, the bondwoman became pregnant and
an infuriated Tigernach ordered that she and Amairgen should
be burned. A fragment from the *Codex Kilkenniensis* states that
Finbarr was illegitimate (*páiste tamhna*) but that his mother was
miraculously saved from execution which was the recognized
punishment for unmarried mothers according to the laws then
obtaining. On the other hand, O'Clery maintains that Finbarr's
parents were married privately shortly before his birth.[6] But
Finbarr seems to have been born in bondage: the Latin and
Irish versions of his *Life* present him as addressing Tigernach
and asking for the release of his parents. The traditional place
of Finbarr's birth is given as *Sean-Mhuileann Cathair Céin*,
which lay to the north of Lisnacaheragh close to a stream known
in its lower course as the Brinny and which joins the Bandon
River near Innishannon. The date of birth was about the mid-
sixth century.[7] Two other children were born into the Amairgen
home, a boy named Modichu who is associated with Lileach in
county Kildare, and a girl who is thought to have been called
Lasair. 'Bairre's own sister' is first on the list of female saints
who were associated with him at Etargabail. The same list
mentions Lasair of Achad Durbcon, but it is O'Clery who first
makes the connection between Lasair, Amairgen and Bairre
when he calls her [*Lassuir*] *ingen Aimirgin derbsiur Barra.*[8]

The Muskerry Mittine of Bairre's *Life* was later known as

---

3 O'Mahony, *A History of the O'Mahony Septs*, p. 11.

4 Plummer, *Bethada náem nÉrenn*, i, 11.

5 Plummer, *Vitae SS Hib.*, i, 65.

6 A letter dated 13 August 1892 and preserved in the Cathedral Archives, Cork,
mentions a 'lithographed copy of the Life of St Finbarr by Brother Michael O'Clery'
which categorically denies Finbarr's illegitimacy.

7 As will be shown subsequently by comparison with the lives of elder contemporaries
of Finbarr.

8 *Geneal. regum Hib.*, p. 59.

Muscraighe Ui Floinn, and from the thirteenth century onwards that part of it which lay north of the Lee constituted the ancient deanery of Muscrylin in the diocese of Cloyne. Today the area is covered by those sections of the baronies of East and West Muskerry which lie north of the river. Achad Durbcon has been incorrectly and tenaciously identified with Gougane Barra, which in Amairgen's time can only have been a wilderness and totally unsuitable for habitation. Achad Durbcon was Macroom, the older name of which is given in the records as Addirpon or Authorpen. Under date 1591 when church property was being confiscated we find reference to *Achad Turpin alias Macroome* and to *Macroome alias Authorpen* on the Royal Visitation List of 1615.[9] Achad Durbcon therefore was at or near Macroom on the Sullane River and less than a mile from the north bank of the Lee. In ancient times, as *Crichad an Chaoilli* (Ancient Topography of Fermoy) shows, townlands or *bailte* were more extensive than at present, and it is a feasible conjecture that the Achad Durbcon of Amairgen included Coulcour and Sleveens to the north of the river near Macroom as well as Farranvarrigane and some other townlands to the south. The original grant given to Amairgen therefore was a shoulder of land extending from the townland of Macroom over the Lee through the pre-Reformation parish of Macloneigh and down to Kilbarry in the present union of Kilmurry. This part of the pre-Reformation parish of Macloneigh appears to have been, after Saint Finbarr's monastery, one of the most important ecclesiastical sites in the early diocese of Cork.[10] References connecting Macloneigh with the later cathedral of Saint Finbarr endorse this supposition.

The earliest diocesan reference is found in the decretal letter issued by Pope Innocent III in 1199, where Cluanachad appears in the list of churches enumerated. The full title of Cluan Achad was more likely *Cluain Achad Durbcon*. In 1281 the place appears as *Clonehyt* and in 1591 as *Cloineighe*, while an annate entry for the year 1493 gives *Maghluaneythe* which, by the seventeenth century, had been resolved into Macloneigh. The annate entry referred to states that in 1493 Matthew O'Mahony, dean of Cork, held Macloneigh and two other vicarages.[11] The visitation

---

9   Murphy, 'The Royal Visitation', p. 205.

10   In the present parochial structure the parish of Kilmichael is a union of the medieval parishes of Kilmichael and Macloneigh. It achieved parochial status in 1493. Before that date Macloneigh was the principal church here (*Matrix ecclesia*), the southern boundary of which was fixed by the stream Morglaisse which runs from near Deshure to the Lee.

11   [Evelyn] Bolster, ed., 'Obligationes pro Annatis Diocesis Corcagiensis'. *Archiv. Hib.*, xxix (1970), 24.

book of 1591 states that the rectory of Macloneigh belonged at
that time to the treasurer, while in that section of the *Civil
Survey* of 1654–56 which deals with Muskerry we read that 'the
tithes of the three plowlands and half of Kilbarry, Kilnarovanagh, Inshynashangane and Faranivarragane belong to the
treasurer of the Diocese of Corke'.[12] Bishop Downes wrote in
1700 that he saw 'Macloneigh Church near the river Lee on the
south side of it; . . . about 40 English acres of glebe lying around
the church, belong[ing] to the vicar; 'tis good land. . . . Farrena-
varagen, being half a plowland containing at least 80 English
acres, belongs to the Bishop of Corke. It lies contiguous to the
glebe of Macloneigh. . . . Some people fancy that this was
formerly a Bishop's See, but I could find no reason for any such
belief.'[13] The townland of Farranvarrigane is obviously an
anglicization of *Fearann Aimhergín*, the land allotted to Amairgen. This townland, which lies within the diocese of Cork less
than a mile south of the Cloyne parish of Macroom, belonged to
the bishop of Cork down to the middle of the seventeenth
century. We find it described under the parish of Macloneigh in
the *Civil Survey* as 'Farranavarragane, by estimation ½ plowland
[containing] 100 acres [plantation measure]. The said lands
belong to the church of the Diocese of Corke, but it is not known
which of the Numbers [? members] of the church is the reputed
proprietor thereof.'[14] The six-inch Ordnance Survey maps
show this townland (on sheet 71, county Cork) situated south of
the Lee and extending from Macloneigh Bridge to Bealahaglaskin Bridge which spans the Lee two miles south-east of Macroom
on the road to Cork. The modern townland includes Macloneigh
(glebe) and church ruin. Its total area in statute measure is 172
acres including 9 acres of water. After the Reformation when
Lord Muskerry appropriated the church lands on his estate,
the only townland which the bishop of Cork and Cloyne retained
was the half-ploughland of Farranvarrigane, which bears out the
premise that the district identified with Achad Durbcon must
have had some special ecclesiastical significance.

Another important townland of this area is Kilbarry in
Warrenscourt; it was once part of the pre-Reformation parish
of Macloneigh and is now in the union of Kilmurry. Kilbarry,
Cill Barra or the church built by Finbarr, may indicate the actual

12   *The Civil Survey, A.D. 1654–56*, vi, 316 (Muskerry barony, county Cork).

13   W. M. Brady, *Clerical and Episcopal Records of Cork, Cloyne and Ross*, i, 211;
hereafter referred to as Brady, *Records*.

14   *Civil Survey*, vi, 317.

site of his home. The extant remains of the site at Kilbarry are as follows:

1. About 300 yards south-west of Warrenscourt House, on the decline toward the stream, is a heap of stones surmounted by a door or window lintel, and now indicated as *Cill Barra* on a plaque erected by the Kilmurry Historical Society.

2. According to tradition, the first *cill* of the saint in his family territory was located on the far side of the glen in the south of the townland and to the west of the laneway leading from the Kilmurry–Poulnargid road. The exact position of the *cill* on this plot of ground which (again according to tradition) has remained untilled, cannot be determined, but it is believed to have been close to the reef of rock which was its northern boundary.

3. Kilbarry graveyard was originally of greater dimensions than its present limits indicate. Two laneways, from the north and south, led to the graveyard. That from the north is said to have been the old road leading from the graveyard through Dromorkan and Kilmichael to Gougane Barra. The laneway from the south, known as *Bóthar Barra*, leads to an enclosure called the Killeen (*cillín*) which is marked as 'Kilbarry Graveyard' on the Ordnance Survey maps.

4. Further south by the stream is the site of an old fort called *Rath Ard an Ghabhail*. One cannot be categorical on the significance of this fort-like mound owing to the diversion of the nearby stream in the time of the Warren family who gave their name to the district. There is a tradition, however, that in earlier times this stream was of considerable size and that it abounded in fish; and from the *Lives* of Finbarr we learn that the saint's daily diet consisted of a salmon caught 'in the fair pool' close to his home.

At baptism Amairgen's son was called Loan or Lochan, a name not previously recorded in the family pedigree. The ceremony, according to the Irish *Life*, was performed by Bishop Mac Cuirp of the Dal Modula sept of Corco Airchind Droma, and according to the later Latin version, by Saint Eolang (Olan) of Aghabulloge. Mac Cuirp, who is one of the most important characters in the life of Bairre, is not introduced in this Latin version until after the completion of Loan's early education at Kilmacahill. It is probable that Mac Cuirp's Christian name was Corbmac (Cormac), and that Cliu was the centre of his activity; his name is also connected with David of Cell Muine (Minevia) and with Pope Gregory the Great. Cliu, where Mac Cuirp's school was situated, was the old name for what is now the diocese of Emly. It lay chiefly in east Limerick and included the Emly and Tipperary town districts also. The family of

Amairgen had certain contacts with the ruling Eoghanacht sept
of this region; consequently there may have been family reasons
for the selection of Mac Cuirp for the baptism of Amairgen's son.

After seven years spent under his parents' tutelage at Achad
Durbcon Loan re-enters the page of history when he attracted
the attention of three clerics or anchorites of Munster who
visited the home of Amairgen. The clerics, Brendan, Lochan
and Fidach, were on their way from Leinster—whither or for
what purpose is not easy to determine, since the Latin *Life* is
stark in its brevity concerning them: *qui aliqua causa cogente ad
regionem suam reversi sunt.*[15] At the sight of Loan one of the
clerics exclaimed, 'Fair is this boy. . . . I know he is the elect of
God and the Holy Spirit dwells within him. Let him come with
us that he may learn (*legeret*), for the grace of God shines in his
countenance.'[16] Loan's parents agreed, and thus it was that
Loan accompanied the hermits on their return journey to
Leinster and received his early education in Ossory. The
journey to Ossory was marked by a ceremony at Sliabh Muincille
near Castlecomer, county Kilkenny, on the Munster side of the
then provincial boundary.[17] Loan complained of thirst, whereupon one of the clerics sent a servant to milk a wild doe which
he noticed grazing on the nearby mountain, assuring him that
Loan's sanctity would tame the wild animal for him.[18] The doe's
submissiveness suggested that the clerics should tonsure Loan
and change his name. 'This is a fit place for his instruction to
commence, for his hair to be shorn and his name to be changed,'
said the senior cleric. Loan was duly tonsured and named
Findbarr or Fair Head from the words 'Fair (*find*) is the crest
(*barr*) on Loan', spoken by the cleric who tonsured him.[19]

At Crosa Brenaind, which is probably Crossbrennan near
Castlecomer, Saint Brendan of Birr is said to have met Finbarr
and to have forecast the extent of the diocese which would one
day be his. 'I had made my request of God', said Brendan, 'for
three estates in Desmond that they might serve my successor
after me; to wit, from the Blackwater to the Lee, from the Lee
to the Bandon and Bearhaven, from the Bandon to Cape Clear.

15   Plummer, *Vitae SS Hib.*, i, 66.

16   Ibid.

17   Patrick Power, *Crichad an Chaoilli*, p. 6, identifies Sliabh Muincille as the southern
boundary of Caoille where there existed a site known as Buncille. Its alternative name,
Ros Coille, may be the *Durrusgaill* of the 1199 decretal list of churches belonging to the
bishop of Cork. *Durrusgaill* was in the district of the Nagle range of mountains.

18   Plummer, *Vitae SS Hib.*, i, 67.

19   Plummer, *Bethada náem nÉrenn*, i, 12.

And God did not grant them to me but God has given them to serve Bairre forever.'[20] Brendan's 'prophecy' may easily be one of the many legend motifs which complicate the story of Finbarr, but Brendan, who died about the year 573, appears to have anticipated the decisions which at the twelfth-century synod of Rathbreasail initiated the establishment of territorial diocesan organization in Ireland. The Latin *Life* adds that Brendan announced that he had come from a border district where strife was recurrent and foretold that Bairre's rule would be over a peaceful territory: *et bene Deus meus sedem pacificam praebuit illi puero, qui ipse multum pacifice vivet.*[21]

After parting with Brendan, Finbarr crossed the provincial boundary into Leinster where he and the three clerics erected the church of Kilmacahill (mac Cathail) in the Gowran Pass. Here Finbarr received his early education and 'read the psalms' under the tuition of the clerics, particularly that of Lochan whom the Irish *Life* represents as the senior of the three.[22] Both Latin and Irish versions call Lochan a Munsterman; the calendars and genealogies of Irish saints make him a native of Leinster. Thus in the *Félire of Oengus* under 31 December there is reference to Lochan and Enda of Cill Manach in south Dublin, 'and of Cill Mac Cathail in Ui Bairrche, that is, at Belach Gabhran'. There is nothing to indicate that the Lochan of this entry had any association with Bairre of Cork, but we cannot overlook the implications which add that extra bit of mystery to the Leinster interlude of the Cork saint's career. Further complications arise concerning Bairre's subsequent education. According to the Irish *Life* he returned to Munster, came to Coolcashin where 'he marked out a church and it was offered to him forever', settled in Aghaboe and then presented himself before Mac Cuirp under whom he completed his studies.[23] The Irish *Life* also depicts Cainneach (Canice) as coming to Bairre at Aghaboe and begging him to relinquish the place to him; but the suggestion that Finbarr was founder of Aghaboe is watered down by a later reference to Cainneach as 'the saint who had been in the church previously'. Cainneach is credited with having foretold a unique privilege for all future rulers of the church in Cork: 'Wherever thy heir and successor assumes the headship, he shall not depart

---

20 Ibid., p. 13.

21 Plummer, *Vitae SS Hib.*, i, 68.

22 Plummer, *Bethada náem nÉrenn*, i, 13.

23 Ibid.

without confession granted him from the heavenly King.'[24] The
Latin *Life* does not mention Cainneach but represents Finbarr
as sent by his masters (*seniores*) on the completion of his term at
Kilmacahill to Mac Cuirp who had recently returned from
Rome. The only place mentioned in his itinerary is Coolcashin
on the Leix–Tipperary border where he marked out a site for a
church, concerning which the Irish *Life* has the statement, *Cill
Chaissin an Ossruidhibh agus as uirthe tugthar Cill Barra . . .
aniugh.*[25] The inconsistencies between the two accounts must be
explained in terms of the growing theory that this section of
Finbarr's life is an interpolation belonging to another Barrfind
whose locale was either the Kilmacahill district of Kilkenny or
the territory of Idrone in the diocese of Leighlin. But while there
is good reason for denying any historical significance to the
Leinster episode in the life of Finbarr of Cork, it is not possible
as yet to venture any definitive conclusion.

At Mac Cuirp's school in Cliu, Bairre studied the Gospel of
Saint Matthew and ecclesiastical subjects generally (*legit
evangelium secundum Matheum apostolum, et regulas ecclesiasticas*)
which Mac Cuirp himself had learned from Pope Gregory (*sicut
ille a Gregorio papa accepit*).[26] Several miraculous episodes
colour this phase of his life: the restoration of sight and speech
to the children of King Fachtna Fergach and the shower of nuts
which Bairre caused to fall while the year was as yet in spring-
time. How long he remained at Cliu is not known, but he seems
to have been ordained there, and Mac Cuirp exacted as tuition
fee that both he and his pupil should be buried together: *Id volo
a te ut in uno loco in die judicii resurgamus.*[27] Mac Cuirp was the
first person to be interred in the cemetery of the Cork monastery.
Leaving Cliu, Finbarr, according to the Latin *Life*, returned to
Achad Durbcon and established a church there (Kilbarry);
but the Irish version tells that he came to Loch Irce where he
founded a school: *Ro aittreabh iar sin Bairri i Loch Irce 7 in
nEtargabhail ris anair, occus is i so scol ro boi occ Bairri insin
Loch.*[28] This O'Clery version of the Loch Irce story varies from
that given by Colgan who has some interesting details to add.
Both accounts follow:

24   Cainneach, who was of the Ciannachta of Glen Geimin in modern Derry, died at
Aghaboe in the year 600.

25   Plummer, *Bethada náem nÉrenn*, i, 13.

26   Plummer, *Vitae SS Hib.*, i, 69.

27   Ibid., p. 70.

28   Plummer, *Bethada náem nÉrenn*, i, 15.

COLGAN

After these things Saint Bairre came to a lake which in the Irish language is called Loch Eirce, near which he constructed a monastery, to which as to the abode of wisdom and receptacle of all Christian virtues, disciples flowed in crowds from every quarter in so great numbers, through zeal of holiness, that from the multitude of the monks and cells it changed that desert, as it were, into a large city. For from that school which he instituted there, numerous men came, remarkable for holiness of life and the praise of learning. Amongst whom were conspicuous:

S Eulang, instructor of
  S Bairre
S Colman of Dore Dhuncon
S Baithin
S Nessan
S Garbhan son of Finnbar
S Talmach
S Finchad of Domnach Mor

S Fachtna Ria
S Fachtna of Ros Ailithir
S Lucer, S Cuman, S Lochin
  of Achad h-airaird
S Carin, S Fintan of Ros
  Coerach
S Euhel of Ros Coerach
S Trellan of Druim
  Draighniche
S Coelchus
S Mogenna
S Modimoc
S Sanctan
S Luger son of Columb.

O'CLERY

After this Bairre dwelt in Loch Irce and in Etargabail to the east (of the lough and) to the west of Ros (in some texts).

Eolang, his tutor

Colman of Daire Duncon
and Baichine
and Nessan
and Garbhan son of Findbar
and Talmach
and Finchad of Domhnach
  Mor
and Fachtna Ria
and Fachtna of Ros Ailithir
Luicer and Coman and
  Loichine of Achad Airaird
Cairine and Finntan and

Eothuile of Ros Caerach
Trellan in Druim
  Draighnighe
and Caelchu
and Mogenna
and Modimmoc
and Santan
and Luiger son of Colum.

And all these and many others who came from that celebrated school, by the merits of holiness and virtue constructed cells in different places and consecrated themselves and all these to S Bairre, their father and master and his successors.[29]

All these offered their churches to God and to Bairre in perpetuity.

The lists, as such, are historically inaccurate, several of the alleged students had died before Finbarr began his life-work and, as already stated, the inclusion of Saint Fachtna of Ross is anomalous. On the other hand, many of these ecclesiastics (whose identification will be found in Appendix A) had foundations in south Munster. Their submission to Bairre and their acceptance of his jurisdiction suggest an early diocesan arrangement in Cork which, in turn, would seem to indicate that from earliest times Cork enjoyed supremacy over a large federation of churches in Munster. Chapter ten of the Irish *Life* follows this list with an account of the holy women who were associated with Bairre's sister at Etargabail: their names, as will emerge from a subsequent chapter, identify them all with south Munster. Following these the tenth chapter gives another and more comprehensive catalogue of saints who offered their churches to Bairre (Appendix B) and shows that the jurisdictional bond between Bairre and these new disciples was cemented by the fact that the donor of each church was given some token-gift of ecclesiastical significance by him. The gifts included reliquaries, the four books of the Gospels, a bronze reliquary containing the Host, an *offertorium* of white bronze, a silver chalice, an altar-chalice of gold and so on.[30] Once again an early diocesan arrangement is implicit in this contractual relationship.

One other reference to Loch Irce is found in an ancient litany of Irish saints which is transcribed into the *Book of Leinster* and which commences by invoking

Seven hundred and seventeen holy bishops in Corcaig Mor with Bairre and Nessan . . .

Seven fifties of holy bishops with three hundred priests whom Patrick ordained . . .

29   Colgan, John, *Acta SS Hib.*, i, 70.

30   Plummer, *Bethada náem nÉrenn*, i, 15. The exchange of reliquaries must be accepted with reserve; as will be shown hereafter the execution of reliquaries did not become common until the eleventh century.

Three fifties of holy bishops in Ailen Arda Nemid . . . [Great
Island] . . .

Seven fifties of holy bishops, seven fifties of priests . . . at
Loch Irchi on the borders of Muscraige and Ui Eachach
Cruada . . .

The enumeration in this litany of all clerical grades from door-
keeper to bishop is once again suggestive of early diocesan
organization.

Where was Loch Irce? The suggestion that it was at the extension of the Lee at Cork must be ruled out if for no other
reason than that the litany just quoted mentions them separately.
Canon Carrigan's guess is that it lay in the neighbourhood of
Coolcashin where there are sites which appear to coincide with
places mentioned in the Irish *Life*. This thesis can only be
admitted if the Leinster interlude of Finbarr's life is to be
accepted in full and without reservation. On the other hand, if
we examine 'Edergole to the east of the Lough, to the west of
Ros' as given in the translation of the Irish version, we discover
on the Ordnance Survey maps that the modern parish of Johnstown in county Kilkenny contains an ancient parish called Erke,
that Erke incorporated the townlands of Lough and Bawn-
ballinlough, that a place called Addergoole lay to the east of
Erke in Aghamacart and that the townlands of Rossdaragh and
Ross or Barrackquarter were also part of the parish of Erke.[31]
The evidence is convincing enough, but what of 'the borders of
Muscraighe and Ui Eachach Cruada'? It is here that Cork's claim
is strengthened. The Muscraighe of the litany is now represented
by the modern baronies of East and West Muskerry, and Ui
Eachach by the present baronies of Carbery, Kinalea and Kinalmeaky; but it is probable that the Muskerry of these early days
extended far beyond its present limits. In fact, there were at
least six territories called Muskerry stretching from the north
of county Tipperary to west Cork; there was a Muskerry in
Leitrim, another in Fermanagh and yet another on the borders
of Meath and Dublin.[32] But there can be no doubt whatever as
to which of these districts was the headquarters of the Ui
Eachach.

About a century ago Dr. Richard Caulfield identified Loch
Irce with the lake of Gougane Barra, and time has proved him
right. The lake is close to the Muskerry-Ui Eachach border, its
name signifies the 'recess of Bairre' and it would appear that

---

31 Carrigan, *The History and Antiquities of the Diocese of Ossory*, ii, 234, 276.

32 Eoin MacNeill, *Celtic Ireland*, p. 79.

this recess or hermitage was situated between the fork, *etar-gabhail*, of two rivers or streams in the townland of Rossalough and in the barony of West Muskerry. The description of the parish of Inchigeela, barony of West Muskerry, as found in the sixth volume of the *Civil Survey*, 1654–56, confirms this solution to the enigma of Loch Irce. The name of the townland in which the lake of Gougane Barra nestles is given in the survey as '*Inshircoongwogane*, 160 acres'.[33] By etymological declension we arrive at *Insh-irco-on-gwogane*, which in turn is probably an anglicization of *Inis-Irce-an-Ghuagáin*, with *Inis* used as a variant for the earlier *Loch*. This townland of Inshircoongwo-gane, which has been absorbed in that of Derreenacusha, is not shown on the modern maps.

In respect of Achad Durbcon the Irish *Life* refers to a *Cuas Barrai*, a cave or hermit's cell, 'and beside it there is a good pool, from which a salmon was taken each night for Bairre, having been caught in a net of one mesh'.[34] Bairre's stay in Achad Durbcon was cut short by the voice of an angel urging him to begin the long trek along the Lee which led to his greatest foundation at the river's mouth; and there can be no doubt but that the real hermitage in his life was Guagane Barra. Tradition tells that an old road led directly from Achad Durbcon to Gougane, and since Bairre must have frequently traversed this road through Kilmichael his selection of Gougane hermitage as his spiritual retreat and powerhouse was logical. Its foundation cannot be accurately dated, but it seems to have belonged to the early period of the saint's life and it was definitely founded before Cork.

The prominence of hermitages in the lives of Irish saints is a pointer to the extraordinary vigour of monasticism in post-Patrician Ireland.[35] The apparently impossible combination of the anchoretic with the apostolic or missionary life was here achieved by Saint Patrick who in the tradition of Martin of Tours stressed the former as the source of religious strength for the latter. Some of Patrick's greatest foundations—Armagh, Trim, Sletty—were semi-monastic seminaries, and the saint himself, while first and foremost a bishop, was at heart a monk fascinated by the call of the wilderness. In time as the monastic idea received impetus from native sources, the tendency to retire became more pronounced and many of the very early Irish

33 *Civil Survey*, vi (Muskerry barony, county Cork). The name *Inshircoongwogane* occurs twice on p. 331 and again on p. 388.

34 Plummer, *Bethada náem nÉrenn*, i, 16.

35 D. D. C. Pochin Mould, *The Celtic Saints : Our Heritage, passim.*

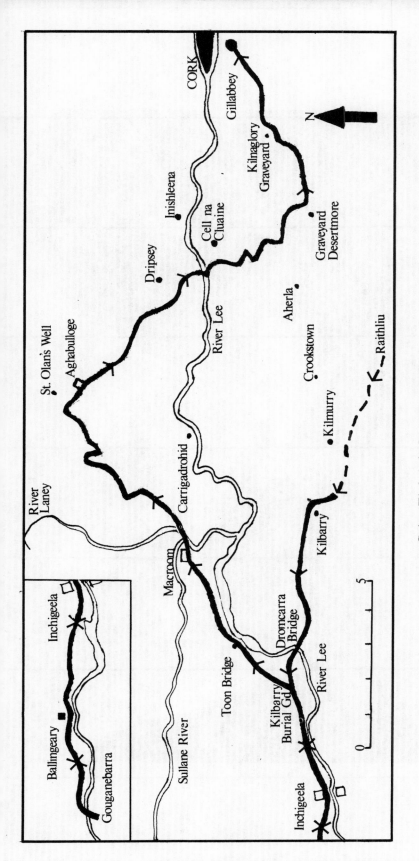

Saint Finbarr's Journey to Cork

Gougane Barra

saints spent part of their lives as hermits. Viewed in this light, Gougane was rather an adjunct to Cork than a distinct monastic site.³⁶ Had it been otherwise it would probably have developed into a distinct parish, but the earliest available list of diocesan property and churches (1199) does not even mention Gougane. Our first reference is found in the *Civil Survey* already quoted which calls it Lough Gouganbarry. The *Books of Survey and Distribution*, dated about 1660, refer to Gouganbarrogh, while Smith gives one of the earliest references connecting Finbarr with it when he writes that 'Gougane Barra signifies *the hermitage of St. Finbarr*, he having (as tradition says) lived there as a recluse before he founded the cathedral of Cork'.³⁷ The inscribed slab which was placed at Gougane in or about the year 1780 endorses Smith's statement by testifying, 'It is said and probable that Saint Finbarry in his sanctuary had recourse to this place, from whom it derived the name Gaggan Barry.' Smith further states inaccurately that Gougane 'since the time of St. Finbar has been frequented by many devotees as a place of pilgrimage . . .'³⁸ The hermitage is not mentioned as one of the eleven Irish pilgrimages indulgenced by Pope Paul V in the early years of the seventeenth century.³⁹ A pilgrimage to Sceilig Mhichíl is recorded in the life of William Tirry, bishop of Cork, 1623–45; he would have opted for Gougane were it recognized as a place of pilgrimage. Gougane did not become a popular pilgrim venue until about the year 1700 when Father Denis O'Mahony, the 'Hermit of Gougane', obtained for it from Rome the privilege of the Indulgence of the Seven Churches. Interesting as it is, this part of the story of Gougane must be deferred until the history of the modern diocese of Cork comes to be written.

From Achad Durbcon Finbarr directed his steps towards 'the

36   A letter written 9 September 1897 by Canon John Lyons of Kinsale to Bishop Thomas Alphonsus O'Callaghan states: 'It is quite certain that there was neither church nor monastery there but a hermitage. I have the tradition from a family of centenarians, one member of whom was contemporary with Father Denis O'Mahony, a.d. 1700, and saw the conical little island which is now the mound at the west end, before Father O'Mahony enlarged on it. On top of this, a heap of stones marked the spot on which Saint Finbarr's hut stood; and smaller heaps of stones marked the stations for prayer around it. This woman was then a young girl. She lived 107 years; her daughter lived 105 and her grand-daughter whom I knew, 103. There are some Irish names which suggest the connection of Saint Finbarr with the place, but neither name nor ruin suggesting the existence of a church or monastery. The place was covered with woods and infested with wolves almost down to the beginning of the [nineteenth] century. There was no arable land there that would support a community of monks.'

37   Smith, *History of Cork,* i, 166.

38   Ibid., p. 167.

39   John Hagan, 'Miscellanea Vaticano-Hibernica, 1580–1631 . . .' *Archiv. Hib.,* iii (1914), 263–4.

place of many waters' which the angel foretold as the place of his
resurrection. Following the course of the Lee over the rough
terrain of its northern bank he came to Cell na Cluaine at the
confluence of the Lee and Dripsey rivers in Inniscarra. Here
was a scene of surpassing beauty in contrast to the wild and
lonely ruggedness of Gougane. Over the Dripsey, a little to the
east, was a nestling inch called Inisluinge where Saint Senan of
of Iniscathaigh had established a monastery shortly after the
foundation of his larger abbey at Iniscarra about the year 532.[40]
To the west was the warm soil of Cronody and in the foreground
over the Lee were the wooded slopes of the Aglish country.
Perhaps it was here that Bairre was given one of the twelve
churches which according to the twelfth chapter of the Irish
Life preceded the Cork foundation. By comparison with Saint
Senan's sojourn at Inniscarra, Finbarr would have arrived at
Cell na Cluaine about the year 600. A local tradition maintains
that the original cell of the saint was at Cronody (*Coradh nOide*,
the enclosure of the religious community) which lay west of the
Dripsey and east of the paper mills, but is now located in
Aghinagh because of a diversion of the river. Here the name
Clais na mBráthar (the Brothers' Ridge) has definite monastic
overtones and, when taken in context with the reference to
Finbarr's crossing the river southwards (*budhes : ba dheis*)[41] to
Cell na Cluaine, it constitutes a significant pointer localizing
the saint on his journey. At low water the Lee was fordable at
many points between Fergus East, Cronody and Inniscarra.
The ford at Fergus East was the main crossing-point linking the
territory north of the Lee with the Aglish country to the south.
Three other fords at Faha-Castleinch, Carrigyknaveen-Curragh-
beg and Inniscarra-Curraghbeg connected Aglish with the
graveyard of Inniscarra. At Carrigyknaveen Finbarr is said to

40   Though now submerged beneath the artificial lake behind the Inniscarra dam, the
abbey of Inisluinge was once a monastery of some importance in the life of Saint Senan
who is also connected with the following Cork sites: Ard Nemid (Great Island),
Ciarraige Cuirchi (Kerrycurrihy), Raithleann and Inniscarra. In *A History of the
Diocese of Killaloe* (p. 18) Dermot F. Gleeson represents Inisluinge as close to the south
side of the Shannon, but for all that the name has lingered on till the present day in the
Lee valley. Tradition tells that sometime around the mid-sixth century some fifty
religious persons (*studentes*) arrived in Cork, of whom ten attached themselves to Saint
Senan at Inniscarra, the remainder being distributed elsewhere, one group going to
Inisluinge about two miles upstream from Inniscarra. Inisluinge or Ennysshelong
belonged later to Gill Abbey at Cork and was mentioned in the leases and grants made
of the abbey lands at the dissolution. In default of evidence showing that it was donated
to the monastery in medieval times, Inisluinge would appear to have been an original
possession of the Cork foundation from the time of Saint Finbarr.

41   Plummer, *Bethada náem nÉrenn*, i, 16.

have viewed the river from a boulder to see which way the water was going and to have taken the decision which led him to make his historic foundation near the southern bank of the Lee at Cork.

The location of Cell na Cluaine like that of Achad Durbcon has evoked wild and fantastic theories. Notwithstanding that it lay on the path of Finbarr's route from Gougane to Cork, it has been identified with Cloyne (*Cluain Uamha*) and with Clonenagh near Mountrath in Ossory, as well as with Killacloyne in Caherlag (Glounthane parish), with Killacloona in Ringrone (Courceys parish) and finally with Kilnaclona in Aglish (parish of Ovens). The claims of Kilnaclona are obvious. It lies to the south of the Lee within easy reach of Desertmore, which as we shall see, loomed large in Finbarr's life, and it has till the present time preserved its original name. In the seventeenth century the townland of Kilnaclona was absorbed in Ballineadig, a townland which lies to the west of Clashanure and extends from the Lee on the north to the old road running from Holly Cross (*Cros a'Chuilinn*) to the river. A church site known locally as *An Teampull* has been identified in a place called Rumley's bog. Its remains consist of a circular mound enclosing a knoll-dotted sward, while a fort-like circle adjoining the church site to the north is believed to have served as a graveyard. The terrain here is marshy, watered on the east by a tributary streamlet, and the approach to the *Teampull* is by way of the old Srelane-Roovesmore road on the south.

Finbarr built a church at Cell na Cluaine which he administered till the arrival of Cormac and Baithin, two pupils of Saint Ruadhan of Lorrha, who had asked of Ruadhan a place for themselves and were directed by him to Finbarr. Finbarr relinquished the church and all its treasures to them and to God: 'Remain here. I shall go in search of another place, for this is not the place of my resurrection.'[42] From Cell na Cluaine Finbarr resumed his trek along the river valley to Cork. Two courses lay open to him: the direct route via the old Srelane road to the east, and the old road from Holly Cross over the Bride to the east of Kilcrea towards Desertmore. He appears to have opted for the latter course and to have tarried for a while at Desertmore, the noted retreat of a hermit named Fiama and one of the more easily recognizable places connected with the life of Cork's diocesan patron. Desertmore was part of the septland of the Ui Criomthann which extended eastwards from the Ui Eachach

---

42 Plummer, *Vitae SS Hib.*, i, 70.

territory of Kilnaglory. The earliest site established at Desertmore was in the marsh near the well to the west of the mound-
shaped plateau of the present graveyard. Tradition states that
Finbarr and the Hermit of Desertmore were intimate friends
who often communed together on the heights of Knockanemealgulla overlooking Desertmore itself. Desertmore was
probably another of Finbarr's twelve churches; at all events
his friendship with Fiama was constant and Desertmore
counted for something important in his life. The medieval
parish of Desertmore became a prebend of the diocese of Cork
in the early fifteenth century.

From Desertmore Finbarr passed through Killumney, Mylane and Kilnaglory, of which the twin townlands of Killumney
and Mylane are still (1969) part of the parish of Saint Finbarr.
The Ordnance Survey map of this district shows a *cill* field in
Mylane bordering the townland of Killumney where there is a
corresponding 'well' field. The *cill* field was originally a graveyard to which roads led from the Desertmore-Cork sector on
the south and from Killumney village on the north. If we assume
that the *cill* owes its origin to Finbarr, the parochial connection
is a logical conclusion. Kilnaglory was another ancient parish
which became a prebend in the diocese of Cork. Its graveyard
which is still in use contains the ruins of an early medieval
church. In its etymological sense, Kilnaglory (*Cill na Gluaire*)
means the 'church of brightness'; and even if it may not be
numbered among the churches built before that of Cork, it may
still claim an honoured place in the history of the saint of Cork.
A legend relating to the radiance of Bairre's hand is recounted
in the Irish *Life*:[43] this hand may have been among the relics
removed to safety from Cork because of Norse incursions.
Kilnaglory may possibly have been the refuge selected for them.

Of the invitations which Finbarr received to settle in the
district around Cork, two call for special notice. First, Aedh,
son of Comgall of the Ui Mic Ciair (Iair), made the saint the
following offer: 'I give thee this place and the cow which God
has led to thee there' (this was referring to a cow that had
wandered away to be delievered of her calf).[44] Finbarr accepted
the offer which was made about the year 606, the year which
Colgan gives as the foundation of the monastery of Cork. After
this, according to the Irish *Life* Aedh Mac Miandach came 'and
he offered to Bairre the place called Foithrib Aedh in Magh
Tuath, and he offered himself and his posterity to Bairre in

43 Plummer, *Bethada náem nÉrenn*, i, 18.

44 Plummer, *Vitae SS Hib.*, i, 71.

perpetuity'.[45] This grant of 'Aedh's Wood' in the 'northern territory' forged an early connection between the diocese of Cork and the territory which stretched from Shandon eastwards to Glounthane, which while it overlaps the diocese of Cloyne has always belonged to that of Cork. Aedh Mac Miandach who donated this land to Finbarr appears in the genealogies as a chieftain of the Ui Cuirb Liathain, a sept which held sway to the east and north-east of Cork city.[46] His place in these genealogies would make him a contemporary of Saint Finbarr.

The land which Finbarr accepted from Aedh of the Mic Ciair was known as *Raithín mac nAeda* and also as Lisheencoonlane, where 'the angel marked out his church and blessed it'.[47] One tradition places the original foundation on the site now occupied by the Protestant cathedral; another equates it with the site upon which the medieval monastery of Gill Abbey was erected. And while it cannot be denied that the Cathedral of Saint Fin Barre occupies a very ancient Christian site, the question as to which is the more ancient—Gill Abbey or the cathedral—has not been convincingly answered.[48] Finbarr's foundation, at its greatest extent, stretched eastwards from the grounds of the present University College to the graveyard of the Protestant cathedral and southwards from the river-bank to the Lough. It is beyond question that Finbarr was a priest when he established his foundation at Cork in 606 but we have no record of the fact. On the other hand, the account given in the Irish *Life* of his visit to Rome with Eolang of Aghabulloge, Maedoc of Ferns and David of Cell Muine, of his meeting with Pope Gregory the Great and of his miraculous episcopal ordination at home must be dismissed as fanciful; but for all that Finbarr was a bishop. One of his first official acts as head of the Church in Cork was the consecration of his new church and cemetery. The church probably served the dual purpose of monastic settlement and first cathedral of the infant diocese of Cork.

In the absence of records descriptive of the monastic building we assume by analogy with contemporary foundations that

45 Plummer, *Bethada náem nÉrenn*, i, 17.

46 *The Yellow Book of Lecan*, p. 415, has the following entry: Fogartach son of Conall, son of Fidhalta, son of Cuimene, son of *Aedh son of Miandach*, son of Aongus, son of Maine, son of Corb, son of Liathan . . .

47 Plummer, *Bethada náem nÉrenn*, i, 17.

48 The presence of a round tower, down to 1760, at the cathedral is held by local historians to support its claim to be the more ancient of the two. The earliest known record of the tower is a map of Cork in 1545, now in the Tower of London, which refers to this tower as 'Ye Watche'. It is also marked on a map of 1602 in Trinity College, Dublin. Sir James Ware, writing in the early part of the seventeenth century, also refers to the tower which Hanmer (1751) says was 'buildeth by the Danes'.

Finbarr's establishment contained a church, an abbot's house, guest house, school, dormitories, refectory, kitchen and out-houses, all encircled within a stone walled enclosure. There would also have been a scriptorium where books were copied— gospels, psalters, liturgical books, commentaries, homilies, extracts from the Fathers[49]—and while we have no annalistic output from Saint Finbarr's monastery it is nonetheless true that Cork continued to be mentioned among the five principal monastic schools of Ireland down to the tenth century. The other four were Clonmacnoise, Armagh, Kildare and Bangor.[50] It would be surprising therefore if some work of copying and illuminating were not executed in Cork. More than likely the students lived in scattered huts, the monastic farm buildings were not in the immediate precincts of the monastery and life within the monastery was rigorous. Finbarr, who was an artisan by family tradition, would have been interested in the construction of the monastery even though this Cork founda-tion was noted more for its founder and personnel than for any architectural qualities. Finbarr, according to the Irish *Life*, had with him a great school of saints who offered their churches to God and to him; and these saints whose names are given in the eighteenth chapter of the *Life* had churches within the confines of county Cork. (Their names and identification will be found in Appendix C). Thus for the third time the idea of an early diocesan arrangement emerges.

The *Lives* do not assign any special name to Saint Finbarr's monastery. It is simply referred to as the 'School of Cork', and while the name *Antrum Bairre* has been loosely applied to it, this designation is more correctly applicable to the twelfth-century foundation of Gill Abbey. The name *Antrum* derives from the cave or hermitage in the limestone cliffs near the monastery to which the saint withdrew for purposes of con-templation. Quarrying operations have obliterated all traces of this *Antrum Bairre* which is believed to have been somewhere beneath the great rock on which the monastery of Gill Abbey was later built.

The blessing of the church was followed by the consecration of the adjoining cemetery which lay to the east of the monastic buildings and probably coincided with the graveyard of the present Protestant cathedral. The ceremony at which Bishop Mac Cuirp and other elders assisted was marked by the prophecy that there would always be an abundance of wisdom in Cork, to

49 Kathleen Hughes, *Irish Monks and Learning*, pp. 61–68.

50 Aubrey Gwynn, 'Irish Monks and the Cluniac Reform', *Studies*, xxix (1940), 414.

which Mac Cuirp added the promise that should his body be the
first to be interred in the new cemetery he would not allow
anyone who died 'within the circuit of Cork' go to hell. Mac
Cuirp *was* the first to go under the soil in Cork, and following
his death Finbarr chose Eolang of Aghabulloge as his confessor
(*anmcarait, anmchara*).[51] Eolang offered his church, his body
and his soul to Finbarr, and asked, as had Mac Cuirp, that their
resurrection should be in the same place. Phenomenology is
again catered for in the next sentence of the Irish *Life* which
states that 'in the presence of the angels and archangels Eolang
placed Bairre's hand in the hand of the Lord . . . that the Lord
took to Him the hand of Bairre . . . released it . . . and from that
day no one could look upon his hand because of its radiance'.[52]

It is presumably as abbot-bishop that Finbarr governed the
infant diocese of Cork, the boundaries of which can then have
but coincided with the possessions of the Ui Mic Ciair from
whom he received the site for his monastery. The last recorded
function of his life is an expedition in search of relics for his
cemetery: an expedition in which he was directed by the voice
of an angel to go to the district of the Ui Criomthann, that is, to
Desertmore. The hermit Fiama promised Finbarr that 'this
place shall be thine with its relics from now until doom', a
gesture in consequence of which Fiama merited to administer
the last rites to Finbarr on the day of his death.[53] Events surrounding the saint's death are contradictory and obscure. From
the Latin version it appears that he informed some of his disciples that he would die in his church in Cork. However, a
footnote to this reference, quoting *Rawlinson* B 484 and 505,
states categorically that he would *not* die in his own city: '*quod
cito esset recessurus, non tamen in civitate sua*'.[54] Latin and Irish
versions tell that he visited Cormac and Baithin at Cell na
Cluaine where he fell ill and was attended by Fiama of Desertmore and then 'sent forth his spirit to heaven by the cross in the
middle of Cell na Cluaine'. The cross in question was of later
erection; hence the Latin version is more correct than the Irish
in this instance. It says that Finbarr died 'where *now* is a cross

51 Plummer, *Bethada náem nÉrenn*, i, 18.

52 Eolang, it will be remembered, is cited in the later Latin version of the *Life* as
having baptized Bairre.

53 Latin and Irish versions follow up this visit by recounting seven major miracles
attributed to Bairre: his speaking from the womb of his mother, his speech immediately
after birth, the offering made to him before his baptism, miracles done for him without
his pleading for them, angels conducting him on his journey, Eolang placing his hand
in the hand of God, the sun shining for twelve days after his death.

54 Plummer, *Vitae SS Hib.*, i, 73, sect. xv and n. 10.

in the middle of Cell na Cluaine'.[55] The year of the saint's death is given as A.D. 623. By that date Finbarr, who according to Colgan had ruled the church of Cork for seventeen years, was aged about seventy-five. We arrive at this date by reverting to the alleged prophecy of Brendan of Birr whose foundation at Birr took place about the year 560. Finbarr was seven years of age when Brendan uttered his prophecy; he was consequently born towards the middle of the sixth century. The saint's remains were taken to Cork for burial presumably via the old Srelane road through Ovens. While the obsequies were being celebrated God did not allow the sun to set for twelve days, during which time 'the synods of the churches of Desmond were busied giving honour to the body of their master' with hymns, psalms, masses and recitation of the hours.[56] Finbarr was buried in the cemetry of his own church in Cork; his grave is believed to have been in the south-east corner of the graveyard of the present Cathedral of Saint Fin Barre.

The Irish *Life* concludes with the burial of Finbarr, but from the Latin version it appears that sometime after the burial the remains of the saint were disinterred and lodged in a silver casket, *in loculo argenteo sunt condite*.[57] We are here confronted with the possibility of a redactor who read his history backwards, and on this point Father John Ryan, S.J., wrote the following observations:

I have no doubt that such a suggestion, if contemplated, is false. The practice of enshrining does not seem to be early, though the removal of the remains of Saint Aidan from Lindisfarne to Iona in 664, and of Saint Columcille and others from Iona to Kells, is an indication that at any time it may have arisen. However, the great period for enshrining was the eleventh century. Sometimes a part of a body—like the arm of Saint Lachtin at Lemanaghan—was thus treated; but in some instances what remained of the body was enclosed in a small silver casket. Most probably the reference in the *Life* of Saint Finbarr is to the placing, in the eleventh century probably, of what remained of the body in such a silver shrine.[58]

In or about the ninth century the remains of Saint Finbarr were reputedly removed from Cork because of Norse incursions and

55 Plummer, *Vitae SS Hib.*, i, 73.

56 Plummer, *Bethada náem nÉrenn*, i, 21.

57 Plummer, *Vitae SS Hib.*, i, 73.

58 Expressed in a letter to Canon P. Cahalane, 26 June 1942.

taken to a place called *Cell na gClerioch*, the church of the clerics, which has been identified as Kilnagleary near Carrigaline. Because of its proximity to Cork harbour and the corresponding hazard of invasion, Kilnagleary can hardly be considered an ideal selection. Kilnaglory near Ballincollig would have been more secure and seems a more likely choice. But even here the precious relics of the saint were not safe; they were destroyed in 1089 during a conflict between the Ui Eachach Mumhan and Dermod O'Brien of Thomond. Only two actual relics of Finbarr are on record. The first was the *Bachall Bairre* which is said to have been at one time preserved in Athlone.[59] The second relic, the Gospel of Bairre, is mentioned in *Cogadh Gaedhel re Gallaibh* about the year 970. The relic is believed to have been given as a pledge of protection by the abbot of Cork to Mahon, elder brother of Brian Boru. When Mahon was killed at the instigation of Maolmuadh, an Ui Eachach chieftain, the relic disappeared from history.

Relatively speaking, the stature of Finbarr of Cork cannot be assessed from comparison with contemporary saints who are associated with him in the *Lives*: Bishop Mac Cuirp of Cliu (d. 606), Brendan of Birr (573), Cainneach of Ossory (598), David of Cell Muine (601), Maedoc of Ferns (626), Eolang of Aghabulloge (620) and Fursa (649).[60] The *Martyrology of Gorman* gives a standard of the saint which is at once short, simple and more inspiring than any that could be framed from comparison: 'May chaste Bairre from Corcach be before me in Heaven, for he was smooth and gentle to the poor.' The *Book of Ballymote* which dates from about the year 1000 preserves for us two stanzas of a poem in his honour which begins: *Bairri breó bithbuadach* . . . We have already seen that Finbarr or Bairre of Corcach Mór heads a list of saints copied into the *Book of Leinster* from the *Martyrology of Tallaght*. More important than any of these references is the inclusion of Saint Finbarr in the *Stowe Missal*, the earliest surviving missal of the Irish church containing the special form of liturgy as used in Ireland in the ninth and tenth centuries. Long lists of early saints, chiefly Irish saints, are inserted into the canon of the *Stowe Missal*; they are given in the genitive and consequently the word

---

59 The Cork Dominicans treasure a monstrance executed in 1669 which embodies the oldest representation of Saint Finbarr. He is depicted in episcopal robes carrying a crozier against a background showing the ancient cathedral with its round tower and the old Dominican priory of Cork, presumably that of Saint Mary of the Island.

60 The above dates, excluding those of David and Maedoc, are approximations.

festus (feast) is understood in each case. The most ancient of
these lists reads as follows:

    . . . sancte brendini . . .

       sancte columba . . . (of Tyrdaglass, one of the Twelve
                            Apostles of Ireland)

       sancte columba . . . (of Iona)

       sancte cainnichi . . .

       sancte findbarri . . .

       sancte nessani . . .

       sancte factni . . .

       sancte lugigi . . .

Professor Kathleen Hughes in her study of *The Church in Early
Irish Society* states that the diptychs of the *Stowe Missal* which
were drawn up between 792 and 812 provide a list of Irish saints
divided into bishops and priests, and points out that liturgical
commemoration began very soon after a saint's death.[61] The
inclusion of Finbarr's name on the most ancient of these lists is
evidence of the growth of an early *cultus* around the Cork patron
and indicates beyond further questioning that a man called
Bairre or Finbarr was endowed with a very definite charism for
what eventually became the diocese of Cork. In itself, this cult
is a weighty counterpoise to Kenney's summary dismissal of the
Lives of Bairre as 'of the late middle ages and quite fabulous'.[62]

Perhaps the most eloquent testimonial to Finbarr came from
his own pupils who carved the name Kilbarry over territories
which even in the saint's day must have owed allegiance to septs
other than the Ui Eachach and the Ui Mic Ciair. In Cork
itself, apart from the Church of Saint Finbarr or the South
Parish, Finbarr is honoured by name in Kilbarry (Blackpool,
cathedral parish of Saint Mary), Kilbarry (parish of Kilmurry),
Kilbarry in Templemartin, Kilbarry (parish of Iveleary), Kilbarry (parish of Dunmanway) and Kilbarry (Kilmoe). The
early cult in honour of Finbarr was probably due as much to
political ambition as to religious fervour and may have developed from the unique politico-ecclesiastical arrangements
then prevailing. (These will be examined in the following
chapter). The saint of the mother church (*matrix ecclesia*) of
any *tuath* became the patron of the *tuath* in such a manner that
the interests of both monastery and local sept became closely
related. It is not unlikely therefore that the growth in prestige
of the Ui Eachach and the cult in honour of Saint Finbarr were
mutually interdependent. And while legend soon busied itself

61   Kathleen Hughes, *The Church in Early Irish Society*, p. 66.

62   Kenney, *Sources*, pp. 401–2.

with the name and fame of Finbarr, such legendary accretion must ever remain extraneous to the abiding work of this great pioneer saint. In Ireland his memory has kept pace with the migration of Corkmen to every part of the country. He is revered as diocesan patron in Caithness, Scotland, whither his fame was brought by missionaries or mariners from Munster, while the Church of Kilbar on the Hebridean Island of Barra is likewise dedicated in honour of the saint of Cork. This island, writes Marjorie O. Anderson, 'seems to have been known by the name of a saint Barr, before Norsemen settled there in the ninth century'.[63] Though commemorated in the seventeenth century on 27 September, the patron of Kilbar is listed as Fymbarrus in the *Breviarum Aberdonense* under date 25 September which is the feast of Finbarr of Cork. Finally, the church of Fowey in Cornwall, which since 1366 has Saint Nicholas as titular, was originally dedicated in honour of Saint Finbarr.[64]

The *Félire Oengussa* indicates 25 September as 'the festival of the loving man, the feast of Bairre of Cork', which according to the *Vision of Mac Conglinne* was preceded by a fast: 'There were the men of Munster in their bands going to Cork for the festival of St. Barre and St. Nessan, in order to fast.'[65] It is probable too that in Cork the medieval custom of singing some Latin verses which embodied an important version of the birth-legend of the saint as found in the Latin and Irish *Lives* was observed.[66] The feast, which was originally celebrated in the monastic church, was subsequently commemorated in the cathedral church of Saint Finbarr which superseded the original foundation in the twelfth century. Here Finbarr was honoured uninterruptedly until the great era of confiscations set in and Catholics were obliged to practice their devotions in secret. The cult of the saint came into its own in 1766 on the establishment of the Church of Saint Finbarr in Dunbar Street, Cork's first post-penal church. Mass on the saint's feast was taken from the common of confessor bishops and special nocturn lessons were sung. In 1805 Dr. Florence MacCarthy, coadjutor bishop of Cork, sought papal sanction for a special Mass in honour of Saint Finbarr; the Mass, he said, was lately

---

63 M. Anderson, 'Columba and Other Irish Saints in Scotland', *Historical Studies*, v (1965), 29.

64 Charles A. Webster, *The Diocese of Cork*, p. 21.

65 Kuno Meyer, ed., *The Vision of Mac Conglinne*, p. 148.

66 The verses which the English historian Meredith Hammer included in his *Chronicle of Ireland* were published in 1633 by Sir James Ware.

found 'in some old missal'. This was probably the missal referred to by the Bollandists who noted 'a Mass for our saint in the Paris Missal for 1734'. The petition described Finbarr as 'patron of the diocese of Cork, and since 1134 titular of the oldest church in the city of Cork, according to the authority of Thomas de Burgo, Bishop of Ossory, in the celebrated work entitled *Hibernia Dominicana*'.[67] Dr. MacCarthy made his request because of a doubt as to whether the Mass in question (a copy of which accompanied the petition) had the sanction of the Holy See. The reply from Rome asked to know the age of the missal referred to, the diocese, church or monastery to which it belonged, and evidence as to the existence of the cult in honour of Saint Finbarr prior to the year 1534. Reference to the 'titular of the oldest church in the city' also called for clarification, since Thomas de Burgo had in mind not the titular church of Saint Finbarr but that built in honour of Saint John the Evangelist (it was called the Abbey *de Antro S. Fymbarri*) at Gill Abbey. The apparent inability of the bishop to comply with these demands of the Holy See explains why the Mass celebrated on the feast of Saint Finbarr is still that from the common of confessor bishops.

Apart from the rather extravagant account of 'seven hundred and seventeen holy bishops of the people of the grace of the Lord in Corcach Mor', comparatively few records remain concerning Saint Finbarr's Cork monastery. Colgan wrote that 'Saint Nessan was educated under Saint Finbarr in a monastery founded by that bishop of Cork.' An old catalogue listing the nine most famous Irish monasteries and their qualifications tells that the School of Cork was renowned 'for the difficult languages of Ireland'.[68] In fact, what Bangor was to Ulster, Cork was to Munster—a guiding light, an oasis in the desert, to which flocked the sons of neighbouring chiefs and many others who were later to attain fame in the church. In spite of its favourable position, however, Cork does not seem to have attracted or catered for any foreign students. Its alumni came mainly from east and west Cork as the appendices to this chapter will show.

67 '. . . quod nuper in veteri quodam missali sit Missa proprie Sancti Barii eiusdem dioecesis patroni, nec non antiquissimae ecclesiae in civitate Corcagiensis, iam ab anno 1134 titularis, juxta Illmum ac Revmum Thomam de Burgo, episcopum Ossoriensen, in celebri opere cui titulus *Hibernia Dominicana*, aliosque scriptores ac indubia testimonia; cumque aliquod dubium exortum sit, an laudata Missa Propria debitam habuerit ab Apostolica Sede sanctionem; idcirco ad omne scrupulum eximendum, humillime supplicet quod Sanctitas Vestra dignetur licentiam concedere cuicumque celebranti, legere propriam illam S Barri Missam eiusdem festo . . .'

68 C. J. F. MacCarthy, 'The Celtic Monastery of Cork', *Cork Hist, Soc. Jn.*, xlviii (1943), 5.

Two of the most outstanding alumni of the School of Cork were Saint Colman Mac Cluasaigh (d. 664) who was known as the sage or *fer legind of Corcaige*, and Saint Cummian *Fota* or *Fada*, son of Fiachra, a west Munster king. To Saint Colman, who became a teacher at the Cork monastery, is accredited the *Sen Dé*, an invocatory hymn which he is said to have composed as a protection against the yellow plague which ravaged Ireland in 664 and to which the saint himself seems to have fallen victim. The *Sen Dé* together with two elegies written by Colman on the death of his friend Cummian *Fada* in 662 constitute Cork's oldest literature. Saint Cummian is described in the *Martyrology of Donegal* as 'the vessel of wisdom of his time'. He received his early education at Saint Ide's school at Killeedy, county Limerick, after which 'he studied at Cork and became a sage'. Later he became abbot of Clonfert and *comharba* of Saint Brendan (*comharba Brendani*). He belonged to the Eoghanacht Locha Lein, the western branch of the ruling race of Munster, and as with other Irish saints has become the centre of a great accretion of legendary matter. Extant texts relating to him are given by Kenney under three headings: (1) a dialogue in verse between Cummian *Fada* and *mac-da-cherda* concerning moral and religious questions and found in the *Yellow Book of Lecan*;[69] (2) part of a cycle of stories connected with Guaire Aidne, king of Connaught, at whose court Cummian shared his versatility as a *segond* or champion with two other Munstermen, one a poet, the other a fool (this is also found in the *Yellow Book of Lecan*);[70] and (3) some anecdotes concerning *mac-da-cherda* and his association with Cummian *Fada*.[71] The *Laudem Apostolorum* which Kenney does not mention is also attributed to Cummian *Fada*, who is likewise author of a penitential which he composed around the middle of the seventh century. The asceticism of this penitential is somewhat milder than that demanded by Saint Columbanus half a century earlier, and Cummian's strictures are applied with more discretion. References in the penitential of Cummian to clerical grades other than those living under monastic discipline prove that monasticism, for all its expansion, had not superseded completely the earlier church organization in which power was vested in the bishops.[72]

69 *Y.B.L.*, col. 335, p. 326.

70 Ibid., col. 797, p. 133.

71 Kenney, *Sources*, p. 420.

72 Hughes, *Ch. in early Ir. soc.*, p. 75.

The ninth century was an unhappy one for the monastery of
Saint Finbarr and for Cork, which was eleven times plundered
in the course of a single century. Still the monastery carried on,
no longer perhaps as a great school but as a community of
religious. Several accounts suggest that the monastery of Saint
Finbarr did not weather the storm of adversity and that the
community made a temporary transfer to the safer northern
sector of the city, to *Foithrib Aedh* in *Magh Tuath*. Traces of
monastic life and names like Clogheen, Kilbarry (near Tober-
barry) and Kilnap (*Cill a nAp*, the church of the abbots) give
support to this theory but cannot be accepted as final criteria.
Whether it was located in the north or south of the city is irrel-
evant; what matters is that the monastery of Saint Finbarr
survived and the various annals indicate—with some unavoidable gaps—that a continuity of episcopo-monastic rulers was
maintained there from the seventh century to the eleventh.
During these centuries the Irish church underwent a great
metamorphosis of structure and administration, the details of
which will be treated in the following chapter, and for a better
understanding of which the final appendix to the present
chapter will serve both as visual aid and reference column.

APPENDIX A

Alumni of the School of Loch Irce

EOLANG   Finbarr's tutor (*aite*). This was Saint Olan of Aghabulloge, who is commemorated in the *Calendars of Irish
   Saints* under 5 September.

COLMAN   Connected with Daire Dunchon according to the
   Lives: probably of Derridonee near Gougane Barra.

BAITHIN   Believed to be one of the disciples of Saint Ruadhan
   whom Saint Finbarr placed at Cell na Cluaine.

NESSAN   This saint's name is linked with that of Finbarr in an
   old litany copied into the *Book of Leinster*, in the *Vision of
   Mac Conglinne* and in Colgan's *Acta Sanctorum Hiberniae*.
   He is believed to have been Finbarr's successor.

GARBHAN   *Garbhan mac Finnbarra*: may be founder of Kil-
   garvan, a parish to the west of Gougane Barra and in the
   diocese of Kerry.

TALMACH   Has no Cork connection, but there is mention of
   Saint Talmach, companion of Brendan the Navigator. He
   is probably connected with Kiltallagh near Castlemaine,
   county Kerry.

FINCHAD   Called Finchad of *Domnach Mór*. Otherwise unknown.

FACHTNA   Called *Fachtnan* in the Latin, and *Fachtna of Cill Ria*
   in the Irish *Life*, this saint is otherwise unidentifiable.

FACHTNA   *Fachtna of Ros Ailithir*: Fachtna Mac Mongaig,
   founder of Ros Ailithir (Rosscarbery), the chief monastic
   centre of the Corca Laighdhe or O'Driscoll tribeland which
   later became the diocese of Ross. From the few extant
   details of his life, Fachtna lived at an earlier period than
   Saint Finbarr. He is chiefly associated with Saint Ita (*Íde*)
   who died in 568 and with Saint Brendan the Navigator who
   died about the year 572. The *Book of Genealogy of Corca
   Laighdhe* makes Fachtna a contemporary of Conall Claon,
   chief of Corca Laighdhe, whose place in the pedigrees puts
   him between the years 500 and 560.

Lucher, Coman, Lochine of Achad Airaird   Saint Coman
is better known as Mocomóg; he was patron of Kilmocomoge or Bantry. The genealogies of the Beanntraighe give his
pedigree. Saints Lucher and Lochine are otherwise unknown.

Carine, Fintan, Eothaile of Ros Caerach   *Ros Caerach* is
identified with Roskeragh or Sheep's Head in Muintervara
(Durrus), lying south of Bantry Bay. Nothing is known of
these saints connected with it.

Trellan   Also called Grellan of Druim Draighnighe; perhaps
of Drinagh.

Caelchú   Unknown.

Mogenna   Simplified to M'Eanna. The name occurs in Kil-
manna at the western end of the Bere peninsula.

Modimmoc   A by-form of Dimma. Saint Dimma, son of
Cormac, brother of Aedh Uargarb, was companion of
Saint Mochua or Carthage of Lismore (d. 637). He in-
structed Dimma as follows: 'Go at once to the land of Ui
Eachach in south Munster. . . . Your tribe shall engage in
internecine warfare if you do not arrive in time to hinder it.'
Dimma went to his own country and 'preaching the Divine
Precept, made peace among them (the Ui Eachach); and
he built a monastery in his own country which he offered
as a gift to Carthage, who did not accept it.' (Plummer,
Vitae SS Hib., i, 183).

Sanctan   Unidentified.

Luiger Mac Coluim   Unidentified.

APPENDIX B

Saints who Offered their Churches to Bairre

Iuran Brit, with Nathi and Breccan of Bairnech Mór in
Muscraighe   Iuran may have given his name to Magourney,
now Coachford, west of Berrings, which is identified with
Bairnech Mór.

Lugaid, son of Fintan, of the Dal Modula of Airthir
Cliach, of the church of Cenn Dromma at Carn Tigernaigh
in the territory of Fermoy   From the Decretal Letter of 1199
it is clear that the bishop of Cork held three churches 'in
the territory of Fermoy', one of which was Cennmuighe,
the modern Kilcanway. *Cenn Dromma* and *Cennmuighe*
may perhaps be interchangeable.

BAETAN MAC EOGHAIN AND MODIMMOC   Two bishops who occupied *Gleann Cáin in Luigdech Éile*, that is, Borrisoleigh, county Tipperary. Otherwise unknown.

SARAN   Described as holding *Druim Eidnech in Ui Luigdech Éile*. Unidentified.

GOBBAN CORR OF FAN LOPAIST   Fanlobbus, now Dunmanway church and parish. Smith's *History of Cork* (i, 42) quotes 'Sanct. Morragh *alias* Gobbancorn de Fanlobbish'. Nothing further is known of this saint.

FINTAN AND DOMANGEN   Mutually connected with *Cluain Fota* (*Fada*) and *Tulach Mín*; otherwise unidentified.

BROGAN   This entry reads: 'Brogan, son of Senan, was a pupil of Bairre, and he offered himself and his church, Cluain Carnai, to Bairre in perpetuity.' Brogan was in all probability founder of Kilbrogan, Bandon.

APPENDIX C

Saints associated with Bairre in the Lives

FACHTNA   Fachtna of Cill Ria, as above.

ELTIN MAC COBTHAIG   Described as of Cell na hIndsi; not mentioned elsewhere as a pupil of Bairre.

FERGUS FINNABRACH   According to the Irish *Life* Fergus occupied *Finnabhair na Rig*, now identified with Finnure in Corkbeg. Corkbeg and the adjoining Aghada belonged to the diocese of Cork in 1199.

CONDIRE   *Conaire* or *Condire mac Foirtcheirn of Tulach Ratha*. If *Tulach Ratha* may be identified as *Tulach Condire*, Tullycondra in the parish of Ballyclough to the northwest of Mallow is suggested. *Tulach Ratha* belonged to Cork in 1199 but has since become incorporated in Cloyne.

LIBER   *Liber of Cell Ia* is associated with Killeagh, county Cork and diocese of Cloyne.

SINNEL   *Silanus* or *Sinnel of Cluain Bruices*, that is, of Clonpriest near Youghal. Killeagh and Clonpriest belonged to the diocese of Cork in 1199.

FINGIN AND TRIAN   Segenus and Trienus (Latin *Life*) were of Domnach Mor Mitine, but there is no proof that Donoughmore in Muskerry, as here identified, ever belonged to the diocese of Cork.

MOCHOLMOC MAC GRILLINE   The Irish *Life* describes this saint as of Ros Ailithir, and he is referred to in *Genealogies of Irish Saints* (Laud MS 610) as 'Colman mac Giriltin from whom

Ros Ailithir is named'. Mocholmoc is a by-form of Colman.
His period is unknown.

FACHTNA MAC MONGAIG   Fachtna of Ross, as above.

COLMAN   Colman of *Cenn Eich* or Kinneigh. He was patron of
the Cinel Laoghaire or O'Donoghue sept. The monastery
of Kinneigh was founded about the year 619 and was situated about half-a-mile west of the present round tower
which dates from about 1014. Little is known of the monastery of Kinneigh; the only relevant annalistic entry comes
from the *Annals of the Four Masters* to the effect that
'Forbasach, son of Maeluidhir, Abbot of Cill-mor-Cinnech,
died, 750.'

MUADAN AND CAIRPRE   Two bishops who, according to the
Lives occupied *Cell Muadan*; otherwise unidentified.

APPENDIX D

Succession-List of the Monastery of Cork

651   Saint Nessan, *comharba Barre*, died.

682   Suibhne son of Maelumha, *comharba Barre* of Corcach,
died (*Chron. Scot.*). Annalistic variations on the date
of his death are: 677 (*Ann. Clon.*); 680 (*A.F.M.*); 681
(*A.U.*); 682 (*Ann. Tig.*). Suibhne is styled *princeps* by
Tigernach and *uasal eascub* in *Ann. Clon.*

687   Russin (Roisen, Roisten), abbot of Corcach-Mor, died
(*Ann. Inisf.* and *A.F.M.*). *Colgan refers to Russinus,
filius Lappain, comharbus S. Barri* (Colgan, *Acta SS
Hib.*, p. 148). The date of Russin's death is given as 683
in *Chronicon Scotorum*.

687–   Void, or at least unaccounted for in the annals. It seems
759   probable that Manchin who is mentioned in the *Vision
of Mac Conglinne* was abbot for a time during this
period.

759   Donat Mac Tuathence, abbot of Corcach-mor, died
(*A.F.M.*).

774   Selbach Mac Cualta, abbot of Cork, died (*Ann. Inisf.*).
The Four Masters place his death at 767.

792   Terog, abbot of Cork, died (*Ann. Inisf.*) The *Annals of
Ulster* state that Teroc, *princeps* of Corcach-mor died
in 791.

816   Conaing (Connmhach, son of Donat), abbot of Corcach-
mor, died (*Ann. Inisf.*).

821   Forbasach (Forbhasach) *comharba* Barre of Cork, died

(*A.F.M.*). The next entry for the same year records the death of Selbach of Inis Pic.

825   Fland Mac Forceallaich, abbot of Lismore, Emly and Corcach-mor, died (*Ann. Inisf.*). The *Annals of Ulster* record his death in 824 and style him abbot of Lismore only.

836   Dunlaing Mac Cathusaigh, *princeps* of Corcach-mor, died without communion at Cashel (*A.U.*). The Four Masters place his death at 832 and style him 'abbot of Corcach'; they give the same name with the title of '*comharba* Barra of Corcach' under 835. Sir James Ware does not mention him.

836   Feidlimid (king of Cashel) 'entered into the abbacy of Cork' (*Ann. Inisf.*).

852   Colum, son of Airechtach, abbot of Cork, died (*Chron. Scot.*). His death is placed at 850 by the Four Masters.

863   Domhnall Ua Laithidhe, abbot of Corcach and Lismore, was mortally wounded (*Ann. Inisf.* and *Chron. Scot.*). The Four Masters record his death in 861.

866   Rechtabhra, son of Murchadh, abbot of Corcach, died (*A.F.M.*). His death is given as 868 in *Chronicon Scotorum*.

875   Domhnall, bishop of Cork, an eminent scribe (*Episcopus Corcaighe, scriba optimus*), died suddenly (*A.U.*). The death is recorded in 874 (*A.F.M.*) and in 876 (*Chron. Scot.*).

891   Saorbreathach, son of Conad, 'scribe, prophet, bishop and abbot of Cork', died (*A.F.M.*). He is called 'sage, bishop and abbot' in *Chronicon Scotorum* under date 896.

892   Airigetan Mac Forandain, abbot of Cork, died (*A.F.M.*).

907   Ailill, son of Eoghan, abbot of Corcach-mor, fell in battle with the King of Ciarraighe Luachra (*Chron. Scot.*).

911   Flann Mac Lughadh, abbot of Cork, 'fell asleep' in this year (*A.U.*). His death is given under 907 in *Chronicon Scotorum*.

928   Fiannachta, abbot and bishop of Cork, died (*Ann. Inisf.*). The Four Masters, who record his death under 926, call him 'head of the rule of most of Ireland.' The *Chronicon Scotorum* in recording his death in 927 does not call him bishop.

951   Ailill, abbot of Cork died (*Ann. Inisf.*). An entry in the *Annals of the Four Masters* for 949 tells that 'Ailill mac Cuirc, abbot of Corcach, died.'

952   Aedh Mac Garbhath, abbot of Cork and Lord of

Dartraighe, was killed by robbers (*A.F.M.*). The entry
in *Chron. Scot.* under 953 reads: 'Aedh, son of Gairbith,
King of Cairbre-mor and Dartraighe *a suis (occisus
est)*'.

958   Cathmhogh, superior of Lismore and bishop of Cork,
      died (*A.F.M.*). The *Annals of Inisfallen* carry the
      entry: 'Cathmog, Bishop of Cork and Abbot of Lis-
      more', while the *Annals of Ulster* call Cathmog
      Airchinnech of Lismore.

978   Cork was invaded and Finnechta, bishop, died (*Ann.
      Inisf.*).

989   Colum Mac Ciaruchain, *comharba* Barre, died (*Ann.
      Inisf.*). The *Annals of Ulster* and of the *Four Masters*
      call him *airchinnech* (later erenagh or herenagh) of
      Cork.

997   Colman of Corcach died (*Ann. Inisf.*). He is not de-
      scribed as either abbot or bishop.

c.1000 'Gilla Patraic ua Enne, *comharba* Bairre': this entry is
      found in the Genealogy of Dal Chais in the *Book of
      Ballymote* (p. 186) and in the *Book of Lecan* (p. 433).

1001 Flaithemh, abbot of Corcach, died (*Ann. Inisf.*).

1006 Ceallach O Meanngorain, *airchinneach* of Cork, died
      (*Ann. Inisf.*).

1009 Diarmaid, *comharba* Barre, died (*Ann. Inisf.*).

1016 Cormac, son of Dunlaing, *comharba* Barre, died
      (*Ann. Inisf.*).

1025 Ceallach Ua Sealbaig, *comharba* Barre, went on pil-
      grimage to Rome (*Ann. Inisf.*).

1026 Niall O Maoldubh (Niall Meiccduib), *comharba* Barre,
      died (*Ann. Inisf.*). The Four Masters give his death
      under 1027.

1027 Art Ua hAirt, *comharba* Barre, died (*Ann. Inisf.*). He
      ruled for less than a year.

1034 Cathal Martyr, *comharba* Barre, died (*A.F.M.*). He is
      styled *airchinnech Corcaighe* in the *Annals of Ulster*.

1036 Oengus, son of Cathan, abbot of Corcach, died
      (*A.F.M.*). The *Annals of Inisfallen* call him 'bishop
      and celibate'. The Four Masters record that he oc-
      cupied the see for only two months.

1036 Ceallach O Saolbach (Hua Selbaig), 'chief anchorite of
      Ireland, *comharba* Barre and learned senior of Munster'
      died (*Ann. Inisf.*). The Four Masters call him *epscop*.

1057 Hua Mutain, *airchinnech* and *fer legind* of Cork, was
      killed in Rosscarbery by the Ui Floinn Arda (*Ann.
      Inisf.*). The entry in the *Annals of the Four Masters* is

to the effect that Mugron Ua Mutain, '*comharba* Barre, noble bishop and lector, was killed by robbers of the Corca Laighdhe after his return from vespers.' The *Annals of Tigernach* states that Mugron Hua Mutain, '*comharba* Barra, *espoc*, was slain by his own community as he was coming from the nocturn'.

1057 Dubdalethe Ua Cinaedha, *airchinnech* of Cork, slept in the Lord (*A.U.*). The *Annals of Loch Cé* carry the same entry.

1085 Clereach Ua Sealbaigh, *ard comharba* Barre, 'the glory and wisdom of Desmond, completed his life in this world'. (*A.F.M.*). He is called *airchinnech* in the *Annals of Ulster*, while the *Annals of Inisfallen* add that 'he was succeeded by Mac Bethad Hua Ailgenain of the Dal Chais'.

1095 Gillachrist O Ruaidhri, anchorite of the Ui Toirdealbaigh (the O'Brien sept), died in Cork (*Ann. Inisf.*).

1096 O Cochlain, a learned bishop and successor (*comharba*) of Barre, died (*A.F.M.*).

1106 Mac Bethad Hua Ailgenain (O Hailgenain), *comharba* Barre, died (*A.F.M.*).

1109 Gilla Padraic Ua Sealbaigh, *comharba* Barre, died (*Ann. Inisf.* and *A.U.*). He seems to have been bishop as well as abbot, and is also referred to as *Vicarius Barri*.

1112 Domhnall O Saolbach was *airchinnech* of Cork.

1118 Diarmait Ua Briain died in Corcach Mor Mumhan after a victory of penance (*Ann. Inisf.*).

1137 Finn, grandson of Celechar Ui Ceinneidig, *comharba* Colum, son of Crimthann, was *comharba* Barre 'for a time' (*A.F.M.*). He became abbot of Terryglass (*Tirdá-ghlas*) and belonged to the sept of Dal Chais. He died in 1152.

1140 Domhnall O Saolbach, *airchinnech* of Cork, died (*A.U.*).

1146 Giolla Padraic MacCarthy was *airchinnech* of Cork. The Four Masters and the *Annals of Ulster* record his death under the year 1157.

II

A Church in Transition

During the fourth and fifth centuries the Christian church in western Europe became organized along the lines of a territorial episcopate in which the bishop, *episcopus*, was the chief depository of sacerdotal functions and of ecclesiastical jurisdiction. The city where his residence (chair, *cathedra*) was established became the centre of administration, and the limits within which the administrative area was confined came to be known as the *dioecesis*. The bishop's assistants in the work of serving the churches and ministering to the people of the *dioecesis* were known as *presbyteri*, or priests, to whom, in course of time and according as diocesan organization was improved and extended, special districts called *parochiae* were assigned. Such a system must have been in the minds of those who in 431 sent Palladius as first bishop to the Irish believing in Christ; it must have been equally in the mind of Patrick when he described himself as 'a bishop, appointed by God in Ireland'.[1] By the seventh century, however, the Celtic church had undergone a major structural change and from then until the introduction of the twelfth-century reform it operated on a more or less closed circuit which was peculiarly Hibernian. Its peculiarities were most marked in liturgy, tonsure, methods of administering baptism and episcopal consecration, the date of celebrating Easter and, above all, the system of church organization and discipline. The foundation in the second half of the sixth century of the great monastic *paruchiae* gave impetus to the change-over in church organization and discipline; henceforward the functional power of a bishop who was not also an abbot was confined almost exclusively to the conferring of orders. His jurisdictional power was practically nil. Our purpose in this chapter is to trace this deviation from continental usage and to assess its effect on the

1 Kenney, *Sources*, p. 291.

diocese of Cork in the centuries between the death of Finbarr and the eventual establishment of a territorial episcopate.

The continental background whence Saint Patrick returned to Ireland in 432 was so impregnated with the monastic traditions of Lerins, Marmoutier and Auxerre that monasticism is regarded as coeval with Christianity in its entry into this country. But Patrick, for all his partiality towards the cenobitic life, executed his work in Ireland as a bishop, and it is becoming daily more apparent through the researches of Irish and non-Irish scholars that in the first era of Irish church history the administration was episcopal and that monastic churches were in the minority. As pointers to the organization of the first-century Irish church we have the canons of the first Synod of Patrick; these canons which are attributed to Patrick, Auxilius and Iserninus are now accepted as dating from the sixth century.[2] Their importance is that they show a church governed by bishops with each bishop exercising jurisdiction within his own *paruchia*, an area coterminous with the *tuath* or unit of secular administration. The bishop had clergy of all grades in his entourage; on these Roman tonsure was enjoined, they were expected to adopt Roman conventions of dress, to attend matins and vespers in the church, those who were married were permitted to cohabit with their wives and to see that they were veiled when they went out.[3] On this matter of clerical marriage Professor Binchy points out that the secular jurists of the seventh and eighth centuries distinguished between the celibate bishop (*epscop óige*) and the married bishop (*epscop óenséitche*), and he recalls a passage from the *Book of Armagh* which depicts Patrick as seeking out as a suitable bishop 'a man of one wife to whom but one child has been born'.[4] Finally, the canons attributed to Patrick, Auxilius and Iserninus show clearly that monasticism was already established in Ireland, but monks seem to have been excluded from all participation in the work of the *paruchia*.[5]

The early eighth-century *Collectio Canonum Hibernensis* is seen to be generally consistent with the earlier canons attributed to Patrick, Auxilius and Iserninus inasmuch as the *Collectio* likewise refers to a church under episcopal jurisdiction, and in describing the duties of the various grades it 'starts with the

2 For arguments on the proposed dates of these canons, see Hughes, *Ch. in early Ir. soc.*, pp. 45–50; for Professor D. A. Binchy's comments on Dr. Hughes's findings see his review of her book in *Studia Hib.*, vii (1967), 217.

3 Hughes, *Ch. in early Ir. soc.*, p. 50.

4 Binchy, Review, *Studia Hib.*, vii, 219.

5 Hughes, *Ch. in early Ir. soc.*, p. 52.

episcopus and moves down through the *sacerdos* (priest) and the rest to the *ostiarius*'.[6] But while the majority of the canons of this *Collectio* are geared to a church governed by bishops, they must be read in context with the acts of the seventh Irish Synod (*Synodus Hibernensis*) which the *Collectio* quotes and which show clearly a swing towards a church in which administration is abbatial and in which the abbot is accorded the title of *princeps*; a church moreover which gains in prestige through the presence of a bishop—living or dead—to whom the highest honour continued to be paid, as may be inferred from three secular law tracts of the seventh and eighth centuries. In *Uraicecht Becc*, which is a tract of the late seventh or early eighth century and which gives the honour-price of all clerical grades from lector to bishop, the bishop, who is usually referred to as *uasal eascub*, is accorded an honour-price equivalent to that of an over-king.[7] In this context we find that Suibhne Mac Maelumha, who was successor or coarb of Saint Finbarr and who died in 682, was described in the *Annals of Clonmacnoise* as such a bishop-prince;[8] similarly with Mugron Hua Mutain in the *Annals of the Four Masters* under date 1057. These two successors of Finbarr commanded the same honour-price as the kings of Munster. The *Crith Gablach*, an early eighth-century tract, while it varies in incidental valuations outlines seven secular grades to correspond, one would imagine, with a similarly gradated ecclesiastical scale. According to this tract the bishop's honour-price would appear to correspond to that of a petty king. Thirdly, an extract from another early eighth-century tract called *Miadshlecta* gives a classification which accords the highest honour-price in Ireland to the celibate bishop.[9]

It is clear therefore that the early post-Patrician church became integrated into Celtic society without any compromise to Celtic tradition and that within this society the higher clergy were accorded a position of dignity equal to that of kings. Bishops, scribes, abbots and priests are all catered for in the secular law tracts, while special prestige attached to the *scriba* or *sapiens*, the later *fer legind* of the Irish monasteries. When first encountered, the *scriba* indicates the existence of a school in which Latin predominated; when later designated as *fer legind*

6 Ibid., p. 48.

7 *Ancient Laws and Institutes of Ireland*, v, 110–112.

8 The *Chronicon Scotorum* records the death of another Suibhne son of Maeluma for the year 891 and designates him as 'anchorite of Cluain-muc-Nois'.

9 Hughes, *Ch. in early Ir. soc.*, pp. 134–6.

he represents a shift in emphasis from Latin to the vernacular in the educational system. This was a post-Viking development. Successors of Finbarr in Cork who fall within this category are: Domhnall, bishop of Cork, whose obituary in the *Annals of Ulster* (875) describes him as *scriba optimus*. He was succeeded by Saorbreathach, son of Conad, whom the Four Masters (891) call 'scribe, prophet, bishop and abbot of Cork' and who is called 'sage, bishop and abbot' in the *Chronicon Scotorum*. The next individual to be so designated was Ceallach O Saolbach who is called *epscop* by the Four Masters and whom the *Annals of Inisfallen* describe as 'chief anchorite of Ireland, *comharba* Barre and learned senior of Munster'. He died in 1036. Other eleventh-century entries tell of Clereach Ua Sealbaigh (1085) *ard-comharba* Barre, 'he was the glory and wisdom of Desmond', and Ua Cochlain, 'a learned bishop' who died in 1096.

The grafting of the new shoot of Christianity on to the older stem of pagan Celtic society eventually generated an imbalance which, in turn, effected a transition from an episcopal to a monastic church. The change-over is not universally traceable— it did not conform to any well-furrowed pattern—but its basic developmental factor is to be found in the tribal and rural nature of Celtic society. Here, amidst the concentration of petty kingdoms, in a milieu lacking central administration and where town-life was unknown, a church organized on more highly developed contintental lines of centralization and organization was completely out of place. On the other hand, monasticism with its stress on the *abbas*, the father, coincided more satisfactorily with the familial nature of Irish tribal life. 'A monastic church', writes Dr. Hughes, 'with its respect for kindred and its ideas of overlordship fitted far more readily into that [legal] framework [of Irish society] than did the Roman-style bishop.'[10] From the sixth century, therefore, to the twelfth, monasticism was the chief characteristic of the Irish church. It was a peculiar type of monasticism: gilt-edged with the asceticism of saints like Columbanus and Cummian *Fada*, riddled with abuses even in the pre-Viking period, operating a highly specialized system of succession and presenting a host of monastic officials and hangers-on whose duties, status and importance continue to pose vexatious problems for the historian.

The second half of the sixth century was the foundation period of the great monastic *paruchiae* or federations, and to this period belong the monasteries of Derry, Durrow, Bangor, Clonmacnoise, Kildare and Iona. From now on authority is

10 Ibid., p. 133.

vested in the abbot, with the administrative transfer being very clearly indicated in the annals. Up to the mid-sixth century episcopal entries predominate; for the remainder of the century bishops and abbots appear in almost equal numbers, but from the seventh century onwards bishops are seen to yield place to abbots. The annals therefore suggest that monasticism was encouraged, and they indicate that some great monastic *paruchiae* were being founded between c. 540 and 615. Applying this annalistic evidence to the church in Cork—its foundation-date, 606, places it in the monastic-*paruchia* period but nonetheless church organization here showed traces of an early diocesan arrangement—we find that apart from Suibhne Mac Maelumha the *uasal-eascub* who died in 682, the successors of Saint Finbarr during the seventh and eighth centuries and for the greater part of the ninth century were invariably abbots. They are described as abbot, *comharba* or *princeps*, and it is not until 875 that the term bishop of Cork, *Episcopus Corcaighe*, makes its appearance in pride of place in the *Annals of Ulster*. This bishop was Domhnall, the *scriba optimus* or eminent scribe, who was succeeded by Saorbreathach Mac Conaid, 'scribe, prophet, bishop *and* abbot of Cork' according to the Four Masters. Thereafter the following successors of Finbarr are listed as both abbots (or coarbs) and bishops: Fiannachta, 928; Cathmog, 961; Finnechta, 978; Niall O Maoldubh, 1026–27; O Cochlain, 1096, and Gilla Padraic Ua Sealbaigh, 1109. In addition to these, Oengus Mac Cathain who ruled for only two months in 1036 is described as abbot in the *Annals of Inisfallen* and as bishop and celibate by the Four Masters.

With the expansion of monasticism and the organization of federated *paruchiae*, the abbot came gradually to supersede the bishop in the hierarchy of ecclesiastical power. The abbot, who might or might not be a bishop, was head of the tribe of his church, his position approximated that of the secular overlord and, like the secular overlord, he had legal responsibilities towards the tribe and in the administration of the church's property. Secondly, he was father of his church, and if in orders himself he was charged with the spiritual formation of his monastic family (*familia*). Thirdly, he was the adviser and protector of the laity. Distinctions were drawn between abbots who were bishops and those who were not, and between priest-abbots and non-clerical holders of the abbatial office. As a rule, church leaders were expected to be in major orders, but abbots, at least in the seventh century, do not appear to have been always obliged to conform to this requirement. On the other hand the prestige of a church was measured against its having a bishop, a *fer legind* and an abbot, and it was not uncommon to find all three offices vested in the one person. Our frequently quoted Saorbreathach Mac Conaid is a classic example of this practice. Where the abbot was not a bishop it was customary to have a resident bishop within the monastery. Under such an arrangement the system in practice in Iona seems to have been generally adhered to. In Iona the abbot exercised jurisdictional power over the internal and external affairs of his monastery and *paruchia*, leaving to the bishop the execution of the functions of order and the duty of officiating at the sacraments reserved to the episcopal office.

But monasticism, while it found its natural habitat in the rural and familial economy of Celtic Ireland, never entirely eclipsed the earlier continental-type of territorial diocesan organization. In the seventh century when the monastic *paruchiae* flourished, when abbots were overlords of monasteries with their property and dependents, when special privileges were accorded to monks and when their properties were safe-guarded by immunities, even then, bishops continued to function outside the monastic system and the secular clergy had their spheres of activity. We have mentioned that the seventh-century *Penitential of Cummian* makes this abundantly clear; so does the eighth-century *Crith Gablach* which vindicates the dignity of bishops in contemporary Ireland.[11] Many of the earlier dioceses, however, found it necessary to conform to the monastic pattern, if only for survival's sake, and in this way Armagh effected a successful transition from the old to the new. So did Clonmacnoise and Kildare, and the development may equally apply to Cork where the contractual relationship effected between Finbarr and the saints who surrendered their churches to him, and the personnel of his school in Cork suggest some pre-monastic type of diocesan arrangement. The preponder-ance of abbots in the succession lists suggests that the change-over must have occurred at an early stage.

The implications of territorial overlordship inherent in Celtic monasticism brought the church into closer fusion with secular society to the extent of effecting far-reaching changes in the system by which monastic succession was determined. The head of the monastery became the ecclesiastical counterpart of the tribal king in his *tuath*, for 'once the church had been assimilated into the native society it was almost inevitable that the native pattern of succession to tribal kingship should be

11 D. A. Binchy, *Crith Gablach, passim.*

applied to Irish monasteries,' as Professor Binchy observes.[12] The Irish aristocracy now wanted to found monasteries, retaining to themselves certain rights over these monasteries and their lands. The system of succession to abbatial dignity was therefore clear-cut. The secular law tracts show that in the first case it devolved upon the 'founder's kin' or the blood relations of the patron saint. Should there be no suitable candidate in this group (as was the case in Cork), selection went to the 'donor's kin' or the descendants of the family who had donated land to the founder. When failure was registered in this group (as seemingly happened again in Cork) the choice was widened to include outsiders. Family succession to abbacies did not always connote that abbots were generally non-celibate, for succession extended to the more distant relationships of nephews and cousins—to all, in fact, who could claim descent from the same common ancestor. It was only natural that the 'donor's kin' of a particular monastery should endeavour to keep up a family interest in its abbacy, and herein lay many abuses. Iona is known to have followed a course acceptable at once to native custom and to the ecclesiastical rule of celibacy, but Iona's procedure did not at all apply to the general run of Celtic monasteries where the predominance of an ecclesiastical kindred became very marked. Family influence in Armagh is seen in the long list of abbots belonging to the Clann Sinnaigh; it is seen in the Ua Rebachain succession in Lios Mór and in the Ua Sealbaigh hegemony in Cork. By the eighth century direct succession from father to son had become common in places, but there is no clear evidence of such a development in Cork, not even in the case of the powerful Clann Sealbaigh who first appear in 1025 with Cellach O Sealbaigh and thereafter at irregular intervals: Clereach Ua Sealbaigh, 1085; Gilla Padraic Ua Sealbaig, 1109; Domhnall O Saolbach, 1140. This, of course, does not preclude the possibility of non-celibate abbots in Cork. One may indeed ask if celibacy was so unusual in the eleventh century that abbot Oengus Mac Cathain's obituary notice in the *Annals of Inisfallen* announced that he was 'bishop *and* celibate'. In the final analysis our evidence is not sufficient to justify a conclusion either way, but it is worth noting that there was no trace of hereditary monastic succession in Cork in the pre-Viking age.

The population content of an Irish monastery of the seventh and eighth centuries was perhaps one of the most intriguing features of Celtic monasticism. Far from being confined to abbots, bishops, clerics and copyists or *scribae*, it comprised a

12　Binchy, Review, *Studia Hib.*, vii, 217.

heterogeneous assembly of inmates nominally called *manaig* who were monastic tenants rather than monks with vows and towards whom the church had certain obligations. These obligations are outlined in the Rule of the Culdees (Céli Dé) which lays down that the church must provide baptism, communion and intercessory prayer for its *manaig*.[13] Furthermore, the secular law tracts indicate the existence of some form of contractual relationship entailing mutual rights and duties as between an abbot and his *manaig*. The *Synodus Hibernensis* makes it clear that these *manaig* or monastic clients were married, that their sons were educated within the monasteries, that while they managed the monastic flocks and lands they paid tribute to the church for lands held from the church and that they passed on their liabilities to their eldest sons. The *manaig* were an accepted part of the ecclesiastical society of their time and as such they were obliged at certain periods to conform to a rigorous code of sexual abstinence. There were instances too when the *manaig* had the right to elect a new abbot.

Exclusive of the *manaig*, the typical Irish monastery comprised three other groups, namely, vowed monks bound to complete chastity *in habitu religioso*, clerics and nuns living in complete poverty and sharing a communal church, and finally, ascetics living under the direction of a religious senior. The picture that emerged in the seventh and eighth centuries, therefore, shows monks living a regular communal life of poverty and celibacy side by side with other married 'monks' who were educated by the church and who held land and stock as clients of the church. The threat to pristine monasticism in such a set-up was realized in the ultimate laicization of the monasteries, but for the time being the client system guaranteed a constant income for the church in the form of tithes, first-fruits, burial fees and the like.

During the seventh century, when monasticism was giving its peculiar stamp to the Celtic church, the Romanizing party within the church was endeavouring to iron out the other peculiarities which, on the resumption of continental contacts, showed that the church in Ireland and in Britain was seriously at variance with continental practice. Of most immediate concern was the Celtic calculation of Easter which varied considerably from that observed elsewhere. The dispute as such goes beyond the ambit of the present study and need not be delayed upon. During its course, the Romanizing party found a champion in Cummian (believed to have been abbot of Durrow), who feared that the stubborn Irish 'who are almost at

13   Hughes, *Ch. in early Ir. soc.*, p. 140, quoting Rule of Céli Dé 57.

the ends of the earth . . . a pimple on the chin of the world'
would be cut off from the body of the church. Unity was the
desideratum on this question much more than on the matter of
liturgy, tonsure and episcopal consecration which was performed in Ireland by one instead of three bishops. The churches
of southern Ireland seem to have accepted the Roman calculation of Easter in the 630s, unlike the north which held out until
704, while Iona with its federated churches did not submit
until 716. Triumph for the Romanizing party did nothing
whatever to halt the development of the monastic *paruchiae*,
nor did it arrest the efforts being made by Armagh lawyers to
achieve precedence for Patrick's church and successor over the
other churches and coarbs of Ireland. The cause of the lawyers
was a lost one. Existing *paruchiae* continued to assert their
autonomy, decentralization was upheld and the effort to achieve
uniformity had to wait until the twelfth century when the monastic foundations yielded place to an episcopal church with
fixed diocesan boundaries and the hierarchy that such a church
presupposed.

The promulgation between 697 and 842 of a series of laws,
cána, some nine in number, illustrates the correlative jurisdiction that had by then been effected between lay and ecclesiastical rulers. Legislation was half-secular, half-ecclesiastical;
the laws (also defined as tributes) entailed that in return for
certain benefits the people were obliged to render certain
payments to the abbot or coarb of the monastic church of the
saint in whose name the law or *cáin* was promulgated. Peace
and the protection of non-combatants seem to have been the
original purpose of many of the *cána*, four of which are listed
on the commentary to the *Félire Oengussa*. These were 'Patrick's
law [*cáin Pátraic*] not to kill the clergy; and Adamnan's law
[*cáin Adamnáin*] not to kill women; Daire's law [*cáin Dáire*]
not to kill cattle and the law of Sunday [*cáin Domnaig*] not to
transgress thereon'.[14] Fines for non-observance of these *cána*
were a valuable contribution to the prosperity of the monastery
from which they were promulgated. In consequence of this
wealth, the church of the late eighth and early ninth centuries,
with its lay abbots, married clergy, hereditary succession to
ecclesiastical appointments, offices held in plurality, had moved
a long way from its apostolic era. An entry in the *Annals of the
Four Masters* for 837 recording the death of Ruaidhri, son of
Donnchadh, 'prior of Cluain Irard and abbot of other churches
too' is typical of annalistic entries of this period. In Cork we

14 Kenney, *Sources*, p. 237.

find two ninth-century pluralists in Fland Mac Forcellaigh who was abbot of Lismore, Emly and Corcach Mor (825) and Domhnall Ua Laithidhe, abbot of Cork and Lismore (863).

For the same period the annalists begin to record inter-monastic rivalry, the inevitable consequence of the autonomy enjoyed by the various monasteries, the lack of central hier-archical control and the increase in numbers registered by the monastic communities—an increase which led the chronicler in the *Félire Oengussa* to complain about the year 800 that 'the little places that were taken by twos and threes, they are Romes with multitudes'.[15] The first recorded battle occurred in 760 between the communities (*muintir, familiae*) of Clonmacnoise and Birr, the second in 764 between Clonmacnoise and Durrow. Monastic fighting forces seem to have been generally drawn from the ranks of the *manaig* or lay clients, but fighting abbots were not unknown and monks and abbots were frequently found in the fighting line. The *Annals of Ulster* make this quite clear for Cork when under the year 807 it records *bellum inter familiam Corcaidhe et familiam Cluain ferta Brendain* [Clonfert], *inter quas cedes innumerabilis hominum ecclesiasticorum et sub-limium de familia Corcaighi*. The 'noblest of the community of Cork' cannot but have included priests and monks with vows as well as monastic clients, and it is probable that Conaing (Connmhach), son of Donat and abbot of Corcach Mor, led his community into battle. We find the Cork community en-tering the lists again in 828 under the leadership (so it would seem) of Dunlaing Mac Cathasaigh, *princeps* of Corcach Mor and *comharba* Bairre. The annalist tells that on this occasion 'the community of Cork again collected the Ui Eachach and Corcu Laigde and Ciarraige Cuirche to Muscraige, and they left two hundred (dead) with them again' (*A.U.*). We are not told what the incident was which provoked the community and its abbot to battle, but participation in this battle may be among one of the reasons explanatory of the sinister obituary notice of Mac Cathasaigh who 'died without communion at Cashel' in 836 according to the *Annals of Ulster*.

The ninth-century reform which is associated with the Culdees was a reaction against the degeneracy of the older religious establishments. The reaction was indicated in a variety of ways, namely, in the increase of anchorites or recluses, in a new and rigorous code of religious ideals and in the rise of

---

15 Kathleen Hughes, 'The Church and the World in Early Christian Ireland', *I.H.S.*, xiii (1962), 112.

the Culdees.[16] The keynote of the reform was ascetisicm, and
while it generated a revival in the church its success was limited
because it lacked organization. For all that, its influence was
wide-spread and it seems to have been particularly successful
in Munster. Strict enforcement of Sunday observance as embodied in the *cáin Domnaig* must have been part of the reform
programme, and assuming that the *Vision of MacConglinne*
which has come down to us as a middle Irish text of the late
twelfth century belongs to an earlier (possibly the eighth)
century, it is possible to infer from it that observance of the
Sunday was a highly organized feature of church service in
Cork in the pre-Viking period. The succession list for Cork
contains a hiatus for the period 687–759, during which Manchin,
who is mentioned by MacConglinne as abbot of Cork, may
have been head of Finbarr's monastery. The *Annals of Ulster*
give *Quies Mancheine Leth-glinn* in 725 and *Dormitio Mancheine
Toma Greine* in 739, and since the holding of offices in plurality
was then common, it is not unlikely that the abbot of Leighlin
and/or the abbot of Tuamgraney (were they one and the same?)
had some connections with Cork. The case is strengthened when
we remember that Cathal Mac Finguine, who is also connected
with the MacConglinne story, died in 737 according to the
Annals of the Four Masters. At all events, Anier MacConglinne,
a vagrant scholar, arrived at the guest house (*taig aiged*) of Cork
shortly before vespers on a certain Saturday evening. Dissatis-
fied with the hospitality he received—'a small cup of the church
whey-water and two sparks of fire in the middle of a wisp of
oaten straw and two sods of fresh peat. . . The blanket of the
guest-house was rolled, bundled in the bed . . . (And there was
no clothing in that house but the blanket) . . . in which lice and
fleas were as plentiful as May dew'[17]—MacConglinne complained and for his trouble was given 'his fill of the muddy water
of the Lee' at the abbot's command. Abbot Manchin also
ordained that MacConglinne should cut his own passion tree
and be crucified on the morrow 'for the honour of me and of
St. Barre and of the Church'.[18] When face to face with the abbot,
MacConglinne renewed his complaint, in answer to which the
abbot left for posterity a verbal account of church practice in
eighth-century Cork. Manchin told MacConglinne that there
were three things about which there should be no grumbling in
the church, namely, new fruit, new ale and Sunday eve's portion.

16   Kenney, *Sources*, p. 468.
17   Meyer, *The Vision of Mac Conglinne,* pp. 14, 10, 16.
18   Ibid., p. 18.

'For however little is obtained on Sunday eve, what is nearest on the morrow is psalm-singing, then bell-ringing, Mass, with preaching and the Sacrament, and feeding the poor. What was a-wanting on the eve of Sunday will be got on Sunday or on the eve of Monday.' Sunday observance in accordance with the requirements of the *cáin Domnaig* was therefore a feature of ecclesiastical life in Cork. So was asceticism, for we read from the same source that 'the men of Munster in their bands were going to Cork for the festival of St. Barre and St. Nessan in order to fast'. MacConglinne's maledictions on the monks of Cork—'ye curs and ye robbers and dunghounds and unlettered brutes, ye shifting, blundering, hanghead monks of Cork'[19]— are consequently to be regarded merely as the vindictive out- pouring of a gleeman who wanted 'a gorging feast of a fortnight' and who resented execution on the heights of *Raithín mac nAeda*. The circumstances of his acquittal and release and his expulsion of the demon of gluttony from King Cathal Mac Finguine make highly interesting reading in Kuno Meyer's edition of the *Vision*.

The monastic 'rules', of which many are known to have been contemporaneous with that of the Culdees,[20] lay down strict norms of discipline and observance redolent of the earlier asceticism. These norms cover the observance of the *opus Dei*, daily recitation of the psalter, prostrations, poverty, care for the poor and the sick, the necessity of work, prayer and study, the avoidance of women and separation from the world. Every- thing, be it prayer or work, must proceed from love, since 'love determines piety' according to the Rule of Comgall. Study was encouraged and anchorites were commonly found acting as masters of the scriptoria which were now (ninth century) a feature of all the major monasteries. The rewards accruing to study were gratifying. The Rule of the Culdees proclaimed that 'the kingdom of heaven is granted to him who directs studies, and to him who studies and to him who supports the pupil who is studying'.[21]

Unfortunately the ascetic reform did not alter the constitution of the church or put an end to inter-monastic rivalries. Fighting abbots continue to stalk the annals, whence it also emerges that the privilege of sanctuary which attached to the church's *termon* lands began to be brushed aside by the laity who, after all, were but following the course mapped out for them by their clerical

19   Ibid., pp. 18–19, 20, 28, 148.
20   Kenney, *Sources*, pp. 144–6.
21   Hughes, *Ch. in early Ir. soc.*, p. 180, quoting Rule of Céli Dé 63.

leaders. Examples of violation of sanctuary are cited for Tallaght in 819, for Kildare in 823, for Clonmacnoise in 834 and for Durrow in 839. The appointment of reigning princes to monastic office was another growing practice, apropos of which the *Annals of Inisfallen* and of the Four Masters record the 'entry of Feidlimid King of Cashel into the abbacy of Cork' in 836. His predecessor, Dunlaing Mac Cathasaigh, ended his days without communion at Cashel. His dethronement and incarceration at Cashel cannot be explained. Was it because of Mac Cathasaigh's part in the battle of 828, or because the revenues of Cork attracted Feidlimid? That it occurred at all is a reflection on the reform movement which by its failure to constitute some central authority left the church at the mercy of unscrupulous princes of the type of Feidlimid (820–47). Notwithstanding that the annalist eulogises him as *optimus Scotorum scriba et anchorita*, Feidlimid violated the churches of Gallen, Clonmacnoise, Durrow and Fore (county Westmeath), and 'occupied the abbot's chair at Clonfert' in 838. By then the Viking terror had struck, the series of *cána* came to an end and the domestic legislation of the previous centuries became swamped in an orgy of wanton killing, monastic spoliation and the abduction of Irish women and children, as the annalists so graphically record.[22]

The Norsemen first appeared in Ireland in 798 and began with isolated raids on coastal areas; then as the potential wealth of Ireland and her monasteries became apparent, they came as settlers. The annals from the 820s onwards make this very clear in their frequent references to the *gentiles*. Historians have given Cork but little notice in their statistical accounts of the Viking raids, despite the annalistic evidence which shows that of all the ancient settlements in Ireland few suffered more severely than Cork which was eleven times plundered in the course of a single century. The monastery of Saint Finbarr was attacked in the years 822, 838 and 845. In 848 the Norwegians established their first foothold in Cork but were forced to yield place to the Danes in 863 in a fierce encounter in which abbot Domhnall Ua Laithidhe (and probably some of his community) was slain. By 867 the Danes were settling on the green islands of the Lee whence there gradually arose the great commercial city of Cork, *Corcach Mór Mumhan*, which with its 'houses and churches' was subjected to raids, as much from local princes as from foreigners, down to the end of the eleventh century

22   *Ann. Inisf.*, *A.F.M.*, and *A.U.*, *passim*.

when the ancient abbey of Saint Finbarr was finally destroyed (1089).

The effects of the Viking invasions were many-sided and far-reaching. For one thing, the church became even more involved in secular affairs, for church leaders began to realize that alliance with secular leaders was their only insurance against annihilation. It is not unusual therefore to find monastic communities of the tenth century assembling in battle array as allies of kings and chieftains and no longer pursuing the strictly inter-monastic rivalries of pre-Viking times. Rejection of the claims of Armagh seems to have been the exception to this rule. In 973 when Dubdaleithe, coarb of Saint Patrick, made his visitation he was resisted by the coarb of Ailbe who refused Dubdaleithe's right to a levy, and it took Mahon (Mathgamhain), king of Munster, to restore peace between them and secure the recognition of Dubdaleithe. In 908 the abbot of Cork and the abbot of Cenn Eitig and the king of Corca Dhuibhne were killed fighting for King Cormac Mac Cuilleanain at Bealach Mughna. The *Chronicon Scotorum* gives the Cork abbot's name as Ailill, son of Eoghan, and adds that Maelmordha, king of Rath-linne, and Maelgorm, king of Ciarraighe-Luachra, with a multitude *to the number* [*sic*] 6,000 were killed there. The clerics seem to have surpassed themselves on the field of Bealach Mughna. The account of the battle as given by Dubhaltach Mac Firbis[23] records the words of one prince whose advice to his colleagues was that they should 'fly suddenly from this abominable battle and leave it between the clergy themselves, who could not be quiet without coming to battle'. Cormac Mac Cuilleanain, who was already a bishop (according to the *Annals of Inisfallen*) when he took the kingship of Cashel in 901, is the first certain instance we have of a bishop-king, and as such he exemplifies a trend confined mainly to southern Ireland whereby churchmen in major orders assumed kingdoms and executed their ecclesiastical and secular duties concurrently. The converse is equally common, i.e., the assumption of ecclesiastical functions by kings and princes in the tradition of Feidlimid who entered the abbacy of Cork. This practice, which became wide-spread in the wake of the Viking invasions, did not affect the church in Cork to the same extent as it did elsewhere. Excluding Feidlimid, the succession list for Saint Finbarr's monastery offers one solitary example in Aedh Mac Garbhaith, whom the Four Masters style 'abbot of Cork and Lord of Dartraighe' (952) and whom the

---

23 *Annals of Ireland . . . Three Fragments Copied from Ancient Sources by D*[ubhaltach] *Mac Firbisigh*, ed. John O'Donovan, p. 206.

Chronicon Scotorum describes as 'King of Cairbre Mor (*Rí Cairbre Móire*) and Dartraighe'. When it came to the point, kings and princes were no respectors of church immunities, and the fact that large monasteries of the ninth and tenth centuries were cities of defence as well as schools, hospitals and alms-houses, made it all the more important that they should not fall into the hands of enemy powers. Churches and monasteries were consequently regarded as forts, places of defence and/or offence, and treated accordingly. Brian Boru's hosting into south Munster in 987 is symptomatic of the general attitude. He took hostages from 'Les Mor, Corcach and Imlech Ibair as a guarantee of the banishment of robbers and lawless people' (i.e., his own enemies) from the *termon* lands of these churches (*Ann. Inisf.*).

It was inevitable that in a milieu of overlapping ecclesiastical and political functions which offered higher clergy tempting inducements to found families of their own, laicization should loom as the greatest threat to the discipline and organization of the church. The traditional name for the monastic ruler, as we have seen, was *abb* or *abbas*, 'the father of the church', a name which alternated with that of coarb or *comharba*, the recognized heir of the founder. In post-Viking times the term *airchinnech* or *airchindic*, anglicized as erenagh or herenagh was more frequently applied. The *airchinnech*—the most elusive of Celtic monastic officials—is difficult to categorize, but he must have been there from the beginning. Professor Binchy's view is that 'this old native word . . . was probably the first term used for the head of a monastic foundation' and that its annalistic debut in the late ninth century was 'merely an index of the increasing use of Irish' in the annals.[24] Kenney holds the same opinion but admits the possibility that the associations of the title *abbas* had become such as to make it seem incongruous when the position was becoming more or less secularized.[25] In the absence of precise data on the inter-relational prestige of abbot, coarb and *airchinnech*, scholars, while they hesitate to equate all three, admit that 'the terms were to a considerable extent interchangeable'.[26] Whatever their origins, however, the preponderance of *airchinnechs* in the annals coincides with and is an expression of the laicization which characterized the Irish church in the period immediately before the twelfth-century

24 Binchy, Review, *Studia Hib.*, vii, 219.

25 Kenney, *Sources*, p. 12, n. 17.

26 John Barry, 'The Erenagh in the Monastic Irish Church', *I.E.R.*, lxxxix (1958), 432.

reform. It is probable that the majority of the *airchinnechs* were laymen whose lay status while tolerated was recognized as a definite abuse;[27] and when reform began to germinate in the twelfth century, the first Synod of Cashel in 1101 by legislating that 'no erenagh of any church in Ireland should have a wife' and that 'a layman shall not be an erenagh', was in reality only underlining those scattered annalistic references which show beyond shadow of doubt that 'the tradition . . . existed in monastic Ireland that the erenagh *de jure* was in orders'.[28]

There were no ninth-century erenaghs in Cork inasmuch as they are not mentioned in the annals. Seven erenaghs are listed between 989 and 1157, some of whom were abbots and/or bishops as well as erenaghs; an indication perhaps, that laicization was not widespread in Cork. The annals give the following statistics:

	Ann. Inisf.	*A.F.M.*	*A.U.*
989 Colum mac Ciaruchain	comharba		airchinnech
1006 Cellach Ua Meanngorain	airchinnech		
1034 Cathal Martyr	comharba		airchinnech
1057 Mugron Ua Mutain	airchinnech and *fer legind*	comharba, noble bishop and lector	
1057 Dubdalethe Ua Cinnaedha			airchinnech
1085 Clereach Ua Sealbaigh		ard-comharba	airchinnech
1140 Domhnall O Saolbach		airchinnech	
1146 Gill Padraic MacCarthy		comharba	airchinnech

In view of the possibility of a faction fight between rival claimants to the church of Cork the overlapping entry for the year 1057 conceals a murder story and calls for comment. Similar instances of monastic strife and murder are recorded for the monasteries of Emly (1052), Armagh (1060), Clondalkin (1076) and for Iona where in 1070 the reigning abbot was slain by the son of his predecessor.[29] The *Annals of Inisfallen* record that Hua Mutain, *airchinnech* and *fer legind* of Cork, was killed in Ros Ailithir by the Ui Floinn Arda. The version given by the Four Masters is that Mughron Ua Mutain, *comharba* Bairre, noble bishop and lector, was killed by robbers of the Corca Laighdhe after his return from vespers. The *Annals of*

27 Aubrey Gwynn, 'The Twelfth Century Reform', in *A History of Irish Catholicism*, ed. Patrick J. Corish, vol. ii, part 1, pp. 14–15.

28 J. Barry, 'The Erenagh in the Monastic Irish Church', p. 426.

29 Hughes, *Ch. in early Ir. soc.*, pp. 242–3.

Tigernach finally claim that Mugron Hua Mutain, *comharba* Bairre and bishop, was slain by his own community on his way out from nocturns. Hua Mutain's probable murder at Ross may have been consequent upon an attempt to gain control of Ross which had been without an erenagh since the death of Colm Ua Cathail in 1055.[30] Ross has never taken kindly to amalgamation with Cork. On the other hand, Hua Mutain's murder at the hands of his own community at Cork assumes feasibility in view of the fact that Hua Mutain and Dubdalethe Ua Cinnaedha were apparently Ross clerics who had made their way into the abbey of Saint Finbarr. Cork may not have favoured a Ross intrusion at a time when a Dalcassian intrusion was already imminent. Next, the omission of Dubdalethe Ua Cinnaedha from the *Annals of Inisfallen* and his inclusion as *airchinnech* of Cork in the *Annals of Ulster* is rather unconvincingly argued by invoking a copyist's error which consigned Dubdalethe to Cork instead of to Trim where the family of Ua Cinaeda supplied at least two erenaghs to the church.[31] As against this theory, the *Annals of Loch Cé* and the *Annals of Ulster* synchronize in placing Dubdalethe in Cork, 'Dubdalethe Ua Cinaetha, *airchinnech* of Corcach, died, 1057'. Finally, the genealogy of the Corca Laighdhe adds weight to the possibility that the controversial *airchinnech* came from Ross. The genealogy shows that the *tuath* or tribeland of O Coinneadh was in the parish of Myross in Corca Laighdhe, and that the *tuath* of O Dubdalethe formed part of the present parishes of Kilmeen and Castleventry where the family of O'Dullea is still in existence.[32] The emergence of a *Dubdalethe O Cinnaedha* from this area is not outside the bounds of possibility and would justify the parallel entries in the annals just quoted.

The Ua Sealbaigh family which supplied abbots, bishops and erenaghs to Cork for over 120 years were likewise installed in the temporary diocese of Kinneigh. Their scholastic accomplishments and asceticism are eulogized in the annals,[33] and while some of them were undoubtedly clerics others must have

---

30   Aubrey Gwynn, 'Bishops of Cork in the Twelfth Century', *I.E.R.*, lxxiv (1950), 21.

31   Ibid., pp. 20–1.

32   John T. Collins, 'Some Recent Contributions to Cork Diocesan History', *I.E.R.*, lxxv (1951), 54.

33   Gwynn, 'Bishops of Cork in the Twelfth Century', p. 109, mentions one Augustine Ua Selbaigh who died as bishop of Waterford in 1182, and ventures the conjecture that since Augustine is mentioned as *magister* in the *Gesta Henrici II* he possibly 'had made his way to Bologna or some other Italian University at a time when neither Paris nor Oxford were fully constituted Universities . . . He is the first Irishman who can be named as a graduate of an European University.'

belonged to the group of lay erenaghs who had established hereditary and even dynastic claims to certain Irish monasteries. Two of the Ua Sealbaigh erenaghs enjoyed exceptionally long tenure: Clereach Ua Sealbaigh who was erenagh from 1057 to 1085 and Domhnall O Saolbach whose tenure spanned the years from 1112 to 1140. The latter was probably a layman who seems to have disputed the claims of Finn Mac Cellechair Ui Ceinneidigh who was *comharba* Bairre for a time in 1137. Finally the obituary notice of Gilla Padraic MacCarthy, erenagh of Cork, in 1146 brings to an end the long series of 'successors of Bairre' as that title had been understood in the period antecedent to the twelfth century.

Notwithstanding the ferocity of the Viking terror the church in the tenth century was powerful enough to attract secular princes to act as her champions. Gradually Irish political power was strengthened, Scandinavian aggression was checked and when the victory of Clontarf was achieved in 1014 Christianity had already percolated through native to Norse society and the Viking settlements throughout the country were undergoing a process of gaelicization. In the eleventh century the church again assumed her role as mediator in the pursuit of peace, for we read that a great assembly of clergy and laity met at Killaloe in 1040 under the presidency of the king of Munster and promulgated 'a law (*cáin*) and a restraint (*cosc*) upon every injustice'. The efforts of Armagh to secure recognition of its overlordship were now encountering less opposition than heretofore— thanks to the earlier patronage of Brian Boru—and consequently Patrick's *comharba* was in frequent attendance at important state occasions throughout the country. If newly-elected, the *comharba* did a circuit of the country and collected a visitation tribute, as did Amalgaid in 1021 when 'he went into Munster for the first time'. Similar Munster visitations were made in 1068 and 1094; a link was being forged between the south and Armagh, and through the recognition thus accorded to the head of the church in Armagh the Irish church in general became acclimatized to the idea of centralization which was intended from the beginning and which was shortly to come into its own.

The eleventh century was likewise a period of intellectual and artistic activity for the church. Anchorites living within or near the churches became numerous, Celleach O Sealbaigh, 'chief anchorite and *comharba* Bairre, 1036' being an example. Monastic scriptoria became centres of devotional and historical compilations—mostly in Irish from Latin originals and indicating the victory of the vernacular after centuries of cultural and linguistic antagonisms. The first part of the *Annals of*

Inisfallen was written by some north Munster scribe in the last decades of the eleventh century, and smiths and metal-workers were expressing their skills through the execution of shrines, reliquaries and the like. This was all part of a post-Viking renaissance which expressed itself in 'a growth of historical consciousness and an impulse to preserve in permanent written collections the old legends, literature and records of Ireland'.[34] Religious observance became again matter for legislation. The *cáin Domnaig* was re-enacted in 1040 and under date 1092 the *Chronicon Scotorum* records the enforcement of laws of abstinence and almsgiving binding for one year. Stress upon the evils consequent upon non-observance of monastic rules, uncelebrated hours, untruthful priests and an inhospitable church[35] shows how close to men's minds was the ideal of a reformed and vigorous Christianity. The re-awakening is best gauged from a comparison of the sentiments expressed in lyrics of the ninth and eleventh centuries. A monk of the ninth century in his distress at the church's embroilment in secular affairs could think of no other balm for his soul than flight to an isolated hut in the woods, known to none but God, where fighting and visiting would no longer trouble him. By the eleventh century the ideal was loftier:

> It were my mind's desire to behold the face of God.
> It were my mind's desire to live with him eternally.
> It were my mind's desire to read books studiously.
> It were my mind's desire to live under a clear rule.[36]

On the political front in Munster during the later Viking period the Eoghanacht dynasty which had been badly shaken by the death of Cormac Mac Cuilleanain at Bealach Mughna in 908 yielded place to the Dalcassian family of Ui Toirdhealbaigh (Toirdhealbhaigh), the chief representatives of which were Mahon and Brian Boru. The defeat of the Northmen at Soloheadbeg (Sulchuait) in 967 and their expulsion from Munster in 971 was followed by the recognition of Mahon as king of Munster in 972. Mahon's reign was short. A confederacy was formed against him and in 976, according to the *Annals of Inisfallen*, 'he was killed by Maolmuadh, son of Bran, king of the Ui Eachach, having been treacherously delivered up by Donovan, son of Cathal, king of the Ui Fidgente' of west Limerick. Colum

34 Hughes, *Ch. in early Ir. soc.*, pp. 227–49.

35 Eleanor Knott, 'A Poem of Prophecies', *Ériu*, xviii (1958), 55–84 *passim*.

36 Gerard Murphy, *Early Irish Lyrics*, no. 26.

53

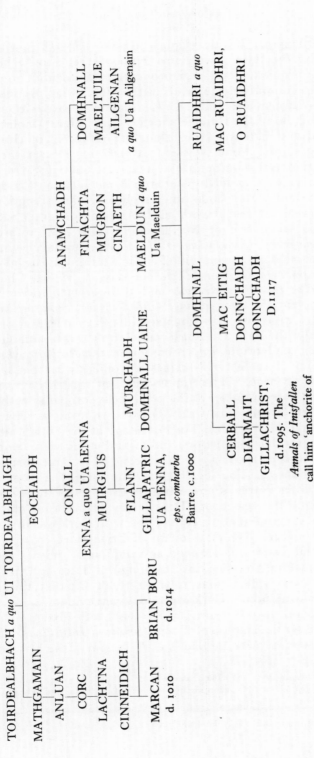

LEABHAR MUIMNEACH, p. 309   *BOOK OF BALLYMOTE*, p. 185.   *BOOK OF LECAN*, p. 433.

GENEALOGICAL TABLE OF THE UI TOIRDEALBHAIGH

Mac Ciaruchain,[37] a Dalcassian, who was *comharba* Bairre and erenagh at the time, gave Saint Finbarr's relic to Mahon in pledge of protection and later pronounced a malediction on all those who compassed the death of the king. Brian avenged his brother's death in 978 at Bealach Leachta to the east of Macroom at the junction of the Sullane and the Lany. Here Maolmuadh was killed 'and there was a great slaughter of the men of Munster' according to the Four Masters. It may have been through participation in this battle that Finnechta, bishop of Cork, died.

Brian became king of Munster after Bealach Leachta and high king of Ireland in 1002 and immediately set about strengthening the Dalcassian interest in Cork. He married his daughter Sadhbh (Sabia) to Cian, son of Maolmuadh—they went to live at Curragheenbrien, *Coradh Ingine Bhriain* close to Raithleann[38]— and he installed his cousin Gilla Patraic Ua Enne as *comharba* of Saint Finbarr's monastery. The genealogies of Dal Chais as found in the *Book of Ballymote* and in the *Book of Lecan* refer to '*Gillapatric Ua Enne, espuicc Cille Dalua 7 comarba Barri*'. The theory which would recognize Gilla Patraic as first bishop of Cork after the Synod of Rathbreasail in 1111 is untenable and based on a tendentious interpretation of the *Leabhar Muimh- neach*, the pedigree list of which synchronizes with that shown on the facing page.[39] The impossibility of this theory is seen when Gilla Patraic's place in the pedigree is compared with that of Gillchrist O Ruaidhri (d. 1095) from whom he is separated by four generation grades. The genealogy of the Ui Toirdheal- bhaigh shows that Brian Boru and Gilla Patraic were contem- poraries, both of them sixth in descent from Toirdhealbach, ancestor of the Ui Toirdhealbhaigh who were located around Killaloe. Gilla Patraic's coarbship of Cork must therefore be dated around the year 1000. The non-inclusion of his name in the annals suggests that his connection with Cork was of a very temporary nature. With the death of Brian Boru in 1014 the power of the Dalcassians waned and the family did not regain pre-eminence in Munster until the reign of Turlough, Brian's grandson, who ruled from 1064 to 1086. By that time the Dalcassian intrusion in Cork was once again evident.

The account of the death of Clereach Ua Sealbaigh in 1085 is followed by the statement in the *Annals of Inisfallen* that 'he was succeeded by Mac Bethad Ua hAilgenain of the Dal Chais'

---

37 The succession-list of abbots and coarbs of Iniscathaigh mentions Finnechta Ua Ciaruchain as vice-abbot who, according to the *Annals of Inisfallen*, died in 994.

38 Tradition connects Sadhbh also with the towland of Lisbanree near Bandon.

39 Gwynn, 'Bishops of Cork in the Twelfth Century', pp. 25–6.

who seems to have attempted to strengthen his position by installing a distant relative in the monastery of Saint Finbarr. This was Gillachrist O Ruaidhri, 'anchorite of the Ui Toirdealbaig', who died in Cork in 1095. Mac Bethad's intrusion suggests the influence of Turlough O'Brien who was then at the height of his power and an ardent advocate of reform. The annals record nothing more of Ua hAilgenain beyond his death in 1106, the year in which Celsus, who had become *comharba Patraic*, was consecrated bishop in Munster on the occasion of his *cuairt* of the southern churches. For the year 1096, however, the Four Masters cite the death of Ua Cochlain, 'learned bishop and *comharba* Bairre', and from an earlier entry given by the same source to the effect that Corcach was burned in 1089 we have evidence of probable strife between rival supporters of Abbot Ua hAilgenain and Bishop Ua Cochlain who was sprung, according to the *Duan Catháin*, from the powerful Clann Sealbaigh. The next recorded instance of Dalcassian contacts with Cork can scarcely be categorized as intrusion but it is nonetheless interesting and relevant. In 1118 Diarmait, son of Turlough O Briain, who had wrested the kingship from his brother Muirchertach and had banished him to Limerick and Killaloe, died in Corcach Mor Mumhan 'after a victory of penance'.[40] Muirchertach died under similar circumstances in Lismore in the following year. The great Dalcassian power now went into decline and the MacCarthy star went temporarily into orbit.

In the mid-twelfth century we find two more Ua Sealbaighs mentioned in the succession list of Saint Finbarr's monastery with a Dalcassian cleric sandwiched between them. The intruder was Finn, son of Cellechair Ua Ceinneidigh, whom the annalists under date 1137 style '*comharba* Barre for a time' (he was presumably expelled) and who died in 1152 as abbot of Terryglass. The final Dalcassian entry for Cork tells that Domhnall Ua Conaing, 'bishop of Killaloe died in 1195 after he had been banished by the legate (Archbishop Matthew Ua hEnna) from his diocese; and he died in the house of Ua Briain's daughter and was buried in Cork'—thus the annalist of Inisfallen. By this time the great reform of the twelfth century was well under way, and a new era in Irish church history was inaugurated. By way of prologue to this great movement it is necessary to explore the extent to which the seeds of reform were sown in the eleventh and earlier centuries. At this point the historian is greatly indebted to Father Aubrey Gwynn, S.J.,

40 *Annals of Inisfallen.*

whose contributions to various periodicals and publications over the years, including a recently published work on the twelfth-century reform,[41] open up vistas hitherto unknown and which show that Ireland in the twelfth century was caught up in a great renewal which rejuvenated the entire church of western Europe.

In Ireland the twelfth-century reform was the brainchild of a small group of zealous churchmen whose work was first codified in the reforming Synod of Rathbreasail in 1111. The reform movement upon which Archbishops Lanfranc (1070–89) and Anselm (1093–1109) of Canterbury exercised immediate influence goes back even beyond them to certain pockets of Irish monastic communities which were to be found at first in Germany and subsequently in Rome, 'in which the programme later advocated by a line of great reforming popes was first formulated and carried into execution'.[42] These Irish monks and hermits are known to have been caught up in the great Benedictine monastic reform of Cluny and in the wider movement for episcopal reform which marked the beginning of the pontificate of Leo IX (1049–54) but which became so influenced by the dynamism of Gregory VII (1073–85) as to be called the Hildebrandine or Gregorian Reform. Tenth-century Germany was the seed-bed of the movement, and in this great Ottonian empire Irish pilgrims made early settlements at Metz, Toul, Verdun, Cologne and elsewhere. Imperial partiality in their regard is seen firstly in the charter of 946 by which Otto the Great confirmed a grant of lands at Waulsort near Dinant in favour of 'certain servants of God coming from Scotia by grace of pilgrimage and wishing to live under the rule of S. Benedict'.[43] A second imperial charter was issued on 22 January 992 by Otto III in favour of 'the Irish monks at Metz and their abbot Fingen' who was also abbot of the monastery of Saint Vannes at Verdun.[44] Irish communities proliferated in Germany during the eleventh century; the most important was that of Saint James at Ratisbon to which the Irish Benedictine communities of Würzburg, Nuremberg, Erfurt, Eichstätt, Constance and Vienna became subject and which was recognized as the head-house of the Irish Benedictine congregation in Germany in 1215.[45] The third

41 Gwynn, 'The Twelfth Century Reform', pp. 1–9.

42 Gwynn, 'Irish Monks and the Cluniac Reform', *Studies*, xxix (1940), 409.

43 Hughes, *Ch. in early Ir. soc.*, p. 253.

44 Gwynn, 'Irish Monks and the Cluniac Reform', p. 420.

45 D. A. Binchy, 'The Irish Benedictine Congregation in Mediaeval Germany', *Studies*, xviii (1929), 197 ff.

abbot of Ratisbon, Christian MacCarthy, founded the monastery of Saint James at Würzburg in 1139. Abbot Christian, whose Cork origins are upheld by Professor Binchy, was a contemporary and probably a relative of Cormac MacCarthy, who had ecclesiastical associations with the monastery of Gill Abbey in Cork and on the towers of whose chapel at Cashel experts detect certain German architectural features.[46] A more exciting link between Ratisbon, Würzburg and Cork county is the dependence of the Benedictine priory of Ross upon the Abbey of Saint James at Würzburg up to immediate pre-Reformation times.

Two of the more renowned Irishmen who made Germany the final goal of their journeyings were Marianus Scottus (Mael-Brigte) the chronicler, and his namesake Marianus who became abbot of the monastery of Weih-Sankt-Peter in Ratisbon. The former Marianus, who was a monk of Moville (Mag-bile), was banished from Ireland in 1052, made his way via Cologne to Fulda where he was ordained priest and spent ten years as an *inclusus* (1059–69), after which he followed a similar pattern of life at Mainz until his death in 1082 or 1083. His chronicle, which comes from the hand of a fellow-exile who acted as amanuensis and which is contained in the *Codex Palatino-Vaticanus* 830, outlines the history of the Irish in Germany in the tenth and eleventh centuries.[47] The other Marianus or Muiredach Mac Robartaig (Mac Roarty or Rafferty of Donegal) left Ireland for Rome in 1057 but was constrained to remain at Ratisbon. His *vita* describes him as 'the ideal scribe of an Irish monastery' and adds that 'many monastic congregations which, recruited from Ireland through faith and charity and the desire to imitate Blessed Marianus, inhabit Bavaria and Franconia "on pilgrimage", are supplied for the most part with the writings of Blessed Marianus'.[48] He died in 1088.

Unrest in France and Italy explains the paucity of Irish contacts with these countries in the tenth century, but Irish pilgrim churchmen were no strangers to Rome even during this period. Royal pilgrimages were remarkably numerous during the eleventh century, more especially after 1027 when free passage for pilgrims was guaranteed through joint mediation of King Cnut and the Emperor Conrad II with Rudolf II of Burgundy. In giving details of these royal pilgrimages (which were interrupted by the events of 1066 in England) Father

46 H. G. Leask, *Christian Art in Ireland*, ii, 81.

47 Kenney, *Sources*, pp. 615–16.

48 Ibid., 617.

Gwynn postulates that many other pilgrims of less noble birth journeyed on the same pilgrim route. Thus in 1025 Cellach Ua Saolbach, *comharba* Bairre, went on his pilgrimage to Rome (*Ann. Inisf.*). He seems to have resigned his abbacy to go on this pilgrimage, but the annals do not make this clear, nor do they indicate that he died in Rome.[49] Another entry in the *Annals of Inisfallen* for the year 1095 tells of Eogan, *cend manach na Gaedil i Róim*, which, coupled with two lists of Irish names found in a Roman manuscript and published by Dom Wilmart, O.S.B.,[50] indicates the existence of an Irish colony in Rome 'during the last years of the eleventh century when the prestige of the Hildebrandine Reform had made Rome once more a centre towards which men came from all parts of Europe'.[51] The Irish community in Rome occupied the monastery of *S. Trinitas Scotorum*, the site of which is believed to have been at the south-east corner of the Palatine Hill a short distance from the church of S. Sebastiano al Palatino.

That the Irish church which still lacked hierarchical organization was nonetheless respectful of and in contact with papal authority is the conclusion to be drawn from a letter addressed by Pope Gregory VII to 'Terdelvacus, noble king of Ireland, and the archbishops, bishops, abbots, noblemen and all Christians who dwell in Ireland'. This letter, which Ussher included in his *Veterum Hibernicarum Epistolarum Sylloge* (1632),[52] impresses the duty of obedience to Saint Peter's successor upon Irish bishops and abbots and urges them to the pursuit of justice, peace and union in charity. Its final exhortation was a personal appeal that 'if any matters arise among you which seem worthy of our help, lose no time in appealing to us, and you shall, with God's help, obtain what you justly ask'.[53] The approximate date of the letter is 1076, by which time Lanfranc's efforts at overhauling the Irish church were two years under way. In 1074 Lanfranc had initiated a correspondence with Brian Boru's grandson Turlough (Toirdelbach Ua Briain), the Terdelvacus of the Gregorian letter, whose designs for ecclesiastical reform were ably seconded by the Dalcassian Domhnall Ua hÉnna who was chief bishop of Munster in the

49   The annals simply state that he 'had been' in Rome.

50   Aubrey Gwynn, 'Ireland and the Continent in the Eleventh Century', *I.H.S.*, viii (1953), 200, quoting *Revue Bénédictine*, xli (1929), 218–230.

51   Gwynn, 'Ireland and the Continent in the Eleventh Century', p. 200.

52   The letter was reprinted by Charles Erlington (1847) in *The Whole Works of Most Rev. James Ussher, D.D.*, iv, 498.

53   Gwynn, 'The Twelfth Century Reform', p. 2.

closing decades of the eleventh century. The occasion for the correspondence was the vacancy caused in Dublin by the death of Bishop Donatus and which Lanfranc filled by the consecration of Bishop Patrick at the request of the clergy and people of Dublin—and according to the traditions of his predecessors (*more antecessorum nostrorum*). The Hiberno-Norse city of Dublin was therefore a suffragan see of Canterbury in the eleventh century and Bishop Patrick had to take an oath of obedience to Lanfranc and his successors as archbishops of Canterbury.

Lanfranc's letter to Turlough, 'magnificent King of Ireland', begins with a diplomatic laudatory passage and develops into a stern denunciation of reported abuses in the Irish church: 'In your kingdom every man abandons his lawfully wedded wife at his own will, without the occasion of a canonical cause . . . and takes to himself some other wife who may be of his own kin or of the kindred of the wife whom he has abandoned, or whom another has abandoned with like wickedness, according to a law of marriage that is rather a law of fornication (*maritali seu fornicaria lege*).' Thus did Lanfranc attack the legal tradition of the brehon law. Other abuses condemned by Lanfranc related to the continued practice of episcopal consecration by only one bishop instead of three, the baptism of infants without chrism, the imparting of holy orders in return for money. He pointed out that these abuses were contrary to the authority of the Gospels and the Apostles, to the prohibitions of the holy canons and to the teaching of the Fathers of the church, and he exhorted the king to order the bishops and all religious men to come together in general assembly over which he (the king) should preside 'and thus strive to banish these evil customs from his realm'.[54] Turlough, who died in 1085, had no opportunity to preside over such an assembly, but his son Muirchertach presided over the synods of Cashel in 1101 and Rathbreasail in 1111.

Following the death of Bishop Patrick in 1084 Donngus (Donatus), who had been selected 'by the clergy and people of Dublin together with Terdelvachus King of Ireland,[55] and the bishops of the region of Ireland', was consecrated in 1085 by Lanfranc, who is said to have marked the occasion by another letter to Turlough Ua Briain. This second consecration (in which Dublin was no longer and unacceptably styled *Metropolis Hiberniae*) endorsed Dublin's dependence upon Canterbury;

---

54 Gwynn, 'The Origins of the Diocese of Killaloe', in Dermot F. Gleeson, *A History of the Diocese of Killaloe*, pp. 100–1.

55 Donatus' authority was in reality confined to *Leath Mogha*.

and while Lanfranc himself had a stormy reign as archbishop of Canterbury, he nevertheless passed on to Saint Anselm the title *Britanniarum primas*, to which however Anselm preferred the less controversial *primas totius Britanniae*.[56] After his consecration in 1093 Anselm, who had previously exchanged letters with Bishop Domhnall Ua hÉnna concerning theological and other matters, appealed for the prayers and co-operation of the bishops of Ireland in the difficulties which he anticipated. Like his predecessor he did not hesitate to condemn the abuses still rampant in the Irish church. His first functional contact with Ireland occurred in 1096 when in answer to an appeal made on behalf of the clergy and people of Waterford he consecrated Malchus, a former monk of Winchester, as its first bishop on 27 December. Signatories to this petition were Muirchertach Ua Briain, king of Munster, his brother and *tánaiste* Diarmait, and Bishop Domhnall Ua hÉnna, *Domnaldus episcopus*, all representing the Dalcassian bloc. Then follow Maol Muire Ua Dúnáin, *episcopus Midie*, Samuel, bishop of Dublin whom Anselm later consecrated in Winchester on Low Sunday in 1097, and finally, Ferdomnach who signed the petition as *Laginiensium episcopus*. He is thought to have been bishop of Kildare.[57]

There were thus three territorial bishoprics (Meath, Dublin, Kildare) in Ireland before the end of the eleventh century, clearly showing that the movement towards the establishment of a territorial episcopate had got successfully off the ground. When Domhnall Ua hÉnna died in 1098 the ecclesiastical leadership which he wielded passed to Maol Muire Ua Dúnáin, *Senóir Leithe Cuind*, and Maol Muire's collaboration with Muirchertach Ua Briain of *Leath Mogha* was one of the outstanding features of the great ecclesiastical metamorphosis of the twelfth century which gave its quietus to every form of Celtic particularism.

56   Gwynn, 'The Twelfth Century Reform', p. 6.
57   Gwynn, 'The Origins of the Diocese of Killaloe', p. 109.

III

The Origins of the Diocese

The jurisdictional area of the early abbot-bishops of Cork would appear to have been determined by two main factors. Firstly, the territorial parallel between the *paruchia* and the *tuath* had its natural consequence in the acceptance of the founder-saint of the *paruchia* as the special patron of the *tuath*. In this way Saint Finbarr became patron of the Ui Eachach, as the *Félire Oengussa* indicates by the entry that 'the Ui Eachach from Carn Ui Neid (Mizen Head) to Cork are under the protection of Bairre'. In the same way the Déise of Lismore, the Corca Laighdhe of Ross and the Osraighe sept of Ossory all had their particular patrons. The list could be extended to cover practically every Irish diocese. The original tribeland of the Ui Eachach lay between the lower courses of the Lee and the Bandon and had its centre or chief seat, as we have seen, at Rath Raithleann. By extension northwards from Raithleann the Ui Eachach annexed the territories of the sept of Ui Floinn Luadh or Ifflanloe which extended along the banks of the Lee from the river Bride to Inchigeela. Pushing westwards, they gradually took in the upper waters of the Bandon and then spread southwards and further westwards to the coast to add to their growing tribeland the Corca Laighdhe peninsulas between Roaring-Water Bay and Bantry. This was the extent of Ui Eachach territory in the eighth century. In the following century they absorbed the minor septland of the Ui Mic Ciair which extended from Cork to the river Bride, and finally, in the period between 971 and 1014 the eastern limits of the Ui Eachach tribeland were set at Cairn Thierna, that is, at Rathcormac near Fermoy. This new extension points to an incursion against the Ui Liathain sept, the western boundary of whose territory lay directly north and east of Cork city. The grant of Aedh Mac Miandach to Finbarr constituted a more ancient basis for the inclusion of this district in the diocese of Cork.

In the second place, it not infrequently happened that a saint or his disciples made important foundations outside the territory with which he was chiefly associated and that the saint's coarbs inherited his jurisdiction over these detached foundations. That this was the case in Cork is clear from the *Lives* of Finbarr; consequently his successors are known to have claimed and exercised authority over churches which lay strictly within the diocese of Cloyne. These places were Finure in Corkbeg, Clonpriest near Youghal, Tullacondra near Ballyclough and finally Donoughmore. We shall see that with the exception of Donoughmore these claims to extra-diocesan jurisdiction were neither unrealistic nor without foundation, and that other areas not mentioned in the *Lives* came likewise within the sphere of Cork diocesan administration. However, the majority of these scattered areas had reverted to Cloyne before the papal taxation of Pope Nicholas IV was announced in 1291. Furthermore, the dioceses of Cloyne and Ross, notwithstanding Ui Eachach expansion, managed to retain their identity, with Cloyne tenaciously holding on to a strip of territory running northwards from the Lee at Macroom to Buttevant, Charleville and Kanturk. Indeed, were it not for a grant of land at Cluain Uamha (Cloyne) made to him by King Cairbre Crom of Munster (d. 580), Colman Mac Lenine might well have confined his activities to mid-Cork and north Cork to the complete exclusion of the eastern area which eventually became diocesan headquarters. The sparse biographical data which we possess connect Colman with Muskerry Mitine between the Lee and the Blackwater and with Muskerry-Donegan in north Cork, while the name *Colman Mitine* as applied to him in the genealogies would seem to indicate Muskerry Mitine as the chief area of his apostolate.[1] As matters came about, however, Saint Colman Mac Lenine held a two-fold territory which covered the greater part of the present county of Cork, and which continued to be held by his successors through the centuries. The same continuity is observable in Cork; for although the Ui Eachach supremacy which dominated Desmond from 845 onwards was superseded by that of the MacCarthys in 1118, the ancient tribal arrangement according to which the coarbs of Saint Finbarr measured the limits of their jurisdiction has remained till the present day basically unchanged.

THE FIRST SYNOD OF CASHEL, 1101

The first Synod of Cashel which was convened in 1101 was an

---

1 *Geneal. regum Hib.*, p. 125.

instrument of capital importance in forwarding the *aggiorna-mento* of the moribund Celtic Church. The account of the synod as given by the Four Masters deserves to be quoted in its entirety: 'A meeting of *Leath Mogha* was held at Cashel around Muirchertach Ua Briain with the chiefs of the laity and the clergy, and around Ua Dúnáin, noble bishop and chief senior of Ireland; and it was then that Muirchertach Ua Briain made a grant such as no king had ever made before, namely, he granted Cashel of the kings to the church without any claim of layman or cleric upon it, but to the religious (*do chraibhdheach-aibh*) of Ireland in general.' Muirchertach was great-grandson of Brian Boru and, like his father Turlough (Toirdelbach) before him, was the recipient of letters from Canterbury on the necessity of correcting abuses in the church. His grant of Cashel of the kings, ancient seat of the Eoghanacht, to the church may not have been entirely altruistic;[2] nevertheless it paved the way for the selection of Cashel as metropolitan see of *Leath Mogha* in 1111. Maol Muire's prestige in both *Leath Chuinn* and *Leath Mogha* was at this time so universally recognized that the genealogical records of *Síol Briain* (the O'Briens of Dal Chais) state his position at Cashel to have been that of 'chief legate, chief bishop and chief senior of Ireland, with authority from the Pope himself', *i núgdarhás on bpápa eiside*.[3] But Cashel was not a national assembly, and it would be more correct to state that Maol Muire's presidency was confined to a gathering representative of *Leath Mogha* rather than of 'the men of Ireland'. The distinction of being 'the first to act as legate of the Apostolic See throughout the whole of Ireland' (*per universam Hiberniam*)[4] belongs to Bishop Gilbert or Giolla Easpoig of Limerick who presided in capacity of papal legate at Rathbreasail in 1111.

In eight important decrees the Synod of Cashel struck at some of the major discrepancies between current Irish practice and conventional Roman usage. Briefly, it enacted:

    1.   'That for all time neither laicized clerk nor cleric should make traffic of God's Church'; a decree aimed clearly at simony and directed towards the making of suitable ap-pointments.[5]

2 Muirchertach's intention may have been to deal the final blow to the centre of Eoghanacht power against which the Dalcassians had fought their own way to supremacy in Munster.

3 Gwynn, 'The Twelfth Century Reform', p. 11.

4 H. J. Lawlor, *St. Bernard of Clairvaux's Life of St. Malachy of Armagh*, pp. xxx–xxxi and 47; hereafter referred to as Lawlor, *St. Bernard's Life of St. Malachy*.

5 For distinctions between laicized clerk and cleric see Gwynn, 'The Twelfth Century Reform', p. 13, and Hughes, *Ch. in early Ir. soc.*, pp. 265–6.

2.   'That neither to king nor chieftain should the church in Ireland pay tribute until doom.' This practice of liberating the church from economic obligations to secular overlords had become common but not universal by the eleventh century.

3.   'That no layman in Ireland shall be an erenagh.'

4.   'That two erenaghs should not be in the one church.' This had for its object the avoidance of possible disputes arising from dual control, and may also have been aimed at reducing the number of *chorepiscopi* in the Irish church.[6]

5.   'That no erenagh of any church in Ireland should have a wife.' The inclusion of non-celibate abbots and bishops is presupposed in this decree.

6.   This decree confirmed the church's right of sanctuary but stipulated that the privilege did not extend to those guilty of murder or parricide.

7.   In this decree the church's freedom from the civil courts (*privilegium fori*) was reaffirmed.

8.   O'Grady's translation of this decree on marriage reads: 'That in Éire none shall have to wife either his father's wife or his grandfather's [i.e., his stepmother or his step-grand-mother]; either his sister or his daughter, or his brother's wife, or any woman at all thus near akin,' *ná ben ar bith chom fogus sin i ngaol.*[7]

Strangely enough the decrees of Cashel were silent on the current Irish practice of concubinage and divorce which Saint Anselm brought to the attention of Muirchertach Ua Briain in 1096: 'It is said that husbands exchange their wives freely and publicly with the wives of others, as a man might exchange one horse for another or any other thing for something given in exchange.' The strictures of Anselm were of little avail against immemorial custom enshrined within the highly codified system of brehon law which made divorce easy and even made allowance for various grades of wives and concubines. Consequently the overthrow of the native Irish marriage law inherent in the eighth decree of the Synod of Cashel was neither speedily nor easily achieved. Seventy years later Pope Alexander IV was given to understand that the Irish 'still marry their stepmothers and are not ashamed to have children by them; that a man may live with his brother's wife while his brother is still

---

6   The *chorepiscopi* were regularly consecrated bishops who had no canonical territorial jurisdiction but who were stationed in large monasteries or attached to certain churches, and whose pastoral duties were subject to the jurisdiction of local abbots or bishops.

7   Gwynn, 'The Twelfth Century Reform', p. 16.

alive; that one man may live in concubinage with two sisters; and that many of them, putting away the mother, will marry the daughters.'[8]

The Synod of Cashel marked a definite breakthrough but its decrees were mainly confined to *Leath Mogha* and it was not until the church of Armagh underwent a major structural re-shuffle that the wished-for reform took on national dimensions. The decade which separated the Cashel assembly from that of Rathbreasail was the period during which this great metamorphosis was effected. The Clann Sinnaich hereditary succession to the coarbship of Armagh was still the determining factor in the ecclesiastical politics of Patrick's church, and it was in virtue of direct descent in this family that Cellach (Celsus) became *comharba Pátraic* in 1105. Cellach's first step after his appointment was to have himself ordained to the priesthood thereby breaking the tradition of the Ui Sinnaich lay abbots. In the following year, 1106, Caincomruc Ua Baigill, bishop of Armagh, died and the way was open for a further innovation. But first Cellach made his *cuairt* or visitation and collected tribute in the lands of Cinel Eoghan and then marched south to Munster, the headquarters of the reform movement. Here he also collected tribute and 'received the orders of noble bishop (*uasal-epscop*) by direction of the men of Ireland', as the *Annals of Ulster* record.[9] It is more than likely that Maol Muire Ua Dúnáin was one of the consecrating prelates and that the ceremony was performed according to the Roman ritual, *more Romano*; but at the same time the consecration did not entail the setting up of a regular hierarchy. The title *uasal-epscop*, however, combined with Cellach's other title of *comharba Pátraic,* marked him out as a bishop with special claims to pre-eminence in the Irish church.[10] Visitations to Connaught and Meath were undertaken by Cellach in the years 1108 and 1110. By that time Limerick had been erected into a bishopric (1106) and its first bishop, Gilbert, who was soon to become papal legate, was consecrated in Ireland by an Irish prelate and not by the archbishop of Canterbury as had been the case with the other Hiberno-Norse bishoprics of Dublin and Waterford. Correspondence between Gilbert and Anselm was nevertheless friendly, and a gift of Irish pearls for the archbishop accompanied Gilbert's announcement of his consecration. At some

8   Maurice P. Sheehy, ed., *Pontificia Hibernica : Medieval Papal Chancery Documents Concerning Ireland, 640–1261*, i, 21.

9   The *Annals of Inisfallen* do not record Cellach's consecration.

10   Gwynn, 'The Twelfth Century Reform', p. 25.

date after 1107 Gilbert had written his treatise *De Statu Ecclesiae* which sounded the death-knell of the monastic *paruchiae* and put an end to the separation of order and administration as hitherto practised in the Irish church.[11] In this important treatise, which became the handbook of the reformers, Gilbert outlined 'for the bishops and priests of the whole of Ireland' his plans for a hierarchically structured church based on European conditions, and at the same time he protested against 'diverse schismatical orders by which almost all Ireland had been deluded in the past'. The church, he said, must be ruled by bishops. Parishes administered by priests and other clergy must be established under episcopal jurisdiction. Monasteries must be governed by presbyter-abbots and these too must come under episcopal control. Bishoprics and dioceses were not to be set up at random; the number of bishops and the size of their dioceses were to be carefully considered, and each bishop was to have a fixed seat and definite powers of jurisdiction. The bishops, numbering at least three and not more than twenty, were to be subject to an archbishop, over whom was the primate, subject immediately to the pope. Archbishop and primate must go to Rome for consecration and to receive the palls (*pallia*). Lay abbots and coarbs were given no quarter in Gilbert's scheme and monks were to confine themselves within the strict limits of monasticism. In other words, participation in parochial work was denied them.

THE SYNOD OF RATHBREASAIL, 1111

The instrument whereby Gilbert's scheme was put into operation was the great reforming Synod of Rathbreasail or Fiad-mic-Aengusa which assembled in 1111. In contrast with the earlier Synod of Cashel this assembly is given extensive coverage in the *Annals of Inisfallen*, the *Annals of Ulster*, the *Annals of Tigernach* and the *Chronicon Scotorum*. All refer to it as the Synod of Fiad-mic-Aengusa, but Keating who took his text from the lost *Annals of Cluain Eidhneach* (Clonenagh) gives Rathbreasail as the venue. An accommodating scribe who inserted an interlinear note in the manuscript text of the *Annals of Inisfallen* resolves the apparent discrepancy by giving Rathbreasail as the alternative name for Fiad-mic-Aengusa. The selection of a southern site—Rathbreasail lay in the central plain of Tipperary near Templemore—is yet another recognition of Munster as the original seed-bed of the

---

11 The text of *De Statu Ecclesiae* (*de usu ecclesiastico*) is printed in Erlington, *The Whole Works of Most Rev. James Ussher, D.D.*, iv, 500–510.

reform movement. Rathbreasail opened under the presidency
of Muirchertach Ua Briain, king of Munster, Gilbert attended
in virtue of his appointment as papal legate representing Pope
Pascal II, Cellach attended as coarb of Patrick and Maol Muire
Ua Dúnáin as 'noble senior of Ireland' (*ard senóir innse Éirenn*).
The *Annals of Ulster* give the attendance as '50 bishops *vel paulo
plus*, 300 priests and 3,000 ecclesiastics (*mac n-ecalsa*), together
with the nobles of *Leath Mogha*' whose purpose was to enjoin
rule and good conduct upon everyone, both layman and cleric.
The *Annals of Tigernach* and the *Chronicon Scotorum* give a
somewhat different enumeration; the scribe responsible for
the *Annals of Inisfallen* gives his information in the form of a
quatrain:

> The number of the pure clerical order
> In the synod of Rath Bresail:
> Three hundred priests—a perfect festival—
> And a fair fifty bishops.

The disciplinary decrees of this great synod must have been
largely repetitive of those issued at Cashel, but these decrees
were summarily passed over by all the annalists who merely
inform us that the synod 'enacted discipline and law better than
any made in Ireland before that time'. The synod's main interest
therefore lies in its scheme of diocesan arrangement, since it was
at this synod, wrote Keating, 'that the churches of Ireland were
given up entirely to the bishops, free forever from the authority
and rent of the lay princes. It was there also were regulated the
sees or dioceses of the bishops of Ireland.'[12]

The hierarchical structure framed at Rathbreasail divided
Ireland into two ecclesiastical provinces corresponding to the
old political divisions of *Leath Chuinn* and *Leath Mogha*.
Armagh was to become the metropolitan of the northern
province, Cashel would control the south and overall primacy
was reserved to the archbishop of Armagh. The parallel between
the arrangement thus drafted and that obtaining in the Anglo-
Saxon church *vis-à-vis* the archbishops of Canterbury and
York was obvious, except that in England the southern metropolitan was primate and in the subsequent development of the
suffragan sees the northern province of York always remained
geographically smaller than its southern counterpart. In Ireland
under the Rathbreasail arrangements the primatial see of
Armagh was to have twelve suffragan bishoprics distributed in
the provinces of Ulster and Connacht and in the kingdom of

12 Geoffrey Keating, *Foras Feasa ar Éirinn: The History of Ireland*, ix, 298–9.

Meath; this would correspond roughly to the modern provinces of Armagh and Tuam. Cashel would represent twelve sees in Munster and Leinster, corresponding to the modern provinces of Dublin and Cashel; and in this way the requirements of Gilbert's *De Statu Ecclesiae* which stipulated that an archbishop should not have less than three and not more than twenty suffragans were fulfilled. The plan looked well enough on paper; its implementation was another matter, and Keating's text which mentions twenty-four but listed twenty-five dioceses shows that the minds of those who framed the diocesan hierarchy were not altogether clear as to what they were about. The statistics given by Keating are as follows:

PROVINCE OF ARMAGH

Ulster	*Connacht*	*Meath*
Clochar	Tuaim	Daimhliag
Ard Sratha	Cluain Ferta	Cluain Ioraird
Doire	Conga	
(nó Raith Bhoth)		
Coinnire	Ceall Aladh	
Dún dá Leathghlas	Ard Carna	
	(nó Ardachadh)	

The inclusion of Armagh brings the total to thirteen. The decree made allowances for changes in Connacht at the discretion of the clergy on condition that they did not increase the number of bishoprics already laid down.

PROVINCE OF CASHEL

Munster	*Leinster*
Lios Mór (Port Lairge)	Ceall Chainnigh
Corcach	Leithghleann
Raith Maighe Deiscirt	Ceall Dara
Luimneach	Gleann dá Loch
Ceall Dalua	Fearna (nó Loch Garman)
Imleach Iobhair	

Including Cashel, the total comes to twelve.[13]

Disapproval of the above arrangement was almost immediate. The exclusion of Dublin even on the pretext of its close association with Canterbury cannot have found favour with the majority of attending prelates at Rathbreasail. The Canterbury associations of the Hiberno-Norse dioceses of Waterford and Wexford do not seem to have created any issue: these dioceses

13   John MacErlean, 'The Synod of Raith Breasail', *Archiv. Hib.*, iii (1914), 3–4.

were incorporated into the Rathbreasail system by the simple
expedient of giving them the alternative titles of Lismore and
Ferns.[14] Gilbert's own diocese of Limerick did not present
any such problem; so for the next ten years Cellach awaited a
favourable opportunity for the incorporation of the diocese of
Dublin in his scheme for an Irish hierarchy. Next, the Rathbreasail settlement for Meath which superseded Ciaran's
paruchia of Clonmacnoise by the new bishoprics of Clonard
and Duleek was not allowed to stand. A rival assembly at
Uisneach at which the influence of the king of Meath and the
clergy of Clonmacnoise was preponderant effected an entirely
new division by which Clonmacnoise became the bishopric of
the western portion of Meath and Clonard replaced Duleek in
the east. But while Clonmacnoise regained its pre-eminence in
Meath, the prestige of the great southern monastery of Emly
was seriously impaired by the emergence of an archbishopric
at Cashel. Cashel, which had never been a monastic site,
benefited immensely by annexation from her suffragans. There
were other annexations with political overtones; all of which go
to prove that nothing could have been more unrealistic than
the Rathbreasail delineations for the south Munster dioceses.
Bearing in mind the prominent part taken in the reform movement by the Ua Briain of Dal Chais, one cannot avoid the
conclusion that the decisions of the synod were in large measure
influenced by Thomond churchmen. The precision with which
the diocesan boundaries of Limerick were delimited must also
be seen as a gesture in favour of Muirchertach Ua Briain who
had made Limerick his capital city. In the immediate pre-
Rathbreasail era there were about fourteen episcopal centres
in Munster, of which Thomond and Desmond had an equal
number. The reduction of this number to seven and the re-
distribution of these seven bishoprics between north and south
Munster is of particular interest: had the boundaries set out at
Rathbreasail been accepted, O'Brien dominated territory
would have had five bishoprics—Limerick, Emly, Cashel,
Killaloe and Ardfert (Kerry), whereas the MacCarthy realms
would have had but two, namely Cork and Lios Mór.

Of the Munster dioceses as enumerated by Keating, Lios
Mór (or Port Lairge) touched Cork on the east and took in a
considerable amount of territory now belonging to Cloyne. Its
limits were 'from Mileadhach on the bank of the Barrow at

---

14 Dublin is not mentioned as part of the diocese of Glendaloch; nor is it given as an
alternative title to Glendaloch. A century after Rathbreasail, however, Glendaloch
became an archdeaconry in the diocese of Dublin.

Cumar na ttri nUisce to Corcach and from the Siuir southward
to the ocean'. The proposed diocese of Raith Maighe Deiscirt
(subsequently Ardfert and now Kerry) touched Cork on the
west and extended 'from Baoi Bheire [Dursey Island] to Ceann
Beara and from the Feil to Dairbhre [Valentia Island]'. This
was the territory of Ua Conchubhair Ciarraighe, a foremost
ally of the O'Briens. Luimneach, which touched Cork on the
north-west, included some parts of the present diocese of
Cloyne, as did also Imleach Iobhair which touched the Rathbreasail boundary for Cork at several points along the Blackwater.[15] Also to be noted is the fact that if the Rathbreasail
decisions were to become effective, certain territories of south
Munster would have to be surrendered to north Munster
dioceses. Cashel, for instance, was to annex a fairly large slice
of the diocese of Lios Mór which lay north of the river Suir and
extended roughly from Cahir to Carrick-on-Suir. By way of
compensation Lios Mór was to get that part of county Cork
which lay between Cork city and Youghal and which belonged
to the diocese of Cloyne, and all the lands of Cloyne north of the
Blackwater were to be annexed to the dioceses of Emly (Imleach
Iobhair) and Limerick. By reference to the southern dioceses
therefore, the ecclesiastical geography of Rathbreasail would
cause Cloyne to be partitioned and Ross to be absorbed in Cork.

The diocese of Cork as envisaged at Rathbreasail but never
fully actualized extended 'from Corcach to Carn Ui Neid and
from the Abhainn Mhór southward to the ocean'. Cork city
was to be the eastern limit of the diocese, Mizen Head its
western terminus, with the dividing line of the Blackwater on
the north and the ocean on the south. Two significant twelfth-
century references indicate, however, that the findings of
Rathbreasail were ignored in Cloyne. In 1139 the O'Healihys
of Donoughmore are described as having their freehold as
erenaghs from the *bishop of Cloyne*,[16] and for the year 1149 the
Four Masters record the death of Nehemius Ua Muirchertaig
uasal-epscop of Cloyne.[17] Nehemius is also mentioned in Saint
Bernard's account of the life of Saint Malachy[18] and in the
Vision of Tundale (*Visio Tundali*) composed by an Irish monk

---

15 MacErlean, 'The Synod of Raith Breasail', pp. 14–15.

16 W. F. T. Butler, *Gleanings from Irish History*, p. 253.

17 John Lynch, *De Praesulibus Hiberniae*, ii, 11, mentions Nehemius as archbishop of
Cashel, but on p. 161 calls him bishop of Cloyne.

18 Lawlor, *St. Bernard's Life of St. Malachy*, p. 89.

in Ratisbon and written about the year 1148–49.[19] Nehemius is mentioned in the Vision as one of the four bishops who were with Saint Patrick in Paradise, and it seems likely that the Irish of south Kerry looked to him as their *uasal-epscop* regardless of the erection of the diocese of Raith Maighe Deiscirt. Diocesan boundaries were still a novelty and the title of *uasal-epscop of Leath Mogha* was certainly in the line of ancient tradition. Nehemius was plainly the holiest bishop of all that area, and the fact that he was also an Ua Muirchertaig was good enough for Kerry. So much for the diocese of Cloyne. As regards Ross, the decline of the Ui Eachach in 1118 and the re-emergence of the Corca Laighdhe made imperative a reconsideration of the Rathbreasail enactments and a recognition of the rights of this small but ancient diocese in south-west Cork.

Next to be considered are the strong traditions that the tribeland of the O'Donoghues (Cinel Laoghaire and Clann Sealbaigh) extending from Murragh westwards to Drimoleague (Dromdaliag) constituted in centuries past a separate diocese of Kinneigh (Cenn Eich) with the ancient church of Saint Colman or Mocolmóg at Kinneigh as its centre. There is no early contemporary reference to this bishopric but it is specifically mentioned in a document from the Archives of Propaganda dated 17 September 1624: '. . . *Unus est Rossensis episcopatus vacans, alter est episcopatus Kinneag qui est Corcagiensi et Clonensi annexus minus necessario utpote capacibus et amplis.*'[20] Bishop Downes who visited Kinneigh in May 1700 states: 'I went to Kinneigh. . . . A high round tower stands in the south-west corner of the churchyard. . . . 'Tis supposed this church was formerly a cathedral. . . . A stone is in the south-west corner of the church of Kineigh, counted very sacred, which the Irish solemnly swear upon. . . . Half a plowland of Kineigh, lying near the church to the west, belongs to the Bishop of Corke and contains about 60 English acres.'[21] Kinneigh, according to Smith, was anciently a cathedral founded by Saint Mocolmoge but united to Ross.[22] We get no clue from these references as to the period when the diocese

---

19 Kenney, *Sources*, p. 742, calls the *Vision* 'an elaborate but crude compilation of cosmopolitan horrors . . . [which] . . . with the exception of the Voyage of St Brendan . . . became the most widely popular of all the stories of mediaeval Ireland'. The *Vision* is reproduced in popular form in C. S. Boswell's *An Irish Precursor of Dante*, pp. 212–19.

20 *Scritture originali riferite nelle congregazioni generali*, vol. 294, f. 41.

21 Brady, *Records*, i, 190.

22 Smith, *History of Cork*, i, 246.

of Kinneigh was in existence, but it seems to have belonged to
the pre-Norman period. Quite a number of small bishoprics
make their appearance in north Munster in the eleventh and
twelfth centuries, chiefly it would seem, as a reaction against
the overbearing conduct of the O'Briens of Thomond, once
the death of Muirchertach and his brother Diarmaid broke
the O'Brien power within a few years of Rathbreasail. The
breakaway bishoprics were Iniscathaigh in the Corca Baiscinn
tribeland of south-west Clare, Kilfenora in the O'Loughlin
territory of north-west Clare and Roscrea in the territory of
Eli O Cearbhaill. Domhnall Mor Ua Briain was strong enough
to bring Roscrea and Iniscathaigh back into the diocese of
Killaloe; but Kilfenora survived, as did Ross and Cloyne in
opposition to Cork in the south. Perhaps it was at this period
and for a like reason that the west Cork diocese of Kinneigh
came into existence consequent upon the intrusion of Dalcassian
coarbs into the Cork monastery in opposition to the local
church families of Ua Sealbhaigh and Ua Cochlain. The proliferation of territorial problems of this nature and the fact that
a mere synodal decree could neither dispossess existing coarbs
nor enforce the jurisdiction of new bishops—let alone provide
revenues for them—made some rectification of the Rathbreasail
decisions imperative.

RATHBREASAIL TO KELLS, 1111–1152

The last years of the reign of Muirchertach Ua Briain were
years of conflict between him and his brother Diarmaid, of
which Toirdelbach Ua Conchubhair of Connacht took advantage by organizing a series of raids against Munster covering
the years 1114 to 1119. The death of Diarmaid Ua Briain in
Cork in 1118 and of Muirchertach in Lismore in 1119 left
Munster open to further attacks from the men of Connacht in
1121 and 1122 by which time Toirdelbach, son of Diarmaid
Ua Briain, had forfeited all hope of regaining the kingship of
Munster. Toirdelbach Ua Conchubhair partitioned the kingdom
of Munster into the old divisions of Thomond and Desmond
and assigned Desmond to MacCarthaigh from whom he
exacted hostages as a guarantee of subservience. Except for
the reign of Domhnall Mor Ua Briain (1168–94) Munster was
henceforth divided into opposing kingdoms in which rivalry
between the O'Briens and the MacCarthys alternated with
mutual alliances against their common enemy Connacht. The
maintenance of this traditional feud with Connacht was to have
important bearings on Cork diocesan history.

Dublin's exclusion from the Rathbreasail enactments claimed

Cellach's attention in the decades following the dissolution of
the synod. The death of Bishop Samuel O Haingli in 1121 followed by the consecration of his successor Gregory at Canterbury
was the turning-point in improving relations between Armagh
and Dublin. Cellach, who had come to Dublin on hearing of
Samuel's death, had his primacy formally recognized by
Gregory, who found himself uncomfortably face to face with
a strong pro-Irish party within his capital. The annalistic entry
which records this submission is understandably exaggerated:
*Cellach comarba Patraic do ghabhail epscopoiti Atha Cliat a
togha Gall 7 Gaedhil.*[23] The real significance of the incident
is that Cellach seized upon Samuel's death as an opportunity
for enforcing the views of Rathbreasail and for breaking
Canterbury's hold on Dublin. The record of Cellach's death
in the *Annals of Ulster* best expresses the prestige that then
attached to him as archbishop of Armagh, 'the one head to
whom the Gaedhil and Gaill, both laics and clerics, were
obedient'. Cellach's title passed in 1134, and not without
opposition, to Malachy (Maol Maodhóg O Morgair), son of
a former master of the school of Armagh, an ascetic, an ardent
reformer, a bishop and a friend of Gilbert and Malchus of
Waterford. Malachy's early reforming campaign had taken him
to Lismore where he became friend and adviser to Cormac
MacCarthy, king of south Munster 'and for a time of all
Munster', whom the nobles of Munster at the instigation of
Toirdelbach Ua Conchubhair deposed in favour of his brother
Donough in 1126. Cormac went on pilgrimage to Lismore 'and
took the crozier (*bachall*) there'; hence his designation as
Espug Ri nÉrenn in the *Annals of Loch Cé*. On Cormac's
deposition Munster was partitioned between Donough Mac-
Carthy and Conor O'Brien of Thomond; but the peace was
short-lived and differences between MacCarthy and O'Brien
resulted in Cormac's restoration as king of south Munster in
1131–32.[24] For the remaining years of his turbulent reign Cormac
was a vital link in introducing into the diocese of Cork the
advance guard of the reform which under Malachy was fast
gaining momentum in the church. Cormac 'loved and always
reverenced Malachy; so much the more because he had learned
more fully in the holy man the things that were worthy of
reverence and affection'.[25] On his restoration he made a grant
of land to Malachy and his exiled community (their reforms

23   *A.U.* and *A.F.M.*

24   Butler, *Gleanings from Irish History*, p. 139.

25   Lawlor, *St. Bernard's Life of St. Malachy*, p. 23.

had been unacceptable in Bangor) and thus was established at
Iveragh (Ibrach) the *Monasterium Ibracense* where Malachy
remained until he returned to Armagh in 1132. Suggested
localities for the *Monasterium Ibracense* are Uibh Rathach in
west Kerry, Sceilig Mhichí off the Kerry coast and Ui
Braccain[26] in the east of the kingdom of Cashel. The monastery's
location at *Templebrakeny* in Barnehely at the mouth of Cork
harbour may yet be admitted.

Malachy's consecration as archbishop of Armagh in 1132
was followed by his *cuairt* of Munster in 1134, the year in which
a hosting into Connacht led by Cormac MacCarthy led to the
unforeseeable establishment of regular diocesan government in
Cork. Cormac's allies included the O'Briens of Tuadh Mumha,
the Gaedhil of Cork, Waterford, Wexford and Dublin, all
reinforced by the sea power of the Ui Eachach and the Corca
Laighdhe.[27] In the course of this attack on the western province
the abbey of Saint Mary at Cong was pillaged and in the
ensuing peace conference at Abhall Ceithernaigh near Uisneach
in county Westmeath over which Muireadach Ua Dubhthaigh
'high bishop of Connaught' presided, a special clause pushed
by Ua Dubhthaigh and by Aodh O hOisin, abbot of Tuam,
obliged Cormac to make reparation for the destruction of
Cong. The reparation was to consist in the erection of an
abbey in Cork dependent upon that of Cong, and concerning
which Sir James Ware has the following entry: 'Cormacc,
King of Munster, or as others say, of Desmond, built this abbey
for Canons Regular of St John the Baptist. It is (unless I err)
the same as that which St Bernard in his Life of Malachy
called *Monasterium Ibracense*, built by King Cormac and
richly endowed by his son and successor, Dermot, about the
year 1173. This abbey, its former name—the Abbey of St
Finbarr's Cave—having been many years antiquated, is called
the Gill Abbey, from Gil-Aeda, an abbot of great name and
afterwards Bishop of Cork, who died A.D. 1172.'[28] Windele
expresses more correctly the work of Cormac in his statement
that the abbey of Cork was 'refounded' and placed under the

26   Edmund Hogan, *Onomasticon Goedelicum locorum et tribuum Hiberniae et Scotiae*,
p. 662.

27   John T. Collins, 'A McCarthy Miscellany', *Cork Hist. Soc. Jn.*, liii (1948), 95,
states 'The Ui Eachach were masters of the coast from Cork Harbour to Timoleague.
The Corca Laighdhe held from Timoleague to Schull and the Ui Eachach again from
Schull to North Kerry. They must have maintained the greater part of the fleet of
Leath Mogha.'

28   Sir James Ware, *De Hibernia et Antiquitatibus eius*, p. 288.

rule of canons regular of Saint Augustine.[29] On the question
of titular we find Ware citing the abbey's dedication to Saint
John the Baptist, whereas a charter known as Dermot's Charter
of 1173/74 gives Saint John, Apostle and Evangelist, as titular.
A transcript of this charter in Wares's own handwriting may
be consulted in the British Museum, and its reconciliation with
Ware's own statement poses an obvious problem. Ware may have
wished to distinguish between the new abbey of canons regular
and a Benedictine foundation in Douglas Street which was similarly dedicated to Saint John the Evangelist.[30] On the other hand
the change of titular may signify the preponderating influence of
the monastery of Tuam which was dedicated to Saint John the
Evangelist and was ruled by Aodh O hOisin, one of the arbitrators
at the conference of Abhall Ceithernaigh and subsequently
archbishop of Tuam. Gill Abbey's dependence on the abbey
of Saint Mary at Cong is clearly seen from the contents of an
old Rental of Cong which Tadhg O Dubhthaig, a monk of Cong,
compiled in 1501 and which contains the following entries:

Item: Cormac MacCarthy, chief of his nation, gave to the
aforesaid monastery (Cong) the parcel of land in his patri-
mony of Birra (Beara) called Inis Cinge (Iniscuinge in Bantry
Bay) and a bell-rope from the ships whatever going out of
the harbour of Dunboith (Dunboy).

Item: That no lay person can levy anything in the city of
Cork without the licence of the Ordinary and of the Church
and Abbey of Cong; and from the day in which he is constituted and appointed, the Abbot of Cork is bound to yield
every year to the Abbot of Cong sixteen half-marks for gilding
the chalices of the monastery of Cong; and on the same day is
bound to hand over all the vestments of the new Abbot of
Cork to the Treasury of Cong. Moreover, the above Cormac
MacCarthy gave to the monastery of Cong a bell-rope from
from every ship whatever going out of the harbour of Cork.[31]

In details of abbatial elections it was the privilege of the
abbot of Cong to confirm an abbot-elect of Gill Abbey and to
remove an existing abbot 'without prejudice to the Bishop of

29 John Windele, *Windele's Cork: Historical and Descriptive Notices* . . . , p. 78;
hereafter referred to as Windele, *Cork*.

30 Arbitrary juggling with titular saints will scarcely explain why pilgrimages in
honour of Saint John the Baptist were, until comparatively recent times, a constant
feature of popular devotion at Gougane Barra.

31 British Museum, Add. MS 4787, f. 1.

Cork, to whom the said monastery of St. Mary [de Antro Sancti Fymbarri *alias* Saint John the Evangelist] is by ordinary right subject'.[32] The electoral rights of the Arroasian abbot of Cong did not, however, necessarily prove a common rule, even though such a common rule is possible; Corkmen are apt to go their own way. There is no evidence for the Arroasian rule in Cork throughout the medieval period; but this does not at all minimize the importance of the canons regular of Gill Abbey in the history of the diocese of Cork.

The first edition of the Ordnance Survey maps of Cork county[33] shows the site of the abbey on the rocky eminence, since called Gill Abbey, overlooking the Lee and close to the traditional cave of Saint Finbarr, whence it derived the name 'Abbey of the Cave' or *de Antro* which occurs in official documents down the years. Other designations of the abbey were the [abbey] of Gillaeda *alias de Antro* without the walls of 'Cork',[34] the abbey of Saint Mary *als* Saint John the Evangelist,[35] *Monasterium Beatae Mariae et Sancti Johannis Evangeliste de Antro Fymbarri*[36] and the abbey of Weym, this last representing a derivative of the Irish *uaimh* of which it seems to be a Latinized version.[37] In later times the monastery was finally called Gill Abbey, a name derived from Giolla Aedh O Muighin who is said to have been appointed bishop of Cork by Saint Malachy in 1140. Cormac MacCarthy, founder of Gill Abbey, was slain in 1138 at Mahoonagh (Magh Tamhnach) near Newcastlewest in county Limerick. His eulogy in the *Annals of Loch Cé* reads: 'Cormac, son of MacCarthaigh, chief king of Des Mumha and bishop-king of Ireland in his time as regards piety, the presentation of jewels and valuables to clerics and churches, and ecclesiastical riches, in books and utensils, to God . . . fell in

32   *Calendar of Papal Letters, 1458–71*, pp. 302–3. The entry from which the above extract is taken represents the first mention in the papal registers of the association of the canon regular of the Lateran congregation with Ireland. The date is 1468–9.

33   O.S. map, Cork county, six-inch sheet, no. 75 (1845).

34   *Cal. papal letters, 1404–15*, p. 203, under date 1410.

35   Ibid., xiii, pt. 1, p. 125, under date 1482.

36   Bolster, 'Obligationes pro Annatis Corcagienses', under date 1465, p. 4.

37   This name appears in Patent Roll 25 Edward I, for the year 1293. *Weyme*, the Abbatia de Antro Sancti Fynbarri of the Roman documents is, according to the late Denis O'Sullivan, but the Latinized version of the abbey's native Irish title, *Mainistir na hUamha*, and he points out that since the Irish word *uaimh* is not pronounced as spelled, it is easy to form an orthographical connection between the various names Weyme, Weym, Wem, Weeme, Lueim and L'Ueim of the Norman copyists and clerks with the native Irish *uaimh*, (See Denis O'Sullivan, 'Monastic Establishments of Medieval Cork', *Cork Hist. Soc. Jn.*, xlviii [1943], 9–18.)

treachery by the people of Tuadh Mumha; and a blessing be with his soul.'

Once a semblance of order had been restored in the northern province of Armagh, Malachy resigned from the primatial see in favour of Gilla Mac Liag or Gelasius and retired to the diocese of Down. He immediately set about reforming the community at Bangor where he had formerly met with concerted opposition, and from Bangor as his headquarters he practically ruled the Irish church for the rest of his life.[38] In 1139–40 he travelled to Rome to secure papal sanction for his reform programme and to seek *pallia* for the archbishops of Armagh and Cashel. 'Pope Innocent II, of happy memory, was then in the Apostolic See,' wrote Saint Bernard. 'He received him courteously and displayed kindly pity for him on account of his long pilgrimage'—but he did not grant him the *pallia*. Malachy was to return to Ireland and 'call together the bishops and clerks and the magnates of the land and hold a general council; and so with the assent and common desire of all shall demand the pall by persons of honest repute, and it shall be given . . .'[39] This council or synod was eventually held at Inis Pádraig in 1148. Meantime Malachy was appointed papal legate in succession to Gilbert of Limerick who wished to resign because of advancing years. Malachy's journey to Rome was marked by a visit to the abbey of Clairvaux which resulted in a close personal friendship between him and Saint Bernard and led to the establishment of Ireland's first Cistercian abbey at Mellifont in 1141/42. Malachy also visited the Augustinian abbey of Arrouaise near Arras 'where he saw for the first time the full observance of the Augustinian rule by a reformed community of canons regular'.[40] Convinced of the potentialities of Arrouaise for the work he had in mind, he introduced the customs of Arrouaise into episcopal sees and many other places in Ireland, and notably into houses of Augustinian canons regular.[41] Herein lay the nucleus of future cathedral chapters.

For the next eight years (1140–48) Malachy pursued his legatine commission throughout the length and breadth of Ireland, and it seems most probable that this was the time when decisions were made as to how many of the new dioceses that

38 Kenney, *Sources*, p. 766.

39 Lawlor, *St. Bernard's Life of St. Malachy*, p. 73.

40 Gwynn, 'The Twelfth Century Reform', p. 48.

41 Hughes, *Ch. in early Ir. soc.*, p. 270.

had come into existence since Rathbreasail were to be given full recognition. Malachy was in Cork in 1140 where the death of the erenagh Domhnall O Saolbach had seemingly led to a dispute over the election of a successor. Malachy 'calling together the clergy and people took pains to unite the hearts and desires of the opposing parties . . . immediately he named to them, not any of the nobles of the land but rather a certain poor man whom he knew to be holy and learned; *and he was a stranger.*'[42] The stranger is believed to have been Giolla Aedh O Muighin, who is represented in the sources[43] as a monk of Saint Muireadach's community at Errew near Lough Conn in the present parish of Crossmolina, county Mayo. The *Miscellaneous Irish Annals* carry a more cogent entry under date 1152 to the effect that 'Aedh O hOisin, the archbishop from whom Gilla Aedh is named, died.' Giolla Aedh O Muighin was probably a canon regular, and his elevation to Cork like that of Malachy to Armagh represented a clean breakaway from adherence to 'founder's kin' and 'donor's kin' in the matter of ecclesiastical elections. Thus in 1140 the Malachian reform had a spectacular triumph in Cork when the offices of *comharba* Bairre and bishop of Cork were conferred on Giolla Aedh O Muighin. Relative to the other commitments of Malachy between 1140 and 1148 Saint Bernard contents himself with the unsatisfactory statement that he held synods in various places. We know of only one from the annals: Terryglass in 1144;[44] but it can hardly have been a mere coincidence that two of the few places mentioned by Bernard as scenes of miracles worked by Malachy are Cork and Cloyne. And it is not unlikely that as papal legate he was called upon to make decisions as to the local claims of Cloyne—claims which were pushed by Nehemius Ua Muirchertaig and finally admitted at Kells.

THE SYNOD OF KELLS, 1152

The *Annals of the Four Masters* record that in 1148 in accordance with the instructions of Pope Innocent II Malachy convened a synod at Inis Pádraig (a small island off the coast of Dublin) at which fifteen bishops and two hundred priests attended 'to establish rules and morals for all, both laity and clergy'.

---

42   Lawlor, *St. Bernard's Life of St. Malachy*, p. 93.

43   *Ann. Tig.* gives 'Airidh Locha Con'. Lynch, *De praesulibus Hib.*, ii, 141: '. . . *quia non in Momonia sed in Connacia natus est, nimirum in Alladensi dioecesi a plebe de Muntirairedh Lochconam accolente.*'

44   *A.F.M.* and *Ann. Tig.*

Unlike the earlier synods of Cashel and Rathbreasail there was no Irish king in attendance at Inis Pádraig. The *pallia* were now demanded in due form and Malachy was commissioned to undertake a second journey to Rome to the court of Eugenius III; but he died *en route* at Clairvaux during the night of 1–2 November 1148. With his death the golden age of the reform movement came to an end, but the *pallia* duly arrived and in March 1152 Cardinal John Paparo convened a synod at Kells over which he presided as *Legatus a latere* in conjunction with Christian Ua Conairche, bishop of Lismore, who was to succeed Malachy as papal legate in Ireland. The synod opened, appropriately, on Laetare Sunday, 9 March 1152. Keating gives the attendance as twenty-two bishops and five bishops-elect; other sources imply a greater episcopal concourse, by reason perhaps of breakaway dioceses like Roscrea and Iniscathaigh and smaller ones like Ardmore and Mungret which sought recognition.[45] By giving four *pallia* instead of two, the synod elevated Dublin and Tuam to official archiepiscopal status, and by finally severing Dublin from Canterbury it set the seal on the work of the earlier reformers. Cardinal Paparo's ruling, which gave ten suffragan sees to Armagh, five to Dublin, six to Tuam and twelve to Cashel, shows that Kells was a synod of redrawn frontiers. The Cashel suffragans were Killaloe, Limerick, Iniscathaigh, Kilfenora, Emly, Roscrea, Waterford, Lismore, Cloyne, Cork, Ross and Ardfert; to which Ardmore and Mungret were postscripted as claiming the right to be bishoprics. Minor rectifications took place subsequently in all provences. In that of Cashel, Iniscathaigh and Roscrea were reabsorbed in the diocese of Killaloe, Mungret never gained recognition and Ardmore after some fifty years of independence was incorporated into the diocese of Lismore. Otherwise, the ecclesiastical geography of Kells has remained permanent (if one excludes the Cork-Ross amalgamation of 18 April 1958). The claims of Cloyne and Ross to independent status were recognized at Kells, and Giolla Aedh O Muighin who attended the synod in company with his immediate episcopal neighbours gave his sanction thereby to those claims. The presence of the representatives of the three southern dioceses at Kells is listed in MS 92 of the Library of the School of Science in Montpellier: *Episcopum de Cluamuama, episcopum de Corchaia, episcopum de Rosailithir.*[46]

45 H. J. Lawlor, 'A Fresh Authority for the Synod of Kells', *R.I.A. Proc.*, xxxvi, sect. c (1922), pp. 16–22.

46 Ibid.

Exclusive of archbishops and bishops, about 300 ecclesiastics —monks and canons—are invoiced on the attendance-list of Kells, 'and they established some rules thereat, namely to put away concubines and mistresses from men; not to ask payment for anointing and baptising; not to take payment for church property and to receive tithes punctually'.[47] Having thus initiated the process of exterminating the remaining abuses in the Irish church, Cardinal Paparo left Ireland towards the end of March 1152. The reform which he sponsored continued to gather momentum under Gilla Mac Liag of Armagh, Christian O Conairche of Lismore and other less prominent ecclesiastics, while the problem of the division of ecclesiastical territory between older coarbs and new bishops was a matter solved by each diocese in its own particular way. In Cork the division seems to have followed soon upon the establishment of Gill Abbey, and even though it is impossible at this distance to venture any definitive statement on the procedure adopted, it may be assumed that Gill Abbey's claims on churches like Durrus, Kilmocomoge, Inchigeela, Kilmichael, Barnehely and others, can only have arisen in or about the thirteenth and fourteenth centuries when monastic impropriators were a common feature of ecclesiastical administration.

Working from the diocesan system as established by the fourteenth century it seems probable that the canons regular set a premium on monastic property contiguous to Gill Abbey and within the ambit of the monastic precinct of Saint Finbarr. To the east of Gill Abbey a site was selected for a cathedral and bishop's residence; and as will be shown in a subsequent chapter, possessions administered immediately by the bishop extended further eastwards to Ringmahon and Douglas, southwards towards Ballyphehane and Turner's Cross and westwards to Ballincollig and Ballinhassig.[48] The abbey property was soon augmented by donations referred to in Dermot's Charter of 1173/74: this is a digest of grants made at different times (between 1152–72) to the abbey by Cormac MacCarthy, founder of the monastery; his son Dermot of Kilbawne from whom the charter is named; Dermot's son, Cormac Lehenagh, and Dermot O'Connor, son-in-law of the elder Cormac. The original charter was lodged in the abbey of Cong where centuries later Sir James Ware copied it. His transcript was subsequently catalogued in the British Museum as Add. MS 4793, f. 70; the original charter has long since disappeared. Harris' edition

47 *A.F.M.*

48 See Chapter vi.

of Archbishop King's *Collectanea* contains a second transcript identical with Ware's save for the following comment: 'It must be understood that the church [mentioned in the charter] is identical with the monastery of St Finbarr's Cave near Cork because it is a monastic house of the Canons Regular, and secondly, because the religious house mentioned in this instrument (*in hoc diplomate*) retains the lands mentioned to this day as it formerly did, and its foundation according to the annals of Ireland took place in the year 1173.'[49] The charter was signed by Christian, bishop of Lismore, legate of the Apostolic See; Donat, archbishop of Cashel; Bishops Gregory of Cork, Bricius of Limerick, Benedict of Ross, Mathew of Cloyne, Eugene of Ardmore, and the abbots of Magio and Cong. With reference to the signatories and their titles, Father T. J. Walsh makes some cogent observations: 'These signatories, seven bishops and two abbots, make no mention of coarbs. They declare their identity by a simple association with canonical sees or areas of jurisdiction. The reforms sanctioned by the Synod of Kells in 1152 are more than implied by these "suitable witnesses" of Dermot's charter. They are taken for granted.'[50]

The grants confirmed by Dermot MacCarthy on Gill Abbey were as follows:[51] 'My glorious father, the king, handed over the said place Lysuctdagh and Cloghan; Dermot O'Connor gave it Killina-Cannigh. . . . I have given . . . the villa of Illae . . . and my illustrious son Cormac . . . has granted to God and St John for the eternal welfare of his own soul and ours, Maduelgi; freely and peacefully and without any secular service.' Of these grants, *Lysuctdagh* remains unidentified, even though it appears in the early fourteenth century as Lyssaghagh, 'a messuage and 60 acres of land', when it was granted by David abbot of Weeme to Daniel Sarresfield for a term of twenty years.[52] *Cloghan* or *Clochán* extended roughly from Grattan Street (present) through the Mardyke to Victoria Cross; the name still occurs in legal documents. Cloghan was a wooded area at the time of the grant and for long afterwards: in 1303 the abbot of Gill Abbey took legal action against 'John Fitzwalter and others . . . for cutting down a number of trees in his wood

49 Walter Harris, '*Collectanea de Rebus Hibernicis*', ed. Charles McNeill, *Anal. Hib.*, no. 6 (1934), pp. 348 ff.

50 Denis O'Sullivan, 'St. Malachy, the Gill Abbey of Cork and the Rule of Arrouaise', *Cork Hist. Soc. Jn.*, liv (1949), 54–5.

51 For the charter in its entirety, see Appendix A.

52 Harris, '*Collectanea de Rebus Hibernicis*', p. 410.

at Cloghan, county Cork, value £100'.[53] The *Villa of Illae* is probably Ballyleigh, a townland near Ballymacadane to which it later belonged. Cormac Lehenagh's grant of *Maduelgi* would appear to be Magooly, Inniscarra, not far from Inish-leena (Inisluinge) where Gill Abbey had some territory. *Killina-Cannigh,* granted by Dermot O'Connor, is presumably Killeens in Saint Mary's parish (North parish) which is mentioned among the later possessions of Gill Abbey and which O'Connor apparently secured as a marriage dowry.

Certain important fisheries on the Lee were also associated with Gill Abbey and with the early bishops of Cork. The episcopal fisheries are given as Uadubgaill and Macmoelpoill and were apparently on the south channel of the Lee: Macmoel-poill may have been located near the present waterworks, the old name of which was the *Bald Weir*. Smith states (without quoting any original source) that 'nearer to the city were large weirs crossing the river Lee, for taking salmon. . . . These [weirs] were first erected by the monks of Gillabbey.'[54] Specific fisheries mentioned in connection with Gill Abbey were Corringraghine and Corincknowpoge, a fourth part of which belonged to the abbey, and which remained in church hands until at least the year 1699 when a rent roll of the diocese mentions 'all the cleevans and weirs called Beallaghkilly, Carrigrone and Carrigonopone'.[55] Two of the many weirs erected by the monks of Gill Abbey remained on the south channel of the Lee until well into the middle of the nineteenth century. The first Ordnance Survey map of Cork (1845) shows the Lower Gill Abbey Weir situated less than two hundred yards below Donovan's Bridge, almost coinciding with the present dam. A second weir, called the Upper Gill Abbey Weir, was erected further up-stream on the expansion of the river opposite the University College.[56]

In determining diocesan property strictly so-called, the decretal letter issued in 1199 by Pope Innocent III to the bishop of Cork[57] is, properly speaking, the foundation charter of the diocese. Its object as expressed in its title, *De Confirmatione*

---

53   Ibid., p. 377.

54   Smith, *History of Cork*, i, 353.

55   Webster, *The Diocese of Cork*, p. 403. From the *Fiants of Elizabeth*, 5566 and 5567, come references to 'two weirs for taking salmon called Cooringraghine and Cornockow-voge, belonging to the monastery de Antro of St Finbar *alias* Gilley'.

56   A. E. Went, 'The Fisheries of the River Lee', *Cork Hist. Soc. Jn.*, lxv (1960), 27–35.

57   Though not named, the bishop in question was probably Murchad O hAodha (1192–1206).

Privilegiorum, is self-evident[58]—the Normans were already in
Cork—and while it adhered in principle to the Rathbreasail
idea of a diocese extending from the Abhainn Mhór to the
ocean, it went beyond this earlier settlement by the inclusion
of (a) certain territories in Ross, (b) territories to the east of
Cork harbour in Cloyne and (c) territories to the north of the
Blackwater towards Limerick. The continued existence of
Cloyne and Ross was recognized, but Cloyne is now bisected
and Ross is practically swallowed up in Cork. The obvious
inference is that Cork in 1199 was regarded as the most important
of the three dioceses into which the county of Cork was divided.
The medieval bishops held thousands of acres in the vicinity
of the ancient church of Saint Finbarr and at other important
church centres throughout the diocese, and it is understandable
that in the change-over from tribal ownership to feudal tenure
much of the church's property would have been jeopardized.
For this reason there is a tendency in the decretal letter to place
special emphasis on lands: *terras Sancti Barri in Ucurp . . .
totum Umacciair in terris, ecclesiis, aquis et possessionibus . . .
terram Sancti Barri in Ciarrigi*. Taken as a whole, the names of
the churches and lands as listed in the decretal and set out below
with identifications where such are possible, show that the
diocese of Cork had assumed its present boundaries by the late
twelfth century. The ambit of the document is clear enough.
Detailed lists of Cork city churches are first given, *cum omnibus
pertinentiis suis et libertatibus intra et extra civitatem*. Eight
churches are mentioned in this section together with twenty-six
other places, mostly identifiable, lying within easy reach of the
city. Three main septs are mentioned in the decretal: *Ucurp*
or Ocurblethan whose tribeland, as we have seen, stretched
from Shandon to beyond Youghal and embraced—as far as the
diocese of Cork was concerned—Glanmire, Watergrasshill,
Glounthane, Currykippane and Saint Mary's Shandon; *Umacciair* (Ui Mic Ciair) extending from Cork to Ovens; *Ciarrigi*
or Kerrycurrihy, whose territory according to the most recent
survey included the present barony of Kerrycurrihy plus the
southern portion of the liberties of Cork, at least as far as a
line between Douglas and Carrigrohane.[59] Also included in
this section is Inispich or Spike Island *cum pertinentiis suis*. The
list next takes in Killanully, Cullen, Nohoval and Kinsale,

58 A decree granted to Cashel was more comprehensive; it embraced protection as
well as the confirmation of privileges and possessions in the archiepiscopal see.

59 Diarmuid Ó Murchadha, 'The Ciarraighe Cuirche', *Cork Hist. Soc. Jn.*, lxxiii
(1968), 60–70.

proceeds along the east bank of the Bandon River to Kilbrogan and Templemartin, then returns along the west bank of the same river to the diocese of Ross where some thirteen places are mentioned (i.e., from Timoleague to Kilcoe). Proceeding to Schull, the list follows the coastline to Bantry and the Bere peninsula, whence returning eastwards it enumerates places from Drimoleague to Kinneigh. Moving in a northerly direction here the list takes in Macloneigh and places along the river Bride to Inishkenny. Next come six churches along a corridor from Rahan near the Blackwater to Limerick, and finally, four on the east of Cork harbour. The full text of the decretal will be found in Appendix B; the identifications follow here:

S. MARIA IN MONTE　This church was situated on the site later occupied by Elizabeth Fort. It was known as the Church of Saint Mary le Nard and its precincts were Barrack Street, French's Quay and Kayser's Hill.

ST. MICHAEL　Probably Ballintemple, the former name of which is said to have been Templemichael.

ST. NESSAN　Situated apparently on the south side of Barrack Street, on or near the site of Saint Stephen's Priory, or else on that occupied by the Mendicity Asylum in 1832.

ST. BRIGID　Situated at the top of Tower Street where later the Cat Fort was erected.

ST. SEPULCHRE　Situated on the site now occupied by the Church of Saint Nicholas (Church of Ireland).

ST. JOHN IN THE CITY　Probably the church of the Knights Hospitallers of Saint John of Jerusalem which stood on the site of the presbytery on George's Quay (the South Presbytery).

HOLY TRINITY　Christ Church, situated as at present on the east of the South Main Street (C. of I.).

ST. PETER　Also as at present, on the west of the North Main Street (C. of I.).

THE MILL OF CORK　Situated between the present Courthouse and the Franciscan Friary of Broad Lane.

UADUBGAILL AND MACMOELPOILL　Fisheries on the south channel of the Lee.

ACHADNANHOS　Probably the cill site in Gurranebraher. Windele mentions the existence of a place off Blarney Road called Ballyhomawse.

DUNCULINN　Situated near Prayer Hill between Shanakiel and Knocknacullen.

CLOCHAN　A district extending from Grattan Street through the Mardyke to Victoria Cross.

NAHULAIN *Na h-Oileáin*: Cork's five islands in the flat of the city, including Saint Maries of the Isle.

DUOLES UCHONDUBAN *Dubhlios Ui Chondhubhain*: believed to be Ballycannon, which is rendered as Ballycanune in the Down Survey. An alternative would be Doughcloyne which was part of the parish of Saint Finbarr.

BALLINAGERRANACH Probably Ballingarranagh or Ballingarrane of the Down Survey maps. In modern survey maps it has become Ballygrohan which lies just north of Ballycannon.

ARDACHAD Killard (*Cill Ard*) in Currykippane, adjoining Ballycannon.

BALIUGIPHAN Currykippane. Ballyphehane as suggested by Risteard O Foghludha appears too much off course (*I.E.R.*, lxxviii [1952], 215–16).

BALIUNDONCHADA Doubtful. May be Ballydonaghy in the parish of Leighmoney.

LESNAEDENAN Referred to in 1296 when the *Custos* of the House of Lepers of Saint Stephen received from Nicholas FitzMaurice the two carucates of Lisneyan and Ballymacgoun. A possible identification is Shandangan in the parish of Cannaway.

BALUFOBEDI Probably Moviddy.

CELL MAGUNCHRINN Read Magunchrum, *Cill Muighe Mochromtha*: probably Macroom.

DUIBETHEIG Probably Knocknabehy in the parish of Grenagh on the Cork-Mallow road.

LESADHDIBECCAM Read *Lios Ratha Bhecain*: probably Rathpeacon in Muskerry East and Barretts.

CELL UDRI Not fully identified; but reading *Cell Vari* for *Cell Udri*, the identification could be Killeenvarra, now Killeen in Matehy, which, like Rathpeacon, is in Muskerry East.

CELLCROMAN Kilcronan in Whitechurch.

CELLCUL Kilcully.

ARDMOR Ardnageehy.

DURUSGUILL The townland of Chimneyfield in the parish of Ardnageehy or Watergrasshill. This was mentioned as *Downresgwyle* in 1599 when it was burned by Hugh O'Neill. The Inquisition of Charles I called it *Downeraskolly*; now Doonpeter beside Glenville.

CELLESCOP MELLAN Killaspugmullane near Riverstown.

CELLESCOPLAPPAN Little Island.

CELLCUNRAN Not identified; may be Kilquane. Alternatively Kilcurfin in the parish of Carrigtwohill.

CULLECHA   Either Culsyl, now Kilcoolishal near Factory Hill, or Coolnacaha, Killaspugmullane.

DUBTULACH   Killahora near Carrigtwohill. O Foghludha states that the former name of Ballyshanegaul or Johnstown in the parish of Carrigtwohill was Dubtulach.

UCURP   The tribeland and later deanery of Ocurblethan.

UMACCIAR   The tribeland of the Ui Mic Ciair.

CIARRIGI   Kerrycurrihy.

INISPICH   Spike Island.

ROSBECH   Templebracknan de Rosbeg, Ringaskiddy; or Rosbeg in Shanbally, Monkstown.

CELLNACLERECH   Kilnagleary, Carrigaline.

CELLIMECLAN   Marmullane, Passage West. O Foghludha gives Kilnicholas in Liscleary.

AESGABRI   Uncertain. The Plea Rolls of 1301 mention Kilgavere near Ballygarvan, which may be the identification of Aesgabri. An alternative suggestion would be Knocknagore, Templebreedy.

HUCURBMACHINO   Perhaps Kilmonoge in Belgooly, or Farranemachen between Liscleary and Carrigaline. O Foghludha suggests Mahon in Blackrock.

CELLINELLAIG   Killanully.

CULLEN   Cullen.

NOCHEONGBAIL   Nohoval.

CENNSALI   Kinsale.

TECHSACHSAN   Tisaxon.

INISEOGANAN   Innishannon.

CELL MOESENOCH   Probably Killhassen on the Castle Bernard Estate near Bandon. We find Kilsassonagh Graveyard on the O.S. map.

CELLBROGAN   Kilbrogan.

CELLMATNAIN   Probably Ballymodan. Also suggested are Templemartin or Templetrine.

MIDISEL   Mishells, Kilbrogan.

ACHADMELEITIG   Killaneetig, Ballinadee; or Ballinveltig in the parish of Inishkenny.

CELLSINCHIL   Probably Kilshinahan or Shanakill in Rathclarin near Kilbrittain.

*TECHMOLAGGI   Timoleague.[60]

*DOMNACHMOR   Donaghmore in the barony of Barryroe.

*CELLSAELEACH   Kilsillagh, also in Barryroe.

*DISERTCRUM   Desert, on the eastern side of Clonakilty Bay.

*INISDUNI   Inchidony Island.

60   Places indicated with the asterisk belonged to the diocese of Ross.

*Magalaid   Probably Templeomalus in Clonakilty. Sheehy in *Pontificia Hibernica*, i, 108–9, suggests Kilmacabea.

*Glenberchin   Castlehaven (Glanbarrahane).

*Cellarchadangli   Killangel, Castlehaven.

*Achaddun   Aghadown.

*Cellmugana   Kilmoon, Tullagh.

*Cluamechi   May be Kilcloonagh in Castlehaven, or Horse Island, *Cluain-echi*, in Kilmocomoge, Bantry.

*Cellcillin   Kilkilleen in Aghadown.

*Cellcohi   Kilcoe.

Scol   Schull.

Cellronan   Later Cill Moronoc, now Kilbronoge, parish of Schull. Sheehy suggests Kilronane in the parish of Fanlobbus or Dunmanway.

Cellmolaggi   Crookhaven, Goleen; anciently known as Cell-molaggi where there was a church dedicated to Saint Molaga.

Cellmua   Kilmoe.

Durrus   Durrus.

Insscuingi   Probably Coney Island, Bantry Bay. Rabbit Island is also suggested.

Cellmochomoc   Kilmocomoge, next to Beara; includes Bantry and Whiddy.

*Cellechdach   Killaconenagh, Castletownbere.

*Cellmana   Kilnamanagh, Beara.

*Cellchattigern   Kilcatherine.

Cellmacceogain   Kilmacowen, Kilcatherine. The present parish of Beara contains Kilcatherine, Killaconenagh (including Bere Island) and Kilnamanagh.

Dramdallach   Drimoleague.

Fanlobais   Fanlobbus, Dunmanway.

Magatia   Probably Murragh. O Foghludha suggests Templemartin near Bandon.

Dissaertsaergussa   Desertserges.

Cennech   Kinneigh.

Cluanachad: Probably Macloneigh. This entry must include Kilmichael and Inchigeela, which do not otherwise appear in the decretal list.

Dunusci   Dunisky.

Cennmugi   Cannaway.

Magalaid   Aglish in the parish of Ovens. O Foghludha suggests 'Magooly, a townland in the parish of Inniscarra which also included Berrings, Dripsey and Magourney'. Magooly belonged to Gill Abbey by grant of Cormac Lehenagh MacCarthy.

DISSERTMORT   Desertmore.

DISSERTANAEDA   Probably Inishkenny, Ballincollig. Brady (*Records*, i, introduction, p. ix), refers to Inishkenny *als* Dissertanaeda.

†RATHEN   Rahan on the Blackwater near Fermoy.[61]

†CLAENNABUR   Clenor in the barony of Fermoy.

†CENNMUGI   Kilcanway in the parish of Carrigleamleary, Fermoy.

†ATHBRUANNI   Kilbroney or Ballybrowney near Rathcormac.

†ARDMACCFAELAN   Probably Kilmaclenine near Kilbroney, or Ardnateampull, Kilbrin. Ardevolan near Kilmallock, as mentioned in the *Black Book of Limerick* (p. 71) is too far off course.

†TULACHRATHA   Probably Tullacondra, Ballyclough. Knockraha in the parish of Kilquane is also suggested.

†CELL-LIA   Killeagh near Youghal in the barony of Imokilly.

†CLUANPRUCHES   Clonpriest, also near Youghal.

†CORCACHBEC   Corkbeg, within Cork harbour.

†ARCHADFADDA   Aghada, at the mouth of Cork harbour.

A careful study of the decretal of 1199 will reveal the extent to which it reflected Norman policy. FitzStephen and de Cogan were already in process of entrenching themselves in east and north Cork, while grants made by the former to Philip de Barry established an important bridgehead from Mallow through Charleville to Glenquin in Limerick.[62] Analogous to this, the decretal shows that Rahan, Clenor, Kilcanway and Kilbroney were stepping-stones connecting the borders of Cork with the diocese of Limerick. It was clearly in the interest of Norman policy to have a strong church in Cork; hence the necessity of linking Cork with the strong base of Norman power in Limerick. Furthermore, FitzStephen had granted Imokilly to the sons of Maurice FitzGerald, and in Imokilly the churches of Corkbeg, Aghada, Killeagh and Clonpriest are confirmed by the decretal as outposts of the diocese of Cork on the eastern side of Cork harbour.[63] Here too Norman influence is suggested in the erection of a strong line of defence against a possible incursion by enemy sea power. The decretal does not mention Muskerry, nor does it carry any reference to the district of Iveleary which was a border district between Cork and Cloyne. A native

61   These final entries marked with a dagger represent places in the diocese of Cloyne.

62   Edmund Curtis, *A History of Medieval Ireland*, p. 93.

63   By his confirmation of the church of Killeagh to the abbey of Saint Thomas in Dublin, Mathew, bishop of Cloyne, shows that he did not recognize the subjection of churches in east Cork to the diocese of Finbarr in 1190.

ecclesiastic would scarcely have omitted these districts in which were situated the hermitage of Gougane Barra and the ancient church of Kilbarry.

The practical absorption of Ross in the diocese of Cork in 1199 cannot be altogether explained in terms of a disputed succession in respect of which the pope in 1198 had mandated the archbishops of Armagh and Cashel and the bishop of Killaloe to take proceedings against D(avid) who was styling himself bishop-elect of Ross.[64] This dispute was soon resolved and the status to which Ross had attained in the period after Kells was such that its summary treatment in the decretal was scarcely justifiable, at least in ecclesiastical terms. An *episcopus Rossensis* took the oath of fealty to Henry II at Cashel in 1171–72; Benedict, Bishop of Ross, witnessed the charter of Dermot MacCarthy to Gill Abbey in 1174, and among the dioceses which paid revenues to the pope in 1192, the diocese of Ross is listed in its own right according to the account given in the *Liber Censuum*: . . . Clonensis, Corcagiensis, Rossensis, Ardfertensis. After 1199 Ross continued to function regardless of the implications of the Innocentian decretal. It is mentioned as one of the suffragans of Cashel in 1212, and the death of Bishop Florence of Ross is calendared for the year 1223 in the *Annals of Inisfallen*. The inclusion of most of Ross in the diocese of Cork must consequently be explained in terms of Norman influence. The Normans had secured a hold on Rosscarbery. They disliked small sees, especially those administered by natives, and a linking of Ross with Cork would have suggested itself to them as important as a linking of Cork with Limerick. It is possible therefore that they took advantage of ecclesiastical confusion in Ross. In the final analysis Norman influence in the framing of the decretal of 1199 moves out of the realm of conjecture when it is remembered that Giraldus Cambrensis who was in Cork in 1183 was in Rome in 1199.

The papal taxations of the early fourteenth century,[65] which represent the Cork diocesan boundaries in approximately their present form, suggest that these boundaries, with the exception of some later rectifications between Glounthane and Carrig-twohill, were established before the end of the thirteenth century; that places originally belonging to Cloyne and Ross had again reverted to their respective dioceses and that the final decision reached made the diocese of Cork once more coter-minous with the ancient tribeland of the Ui Eachach. Following

64 *Cal. papal letters, 1198–1304*, p. 3.

65 These taxations will be treated in detail in Chapter xii.

the list of parishes as given in 1302 one finds along the north and east the parishes of Kilcully, Dunbulloge, Ardnageehy, Kilshinahan, Kilquane, Ballydeloher, Caherlag and Little Island. Parishes indicated along the Lee are Ovens, Aglish, Cannaway and Kilmurry. Boundary parishes between Cork and Ross as then given are Burren, Rathclarin and Kilbrittain. The present position as occupied by the parishes of Kilbrittain, Bandon, Caheragh, Enniskeane, Dunmanway, Drimoleague and Schull is not indicated, but by reference to the Ross boundaries as delineated in the same year (1302) we find that the diocesan boundary as presently known was already in existence.[66] Parishes from Murragh and Enniskeane to Durrus and Schull are omitted from the fourteenth-century taxation records for Cork, for which omission the poverty of this part of the diocese has been argued as an insufficient justification for the outlay entailed in levying the tax. On the other hand Ross— parts of which were at least as poor as the missing areas of Cork—was taxed in 1302; consequently it is probable that the political turmoil which destroyed the geographical unity of the Ui Eachach tribeland after 1118 is responsible for the omission of the western parishes from the taxation lists.[67] Such omissions to the contrary, it may be maintained that the diocese of Cork as charted in the fourteenth-century records is still the old Ui Eachach diocese extending from Cairn Thierna to Carn Ui Néid; the territories upon which its deaneries were later erected had been a long-standing possession of the O'Mahony clan, and its absorption of territories (from Kinneigh near Bandon to Drimoleague) represented by the ancient see of Kinneigh was probably sanctioned by immemorial custom. Districts in the Bere peninsula, as outlined in 1199 and which could not stand this test, were restored to Ross, as were likewise most of the places in dispute between Cork and Cloyne.

Apart from the principle of immemorial custom, however, several details of the Cork-Cloyne diocesan boundary appear to have been the result of friendly compromise. For instance, the Cloyne parish of Whitechurch contains several townlands which lie within the barony of Cork and which the *Books of Survey and Distribution* for 1657 show to have belonged to the

---

66   In 1302 Ross included the Bere peninsula, which in the confusion of later penal times was administered and ultimately incorporated in the diocese of Kerry.

67   That part of the tribeland represented by the ancient bishopric of Kinneigh had been invaded by the MacCarthys and other septs. Political unrest prevailed also in the district between Kilmurry and Inchigeela. Between 1259 and 1330 the chief of Kinalmeaky bestowed portions of territory in this locality on young relatives, thereby establishing the minor septs of the O'Mahonys of Ifflanloe, Clan Conogher and Clan Finín.

parish of Kilcully, and by analogy to the diocese of Cork. No indication is given as to when or how the change took effect. Part if not the entire parish of Blarney is believed to have belonged at one time to Cork but was ceded to Cloyne in return for concessions elsewhere. On the eastern boundary between the two dioceses is the bisected townland of Killacloyne, of which Caherlag owes spiritual allegiance to the diocese of Cork and Carrigtwohill to that of Cloyne. The entire townland belonged originally to Cloyne; the present arrangement which dates from about 1785 is believed to have been the suggestion of Bishop McKenna of Cloyne for whom the advantage of a river frontier had some special appeal. On the other hand, the tradition which made a diocesan boundary of the Lee and allocated all territory south of the river to Cork has its own problems. The parish of Iveleary, part of which lies north of the Lee and yet belongs to Cork is the least provocative anomaly here, and may be explained by reference to Gougane Barra, the inclusion of which in the diocese of Finbarr was a *sine qua non* of any ecclesiastico-territorial arrangement. A similar anomaly occurs in the parish of Macloneigh, referring to which Bishop Downes noted that 'half ye tithes of the lands of Coulcour and Slevins, *lying north of the river Lee,* belongs to the vicarage of Macloneigh', that is, to the diocese of Cork.[68] The townlands of Sleveens and Coulcour, now in the parish of Macroom (Cloyne) were apparently connected with Macloneigh by the ford called *Ath an Teampuill* which served as a bridgehead for Macloneigh, and it seems feasible that the adaptation of some tribal arrangement led to a compromise of sorts between Cork and Cloyne as suggested by the division of tithes. Again, the townlands of Fergus East and Cronody in the parish of Ovens, though north of the Lee, belong to the diocese of Cork. Local tradition tries to explain this deviation by connecting the townlands with the abbey of Kilcrea, but it is doubtful if Kilcrea ever held land north of the river. Here too the existence of the ford at *Cros a' Chuilinn* suggests a bridgehead between Aglish and the north bank of the river, and it was probably some friendly arrangement which finally divided the townlands, allocating Fergus West to Cloyne and the rest to Cork.

The need for friendly compromise does not seem to have arisen in the case of Spike and the islands in Cork harbour. While never a parish in its own right, Spike (*Inispich*) was mentioned in the decretal of 1199, though not in the papal taxations of the fourteenth century. Its inclusion with that of

68 Brady, *Records*, i, 211.

the islands in the diocese of Cork is based on the early foundation of Saint Mochuda or Carthage. Cathal Mac Aedha, king of Munster, who met the saint in the region of Kerrycurrihy and was cured by him of a grievous ailment, bestowed on him a special grant of lands which included *Hillian Kathail, Ross Beg, Ross Mor* and *Insulam Pic;* in other words Rocky Island, Ballybricken, Ringaskiddy and Spike Island.[69] The monks of Saint Carthage established a cell in Rosbeg and in this way forged the connection between the island of Spike and the Cork diocesan mainland.

There is, finally, a case of overlapping on the boundary between the dioceses of Cork and Ross. The townland of Greenmount, situated to the west of Roaring-Water Bay on the mainland forming the parish of Schull, is reckoned as part of the Ross parish of Kilcoe, and may even be reached directly by water without the necessity of traversing Cork diocesan territory. A vague tradition connects this anomaly with a tribal marriage arrangement according to which a lady from Greenmount with the townland as her dowry married some local tribesman from Kilcoe. In all other respects the boundary which separates Cork from Ross coincides with the delineation of Ross as defined in the taxation returns of that diocese in 1302. Instances of territorial encroachments, however, are not confined exclusively to the dioceses of Cork, Cloyne and Ross, but are rather a feature of Irish ecclesiastical geography. Waterford encroaches on Cashel, Ossory on Killaloe, Ardagh and Clonmacnoise on Kilmore, Tuam on Clonfert and Achonry, while five of the northern dioceses claim territories on both sides of the border which separates Northern Ireland from the Republic.[70] Basically the ecclesiastical subdivision of Ireland is such that church and civil provinces do not coincide except partly in Connacht; nor can natural boundaries be taken as infallible guides to diocesan limits, as the diocese of Cork so clearly illustrates. Irish dioceses presently number twenty-six, none of them haphazardly arranged but all having deep and penetrating roots in ancient tribal settlements and migrations that are nearly as old as Irish time. So with the diocese of Cork. Its limits as we know them date from the thirteenth century but its roots are embedded in a remote past when Cork was a centre of learning, a home of culture and a nursery of saints. Its tribal

---

69   For identifications, see Diarmuid Ó Murchadha, 'Some Obsolete Place-names in Cork Harbour', *Cork Hist. Soc. Jn.*, lxv (1960), 18–23. The suggestion that Haulbowline was the Hillian Kathail is untenable by reason of the fact that Bishop Downes mentions Rocky Island and Haulbowline separately.

70   Jean Blanchard, *The Church in Contemporary Ireland*, p. 5.

patrons, the Ui Eachach, were for a time the mightiest of all the southern septs, while the vicissitudes of other tribes— Ui Floinn Luadh, Ui Liathain, Ui Mic Ciair, Corca Laighdhe, Ui Mic Caille and others—are also interwoven in the history of this ancient diocese which once stretched from the Blackwater to the southern sea.

It is characteristic of the paucity of our records that nothing further is known concerning Giolla Aedh O Muighin who stands silhouetted between the sunset of monastic and the sunrise of episcopal Cork. His death in 1172 merited not more than a single line in the annals, but the monastery which took its name from him enjoyed considerable prestige in medieval Cork. Its community of reformed canons regular undertook pastoral work in the outlying parishes of the diocese; its capitular organization afforded a standard upon which the diocesan chapter was modelled; its abbots, like those of the Cistercian Abbey of Tracton, were frequently mandated by the Holy See to enforce decisions (not always easy ones) on matters of ecclesiastical discipline and administration;[71] while its salmon weirs and fishing pools, its vast acres of arable land and pasture, its forests and its mill made it a highly self-contained social unit with unlimited potentialities. The failure of the later monks and abbots of Gill Abbey to develop these potentialites brought its retribution in their complete annihilation in the sixteenth century. Even the annals disappeared; consequently details of the history of Gill Abbey are confined to the *Calendars of Papal Letters* and to various state records, calendars of patent and close rolls, justiciary rolls and reports of the deputy keeper of records. From these combined sources we get a reasonably

---

71 *Cal. papal letters, 1431–47*, p. 197, under date 1441 and in the pontificate of Eugenius IV; Mandate 'to the abbots of Tracton (*de Albo Tractu*) and Gill Abbey (*de Antro Sancti Fynibarri*) in the diocese of Cork, and the official of Cork: the Pope having been informed by John Walsche, dean of Cork, bachelor of Canon Law, that Thomas Tyrri, rector of the parish church of Little Island (*Sancti Lappani de Inysmele alias parve insule*) in the diocese of Cork, has remained for several years under sentence of excommunication . . . and although publicly proclaimed excommunicated has celebrated Mass and other divine offices and has committed perjury . . . orders the above three . . . to summon Thomas before them, and if they find the above or enough thereof to be true, to deprive Thomas, and in that event to collate and assign the said rectory . . . to John . . .'

   Cal. papal letters, 1471–84, pt. 1, p. 393, under date 1474 and in the pontificate of Sixtus IV: 'To the abbots of Tracton (de Albo Tractu) and St Mary's *als* St John the Evangelist's *de Antro Sancti Fimbarri*, in the diocese of Cork, and the official of Cork. Mandate to collate and assign to Donatus Murphy (Omorchw), rector of Moilla in the diocese of Cloyne . . . the treasureship of Cork, a non-major dignity . . . so long void that its collation has lapsed to the Apostolic See, although Patrick Lawles, priest, who is to be summoned and removed, has without any title detained it for between twelve and thirteen years . . .'

comprehensive survey of the abbatial succession from the death of Giolla Aedh O Muighin in 1172 until the closing years of the fifteenth century. Gill Abbey history as culled from these sources is tabulated in the final appendix to this chapter.

APPENDIX A

Dermot's Charter

'Dermot, by the favour of divine clemency, King of Munster, to all the faithful of Christ, as well present as future, peace for ever and greeting. Having experience of the fleeting memory of mortals and the unstable pomp of a world passing away, We have therefore thought it worthy to commemorate in charters the great zeal of love which my father, Cormac, King of Munster, of blessed memory, built the church of St. John, Apostle and Evangelist, at Cork, for Archbishop Maurice, and for Gregory, and for their successors the pilgrims from Connaught, compatriots of St. Barry, and commended in defence to his descendants. But now having been called to my paternal kingdom, relying on divine aid, I have undertaken, as becomes royal magnificance, to defend the said church for the welfare of my own soul and the souls of my parents; and I have proposed to elevate and enlarge it for the honour of the Saints whose the same place is known to be. Therefore let the whole body of the faithful know that I [confirm] all things which the said place justly at present possesses, either by the presentation of my father, or by the donations of other Kings. For my glorious father, the King, handed over to the said place, Lysuctdach and Cloghan; Dermot O'Connor gave it Killina-Cannigh; which I by the following confirm. And be it known that I have given and by this my charter have confirmed the villa and church of Illae to the said pilgrims. Moreover, my illustrious son, Cormac, at the request of Catholicus, Archbishop of Tuam, has granted to God and St. John, for the eternal welfare of his own soul and ours, Maduelgi, freely and peaceably and without any secular service; which royal land we have confirmed by grant. Finally, the Monastery itself, with all the aforesaid lands, we have taken under our protection, and have secured from all secular rent, and grant it peaceably and freely for ever to God. But lest anyone, either about some other or about these things, should presume [to question the matter], We have authenticated this charter with the impression of our seal, and [have delivered it] to be preserved by the pilgrims from Connaught before fitting witnesses. These are the witnesses from the clergy and people:

95

Christian, Bishop of Lismore and Legate of the Apostolic See
Donat, Archbishop of Cashel
Gregory, Bishop of Cork
Bricius, Bishop of Limerick
Benedict, Bishop of Ross
Mathew, Bishop of Cloyne
Donat, Abbot of Magio
Gregory, Abbot of Cong
Eugene, Bishop of Ardmore.'

Appended to the above transcript in the British Museum are the following notes (made in all probability by Sir James Ware), written in Latin and lettered (A), (B), (C), (D). Note (A) refers to King Dermot who granted the charter; note (B) to his father, Cormac MacCarthy; note (C) deals with the question of the site of the church to which the charter was granted; and note (D) discusses the establishment of archbishoprics. An anonymous final note gives precise data for ascertaining the date of the charter.

Note (A):   'Him the Irish Annals call Dermot of Kilbawne, from the place he was slain at, the beginning and end of whose reign are recorded in the succeeding note: Anno 1150, Dermot, son of Cormac of Muighannugh, was made King of Munster; he was slain by the foreigners at the green of Kilbawne afterwards.'

Note (B):   'He it is whom the Annals call Cormac of Muighannugh, the beginning and end of whose reign they note thus:

Anno 1123.   Cormac, son of Muriagh McCarthy, was made king;

Anno 1126.   Cormac, son of Muriagh McCarthy, was reconciled (?) . . . to Lismore on pilgrimage and took the crozier there also;

Anno 1134.   The Church for the Synod [built by] Cormac, son of Muriagh McCarthy, at Cashel, was consecrated by the high-bishop of Cashel and by the bishopry of Munster . . .'

Note (C):   'Some will have that this church was situate outside the south gate of the city of Cork, though it is not apparent from the ruins; they say nevertheless it was the monastery which at the end of this charter is called the cell, and the common tradition makes a monastery to have been there. But now hardly any traces of the monastery appear, for Thomas Ronain, Mayor of the City of Cork in the year 1630, took care to build the Hospital of the poor on this foundation of that church or monastery. But we believe rather, that by this church is meant the monastery of the cave of St. Finbarr, near Cork, as well because the monastery of the Canons Regular is there, as also because that foundation to this day possesses the lands mentioned in this charter. These things happened according to the Irish Annals:

'Anno 1137. The Monastery of the Cave was built for the Bishop O'Duffy under the protection of Barri, at Cork (?): Now commonly called Gill-Abbey, from St. Gilla-Ada, Abbot of that monastery, and afterwards Bishop of Cork, who died 1173.'

Note (D) : 'As this charter was issued after the year 1150, it appears to be evident that the said Archbishop was here before the advent of Christian, the Legate, or of Papiron, who is said to have instituted four Archbishops for Ireland. For as this grant was made by Cormac of Muighannuig, who died in the year 1138, many years before the advent of Christian into Ireland, it appears that Maurice, to whom the grant was made, preceded the advent of Christian. Moreover, concerning this Maurice the Archbishop, the Annals of Ireland thus record:

'Anno 1134. Muireadach O'Duffy, High Bishop of Connaught, went on behalf of Turlough, son of Roderick O'Connor, and made peace between Leath Chuinn and Leath-Mogha, and Turlough gave Cormac, son of Murriagh, peace at the request (?) of the high-bishop. This charter very likely was also made on account of that peace.'

It was a common custom in Ireland long before the Synod of Kells to apply the term *ard-epscop* or *uasal-epscop* (archbishop) to any bishop who had become remarkable for piety and/or ability. Such titles of dignity did not convey any official ecclesiastical significance in terms of jurisdiction. Muireadach O'Duffy was therefore high-bishop of Tuam from 1128 until 1150 according to popular acclaim; but the first canonically instituted archbishop of Tuam was Aodh O hOisin who received the pall (*pallium*) from Cardinal Paparo in 1152. On his death in 1180-1, he was succeeded by Cathal Ua Dubhthaigh, the signatory *Catholicus* mentioned in the charter of Dermot MacCarthy.

Final Note to Charter

CHRISTIAN   Bishop of Lismore and Legate of the Apostolic
See. Raised to the see of Lismore, 1150; appointed joint
legate with Cardinal John Paparo; held the see of Lismore
at the time of Dermot's Charter, but resigned shortly
afterwards; he died in 1186 and was buried in the Cistercian
Abbey of O'Dorney (Abbeydorney) in Kerry.

DONATUS   Archbishop of Cashel. Donnell O'Hullachan
reigned as archbishop from 1158 until 1184.

GREGORY   Gregory O hAodha who succeeded Giolla Aedh
O Muighin as bishop of Cork in 1172 and died in 1182.

BRICIUS   Bishop of Limerick. He occupied the see in 1174
and may be identified as Brictius who attended the Third
Lateran Council.

BENEDICT   Bishop of Ross; occupied the see in 1174.

MATHEW   Mathew O Mongagh who ruled as bishop of Cloyne
from c. 1168 to 1192, at which date his death is recorded
in the *Annals of Inisfallen.*

DONATUS   Abbot of the Cistercian Abbey of Maigue or
Monasternenagh in the barony of Pobal Briain in county
Limerick. The monastery was founded by an O'Brien of
Thomond in 1148 or 1151.

GREGORY   Abbot of Cong; probably Gillebard Ua
Dubhtaing, whose Christian name is latinised as *Gregorius.*

EUGENE   Bishop of Ardmore, of whom no further details are
available.

APPENDIX B

Decretal Letter of Pope Innocent III, 1199 :
Reg. Vat. Vol. 4, f. 150r–150v

The section between asterisks (*) is omitted in the original bull.
Such clauses were common and were accordingly inserted from
one bull to another.

. . . Corcaiensi episcopo eiusque successoribus canonice
substituendis in perpetuum.
Ex iniuncto nobis apostolatus officio* et licet immeriti de
universis ecclesiis solicitudinem habere tenemur et earum
utilitatibus auctore Deo diligenter imminere. Eapropter venera-
bilis in Christo frater tuis iustis postulationibus clementer

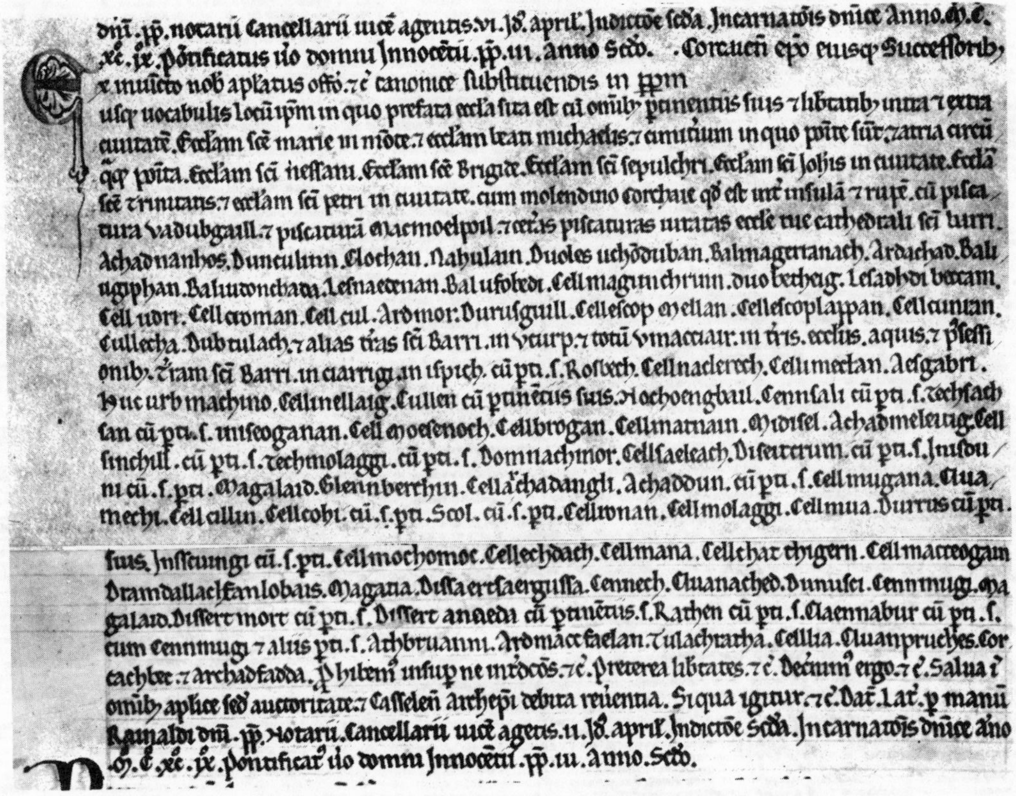

Decretal Letter, 1199

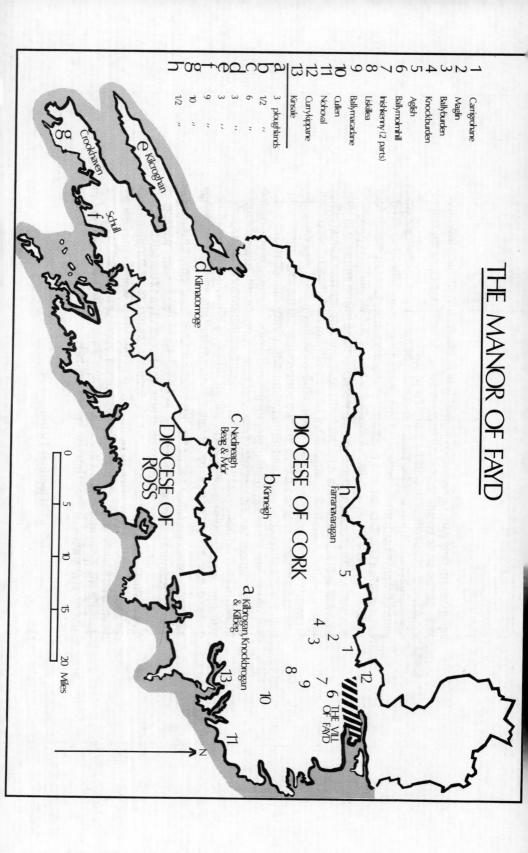

THE MANOR OF FAYD

1 Carrigohane
2 Maglin
3 Ballyburden
4 Knockburden
5 Aglish
6 Ballymolnrihill
7 Inishkenny (2 parts)
8 Liskillea
9 Ballymacadane
10 Cullen
11 Nohoval
12 Currykippane
13 Kinsale

a 3 ploughlands
b ½ "
c 6 "
d 3 "
e 3 "
f 9 "
g 10 "
h ½ "

DIOCESE OF CORK

DIOCESE OF ROSS

h Farahavaragan

b Kinneigh

C Nedineagh
  Beag & Mór

a Kilbrogan, Knockbrogan
  & Killceg

d Kilmacomoge

e Kilcroghan

Crookhaven

Schull

12 6 THE VILL
      OF FAYD

N

0 5 10 15 20 Miles

annuimus et Corcaiensem ecclesiam cui auctore Deo preesse dinosceris sub beati Petri et nostra protectione suscipimus et presentis scripti privilegio communimus, statuentes ut quascumque possessiones quecunque bona eadem ecclesia in presentiarum iuste et canonice possidit aut in futurum concessione pontificum, largitione regum vel principum, oblatione fidelium seu aliis iustis modis prestante Domino poterit adipisci, firma tibi tuisque successoribus et illibata permaneant, quibus haec propriis duximus exprimenda vocabulis:* locum ipsum in quo prefata ecclesia sita est cum omnibus pertinentiis suis et libertatibus intra et extra civitatem, ecclesiam sancte Marie in Monte et ecclesiam beati Michaelis et cimiterium in quo posite sunt et atria circumquaque posita, ecclesiam sancti Nessani, ecclesiam sancte Brigide, ecclesiam sancti Sepulchri, ecclesiam sancti Johannis in civitate, ecclesiam sancte Trinitatis et ecclesiam sancti Petri in civitate, cum molendino Corchaie quod est inter insulam et rupem cum piscatura Ua Dubgaill et piscatura MacMoelpoill et ceteras piscaturas iuratas ecclesie seu cathedrali sancti Barri, Archadnanhos, Dunculinn, Clochan, Nahulain, Duoles Uchonduban, Ballingerranach, Ardachad, Baliugiphan, Baliudonchada, Lesnaedenan, Balufobedi, Cell Magunchrinn, Duobetheig, Lesadhdibeccam, Cell Udri, Cellcroman, Cellcul, Ardmor, Durusguill, Cellescop mellan, Cellescoplappan, Cellcunran, Cullecha, Dubtulach et alias terras sancti Barri in Ucurp et totum Umacciair in terris, ecclesiis, aquis et possessionibus; terram sancti Barri in Ciarrigi, Inispich cum pertinentiis suis, Rosbech, Cellnaclerech, Cellimeclan, Aesgabri, Hucurbmachino, Cellinellaig, Cullen cum pertinentiis suis, Nochoengbail, Cennsali cum pertinentiis suis, Techsachsan cum pertinentiis suis, Iniseoganan, Cell Moesenoch, Cellbrogan, Cellmatnain, Midisel, Achadmeleitig, Cellsinchill cum pertinentiis suis, Techmolaggi cum pertinentiis suis, Domnachmor, Cellsaeleach, Disertcrum cum pertinentiis suis, Inisduni cum pertinentiis suis, Magalaid, Glennberchin, Cellarchadangli, Achaddun cum pertinentiis suis, Cellmugana, Cluamechi, Cellcillin, Cellcohi cum suis pertinentiis, Scol cum suis pertinentiis, Cellronan, Cellmolaggi, Cellmua, Durrus cum pertinentiis suis, Insscuingi cum suis pertinentiis, Cellmochomoc, Cellechdach, Cellmana, Cellchatthigern, Cellmacceogain, Dramdallach, Fanlobais, Magatia, Dissaertsaergussa, Cennech, Cluanachad, Dunusci, Cennmugi, Magalaid, Dissertmort cum pertinentiis suis, Dissertanaeda cum pertinentiis suis, Rathen cum pertinentiis suis, Claennabur cum pertinentiis suis, cum Cennmugi et aliis pertinentiis suis, Athbruanni, Ardmaccfaelan, Tulachratha, Cell-lia, Cluanpruches, Corcachbec et Archadfadda.

APPENDIX C

The Abbots of Gill Abbey (de Antro)

1172   Giolla Aedh O Muighin died.

1248   An unnamed abbot of Gill Abbey paid a fine of £20 to the Exchequer.

1285   R(obert) died. On 17 May the prior and convent of Weeme, Cork, of the Augustinian Order, having notified that their church was vacant by the death of Brother R., late abbot thereof, prayed licence to elect: the king granted licence accordingly, commanding them to select an abbot who would be devout, fit to rule their church, and useful and faithful to the king and to Ireland. Power was given to the justiciary to give the royal assent to the election, and on confirmation to restore the temporalities, 'previously, however, taking from the elect letters sealed with his seal and that of the Chapter, that this grace shall not tend to the King's prejudice, nor be converted into a precedent' (*Cal. doc. Ire., 1285-92*, p. 51).

1293   Gilbert O'Brogy was deposed. On 21 April, Brother Thomas, canon of the Church *de Antro Barre*, near Cork, announced to the king the deposition from the abbacy of Gilbert O'Brogy. The king wrote to William de Vesey, justiciar of Ireland, granting licence to elect, despite the lack of evidence as to why the church became vacant. The king also empowered the justiciar to receive the customary fealty and restore the temporalities in the king's name, if and when the election would be canonically confirmed.

1297   Alan O'Millanagaly. The king gave his consent to his election as abbot and the bishop of Cork was asked to do his part as diocesan (*Cal. justic. rolls Ire., 1295-1303*, p. 130).

1300   Gilbert O'Brogyd, canon of Gill Abbey, presented letters . . . 'which testify that the prior and convent unanimously elected him Abbot.' He is apparently the abbot who was deposed in 1293. In the year of his election O'Brogyd was indicted for harbouring thieves and felons, but was acquitted by reason of his representation that he had formerly paid a considerable fine for a similar offence to John Wogan, justiciar of Ireland (*Cal. justic. rolls. Ire., 1295–1303*, p. 303).

1303   Thomas O Ffyn became abbot.

1311   Thomas, abbot of Weyme Abbey, sued Owen, abbot of the Cistercian Abbey of Tracton, for possession of one acre of turbary and forty acres of pasturage at Kilmoney.

1318   David de Onega (?de Cogan) was abbot (*P.R.I. rep. D.K. 42*, p. 17).

1324   Thomas O Ffyn, canon of Gill Abbey, was re-elected abbot.

1355   Maurice McDughy, was abbot *de Antro* (*Anal. Hib.*, no. 4, p. 399).

1365   William succeeded on the resignation of Maurice (Windele, *South of Ireland*, p. 78).

1377   Nicholas was abbot, 1377-1403.

1418   Thady O'Cally was elected abbot.

1465   Donald O'Kellycharn died.

1465   Eugene O'Modagain *alias* Saygs who was transferred from the Order of Preachers to that of Saint Augustine became abbot of Gill Abbey. A papal mandate of 1474-5 describes him as a canon of Saint Mary and Saint John the Evangelist, and provided him to the monastery of Saint Mary *de Portu Puro*, Clonfert (*Cal. papal letters, 1471-84*, pt. 1, 389).

1468-9   Cornelius O'Flyn (Ylayn) was provided to the abbacy. In 1482-3 he was granted the chancellorship of Cork for life (*Cal. papal letters, 1471-84*, pt. 2, p. 124).

1482-3   Donald Machardich. Because of strife between Cornelius O'Flyn and Donald Machardich, Richard, Abbot of Cong, removed Cornelius and a papal investigation was instituted. Cornelius O'Flyn was reinstated and was still ruling in 1488 when he witnessed a grant of land made by John Barrett (son of Richard, son of Symon de rede Bared) of Cloygh Phylyb in favour of Eugene, son of Thadeus, son of Cormac MacCarthy.

IV

The Norman-Irish Church

The effects of the Anglo-Norman invasion (1169) on the political, social and economic structure of medieval Ireland call for nothing more than a passing reference here punctuated by a re-emphasis of Professor Otway-Ruthven's statement that the fragmented nature of Irish society made it impossible for either the Normans to consolidate their conquests or for the Irish to resist them effectively.[1] The failure of the Norman takeover in Cork is symptomatic; consequently, something must be said concerning the impact of the invasion on the affairs of Munster in general and of south Munster (*Desmumha*) in particular. When Henry II landed near Waterford on 17 October 1171, Dermot MacCarthy, king of Cork (or of Desmond), was the first to offer his submission: he did homage, swore fealty and gave hostages in token of his willingness to pay regular annual tribute to Henry. Shortly afterwards according to the *Miscellaneous Irish Annals*, 'Domhnall Mor O Brien and Donchadh, son of Cian O'Mahony (of the Ui Eachach) went to meet Henry on the banks of the Suir and made submission to him.' This submission of the kings of Desmond and Thomond gave Henry opportunity to garrison the cities of Cork and Limerick. After these initial submissions the king made a partial circuit of the country, he returned to Dublin for Christmas and entertained many Irish princes there. Next, the Irish bishops in session at Cashel in 1172 under the presidency of Christian of Lismore swore fealty to Henry: he had been invested with the lordship of Ireland by Pope Adrian IV and came in quality of a reformer of abuses, and it was possibly for these reasons that each bishop gave Henry confirmatory sealed letters which were

---

1   A. J. Otway-Ruthven, *A History of Medieval Ireland*, pp. 35–6.

later transmitted to the pope.[2] Thus within a single year Henry secured ecclesiastic and secular acceptance in Ireland. His status *vis-à-vis* the church was to be further endorsed by the year 1175.

The events of the years immediately following Henry's visit left no doubt as to the aims of the king's Irish policy, namely, the introduction of the institutions of English law into Ireland, a policy enunciated in the reign of King John by the famous writ of 1253 which stated: *cum eadem leges et consuetudines sint in Hibernia et in Anglia*.[3] The parcelling out of Irish land was initiated by Henry whose Norman subjects paid scant heed to the rights even of those princes who had submitted to the king. In 1173 Raymond le Gros led a hosting into Offaly, whence he plundered as far south as Lismore where his followers commandeered ships for the conveyance of their booty to Waterford. Here, a fleet led by Gilbert, the Ostman mayor of Cork, encountered the freebooters, but the men of Cork were defeated and some of their ships were appropriated for the enemy by Adam de Hareford. Dermot MacCarthy, who was in Lismore at the time, beat a speedy retreat on the arrival of le Gros, to whom according to Giraldus Cambrensis he abandoned four thousand animals.[4] Dermot's son Cormac Lehenagh now revolted against his father in protest at the establishment of a Norman garrison in Cork, but Dermot sought and secured the assistance of le Gros against his son. Cormac was beheaded[5] and in 1176 Dermot MacCarthy bestowed upon le Gros a princely inheritance in Kerry. This was handed over by le Gros to his son Maurice who married Catherine, daughter of Milo de Cogan, and from whom were descended the powerful FitzMaurice chieftains and barons of Lixnaw, county Kerry.[6]

The extension of Norman power in Munster was facilitated by feuds between the O'Briens and the MacCarthys which devastated the country from Cork to Limerick and from Waterford to Mount Brandon between the years 1174 and 1177. This caused the Ui Mic Caille to flee southwards across the Lee into Ui Eachach, the Ciarraighe Luachra into Thomond, the Ui Chairbre, the Ui Chonaill and the

2   Sheehy, *Pontificia Hib.*, i, nos. 5 and 6.

3   Geoffrey J. Hand, 'The Church and English Law in Medieval Ireland', *Ir. Cath. Hist. Comm. Proc.* (1959), p. 10.

4   *Expugnatio Hibernica: Giraldi Cambrensis Opera*, v, 308–9, ed. J. F. Dimock.

5   Smith, *History of Cork*, i, 24.

6   C. B. Gibson, *The History of the County and City of Cork*, i, 24.

Ui Dhonnabhain into Eoghanacht Locha Lein and to the
country around Mangarta.[7] On top of this confusion came
the migration from Tipperary of the MacCarthys and the
O'Sullivans, and from west Limerick of the Collinses and
others, and on all the lands thus vacated the Normans soon
had castles built in south Tipperary, on the plains of Limerick
and in most of north Kerry.[8] Thomond was at this time
licking the wounds received in recent clashes with the king
of Connacht. In Desmond, Dermot MacCarthy was in strife
with the Ui Eachach and the Ui Mic Caille; therefore both
kingdoms presented an easy prey for exploitation according
to the norms laid down by Henry II at Oxford in May 1177.

By the Council of Oxford, Henry with papal approval made
his son John lord of Ireland, *Dominus Hiberniae*, a title which
according to Orpen expresses the feudal and territorial
relationship which it was desired to create.[9] Henry then
proceeded to a division of the land of Ireland on a basis calculated to curb any pretensions to power on the part of his
vassals. The grantees—Strongbow, de Lacy, FitzStephen,
de Cogan and others—were to conquer, organize and settle
the lands allotted to them. Under these arrangements Henry
bestowed the kingdom of Cork or Desmond on Robert Fitz-
Stephen and Milo de Cogan at service of sixty knights, reserv-
ing to himself the city of Cork and the cantred of the Ostmen
(*cantredus quod est Hostmannorum*).[10] Limerick was given to
three courtiers but they surrendered the grant later in the year
and Limerick then fell to Philip de Broase.[11] With reference
to the Cork grants Giraldus says that 'FitzStephen and Milo
divided seven cantred between them which were contiguous
to the city and which they held in great security; three of
which eastward fell to FitzStephen's lot and the four westward to Milo's. . . . The government of the city remained
common to them both and the tribute of the other twenty-four
cantreds, which remained undivided, was to be equally distributed between them, when they should be brought under
subjection.'[12] From the foregoing it would appear that the
kingdom of Cork, counting the cantred of the Ostmen, em-

7 O'Mahony, *A History of the O'Mahony Septs*, p. 64.

8 Butler, *Gleanings from Irish History*, pp. 161–2.

9 G. H. Orpen, *Ireland under the Normans, 1169–1333*, ii, 31.

10 This phrase occurs in most of the calendared records of the period, more especially
in *Gesta Regis Henrici Secundi Benedicti Abbatis*, ii, 173.

11 Ware, *De Hibernia et Antiquitatibus eius*, p. 194.

12 *Expugnatio Hibernica*, p. 346.

braced thirty-two cantreds. The task of taking possession of the new fiefs in Desmond was eased for the grantees by Murtough and Domhnall O'Brien who 'accompanied Fitz-Stephen and de Cogan to Cork where they committed many depradations'[13] and burned and destroyed many churches on the plain of Munster.[14] Cork city was already held by a Norman governor, Richard of London (de Londres), and was therefore easily taken possession of,[15] thus giving the Normans a strong base of operations in the south.[16] There must have been a conflict of sorts with Dermot MacCarthy, and subsequently an agreement by which FitzStephen and de Cogan got seven cantreds while the remaining twenty-four which presumably remained in MacCarthy's hands, were to pay tribute to the grantees, with FitzStephen and de Cogan acting jointly as the king's representatives in the city and in its Ostman cantred. The term *cantred* which is apparently of Welsh origin signified a feudal unit equivalent to the 'hundred', and in the time of Giraldus Cambrensis was designated as the equivalent of one hundred holdings (*tanta portio terrae quanta centum villas continere solet*). The cantred of the Ostmen included the north liberties of the city of Cork and portion of the barony of Kerrycurrihy. Certain lands in this barony, namely, Murivechimelane and Balilanocane near Marmullane (Passage West), were granted jointly by FitzStephen and de Cogan to the abbey of Saint Nicholas at Exeter; it seems likely that this area belonged neither to FitzStephen's moiety nor to that of de Cogan, but that it formed part of the cantred of the Ostmen which Henry had placed under their joint governorship.

In the subdivision of the kingdom of Cork FitzStephen took three cantreds to the east of Cork harbour and de Cogan four to the west. FitzStephen's cantreds were Olethan, Muscrie-Donegan and Killede, concerning which Edmund Barry's *History of Barrymore* states that they were coextensive with the ecclesiastical deaneries of Olethan and Muskerry-Donegan in the diocese of Cloyne and the deanery of Ocurblethan in the diocese of Cork.[17] He modifies his statement

13 *Ann. Inisf.*

14 *Ann. Tig.*

15 *Expugnatio Hibernica*, pp. 347–9: A civibus et milite quodam, Richard scilicet Londonendi, tunc ibi sub Adelini filio custodiam agente, cum honore recepti.

16 Unlike Limerick which had to be temporarily abandoned.

17 Edmund Barry, *A History of Barrymore*, p. 18.

later to identify Killede with the barony of Glenquin in county Limerick.[18] Gibson puts Killede in the present barony of Imokilly, thus placing it near the Cork deanery of Ocurblethan which extended eastwards from the north liberties of the city to the ancient parishes of Glounthane, Glenville and Carrignavar. In terms of physical rather than of ecclesiastical geography, the cantred of Olethan (Ui Liathain) extended eastwards from Cork harbour towards Youghal; Muskerry-Donegan represented the baronies of Orrery and Kilmore in county Cork, and consequently FitzStephen's grants are easily identifiable. De Cogan's cantreds are more problematic. From Sir Richard Cox's *Regnum Corcagiense* we learn that de Cogan had a footing in Muskerry. A confirmatory grant of Kilmohanoc (Kilmonoge at Oysterhaven near Kinsale) shows that he also had Kinalea. His remaining cantreds were Kerrycurrihy and Rosailithir (Rosselithir). The plea rolls of 1301, which are a close approximation of the foregoing, show four cantreds (not including Kerrycurrihy) in south and west Cork: Kinalea in two parts, Kinalbek or Kinalmeaky, Muskerry Mitine and Ibathan or Ibawne. Very probably these divisions represented the original de Cogan cantreds to the west of the city, though by 1301 Ibathan extended only as far as Rathbarry, while Rosscarbery (Rosailithir) and the coastal district had been reconquered by the Irish.[19]

For five years FitzStephen and de Cogan exercised joint governorship of the kingdom of Desmond. Entries in the *Register of the Abbey of St. Thomas the Martyr* for these years indicate a co-operation between the grantees and the early post-Norman bishops of Cork, notably Bishops Gregory (1172–82) and Reginald (1182–87), in endowing the Norman-sponsored Dublin abbey with lands and churches in Cork city and its vicinity. The same co-operation is seen in grants made to the church of Saint Nicholas in Exeter. Marriage alliances gave family cohesion to the adventurers. Ralph, illegitimate son of Robert FitzStephen, married Margarita, heiress presumptive to the de Cogan grant. Following this marriage FitzStephen conferred on Margarita one-half of the Great Island in the harbour of Cork, and she, in turn, made a grant of the church of Clonmel on the island to the abbey of Saint Thomas.[20] She also granted twenty carucates of land at

18   Ibid., p. 71.

19   *Plea Rolls*, 1301, viii, 76–91.

20   *Register of the Abbey of St. Thomas the Martyr*, ed. J. T. Gilbert, pp. 226–7.

'Crimdarin in Rosailithir' to the abbey of Saint Mary in Dublin, a circumstance which shows that de Cogan's cantreds were connected with the two most important religious houses in Dublin. Milo de Cogan, Ralph FitzStephen and five other knights were killed in 1182 by Mac Tíre, the dispossessed chief of Imokilly. The *Annals of Loch Cé* carry a detailed account of the incident: 'Milo de Cogan, after assuming the kingship of Corcach and Des Mumha, and after plundering Ath Cliath and Port Lairge, and after destroying all Erin with church and territory, was slain by Mac Tíre, King of the Ui-mic-Caille, and a great slaughter of foreigners along with him.' The massacre seems to have heralded a general uprising under Dermot MacCarthy and it was only the timely arrival of le Gros from Waterford that saved the position for Robert FitzStephen. In February 1183 Philip de Barry, FitzStephen's heir, came to Cork accompanied by his brother, Giraldus Cambrensis, whose account of the conquest of Cork has the benefit of being an eyewitness report. FitzStephen, who died shortly after their arrival, settled on Philip de Barry, 'my nephew, three cantreds in my land of Cork, *viz.*, Olethan and two other cantreds in the Kingdom of Cork [Muscrie-Donegan and Killede] just as they shall come to him by lot'.[21] The Barrys established their chief seat at Carrigtwohill (Barryscourt), with outlying castles at Castlelyons and Buttevant. Dermot MacCarthy continued to engage in intermittent scuffles with the Normans until 1185 when 'he was slaine neere unto Cork in a parley between the citizens and some of Theobald Walter's party.'[22]

The extent to which the early subinfeudation of the kingdom of Cork was carried out in the lifetime of the early grantees cannot be ascertained. FitzStephen, besides making large grants of the territories allotted to him, is also known to have made speculative grants of lands not included in his three cantreds. In addition to Philip de Barry five other subgrantees of FitzStephen are mentioned, namely, Alexander, son of Maurice FitzGerald, who became the first FitzGerald occupant of Imokilly, Raymond Magunel and Thomas des Auters who likewise held land in Imokilly, and Alexander and Raymond FitzHugh who settled in Fermoy. When FitzStephen died without direct male issue in 1183 his lands which were held in fee from the crown passed by a devious and thoroughly

21 *Expugnatio Hibernica*, pp. 350–1.

22 B.M., Clarendon MS 4783, f. 97.

confusing process to the Carews. The inheritance seems to have first passed to FitzStephen's half-brother Raymond le Gros de Carew, and from him to Richard de Carew who was a leading figure among the Anglo-Normans in Cork about the year 1200 and whose wife, Raghenilda, was the daughter of a MacCarthy chief. Richard de Carew is believed to have been an illegitimate son of Raymond le Gros or of le Gros' elder brother, Odo de Carew, who had settled in east Cork and from whom the Garryvoe Carews were descended. He was succeeded by his son Robert, of whom we read that in 1216 'Robert, son and heir of Richard de Carew, was fined £100 for his relief.' He was therefore a chief tenant to the crown. Robert was succeeded by his son, another Richard whose death is recorded in the *Annals of Inisfallen* for the year 1272: 'Richard de Kerreu died in Cork, a great noble baron and Seneschal of Desmond.' When his son Maurice reached his majority in 1276 he was given the manor of Corth Castle or Ballinacurra, Midleton, with subsidiary manors at Mogeely and Aghada.[23] *The Pipe Roll of Cloyne* mentions a Thomas de Carew in connection with Castlecore or Ballinacurra in 1376, but the family fell into obscurity shortly afterwards. Thomas surrendered the manors of Olethan and Muscrie-Donegan to David de Barry, and later in the century the ancient FitzStephen lands fell entirely to the Barrys and the FitzGeralds who held them as tenants-in-chief of the crown.

The de Cogan estates, which were more enduring as a family possession than was the grant made to FitzStephen, underwent their own changes of ownership through female succession in the immediate post-Norman period. Milo de Cogan's daughter and heiress was thrice married. Her first husband was Simon le Poer.[24] When he died she married Ralph FitzStephen whose death at the hands of the Mac Tíre chief of Imokilly widowed her for the second time. Her third husband was Patrick de Courcey of whom little is known beyond that he died before 1236; but it was through this marriage that Milo de Cogan's moiety of the kingdom of Cork passed to the de Courceys of Kinsale. Their chief castles were at Ringrone, Kinsale and Kilbrittain.

It was apparently in an endeavour to ease a situation which was becoming progressively more complicated that King John issued three new grants on 8 November 1207. By the first Philip de Prendergast was given a grant of forty knights' fees,

23   *Calendar of the Justiciary Rolls, 1295–1303*, pp. 383–5.

24   *Chartularies of St. Mary's Abbey*, ed. J. T. Gilbert, ii, 4, 21.

fifteen between the port of Cork and the port of Insovenach and twenty-five elsewhere. The second gave Robert Fitz-Martin a grant of twenty knights' fees in the cantred of Insovenach and twenty fees elsewhere. By the third grant Richard de Cogan got the cantred of Muscry-Omittone. If we study these grants we find that de Prendergast's share included the ancient tribeland of Kerrycurrihy which lay between Cork city and Crosshaven, with its principal stronghold at Carrigaline or Beaver (*Beauvoir*). An inquisition taken in 1251 into the possessions of Gerald, son of Philip de Prendergast, showed that he held lands at Belnar (Carrigaline) and Dufglas (Douglas) directly of the king.[25] Robert FitzMartin's cantred of Insovenach lay around Cork harbour and may have included the Great Island, or may have had some bearing on the island of Inis Mheadhonach. All that can be said about Insovenach is that it seems to be identical with the 'island of Inysewenagh within the port of Cork' which Philip FitzWilliam de Barry of the Great Island granted Edmund Tyrry in 1442.[26] Little is known of the grantee, Robert FitzMartin; the only other reference to him is found in a grant of the cantred of Rosselithir to David de Rupe, and it seems likely that his lands were ultimately acquired by the Barrys. Finally, the cantred of Muscry-Omittone which went to Richard de Cogan comprised the baronies of Muskerry and Barretts in mid-Cork. The cantred's chief stronghold was at Dundrinan, now Castlemore near Crookstown. Richard de Cogan's son married Maria de Prendergast. Thus the lands around Carrigaline reverted to the de Cogan's and the castle of Carrigaline became the principal de Cogan stronghold of this thoroughly Normanized area. By 1439, however, the de Cogan lands in Muskerry, Dundrinan and Kerrycurrihy were granted to James FitzGerald, earl of Desmond, by Robert FitzGeoffrey de Cogan.

From the late twelfth century onwards the eastern half of the diocese of Cork, the city included, was in the power of the Anglo-Norman settlers. The grantees were also powerful in places like Bandon, Innishannon and Kinsale and thence to Rosailither (diocese of Ross), but they never penetrated the extreme limits of the diocese which remained in Irish hands down to the seventeenth century. As will be shown in a subsequent chapter, the bishop's manorial rights were early recognized within the Normanized area, even though he was

25 *Calendar of Inquisitions Post Mortem, Hen. III*, i, 254.

26 Diarmuid Ó Murchadha, 'Where was Insovenach?', *Cork Hist. Soc. Jn.*, lxiv (1959), 57–62.

obliged to account for his profits and pay certain rents to the
king. He had his own Manor of Fayd and a subsidiary manor
at Kilbrogan and he exercised all the rights of a feudal lord
within the territories under his jurisdiction. His adoption of
feudal status under the crown was his best safeguard against
the encroachments of his over-mighty Anglo-Norman neighbours, a safeguard which was further strengthened by the
decretal letter of 1199. Clashes and over-lappings of jurisdiction proved perennial, however, for as Father Dunning has
pointed out,[27] one great problem which arose as a result of the
conquest was the status of ecclesiastical property in conquered
areas and the partial application of feudal tenure to ecclesiastical
property in a country which had little or no experience of feudal
practices. Even Giraldus is loud in his condemnation of the
invaders for their usurpation of church property,[28] while the
letters of Innocent III carry occasional nuances regarding the
same problem. Clashes of jurisdiction in Cork will be considered
in the chapter dealing with the diocesan episcopacy of the
twelfth and thirteenth centuries. Our present purpose is to
penetrate the impact of the Norman invasion on the Irish
church generally.

When in 1171 Henry II came to Ireland ostensibly 'for
purposes of reform' the great reform movement of the twelfth
century was already well under way. A territorial episcopate
had been established, cathedral chapters were being formed
and abuses connected with ecclesiastical dynasties and with
church administration and discipline were being effectively
eliminated. But there were still problems clamouring for attention and it was probably in an effort to secure secular support
for the reform movement that the Irish clergy took to the king
and his Anglo-Norman entourage. For this reason the Synod
of Cashel, 1172, which Giraldus says was summoned by
Henry II, is to be regarded as the first instrument towards
forwarding the ecclesiastical policy of the king. Christian
O Conairche, bishop of Lismore and papal legate, presided
at this synod; also present were the archbishops of Cashel,
Dublin and Tuam, a majority of the Irish episcopate and a
representative gathering of dignitaries. The archbishop of
Armagh, who was unavoidably absent, consented later to all
the synodal enactments. The bishops after swearing fealty to

27 P. J. Dunning, 'Irish Representatives and Irish Ecclesiastical Affairs at the Fourth
Lateran Council', in *Medieval Studies presented to Aubrey Gwynn, S.J.*, p. 93.

28 *Expugnatio Hibernica*, p. 293.

the king, set about the more pressing matter of reform, and the constitutions of Cashel produced by them covered a comprehensive variety of subjects. Marriage customs of the brehon laws were condemned; tithes were declared payable only to parish churches; Irish kings and chieftains were denounced for exacting hospitality from the churches; regulations were set for the making of wills and, finally, the bishops, according to Giraldus, drew up a statement 'of the enormous offences and foul lives' of the people.[29] A decree also stipulated that in future divine offices were to be celebrated in every part of Ireland according to the forms and usages of the church of England. This meant that the Sarum use of the Mass, as approved by Rome, was to be henceforth the one and only orthodox usage in Ireland. Giraldus, who enumerates this with the other decrees of the synod, adds, 'for it is right and just that as by Divine Providence Ireland has received her Lord and King from England, she should also submit to a reformation from the same source'.[30] Giraldus's pronouncement cannot be accepted without reservation since it obviously betokens his own wishful thinking. An examination of the constitutions of Cashel has shown that in the decisions of the synod there was 'nothing relative to religious dogmas, to matters of faith or to points of ecclesiastical discipline; and some of these decrees refer to matters of a political rather than of an ecclesiastical nature'.[31]

The constitutions of Cashel received royal confirmation and were promulgated in the king's name, and when Henry II left Ireland on 17 April 1172 he did so with the conviction of having strong clerical support for his policy in Ireland. Pope Alexander III's reply to the letters he had received after the convocation at Cashel was expressed in letters to the archbishops and bishops of Ireland, to Henry II and to the kings and princes of Ireland. In the first and second letters the pope referred to the crimes and excesses of the Irish, and in that addressed to the bishops they were ordered to assist Henry in maintaining possession of the land of Ireland and in eliminating all abominations. They were furthermore to invoke the censures of the church against any person of whatever rank who broke his oath of fealty to the king. Henry II was commended and urged to greater efforts in the praiseworthy reform which he had undertaken, and kings and princes who had submitted to

29   Sheehy, *Pontificia Hib.*, i, nos. 5 and 6.

30   *Expugnatio Hibernica*, chap. 24 *passim*.

31   J. Lanigan, *An Ecclesiastical History of Ireland*, i, 32.

him were advised to be true to their sworn fealty.[32] The publication of Pope Alexander's threefold reply seems not to have taken place until 1175 at the Synod of Waterford. The powers of the English kings over the Irish church were subsequently strengthened by letters from popes Innocent III and Honorius III enjoining on the Irish bishops the duty of respecting the royal rights. One important consequence of the Norman invasion therefore was the inauguration of a new church-state relationship in Ireland. Coupled with this were the introduction of continental religious orders and the beginnings of parish organization.

The ecclesiastical policy of Henry II was geared towards bringing the church in Ireland into conformity with that of England, or to quote Giraldus Cambrensis: *Ecclesiae illius statum ad Anglicanae ecclesiae formam redigere modis omnibus elaborando.*[33] The king was to hold the same position in respect of the Irish as of the English church, concerning which a recent study has pointed out that 'the principle of the adoption by the Irish Church of the institutions of the English Church was logical enough in itself, being the ecclesiastical complement of the extension to Ireland of English law and institutions in the secular sphere, and it enjoyed papal approval.'[34] This extension meant royal control over episcopal and abbatial elections, which in turn involved the threefold process of obtaining the *congé d'élire* or licence to elect, followed by royal assent and mandates for the restoration of temporalities which were to be retained in the king's hand (*in manu regis*) during times of vacancy. It meant also that cathedral chapters according as they were set up tended to be flooded with Anglo-Norman ecclesiastics. Cork's first-known archdeacon was such an Anglo-Norman.

In the early years of the Anglo-Norman administration the common law area, that is the area under English control, was small, and it was only within this restricted belt that the new church-state relations became really operative. Surviving Irish records of the period are so fragmentary that a workable conclusion commonly applicable is out of the question. Edward Tresham's *Rotulorum Patentium et Clausorum Cancellariae Hiberniae Calendarium*, which covers the period from Henry II to Henry VII, is an example of the unsatisfactory documentation to hand. A complementary source enshrined in the series of

32   Sheehy, *Pontificia Hib.*, i, nos. 5 and 7.

33   *Expugnatio Hibernica*, pp. 280–1.

34   J. A. Watt, 'English Law and the Irish Church: The Reign of Edward I', in *Med. Studies presented to A. Gwynn*, p. 134.

Irish pipe rolls perished in the burning of the Irish Record Office in 1922. To offset this loss, however, we have the *Calendar of Justiciary Rolls, 1295–1307,* in three volumes and Sweetman's five-volume *Calendar of Documents relating to Ireland 1171– 1307,* which with the escheatry accounts throw some light on an otherwise elusive situation. Still, the overall result is far from satisfactory. King John and King Henry III are known to have made determined efforts to control Irish episcopal elections, but royal jurisdiction did not become fully operative until the reign of Edward I (1272–1307). By that time the common law area embraced practically the entire country, and because this period represents the zenith of the English lordship of Ireland it is understandably well documented. Consequently an appreciation of the problems and difficulties of the time is possible. Notwithstanding the strength of the English power in the first Edwardian era, local peculiarities, provincial differences and a varied population balance made the carrying out of the royal decrees difficult and at times impossible. For ecclesiastical purposes the royal power was confined to the provinces of Dublin and Cashel and to the diocese of Meath. Because of longstanding anglicization Dublin presented little difficulty. The situation in the province of Cashel, on the other hand, was kaleidoscopic. During the course of the thirteenth century an English succession was maintained in the dioceses of Limerick and Waterford; an exclusively Irish succession in Cashel itself as well as in Ross and Kilfenora; the dioceses of Killaloe and Ardfert had each only one non-Irish bishop, and there was a mixed succession in Cork, Cloyne and Emly.[35] Dioceses within the provinces of Armagh and Tuam were, with some exceptions, ruled by native clergy throughout the thirteenth century, all going to show that the situation was far from being standardized. There were actually sharp divisions as between English and Irish areas within individual dioceses where a distinction was clearly drawn between clergy *inter Anglos* and clergy *inter Hibernicos.*[36]

The racial division within the Irish church of the thirteenth century was only one of many problems confronting the episcopate. There were disputes about diocesan boundaries and about ecclesiastical jurisdiction, particularly about the primacy, as well as strained relations between bishops and their chapters, conflicts between metropolitans and their suffragans, disputes with secular authorities over ecclesiastical liberties, and so on.

35 Ibid., p. 135.

36 F. M. Powicke and E. B. Fryde, eds., *Handbook of British Chronology,* pp. 305 ff.

And it was from this racially and internally divided episcopacy that Edward I sought 'that co-operation with the state which all medieval political theory held to be divinely ordained and which all medieval kings needed in some degree for the maintenance of political stability'.[37] A satisfactory *modus vivendi* involved control of episcopal appointments, taxation and the delineation of the respective jurisdictions of ecclesiastical and royal courts. During the regency of Henry III the pattern of episcopal appointments laid down by common law and approved by Innocent III gave the king an important place in the electoral formalities, as well as custody of temporalities during times of vacancy; and while this concordat between the claims of canon and civil law cannot have seemed an ideal situation to Innocent III, it was confirmed by Gregory IX in 1227 and by Innocent IV in 1246 and remained more or less the standard practice down to the Reformation. But the extension to Ireland of a system which sought to secure the election of English clerics to Irish benefices was opposed locally and was abrogated, temporarily, by Honorius III who in 1220 condemned this racial exclusiveness as an *abusus tante temeritatis et iniquitatis*.[38] The solution finally accepted was that the diocesan chapter should notify the king on the death of a bishop and should solicit the *congé d'élire*. The elect had to receive royal approbation *before* he was canonically examined by his metropolitan (or by the pope if the elect was a metropolitan), and he was to swear an oath of fealty to the king. He was then given the temporalities which the escheator had held during the vacancy. The escheator was one of the most important of the royal ministers in Ireland, his importance deriving from the fact that when Henry III conferred the lordship of Ireland on his son Edward in 1254, he reserved to himself the revenues arising from vacant bishoprics and abbacies. During vacancies these revenues were administered by the escheator who, because of his contacts with the higher clergy, became the principal representative of the king in Ireland. The interval between the actual restoration of temporalities and the royal mandate ordering restoration was usually only a matter of weeks, except in case of disputed elections when delay was inevitable.

Variants introduced into the electoral procedure by the subterfuges of chapters and metropolitans were sternly checked, and as the reign of Edward I progressed and English power in Ireland was consolidated, the threat of seizure of temporalities

---

37 Watt, 'English Law and the Irish Church', p. 137.

38 *Calendar of Documents relating to Ireland, 1171–1251*, nos. 736, 739.

was an effective instrument for keeping bishops and chapters obedient to the royal will. In 1278 Richard of Wexford, bishop of Ossory, had his temporalities confiscated for going abroad without a licence. Richard Cheeves, bishop of Leighlin, was similarly punished in 1295 on a charge of harbouring felons.[39] Threat of seizure was invoked against Bishops Robert Mac Donnchada of Cork and Nicholas de Effingham of Cloyne in 1297, and in 1299 the bishop of Emly had his temporalities withheld because of debts he incurred during his tenure of an English escheatry.[40] It must also be borne in mind that secular interference with episcopal elections was not confined to the English king and his immediate representatives in Ireland. From the letters of Innocent III we learn that the king of Cork opposed the candidate D(aniel) in a disputed election in the diocese of Ross,[41] from which it may be inferred that individual Irish kings must have exercised considerable control in church affairs in areas not immediately under Anglo-Norman influence. It was not without reason therefore that the council of Cashel issued a condemnation of the exactions which Irish kings and chieftains levied on the church.

The electoral system did not become immediately stabilized and there were evasions of the royal prerogative in many places. Electoral proceedings which ignored the king were initiated in Leighlin, Emly, Meath, Killaloe, Elphin, Kilmacduagh and Cork. The archbishops of Cashel are known to have confirmed and consecrated several suffragans who had not complied with the procedural regulations and in 1250, that is, during the reign of Henry III (1216–1272), the native clergy decreed the exclusion of Englishmen from canonries in Irish cathedral churches. Pope Innocent IV condemned this decree, but there is no evidence to prove that papal intervention made any material alteration in the situation. On the other hand, we find quite a number of dioceses with predominantly native chapters and whose bishops were certainly native, making regular applications for the *congé d'élire*. Taken all in all, it seems that the political attitudes of the Irish bishops could and did vary according to the geographical fluctuations of the common law area. Taking the four provinces separately, we find that holders of the bishoprics in Dublin were usually compliant; parts of Cashel which lay within the common law area found that

---

39 *Cal. justic. rolls Ire., 1295–1303*, pp. 66, 73.

40 Ibid., pp. 253, 255.

41 Augustin Theiner, ed., *Vetera Monumenta Hibernorum et Scotorum*, p. 1. The pseudo-bishop is called D(avid) in *Cal. papal letters, 1198–1304*, p. 3.

co-operation with the crown was essential even though only Irish born prelates were elected to Cashel during the thirteenth century; Armagh, in an endeavour to protect traditional primatial rights, had to compromise in order to avoid further encroachments by royal officials; Tuam was sufficiently far removed from the main centre of English power to follow its own way with but few limitations. Dr. Watt's summing-up of the situation is that 'the political attitudes of bishops in Ireland was decided not so much by the national origins of the individual bishop as by his proximity, geographical or functional, to the civil administration.'[42]

About fifty bishops, half of whom were Irish, were elected in the approved fashion during the reign of Edward I. Surviving escheatry accounts of the period show those dioceses the temporalities of which were *in manu regis* during vacancies. Twenty-two of the thirty-four Irish dioceses are represented in these accounts, and two of the accounts show returns from the diocese of Cork. These were the escheatry returns of John de Sanford in 1282 and those of Walter de la Haye in 1302.[43] The dioceses listed in the earlier account are Cork, Kildare, Lismore, Dublin and Meath; the second account lists the returns from Limerick, Ossory, Cork, Cashel and Kildare. A characteristic feature of the accounts is that in the twenty-two dioceses in question only a part, and sometimes a negligible part, of the possessions of certain sees is accounted for. Even in the reign of Edward I (1272–1307) when English power was at its peak, the escheator found it difficult to penetrate certain areas and was completely excluded from others. Such obstacles to the contrary, the escheatry through custody of temporalities made a very valuable contribution to the exchequer in the period under consideration.

By and large, the system of royal control over episcopal elections worked harmoniously enough in the reign of Edward I. Good relations with the chapters were maintained by the king's delegation of his electoral rights to his justiciar, and this while satisfying the chapters had the extra advantage of economy. Certain dioceses, however, were reserved for special action by the king, as is clear from a royal mandate of 21 May 1227 in which the king granted Geoffrey de Morisco power to issue formal licence to elect in place of the king in all Irish sees with the exception of eleven: Kildare, Ossory, Leighlin, Ferns, Meath, Emly, Limerick, Killaloe, Cork, Waterford and

---

42 Watt, 'English Law and the Irish Church', p. 163.

43 A detailed account of these escheatry returns will be given in Chapter VI.

Lismore.[44] Edward I's *modus vivendi* entailed on the one hand the recognition by the chapter of the king's electoral rights, and on the other an appreciation by the king of the power of the local forces which an individual chapter represented.[45] The chapter therefore was of paramount importance in the structure of the medieval diocese. Its control of electoral procedures was practical as well as theoretical, the papal role being more or less confined to the exercise of appellate jurisdiction, notwithstanding which the papacy, through its lawyer popes of the calibre of Innocent III, managed to achieve a reasonable balance between the royal power, the capitular body and the nominees. How far the chapters were free to elect whom they wished is a subject not yet fully explored, but from the constant stream of requests for licences to elect and for royal assent which marks the thirteenth century the English kings seem to have been willing to allow a free hand to the chapters and not to have pushed the appointment of their own nominees. Edward I's proposal of Stephen Fulbourn to Waterford in 1273 would seem to be the only recorded instance of its kind— and the Waterford chapter accepted it. Edward, however, appointed to vacant canonries in Dublin during archiepiscopal vacancies. He also exacted fines for breaches of electoral procedure in Clonmacnoise, Killaloe and Ossory; whereas for a breach in Cork in 1248 Henry III only exacted a promise that there would be no further deviation.[46] Direct papal intervention in thirteenth-century Ireland was negligible—there are only twelve episcopal provisions recorded during the reign of Edward I—and it is noteworthy that where papal intervention was invoked, the kings accepted the papal solution without demur; which goes to prove that while the popes were ready to respect the electoral rights of the English kings they were adamant in upholding the candidacy of any cleric who had been canonically examined and found suitable for promotion to the episcopacy. In cases which involved compromise on the part of the king (and these became more frequent with time), the temporalities were restored to the papal providee but he had to make formal repudiation of anything prejudicial to the king in his letter of appointment. Placing this alongside the king's other weapon of control and/or confiscation of temporalities it would seem that there were limits beyond which the pope could not pursue his policy.

44   *Cal. doc. Ire., 1171–1251*, no. 1519.

45   Watt, 'English Law and the Irish Church', p. 144.

46   See Chapter vii, section on Bishop Lawrence (1248–65).

Papal policy in respect of thirteenth-century episcopal appointments in Ireland may be summarized as follows: Insofar as the English kings, Henry III and Edward I, did not contravene the 'law of the canon' in their electoral procedures, they were upheld by papal approval. They were not permitted to exercise racial discrimination. Neither could they reject for political reasons a candidate who was adjudged canonically suitable. Disputed elections were referred to Rome where the decision given usually reflected that of the local chapter. When direct provision by the pope was the only viable solution of a deadlock, the popes wherever possible again gave consideration to the wishes of local bodies. As we shall see, this deference to local needs and peculiarities was outstandingly characteristic of the whole system of papal provisions when such provisions became the normal method of appointment to vacant benefices.

As to King Edward's ruling on taxation and his attitude towards the legal position of the Irish church, he insisted that the custom obtaining in England should be extended to Ireland. His reply to an episcopal complaint against alleged encroachment on ecclesiastical jurisdiction was precise and unyielding: *Fiat eis secundum quod sit prelatis in Anglia.* Episcopal opposition to such royal control as expressed in the *Articuli Cleri* of 1291 was ineffective because of lack of unanimity among the bishops, and there is every indication that the relationship between common law and canon law became uniform in Ireland as in England. Matters of taxation, of the workings of ecclesiastical courts and of the application of the *congé d'élire* in Cork will be treated in the following chapters. What follows immediately as an appendix contains (a) a list of unpublished charters relating to Ireland, 1172–82, from the archives of the city of Exeter giving a clear account of Norman families in Cork and of the lands and churches of the diocese which came under Norman influence; (b) a digest of grants in lands and churches to the abbey of Saint Thomas, Dublin.

The reasons why the priory of Saint Nicholas at Exeter should have been singled out as an object for largesse by FitzStephen and de Cogan are not as apparent as the factors urging their liberality to the Dublin abbey of Saint Thomas. It has been proved that there was no real connection binding these Anglo-Normans to Devonshire, at least when the grants here recorded were made. In spite of this obscurity regarding the choice of the Exeter priory, one very important result of the transactions of FitzStephen and de Cogan was a change of titular in one of Cork's city churches in the early post-invasion period. This was the church of Saint Sepulchre which occupied the site of the later church of Saint Nicholas and must have been its original name.[47] It is possible that the change of titular was effected under Bishop Gregory O hAodha (1172–82) who placed monks of Saint Nicholas in the church of Saint Sepulchre. The church, which 'lay waste' when the monks were introduced, became the centre of the Exeter priory's possessions in Cork. Its importance may be gauged from the fact that one of the grants calendared in the Exeter archives was made out 'not to St. Nicholas of Exeter . . . but to St. Nicholas of Cork and the monks there'.[48] When or how the connection between Exeter and Cork was dissolved is not known, but it must have occurred at an early date, perhaps during the episcopate of Reginald (1182–87) who confirmed Roger of Oxford's grant of the chapel of Saint Nicholas to the abbey of Saint Thomas in Dublin.[49] This abbey, commemorative of Saint Thomas à Beckett, was founded in Dublin in 1177 by William FitzAudelm (Fitz-Aldelm), representative of King Henry II in Ireland. The abbey's foundation charter was executed by FitzAudelm in presence of Cardinal Vivian, the papal legate, and of Archbishop Laurence O'Toole. The alleged objects of the new foundation, as set down by King Henry, were to promote his own spiritual welfare as well as that of his sons, his parents, the Earl of Anjou and the Empress Matilda. The abbey was administered by the Augustinian Canons of Saint Victor and for its upkeep the king granted the monks the returns from certain tolls, rights and privileges. These were soon supplemented by endowments of lands and churches made by the Anglo-Norman grantees and by some of the early post-Norman bishops. King John confirmed the Augustinian Canons in their possessions and conferred several new concessions, principally tithes of salmon, fishing rights and tolls from ale and metheglin, upon them.[50] As a royal foundation Saint Thomas's Abbey was immediately under royal protection and its abbots could only be appointed subject to the approval of the king. When appointed, the abbots became *ipso facto* members of the king's council in Ireland, they sat is parliament and administered justice in the court of the abbey.

The *Register of the Abbey of St Thomas* is the oldest recorded extant account of the Anglo-Norman settlement in Ireland. Its

47 Eric St. J. Brooks, 'Unpublished Charters relating to Ireland, 1177–82, from the Archives of the City of Exeter', *R.I.A. Proc.*, xliii, sect. c (1936), pp. 313–66.

48 Ibid., p. 337.

49 See Charter 248 in Appendix B.

50 *Reg. St. Thomas, Dublin*, introduction, *passim*.

contents show the churches, lands, possessions and rights acquired by the abbey during the first hundred years of its existence. After kings Henry II and John the principal bene-factors of the abbey were the Anglo-Norman adventurers, aspects of whose careers are exemplified in the documents of the *Register*. Over and above the lavish donations of these Anglo-Normans, the abbey received extensive grants of churches and tithes from the archbishops of Armagh, Dublin, Cashel and Tuam, and from about seventeen suffragan bishops. Abbots and priors are also enumerated among its beneficiaries. In view of the Cork grants enumerated below it is conceivable that a considerable amount of money was siphoned off from the diocese of Cork towards the upkeep of this Norman-sponsored establishment. It is somewhat difficult to determine the length of time during which this contact with the Dublin abbey was maintained, but the bishops of Cork seem to have regained control at an early date of all diocesan grants made to Saint Thomas's. Not a single grant of those outlined in the following appendix appears in the document listing the possessions of the abbey at the time of the confiscations, 1540–41.

APPENDIX A

Grants to the Church of Saint Nicholas, Exeter

Charter 4   Grant from RICHARD DE COGAN, with the consent
of his lord, Milo de Cogan, of the *church* of Chilmahanoc,
along with a carucate of land and tithes of the vill, and three
other carucates in another suitable place; and also the tithes
of the fisheries pertaining to the vill.
Witnesses : Milo de Cogan, Robert FitzStephen and his son
Radulph (Ralph), Roger de Chiricelle, William de Brideshale,
Gunfrei (Gargate), Hugh de Tilli, Oein de Cantilo, John de
Lyditon, Roger de Oxeneford, Gunmore, Roger de Bodmin,
Alexander, and many others (*et multis aliis*).
Note : Chilmahanoc is Kilmonoge at Oysterhaven near
Kinsale.

Charter 5   Grant from MILO DE COGAN of the *land* which is
between the Cross of Cameleire upon the water up to the
curtilages of the burgesses of the city (of Cork), and on the
other side the road . . . to the church of St. Sepulchre.
Witnesses : As above with the following additions: Richard
Hundethin, Lucas de Lundoniis, John Hundethin, Brother
Philip of the Hospital of Jerusalem, Brother Thericus,
Reginald the monk, and Stephen and John, clerics.

Charter 6   Grant from ROBERT FITZSTEPHEN and MILO DE
COGAN of the *church* of St. Sepulchre outside the vill of Cork.
Witnesses : Raymond (le Gros), nephew of Robert Fitz-
Stephen, Richard de Cogan, William de Waleis, Roger de
Conditon (Condon), Thomas de Altirs, Raymond Beg,
Roger de Oxeneford, Roger de Bodmin.

Charter 7   As the preceding charter but with different
witnesses: Gregory, Bishop of Cork, 'who placed the said
monks of St. Nicholas in the church of St. Sepulchre because
it lay waste'; Reginald, archdeacon; Robert, chaplain; John
and Stephen, clerics; Alexander FitzMaurice, William le
Waleis, William de Brideshale; Walter, cleric.

Charter 17   (Inserted here because of its connection with
land at Saint Sepulchre as in Charter 5 above).
Grant from MILO DE COGAN of the *land* which is between
the Cross of Cameleire and the little harbour, which land is

(?outside) the vill (of Cork), where small ships and boats put in; that is, between the curtilages of the burgesses and the water, and on the other side by the way which leads up to the church of St. Sepulchre and the great water. Also of the land between the cemetery of St. Sepulchre and the way behind . . . Grant also of the land on the eastern side of St. Sepulchre by the road which lies next to the court of the Hospital of St. John of Jerusalem—the land to be as wide on the east as it is on the western part.

Note : This grant shows that Saint Sepulchre must have been on the site of the later (and present) church of Saint Nicholas. The Hospital of Saint John of Jerusalem lay to the east of Saint Sepulchre; the little harbour or cove was near Mary Street and *Cove* Street adjoined it. The curtilages of the burgesses were probably those outside the South Gate at Barrack Street.

Charter 8   Grant from ROBERT FITZSTEPHEN and MILO DE COGAN of the *land* called Murivechimelan and the *land* called Balilannocan, with all appurtenances in churches, fisheries, meadows, etc., quit of all temporal service.

Witnesses : Richard de Cogan, Geoffrey de Cogan, Ralph FitzRobert, Raymond le Gros FitzWilliam, Alexander FitzMaurice (?FitzGerald of Youghal), Raymond Bec, Roger de Conditon, Turold, Gunfrid, Roger de Oxeneford, Stephen FitzBertram, William de Brideshale, Richard and John Hundethin, Gunnore and others.

Note : Murivechimelan is evidently Marmullane, Passage West, which appears as Killmurrymalane and Kilvoryomilane in later documents. Balilannocan may be Ballinaknockan, now Hilltown in the parish of Carrigaline.

Charter 9   Identical with Charter 8, even as to witnesses, except for the inclusion of Raymond FitzHugh of Fermoy. He was slain in 1185.

N.B. Charters 1 to 11 in the above arrangement are all originals. The remaining charters, 12 to 43, are written on a roll which is said to belong to the time of Edward I (1272–1307).

Charter 12   Grant and confirmation of Murivechymelan and Ballilannokan, as in Charter 8.

Charter 13   Grant and confirmation of land between the Cross of Camelyere, as in Charters 5 and 17.

Charter 14   Grant and confirmation from ROBERT FITZSTEPHEN of the grant which his nephew (?Philip de Barry) gave of (the tithe of the land which is) outside the vill of Cork, on the north side of the land of St. Thomas's Abbey, Dublin; and one carucate of land for the salvation of his lord, for the salvation of himself and his son Radulph. Confirmation also of the tithe (?of the mill of St. Nessan and the tithes of) the fishery which belonged to Humeolhuri.

Note: Mouse-eaten portions of this charter (righthand side) have been restored in brackets by reference to Charter 23, which for purposes of simplification is next quoted.

Charter 23   Grant from PHILIP DE BARRY of a carucate of *land*, with the tithe of the land between the road which divides the land . . . (?of St. Nessan's and) the water which leads to the mill of St. Nessan, for the salvation of King Henry II etc. Grant also of the tithes of the mill of St. (?Nessan) and the tithes of the fishery formerly belonging to Rutherwcharany, and the tithes of another fishery formerly belonging to Humeolhury. (The *Register of the Abbey of St Thomas* has a grant from Philip de Barry in the same area; this grant mentions the mill of St. Nessan).

Witnesses: Robert FitzStephen, Robert de Barry (son of Philip the grantee); Hugh, chaplain; Brother H.; William Fossard; William, presbyter; S. FitzOdo, Geoffrey de Exonia, Roger de Oxeneford.

Note: Places mentioned in this charter lay around the Kiln River and Shandon on the north side of the city.

Charter 15   Grant from ROBERT FITZSTEPHEN of the *land* . . . and the land of Baldwin Minerby in the city of Cork, with one burgage and all appurtenances, both land and sea . . . quit of service except the duty of watchman attached to one burgage. (This would probably mean a grant of 'land between a certain land and the land of Baldwin Minerby').

Charter 16   Grant and confirmation from ROBERT FITZ-STEPHEN of a *burgage* formerly of Galgepall in the vill of Cork . . . Grant also of the *land* formerly belonging to Gilbert son of Hurg, quit of all service except watchman's duty.

Note: The reference here is to Gilbert, son of Turgerius, Ostman mayor of Cork under MacCarthy.

Charter 18   Identical with Charters 6 and 7.

Charter 19   Grant from MILO DE COGAN of (the *church*) of Kilsale (Kinsale) with two carucates of land . . . with all appurtenances and other alms which pertain to the church. Grant also of all tithes (?of the lands) which pertain to the grantor's lordship of Kilsale.

Witnesses: Richard de Cogan, Radulph son of Robert, etc.

Charter 20   Identical with Charter 4.

Charters 22, 24   Variants of Charter 4. Charter 22 has a witness not encountered in any of the other charters, namely, Richard de Pyncheny.

Charter 25   Grant from WILLIAM NOT of half the *land* which
(? he holds of the church of St.) Fymbary, and of the Archdeacon of Cork; that is to say, half of the vill called Balivfian
(? Ballyphehane), and half of another which (belonged to)
Macyseanyh (*Mac Uí Seanaigh*) and Seacht Injenay Seanyh
(? *Seacht(ar) Inghean Seanaigh*) . . . to be held of the grantor
and his heirs by the same service as (? the grantor holds them
of) the church of St. Fymbary and of the Archdeacon of
Cork.
Witnesses : Robert FitzStephen, Robert FitzHelidore (he was
ancestor of the Stackpoles), Richard FitzGodebert (ancestor
of the Roches), Haymon Not, Walter Not, Stephen Fitz-
Robert, G. son of William le Waleis, Nicholas FitzG . . . de
Exonia, John Hundethin, Gunnore and his brother Odo,
Bartholomew and Roger Palmer.

Charter 26   Grant from GEOFFREY DE ARGENTON of the *land*
in front of the gate of St. John's.
Witnesses : Alexander FitzMaurice, William le Waleis, Robert
de la Marchall, T. Cantares, T. Alynne, etc.

Charter 27   Grant from ALEXANDER DE ST. ELENA to *St.
Nicholas' Cork*, and the monks there, of the *church* of his
lordship, of half a cantred with all (? ecclesiastical benefices
pertaining) and one carucate of land, for the salvation of the
grantor's soul etc.
Witnesses : John FitzBernard, John le Nories, Gounfrey
Gargate.
Note : Alexander de St. Helena is said to have founded the
Preceptory of Mourne (Mourneabbey) for the Knights
Hospitallers of St. John of Jerusalem.

Remaining charters on the roll relate to east Cork, to Wexford
and Kilkenny, and have no further relevance for the diocese
of Cork.

APPENDIX B

Charters relating to Cork
from the
Register of the Abbey of St Thomas

Charter 237   Grant from MILO DE COGAN to the church of
St. Thomas the Martyr outside the west gate of Dublin, the
service of one knight's fee in my land of Cork, namely
Crimdarin, with all its appurtenances . . . to be held of me
and my heirs in churches and ecclesiastical benefices, towns,

gates, woods, valleys, roads, paths, meadows, pastures, waters, mills and fisheries.

Witnesses : Gregory, Bishop; Reginald, Archdeacon; Robert FitzStephen, Ralph son of Robert, Merachu, T. Tancart, Geoffrey de Cogan, Hubert de Humframville, John Fitz-Bernard and many other knights (*multisque aliis militibus*).

Note : Crimdarin is identified as Kinnure near Kinsale.

Charter 238 Grant from MILO DE COGAN: Know that I have given and conceded, and by this charter have confirmed . . . to God and to (the church of) St. Thomas the Martyr, a quarter of a weir under the bridge of Dungarvan on the east (*orientalem partem*) of Cork, and a tithe of the value of that weir which is in my power to give . . .

Witnesses : Richard de Cogan; Roger, Seneschal; Richard de Pincheni; William de Brideshale, William FitzGeoffrey, Lucas de Londoniis, Roger de Oxeneford, Stephen, cleric, and Brother Tierri.

Note : See Charter 242 below.

Charter 241 Grant from MILO DE COGAN confirming the gifts which his people had given or would give to the Abbey of St. Thomas, 'of my lands within the kingdom of Cork', with churches, tithes, lands, vills, fisheries, mills . . . ,' for Henry, King of England . . . for John, his son, for the souls of their ancestors and for me and the souls of my own ancestors, in perpetual alms.'

Witnesses : Richard de Cogan, Richard FitzGodebert, Geoffrey de Cogan, Richard de Pincheton, William de Brideshale, William son of Galfrid, Engelramo and many others.

Charter 242 Grant from PHILIP DE BARRY: Know that I have given and conceded, and by this charter have confirmed, to God and to the Church of St. Thomas at Dublin . . . the two carucates of land near the bridge of Dungarvan, with the adjoining meadow lower down the river as far as the great water. Which meadow is to be included (*mensuratum sit*) in these two carucates. And the site of one mill near the river which flows from the mill of St. Nessan near the ancient castle; that is, between the great water and the last site (*ultimam sedem*) of the ancient sites of the mill. And three acres near the above-mentioned castle from the great road to the site of the mill. *Witnesses :* Gerald, archdeacon (Giraldus Cambrensis); Adam, monk; Robert de Barri, Alexander Fitz-Maurice, Alexander and Raymond FitzHugh, Raymond Magunel, Stephen FitzOdo, Adam de Cantiton, Roger de Oxeneford, William de Cantiton, Geoffrey de Exonia and many others. *Note:* Dungarvan, Saint Nessan's Mill, etc., were all near the Kiln River and John Street. The ancient castle (*vetus castellarium*) was probably Shandon (*Seandún*). Alexander FitzMaurice held Killeagh and Youghal; he was brother of Gerald, ancestor of the Earls of Kildare, and of Thomas, ancestor of the Earls of Desmond. Stephen FitzOdo was the son of Odo de Carew, elder brother of Raymond le Gros. Alexander FitzHugh founded Bridgetown Abbey (*de Villa Pontis*). Giraldus, the first witness, was in Cork in 1183.

Charter 243　　Grant from STEPHEN FITZODO DE CAREW to the church of St. Thomas the Martyr near Dublin . . . the church of Trummor with the tithes of one knight's fee around that church, and all other ecclesiastical benefices (revenues).

Witnesses: Robert de Barri, Walter de Barri, John Fitz-William, Robert FitzHugo, Walter FitzRobert, Gilbert Flandrensi, Geoffrey Exonie and others.

Note: Trummor of this charter is Drummer *alias* Temple-bodan, eight miles north of Midleton, county Cork.

Charter 244　　Grant from ALEXANDER FITZMAURICE of the church, tithes, fruits and all ecclesiastical revenues of my vill called Killie, and two carucates of land in the vicinity of the same vill adjoining the aforesaid church.

Witnesses: Robert FitzStephen, Raymond FitzHugh, Raymond Cantiton, Paganus Mansel, Robert de Barry, Walter de Barri, Ralph and Reginald de Altaribus.

Note: The vill of Killie is identified as Killeagh near Youghal.

Charter 245　　Grant from PAGANUS MANSEL (at Cork), the church of St. Mary de Ratcartne, with half a carucate of land and half the ecclesiastical revenues of the entire grant.

Witnesses: Alexander FitzMaurice, Robert de Altaribus, Ralph his brother, Raymond Magunel, Walter, cleric; Roger de Oxeneford, Geoffrey Exonie, Herbert Walensi, Roger de Bodmin, Peter Whyte, Stephen Walensi and Alan, cleric.

Note: Ratcartne is probably Rath, now Garranekennifick, near east Fermoy, county Cork.

Charter 246　　Grant from LEUKI FITZROBERT of all churches and tithes and fruits (*oblaciones*) and all ecclesiastical revenues of my entire territory which I hold in my region of Cork; and especially of the entire territory which my sponsor, Lucas de Londoniis, gave me in his old age, namely a third part of his conquest. And I give to the above church (of St. Thomas) one carucate of land in the district of Yahmarcat Ukoneidi. These churches and ecclesiastical revenues and this carucate of land I grant to the church of St. Thomas near Dublin; to be held of me and my heirs freely, peacefully and honourably in proper (*puram*) and perpetual grant.

Witnesses: Robert FitzStephen, Raymond FitzWilliam, Richard de Cogan, Geoffrey de Cogan, Raymond de Cantiton, Raymond FitzHugh, Raymond Magunel, Paganus Mansel, Robert de Altaribus.
Unidentified.

Charter 248 *Confirmation of Reginald, Bishop.*
Confirmation to God and to the church of St. Thomas the Martyr at Dublin . . . the chapel of St. Nicholas in the city of Cork . . . which chapel Roger de Oxeneford gave in perpetual gift to the above-mentioned church. And (? the brethren of) the above church of St. Thomas will give five English coins and one pound of wax each year on the feast of St. Nicholas to the church of St. Finbarr for every service pertaining to the bishopric.

Charter 249 Confirmation to the church of St. Thomas the Martyr near Dublin, by Bishop Reginald of every grant which the faithful have granted or may in future grant in the territory of Cork and 'in our diocese', namely, in lands, tithes, fruits, churches and ecclesiastical revenues. And the brethren of the aforesaid martyr will give every year to our church on the feast of St. Finbarr one *sextarius* of wine or its price in *denarii* for the celebration of the divine office, for every affliction (*quaerula*) threatening us, and for every episcopal service (*consuetudine*).
Witnesses: Adam, monk of St. Sepulchre; Brother Philip, Hospitaller; Robert FitzStephen, Richard de Cogan, Alexander FitzMaurice, Raymond FitzHugh, Robert de Barry, Stephen FitzOdo, Robert de Altaribus, Gilbert ** Flandrensi, William Fossard, and Alan, cleric.
**At this point, on the margin of the charter, the words *'ante annum* 1184', are written in a later hand.

Charter 250 *Confirmation of Bishop Gregory.*
This is a repetition of Charter 249 except that Robert Fitz-Stephen and Milo de Cogan are cited, not as witnesses, but as ratifying the decision of Bishop Gregory.
Witnesses: Reginald, archdeacon; Ade, monk; Aggiro, priest (*presbyter*); Brother Andrew of the Hospital of Jerusalem; John, cleric, and many others.

Charter 251 Grant from WALTER DE BARRI . . . of the church near to my castle . . . in my land of Dunlobbes, and the tithes, offerings and all ecclesiastical revenues pertaining to the said church, and a carucate of land contiguous thereto.
Witnesses: Robert FitzStephen, Richard de Cogan, Robert de Barri, Alexander FitzMaurice, Paganus Mansel, Raymond FitzHugh.
Unidentified.

Charter 252   Grant from WALTER FITZROBERT . . . of the
church, tithes and fruits and all ecclesiastical revenues of
one vill in my tenement (*tenemento meo*), which I hold in
the district of Occulan; and two carucates of land adjoining.
Witnesses: Alexander FitzMaurice, Raymond FitzHugh,
Raymond Cantiton, Pagan Mansel, Robert de Barri, Robert
de Altaribus.
Unidentified.

Charter 254   Grant from RICHARD DE CAREW . . . of one
burgage in Dungarvan, namely that nearest to the bridge
which is between the city and Dungarvan in the east. Furthermore, I have given to them (the brethren of St. Thomas)
certain land in Dungarvan, near the land of David de Drihille,
extending in breadth one hundred and twenty feet from
(*versus*) the city, and in length as far as the river to the east.
Witnesses: Philip de Prendergast, Alexander FitzHugh,
Ralph de Sommeri, John and Walter, clerics; David de
Drihille, Robert FitzGodebert, Geoffrey de Net, Bartholomew
de Bristollia, Jordan, son of Bartholomew.

Charter 256   Grant from MILO DE COGAN and ROBERT FITZ-
STEPHEN, confirming to the brethren of St. Thomas one
part of a mill between the city of Cork and Dungarvan, and
one burgage near the gate of Cork.
Witnesses: Dominus Reimundus, Richard and Geoffrey de
Cogan, Raymond Magunel, Richard FitzGodebert, Richard
de Pincheton, Thomas and Ralph de Altaribus, Ralph
FitzStephen, Lucas Londonie, Drin *filius* . . . , and Thomas
his brother.

Charter 257   Grant from ROBERT FITZSTEPHEN . . . of one
island outside the city of Cork on the east of the city, namely
that island which is between the city and the king's mill, and
one site of a mill near the same island.
Witnesses: Alexander FitzMaurice, Raymond de Cantiton,
Raymond FitzHugo, Robert de Altaribus and Ralph, his
brother, Raymond Magunel, Roger de Oxeneford, Walter,
cleric; Roger de Bodmin, Bartholomew de Bristonia, William
Coterel, Cunnare and Alan, cleric, who composed and wrote
this charter.
Unidentified.

Charter 258   Grant from RAYMOND MAGUNEL . . . of the
mother church of Ynespic, with the tithes, offerings and
revenues of the entire island which belong by right to the
said church. Likewise the church of Kairultan, with the
tithes, offerings and revenues pertaining by right to the
church, in perpetual gift, for me and my wife, for her descend-

ants and mine, and for our souls and the souls of our ancestors.
Witnesses: Robert FitzStephen, Milo de Cogan, Ralph
FitzRobert (FitzStephen), Robert, Thomas, Reginald and
Ralph des Auters, Stephen, parson of Holy Trinity and
many others.
Note: Ynespic is identified as Spike Island; Kairultan as
Caherultan, Castlemartyr.

Charter 259   Grant from ALEXANDER and RAYMOND FITZHUGO
. . . of half the church of Chiltumer and one carucate of land,
with all the tithes and fruits pertaining thereto.
Witnesses: Raymond FitzWilliam, Alexander FitzMaurice,
Robert, son of Philip de Barry, Jordan Cantiton, Robert and
Reginald des Alters.
Note: Chiltumer is identified as Kilcummer, which was not
far distant from Bridgetown Abbey founded by Alexander
FitzHugo.

Charter 260   Grant of GEOFFREY DE EXONIA (D'EXETER).
Know that I have granted . . . to the church of St. Thomas
of Dublin, the church, tithes and fruits of Inhismacnel, and
half the church of Hismaclot, with half the tithes and fruits
of the said island . . .
Witnesses: Robert FitzStephen, Alexander FitzMaurice,
Paganus Mansel, Robert de Barri, Walter de Barri, Stephen
FitzRobert, and Ralph, *filius Codi.*
Note: Inhismacnel is Little Island: Hi(ni)smaclot may be
Harper's Island to the east.

Charter 262   Charter of REGINALD, ARCHDEACON.
Know that I have given and conceded, and by this charter
have confirmed every liberty which Gregory, Bishop of
Cork, gave to the church of St. Thomas at Dublin . . . And
if any person, under the inspiration of the devil, wishes to
take from the above church the liberty which Bishop Gregory
conferred on it, let him be accursed unless he justly restore
to the church all that he had taken away. This (charter) has
been made in the presence of Brother Simon, Brother Philip
and the monk Ade.
Witnesses: William, presbyter; Henry, presbyter; John,
deacon, and many others.

Charter 263   *Continuation of above:* And in order that the
church of Cork should have a share in the benefits which the
ministers of the said church (of St. Thomas) make available
through psalms, hymns and prayers, Gregory, by the grace
of God, Bishop of Cork, with the consent of the entire
Chapter (*tocius capituli ecclesie sue consilio*), granted the
church of St. Nessan as a perpetual alms to the church of the
martyr Thomas at Dublin.

Charters 265, 266   Charters of MARIANUS UA BRIAIN, BISHOP
(1207–1224)

Let all know that we have given and conceded and by this
charter have confirmed . . . all the ecclesiastical revenues of
Duneglas and Cridarin and Balimakin and all other revenues
which have been granted or will be granted from our diocese
to the aforesaid canons (of St. Thomas).

Witnesses : Richard de Carew, Philip de Prendergast, Alex-
ander FitzHugo, Robert FitzRobert, Reginald de Altaribus,
Ralph de Sommeri, David Drihille, Ralph FitzGodebert;
Walter, cleric; John, cleric, and many others.

Note : Duneglas may be identified with Douglas; Cridarin
with Kinnure near Kinsale; Balimakin with either Mahon,
Blackrock, or with Ballymacus, Kinsale.

Charter 270   Grant from GEOFFREY FITZODO . . . of the church
of Clonmel with its lands, all its appurtenances and tithes,
and the revenues of the church(?) of Ynesmor.

Witnesses : Philip de Prendergast and Geoffrey, his son;
Richard de Cogan, Jordan, Bartholomew and Walter de
Gallenatan; Thomas, cleric, and many others.

Note : Clonmel is identified as Old Church, Cobh; Ynesmor
with the Great Island.

Charter 271   Grant from MARGARITA DE COGAN . . . of my
church and the land which lies near the church of Cloedmedli
(Clonmel), together with all the tithes and fruits of half the
island of Inhismor which is my dowry (*matrimonium meum*).

Witnesses : Robert FitzStephen, Alexander FitzMaurice,
Lucas de Londres, Robert de Altaris, Raymond Magunel,
Roger de Oxeneford, Geoffrey de Exonia, Adam, monk of
Exonia, and many others.

Charter 272   Another grant from MARGARITA DE COGAN of
the church of Cloen Medli and the tithes of Inhismor.

Witnesses are the same as in the preceding charter, except
that Adam, monk of Exonia, is here called '*Adam de Sancto
Nicholao, qui scribit ipsum scriptum*'.

V

Early Post-Norman Religious Foundations

The Knights Hospitallers of Saint John of Jerusalem and the Benedictine monks of Saint John the Evangelist were an important feature of the socio-ecclesiastical structure of medieval Cork. Both establishments were located in the southern suburbs, both were extra-diocesan foundations (in the sense that they were cells of other houses not established in Cork), both came in the immediate wake of the Norman conquerors, and neither order weathered the sixteenth-century storm of confiscation and dissolution. The Hospitallers came into the diocese between 1173 and 1182, the Benedictines were established in 1192, and like the religious orders of later centuries these early foundations had their own special contribution to make to diocesan history. Another important foundation of the immediate post-Norman era was the Cistercian Abbey of Tracton which achieved greater prominence than either the Hospitallers or the Benedictines, but which like them was destined to be swallowed up in history after 1541.

THE KNIGHTS HOSPITALLERS

Of all the great medieval military orders the most important, in terms of duration and expansion, was that of the Knights Hospitallers of Saint John of Jerusalem, the long annals of which extend from the chivalrous days of the Crusades down to our times. The order owes its origin to one Peter Gerard whose family and birthplace are unknown but whose title to founder is proved from a bull of Pope Paschal II, dated 1113 and addressed to *Gerardo, institutori ac praeposito Hierosolmitarii Xenodicii*.[1] Profiting by the presence of crusaders in

---

1 K. J. von Hefele, *Histoire des Conciles*, v, 322. A hospital founded in 1023 by Amalfi merchants for the care of the poor and sick Latin pilgrims has been erroneously regarded as the origin of the Hospitallers. This earlier hospital had Saint John of Alexandria as its patron and its members followed the Benedictine Rule, whereas the Hospitallers adhered to the Rule of Saint Augustine.

Jerusalem, Peter Gerard secured the adherence of many who in later years enriched the order by grants of vast estates in many parts of Europe. Knights were first introduced under Gerard's successor, Raymond of Provence (1120–60), who, because of increasing numbers of pilgrims, defrayed at his own expense the cost of an armed escort which in time developed into an organized army recruited from among the bravest of the crusaders. Gradually a military order emerged. Under Alphonso of Portugal, ninth grand master, we find three distinct types of members: military brothers, infirmarians and chaplains to whom divine service was entrusted. The Hospitallers were distinguished by a black mantle emblazoned with a white cross.

Many nobles of western Europe conferred vast grants upon the order. In France, Guy de Forcalquier gave them many castles and lands. In Spain, Don Pedro Dartel, first baron of Aragon, surrendered a city with its dependencies to them. Some of the finest castles in Naples and Sicily were similarly handed over to the Knights, who in consequence of such rapidly increasing wealth found it necessary to organize some form of financial administration for the order. A new office, that of preceptor, to whose care the lands of each manor were entrusted, was created in 1270 under the Grand Master Hugh de Rane. By that date the Hospitallers were a streamlined organization with a hierarchical personnel and an ever increasing proletariat of members.

The Order of Hospitallers was introduced into England early in the reign of Henry I (1100–35). The first priory, which was founded at Clerkenwell in 1100 by Jordan Brisset, retained its status as the English central house down to the days of the first Elizabeth. The original foundation at Clerkenwell was destroyed in 1381 by Wat Tyler's mob, and from the fact that the buildings of the Hospital of Saint John of Jerusalem were burning for seven days after this attack, we may presume that the buildings were fairly extensive.[2] At the suppression the Hospital ranked fourth in the list of England's wealthiest monasteries, with an estimated valuation of £2,385 19s 8d.[3]

The Knights Hospitallers are not met with in Ireland prior to the Anglo-Norman invasion. It is beyond question that they were here in the time of Strongbow from whom they got a site

2   John Capgrave, *Chronicle of England, 1328–88*, p. 289: '. . . et amplius . . . illam domum nobilem hospitalis Sancti Johannis de Clerkenwell imisso igne ardere fecerunt per continuos septem dies.'

3   Thomas Fuller, *A Church History of Britain from the Birth of Jesus Christ until the Year 1648*, p. 329.

for a priory at Kilmainham near Dublin, their first settlement on Irish soil.[4] From kings and nobles the Hospitallers subsequently received grants of land in various parts of Ireland, as far north as Down and as far south as Cork, and while yet in their Irish infancy the Hospitallers occupy in our records a position among bishops and others as witnesses to certain deeds and charters.[5] In the county of Cork their main preceptory was at Mourne on the river Clyda about five miles south of Mallow; in Cork city itself they had the Hospital of Saint John together with territories embracing the Boreenmanna Road, Monarea, Westerfield *alias* Terenure *alias* Ballinure[6] and Carrigeen near the present South Infirmary. Within the diocese of Cork the Knights Hospitallers or Military Monks of the White Cross had claims on the rectories of Inchigeela, Kilbrogan, Macloneigh, Moviddy,[7] portions of the churches of Dundrinan and Athnowen (Ovens) and the church of Kilmurry.

The Hospital of Saint John of Jerusalem was situated a little to the east of the Benedictine Priory and Hospital of Saint John the Evangelist. It stood on that part of the Red Abbey Marsh now known as George's Quay where its actual site was later occupied by the recently-evacuated presbytery of Saint Finbarr's South. By deduction the date of the foundation can be placed between 1172 and 1182. In the former year the priory of Kilmainham was founded; in the latter year Bishop Gregory of Cork died, and it was during his episcopate that Brother Andrew of the Hospital of Jerusalem witnessed a confirmatory grant to the abbey of Saint Thomas in Dublin. It appears that the preceptory of Mourne granted to the hospital one messuage and two crofts on an annual return. In 1212 the foundation was referred to as *Sancti Johannis de Corcag*, with the suggestion that 'it does not seem to have had the standing of a preceptory', but that it was a cell of some other house of the order in Ireland.[8] The house in question was most likely the preceptory of Mourne. By 1241 or 1242 the Templars and the Hospitallers, whose extensive privileges and liberties aroused and provoked jealousies and disputes, were reduced to having 'but one man or one messuage quit of the common customs of the city'.[9]

4 It is more than probable that they came in Strongbow's entourage.

5 *Reg. St. Thomas, Dublin*, p. 210.

6 Brady, *Records*, i, 275.

7 Ibid., pp. 120, 139, 210, 218. These claims all belonged to the preceptory of Mourne.

8 *Registrum de Kilmainham*, ed. C. McNeill, pp. 140–1.

9 *Cal. doc. Ire., 1171–1251*, no. 2552.

The confusion engendered by the existence of two contemporaneous foundations dedicated to Saint John in the locality of Douglas Street may be dissipated as follows: The *church* of Saint John as it appears in the records is usually connected with the Benedictines. Near this church was a *Liber Hospes* or guest house where the Knights of Saint John of Jerusalem were housed and entertained after their travels. This *Liber Hospes* belonged to the Hospitallers who seem to have confined their activities in Cork to catering for travelling brethren and stranded mariners. Tradition connects the Cross of Cameleire with the Knights Hospitallers. The cross, which was erected as an aid to navigation on the south channel of the Lee near the present Parliament Bridge, indicated the tiny inlet or cove where ships could find anchorage and their crews hospitality. Hence the origin of Cove Street.

A rather tenuous tradition which connects the Knights Hospitallers with Christ Church can only be accepted insofar as the Hospitallers may have taken over from the Templars after that order's suppression in 1312. Windele states incorrectly that the Knights Templars were in Christ Church and in Ballintemple in the year 1392: the order had been dissolved by a decree of the Synod of Vienne on 16 October 1311 and by the bull *Vox clamantis* of Clement V on 22 March 1312. The connection of the Hospitallers with Ballintemple may be assumed by the fact that the bulk of their territory was in the Blackrock area. A *Liber Hospes* in Blackrock is consequently a feasible suggestion which is strengthened by monastic remains in the Blackrock–Ballinlough–Boreenmanna Road sector. Springville with its piscina holy water fonts and Citadella are here indicated as sites of a guest house and stronghold (*citadel*) of the Military Knights.

Reference to the churches of Saint John the Baptist and Saint Anne as parcels of the possessions of the Hospital of Saint John has also bred confusion. The grant from which this supposition has arisen deserves to be quoted in full to show that its interpretation need not entail any inclusion of Saint John the Baptist and Saint Anne as parcels of Saint John of Jerusalem: 'Demise to Thomas Lynch . . . church of Saint John the Baptist, and the chapel of Saint Anne near Cork; in the county of Cork, 5 acres [of] arable [land] in the Maseres field; 3 little parks; one acre arable, called Grobnogclothe; several chief rents; and also the reversions, rents, and profits of all the premises of the said late church [?] or chapel belonging [to the] parcel of the possessions of the late monastery of St.

John of Jerusalem.'[10] Not a single other document connects the Hospitallers with possessions on the north side of the city.

We have no details of the internal history of the Hospital of Saint John of Jerusalem but the establishment seems to have achieved semi-parochial status for a time, and before the dissolution the prior and brethren leased their property (except for a garden occupied by William Lombard) for thirty-one years at £3 13s 4d per annum.[11] An inventory of their property in 1541 showed that they then possessed a church which was in decay, several gardens which they had leased, a hostel or frank-house and a manor field. This final item would suggest that at some stage of its history this Cork house of the order of Hospitallers had acquired free status for itself and its tenants.

SAINT JOHN THE EVANGELIST

The priory of Saint John the Evangelist was founded as a cell of Saint Peter's, Bath, about the year 1192 and was endowed by John, lord of Ireland and earl of Morton. It stood on the south side of Douglas Street on the site presently occupied by the South Monastery and the South Presentation Convent, while the burial vault of its priors may still be seen in the disused graveyard of Saint John to the rear of a terrace of houses which has replaced the ancient priory. Sir James Ware in his *De Hibernia et Antiquitatibus Eius disquisitiones* and Broudine in *Propugnaculum Catholicae Veritatis* concur in recording that 'John . . . founded near Cork a monastery for Benedictine monks, *sub titulo* of St. John the Evangelist . . . and made it a cell to the Abbey of Bath in England.'[12] An *Inspeximus* taken in 1358 at the request of Prior John Istod of Bath gave the endowments of the original grant, namely, 'two carucates of land called Culmore and Balliofulin; and all the ground from the land of John, Bishop, which lay at the head of the south(gate) bridge of Cork, extending to the narrow pass or inlet of the road to the east, and two burgages in Dungarvan at the head of the bridge opposite the south [i.e., the North Gate Bridge], one to the east and the other to the west; and the more desirable mill-site beyond the mill belonging to the Earl himself.'[13]

10   *Calendar of Patent Rolls, 1225–32*, pp. 561–2.

11   Fiants of Elizabeth, no. 1385, from the *Eleventh* to the *Sixteenth Reports of the Deputy Keeper of the Public Records in Ireland*, p. 206.

12   Denis O'Sullivan, 'Monastic Establishments of Mediaeval Cork', p. 11.

13   B.M., MS Rawlinson B 479; ex Rot. Pat., anno 12 Edward III in Turri Bermingamiana. See Appendix B (i).

The bishop mentioned in the *Inspeximus* but not in the original grant[14] was John Roche, whose name was probably inserted by the scribe responsible for the document. The placenames of Culmore and Balliofulin are identifiable from a civil action taken in August 1226 which resulted in an agreement between Philip de Prendergast who claimed the lands and the then prior of Saint John's.[15] The disputed carucates of land were the townland of Coolmore in Shanbally (civil parish of Carrigaline) and the townland of Ballyfouloo in Monkstown. Coolmore was apparently retained by de Prendergast since it does not again appear in any document referring to the Cork property of Saint Peter's, Bath, or to that of Saint John's. On the other hand, it is probable that the prior received other townlands near Ballyfouloo as compensation for the loss of Coolmore. By 1330 Saint John's possessions in the vicinity of Ballyfouloo had increased to five acres.

The mill and burgages of the grant were also in dispute in 1226 between Thomas FitzAnthony and the prior. The latter represented that 'whereas he holds a mill and two burgages in Cork, of the gift of King John when Earl of Morton, Thomas FitzAnthony, to whom the same king afterwards committed on lease the county of Cork, disseised him.'[16] The justiciar was ordered to ensure justice for the prior 'unless the mill and burgages are in the king's demesne'. The mill in question was probably Saint John's Mill which stood near the Kiln river and is believed to have been erected in the year 1020. The burgages in Dungarvan lay near Shandon in the northern suburbs. The 'one to the east' which is more frequently referred to as the messuage of Saint John the Baptist is here clearly associated with Saint John the Evangelist: this Johannine enigma is only one of many insoluble problems presented by medieval Cork. The land allotted to the Benedictines outside the south gate, though not precisely defined in the grant, lay somewhere to the east of the Augustinian Red Abbey between Douglas Street and Evergreen Street. An earlier grant to the monks of Exeter covered this same area,[17] and the suggestion that the monks of Exeter may have surrendered their title to the Benedictines is corroborated by the fact that the rectory of Kinsale, which was also granted to the English monks, became subsequently a Benedictine possession.

14   The reigning bishop then was Murchad O hAodha (1192–1206).

15   *Cal. doc. Irè.*, 1171–1251, no. 1436.

16   Ibid., no. 1437, dated 19 August 1226.

17   See Chapter IV, Appendix A.

The Benedictine priories of Saint Catherine's, Waterford, and Saint John's in Cork were endowed as distinct foundations and presumably as cells of Bath, but relations between Waterford and the parent house and with Cork were not always harmonious. At one time Waterford asserted its independence of Bath and maintained a separate existence until 1204 when unity was again restored.[18] Administratively speaking, the greatest confusion prevailed. At times Cork and Waterford were governed by the same prior without reference to Bath; at other times both were described as subject to Bath. References extracted from records and calendars will best illustrate the situation:

1225–26	The prior and monks of the Hospital of Saint John of Waterford and Cork.[19]
1235–36	The prior of Saint John the Evangelist in Ireland.[20]
1284	Brother Richard de Lucy of Warwick, custodian of the Hospital of Saint John the Evangelist of Waterford and Cork.[21]
1290	Brother John de Compton is keeper of the Hospital of Saint John the Evangelist of Waterford and Cork.[22]
1335	Thomas de Foxcote, prior of Waterford and Cork.[23]
1344	Mandate to the precentor of Cork to make provision to John de Axebrugge, monk of Bath, of the priory of Saint John the Evangelist in the diocese of Waterford and Cork, value twenty marks, subject to the church of Bath.[24]
1380	John Horsington is prior of Cork.[25]
1386	Brother Thomas de Wylton, prior of Waterford and Cork.[26]
1455	John Lambert, prior of Waterford and Cork.[27]
1463	John Mac Clanchy, prior.[28]

18 *Cal. doc. Ire., 1171–1251*, no. 1220.

19 Ibid., no. 1343.

20 Ibid., no. 2343.

21 *Cal. doc. Ire., 1252–84*, no. 2302.

22 *Cal. doc. Ire., 1285–92*, no. 728.

23 A. E. Hurse, 'Monkstown and Passage West, County Cork', *Cork Hist. Soc. Jn.*, xxx (1925), 16.

24 *Cal. papal letters, 1342–62*, p. 97.

25 Hurse, 'Monkstown and Passage West', p. 16.

26 Quoted in *Rot. Pat. 10 Richard II*.

27 Hurse, 'Monkstown and Passage West', p. 16.

28 Ibid., pp. 16–17.

1536   Nicholas, professed monk of Bath, prior or keeper of Waterford, is seised of property in Cork.[29]

The specific object of the Benedictines of Saint John the Evangelist is outlined in a document dated 1330 which states that the priory was established for the 'sustenance of four chaplains performing divine service daily at Cork for the souls of the King's ancestors, and of all the faithful deceased yearly, and twelve beds for paupers, and sustenance for two brethren and two [nursing] sisters there, forever'.[30] We find this statement of the works and objects of the order confirmed and in part qualified by an inquisition taken in 1381, the returns of which stated that the premises were given to the prior of Bath 'to relieve there [in Cork] the blind and the lame and to find a monk [not four chaplains] who ought to perform the said alms for the souls of the progenitors and heirs of the King forever'.[31] More than likely the Benedictines, like other orders dedicated to the care of the blind and the infirm, benefited by charitable bequests and endowments even though only one such bequest has been recorded. This was the will of John de Wynchedon who in 1306 bequeathed 'to the infirm of St. John the Evangelist a half-mark and a feather bed with its habiliments'.

The fourteenth-century taxations show that the *spiritualia* of Saint John the Evangelist carried a valuation of forty marks and that its temporalities (*temporalia*) which included the infirmary and the manor of Legan were rated at ten marks. The inquisition of 1381 outlined the material possessions of the Benedictines in greater detail: a messuage and eighty acres of land; twenty acres of pasture; thirty acres of wood and twelve acres of a bog in Legan; a messuage and sixty acres of land in Ballyglannagh, the like in Hammondeston and forty acres in Malbawne.[32] Failure to pursue the objects of the order was punishable by confiscation of property, as happened temporarily in 1330 when Prior John de Compton was charged with neglect. A more serious confiscation is recorded in the late 1370s, but on this occasion the prior 'by John Horsington his attorney pleaded that the offence was not sufficient to justify the seizure and begged an amoveas manus and restitution of the property'.[33] The formal release appears to have been

29   P.R.O.I., Lodge MS.

30   *P.R.I. rep. D.K. 44*, p. 30.

31   Quoted in *Rot. Pat. 5 Richard II.*

32   See Appendix B (ii).

33   B.M., Roche MSS (abstracts).

made when the king 'on the security of Richard Wynchedon
and William Gordon granted to John Horsington, procurator
of the house of SS Peter and Paul of Bath in England, guardian-
ship of the revenues of the churches of Kinsale, St John the
Evangelist in *Le Fairgh* near Cork, and the rectory of the
church of Legan in the said county'.[34] The tenor of the document is indicative of Saint John the Evangelist's dependence
upon and enfeoffment to the priory of Bath.

Legan, which medieval documents place eight miles from
Kinsale, is now identified with Monkstown where the Benedictines are known to have had fishing tithes and a fishing weir.
Monkstown was a Norman foundation and was established
before 1226 by King John, by de Cogan or by de Prendergast.
Traditions of an earlier Irish foundation at Legan are supported
by the researches of Dom Patrick Nolan, O.S.B., and by the
late Canon Patrick Power who considered it 'extremely likely
that there was an earlier monastery there which was made over
to the Benedictines'.[35] A quotation from the *Dublin Penny
Journal* does not help to clarify matters: 'The parish and village
of Monkstown derive their value from a monastery of Benedictine
monks belonging to the Priory of St. John's [*sic*] Waterford,
who laid the first foundation of their small residence in the
fourteenth century upon a grant of land made by the MacCarthys
to their parent establishment. Three or four of these clustered
inhabitants remained on the then wild and lonely hills of the
parish. But from causes now concealed . . . the little Benedictine
settlement was deserted and soon became a ruin.'[36] All that
can be stated with certainty is that the monastery of Legan
stood in what is now locally termed the Coffin Field. The
term Monkstown, though obviously derived from the
Benedictines, was not introduced as a placename until long
after the departure of the monks.

One of the most illuminating accounts of Saint John's (the
property of Dr. Caulfield) was unhappily lost in the destruction
of the Four Courts in 1922. An indifferent copy of this document—undated but probably of late fifteenth-century compilation—may be consulted among the Windele Papers in the
Royal Irish Academy under the heading, 'A Copy of all such
as belongeth to St Katherine and to St John the Evangelist
neere the South Gate of Cork, which church and its appurtenances belongs to Maurice Ronayne of Cork'. Then follows

34 *Rot. Pat. 5 Richard II*, 1381.

35 Cahalane Papers; letter dated 1 February 1923.

36 Hurse, 'Monkstown and Passage West', p. 17.

a description of the 'Hospital of St John . . . the Manor of Legan', from which we learn that the prior of Bath had at Cork a parochial church and chapel of Saint Leonard (probably the infirmary chapel), a hospital or infirmary and a court for his tenants in Saint John's Street, i.e., in the northern suburb of Dungarvan where the Benedictines held two burgages. The prior of Bath also held a church at Kinsale and some small property in Youghal. Robert de Cloprote, formerly prior of Bath, levied six marks on the city of Cork for the upkeep of the infirmary which was also entitled to tithes, great and small, from the produce of the grange at Legan according to the custom of the manor there. At Grange, in addition to the priory, there was a monastic farm with living apartments, ovens, kitchens and cellars for the resident farmer together with outhouses for horses, sheep and cows. Apart from the lands of the tenants, two extra carucates were attached to this farm.

Saint John's Priory in Douglas Street seems to have attained parochial status at an early stage. A fifteenth-century procuration list of the city and suburbs rated it at twenty shillings and quoted the prior of Bath as holding both its rectory and vicarage. By inquisition taken in 1536 the Benedictines still administered the property at Legan but had lost their parochial status in the southern suburbs where the Knights Hospitallers were likewise functioning. The belief is that the Benedictine foundation was somehow absorbed by the Hospitallers who seem also to have succeeded to semi-parochial status in the district. The pre-eminence of the Hospitallers over the Benedictines is borne out by the complete absence of Benedictine signatories to the many medieval deeds and charters in which the history of the Knights Hospitallers is enshrined.

Our final reference to the medieval priory of Saint John the Evangelist comes from Archdall and bears out the theory that the house in Douglas Street had depreciated in status and that the interest of the Benedictines had veered towards their possessions in Monkstown: 'The prior (of St John's) was seized of three carucates of land in Ballinvannegh (*Baile na Manach*, Monkstown), two carucates in Ballaneghe (Ballyglannagh) and the monastery of Legan, with the tithes of the said lands, the site of the monastery and sixteen messuages held from the king, situated and lying in the county of Cork, of the annual value of twenty shillings.'

THE CISTERCIAN ABBEY OF TRACTON

About four miles to the south of Carrigaline on the north bank of a stream close to the tidal estuary of Ringabella Bay, the Cistercian Abbey of Tracton occupied a site in the ancient townland of Tubrid in the barony of Kinalmeaky. To the north and east were hills; to the south and west stretched rich alluvial flats; on the south-east was an elevation called Knocknamanagh, the entire area being geographically suited to Cistercian isolationism and withdrawal. The name of Tracton like that of many other Irish Cistercian abbeys is evidently un-Irish; nor did the community of Tracton ever blend into the local way of life as did other foundations, particularly those belonging to the filiation of Mellifont.[37] In point of fact, the traditions of Tracton were foreign to the general run of Irish Cistercian monasteries, the origins of which could be traced to either Mellifont or Saint Mary's Abbey, Dublin.[38] Thus, while the abbots of Tracton were lords of parliament and papal mandatories, the abbey itself continues to be one of the lesser-known foundations of the Cistercian Order in Ireland. Its official designation was *Albus Tractus*, hence *de Albo Tractu*, derived from its parent house of Alba Landa, now Whitland, Caermarthenshire, Wales. Alba Landa itself was founded by Rhys ap Griffin at the time of the conquest.[39]

The identity of the founder of Tracton has long been a matter of controversy in which historians of repute have been singularly blind to Tracton's Welsh affiliation. Sir James Ware, quoting 1224 as the foundation date, does not attempt any identification of the founder. Hartry, Allemand and Janauschek incline to a MacCarthy patron but are strongly contradicted by Canon O'Mahony who wrote that 'Kinalea was the old original possession of the Cinel Aedha. . . . There is not the shadow of a proof that it ever passed to the MacCarthys. Robert FitzMartin was in possession in 1207, and the Barrys who obtained it from him, were in occupation in 1240. . . . Some one of those families was, therefore, the occupier when Tracton Abbey was built in 1224. . . . The monks were brought from Alba Landa in Wales, the country of the FitzMartins and the Barrys.'[40]

Orpen's theory is that 'early in the thirteenth century, the eastern part of the present county of Cork as well as the present

---

37 B. W. O'Dwyer, 'Gaelic Monasticism and the Irish Cistercians, c. 1228', *Ir. Cath. Hist. Comm. Proc.* (1965–67; published 1968), p. 24.

38 As will appear, Tracton had a rather tenuous connection with Inislounaght and Maigue.

39 Denis O'Sullivan, 'The Cistercian Abbey of Tracton, County Cork', *Cork Hist. Soc. Jn.*, xliv (1939), 2.

40 O'Mahony, *A History of the O'Mahony Septs*, p. 64 n.

county of Limerick seems to have been in the hands of the English landholders, and to have been entirely settled by them. . . . In 1207 however, Philip de Prendergast and Richard de Cogan received extensive grants of lands from the Crown, the former in the district between Cork and Inishannon, where the important manor of Beuver (Beauvoir) or Carrigaline was afterwards formed. . . . From the Inquisition taken on the death of Gerald, son of Philip de Prendergast, in 1251, we can gauge the importance of the manor of Beuver. There were eleven tenants . . . at rents, and there were two market-towns, Carrigaline and Douglas, each with a large district of burgage lands. In 1224 the Abbey de Albo Tractu was founded for Cistercians at a place about two miles south of Carrigaline. The monks came from Ty Gwyn or Alba Landa, now Whitland[41] near Tenby, and the foundation may confidently be connected with the settlers from South Wales.'[42]

Chancellor Webster, writing in 1920, comes to practically the same conclusion when he says that 'the Barrys were in possession . . . in 1240 and appear to have been preceded by Robert FitzMartin. Moreover, the abbey [of Tracton] was founded for monks of the Cistercian order who were brought from Whitland, the Welsh Ty Gwyner Daf, and the Latin Alba Landa, an abbey situated on the western border of Carmarthenshire . . . in the diocese of St. David. It was from the name *Alba Landa* of the Welsh Abbey that the house erected in this diocese got its name, *Abbatia de Albo Tractu*. A MacCarthy would have sought the first members of his new community nearer home.'[43]

The publication of the second volume of *Analecta Sacri Ordinis Cisterciensis* in 1946 and of the second volume of *Statuta Capitulorum Generalium Ordinis Cisterciensis* provides the final solution to the problem. Here we discover that in 1222 Odo de Barry petitioned through the abbots of Inislounaght and Maigue for the establishment of a Cistercian abbey on his lands.[44] In the following year the petition was granted with the stipulation that the foundation should be made from

---

41   *Chartularies of St. Mary's Abbey*, ii, 235: 'Brut y Tywys, 1224'.

42   Orpen, *Normans*, iii, 117–19.

43   Webster, *The Diocese of Cork*, p. 188.

44   Joseph Canivez, *Statuta Capitulorum Generalium Ordinis Cisterciensis*, ii (1221–61), 20, has the following entry under date 1222, no. 34: 'Petitio Odonis de Barris in Hibernia de construenda abbatia, committitur abbatibus de Surio et de Magio qui personaliter accedant ad locum et circumspectis omnibus quae necessaria sunt ad abbatiam construendam, sequenti Capitulo quod invenerint studeant nuntiare.'

the *Abbey de Blancha Landa*.[45] Thus safeguarded from tendencies to gaelicization, the abbey of Tracton was founded in the year 1225.[46]

The first official account of the activities of the Cistercians of Tracton is found in the report of Abbot Stephen of Lexington who in 1228 was sent by the abbot of Clairvaux as visitator-general of Irish Cistercian monasteries which were then reported as being in a state of decadence, financial mismanagement and dilapidation. Abbot Stephen's report recounted instances of alienation of monastic property, robbery, grave breaches of monastic discipline and racial animosity so bitter as to make him legislate against the admission of subjects who could not accuse themselves of their faults in either French or Latin. The Irish language, which to the visitator was a barbarism, a medium for plotting conspiracies and a sign of ignorance, was to be superseded by French, so that on future visitations the abbot of Clairvaux (who was entrusted with the task of reforming the order in Ireland) or his delegate might be able to communicate coherently with the monks.[47] Abbot Stephen's reforms were fiercely resisted, especially in Inislounaght and at Maigue where he was confronted by armed abbots and belligerent monks.[48] Tracton, though it cannot have so quickly succumbed to the abuses rampant in the other Irish houses—its abbot is described as *vir strenuus et religiosus*[49] —was nevertheless subject to visitation. The only fault found with it was on the score of language, not Irish but Welsh, and Abbot Stephen complained the monks of Tracton for defying the authority of the General Chapter in their insistence on the Welsh tongue (*ne aliqua ratione dictum abbatem et conventum aut formam ordinis inibi inchoatam et auctoritate capituli generalis impositam audeant perturbare*).[50] It is not known when Welsh became extinct at Tracton Abbey, but it may be safely hazarded that the native Irish tongue was never popular in the White Tract Vale.

In contrast with other Cork foundations, state references to

45   Ibid., no. 35, p. 29: 'Petitio Domini Odonis de Barri exauditur, de mittendo conventu committitur Claraevallensi et abbati de Blancha Landa.'

46   P. B. Griesser, ed., *Analecta Sacri Ordinis Cisterciensis*, ii, 91: 'Alba Domus—Albalanda in Wallia, diocesi Menevensi, cuius filia erat Albus Tractus in comitatu et diocesi Corcagiensi, fundata 1225.'

47   Otway-Ruthven, *Med. Ire.*, p. 137.

48   O'Dwyer, 'Gaelic Monasticism and the Irish Cistercians', p. 26.

49   Griesser, *Analecta Sacri Ordinis Cisterciensis*, ii, 91.

50   Ibid.

Tracton are plentiful for the medieval period. In 1251 the abbey, through default of its abbot, lost half a carucate of land at Kilmeaton.[51] On 30 July of the following year a gift in frank-almoign of half a carucate of land at Killenekolm was granted to the abbot and convent of *Albo Tractu*, and it was stated in the gift that the king had recovered this land 'in his court before the justices at Dublin against the said abbot and convent by default made by the said abbot in the said court'.[52] On the same occasion a mandate issued to J[ohn] FitzGeoffrey, justiciar of Ireland, ordered him to take security from the abbot of Tracton for the payment of sixty marks to the king at the exchequer of Dublin; half the sum (*mediatam*) was to be paid at Easter in the thirty-seventh year of Henry III and the remainder at Michaelmas.[53] In the taxation rolls of Pope Nicholas IV (1288–91) the abbey of Tracton was taxed at ten marks, but this taxation never became effective. In 1297 the abbot of Tracton recovered from Philip Mac Owen Barry the right of presentation to Clontead. The abbot was indicted and fined £40 in 1301 for receiving and harbouring his nephew Maurice Russell, against whom a charge of rape had been preferred (*qui rapuit quandam mulierem Anglicanam*), and in the same year when the chapels of Grenagh (Granig townland north of Tracton), Kresdynre (? Kinure) and Clonmede were alienated according to statute the abbot of Tracton paid five marks for respite until the octave of the feast of Saint Michael when he presumably redeemed the alienation. In 1311 Audeon or Owen, abbot of Tracton, was sued by Abbot Thomas of Weyme for one acre of turbary and forty acres of pasturage at Kilmoney.[54]

Because of the insecurity of the fourteenth-century English lordship of Ireland, rumours as to the activities of certain religious persons in fomenting hatred against the usurpers led to the passing of strict preventative legislation. All members suspected of Irish sympathies were to be removed from monasteries in affected districts, and in future only select English religious with English companions were to minister to the native Irish. An enactment issued at Kilkenny in 1311 stipulated that neither Irishmen nor enemies of the king should be admitted to profession in any of the English religious houses

---

51   *Cal. doc. Ire., 1171–1251*, no. 3151.

52   O'Sullivan, 'The Cistercian Abbey of Tracton, County Cork', p. 3.

53   Ibid., citing Charter Roll 36 Henry III, m. 7, p. 400.

54   T.C.D., MS F1.16.

established in Ireland.[55] A list of these English foundations was appended to the enactment; it included the monastery *de Albo Tractu*. This enactment of 1311 was revised and amplified in 1367 and has come down in history as part of the Statutes of Kilkenny.

The possessions of Tracton Abbey were confirmed by King Edward III in 1375 who took 'the abbot *de Albo Tractu*, men, lands, possessions and goods of whatever kind into special protection and defence'.[56] From then on the abbot was accorded manorial status and was entitled to sit in parliament as a spiritual peer.[57] Tracton's prestige is seen in the frequency with which papal and royal commissions were entrusted to its abbot; and royal mandates were no less demanding than were those papal mandates involving the abbots of Gill Abbey and Tracton which have been quoted in Chapter 3. In 1375 a mandate from Edward III ordered the abbot of Tracton to attend in person (*in propria persona*) at a parliament in Dublin on the Saturday within the octave of Saint Hilary. He was not to send his proctor in his stead.[58] The abbot was again commanded to be present at parliament in Tristledermot in the first year of the reign of Richard II.[59] Similar mandates were issued in September 1380 and in April 1381. At the parliament of 1381 the abbots of Tracton and Gill Abbey were appointed collectors of a special levy for the king.

An extract from Rental and Surveys Roll 936 in the British Museum suggests that the abbot of Tracton was parish priest of the district controlled by the abbey and that the abbey church was a parish church even from the time of its foundation: 'The church of the said monastery from time immemorial was and is the parish church of Tracton.' This being so, the list of abbots of Tracton is likewise the list of its parish priests. Excluding anonymous entries for the years 1251, 1297, 1301 and 1340, this list reveals several stormy episodes in the history of Tracton Abbey.

1311   Owen.

1347   Roger Codd was deposed.

55   Quoted in Statutes 5 Edward III.

56   *Rotulorum Patentium et Clausorum Cancellariae Hiberniae Calendarium*, no. 215, p. 96.

57   Ibid.: 'Abbas de Tractona locum habuit et suffragium inter regnis proceres comitiis Parliamentariis.'

58   *Rot. pat. Hib.*, p. 109, no. 116.

59   Ibid., p. 104, no. 73.

1347 David Furlong became abbot.

1350 Richard Brayghnock.

1363 Abbot Thomas died.

1363 Richard Graynell was deprived. Richard Fleming was appointed by papal provision, but was not finally installed until 1368 when he was re-appointed.

1450 John Flemyng, John Culthan and Miles Roche were 'pretended abbots'. All three were superseded by John Barry.

1464 Milo Roche, one of the pretenders in 1450, became abbot of Tracton this year and subsequently bishop of Elphin.

1467 Robert O'Callaghan (or Ohuallachayn), a monk of Maure Abbey (*de Fonte Vivo*), was appointed abbot of the monastery *Beatae Mariae de Albo Tractu*.

1482 Raymond Barry.

1499 John Barry.

1501 James Barry.

1542 John Barry.

As well as being rector of the parish of Tracton, the abbot was responsible for the provision of vicarial services to churches which were impropriate to the abbey, namely Ballyfoyle, Ballyfeard, Clontead, Ballymodan, Ballyspillane (Cloyne), Kinure and the parcel of Belgooly. Annate entries for the years 1489 and 1493 show that Raymond Barry bound himself for the rectories of the parish churches of Innishannon and Dunderrow.[60]

Land and its administration featured as largely in the history of Tracton as in that of other Irish Cistercian houses, with the difference, however, that the records of Tracton do not carry references to any evidence of extreme financial disorganization or too close a liaison with or adaptation of local customs. References already quoted show that the abbots of Tracton were constant litigants for land right through the thirteenth century. They were no less active in the fourteenth. In 1340 the abbot sued Philip de Midia (Meade) for having devastated the woods of Leighmoney which Owen, the former abbot, had leased to him. Ten years later, 1350, when the chapel of Clontead, the church of Krendre [*sic*] and the chapel of Granath (Granig) were again alienated by statute of mortmain as in 1311 the abbot paid the king five marks respite until the octave of Saint Hilary when he once again redeemed what had been alienated.

60 Bolster, 'Obligationes pro Annatis Diocesis Corcagiensis', pp. 19, 23.

Domestic affairs at Tracton Abbey in the fourteenth century reflect what was apparently a normal situation among contemporary Cistercian houses where religious discipline was lax and the spirit of Clairvaux a dead letter. In 1350 Richard Brayghnock, prior or abbot of Tracton, was indicted for having murdered one of his monks. Brayghnock's previous history as outlined in his decree of acquittal is revealing. The acquittal was accompanied by pardon 'for all transgressions, felonies and breaches of the king's peace in Ireland committed by him up to the 13th of August in the 24th year of the reign of Edward III', that is, up to 1350.[61] That there were others like Brayghnock in Ireland is to be inferred from the petition filed in 1363 by Nicholas, son of Abraham, Cistercian monk of Chore (*de Choro Benedicti*, Midleton), who sought 'dispensation that he may be promoted to the dignity of abbot, seeing that there is in Ireland a very great lack of fit persons for such dignities'.[62]

From 1350 until 1363 the first of many gaps in the history of Tracton occurs. Richard Graynell who was appointed abbot in 1363[63] was deprived in the same year under somewhat unusual circumstances. David de Cornwalshe, abbot of Dunbrody, was commissioned by the abbot of Alba Landa to visit the abbey *de Albo Tractu* for purposes of investigating and reforming abuses there. On his arrival at Tracton Abbey David found the monks in open rebellion against their abbot, Richard Graynell, who was far from being of the character and integrity of his predecessor in Stephen Lexington's time. Graynell entreated the visitator to advise and correct the monks and, the better to purchase his support, he presented him with the sum of ten pounds and a horse valued at twenty marks. But the irate community would not be denied, and drawing from some surreptitious source (*peculium*) they gilded their complaints with a sum of twenty pounds. The visitator, having decided in their favour, departed from Tracton astride the horse he had received from the now-deposed Richard Graynell.[64] Two years later (1365) and not surprisingly, the abbot of Dunbrody was convicted on a charge of bribery arising from the visitation of Tracton, but he was pardoned by royal mandate on payment of a fine of one mark.

61   T.C.D., MS F1.16, p. 326.

62   *Calendar of Entries in the Papal Registers Relating to Great Britain and Ireland: Petitions to the Pope, 1342–1419*, p. 469.

63   Theiner, *Vetera Mon.*, p. 326, no. 633: 'Richardus Monasterio de Albo Tractu in abbatiam praeficitur.'

64   T.C.D., MS F1.16, p. 326.

Despite gaelicization in other communities in the fourteenth century Tracton appears to have continued staunchly loyal to its English connection, for which the confirmation of its privileges by Edward III in 1375 may have been the expression of royal gratitude as well as of royal protection. Such favours notwithstanding, the abbot of Tracton was fined £10 in 1377 for non-attendance at parliament. Pleading ill health as his excuse and protesting that he had delegated William Ilgar, his lawyer, to represent him, the abbot asked for and was accorded a respite of fifteen days to enable him to file legal suit for pardon either before the Privy Council or at the next sitting of parliament.

From 1377 to 1389 another hiatus occurs in the history of Tracton; by the latter year, however, the abbey reappears in the records in full enjoyment of royal patronage. In this year Richard II by special mandate ordered his bailiffs and other officials to protect the community and particularly the abbot of Tracton whom he wished to have under his special favour (*quem favore prosequi vult*).[65] After 1389 the annals are again silent and from then on the papal registers are the only sources of reference to the abbey of Tracton. Most of the references for the period 1418–83 are pointers to the prestige attaching to the abbacy of Tracton in the fifteenth century, though it is clear that by 1450 a grievous deviation from Cistercian and monastic ideals had set in among the community. The monks were simoniacs and excommunicates who celebrated Mass and the divine office in defiance of the power of the keys. Abbot Miles Roche had dilapidated the goods of the abbacy, had committed simony and was a notorious fornicator. The dean of Cork was ordered to investigate the matter, to depose Roche, and to install John Barry, a monk of Whitland in Wales, 'who though illegitimate, by his own temerity and without canonical title and by force and power of his friends and kinsmen intruded himself into the rule and administration of the Cistercian monastery of Midleton (*de Choro Benedicti*) in the diocese of Cloyne and detained it for seven years'. John Barry was by the same papal mandate confirmed as abbot of Tracton and was permitted to retain any other dignities of his order and to exchange them as often as he pleased.[66] An entry dated 1463 throws light on the manner in which Belgooly became attached to the abbey of Tracton. The archdeacon and

65   *Rot. pat. Hib.*, p. 96, no. 125.
66   *Cal. papal letters, 1447–55*, p. 510.

treasurer of Cork were mandated by Pope Pius II to bestow upon investigation the benefice (without cure) of Belgooly on Miles Roche, who had again become abbot of Tracton. Roche had represented that although the monastery of Tracton was richly endowed at its foundation 'and used to abound in fruits' its assets were now reduced to sixty marks sterling which he declared to be insufficient to 'keep up his estate and that of the convent, repair its buildings and bear its other burdens, on account of the abundant hospitality which is given to princes, dukes, barons, knights and other noble guests and also to the poor without distinction of persons'.[67] Belgooly, which was described as a parcel (*particula*), was a perpetual benefice and was in lay patronage. Andrew Low and William Hodyne, who were behaving as parcellers (*pro particulariis*), had usurped and divided its fruits and held possession without canonical title or tittle of right. The pope ordered the mandatories to unite and to appropriate the benefice of Belgooly to the monastery of Tracton in perpetuity and decreed that all future abbots might convert its fruits to the use of the monastery without the necessity of renewing any licence to do so. References citing the abbots *de Antro* and *de Albo Tractu* as joint mandatories are of constant occurrence in the papal registers; the final citation of the abbot of Tracton in this capacity is connected with the canonical erection of Kilmichael to parochial status in 1493.

A papal mandate of 1481 styles the abbot of Tracton as abbot *de Arbo Tractu*, and in 1483 he is erroneously called abbot of Holy Cross *de Albo Tractu* in a mandate addressed to him and to the abbot of Chore Abbey, Midleton. Tracton's titular was the Blessed Virgin. Sir Richard Cox gives an unsatisfactory explanation of the anomaly in his *Regnum Corcagiense*. Tracton Abbey, he states, was 'made anno 1224 and confirmed by King Edward III, wherein they pretend to have a piece of the Crosse (which Barry Oge at a great price obtaind and gave to the Abby); and this is so firmly believed that on every Holy Thursday vast multitudes from far and near resort to pay their devotion to this relick.'[68] Cox's liturgical perceptiveness was nothing if not unchronological.

As might be expected, the loyalties of Tracton Abbey remained staunchly English right up to the dissolution. It could hardly have been otherwise considering that its abbots

67 *Cal. papal letters, 1458–71*, p. 180.

68 Richard Cox, '*Regnum Corcagiense or a Description of the Kingdom of Cork*', ed. R. Day, *Cork Hist. Soc. Jn.*, viii (1902), 163.

were lords of parliament and that the admission of Irishmen into its community was discouraged. With the single exception of Robert Ohuallachayn who became abbot in 1467, all other abbots were either English or of English extraction, and from 1483 onwards the abbacy became the exclusive preserve of the Barrys, descendants of Odo de Barry who was instrumental in bringing the Cistercians from Alba Landa to Cork in 1225. One of the few known seals of the medieval diocese of Cork was that used by John Barry, last abbot of Tracton. The impression of this seal, *Sigillum Johannis Monasterii de Albo Tractu, 15 Octobris 1542*, was seen by Dr. Caulfield on a grant of the rectory of Innishannon. The device showed a (dexter) sleeved hand holding a pastoral staff which a kneeling cleric receives. Except for the kneeling figure, the seal of Tracton's abbot was identical with that of Saint Bernard of Clairvaux.

The enormous wealth of Tracton Abbey may be gauged from the final inventory of its possessions which was drawn up on the eve of its dissolution and which shows Tracton to have held an acreage far in excess of anything owned by any other religious order in medieval Cork. The possessions as listed included the abbey and precinct with its immediate demesne lands which amounted to three gardens containing 2 acres; other demesne lands containing 100 acres of arable land and 60 acres of pasture; 720 acres in the townlands or hamlets of Tracton, Derva and 'other places' (probably Kinure, Clontead and Belgooly); 300 acres in Ballinamanaghe; 400 acres in Balliespellan and the rectories of Tracton, Ballyenhill, Ballyfeard, Clontead, Ballymodan, Kylmory[69] and Ballyfewan (probably Ballyfoyle), with all chapels, tithes, etc., pertaining thereto.[70] The process whereby the abbot and community of Tracton were thrown into irredeemable anonymity after the fashion of the Hospitallers and the Benedictines belongs to a later stage of the evolution of the history of the diocese of Cork.

69 If Kilmurry, this is patently incorrect; Kilmurry was impropriate to *de Antro*.

70 *Extents of Irish Monastic Possessions, 1540–41, from Manuscripts in the Public Record Office, London*, ed. N. B. White, pp. 143–4.

APPENDIX A

Saint John of Jerusalem
(Lands and possessions as listed in 1541)

1 church, roofed with tiles, ruined and in decay.

5 acres called the Manor Field, occupied by Richard Newgent, Clement and Michael Tyrre.

3 small parks of 1 acre, occupied by Richard Newgent &c.

1 acre called Gortnoglogh, occupied by Richard Newgent &c.

7 gardens.

3 gardens and 4 acres [twice]; occupied by Walter Galwey and William Tyrre.

6 acres called Necarrykgynne, occupied by Walter Galwey, Richard and James Roche.

2 acres, occupied by Patrick Roche as free tenant.

1 messuage in Cork called a Frankhouse.

APPENDIX B

Saint John the Evangelist

(i) Inspeximus, 1358.

Inspeximus etiam quandam aliam chartam ejusdem Johannis in haec verba. Johannes, dominus Hiberniae, comes Moreton, Archiepiscopis, Episcopis . . . . salutem. Sciatis me dedisse et concessisse et hac presenti charta confirmasse Deo et domui eleemosynae meae Beati Johannis de Corcagia et fratribus in ea servientibus: Culmo..e, Balliofulin et omnem terram a terra Johannis Episcopi quae est ad caput pontis Corcagiae del Sud usque ad forcias viae orientis, et duo Burgagia apud Dungarvan ad caput pontis contra miu [sic] ad orientem, et aliud ad occidentem, et unum locum molendini meliorem post molendinum meum, in puram et perpetuam eleemosynam, pro anima patris mei et pro animabus fratrum meorum. Quare volo et firmiter precipio quatenus fratres domus Beatae Johannis de Corcagia et eorum successores habeant et teneant predictas terras, bene et in pace libere et quiete, honorifice et integre plenarie et rationabiliter in bosco et plano, in viis et in semitis, in pratis et in pascuis . . . . cum omnibus libertatibus et liberis consuetudinibus iisdem terris pertinentibus. Testibus Willelmo de Wendewall, Reginaldo de Damartin . . . . . Nos autem tenores chartarum illarum ad requisitionem dilecti nobis in Christo fratris Johannis Istod nunc Prioris Bathon tenore presentium duximus exemplificandos. In cujus Rei &c. Almarico de Sancto Amando, Justiciario &c., apud Cork, Decimo die Aprilis. (MS Rawlinson B. 479, ex Rot. Pat. 32 Edward III, *in turri Berminghamiana*).

(ii)   *Extent of possessions, 1381*

'Prior of Bathe, Co. Cork.' [In margin.] 'The King, being willing to be certified of the manner and cause of taking into his hands a messuage of 80 acres of land, 20 acres of pasture, 30 acres of wood and 12 acres of bog in Legan, a messuage and 60 acres of land in Baltgolgh, the like in Hamondeston and 40 acres in Malbane, which was the estate of the priory of Bathe in England, directed John FitzRery, Escheator, to certify same into Chancery; who returned that it was found by Inquisition that John, late King of England, enfeoffed the prior of Bathe of the said premises, with the church of St John the Baptist [*sic*] near Corke, to relieve there the blind and the lame and to find there a monk who ought to be presented by the said prior to the Chancellor of Ireland, who ought to perform the said alms and service for the souls of the progenitors and heirs of the said King forever; to hold the said church and premises by the said services.' (Abstract, Roche Papers, British Museum).

VI

The Feudal Bishop of Cork

Whether it is considered as an ecclesiastical or a civic unit early medieval Cork was not the city-within-the-walls into which it developed in the later Norman period. Its history was mainly the history of the southern sector where the cradle of the city was situated and which developed from a thriving monastic centre into a relatively flourishing commercial centre with a special Ostman cantred. The Anglo-Normans who came in 1169 came from a country where the communal movement was already well organized, consequently it is not surprising to find them introducing this communal element into the civic structure of Irish life. Before the Norman period Cork under MacCarthy had a mayor named Gilbert, but the citizens lacked the privileges and monopolies commonly associated with the Normans, and even though Cork received its first grant of autonomy in 1199 from John, lord of Ireland,[1] the city was not to have a mayor of its own until the reign of Edward II (1307–27). John's charter, which conferred on Cork 'the liberties of the men of Bristol', contains no allusion to the Ostmen who had by this time lost their earlier status; and while these Ostmen continue to appear in the official registers as the 'Burgesses of Schendone', evidences of a separate Ostman community in Cork begin to decrease in the thirteenth century and disappear altogether in the fourteenth. Their non-recognition and non-acceptance by the citizens of Cork is shown in a petition addressed by the Ostmen in 1290 in which they complain that 'owing to the citizens of Cork who hold the vill to farm, . . . [the

---

1 William Lynch, *A View of the Legal Institutions, Honorary Hereditary Offices and Feudal Baronies Established in Ireland during the Reign of Henry II*, p. 168: 'John deemed it prudent to grant the inhabitants of cities and other fortified places charters of privileges which, elevating them above the level of the great body of tenants and vassals, might secure their attachment to the government.'

Burgesses of Schendone] dare not trade as they were wont to, . . . as they are much impoverished thereby.'[2]

By the liberties of Bristol as granted by King John to Cork in 1199 (they were granted to Dublin in 1192, to Limerick in 1199 and to Waterford in 1215)[3] the citizens were given the privilege of self-government by being permitted to elect their own council and administrative officers and by the establishment of their own judiciary within certain specified limits.[4] The commercial privileges contained in the charter guaranteed exemption from certain tolls and placed restrictions on the trading activities of outsiders within the area of corporate jurisdiction. But John's charter was vaguely worded and Cork had to wait until the reign of Henry III (1216–72) for a specific definition of her liberties. Charter 16 Henry III in 1241 granted major concessions to the city of Cork. By its terms (1) the fee farm of the city was fixed at eighty marks. This fee farm was a stipulated rent exacted in return for favours conferred, the levying of which provoked considerable opposition in times of stress and war. Statistics show that in 1241 Cork ranked third in importance among Irish cities: the fee farm for Dublin was 200 marks,[5] for Waterford 100 marks and for Limerick 60 marks.[6] (2) The citizens were given the prisage of wines, and even though only briefly mentioned in the charter this prisage constituted in later years a substantial contribution to the revenue. Duties on wine were levied on all merchants, native as well as foreign, and were originally levied in kind and in proportion to ships' lading. When the prisage became a money payment and when attempts were made to gather it as crown revenue, clashes between collectors and bailiffs were of frequent occurrence in Cork. (3) Citizens were 'to be quit of toll, lastage, passage and pontage' and all other customs within the king's realm. *Lastage* was a transport permit exacted at fairs and markets; *passage* was either a fine or scutage exacted from a feudal tenant to defray costs of his lord's overseas travel, or it could be interpreted as the price of permission to travel over river or sea; *pontage* was a toll levied for the maintenance and repair of bridges. (4) Heavy restrictions on foreign traders

2   *Cal. doc. Ire., 1285–92*, no. 622.

3   Otway-Ruthven, *Med. Ire.*, p. 123, n. 69. For discussion as to the date of Waterford's charter see Orpen, *Normans*, ii, 314.

4   J. J. Webb, *Municipal Government in Ireland*, pp. 2–5.

5   *Historic and Municipal Documents of Ireland, 1172–1320*, ed. John T. Gilbert, p. 63.

6   William O'Sullivan, *The Economic History of Cork City, from the Earliest Times to the Act of Union*, p. 22.

guaranteed for merchant princes of Cork the monopoly of trade within the borough. (5) The burgesses were freed from villein status and external courts, and they were given a hundred-court, a merchant guild and a council of twenty-four. The guild had its headquarters in the Guildhall where the sheriff and the officials of the hundred-court were also quartered. The powers of the court, though extensive, were effectively shackled by the reservation of certain places to the justiciary whose peripatetic court netted a constant and sizeable revenue for the king.[7] (6) The privilege of self-government was re-affirmed, concessions of social value were accorded, assizes of bread and beer ensured a proper standard in these commodities, and residence within the city limits was the principle upon which all privileges were granted. The privilege did not pre-clude the burgesses from acquiring lands and tenements outside the city.

As yet, no power was granted for the election of a chief officer; he was still chosen by the king and his duty was to ensure that the rent or fee-farm of the city was paid regularly to the exchequer in Dublin. At times the justiciary was mandated to see after the payment, and in 1223 we find the archbishop of Dublin appointed as collector: 'The K[ing] commits the custody of the counties of Waterford and Desmond and of the city of Cork to Henry Archbishop of Dublin, Justiciary, and commands the K.'s bailiffs and subjects, as well English as Irish, to be intentive and respondent to the Archbishop as the K.'s bailiff.'[8] Later, the duty of collecting the fee-farm of the city devolved entirely upon bailiffs. The bailiffs, two in number, also collected fines and other items of casual revenue from which they paid any sums owed by the king. The duties of the sheriff, as distinct from those of the bailiff, were directed mainly towards the administration of justice, in pursuance of which he worked in collaboration with the justiciar.

Taking the charter as a whole we find that the revenue of Cork city came from rents, from the proceeds of the courts, from the prisages of wine and from the assize of beer and bread. The city's outlay involved the payment of the fee-farm and all expenses entailed in the maintenance of the city and its defence against the attacks of its hostile Irish neighbours. It would appear that the Irish *qua* Irish were excluded from benefits conferred upon the citizens and that consequently the privileges of the latter could only be enjoyed subject to frequent

7   *Cal. justic. rolls Ire., 1305–07*, pp. 360, 362.

8   *Cal. doc. Ire., 1171–1251*, no. 1060.

and violent attacks. In time it became necessary to enclose the city.

The expansion of Norman power within and around the city and the establishment of the feudal form of government and land tenure was bound to affect the status of the bishop of Cork as well as that of local secular landlords. The diocese, of its very nature, was intimately connected with lordship and with land, and when an ecclesiastic was raised to the episcopate he became *ipso facto* a landowner on a considerable scale. As such, he was bound to accept the responsibilities which the ownership of land entailed. He was also prone to involvement in disputes over land which were inevitable considering the litigious tendencies of the medieval mind and the territorial structure of medieval society, built as it was on the feudal system with its concept of land as the only wealth that mattered. From the late twelfth century onwards the city and the eastern portion of the diocese of Cork were (as we have already stated) in the power of the Anglo-Norman settlers and subject to feudal tenures. Within this area the bishop of Cork possessed certain lands and properties and, the better to secure these estates under the new regime, it was inevitable that he should seek the status of a feudal lord and hold his property under feudal tenure. The change in the temporal position of the bishop, which seems to have taken place in the early years of the Anglo-Norman settlement, may have been effected in circumstances similar to those obtaining in Dublin, where John Comyn, who became archbishop in 1181, 'had the Archiepiscopal estates granted to him in *barony* with power of holding courts, etc., by which means he and his successors, holding their possessions by that tenure, became bound to attend the *Curia Regis* and were invested with the dignity of Parliamentary Barons'.[9] The origins of other spiritual peers of parliament—bishops, abbots and priors, might be similarly traced.

Faced with the alternative of becoming a feudal lord under the king or of being the vassal of a Norman adventurer, the bishop's choice was clear. As a feudal lord he could secure the ecclesiastical property of the see, for had this property not been legally secured, the bishop's spiritual position as such might not have prevented encroachment on his possessions by the city of Cork. In view of the fact that in 1220 the archbishop of Dublin found it necessary to secure from King Henry III a charter of protection against the city of Dublin,[10] the adoption

9   Lynch, *Legal instit. Ire.*, p. 167.
10   *Cal. doc. Ire., 1171–1251*, no. 935.

of feudal status by the bishop of Cork is self-explanatory. Unless the bishop became a feudal lord, his vassal status under a Norman seigneur would enable the latter to present his own candidate for the bishopric in time of vacancy. On the other hand, manorial status had its own inherent dangers, for since the king or his representative held the temporalities of the see during a vacancy, there was always the possibility of an abuse of privilege here, coupled with the dangers of a church-state conflict. Born of this situation was the custom by which the dean and chapter informed the king of the vacancy and solicited the *congé d'élire* or licence to elect. Quite apart from this royal control, feudal lords exercised considerable patronage within their own territories by their right of advowson, that is, they presented a candidate for a benefice, which presentation was normally followed by induction by the bishop or his official (*officialis*). Thus Sarsfield presented to Templeusque, Barry Oge to Innishannon, Meade to Liscleary, Roche to Templetrine and so on.[11] The practice led to many abuses in the medieval period, an echo of which was heard in comparatively modern times when the Coppingers tried unsuccessfully to vindicate their patronage of Saint Mary's, Shandon.

By virtue of his position as landowner, the early feudal lord was civil governor of those living within his demesne lands. As yet there was no central government such as evolved in later centuries; consequently the feudal lord was charged not merely with defending his territory but with the maintenance of law and order by holding courts within the area under his jurisdiction. The feudal unit of administration was the manor: in Cork there were manors at Shandon, Sarsfield's Court, Douglas, Carrigaline, Ringrone, Rincurran, Kinsale, Kilcrea and so on. The territory of a feudal lord was usually subdivided into a number of manors, with the lands about each castle forming a separate unit. Because these areas of jurisdiction were of moderate porportions, each manor was administered from the castle or central residence which in feudal terminology was called the *caput*. Ecclesiastical manors (a diocese without a manor was unthinkable) were organized on a system similar to that of the ordinary secular manors. The only difference was that the lands comprising the bishop's manor were widely scattered whereas secular manorial lands were contiguous. For all that, the bishop of Cork as feudal lord was in the same position as that of a lay lord in all matters relative to manorial status and

---

11 Such a church is described as follows in the annates: 'quae de jure patronatus laicorum existit.'

administration. Vassals of the bishop are therefore referred to in terms similar to those applied to the vassals of the lay magnates.

The fourteenth-century *Pipe Roll of Cloyne* which portrays details of the organization of the estates of the bishop of Cloyne offers the best example of the arrangements of the temporalities of an Irish diocese under feudal tenure. From the early thirteenth century the entire area covered by the diocese of Cloyne was in Anglo-Norman hands. For *ecclesiastical* purposes the diocese was divided into five deaneries, corresponding to and named after the five ancient tribal territories of which the diocese was constituted. Following this pattern, the bishop's lands in each deanery were erected into separate manors, each administered from and named after the castle or chief residence attached to the principal church of each deanery. In this way the bishop's lands in the deanery of Imokilly which lay between Midleton and Youghal constituted the manor of Cloyne, with the bishop's residence which stood near the cathedral of Cloyne as *caput* or administrative centre. The estates in the adjoining deanery of Olethan extending from Carrigtwohill to Castlelyons became the manor of Coul, the administrative centre of which was the church of Coul near Castlelyons. Similarly with the other deaneries.

A somewhat different arrangement obtained in Cork. The only part of the diocese governed by the Anglo-Normans lay to the east, and within this area the deaneries which were contiguous to the city—Kerrycurrihy, Kinalea *ultra*, Kinalea *citra* and Ocurblethan—were comparatively small in size and were within fifteen to twenty miles of the city and of the bishop's residence. These lands were accordingly erected into a single manor, the manor of Fayd, so named from the townland on the south side of the city on which stood the cathedral of Saint Finbarr and the episcopal residence. The bishop's court and residence at Cork, at least from the early fourteenth century, stood to the west of the cathedral on the site now occupied by the Protestant bishop's palace. Its position is indicated in the text of a grant made in 1328 by Bishop Walter le Rede to the vicars choral of the cathedral church by which he conveyed to them a plot of ground 204 feet in length by 200 feet in breadth, bound 'by the said [cathedral] church on the east and the bishop's court on the west'.[12] The word Fayd—also rendered as Faythe, Faigh, Fairgh, Fath, Fayhe and Fathie—is a derivation of the Irish *faithche* or green, the *Faithchi Chorccaige* as

<hr>

12 Smith, *History of Cork*, i, 40. It seems probable that some remains of the earlier bishop's court existed when William Lyon became Protestant bishop of Cork in 1583.

mentioned in the *Vision of Mac Conglinne*.[13] The original *faithche* referred to by MacConglinne is understood to have embraced the precincts of Saint Finbarr's Monastery, Crosse's Green, Greenmount and Ballyphehane. Such a *faithche* was the centre of civic life, of assemblies, court proceedings, fairs, markets, religious processions and executions. Each town's *faithche* enjoyed specific rights and amenities. Visitors were free to go upon it and could not be sued for trespass, 'for every *faithche* is free to all comers'.[14] Animals, and more especially sheep, were kept grazing on the *faithche* 'which was not to remain profitless', and in the last analysis the green was a popular venue for athletic pursuits and for every type of game.

Though frequently mentioned in the state papers the actual boundaries of the green of Cork are nowhere defined. Part of it, lay within the bishop's manor of Fayd, and for it the bishop received a yearly rent of six marks. The *faithche* extended also to Kilreendowney (Killeenreenowney) where there were 'some small fields and a small street which . . . [were] not in the Manor of St. Barry's [the manor of Fayd] but in the city.'[15] A map of Cork published in 1774 shows Gallows Green to the north-east of the Lough and on the high ground above it and having a 'pound' at its north-eastern corner. More than likely this was the last vestige of the ancient green of Cork where MacConglinne, having cut his passion tree, was to die. Assuming therefore that the locality mentioned in the *Vision* is correct, it is possible that the *Imaire an Aingil* or 'the Angel's ridge on the green of Cork which is never a morning without dew' may be identified with the ridge overlooking the Lough on which stand the schools of the Presentation Brothers at Greenmount. After the Norman conquest, when the amenities of the *faithche* which for so long had been at the disposal of the citizens became crown property, a yearly rent for its use was levied. Because of this, many references to the green of Cork are to be found in the medieval records of Cork and in the pipe rolls of the Irish exchequer. The discharge of the rent for the *faithche* was one of the heaviest impositions laid upon the citizens of medieval Cork, and one from which they constantly sought exemption.

---

13   *Cogadh Gaedhel re Gallaibh : The War of the Gaedhil with the Gaill*, ed. J. H. Todd, p. 151, relates that Brian Boru and his army came to the green of Dublin, *co fachi Atha Cliath*, and that the troops encamped there again after the battle (p. 211). The *Annals of of Ulster* record a hosting by Muirchertach Ua Briain to the *faithche* of Luimneach in 1157.

14   John T. Collins, 'Where Was the Green of Cork?', *Cork Examiner*, 6 January 1934.

15   Brady, *Records*, i, 265.

But to return to the bishop's manor and townland or vill of Fayd.

As a townland, and townlands were extensive in those days, the Fayd would have included lands about the cathedral and the bishop's residence and would have extended westwards towards Bishopstown, Inchigaggin and Farranmacteige which were part of the property of the bishop as later records indicate.[16] We get the boundaries of the vill to the east and the south from a report of a law case heard in Dublin in 1337. The report tells that the bishop of Cork (John de Ballyconingham) and his chaplain, Adam Mansell, seized a cow belonging to Adam Coppinger at 'Corragh in a place called Maghy lying between Kilmahallock and Duffglass (Douglas) and carried her to the bishop's manor of Faiagh'. Adam Coppinger held one messuage and one carucate of land of the bishop at Corragh, subject to twenty shillings per annum and to suit of court at the bishop's manor of Fayd. Delayed judgement in this case was not given until 1340 when it was stated that the land called Maghy was part of the lands called Corragh, it lay between Kilmahallock and Duffglass, and was within the bishop's manor of Faiagh which he held in right of his church of Saint Finbarr.[17] Corragh is very probably the present townland of Ballincurrig to the north-west of Douglas. Kilmahallock lay between Douglas and Crosshaven. Maghy may be identical with Maghan or Mahon, the townland upon which Blackrock is situated. It is significant that Curraghconway which lies south of Douglas paid rent to the Protestant bishop in 1584. Putting our fragmentary documentation together we now discover that the feudal vill or townland of Fayd extended from Bishopstown to Douglas and Blackrock. The manor as distinct from the townland of Fayd, included the bishop's estates in that part of the diocese which was under Anglo-Norman domination and which embraced places as far distant as Kinsale, Kilbrogan (Bandon) and Moally or Aglish. Outside of this area, in the western extremities of the diocese which remained under Irish tribal rule, the vast estates of the bishop would seem to have been held and administered according to Irish tenure.

A thirteenth-century revenue account known as the Sanford Account[18] is our first available documentary evidence concerning the feudal position of the bishop of Cork. The account

16   To be quoted subsequently.

17   Webster, *The Diocese of Cork*, p. 405, quoting a record in the court of common pleas held at Dublin before Simon FitzRichard and his companions, 2 Edward III.

18   B.M., Add. MS Ascough 4784, f. 77v.

of the returns of the see during a vacancy lasting from December 1276 to June 1277 was submitted by John de Sanford, king's escheator, to whom the revenues of the see were customarily directed. In it the escheator acknowledged the receipt of £32 13s 10d for the interim period from the death of Bishop Reginald to the appointment of Robert Mac Donnchada. The money received came from the returns of 180 acres in the manor of Fayd with its meadows and pastures; from rent received from its farmers, its free tenants and its burgesses; from the profits of the mill, fisheries and warrens and from the perquisites of the court and the hundred. Also included were the rents of the lord bishop's thirty-six acres at Kilbrogan, the rents of the *betagii* of the same place, the profits of the fishery and the perquisites of the court. The distinctly feudal terminology of the document cancels any doubt respecting the feudal status of the bishop of Cork.

Lands which lay about the bishop's residence and which were retained in the bishop's own hands were customarily rented to and tilled by the farmers. Such lettings were usually short-time arrangements. The greater part of the bishop's possessions throughout the manor was in the hands of freeholders, gentlemen proprietors like the Cogans, Rochfords, Goulds, Frenches, Wynchedons and de Courceys. These freeholders had a hereditary right in their estates and were closely associated with the bishop in the administration of the manor. For lands thus held they paid a head-rent and were bound to suit of court, homage and fealty. Finally, burgesses were those gentlemen and merchants who held lands and houses within the borough or townland which lay about the bishop's residence. Burgage tenure under which they held would seem to have been equivalent to that of the freeholders, in that the burgesses would be liable for rent but would be free of services for which lesser tenants would be answerable. Circumstances altered the status of burgesses in towns or cities which did not enjoy charters of liberty; for this reason we find references to chartered and unchartered burgesses. Generally speaking, burgesses had a definite status of freedom in chartered cities, but the incongruity of burgage tenure is shown in the decidedly archaic social structure of the episcopal lands of Cloyne where certain burgesses of Kilmaclenine who were described as *betagii* were so circumscribed in their movements that they might not remove from the villa except for pasturing on the lord bishop's demesne lands.[19]

19 Richard Caulfield, *Rotulus Pipae Clonensis ex Originali in Registro Ecclesiae Cathedralis Clonensis* (The Pipe Roll of Cloyne), pp. 15, 18, 20–1.

In Kilbrogan where the bishop apparently held an estate
as an adjunct of the manor of Fayd, we find this class of unfree
tenants, *betagii, biadtachs* (betaghs), or food-rent payers who
have been described as 'laymen using glebe lands'.[20] They
were sometimes described as natives (*nativi*), even *hibernici*
or serfs because they were tied to the soil and were obliged to
works and services unworthy of freemen. The *Pipe Roll of
Cloyne* affords many examples of such services: working on
the lord's demesne at certain seasons of the year, carting his
produce to market, delivering his letters, providing fish at low
cost for his table and so forth. They might not leave the manor
and could be recovered in the sheriff's tourn or court if they
fled.[21] Still, when one considers that their property consisted
mainly of cattle, escape must have posed no great problem for
those living near the marches.[22] In many ways the Irish betagh
was the counterpart of the English villein, and in some instances
he was in theory completely at the disposal of his lord, as for
instance were 'the men of Saint Colman', betaghs of the
bishop of Cloyne. And while it is probable that most Irish
dioceses had betagh populations of similar status with the men
of Saint Colman, it is only for the diocese of Cloyne that we
have a detailed rental. But for all that, John de Sanford's
escheatry account for Cork makes it clear that betaghs were a
definite feature of the social structure of the medieval see lands
of Cork.

The betaghs, who were common in most manors in the
centuries following the Anglo-Norman invasion, were remnants
of the native Irish tribesmen who before the invasion had owned
and ruled the lands which went to constitute the Anglo-Norman
manor, a small portion of which they were permitted to retain.
An inquisition taken in 1288 concerning the manor of Inchiquin,
that is, of the district covering Youghal, Killeagh and Ballymacoda, showed that of a total of about 140 ploughlands, only
$20\frac{1}{2}$ ploughlands were set aside for the betaghs, forty-four in
number, who bore the ancient names of O'Cunnyl, O'Kenach,
O'Mulondony, O'Glassiny and so on. Because this was an
area without township or burgesses, the terms upon which the
betaghs were accepted are not known. Their status may have
been parallel to that of the betaghs of the manor of Douglas
who held one and a half carucates of land at a specified rent

20   *Cal. doc. Ire., 1171–1251*, glossary.

21   Ibid., p. 120.

22   *Cal. justic. rolls Ire., 1305–07*, p. 379.

but for whom other services were commuted.[23] When betagh services were thus commuted for a money rent we may say that the emancipation of betaghs or villeins was in sight.

The Kilbrogan estates of the bishop of Cork which were tenanted by betaghs lay in the O'Mahony territory of Kinalmeaky. With the exception of its south-eastern sector near Innishannon, this district was never firmly under Anglo-Norman control. Still, the revenue account under consideration mentions that John de Sanford collected 23s 6d from the *betagii* of Kilbrogan, and the plea rolls of 1301 give a list of townlands in Kinalmeaky which were subjected to fines in that year. It is likely, therefore, that some traces of Anglo-Norman tenure and custom penetrated into the sub-manor of Kilbrogan. Mention of betaghs in ecclesiastical lands continues till the end of the Middle Ages, while *nativi* are known to have existed on the archiepiscopal lands of Dublin down to the year 1531.[24] Ten years later, however, when Irish monastic lands were surveyed it was found that 'though everywhere there are small tenants owing labour services and rents in kind, all valued in money, the only reference to unfree tenants is the statement on several manors: *Here there are no nativi.*'[25]

Reference to the court and the hundred in the Sanford Account shows that the feudal bishop of Cork was charged with the administration of justice within his manor of Fayd. The court was presumably the manor court or court baron which was held every three weeks under the presidency of the bishop's steward. It dealt with matters like rent, boundaries, entry fees, the deaths of tenants, the surrendering or assumption of holdings—all of which necessitated the payment of feudal dues. A second court known as the leet court or court of record, was presided over by the seneschal. It dealt with civil and criminal offences and had sittings twice a year, at Easter and at Michaelmas. From the manor of Ringrone near Kinsale comes an instance of both manor and leet courts in operation. According to an inquisition taken at Kinsale in 1372 John, Lord Courcey, and his son Gerald passed patent for the castle and manor of Ringrone and several other lands, advowsons of churches, etc., with the liberty of a park, free-chase and free-warren, goods of fugitives, wrecks of the sea, a court leet and a court baron, with fairs, markets and several other privileges in

---

23   *Cal. doc. Ire., 1171–1251*, no. 3203.

24   A. J. Otway-Ruthven, 'The Native Irish and English Law in Medieval Ireland', *I.H.S.*, vii (1950), 10.

25   Ibid., quoting *Extents Ir. mon. possessions, passim.*

the town of Ballinspittal in the said manor.[26] The churches mentioned in this patent were Ringrone, Kilroan, Garinoe (?) and Killowen. In the same way the leet court of Shandon gives an exhaustive list of offences falling within its jurisdiction.

The Sanford Account does not clarify the situation as between the leet court and the hundred which also dealt with civil and criminal offences, with pleas of debt and trespass and with offences against the assizes of bread and ale. Profits accruing to this court in the form of judicial payments from fees and fines imposed upon offenders and litigants were always an important source of regular revenue. However, the term *hundred* varied according to locality, and its signification in the present context is not easy to assess. Strictly speaking, the hundred presupposed a burgage, and very little reference to hundreds as distinct from burgages is found outside townships and other fortified places. John de Sanford may have used the term by way of reference to subjects of the bishop of Cork living in a town or burgage near the cathedral church of Saint Finbarr. The origin of the hundred court as applied to the bishop's manor is no-where accounted for; it may have been granted by patent in 1241 when the city of Cork got its hundred. Another unanswered question is whether or not the bishop's patent extended to the sub-manor at Kilbrogan. The area over which he exercised immediate civil jurisdiction was the townland or vill of Fayd exclusive only of subjects belonging to the Benedictine Church of Saint John the Evangelist which achieved manorial status as a cell of Bath and paid its dues accordingly. In time the term hundred as applied to manors was replaced by other designations. For the diocese of Cork the only references to this court come from the Sanford document of 1277 and from another revenue account submitted in 1302. Later again the steward and seneschal of Saint Finbarr's (that is, of the manor of Fayd), were appointed, according to Windele, 'to hold in and for the said manor Courts of leet or of Frankpledge',[27] and it is interest-ing to find this terminology retained until the beginning of the eighteenth century. Brady records that in 1700 there was 'a particular constable for the verge chosen at the Court Leet of the Manor' and there were 'two other constables in the manor chosen at the Quarter Sessions of the city'.[28]

Side by side with and complementary to these civil courts of the Middle Ages were the church courts which had precedence

26 Smith, *History of Cork*, i, 214 n., quoting *Rot. Canc.* [*sic*].

27 R.I.A., Windele MSS, ii, 291.

28 Brady, *Records*, i, 265.

in certain fields of law[29] and the privileges of which were recognized under the two main headings of benefit of clergy (*beneficium cleri*) and the right of sanctuary (*privilegium fori*). By virtue of the former privilege, clerks were entitled to have cases charged against them referred to the ecclesiastical courts. Without exploring the procedural intricacies inherent in the indictment of the clergy before the justiciar's court, a few instances from medieval Cork will exemplify the workings of the system. At a delivery of gaol in 1295 Richard Clok, clerk, was charged with having stolen a cow worth half a mark from William de Rupe. He was found guilty but not degraded, and consequently no sentence could be executed against him; but because no prelate claimed him by authority of the bishop, he was committed to prison. Later, Geoffrey, the vicar of Holy Trinity, and John de St. Patrick demanded his release in the name of the bishop.[30] Under the same date the following clerks were also handed over to the bishop's commissaries: Adam Onel, a housebreaker and a thief; Maurice, who stole a pig from William de Stanton; Philip le Graunt, who was declared guilty of the murder of William de Loges; John Bernard, vicar of the church of Saint Catherine, who was charged with the theft of a hood valued at two shillings from Magina, wife of Richard Ultach; Nicholas Omongenan, who stole a pan and a trivet. In 1297 the bishop himself, the Cistercian Robert Mac Donnchada, was charged with having stolen from Andrew de Arundel 'a stack of wheat and a stack of oats, value £20, to his [Arundel's] damage of £30.'[31] The sequel to the foregoing charges has not been put on record.

A more clear-cut instance of the overlapping of church and civil courts is recorded for the year 1313 when Simon Penrys, who was charged with the death of Richard Sinahit, declared that he was a clerk and claimed exemption from the court of common pleas in Cork. John Bernard, vicar of Saint Catherine's who in 1295 had been cited before the court on a charge of theft, now demanded that Penrys be delivered over to his custody. Upon investigation by special juries it was found that Sinahit had accosted Penrys on the highway and would have killed him had not Penrys drawn his knife in self-defence and so killed his assailant. What makes this case noteworthy is that

---

29   For instance, the consistorial court (episcopal court) of Cork had power of probating wills relating to movable property.

30   *Cal. justic. rolls Ire., 1295–1303*, p. 33.

31   Ibid., p. 162.

though the jury acquitted Penrys, his chattels were confiscated because he had 'refused the common law'.[32]

By the legal privilege of sanctuary an uncondemned criminal might take refuge in a consecrated church and remain there unmolested for a period of forty days, after which, if he had not abjured the land, he could be starved out but not forcibly removed. In 1295 an unusual instance, the only one of its kind on record, occurred in Cork, whereby Thomas de Cauntiton, a clerk who had escaped from the king's prison sought sanctuary in the church of Saint Peter and eventually fled the country. He returned later and when duly apprehended, successfully claimed benefit of clergy upon which he could have relied at the start and so have avoided his self-imposed temporary exile.[33] Another interesting case was that of Stephen le Waleys whom twelve jurymen accused in 1311 of hitting John Bederne on the head with an axe. Le Waleys took sanctuary in the church of Holy Cross del Nard from where he issued his 'no surrender' to the coronors and keepers of the pleas in Cork. He remained in the church for over three weeks and then escaped through negligence of the guard, but his goods were ordered to be confiscated, and from them John Bederne, who had recovered from his wound, was to be compensated. The justices also agreed that William de Neuhaus of Cork should get half a mark for the losses he sustained because the justices in that and previous sessions had held pleas of the crown in his house.[34]

The revenue account submitted by Walter de la Haye in 1302 is our second indication of the feudal status enjoyed by the medieval bishops of Cork. This escheatry account registers £23 15s 11d derived from the temporalities of the diocese during the three months' vacancy from the death of Robert Mac Donnchada on 6 March 1302 to the restoration of the temporalities to John McCarroll on 12 June of the same year. The account included 'rent of pasture and meadow of the manor of the Bishopric . . . rent of the gavellers . . . of the free tenants . . . issues of mills, fisheries, weirs, and gardens . . . and . . . perquisites of [the] Court and Hundred there'.[35] The gavellers here referred to were sometimes known as customary

---

32   *Cal. justic. rolls Ire., 1308–14*, p. 288.

33   *Cal. justic. rolls Ire., 1295–1303*, p. 34.

34   *Cal. justic. rolls Ire., 1308–14*, pp. 197–8.

35   *P.R.I. rep. D.K. 38*, p. 83, containing Pipe Roll 31 Edward I which is the 'Account of Walter de la Haye, Escheator of Ireland, of the issues of certain bishoprics in the king's hands, from the morrow of the close of Easter, a.r. 24, to the morrow of the Purification, a.r. 32.'

tenants who held land by the custom of the manor. At other times they were referred to as copyholders because they were furnished with a copy of the court record.[36] Copyholders appear to have been distinguished from free tenants by insecurity of tenure and higher rents. Free tenants, as we have seen, enjoyed a hereditary right, whereas copyholders held *ad voluntatem* or *per scriptum domini ad terminum*.[37] This was ultimately extended to cover a period of three lives.[38]

By 1302 the city over which the bishop was spiritual head had undergone many changes. In July 1218 it had been enclosed, and by order of Henry III a three years' farm of the city was to be paid to Thomas FitzAnthony for purposes of defence. For the years 1262, 1269 and 1284 we find references to the fee-farm of the city and the rent of the Fayth; in 1275 the citizens lent money to maintain war against Irish enemies[39] and in 1284 King Edward I granted to the citizens certain customs for five years to aid them in enclosing their vill of Cork. Such grants, known as murage grants, were the usual means employed towards defraying the cost of maintaining and extending city walls. From the date of the enclosure of the city the attacks of the Irish are constantly given as excuses for the citizens' inability to pay the fee-farm and the rent of the Fayth. Such excuses were not always accepted, for in 1284 the full total of '80 marks as fee farm and 6 marks for the rent of the Fayth' was exacted from the citizens notwithstanding alleged local disturbance.[40] Guilds began to appear in the city before the end of the thirteenth century when we find references to masons, carpenters, smiths, tailors, tanners and dyers, representatives of the principal trades being pursued in Cork up to that time.

No comprehensive estimate can be given of the trade of Cork—its content, direction or extent—for the pre-Norman period, and available records for the early post-Norman period are at best vague and unsatisfactory. The murage grant of 1284 enumerates what must have been the more usual items

36   Edmund Curtis, 'The Court Book of Esker and Crumlin', *R.S.A.I. Jn.*, lx (1930), 38–51 ff.

37   *The Red Book of Ormond*, ed. N. B. White, p. 32.

38   In R.I.A., Cork Inquisitions, i, 160, one reads that 'on 7 January 1611, John Joannes is likewise seised of one copiehold which consists of one house and garden, parcell of the said seignory [Mallow]. George Herbert is likewise seised of one copiehold which consists of one house and garden for the tearme of three Lyves, parcell of the said seignory.' Though a post-Reformation document, the arrangement outlined would appear to be the extension of a more ancient settlement.

39   *Cal. doc. Ire., 1252–84*, no. 842.

40   Ibid., no. 2329.

of trade, viz., wine and honey, timber, hides and skins, wools, Irish cloth, dyed and undyed English cloth, French cloth, canvas and wax, pepper, almonds, rice, tallow, cheese or butter, onions, garlic, wheat and oatmeal, cattle, fish (salmon, conger, ling and hake), mercury and kitchen utensils.[41] Thus emerges a scale of imports and exports from thirteenth-century Cork. Wine, the most important of all commodities then imported, apparently paid high dividends through the prisage rights enjoyed by the merchants. French rather than Spanish wines comprised the bulk of the intake which came from Gascony, Bayonne, and Bordeaux.[42] It is probable that a re-export trade was also exercised and that the king's purveyors who requisitioned wine for the armies in Scotland, Wales and France paid occasionally for their purchases. Little can be ascertained, however, as to the bulk of this two-way traffic in wine; the probabilities are that it was relatively small. Provisions—wheat, oatmeal, meat, fish and malt—ranked high on the export list and were dispatched through Bristol and Carlisle for consumption in England and Scotland.[43] Gascony was another consumer. On occasion, provisions were accepted in lieu of money payment for the fee-farm of the city. Hides, wool and wool-fells were other important exports, but these became dutiable under an impost called the New Custom which was levied in 1275 at the rate of half a mark on every sack of wool and on every lot of three hundred wool-fells, and of one mark for each last of hides (that is, on every 200 hides).[44] Legislation issued in 1294 prohibited the export of these commodities to France or to French dominions.[45] Stag, goat and horse hides were other main items of trade, and though a smaller venture in rabbit, squirrel, fox and marten skins was undertaken locally it seems to have languished at an early date. Exports of Irish cloth from Cork can only have been on a small scale,[46] and butter, while it is mentioned in the murage grant, seems a dubitable export because of its perishable nature and the lack of preservation facilities. Timber, whether required for domestic or maritime purposes, was got locally and only rarely exported. Taken all in all, inland trade in the city and county of Cork fed on and

---

41   Ibid., no. 2248.

42   Rowley Lascelles, *Liber Munerum Publicorum Hiberniae*, i, pt. 1, p. 34.

43   *Cal. doc. Ire., 1171–1251* and *1252–84, passim.*

44   *Cal. doc. Ire., 1252–84,* nos. 1116 and 1429.

45   *Calendar of the Close Rolls, 1288–96,* p. 405.

46   *Cal. doc. Ire., 1171–1251,* nos. 462 and 500.

was supported by a large European commerce, and Kinsale, Youghal, Bantry and Baltimore had their trade connections with the continent and with Cork.

As owner and administrator of a feudal manor with its mills, fisheries, warrens, pastures, meadows, gardens and woods, the bishop of Cork through his stewards and bailiffs must have participated to some degree in the fast-growing volume of trade and commerce which was bringing such wealth to his cathedral city. Considering the formidable entourage of a medieval bishop, his household requirements cannot have been adequately supplied locally and consequently some system of exchange or barter is not unlikely. In fact, the status of the medieval bishop of Cork within his own city and vill cannot have differed greatly from that of baronial ecclesiastics elsewhere.

Apart from important details concerning the vill or townland of Fayd the revenue accounts of Sanford and la Haye contain no references whatever to episcopal lands outside this area. A more satisfactory account of the bishop's possessions in the Anglo-Norman sector of the diocese is furnished by a document believed to have been compiled in 1456 during the episcopate of Jordan Purcell, first bishop of the united sees of Cork and Cloyne. This document, which could be regarded in a sense as the pipe roll of Cork, gives details concerning tenants, the names of townlands held by each and statistics of rent payments, but it does not record any areas of holdings as does the *Pipe Roll of Cloyne*. Personal names recorded in Bishop Purcell's rent roll are all Anglo-Norman, the tenants are tenants-in-fee, the amounts mentioned are chief or head-rents, and many of the places mentioned are prebendal parishes.

Terrae et Redditus Epi. Cork.[47]

De civitate et de la Fath de Cork	6 marks
De Petro de Cogan pro Carrigrohan	28 s.
De Richardo de Cogan de Maogillin	2 m.
De David Burden	1 m.
De Comite Ultonie pro eclonine	20 s.
De Galfrid de Cogan pro Moally	10 s.
De Edwardo Redisford de Ballimolimihill	20 s.
De Nicholas Gold de Inscriny	6s.8d.
De David Cogan de Lisgille	2 m.
De Henry Gold de Inscrinybeg	10 s.
De David Gold de Ballimakedan	10 s.

47   B.M., Add. MS Ascough 4787, f. 78v.

Odone de Fraxinet de Cullen	20 s.
De Johanne Winchedon de Noffale	6 m.
De Willelmo Coggan de Correkeppan	2 m.
De Nicholas de Curcy de Kinsale	£31.12s.11d.[48]

From the above we find the bishop of Cork enjoying a rent of six marks for that part of the *faithche* in Cork city which overlapped his own townland of Fayd. He also held lands in Carrigrohane, Maglin, Ballyburden and Knockburden near Ballincollig,[49] Ballymolmihill (now Rochfordstown *alias* Castle-white), Inishkenny in two parts, Ballymacadane or Oldabbey near Waterfall, and Liskillea. Thus there emerges a continuous block of townlands extending from the cathedral westwards to Ballincollig and southwards to Liskillea and Ballinhassig. The bishop is also shown as possessor of other estates at Curry-kippane, Moally or Aglish, Cullen or Riverstick, Nohoval and Kinsale. The estate known as 'eclonine' and held by the earl of Ulster[50] has not been identified, unless it could be equated with Killumney which was within the parish of Saint Finbarr. The omission of the bishop's lands at Kilbrogan from this rent roll may have been due to the fact that Kilbrogan was no longer within the area under feudal tenure.

Casual references to some of the properties outlined in the rental of 1456 occur in other pre-Reformation documents. Caulfield's *Annals of Kinsale* record of Nicholas de Courcey who died in 1474 that 'in an ancient Roll in the custody of ye Bishop of Cork, dated a.1278 [*rectè* 1456] is mentioned that Nicholas de Curcy of Kinsale did divide ye chief rents of Kinsale with ye Bishop of Cork, and Gerald de Courcy did make ye like partition with ye Bishop of Cork by Richard Roche his deputee, and kept Court Barron in ye said town of Kinsale.' A Latin document quoted by Smith as being in the possession of George White of Castlewhite or Rochfordstown, deals with a family dispute among the Rochfords concerning the lands of Castlewhite in 1514. The deed describes the Rochfords as 'vassals of the Bishop of Cork (*vassali Episcopi Corcagen.*)', that is, his tenants-in-fee.[51]

It appears almost certain too that the medieval bishop of Cork held territory in Ringaskiddy, since in 1547 a document

48 Taking a mark to be the equivalent of 13s 4d, the above returns would realize the sum of £50 10s 11d.

49 *De David Burden* in the document.

50 Richard Plantagenet, who was earl of March and earl of Cork (1449) as well as being earl of Ulster.

51 Smith, *History of Cork*, i, 363.

was drawn up to prove that the lands of Richard Skyddye, 'chief of his nation', called by his old deeds Rossbegge and Skyddye's Poynte, were free of all rents and impositions 'excepting only certeyne chief rents to the busshoppe of Corcke'.[52] The lands in question, then known respectively as Templebrettayne and Rynnyskydde, represented the modern townlands of Ballybricken and Ringaskiddy.

Further details on episcopal holdings in the medieval diocese of Cork are to be had only from post-Reformation rent rolls and surveys which, though outside the ambit of the present study, must nevertheless be considered as contextual. The first of these is an inquisition taken in 1584 and shows that the Protestant bishop of Cork fared badly as regards lands in the Anglo-Norman area near the city. At the death of Matthew Sheyne in 1582 the see had three ploughlands in Ballinaspick (modern Bishopstown) and the rents of Rochford's lands, Carickanway (Curraghconway), Ringaskiddy, Canaboy, Killanully and some districts in the diocese of Cloyne. Bishop Sheyne also retained the ploughlands of Inchigaggin and Farranmacteige, but the possessions of the see at Carrigrohane, Ballincollig, Inishkenny, Currykippane, Aglish, Cullen, Nohoval and Kinsale were lost. Evidence of seventeenth-century documents, however, shows that the bishop fared better as regards estates in the Irish territories to the west which remained outside Anglo-Norman domination. These estates are enumerated in a *Rent Roll of the Diocese of Cork* which was compiled in 1699 by the officials of the Established Church. The rental is of particular interest in that the western territories which it enumerates were not mentioned in any of the earlier feudal rentals of the diocese. Briefly, these estates were:

	ploughlands
Kilbrogan, Knockbrogan and Kilbeg, near Bandon	3
Kinneigh	$\frac{1}{2}$
Nedinagh Beag and Nedinagh Mor, lying about Fanlobbus Church (Dunmanway)	6
Kilmacomoge or Bantry	3
Kilcroghan in the parish of Muintervara	3
Schull	9
Crookhaven and Kilmoe	10
Farranavaragan or Macloneigh near Macroom	$\frac{1}{2}$

52 Richard Caulfield, *The Council Book of the Corporation of Kinsale*, appendix N.

Notwithstanding the absence of written references earlier than the seventeenth century, most if not all of the lands listed in the foregoing rent roll lay around important early church sites and must have been ecclesiastical property from the earliest times. Taking these possessions in their entirety and remembering that in medieval times land was the only wealth that mattered, the feudal bishop of Cork cannot but have been a person of significance in the socio-economic as well as in the ecclesiastical affairs of the diocese. Even granted that the lands listed in the rent roll of 1699 were in the bishop's hands at the time of the earlier rental (1456), the income from these far-flung estates was more than counterbalanced by commitments— religious, social and educational—which it was his duty to discharge. When these extensive episcopal lands were taken over by the Protestants, they were taken not as diocesan but as the personal property of the Reformation bishops, and they were used regardless of all such traditional religious obligations.

The names of the great families of Rochfords, Cogans, Courceys, Goulds and others who were tenants of the medieval bishops are conspicuously absent from the rental of 1699, from which it may be inferred that the status of other tenants on the manor of Fayd had also deteriorated. Some writers, however, maintain that the condition of tenants as under the medieval church improved under the new regime, that 'by the sixteenth century . . . servile tenure was rapidly coming to an end and was formally abolished in 1605 . . . [that] it survived longest . . . on the Church lands, and hence when the monasteries were dissolved was brought to an end under the new landlords.'[53] As against this rather biassed view, the fact remains that servile tenure was a feature of all manors, both secular and ecclesiastical, and that the change in the status of villeins or *betagii* was a gradual process which was greatly hastened by the Black Death when labour became scarce and services were commuted. Where other tenants were concerned, a notable deterioration in their condition was effected under the new regime as may be seen from a comparison of rent rolls. The revenue accounts of 1277 and 1302 show that the majority of tenants on the episcopal manor were free or hereditary tenants. The rental of 1699 mentions no free tenants whatsoever. The status of the free tenants as such had changed to that of farmers or lease-holders to whom leases were granted for short periods only. The trend was therefore retrogressive rather than progressive.

53 Curtis, 'The Court Book of Esker and Crumlin', p. 143.

VII

The Diocesan Episcopacy : Twelfth and Thirteenth Centuries

GREGORY O HAODHA, 1172–1182

As immediate successor to Giolla Aedh O Muighin whom Saint Malachy appointed to Cork in 1140, Gregory O hAodha occupies an important position in Cork diocesan history. The first year of his episcopate coincided with the Synod of Cashel which, while it endorsed with ecclesiastical approval the position of Henry II in Ireland, was at the same time, through its legislation on tithe-paying, the starting-point of parochial organization in this country. In spite of the lack of confirmatory evidence, it is a plausible supposition that the delineation of parochial geography in Cork had its beginnings under Gregory O hAodha. As a likely inheritor and advocate of the twelfth-century reforming ideals he belongs to that group of ecclesiastics who, to quote Kenney, 'selected cathedral churches, established diocesan chapters and founded new monasteries occupied by branches of foreign religious orders'.[1] Our first evidence of a cathedral chapter in Cork is the existence of an archdeacon during Gregory's episcopate. The absence of all reference to other capitular personnel does not preclude the possibility that by 1180 or thereabouts a secular chapter was already in process of erection. And while the existence of an archdeacon could be dismissed as nothing more than an appointment made by Bishop Gregory under Norman pressure and most probably with right of succession,[2] it is nevertheless the coping-stone upon which our evidence for the origin of the diocesan chapter is based. Another noteworthy aspect of Gregory O hAodha's episcopate was the arrival in Cork of the Norman-sponsored Knights Hospitallers of Saint John of Jerusalem between the years 1172 and 1182.

1 Kenney, *Sources*, p. 749.

2 Gwynn, 'The Bishops of Cork in the Twelfth Century', p. 105.

To Gregory O hAodha likewise fell the task of controlling the destinies of the diocese of Cork during the opening years of the Anglo-Norman occupation. We have noted that Henry II granted joint governorship of the kingdom of Cork to Robert FitzStephen and Milo de Cogan in 1172; even though the Norman hold over this area did not survive the lifetime of the original grantees, the years of Gregory's episcopate cannot but have been punctuated by attempts to extend Norman influence over the church in Cork. Judging from existing records, Bishop Gregory's principal administrative function was the witnessing and granting of charters. In fact, his liberality to the abbey of Saint Thomas in Dublin and to the priory of Saint Nicholas in Exeter suggests that despite his Gaelic surname he was in close collaboration with the newly-arrived adventurers.[3] The churches and church lands alienated by him were (a) the grant of Kinure which Milo de Cogan made about the year 1174 to the canons of Saint Thomas, Dublin;[4] (b) the church of Saint Nessan, c.1180, and a confirmation by special charter of all grants of churches in the bishopric of Cork 'which righteous men had made to the abbey of St Thomas'; (c) the church of Saint Sepulchre in Cork city which was granted to the monks of Saint Nicholas, Exeter, by FitzStephen and de Cogan. Bishop Gregory confirmed this charter c.1182; his purpose in ratifying this grant may have been his inability to preserve or restore the church of Saint Sepulchre which was then lying waste (*quia vastata erat*).[5] The grants were not altogether gratuitous: some of those in favour of the abbey of Saint Thomas carried a stipulation binding the community to provide for the celebration of Mass on Saint Finbarr's Day.[6]

One other document preserves the name of Gregory O hAodha. This is the charter of Dermot MacCarthy who in 1174 confirmed to the monks of Gill Abbey all grants and privileges bestowed on them by his father Cormac MacCarthy in 1134, which grants were augmented by donations from other MacCarthy and O'Connor relatives.[7] Gregory's name on this charter occurs immediately after those of Christian O Conairche, papal legate and bishop of Lismore, and Donatus O'Hullachan,

---

3 Webster, *The Diocese of Cork*, p. 38, suggests that Gregory was a foreigner.

4 *Reg. St. Thomas, Dublin*, p. 201.

5 Brooks, 'Unpublished Charters relating to Ireland, 1177–82, from the Archives of the City of Exeter', pp. 324–5.

6 *Reg. St. Thomas, Dublin*, p. 210. See Charters 248 and 249 in Appendix B, Chapter IV above.

7 See Appendix A, Chapter III above.

archbishop of Cashel. The bishops of Limerick, Ross, Cloyne, and Ardmore follow, as do also the abbots of Magio and Cong. Assuming that the list so arranged indicates priority, the diocese of Cork and its bishop ranked high according to twelfth-century reckoning. The *Annals of Loch Cé* carry the account of Bishop O hAodha's death under the year 1182 and in this way supply for the hiatus occurring in the *Annals of Inisfallen* for the years 1181–89.

REGINALD, 1182–1187

Reginald, who was archdeacon of Cork under Gregory O hAodha, is Cork's first-known archdeacon and was possibly the first cleric to have attained archidiaconal status in the diocese. His Anglo-Norman parentage is beyond question, and if, as seems likely, he was appointed under Anglo-Norman pressure, his appointment is proof of great changes wrought and attempted in the diocese after the arrival of FitzStephen and de Cogan in Cork. The trend was everywhere the same. Dublin got its first Anglo-Norman bishop in 1182, the year of Reginald's appointment in Cork. The appointment of John Comyn (Cumin) to Dublin was followed by the erection of a diocesan chapter, strongly Anglo-Norman in personnel, in Saint Patrick's Cathedral. Within the next twenty years— that is, about the year 1205—a similar development 'considering English custom' was apparently forced upon Bishop Donnchad Ua Briain of Limerick.[8] Events in Cork occupy a position closer in time to what was happening in Dublin, and in both places the secular chapter appears to have grown up alongside an existing monastic chapter: the Arroasian canons of Christ Church in Dublin and the Augustinian canons regular of Gill Abbey in Cork.

Like his predecessor, Reginald's main administrative functions were connected with the abbey of Saint Thomas and the priory of Saint Nicholas. As archdeacon he witnessed one grant to the Exeter priory and three to the Dublin abbey. A statement in one of these charters to the effect that Bishop Gregory had made the grants in question *with the consent of the entire chapter of his church*[9] suggests that before 1182 Cork was beginning to move away from the purely monastic type of chapter which Saint Malachy is thought to have established under Giolla

---

8 *The Black Book of Limerick*, ed. J. MacCaffrey, no. cxlii, p. 117: . . . anglicanam considerantes consuetudinem . . .

9 *Reg. St. Thomas*, Dublin, p. 219.

Aedh O Muighin. In his capacity as bishop, Reginald confirmed the grant of the chapel of Saint Nicholas 'which Roger de Oxeneford gave in perpetual gift to the aforementioned church [of Saint Thomas] through the hands of my predecessor, Bishop Gregory'.[10] By a second charter he confirmed all previous grants which had been or would in future be made to the canons of Saint Thomas by the faithful of his diocese (*in nostro episcopatu*). A stipulation attached to the former charter obliged the monks of Saint Thomas to give five English coins and one pound of wax each year on the feast of Saint Nicholas to the church of Saint Finbarr in Cork. The second demanded of the Dublin community an annual gift on the feast of Saint Finbarr of one *sextarius* of wine or its equivalent in denarii for the wants of the church and the needs of the bishopric.

Nothing further is known of Bishop Reginald's activities in Cork, but it may be safely assumed that his episcopate was marked by an appreciable influx of Norman clerks and monks into the diocese. Not a single annalist records his death in terms of personal reference. The *Annales Buelliani* record the death of a bishop of Cork in 1187, *Episcopus Corcaigi quievit*, while the *Western Annals of Boyle* have entered the death of Acher, bishop of Cork, under the year 1188: *Acher, episcopus Corcaigi quieuit*.[11] The hopeful supposition that Reginald and Acher are identical would be too facile a solution to this type of problem which turns up in every diocese. More probably, Acher was the priest Aggirus (*Aggiro presbytero*) who with Archdeacon Reginald witnessed one of Gregory O hAodha's charters.[12] It seems therefore that between 1182 and 1188 two short-lived Anglo-Norman bishops ruled the see of Finbarr. Lynch's identification of Reginald with an O Selboic who died in 1205 is too far off the mark to merit consideration.[13]

MURCHAD O HAODHA, 1192–1206

From the death of Bishop Reginald in 1187 the see of Cork remained vacant until at least 1192, and though the vacancy was filled about this time we are nowhere given the appointee's name, Murchad O hAodha, until his death is recorded in both the *Annals of Inisfallen* and the *Annals of Loch Cé*. The years

10   Ibid., pp. 218–19.

11   Gwynn, 'The Bishops of Cork in the Twelfth Century', p. 108.

12   *Reg. St. Thomas, Dublin*, charter no. 250.

13   Lynch, *De praesulibus Hib.*, ii, 141.

from Reginald's death to the turn of the century were a time of ecclesiastical obscurity and political confusion bound up with the course of Norman expansion in Desmond. Because of prevailing turmoil we get no more than a few scattered fragments of diocesan history for these years and are in the realm of conjecture for the greater part of Murchad O hAodha's reign. An unnamed bishop of Cork seems to have been administering the diocese of Ross before the summer of 1198 when one of two other claimants filed a complaint against him to Pope Innocent III. The intruder seems most likely to have been a member of the powerful Ua Sealbaigh family which gave so many abbots and erenaghs to Cork. Under the year 1205 the *Annals of Inisfallen* record the death of a Bishop Ua Sealbaigh in Cork: *in t-espuc Ua Sealbaic i Corcaig q. in Xto*.[14] The entry does not call him 'bishop of Cork', therefore the obvious inference is that he died as a pilgrim in Cork, the last scion of the ecclesiastical dynasty of Ua Sealbaigh.[15] Political interference was also a feature of this disputed Ross election as is clear from the letters of Innocent III which mention the opposition of the king of Cork towards the candidate who obtained election.[16]

In 1199 the bishop of Cork, who was still unnamed, received from Pope Innocent III the famous decretal letter confirming him in possession of the churches and properties of the see. The liberties of Bristol were conferred on the city in the same year by King John; consequently it would appear that Cork set out on the road to civil autonomy during the episcopate of Murchad O hAodha. In 1202, according to the *Register* of Saint Thomas's Abbey, 'M. Bishop of Cork' made two agreements with Brother Simon, prior of Saint Thomas's relative to certain payments due to the bishop,[17] and in 1205 'M. Bishop of Cork' was witness to the charter by which Bishop Donatus of Limerick established a secular chapter in his

---

14 *Ann. Inisf.*, f. 43c.

15 Lynch, *De praeseulibus Hib.*, ii, 141–2, contains a highly confused entry concerning the diocese of Cork in the last years of the twelfth century and the opening years of the thirteenth: Reginald successit, sed quando consecratus aut mortuus fuerit non comperi. In *Annalibus Innisfallensis Coenobii* ad annum 1205 fit mentio cuiusdam O Selboic episcopi Corcagiensis, qui anno 1205 vivere desiit. Non possum non [nunc] suspicari hunc eundem esse cum Reginaldo supra memorato, qui episcopus fuit 1199 et confirmationem tunc impetravit omnium possessionum sedis Corcagiensis ab Innocentio III, quarum cathalogus in eiusdem Innocentii epistolis habetur.

16 Dunning, 'Irish Representatives and Irish Ecclesiastical Affairs at the Fourth Lateran Council', p. 93, n. 13.

17 *Reg. St. Thomas, Dublin*, pp. 220–1.

diocese.[18] The final recorded act of Murchad O hAodha's episcopate is as enigmatic as the rest of his career. The account of his death in the *Annals of Inisfallen* states that he died at Sliabh gCua on a hosting: *in tescub Ua hAedha do agail báis issléibchua ar slugid*. The hosting, which may have been launched against encroachments on the north-eastern boundaries of the diocese, would suggest that a satisfactory *modus vivendi* had not yet been achieved between the old inhabitants and the new Anglo-Norman arrivals in Cork.

MARIANUS UA BRIAIN, 1207–1224.

Here again we are confronted with a controversial figure, the date of whose accession can only be ascertained by deduction from data relevant to the canonization of Laurence O'Toole. The process for canonization, which is catalogued as MS 1832 in the Bibliothèque Sainte Geneviève in Paris, contains a testimonial letter from *M. Corcagiensis*. The signatory could not be that of Murchad O hAodha, as has been suggested, because the signatory was a canon regular of Christ Church and as such a witness to the daily life and virtues of Laurence O'Toole.[19] Legris' *Life of Laurence O'Toole* states that Marianus Ua Briain was an Arroasian canon. The documents collected for the process cover the years 1206 and 1207 and the proceedings were opened in 1208 after the consecration of Eugene, archbishop of Armagh, who was also a witness to the documents. Assuming that Marianus Ua Briain is *M. Corcagiensis*, his election must have occurred shortly after the death of Murchad O hAodha. Sweetman's *Calendar of Documents relating to Ireland* introduces a further complication by listing Marianus as Maurice,[20] but as Sweetman's inaccuracies are notorious, a copyist's error in the case of Marianus Ua Briain cannot be ruled out. A final difficulty is posed in the *Handbook of British Chronology* which catalogues an anonymous entry for the see of Cork after the death of Murchad O hAodha, and which dates the accession of Marianus as c.1215.[21] This is probably due to the compiler's over-reliance on Lynch who admits his inability to discover who

18 *The Black Book of Limerick*, no. cxlii, p. 117.

19 M. V. Ronan, 'The Diocese of Dublin', *I.E.R.*, xliii (1934), 508. Aumonier Legris's *Life of Saint Laurence O'Toole, Archbishop of Dublin, 1128–1180* (Dublin 1914), pp. 38, 92, states that Marianus was an Arroasian canon of Holy Trinity.

20 *Cal. doc. Ire., 1171–1251*, no. 1209. Lynch, *De praesulibus Hib.*, ii, 142, mentions that Marianus is called Mauricius in the archives of the Tower of London.

21 Powicke and Fryde, *Handbook of British Chronology*, p. 325.

succeeded Bishop Reginald in the see of Cork.[22] Finally, a Rawlinson document[23] postulates a vacancy in Cork in 1215 for which King John unsuccessfully urged the candidacy of Geoffrey White, a cleric in the household of Archbishop Henry de Londres of Dublin. It is extremely doubtful that White was ever consecrated. The accumulated contradictions may be explained in terms of the translation of Marianus Ua Briain to Cashel which was not effected until 1224 but was apparently postulated at an earlier date, probably in 1215.

The year 1215 is particularly memorable by reason of Pope Innocent III's convocation of the Fourth Lateran Council, the twofold object of which was the proclamation of a crusade to the Holy Land and the furtherance of reform in the church. To facilitate the latter, bishops everywhere were instructed to draw up programmes of reform relevant to their own dioceses, and metropolitans were told that they should 'personally and by discreet agents . . . enquire precisely about all matters which seem to call for energetic correction and reform' and then submit their written reports to the council.[24] Irish attendance at the council amounted to eighteen bishops and two bishops-elect, a mixed gathering representative of the then Irish episcopate. The absence of the bishop of Cork may have been due to uncertainty and confusion arising from the supposed vacancy of 1215. On the other hand, the bishop of Cork with his neighbour of Cloyne and the bishop of Killaloe may have been administering the affairs of the province during the absence of the archbishop of Cashel who was accompanied by the bishops of Ross, Limerick, Emly and Waterford and the bishop-elect of Lismore.

The problems of the contemporary Irish Church were mostly the offshoot of difficulties consequent upon the Anglo-Norman invasion: secular interference in ecclesiastical elections, feudalization of church property, the unfinished character of the twelfth-century diocesan organization stemming from Rathbreasail and Kells. Other perennial problems dealt with non-payment of tithes, the difficulty of enforcing the marriage laws of the church, the lingering custom (in places) of hereditary succession to ecclesiastical benefices. The raising of these

22 Lynch, *De praesulibus Hib.*, ii, 142: 'Quis ille [Reginaldus] successerit traditum non reperi. Sede autem anno 1215 vacante . . .' He adds that Henry III proposed Geoffrey White for the vacancy. Henry's regnal dates are 1216–72.

23 B.M., Rawlinson MS B 479, f. 14.

24 Dunning, 'Irish Representatives and Irish Ecclesiastical Affairs at the Fourth Lateran Council', p. 92.

problems by the Irish prelates at the council 'give an insight
into the state of the Irish Church and throw some light on how
after almost half-a-century the coming of the Normans was
affecting the ecclesiastical situation'.[25] The canons of the council,
seventy in number and mostly disciplinary, condemn most of
the abuses prevalent in Ireland, but this legislation must not
be regarded as aimed directly at Irish abuses; similar abuses
abounded on the continent. But the council legislated specifically
against lay encroachment on clerical appointments and decreed
that whoever accepted election by the secular power was not
elected, and that acceptance of such election would entail
forfeiture of future preferment. If a chapter failed to elect
within three months of the death of a bishop, the right and
duty of election were to pass to the metropolitan, but if he
confirmed an unsuitable candidate, the confirmation was invalid
and the offending archbishop was to be suspended until absolved by the pope. The council ordered a lectureship in theology
to be established in every cathedral and legislated on the
necessity of the Easter Duty, the need to curb clerical avarice
(apropos of which convents were forbidden to demand a
premium, on the plea of poverty, from would-be aspirants),
the treatment of heretics, judgements as between bishops and
religious orders in their disputes, rules for the trial of clerics,
the right of chapters to correct their own members and regulations governing the resignation of benefices. Relations between
Jews and Christians were another item on the agenda of the
council, as was also the approval of the mendicant movement.

In 1216 King Henry III in what must have been one of the
earliest statutes of his reign announced that 'we have granted
to God (and) by this our present Charter have confirmed for
us and for our heirs forever that the Irish Church shall be free,
and have all her rights entire and [her] liberties inviolable.'[26]
The same instrument, a statement guaranteeing the restoration
of lands to minors when they came of age, concluded with the
assurance that 'all these things shall be observed in regard to
the custody of vacant archbishoprics, bishoprics, abbacies,
priories, churches and dignities.' The hopes aroused by Henry's
bounty were short-lived; before the century was out (1291)
the sentiments of Henry's son Edward were to be expressed
as follows: 'If anyone shall have presented someone to any
church, and the prelate [presumably the bishop] wishes to

25   Ibid., p. 93.

26   *Statutes, Ordinances and Acts of the Parliament of Ireland, King John to Henry V,*
p. 7 (1 Henry III).

make due enquiry, according to the approved manner and custom, it is not permitted him, but unless he immediately admit the person presented, he is attached by the King's officers, as in the diocese of Ossory.'[27]

The extension of Norman influence within the diocese of Cork during the episcopacy of Marianus Ua Briain in seen in a grant made out in July 1215 to Thomas FitzAnthony which secured to him and to his heirs 'custody of kingdom of Desmond with the city of Cork as far as it belongs to the king; all the king's demesnes in that county, all escheats in Desmond now in the king's hand, with the issues of those escheats for the safe keeping of bailiwicks and the king's castles'. FitzAnthony in return was to pay 250 marks a year at the exchequer of Dublin 'for the counties of Waterford and Desmond and the city of Cork, as far as it is the king's'.[28] On 8 July 1218 the king, on being informed that it would tend to the security of his majesty if the city of Cork were fortified, ordered that three years' farm of the city should be paid to FitzAnthony for that purpose.

What of Marianus Ua Briain's dealings with the king and the colonists? Our only indication is a double entry in the *Register* of Saint Thomas's Abbey by which he confirmed all the ecclesiastical revenues of Douglas, Kinure and Balimakin, and all other revenues which had been or would be granted from the diocese of Cork to the canons of Saint Thomas. Marianus was therefore an accommodating cleric. Like Archbishop Ua hEnna of Cashel and Bishop Donatus Ua Briain of Limerick he enjoyed the confidence of the king and gave him in return his loyalty and co-operation. The preponderance of non-Irish clerics in Cork in the opening decades of the thirteenth century shows that Marianus was not averse to the intrusion; it was during his episcopate that the archbishop of Dublin was appointed king's bailiff in Cork.[29]

On the voidance of the see of Cashel in 1223, Henry III granted royal licence to the dean and chapter to proceed with the election of an archbishop.[30] Marianus Ua Briain was postulated by the chapter, appointed by the pope and confirmed by the king—in that order. The *Calendar of Close Rolls*, 9 Henry III, is incorrect in stating that the election was confirmed by the pope. The correct form of the papal appointment

27   Ibid., p. 187 (19 Edward I).

28   *Cal. doc. Ire., 1171–1251*, no. 842.

29   See Chapter VI.

30   *Cal. doc. Ire., 1171–1251*, no. 1133.

is given by Theiner: *Venerabili fratri Mariano . . . Casselensem electo . . . te . . . ex officio nostro providemus ad eius* [*archiepiscopatus*] *curam . . .*[31] In June 1224 the pope wrote to Henry III asking for his 'easy and gracious assent' to the election of Marianus, and Marianus was advised to go with the pope's letters to the king of England and obtain permission to proceed to Rome for the *pallium*, since 'Master M. Scot [the former archbishop], being ignorant of Irish [had] resigned.'[32] Michael Scot, who was apparently a papal official of sorts, had been appointed to Cashel early in 1224, but his appointment did not take effect, and it is doubtful if he was ever consecrated. Marianus Ua Briain was translated to Cashel on 20 June 1225. In the following year, in conjunction with the bishops of Limerick and Cloyne, he received a papal mandate to settle a dispute over succession to the see of Killaloe, the rival claimants to which were Robert Travers and David, archdeacon of Killaloe. On a journey to Rome in 1231 Marianus Ua Briain fell ill and, believing himself to be dying, sought refuge in a Cistercian monastery, but he recovered and resumed his journey and eventually returned to Ireland. He died in 1236 and was buried in the Cistercian monastery of Inislounaght, a circumstance which has given rise to the belief that he was a Cistercian.

GILBERT, 1225–1238.

Gilbert, who succeeded Reginald as archdeacon in 1182, became bishop in succession to Marianus Ua Briain. King Henry III assented to the election on 5 June 1225 and even though the papal record of the proceedings is not extant, there is no reason for doubting any departure from customary procedure. At all events the king ordered his justiciary 'to give seisin to the Elect [of Cork] of all the lands, rents and possessions belonging to the bishopric'.[33] First among Gilbert's official functions was his attendance at the consecration of Tracton Abbey in the year of his own consecration. In the same year the bishop was mentioned in a deed referring to the Benedictine priory of Saint John the Evangelist in Douglas Street. The fact that the Benedictines were litigating against Philip de Prendergast concerning proprietorship over the vills

31　Theiner, *Vetera mon.*, p. 23.

32　*Cal. papal letters, 1198–1304*, p. 97.

33　*Cal. doc. Ire., 1171–1251*, no. 1303.

of Culmore and Ballyfouloo indicates the threat still attaching to ecclesiastical property at the hands of the settlers.[34]

We have seen that in 1227 Geoffrey de Morisco was entrusted with power to grant on his own initiative formal licence for election to vacant sees in places where clerical poverty warranted such a procedure. Cork with ten other dioceses—Kildare, Ossory, Leighlin, Ferns, Meath, Emly, Killaloe, Limerick, Waterford and Lismore—was specifically excluded from this arrangement.[35] The diocesan economy of Cork was therefore relatively buoyant when Gilbert took over, and sufficiently attractive to warrant continued personal control by the king. In 1223 Henry III made his influence more oppressive when he commanded all archbishops, bishops, abbots, priors, arch-deacons, deans and all prelates and ecclesiastical persons to presume not to hold pleas of advowsons and lay fee (which are not connected with testamentary or matrimonial matters)[36] in Court Christian as they were against his crown and dignity.[37] Furthermore, the justiciary was ordered to ensure that the royal dignity would not suffer detriment by any overlapping between ecclesiastical and civil courts, and to have letters patent to this effect read and kept.

At some date between 1228 and 1236 Bishop Gilbert witnessed a deed by which Bishop Hugo de Burgo of Limerick granted the township of Sengol to the canons and vicars of Saint Mary's, Limerick.[38] During these years too he admitted the mendicant friars into the diocese, the Dominicans (in 1229) who estab-lished themselves at Saint Mary of the Island, and the Franciscans who founded the Grey Friary of Shandon in 1231. A royal mandate issued on 5 October 1237, shortly before Bishop Gilbert's death, throws light on a custom whereby the matrimonial expenses of the royal family were to be met by taxation of the 'king's lands' in Ireland. In the present instance Henry III hoped to induce his subjects in Ireland to help him pay the dowry required by his sister on her marriage to the German emperor. To meet the costs, earls, barons and other magnates were required to pay a scutage of two marks, while archbishops, bishops, abbots, priors and 'other men of religion' were expected

34   Ibid., no. 1436.

35   Ibid., no. 1519.

36   G. J. Hand, 'The Church and English Law in Medieval Ireland', *Ir. Cath. Hist. Comm. Proc.* (1959), p. 16. Ecclesiastical jurisdiction was undisputed in the matri-monial sphere.

37   *Stat. Ire., John–Hen. V*, p. 25.

38   *The Black Book of Limerick*, no. lii, p. 46, mentions 'G. Corcagiensi'.

to contribute one-thirtieth of their movables as the prelates of England had already done. The archbishops of Armagh, Dublin and Tuam were mentioned by name in the mandate, together with the dean and chapter of Cashel and sixteen bishops, among whom the bishop of Cork, presumably Gilbert, was cited.[39]

The final official record of Gilbert's episcopate states that in 1237 with the assent of the chapter he 'granted in fee farm to Michael de Druille one ploughland . . . lying between Kilmohallock and the land of Dufglas [Douglas] . . . at the rent of sixteen pence'.[40] Gilbert, who is believed to have died about the year 1238,[41] was recognized as a free citizen of Dublin shortly before his death.[42] He was undoubtedly an Anglo-Norman.

LAURENCE, 1248–1265

The ten-year vacancy following the death of Bishop Gilbert admits of two explanations: an incorrect obituary entry for Gilbert or (and more likely) a power struggle between the king of England and the chapter of Cork. The election which raised Laurence, dean of Cashel, to the episcopal chair of Cork on 5 May 1248 is noteworthy as representing the independent action of the dean and chapter of Cork who, in contravention of a royal decree of 1227, conducted electoral proceedings without securing the necessary *congé d'élire*. A parallel case occurred simultaneously in the diocese of Kilmacduagh where the canons, independently of royal permission, elected their archdeacon Gilbert as bishop, and the king, faced with the *fait accompli*, gave 'of his special grace' assent to the election 'considering the merits of the elect'. Royal prerogative against future attempts at independence was safeguarded by demanding letters from the chapter and canons of Kilmacduagh undertaking that they would not again contravene existing electoral laws. A similar solution was attempted in Cork. The election of Laurence was recognized on 14 September 1248, and the justiciary was advised 'not to impede the confirmation of Laurence, elected bishop of Cork'. Then came the rub: the

39 *Cal. doc. Ire., 1171–1251*, no. 2410.

40 Ware, *De Hibernia et Antiquitatibus eius*, p. 558.

41 Conrad Eubel, *Hierarchia Catholica Medii Aevi*, i, 211.

42 *Historic and Municipal Documents*, no. xxxviii, p. 116.

temporalities were to be restored only on condition that the chapter would not again initiate electoral proceedings without first soliciting *and obtaining* the royal licence to elect.[43] The Cork canons were uncompromising and objected to the demand that the king's licence should not only be sought but secured— and they won their point. The only future requirement laid down for them was that they would never again 'proceed to election of this kind without first at least *praying* licence to elect'.[44]

Between 1248 and 1254 Laurence was cited as papal mandatory to exercise judgement in cases occurring in the dioceses of Annadown and Ross. In March 1251 Laurence of Cork, the archbishop of Cashel and the bishop of Kilfenora were mandated to investigate the case of Concord, canon of Annadown, whose postulation for the see of Annadown was being impeded by the archbishop of Tuam. The archbishop, who had been ordered in January 'to receive in place of the pope the postulation of Concord, canon of Annadown, to that see', appears to have neglected the charge entrusted to him.[45] The sequel to the mandate of 1251 is not recorded, but since Concord secured his appointment to Annadown the mission of Laurence and his co-mandatories was successful. In March 1254 Laurence, with the bishops of Cloyne and Lismore, was appointed to examine the postulation by the chapter of Ross of Maurice, precentor of Cloyne. The mandatories were authorized to decide on Maurice's qualifications and to determine the validity of the postulation. If satisfied, they were to dispense Maurice on account of illegitimacy, confirm the postulation and consecrate him without prejudice to the metropolitan see of Cashel which was then vacant.[46] Finally, Laurence is listed in an entry in the *Black Book of Limerick* under date 1255 which recounts that the archbishop of Cashel bound himself to approve the decisions of his suffragans in matters of suspension, interdict and excommunication, provided their regulations redounded to the advantage (*ad favorem*) of the church and were in keeping with the liberties and customs of the province of Cashel.[47]

Later in 1255 Bishop Laurence took up duty as substitute

43   *Cal. doc. Ire., 1171–1251*, no. 2933.

44   Ibid., no. 2967.

45   *Cal. papal letters, 1198–1304*, p. 267.

46   Ibid., p. 297.

47   *The Black Book of Limerick*, no. lvi, p. 48.

for Aymer, bishop-elect of Winchester. His departure without any apparent provision for the administration of his diocese during his absence has led to the belief that he was an Englishman. The prolongation of his sojourn in England was soon cause for complaint at home, but a royal decree issued before the end of 1256 stated that he was remaining in England at the king's instance and ordered John FitzGeoffrey, the justiciar, 'to respite till the feast of St. John the Baptist [24 June] all personal plaints against Laurence in that country'.[48] Subsequent letters issued by Henry III to the tenants of the bishop of Cork 'touching an aid being made to him' suggest that the English king was well repaid for any favour shown to Bishop Laurence.[49] Obscurity veils the bishop's movements from 1258 until his death which occurred before 27 March 1265.

The aid levied by Henry III in 1256 on the bishop's tenants was only one of many incidental customs and imposts demanded of the citizens of Cork in return for the accumulated privileges of their charters. Other demands on them included levies of money, provisions, ships and personnel to support and supplement the army. More specifically, we find that in 1234 Richard Curteis, a burgess of Bristol, was licensed to ship to Cork 100 quarters each of wheat and oatmeal for export to England.[50] Ten years later (1244) King Henry III sent to Cork for 200 crannocks of wheat and required that Cork together with the other provisioning centres—Dublin, Waterford and Drogheda —'shall retain in their port[s] all the ships and boats capable of carrying 40 men and shall send them to Carlingford . . . to transport the K[ing]'s army of Ireland'.[51] When in August 1255 the expedition destined for the Scottish wars ran short of provisions at Grannock, the king commanded the men of Dublin, Waterford, Drogheda, Limerick, Cork and Carrickfergus 'to send all the provisions they can collect together with the merchants of those provisions', and the justiciary at the same time was ordered 'to raise on loan or on the Michaelmas rents of Ireland, or out of the K[ing]'s treasure on hand, 500 marks to purchase corn and flour, which he shall send as quickly as possible, . . . [and to cause] as many wine and provision merchants as he can [to come] with masons and other workmen'.[52] Early

48   *Cal. doc. Ire., 1252–84*, no. 481.

49   Ibid., no. 1256.

50   *Cal. doc. Ire., 1171–1251*, no. 2226.

51   Ibid., no. 2687.

52   Ibid., no. 2768.

proof this of the traditional English blunder of engaging in warfare without realizing the necessity and importance of a properly-functioning commissariat.

WILLIAM OF JERPOINT, O.CIST., 1266–1267

On 27 March 1265 Geoffrey O'Brennan and David de Lang, treasurer and precentor of Cork, were deputed to announce the death of their bishop and secure royal licence to elect. Their failure to exhibit the customary letters patent from the chapter provoked the king's disapproval and the *congé d'élire* was accompanied by the proviso that the dean and chapter 'Shall transmit by the person to be elected letters patent testifying that licence to elect had been demanded'.[53] The dean and chapter were furthermore exhorted to elect a bishop who would be devout to God, useful to the church and faithful to the king and his kingdom. Capitular choice fell upon William, monk of the Cistercian abbey of Jerpoint in the parish of Thomastown, county Kilkenny. His election was confirmed by James, cardinal-bishop of Porto and Saint Ruffina, but the temporalities were not restored until 28 November 1266.[54] No explanation is given in the records for the long delay in restoration of the temporalities: the normal period between election and restoration was about three months. A protracted vacancy between the death of Laurence and the election of William was probably the cause of the delay. William of Jerpoint had such a very short episcopal reign that Sir James Ware and John Lynch doubt his consecration,[55] but this doubt is removed by the fact that on 8 July 1267 the Cork chapter again announced the death of their bishop and secured the necessary royal permission to elect a successor.

Though William of Jerpoint's episcopate was too short and uneventful to merit inclusion in either papal or state records, this elusive Cistercian occupies a unique position in the annals of his own monastery. In an age when Cistercians were more actively participant in church affairs than at present, he was the only monk of the abbey of Jerpoint to achieve episcopal status.[56] He was the first of two Cistercian monks to rule the

53   *Cal. doc. Ire., 1252–84*, no. 767.

54   Ibid., no. 806.

55   Lynch, *De praesulibus Hib.*, ii, 142, states: 'Guillelmus de Ieripont, monachus Cistertiensis coenobii Ieripontis in agro Kilkeniensi, sedis huius temporalia 28 Novembris 1266 consecutus est. *Si consecratus fuerit*, episcopatum exiguo tempore gessit . . .'

56   Carrigan, *The History and Antiquities of the Diocese of Ossory*, iv, 284–96, where the annals of Jerpoint are outlined.

see of Finbarr and he is the earliest known bishop of Cork the representation of whose features has been, however imperfectly, preserved for posterity. A recent article on the sculpture of the cloister of Jerpoint Abbey contains the following relevant observations:

> On the back of the slab [called Pier 2, on the front of which an abbot is depicted] is one of the best known of the Jerpoint figures: an enthusiastically blessing cleric usually referred to without hesitation as a bishop. Such he probably is, although the absence of a mitre is most unusual in Irish bishops who are portrayed giving a blessing or benediction. The figure appears to wear an alb, amice, chasuble, stole and foot-gear. His foliate crozier turns outward, but the notion that the crozier of a bishop faces always away from him, that of an abbot toward himself, has too many exceptions to have any real value in an attempt to differentiate between the two. The close resemblance between this figure and that on a tomb slab in the chancel of the abbey has often been remarked. Here, too, the mitre is lacking. But the contrast between the two figures on Pier 2 indeed seems to be that of abbot versus bishop. The possibility that the bishop may be a reference to Bishop William, who had been a monk at Jerpoint and died in 1267, soon after his elevation to the episcopal chair, must be considered. At any rate, the occupants of Pier 2 make us aware of the presence of both regular and secular clergy of importance, and of the blessings of the church.[57]

REGINALD, 1267–1276

In Reginald we encounter another semi-anonymous cleric from the diocese of Cashel who, like Bishop Laurence (1248–65), makes his entrance and exit on the page of history without either pedigree or surname. David de Lang and Geoffrey O'Brennan were again chosen on 8 July 1267 to announce the death of their bishop (William) and to petition royal licence to elect a successor.[58] In due course Reginald, treasurer of Cashel, became bishop of Cork and the king commanded William de Bakepuz, his escheator, to restore the temporalities 'when the elect shall have been confirmed and his fealty according to custom received'.[59] Bishop Reginald's appointment was

---

57 E. C. Rae, 'The Sculpture of the Cloister of Jerpoint Abbey', *R.S.A.I.* Jn., xcvi (1966), 71.

58 *Cal. doc. Ire., 1252–84*, no. 824.

59 Ibid., no. 829.

duly confirmed by the metropolitan and the temporalities were restored to him on 5 August 1267. Little is known of Reginald's activities as bishop of Cork beyond that in 1270 he recovered from Prince Edward the patronage of the churches of Kilmonoge, Saint Mary le Nard and the chapel of Saint Peter's, Dungarvan. The grant was to lead to litigation during the reign of his successor. The church of Kilmonoge had been granted by Richard de Cogan to the monks of Saint Nicholas, Exeter, while grants in Dungarvan in the northern suburbs had been confirmed on the abbey of Saint Thomas at Dublin by Milo de Cogan and Robert FitzStephen. By inference, therefore, contacts between Cork and these extra-diocesan houses were already severed. The recovery, however, in no way compromised royal control over ecclesiastical appointments in Cork, since in 1275 Edward I presented Richard le Blund to the church of Fersketh (?) in the diocese of Cork which was declared to be 'in the king's gift by reason of the custody of the lands and heir of John de Cogan, the younger, deceased, tenant-in-chief'.[60]

Richard de Carew died in Cork in 1272 and state records of the period show that the situation in Cork was then greatly overcharged. At Easter 1275 the inhabitants were obliged to lend money 'to maintain war against Irish enemies and citizens' who showed determined opposition to additional imposts placed upon them in order that town dwellers might enjoy extra liberties.[61] In the midst of this confusion Bishop Reginald died on 16 December 1276, and according to custom the temporalities of the diocese reverted to the king's escheator whose receipts have already furnished us with the earliest indication of the sources from which the medieval bishops of Cork derived their revenue.

ROBERT MAC DONNCHADA, O.CIST., 1277–1302

In striking contrast to his predecessors, Bishop Robert Mac Donnchada, Cork's second Cistercian bishop in ten years, is presented in the calendared records with a notoriety unsurpassed by any of his contemporaries. Licence to elect was issued to the dean and chapter of Cork on 24 January 1277,[62] royal assent was given on 8 May and on 11 June the king 'having learned by letter of David, archbishop of Cashel, that he had confirmed the election of Brother Robert, monk of the

60   *Cal. pat. rolls, 1272–81*, 4 Edward I, m. 10.

61   *Cal. doc. Ire., 1252–84*, nos. 904, 931.

62   Ibid., no. 1315.

Cistercian Order, as Bishop of Cork', accepted the confirmation, acknowledged the fealthy of the elect and restored the temporalities to him.[63] The pipe rolls of Edward I make it clear that the returns from the temporalities dating from the death of Reginald to the appointment of Robert Mac Donnchada realised £32 13s 10d, and that this sum *was delivered to Robert the monk*.[64] Only one other bishop of Cork, Roger Ellesmere (1396–1406), was to share with Bishop Mac Donnchada the distinction of receiving back payment of temporalities which had accumulated during a vacancy. As a bribe (if it was such) this liberality failed, for during the course of the thirteenth century the authorities had no more uncompromising cleric to deal with than this Cistercian bishop of Cork.

Robert Mac Donnchada was in England in 1287 and exercised episcopal functions there to the extent of granting an indulgence of forty days to all who visited the Lady chapel in the priory of Maiden Bradley in Wiltshire. On his return to Cork he received the Austin friars into the diocese about the year 1288, but he went to England again in 1291 and in 1292 he was acting as suffragan in Winchester under special protection from Edward I.[65] Once again he granted an indulgence (of twenty days this time) to persons visiting the same Lady chapel and praying for the soul of Richard de Piperharewe.[66] A letter written as recently as April 1909 carries confirmation of this indulgence. The writer, Rev. Arthur Stanley, states, 'I have copies of two indulgences dated at Maidenbradley, Wilts, one in 1287 and the other in 1292, granted by *Frater Robert, Episcopus Corcagensis* to all who visited the tomb of Richard de Peperharow buried in the cemetery of the priory of Maidenbradley, and pray for his soul and all the faithful departed. *Noster patronus beatus Finbar* is mentioned . . .' The original of this letter may be seen in the reference department of the Cork County Library interleaved in the third volume of Brady's *Records of Cork*.

Even during the period of his English mission, Robert Mac Donnchada's career was chequered by almost unbroken conflicts with the civil authorities, and he may well be regarded as the earliest personification of the growing self-determination of the Irish church against the claims of the English kings. The roll

63   Ibid., no. 1360.

64   As stated in patent 10 Edward I.

65   *Cal. doc. Ire., 1285–92*, nos. 971, 1147.

66   Ibid., no. 215; also in *Cal. pat. rolls, 1281–1303*, pp. 447, 506.

of receipts for the Easter term of 1286 shows that Bishop Mac Donnchada was fined £6 for trespass. He was fined £21 for contempt on 25 June and £7 13s 0½d for the same offence on 30 September. All such offences to the contrary he was appointed by Edward I in 1287 to investigate local disturbances by means of which certain merchants of Kilmehalok (between Douglas and Crosshaven) 'had impeded the citizens in freely buying and selling by wholesale or retail, their merchandise in the town of Kilmehalok' as had been their custom.⁶⁷ The bishop, whose initial is incorrectly given as 'P.', was to receive the attorneys of the mayor and bailiffs of Cork and certify their names to the king. The sequel to this inquiry is not recorded, but the integration of the native Irish into the corporate life of the city may be explained by analogy with developments elsewhere. Because of the immunities and privileges enjoyed by them, the corporate towns were a consistently loyal English element in Ireland, but it was not until they became oligarchic they they became anti-Irish in sympathy. The earliest civic records of many towns contained many Gaelic names, civic freedom was frequently granted to the Irish and the medieval rule of 'a year and a day' enabled many of the betaghs and poor tenant class to escape from feudal servitude into urban freedom. There were openings in all cities for law-abiding and industrious Irishmen, charters of whose admission to English law and liberty are recorded by Gilbert in his *Historic and Municipal Documents*. The main source of native resentment, in the thirteenth century especially, appears to have been the belief that the immunities enjoyed by a city had to be balanced by imposts laid on goods produced outside the walls. Apart from the incident just quoted and one isolated eruption under Bishop Reginald in 1275 there is little evidence to suggest that the presence of the native Irish proved too great a hindrance to peaceful commercial relations between colonists and natives in thirteenth-century Cork, although the citizens in later centuries used the alleged attacks of the Irish as an excuse for avoiding payment of the fee farm of the city.

Bishop Mac Donnchada was again fined £16 13s 9d for contempt in 1288. In December 1291 he was amerced before Stephen, archdeacon of Tuam and justiciary of Ireland, 'in £100 for contempt' and he was fined £40 by the same justiciary for having held pleas in the ecclesiastical court 'touching the king's crown and dignity'.⁶⁸ Because of his

67 *Cal. doc. Ire., 1285–92*, nos. 251, 271, 310.

68 Ibid., nos. 403, 1000.

refusal to pay, the authorities levied £45 5s 10d on his goods and chattels, and even though he was pardoned a balance of £94 14s 2d, which represented arrears of amerciaments, he was reported in 1294 as owing £54 14s 2d for contempt, £40 for holding pleas in Court Christian concerning chattels and debts having no bearing on testaments or matrimony, and 40 shillings 'because he did not come when summoned'.[69] Three years later (1297) Bishop Mac Donnchada acknowledged in presence of John Wogan, justiciary, that he owed Master John Lovel an annual rent of 40 shillings together with £20 arrears,[70] and in 1298 he was still £54 14s 2d in debt.

Two important issues led to a confrontation between Bishop Mac Donnchada and Edward I in July 1297. The king caused four writs to be promulgated against the bishop demanding the advowsons of the churches of Kilmonoge, Saint Mary le Nard, Saint Peter's, Dungarvan, and the advowson of the church of Nohoval (Nothynual). For the three city churches the bishop referred to King Edward's earlier grant to Bishop Reginald, and he invoked a charter by which King Henry III had granted these churches to the bishop of Cork and to his successors in perpetual alms. Consequently King Edward had no present right to the churches. But judgement was given against the bishop on the plea that when Edward made the grants to Bishop Reginald he had no real right to the advowsons seeing that his father, Henry III, was still alive. It would seem that notwithstanding his father's donation of Ireland to him in 1254, Prince Edward's status was merely that of a viceroy, and that this status precluded all independent action on his part. As to the church of Nohoval, Bishop Mac Donnchada denied the validity of the king's right to base his claim on the fact that 'King John had held Nohoval', and he insisted that the continuance of the confirmatory charter of Henry III 'ought not to hurt the King' because 'at the time of its making no right descended to the King.'[71] The bishop's remonstrances fell upon deaf ears, and by 1299 the king had recovered the advowsons of all four churches.

The second confrontation revolved upon the problem of taxation. From the beginning of his reign the exigencies of King Edward's wars in Scotland and Gascony made such insupportable demands on Cork that bishop and king were

---

69   Cited in *Pipe Roll, 20 Edward I*.

70   *Cal. justic. rolls Ire., 1295–1303*, p. 97.

71   Ibid., p. 143.

inevitably drawn into bitter conflict. In 1278 certain merchants from Lucca were appointed 'to receive to the K[ing]'s use half-a-mark for each sack of wool . . . from each 300 wool fells . . . and one mark from each last of hides leaving Ireland'.[72] By March 1295 royal writs commanded the treasurer, William de Estdene, to provide with all speed from merchants and others in the country about Cork and Youghal 'ten or twelve or more shiploads of good wheat and oats and send them to Bayonne, Lyons, Bourg-sur-Mer and those parts'.[73] An extraordinary levy on corn was ordered in Cork *only* in 1297 and was extended to the clergy who were believed 'to have quantities beyond their reasonable sustenance'. Bishop Mac Donnchada, Bishop Nicholas de Effingham of Cloyne and Philip Oshefeth, dean of Cloyne, resisted the king's collectors and 'caused to be excommunicated all who put hand on that corn, . . . so impeding the ministers of the King and the execution of the business which he had at heart'.[74] When William de Muenes, whom Edward had presented to Holy Trinity in 1295, seized corn at Caherlag and other corn outside the walls of the town, Bishop Mac Donnchada and Thomas de Lang 'caused the corn so seized for the expedition to be threshed for their own will'.[75] At a special court summoned in Cork John Wogan sentenced Thomas de Lang and the dean of Cloyne to jail and threatened confiscation of temporalities against the two bishops. The confiscations were later commuted to a money payment. The bishop and dean of Cloyne were fined twenty and fifteen marks respectively; Bishop Mac Donnchada was fined fifteen marks, his payment of which is extremely doubtful. Judging from the fines levied, the temporalities of Cloyne seem to have been greater than those of Cork in July 1297. The final charge invoiced against Robert Mac Donnchada was that at Lenoun in 1297 he took a stack of wheat and a stack of oats thereby inflicting damage to the tune of thirty pounds on Andrew de Arundel.[76] It was during these final years of Bishop Mac Donnchada's episcopate that the famous *Clericis laicos* of Boniface VIII was issued (1296) forbidding secular rulers to exact or ecclesiastical rulers to pay taxation without papal consent. Oddly enough, the bull, which was directed mainly at Philip the Fair of France,

72 *Cal. doc. Ire., 1252–84*, no. 1429.

73 *Cal. doc. Ire., 1293–1301*, no. 197.

74 *Cal justic. rolls Ire., 1295–1303*, p. 95.

75 Ibid.

76 Ibid., p. 162.

was effectively invoked in Ireland against the exactions of
native Irish chieftains and petty kings in the northern province,
and while there is no supporting evidence from the provinces
of Tuam and Cashel where similar problems must have existed,[77]
Bishop Robert Mac Donnchada of Cork stands out as an uncompromising advocate of the implications of *Clericis laicos*,
not indeed against the encroachments of any local prince, but
against the importunate demands of the English king.[78]
Episcopal opposition notwithstanding, appeals and demands
continued to pour in from England. Various sums were passed
in 1298 as payment for the provision of wheat, oats, wines, fish
and other supplies at Cork, Waterford and other places in
Munster for the king's expedition to Scotland.[79] The army was
again so reduced in January 1300 that the king asked that men
and provisions be collected in Ireland and that merchants in
Dublin and Cork should send supplies to Carlisle 'for the salvation of the K[ing]'s crown'.[80] Fines collected on this occasion
included huge sums for wine for the king's castles.[81] The
fourteenth century opened with an appeal from Edward I to
the merchants of Cork for two ships 'to totally suppress the
malice of the Scotch'.[82]

In April 1301, that is, during the final year of Robert Mac
Donnchada's episcopate, a case arose in Cork concerning the
petition of 'Agnes de Hareford and the nuns of the house of
St. John the Baptist [in a street called] Saint John Street in the
suburbs of Cork'.[83] An inquisition taken at Cork on 21 August
1301 before Prior William de Ross of the hospital of Saint John
of Jerusalem, *locum tenens* of the justiciary, returned that it
would not be prejudicial to the king to grant licence to this
recluse for certain lands petitioned in her behalf. The lands
were:

1. One carucate in Clenboly in Inysmore (probably
    Clonmel on the Great Island) and the advowson of the
    church of Dungourney. Grantee: William de Barry.
2. Twenty librates of land in Muscry, Olethan and Obaun:
    the land in Muscry (Muskerry-Donegan in Buttevant)

77   Otway-Ruthven, *Med. Ire.*, pp. 135–6.

78   Details of clerical opposition to taxation will be outlined in Chapter 13.

79   *Cal. doc. Ire., 1293–1301*, nos. 523, 534, 589, 632.

80   Ibid., nos. 716, 717, 754.

81   *Cal. doc. Ire., 1302–07*, no. 56. The combined takings were £237 4s 5d.

82   Ibid., no. 777.

83   *Cal. doc. Ire., 1293–1301*, no. 801.

and Olethan (Barrymore, east Cork) by service of £10 a year to be paid to Maurice de Carew of Castlecore, Ballinacurra, tenant-in-chief; the land in Obaun (Ibawne and Barryroe around Timoleague) to be held of Thomas de Multon free of service. Grantee: Sir John de Barry.

3. A carucate and a half of land in Garrancor, Obaun (Garrancore in the parish of Kilgarriff near Clonakilty) and Kyllynleth in Funerthrach (now Killeenleagh in the parish of Caheragh in the ancient deanery of *Fonn Iartharach*); the advowson of the church of Saint Mary de Karatha (Caheragh); two acres in Kilcoan (Kilquane) and the advowson of the church there; all of the fee of Gerald FitzMaurice. Grantee: John FitzGilbert who holds by service of one penny a year.

4. Two acres in Kylmyde in Kynalletha (Ballymartle in the barony of Kinalea) and the advowson of its church; two acres in Katherlaga (Caherlag near Little Island) and the advowson of the church; and two acres of land and the advowson of the church of Le Chyrcheton in Ynismatnel (now Wallingstown, Little Island). Grantee: Philip FitzRobert.

The only exception to Agnes de Hareford's petition were the twenty librates offered by Sir John de Barry in Muscry, Olethan and Obaun which were ordered to be withdrawn. The king's agreement to the remaining grants was based on the realization that in the four neighbouring counties and five adjacent bishoprics there was no house for women of religion 'save the said house of St John which is not yet built up nor established according to its rule'.[84] In support of the foundation it was stated that it would redound to the convenience of the country if the house could be endowed, 'for there is no other house of nuns where knights and other free men in those parts may have their daughters brought up or maintained, nor in [the] three counties adjoining'.[85]

It was on this note that Bishop Robert Mac Donnchada's career terminated. The *Annals of Loch Cé* carry a simple record of his death: 'The Bishop of Cork, a Grey (Cistercian) Monk, rested in Christ, 1302.' The new century ushered in a great native resurgence which was destined to have important bearing on the Irish church. Before passing to a consideration of this native revival however, several important details of diocesan

---

84 Ibid.

85 *Cal. justic. rolls Ire., 1295–1303*, pp. 154–5.

organization claim attention; firstly, a survey of female religious establishments in Ireland by way of elucidation and elaboration of Agnes de Hareford's petition for a nunnery in Cork in the opening years of the fourteenth century.

NUNS IN CORK

Records dealing with female religious establishments are more meagre than those for communities of men. Indeed, in many cases details of religious houses for women are non-existent for several centuries before the general suppression in Reformation times. For this reason it is impossible to assess the size and state of many communities of nuns in the early sixteenth century; by that time several had already become extinct or were beginning to decline. Many early Celtic abbeys of women died out long before the Synod of Rathbreasail (1111); others again before the Anglo-Norman invasion (1169), so that only a few continued into the medieval period, and many of these became Augustinian houses in the twelfth century. Kildare and other Celtic abbeys had communities of men and women living under a common rule but strictly separated as regards even visual intercourse. In such cases the abbess was usually the common superior, and in Kildare the men's community appears to have been relegated to a secondary position by the twelfth century. The line of Kildare abbesses can be traced from about the eighth century to 1171: the early title of abbess was *Banairchinneach* or *Dominatrix* which from the middle of the tenth century yielded place to *comharba Brighde*. Establishments of the Kildare type were also to be found on the continent, particularly at Fontevrault in France and also in England where double monasteries for nuns and regular canons were founded about 1130 by Gilbert of Sempringham. The Gilbertines continued as a double order until the suppression of English monasteries in 1538. Other double monasteries in England were destroyed in the ninth and tenth centuries, and among the Premonstratensians such double monasteries were discouraged after 1140. It is of particular significance for Irish history, however, that Abbot Gervase of Arrouaise (1121–47) admitted both men and women to the religious life and that Arrouaise became the motherhouse of a mixed order.

Saint Malachy's visit to Arrouaise in 1139–40 was followed by the introduction of the rule and observances of Arrouaise into many places in Ireland, while from *La Vision de Tondale* it is clear that the great reformer established Irish houses for nuns in 1144.[86] The first of these, Saint Mary's Abbey, Clonard, continued to be the Irish motherhouse for all Arroasian Augustinian canonesses until 1224 when it was superseded by Kilcreevanty. Its possessions as confirmed by Pope Celestine III pertain also to churches of canons regular and suggest that the churches were shared by canons and canonesses alike. The nuns may have formed small communities which were attached to the monasteries of canons, but they had their own special residences and were assigned special duties in the almonries. References to sisters in connection with the Cistercian abbeys of Mellifont, Inislounaght and Jerpoint in the visitation of Stephen of Lexington in 1228 are somewhat difficult to explain in view of the Cistercian prohibition of contacts between monks and women. It is possible that here too the sisters were introduced to serve in the almonries and lay infirmaries, but they were denied admission into the cloisters. Irregularities and scandals led to the removal of sisters from these Cistercian abbeys shortly after 1228. Sisters as well as brothers were to be found in at least three of the Augustinian priory hospitals of the *Fratres Cruciferi* in Ireland which were founded after 1185. It is beyond question too that there were sisters in the Benedictine monastery-hospitals of Waterford and Cork, but these were among the many which became extinct before the Reformation.[87]

The earliest reference to a nunnery in Cork is the sixth-century monastery built at Boirneach *als* Ballyvourney for Saint Gobnait.[88] Its existence after 1172 is extremely doubtful. Of far greater significance is that section of chapter 10 in the Irish *Life of Saint Finbarr* which describes a community of holy women at Etargabail. The identification of these holy women proves beyond doubt that the nunnery of Etargabail· (not to be confused with another place of the same name in upper Ossory) was in west Munster not far from the saint's own hermitage of Gougane Barra. First on the list is *Derbhshiur Bairri* or, more precisely, Lasair, daughter of Amairgen, sister of Bairre, also referred to as Lasair of Achad Durbcon.[89] The Kilbarry-Macloneigh-Macroom district is therefore implicit.

86   V. H. Friedel and Kuno Meyer, *La Vision de Tondale*, p. 56: 'St Malachias qui fu après lui qui vint a Rome au temps Pape Innocent . . . fonda en se temps xliiii aneies de moinnes de chanoinnes et de nonnains.'

87   I am indebted to Father Aubrey Gwynn, S.J., for this summary, extracted from a survey completed by him and Mr. Neville Hadcock, the manuscript of which I was permitted to read.

88   Colgan, *Acta SS Hib.*, p. 315.

89   *Genealogiae regum Hib.*, p. 59.

After Lasair comes Crothru, daughter of Conall, a well-known saint of the Corca Laighdhe who is listed in the *Martyrology of Donegal* as Clothre of Inse Duine, that is, Inchidony Island near Clonakilty. Crothru's father, according to the ancient genealogies, was a contemporary of Saint Finbarr. Next on the list are the three daughters of Mac Carthain: Coch, the nun of Rosbanagher, Moshillan of Rath Mor and Scothnait of Cluain Bec. The church of Kilcoe, situated about four miles west of Skibbereen and in the diocese of Ross, preserves the memory of Coch (*Cill Coiche*); this is the Cell Cohi mentioned in the decretal letter of 1199 as belonging to the diocese of Cork.[90] Scothnait of Cluain Bec, who has been confused with Scuithin, a man-saint of Cluain Beg in the Glen of Aherlow, has probably some connection with Kilscohanagh, an old church site near Drimoleague, which is mentioned in the patent rolls of James I and in the Down Survey.[91] No trace remains of the holy woman named Moshillan of Rath Mor, although there is a Rathmore in the parish of Tullagh, south-west of Skibbereen.

The Etargabail list concludes with the three daughters of Lugaid, 'Duine, Her and Brighit of Airnidhe', who have been identified by Hodges and Smith[92] as 'Duineda of Achad Duin, Echtach and Brigit of Tipranandhe'. Achad Duine is the modern Aghadown in the diocese of Ross. No other reference to Her is known to be extant, but Brighit of Airnidhe may be identical with Brigh of Ernaidhe who is mentioned in the *Book of Leinster*. Ernaidhe is the more common form of Airnidhe, which written as *Oirnidhe* was another name for Saint Gobnait's church at Ballyvourney.[93] Another clue may be found in the linguistic distinction between Brigit (Brigid) and Brigh (Brighit). Churches named after Brigit were called Kilbreedy or Kilbride; foundations of Saint Brigh appear as Kilbree (*Cill Brighe*). By analogy, Kilbree near Inchidony and Kilbree (Kilbreagh) in Durrus may well have some connection with the Brighit or Brigh of Airnidhe who features on the Etargabail list. Like the Etargabail of upper Ossory this early Cork nunnery may have originally followed the rule of Saint

---

90 The compiler of the Etargabail list identifies Coch with Saint Cochae of Rossbanagher near Ennis, county Clare, who was a friend of Saint Ciaran of Cape Clear, situated not far distant from Kilcoe. Assuming this to be correct, Coch would have been earlier than Saint Finbarr.

91 In modern Ordnance Survey maps the final -t has been dropped.

92 R.I.A., MS No. 12.

93 D. Ó hÉaluighthe, 'St. Gobnet of Ballyvourney', *Cork Hist. Soc. Jn.*, lvii (1952), 45.

Brigid, and like the Ossory foundation it may have become Augustinian some time during the twelfth century, if indeed its span of life extended that far.

From the sixth century, therefore, until the petition of Agnes de Hareford at the beginning of the fourteenth century, there are no references to female religious communities in Cork apart from the sisters attached to the Benedictine priory of Saint John the Evangelist. Dugdale's statement that the nunnery of Saint John the Baptist was a Benedictine foundation is not in accord with another theory which maintains that the nuns were Augustinian. From this complete lack of evidence as to the existence of educational establishments administered by nuns the contention that Agnes de Hareford's nunnery was the only one of its kind in Cork and the neighbouring counties appears to have been true, notwithstanding the tradition which connects some kind of teaching centre with the church of Saint Brigid. Here, as in other aspects of diocesan history, lack of records makes any satisfactory assessment of existing conditions virtually impossible. It would appear, however, that with the possible exception of Ballymacadane, which is said to have been founded about the year 1450 for 'Austine Nuns',[94] there was no convent for female religious in the pre-Reformation diocese of Cork.

---

94 Smith, *History of Cork*, i, 154. The abbey of Ballymacadane will form the subject of a later chapter.

VIII

The Coming of the Friars

Positively and negatively the thirteenth century is rightly considered a nonpareil in the history of the Catholic Church and of Europe generally. On the negative side it began with the turbulent reign of King John of England and ended with sounds of the first remote rumblings of the Hundred Years' War. In Ireland it saw the progressive Normanization of conquered territories and sowed the seeds of future troubles which aggravated Anglo-Irish relations in the following centuries. On the continent it witnessed the debacle of the Fourth Crusade, the bitter struggle between Empire and Papacy and the failure to bring about reunion with the Eastern Church at the Second Council of Lyons in 1274. Positively, this was the century of centralization and reform in the church; the century of the great Pope Innocent III and of the Fourth Lateran Council of 1215. All through the century, thanks to the growing centralization of the church under the papacy, the pope's *plenitudo potestatis* became every day more operative in areas of legislation, judicial appeals and finance. The thirteenth century saw the great cathedrals of Europe go spiralling heavenwards, and it was a century of intense intellectual activity in which the newly formed universities, the lectures of cathedral chancellors and theologians and the grammar and parochial schools provided new and attractive educational opportunities for the clergy. The pity is that those who availed themselves of the opportunities offered were in the minority. Finally, the thirteenth century was pre-eminently the century of the friars and of the mendicant ideal, for the friars revolutionized the technique of the pastoral ministry, they were a challenge and an answer to the moral and social ills of the time, and they aimed at rekindling the embers of love in a world that had gone cold.

The mendicant ideal of voluntary poverty which was the actualization of the dream of Francis of Assisi (1182–1226) was a protest against the traditional concept of monastic life hitherto characterized mainly by a withdrawal from the world for purposes of personal sanctification. The friars aimed to live entirely among men, to share in the hardships and sufferings of the poor and by so doing to propagate the message of the Gospel. The new movement had its critics as well as its supporters, but efforts to wean Francis from his experiment were unsuccessful. 'The Lord hath called me by the way of humility', he said, 'and He has shown me the way of simplicity, and I do not want you to mention to me any other rule, neither that of S. Augustine, nor of S. Benedict, nor of S. Bernard. And the Lord told me that he wished me to be a new fool (*novellus pazzus*) in the world and that He did not want to lead us by any other way than by that wisdom.'[1] It was Francis of Assisi's good fortune to live during the pontificate of Innocent III, the reforming pope who realized that old methods would no longer suffice and who sought a body of men inspired with lively faith and the evangelical ideal, unencumbered by worldly goods, who would approach the people with open arms proclaiming anew the words of love and truth.[2] By 1210 when Francis visited Rome and won the pope's verbal approval, the Order of Friars Minor[3] was born and a new and glorious page was opened in the annals of the church. Further confirmation came at the Lateran Council of 1215, and by 1221 the friars were re-evangelizing Europe and the East, travelling everywhere with that freedom wherewith Christ had made them free. Saint Francis had truly supplied the church with a new force perfectly tailored and adapted to contemporary needs. Final confirmation of the order came in 1223 from Pope Honorius III.

On the reverse of the mendicant coin was the experiment of Dominic Guzman (1171–1221) whose Order of Preachers was the solution to the parochial ills and heresies of the time. He considered that the parochial clergy were too ignorant and the regulars (Benedictines and Cistercians) too exclusive and remote from the needs of everyday life. He wanted an organization which would be neither monastic nor secular, and while his followers would be 'regulars' by their submission to discipline and their training, they were to enjoy the same liberty of movement as the Franciscans, and like them were to proclaim the truth of the Christian faith at every opportunity.[4] The

1 John R. H. Moorman, *Church Life in England in the Thirteenth Century*, p. 366, quoting *Verba S. Francisci*, cap. v, in *Documenta Antiqua Franciscana*, ed. Lemmens, i, 104.

2 Henri Daniel-Rops, *Cathedral and Crusade*, p. 178.

3 The Franciscans were not officially called Friars Minor for another six years.

4 A. G. Little, 'The Mendicant Orders', in *Cambridge Medieval History*, vi, 757–61.

Order of Preachers received papal approbation and confirmation at the end of 1216.

Initially, Francis and Dominic shared the same ideal of launching a new type of religious life unfettered by the conservatism of the older monastic system. From the *poverello* of Assisi the founder of the Friars Preachers imbibed the mendicant ideal, not perhaps with the same sense of total abandonment to divine providence but in a manner at once evidently in contrast with the luxurious living of contemporary society both secular and ecclesiastical. Dominic's formal object was to save the church from the assaults of heresy, more particularly the Albigensian heresy then prevalent in Languedoc; hence his insistence on an educated clergy capable of disputing on equal terms with the adversaries of truth. Study held pride of place in the Dominican *horarium*; even the divine office was to be recited *breviter et succincte* so that its length would not impede the studious. Francis of Assisi, on the other hand, had no formal policy save that of literally following the Gospel's precepts, thereby—in the words used by the council fathers of Vatican II—radiating before all men the loveable features of Jesus Christ. But while both founders differed in incidentals each assimilated something from the other—the Dominicans accepted poverty as a necessity of their lives, and the Franciscans were soon to be found holding their own with the Friars Preachers in the university centres of Europe.

The success of the mendicant movement was phenomenal. It came at a time when the growth of urban life was creating new problems for the church, and the friars became immediately popular with the town and city dwellers who flocked in steadily increasing numbers to their sermons,[5] for a sermon in the thirteenth century was something unusual. Most of the early friaries were built, if not within, at least close to the walls of medieval towns, and in many places the wall itself served as part of their boundary. Franciscans and Dominicans had early foundations in Cork. The Augustinian eremites or Austin friars who also adopted the mendicant ideal were of later

---

5   Moorman, *Church Life in England in the Thirteenth Century*, 400–1, has the following eulogy on the friars as representing the purest and strongest element in the life of the thirteenth-century church: 'They brought new life into the parishes, stirring up the minds and the affections of men and women. They aroused even the clergy to a deeper sense of responsibility and encouraged them to give more help to their people. They captured the Universities, forcing them to look higher than mere academic discussions of trivialities, and to see the part which the lecture-rooms could play in meeting the spiritual and mental hunger of men. They built up a whole network of schools from which all could benefit. Above all, they provided a system, full of life and vigour and austerity, in which those who were prepared to forsake all for Christ's sake could find their spiritual home.' John Moorman is Anglican bishop of Ripon in England.

vintage, as were also the Carmelites.[6] Each order had its own contribution to offer as a spiritual leaven in the diocese.

THE FRIARS PREACHERS

Arriving within sixty years of the Norman conquest, the mendicant friars who came from England to this country in the early decades of the thirteenth century were sponsored in most instances by Norman overlords; consequently, their early dispersal throughout the newly-settled areas was but natural. First to arrive were the Dominicans, although a persistent Franciscan tradition maintains that 'in 1214, while St. Francis yet lived, certain Franciscans who had left Compostella, while a convent was being built, landed in Ireland.'[7] The first Dominican foundation in Ireland was established in Dublin in 1224 under the auspices of Maurice FitzGerald. Shortly afterwards the Black Friars moved to Drogheda, thence to Kilkenny (1225), Waterford (1226) and Limerick (1227). They reached Cork in 1229. The patron of the Cork foundation was Philip Barry, a Welsh nobleman and ancestor of the Barrymore family in the county of Cork. The priory was situated outside the city wall on one of the marshy islets to the south-west and close to the cathedral church of Saint Finbarr. Thereafter called Saint Dominic's Island or Abbey Island, the site of which is fairly well defined in many of the early maps of Cork, the area covered by the precincts of the priory is now included in the district of Crosse's Green. The title chosen for the new religious house—Saint Mary of the Island—was a happy choice.[8] Its patroness was the Blessed Virgin Mary, its location was insular and it was necessary to distinguish it from the churches of Saint Mary le Nard and Saint Mary Shandon. The title of this first Dominican house in Cork is still preserved by the Sisters of Mercy; the boundary wall of their convent of Saint Maries of the Isle contains two closed-up window niches which are believed to have formed part of the thirteenth-century priory.

Although it is described in the annals of the Dominicans as

6 The Carmelites were established in Kinsale in 1334 under their prior Stephen Prene who received a quarter of land in Liscahan from their patron Robert FitzRichard Balrain. Very little of the early history of the priory is known, but tradition maintains that the friars looked after a leper settlement in the spittal lands close to Brown's Mills. The history of the Carmelites of Kinsale therefore belongs to a period later than that catered for in this volume.

7 E. B. Fitzmaurice and A. G. Little, *Materials for the History of the Franciscan Province of Ireland*, p. xii, n.

8 Thomas de Burgo, *Hibernia Dominicana*, p. 214.

magnifica Ecclesia and a state record of James I in 1616 refers
to 'the church, steeple and monastery', no further details remain
concerning the structure of the abbey or the lives of its inmates.
All that has come down to us is the fact that the Dominicans
in their island home had two treasured possessions, viz., a
highly-venerated image of Saint Dominic and an equestrian
statue of their patron, Philip Barry. Apart from the two window
niches in the rear wall of Saint Maries of the Isle, other extant
remains of the foundation are scanty. They include stones
inserted in the walls of the present priory on Pope's Quay and
a stone inscribed *In hoc signo vinces*, which was found in the
wall of a mill in Crosse's Green; but the fact that this stone
bears a recent date casts doubt on its authenticity as a relic of
the thirteenth-century friary. The ancient doorway forming
the dean's entrance in the south wall of Saint Fin Barre's
Cathedral is also believed to have belonged originally to the
Abbey of the Island,[9] but at this distance of time it would be
impossible to verify the truth of this claim.

A picture of Dominican life in medieval Cork may be gauged
by application to Cork of the features characteristic of Dominican
life elsewhere. The Dominican liturgy was introduced with
special emphasis on the evening devotion of compline through
which the Dominicans exercised an energetic apostolate among
the laity. The shrine containing the image of Saint Dominic
would have been a centre of devotion, particularly on the saint's
feast day; and there would have been Marian devotions likewise.
Preaching was presumably an outstanding feature of the friars'
activities, accompanied by the apostolate of the confessional
and possibly by that of teaching whenever opportunity presented
itself. The friars would also have extended their sphere of
action outside the precincts of their island home. The Abbey
of the Island, however, remained their only foundation in the
diocese of Cork; and while they established three monasteries
in the neighbouring diocese of Cloyne—Youghal in 1268,
Glanworth in 1474 and Castlelyons at some intermediate date—
they did not penetrate at all into the diocese of Ross.

For maintenance the Dominicans had various sources on
which to rely apart altogether from the continued liberality of
their patron's family. Saint Dominic's legislation on poverty
was never absolute, certain modifications were early introduced
and consequently we find the Dominicans accepting grants of

9   D. P. Fitzgerald, 'Old Cork Churches', *Cork Weekly Examiner*, 4 July 1925. More
likely, this door formed part of an earlier church of Saint Finbarr and was incorporated
in the later building.

land from private individuals. They also owned mills and
fishing rights, and while these might provide food for the
community there must have been a constant surplus which
added up to a steady income for all houses of the order in
Ireland. The Cork foundation seems to have fared well in this
respect, and while it could not compete with the Cistercian
abbey of Tracton, its landed property, its mills and its weirs,
according to an inventory taken in the sixteenth century, were
reasonably extensive. They added up to 'three small gardens
containing 1½ acres; two stangs of land [a stang was the
equivalent of one acre]; a fishing pool; half a salmon weir;
three acres of land called the half Skeaghbegge [Skehabeg];
ten acres of arable land and a mill at Rathmyny [Raheen];
twenty acres of arable land and twenty acres of pasture in
Galveiston',[10] that is, in Killeenreedowney, Ballyphehane,
which is given given as Galweyston *alias* Killen in a lease dated
1547.

In addition to the gifts of private individuals the Dominicans
in the royal cities of Dublin, Cork, Waterford, Limerick and
Drogheda were recipients of annual alms donated by English
kings. Such donations were commenced by Prince Edward I
before 1272, they can be traced to the year 1435 and there is no
indication of their discontinuance after the latter date. The
alms as such are interesting. On 30 June 1285 King Edward I
in a letter to the justiciar of Ireland and the treasurer of Dublin
stated that 'having ere he assumed the reins of government,
granted to the Dominican Friars of Dublin, Cork, Waterford,
Limerick and Drogheda, twenty-five marks a year at the
Exchequer of Dublin, the K[ing] . . . wishes to continue and
amplify this grace . . .'[11] From 1295 to 1302 seventy marks
or £46 13s 4d were equally divided between the Dominicans
and the Franciscans[12] except for the year 1298 when the alms
granted was only £30. Similar alms were continued for the
years 1305, 1306 and 1307.[13] These annual grants are still
traceable during the fifteenth century, and though there is a
noticeable diminution in the allowance,[14] Dublin and Drogheda
seem to have received continual alms from the English kings
until the Reformation.[15]

10   B.M., Rentals and Surveys Roll 936.

11   *Cal doc. Ire., 1285–92*, no. 97.

12   *Cal doc. Ire., 1293–1301*, nos. 273, 328, 346, 565, 682.

13   *Cal. doc. Ire., 1302–07*, nos. 475, 557.

14   *Cal. pat. rolls, 1299–1401, 1429–35, passim.*

15   D. D. C. Pochin Mould, *The Irish Dominicans*, p. 52.

For more than three hundred years the Cork Dominicans enjoyed certain important municipal privileges and immunities. In the early days of the foundation the privilege of sanctuary which applied to all medieval churches was extended in their case to embrace the entire island. The surrounding locality was also tax free; hence many people took up residence on the island in order to enjoy exemption from the *sessa* of soldiers and from other burdensome public levies. (The island's immunity was acknowledged even as late as the seventeenth century.) Another important privilege bestowed on the Dominicans of Saint Mary of the Island was the custody of the key of the south gate of the city which lay 'next the house of the Preaching Friars'. In former times custody of the city gates was committed to the mayor, bailiffs and other honest men of the city with free passage to and fro accorded to the friars and to good citizens recommended by them. In 1317 Sir Roger Mortimer and his council relieved the mayor of his charge which was then conferred as a favour on the Dominicans. Another connection between the house of Mortimer and the Dominicans of Cork is recorded for the year 1381 when the lord-lieutenant, Edmund Mortimer, earl of March and Ulster, lodged in the abbey of Saint Mary of the Island. He died there on 26/27 December from an ailment contracted while crossing the river in mid-winter and was, according to tradition, buried within the precincts of the priory. Gilbert, however, gives the church of Holy Trinity as his resting-place: *Edmund Mortimer . . . die Sancti Johannis Evangelistae, non sine magna mirore, omnium pacem Hiberniae diligenc (ium), apud civitatem Corcagiam diem clausit extremum, sepultusque est in ecclesia Sanctae Trinitatis ejusdem civitatis . . .*[16] The sudden death of Mortimer exposed the city and county of Cork to the attacks 'of the nations of the Barrets and other Irish enemies and rebels then at war', and to allay the general unrest a council was called at Cork on 9 January 1382.[17] At this council John Colton, dean of Saint Patrick's, Dublin, was sworn in as governor 'at the convent of the Preaching Friars'.[18] On 24 January Roger Mortimer, the new earl of March and then only seven years old, was appointed lord-lieutenant; the appointment was followed by the nomination of his uncle Sir Thomas Mortimer as deputy at an assembly held in Naas in the following March.

Shortly after their arrival in Ireland the Dominicans began

16   *Chartularies of St. Mary's Abbey*, ii, 285.

17   Otway-Ruthven, *Med. Ire.*, p. 315.

18   Lascelles, *Liber Munerum Publicorum Hiberniae*, ii, 198–9.

to be appointed to Irish bishoprics and were reasonably well represented in the episcopate during the thirteenth and early fourteenth centuries. To this period belongs Philip of Slane, a member of the community of Saint Mary of the Island, a scholar and a king's clerk who became bishop of Cork in 1321 and was later appointed to the king's council in Ireland. Another friar, John le Blound, ex-dean of Cloyne, was prior of Saint Mary of the Island in 1341, was appointed attorney by Philip of Slane but was defeated when proposed for the bishopric of Cork. A third member of the Cork community, who is known somewhat anonymously as *Johannes Corcagiensis*, was archbishop of Cologne in 1461.

Although the Dominicans first entered this country in the wake of the Anglo-Normans they owned several houses under Irish patronage, and Dominican foundations generally contained members of the Irish as well as of the English nation. Herein lay the seeds of friction and disorder which surfaced in accordance with current political trends and which led to inevitable tensions and hostilities within the various communities. Subjection to the English province until 1536 despite several efforts at autonomy made matters more difficult for the Dominicans than for the Franciscans who erected an Irish province at the outset of their mission, but whose history for the medieval period was particularly turbulent notwithstanding this autonomy. Racial disturbances coupled with the clash of loyalties involved in the Bruce invasion and subsequent conflicts produced in Cork as elsewhere relaxations in religious observance which finally attracted the notice of the Dominican superior general, who in 1484 took immediate steps to ensure that strict observance would be restored in Coleraine, Drogheda, Cork and elsewhere in Ireland. Thus was inaugurated the reform of of Raymond of Capua which gave a new look to Irish Dominicanism as will be shown in a subsequent chapter.

THE FRIARS MINOR

'This province of Ireland . . . had as its founder one of the companions of the seraphic father Francis . . .' wrote Francesco Gonzaga in his sixteenth-century *De origine Seraphicae Religionis Franciscanae*. From this statement was born the tradition, otherwise unsubstantiated, that the Franciscans came to this country in 1214. Franciscan annalists from Luke Wadding to the present time give the date of arrival as in or about 1231, perhaps even before that date, and maintain that the first Franciscans to reach Ireland came from England under Richard

of Ingewurde or Ingworth as provincial minister.[19] The Friars
Minor, like the Dominicans, were in many instances Norman-
sponsored, and like the Friars Preachers they too opted for
port towns and travelled along the major river valleys. The
only difference was in point of direction. From Dublin the
Dominicans spread southwards and westwards, while the
Franciscans, starting from Youghal and Cork, extended their
influence with almost phenomenal rapidity into the major
cities and towns throughout the provinces. Their Dublin
foundation was made within two years of their arrival from
England (1232), and by the mid-year of the thirteenth century
and within a quarter of a century of their first arrival the Friars
Minor were firmly established in the country from Cork in the
south to Carrickfergus in the north and with a bridgehead to
the west at Athlone.[20] It is unfortunate that no names have
come down to us from this early period.

According to Wadding, Archdall and others the Friars
Minor had nine houses in Cork county, four of which were
within the diocese of Cork, namely, the Grey Friary of Shandon
and the rural friaries of Bantry, Ballymacadane and Kilcrea.
The first house of the friars in Cork was the Grey Friary of
Shandon, a stately monastery and church dedicated to the
Blessed Virgin and sometimes designated as *Sancta Maria
in monte*. There is still much controversy as to the date of its
foundation and the identity of its founder. Brussels MS 3410
as quoted in *Analecta Hibernica*[21] has the following entry for
the year 1229: *Mainistir do thóccbháil a ccorcaigh do bhráithribh
S. Froinséis lá Mag cárthaigh mór Rí mumhan Diarmaid a ainm.*
Supporters are not wanting for the year 1240, but, as mentioned,
the Franciscans themselves give the date circa 1231 for their
earliest Irish house, the friary at Youghal with which the Cork
foundation was coeval. Dermot MacCarthy Mor of Dundrinan
is generally acclaimed as the founder of the Cork friary, a
claim strengthened by the fact that since the Friars Minor came
to Ireland in the wake of the conquering Normans, MacCarthy
Mor through his Norman wife, Petronilla Bloet,[22] may have
acquired certain interests in lands around Cork city which had
already come under Norman influence. The place of honour
accorded to the MacCarthy tomb in the Franciscan church is

19 Fitzmaurice and Little, *Franciscan province Ire.*, p. xi.

20 Canice Mooney, 'The Franciscans in Ireland', *Terminus*, June 1954, p. 127.

21 Joseph Moloney, 'Brussels MS 3410: A Chronological List of the Foundations of
the Irish Franciscan Province', *Anal. Hib.*, no. 6 (1934), pt. 3, p. 193.

22 *Cal doc. Ire., 1171–1251*, no. 766.

another indication of MacCarthy Mor's patronage of the early friars in Cork, while the reservation of special apartments within the monastery for MacCarthy's use tells its own story.

Other suggested founders of the Grey Friary are MacCarthy Reagh, Viscount Barry of Shandon and Philip Prendergast.[23] Of these, Philip Prendergast because of his many benefactions to the order was accorded the title of *second* founder, while his signature to an ancient document makes it possible to locate the exact site of the ancient friary. The document, dated 1371 and signed with the great seal of the kingdom, was transcribed in 1520 by Father William O'Magram, the Observantine provincial, but as the document is obviously a copy of an earlier scroll (dated tentatively 1300) it may well be a confirmation of the original grant made by MacCarthy Mor. It reads as follows: 'Let those present and to come know that I, Philip Prendergast, have donated, granted, and by this my charter have confirmed to the Friars Minor of Shandon, in honour of the Blessed Virgin and of Blessed Francis, the tract of land which extends in length from the tenement of the burgesses of the said township [Shandon] on the East, as far as the Tobair Brenoke on the west; and in breadth from the Rock on the north to the water of the Lee on the south, together with the fishery of that river situated near the said place.'[24]

The site of the friary therefore lay outside the city wall along and to the north of the North Mall; the friary itself stood a little to the rear and west of the present Franciscan Well Mineral Water Factory. The *Tobair Brenoke* or Well of Eloquence or Learning was at the end of Wise's Hill where its location is marked by a carved stone inserted in the western wall of the hill in 1810 when the well was being closed. Tradition recalls another well, the Holy Well of Saint Finbarr, which was situated in the centre of the courtyard leading to the friary church. The medicinal waters of this well were particularly efficacious as a cure for ophthalmia. Father Wadding, in his *Annales Minorum*, records that at the suppression the person who received the property blocked up this well in order to keep out the crowds.[25]

In time the property of the friars extended beyond the limits

23 Canice Mooney, 'The Mirror of All Ireland', in *Franciscan Cork*, p. 5, quoting Luke Wadding, *Annales Minorum*, ii, 310.

24 Denis O'Sullivan, 'The Franciscan Friary of Medieval Cork', *Cork Hist. Soc. Jn.*, xlv (1940), 14. Tobair Brenoke is also rendered *Tubber-na-Brinnah* and *Tubbar Vrian Oge*. Another variant appears in leases of the sixteenth and seventeenth centuries. In 1608, for instance, a lease was given to Thomas Yorke '. . . of a garden next Cork being by west the moore of Shandon Abbey freers by the well called Tobiervrianogy'.

25 Luke Wadding, *Annales Minorum*, ii, 310.

of the original grant (which was comparatively small) and included a mill and gardens in Reilly's Marsh. Legend also connects the friars with Gurranebraher (*Teampull na mBráthar*), and they enjoyed as well the fishing rights of Goul's Weir above the Lee mills together with a second mill known as the Friars' Mill. The location of the cemetery, church, mill, weir and fishery of the friars may still be indicated, while traces of the friary buildings remain at the rear of houses on the North Mall. These remains include some stone mullions and inscribed stones and the cut-stone head of a dual lighted window from the abbey which is now built into the east wall of the distillery. The letters S.M.B.C. which are distinctly legible on this stone are taken as signifying *Sancta Beata Mater Christi*. Another inscribed stone bearing the legend *(G)LORIA*/I.M. and dated 1590 was discovered near the abbey site and is preserved in the North Monastery,[26] while in 1804 the removal of some old ruins to make room for the present brick houses on the North Mall revealed many stone coffins containing the remains of what were obviously church dignitaries and nobles. Apart from the place of honour accorded to the founder's tomb in the choir, two other MacCarthys, Diarmaid's son Finghen and his brother Cormac, are believed to have been buried here before the general permission for such burials was granted. Then followed Dermot MacCarthy the Fat who was killed in 1275; Regnailt (d. 1298) who is conspicuous as the only lady on record to have penetrated the enclosure, and Donell Rua MacCarthy, king of Desmond, who after a victorious career against his enemies and after a greater victory of piety and repentance died in 1302 clothed in the Franciscan habit: '*iar mbuaidh chrabhuydh 7 aithrigi d'ec 7 a adnacul i n-ecusc na mBrathar [sic] Coslomhnachta [sic] i Corcaich ar lar choradh na mbrathar [sic]*.'[27] The Friary received the remains of Dermot MacCarthy in 1359, of his son Domnall Og in 1390 and of his son again in 1426. Fourteen knights of the Barrymore family, the Coppingers and members of other prominent Cork families were also interred in the friary of Shandon or in its adjacent cemetery. The damaged lid of one of the coffins excavated in 1804 revealed a sculptured sceptre and an inscription in Norman French.[28]

The friary of Shandon is clearly indicated in several old

---

26 D. P. Fitzgerald, 'The Friary of Shandon', *Cork Examiner*, 27 June 1925, suggests that the letters I.M. stand for the names of Jesus and Mary.

27 *Ann. Inisf.*, second entry for 1302.

28 Windele, *Cork*, p. 72.

maps and drawings of the city, and a plan of the abbey is given
in the earliest known map of Cork, circa 1545. It is also indicated
in a map dated 1585 in Trinity College, Dublin, and in one
dated circa 1600 in *Pacata Hibernia,* while Wadding describes
it as 'a notable church, divided in two by high columns and
adorned by an exquisite choir'. It appears to have been among
the first of the Irish Franciscan friaries marked out for spoliation
in the sixteenth century when the church and belfry were
ordered to be thrown down. All the other buildings, 'with the
chambers, in the precinct [were judged to be] suitable for the
necessary uses of the farmer dwelling there'.[29] Unlike other
instruments of dissolution, that relating to the friary of Shandon
does not contain any detailed description of the general layout
of the building.

The pastoral ministry of the Franciscans in Cork as elsewhere
was in all probability devoted to preaching and the confessional.
In the thirteenth century when clerical education was in the
doldrums and when a sermon was a rare event, the formal
and specific training of the friars equipped them for the demands
of the preaching apostolate. Not that the parish clergy were
entirely illiterate: many of them, later in the century, held
degrees. Unfortunately such degrees did not guarantee any
training in religious knowledge, and therefore the work of
preaching devolved mainly upon the friars. Their success as
preachers in Cork was acknowledged in the continuance until
the early decades of the nineteenth century of their weekly
assignment to preach in the North Chapel—a practice which
terminated during the episcopate of Bishop John Murphy
(1815–47). The organization of pilgrimages to the Holy Well
of Saint Finbarr, the popularization of devotion to their founder
and to the Blessed Virgin, the visitation of the sick and allied
works of mercy were all activities characteristic of the
Franciscans. Their role as itinerant preachers throughout the
dioceses cannot be over-emphasized, nor can their special
Third Order apostolate be overlooked. The Third Order (we
hear of it first in Florence in 1224) developed from Saint
Francis's *Letter to all Christians* which, to quote Father Canice
Mooney, 'became for those who adopted it as a sort of charter
of their association with the great Franciscan family'.[30] It is
incontrovertible that the tertiary idea came to Ireland almost
as soon as the Franciscans themselves, while among the deeds
of Christ Church in Dublin a bull of Martin V dated 3 May

29 *Extents Ir. mon. possessions*, pp. 138–9.
30 Mooney, 'The Franciscans in Ireland', *Terminus*, February 1956, p. 15.

1428 and addressed to the brothers and sisters of the Third
Order, embodies an *inspeximus* of a bull of Nicholas IV, dated
18 August 1289, which hints that Irish tertiaries were already
interesting themselves in the development of a Third Order
Regular.[31] The tertiary idea stressed the love of God and His
Blessed Mother; it exhorted to moderation, to frequentation
of the sacraments and the practice of brotherly love, mercy,
humility and meekness. By personifying these virtues themselves the friars rescued their hearers from the doldrums of
spiritual lethargy and malnutrition. An apostolate of this
nature was bound to have its opponents, particularly in clerical
ranks, but though there is no evidence that the friars were
oppressed in Ireland in the thirteenth century, the reissuing
in 1245 of their right of self-government and their freedom
from episcopal control was an added safeguard to the autonomy
on which Saint Francis set so high a premium.

For their daily needs the Friars Minor had resources similar
to those enjoyed by the Friars Preachers, namely, the patronage
of benefactors augmented by gifts in kind from other generous
individuals, and though their original endowment was somewhat enlarged they never acquired extensive landed property
as did other orders. The bulk of their financial support came
by way of royal grants which at times were issued for specific
purposes but more frequently with no qualifications attached.
The first grant on record is dated 15 October 1245, when
Henry III ordered an annual sum of twenty pounds to be paid
on the feast of All Saints from the Dublin exchequer to buy
one hundred habits (*tunicas*) for the Friars Minor of Dublin,
Waterford, Drogheda, Cork, Athlone and Kilkenny.[32] The
amount would postulate an average of fifteen or sixteen friars
in each of the houses mentioned. The grant, which proved
inadequate to the purpose, was increased within a few weeks to
35 marks or £23 6s 8d and the money was then channelled
for two years towards meeting the costs of enlarging the
Waterford friary. These royal grants, ranging in liberality,
continued to be paid at irregular intervals until 1372. By 1292
the friars of Cork shared equally with Dublin, Waterford and
Drogheda an annual grant of twenty-five marks; by 1311 their
quota was reduced to five and a half marks, and there are no

---

31   In Cork, the Franciscan friary of Ballymacadane was a foundation of the Third
Order regular. See Chapter XVII.

32   *Cal. doc. Ire., 1171–1251*, no. 2776.

records of royal gifts in kind to the Cork friary such as were granted to other friaries at varying intervals.[33]

In 1244 the first Irish provincial assembly of Friars Minor was held in Cork. The selection of Cork as venue for this important assembly is regarded as indicative of the size and importance of the Grey Friary which the records describe as the most commodious and well-to-do Franciscan house in Ireland at the time. Relatively speaking, such a statement can have but limited significance since there were scarcely more than eight friaries in Ireland by 1244. In fact, austerity seems to have been the key-note of Franciscan life in medieval Cork: Luke Wadding tells that the strict observance, regular life and piety of its inmates caused the Grey Friary of Shandon to be called the 'mirror of all Ireland' (*Speculum totius Hiberniae*).[34] By 1252 the Irish Franciscan province was divided into custodies, and shortly after that date comes a reference to Friar John of Kilkenny, 'formerly custodian in various custodies in Ireland, at one time of Drogheda, at another of Cork'.[35] Cork, which was erected into a custody (*custodium*) in or about the year 1260 in the general chapter at Norbonne, is listed in 1282 as the third of four custodies of the Irish province. By this time also it had become customary for Friars Minor to be raised to the Irish episcopate, but in the long annals of Cork bishops only two Franciscans are encountered, neither of whom ever administered the see. In 1329/30 Pope John XXII authorized the archbishop of Armagh to translate Ralph de Kilmessan, O.F.M., from the see of Down to that of Cork, but the translation never took place owing to the appointment of John de Ballyconingham to Cork. Later, Lewis McNamara, O.F.M., was provided to the see on 24 September 1540, but he died before consecration.

By the late thirteenth century the admission of Irish subjects proved a turning-point in the history of the Irish Franciscan province, for in a country so bedevilled by racial conflicts peaceful coexistence within monasteries was found to be virtually impossible. To racial hatred was added linguistic division, and in 1285 both Franciscans and Dominicans were accused of making much of the Irish language. The clash of loyalties was high-lighted and possibly affected by contemporary

---

33 Fitzmaurice and Little, *Franciscan province Ire.*, p. 222, relates that sixteen crannocks and thirteen pecks of oats were granted to Drogheda in 1324–25, and that cows and beer were granted to the Wicklow friars in the same year (p. 224).

34 Wadding, *Annales Minorum*, ii, 310.

35 Fitzmaurice and Little, *Franciscan province Ire.*, p. xx.

events in Wales and Scotland, and though Irish sources divulge little of the real troubles of the period in general, we get very precise details of events in Cork. A Worcester annalist records that 'On the 10 June [1291] at Cork in Ireland there was a general chapter of the Friars Minor, where the Irish Friars came armed with a papal bull: a dispute having arisen regarding this, they fought against the English friars; and after many had been killed and wounded here and there, the English at length gained the victory by the help of the city and with scandal to the Order.' A second English annalist, a monk of Norwich, amplifies the former statement by stating that 'sixteen friars with their fellow-friars were killed, some were wounded and some of them imprisoned by the King of England.'[36] The Cork friary by its proximity to Norman city and Gaelic territory could hardly have come unscathed through the political upheavals of the times. Later in the year (17 September 1291) Edward I instructed his justiciar, sheriffs and other officials in Ireland to restrain the rebellious friars and restore peace and concord. In consequence of the racial strife evoked at the chapter of 1291 the Irish Franciscan province lost the right of electing its own provincials who were in future to be appointed by the minister general with the advice of the good men of the order. The constitutional change thus effected was embodied in the decretal *Exivi de Paradiso* of Clement V which was issued on 6 May 1312.[37] This situation obtained until 1469 when at the chapter of Waterford Father William O'Reilly, the first Irishman of native stock to hold office, was elected. As well as being subject to external influences in the appointment of provincials it would also seem that during the first two centuries of their Irish existence the friars had to secure the approval of the king of England before any form of election or appointment could take place.[38]

The Bruce invasion, which scarcely affected Cork but which caused rifts in other friaries, was preceded and followed by legislation excluding Irishmen from religious houses within the 'English land'. In 1324 the Franciscans came in for heavy flagellation when inquisitions disclosed that the friars in the cities of Cork and Limerick as well as in the towns of Buttevant, Ardagh, Nenagh, Clare, Galway and Athlone were gravely suspect, a danger to the king's peace and to the state of the realm. Suspect friars were to be distributed throughout the

36   Ibid., pp. xxiii, 64.

37   Ibid.

38   Mooney, 'The Franciscans in Ireland', *Terminus*, July 1954, p. 152.

other houses of the order in Ireland, not more than three or four being permitted in each house, 'in order that a mutual cohabilitation of friars of English and Irish blood shall be brought about'. Irish friars under this censure were not to be appointed guardians in any of the eight houses named, and all Irish friars were 'to take corporal oath . . . that for the future they will make no suggestions, incitements or secret factions by which the peace of the land can be disturbed'.[39]

All such upheavels to the contrary, the Franciscans had a second foundation in the diocese of Cork by the year 1320, this time a semi-rural friary at Bantry, the most elusive of all Franciscan houses in Ireland. A chronological list of Irish foundations (Brussels MS 3410) has the following entry which seems definite enough: 'A.D. 1320, *Mainistir Bheanntraighe a ndúthaigh í Shúilleabháin in easpuccóideacht Ruis do thógbháil, do bhráithribh S.F. la Húa Súilleabháin . . .*'[40] The seventeenth-century *Brevis Synopsis* states that the convent of Bantry in the diocese of Ross [*sic*] was begun in 1320 by O'Sullivan and was reformed by Father David Herlihy in the year 1482. A third opinion quoted by Windele maintains that the abbey was founded either in 1420 or 1460 by Dermot O'Sullivan for Franciscan friars. Seeing that the weight of evidence favours 1320 as foundation date, this final reference may be nothing more than a confirmation of O'Sullivan's protection or patronage of the friars. Scarcely any details of the early history of Bantry Abbey have survived, but from the researches of the late Canice Mooney, O.F.M., supplemented by an old map printed in Caulfield's *Council Book of Kinsale* there emerges some idea of its layout and architectural style.

The abbey, according to Father Mooney, was a beautiful collection of buildings, smaller but somewhat more ornate than Kilcrea (1465). Caulfield's map, which is copied from an original in the Public Record Office, London,[41] depicts the abbey as conforming to usual Franciscan lines, but instead of the strong belfry tower which distinguished Irish Franciscan architecture, it had a slender tower and spire with parapet and transept on the north side. The domestic buildings lay apparently to the south of the church, and the enclosure wall with its gateway to the north ran right down to the edge of the bay. The fragmentary

39 *Calendar of Ormond Deeds, 1172–1350*, deed no. 575, p. 237.

40 Moloney, 'Brussels MS 3410', p. 195. See also in the same issue (*Anal. Hib.*, no. 6 [1934], pt. 2, p. 156) Father Brendan Jennings's 'Brevis Synopsis Provinciae Hiberniae FF. Minorum'.

41 The original is catalogued as M.P.F., 94.

remains of the abbey comprise an ogival window-head, the moulded base of a large pillar or pier and 'a large moulded stone terminating at one end in a well-carved rather classic human face with closed eyes, very high forehead and rather long thin nose'.[42] The features were probably those of the original founder of the abbey. Nothing further is known concerning the medieval abbey of Bantry, which does not again appear on the page of history until 1580, and consequently belongs to a later period in the history of the diocese.

Continued discord among the friars led in 1325 to a division of houses between the Irish and the English. A re-shuffle of custodies enacted by the general chapter of Lyons erected Cork into a separate English custody which was to include Buttevant, Limerick, Ardfert and subsequently Timoleague. There were now five custodies—the original Cork custody had been handed over to Cashel—but the arrangement fluctuated and by 1345 the Cork custody was abolished.[43] Even before that date the system of apartheid does not appear to have produced results, and in 1337 Edward III found it necessary to reverse the decision of Edward II by ordering that Irishmen, 'faithful subjects of the king and living among the English', should be admitted into religious houses among the English in Ireland.[44] From this date forward, references to the Cork friary, apart from those detailing the grant of royal alms, are meagre. The *Annals of Inisfallen* carry an obscure entry for the year 1317 to the effect that the Cork friars were indicted for some unspecified offence to which they objected on the grounds that their citation before the king's court was illegal from the point of both civil and ecclesiastical law (*contra commune ius et speciale*). Very few names of these early friars have been preserved. During the thirteenth century Friar Nicholas de Aquis who was conducting a visitation of the Irish province spent some time in Cork, while the compiler of the thirteenth-century *Liber exemplorum* was at one time teaching in Cork. This would presuppose the existence at an early date of a *studium particulare* at the Grey Friary, but the records throw no further light on the matter. In 1306 Adam Wynchedon, son of a prominent city merchant and church benefactor, is mentioned in his father's will as a Friar Minor, and at the close of the century, 1399, the

42   Canice Mooney, 'Franciscan Architecture in pre-Reformation Ireland', *R.S.A.I. Jn.*, lxxxvii (1957), 123, 136.

43   Fitzmaurice and Little, *Franciscan province Ire.*, pp. 120, 133–4, 138–9, 163–4.

44   Thomas Rymer, *Foedera, Conventiones, Litterae et Cujuscunque Generis Acta Publica*, ii, 964.

death of Friar Dermot MacCarthy is recorded. Brother Dermot, who was nicknamed 'the Thin' because of his many austerities, was buried in the chapter room.[45] Two of the last pre-Reformation provincial chapters of the Franciscans were held in Cork in 1521 and 1533. By then the Grey Friary of Shandon had accepted the Observant reform which with its contemporary Dominican and Augustinian manifestations was to prove a redeeming feature of the Irish church on the eve of the sixteenth-century religious revolt.

THE AUGUSTINIAN EREMITES

The Augustinian eremites trace their origin to the year 388 when Saint Augustine and a few followers formed themselves into a society of hermits at Tagaste in North Africa. Augustine's ordination in 391 coupled with his decision to live at Hippo wrought a significant change in the infant foundation. At Hippo the Rule of Saint Augustine took definite shape and Augustine's episcopal residence became a monastery where he lived a community life with his clergy who pledged themselves to follow the rule he had drafted.[46] After his death in 428 the eremites continued to extend and flourish in Africa and, after early foundations in Sardinia, Naples and Languedoc, began to infiltrate into other European countries. From the sixth to the eleventh century eremitical foundations were made in secluded places in a manner prohibitive of any union between houses. Consequently these scattered groups adapted themselves to their varying environments, they all bore the common name of Hermit Friars of Saint Augustine and conjointly formed the Order of Saint Augustine, but they remained independent until 1256.[47] At the beginning of the thirteenth century there were three distinct groups of hermits known respectively as Hermits, Augustine Hermits and Hermits of the Order of Saint Augustine. At the Lateran Council of 1215 Innocent III recognized the antiquity of the third group whom he admitted with the Carmelites to the privileges of the mendicants. Acceptance of the mendicant ideal did not, however, derogate from the original character and status of these older orders, though it contributed greatly to their diffusion. In 1244 at an assembly held at Rome an amalgamation of Augustinian houses in Italy ordered by Pope Innocent IV

45 Jennings, 'Brevis Synopsis Provinciae Hiberniae FF. Minorum', p. 182: 'Fr Dermitius Cartheusa, nimia abstinentia cognomento macer, vir summae humilitatis . . .'

46 A. J. Goodman, *Who Are the Augustinians?*, p. 16.

47 D. J. Kavanagh, *The Augustinian Order*, p. 37.

led to the creation of an Augustinian Congregation which in turn
paved the way for the Grand Union of 1256. The union was
confirmed and ratified by bull of Alexander IV who also
granted to the Augustinians the privilege of exemption from
episcopal jurisdiction which had been already granted to the
Franciscans and Dominicans. From this date the reconstituted
Augustinian eremites or Austin friars were governed by a
resident superior in Rome who now governed some 122
monasteries of the order in Italy, France, Belgium, Germany
and England. Like the Franciscans and Dominicans, these
Austin friars had much to offer to the thirteenth-century
church.

From England the Augustinian Order was introduced into
Ireland toward the close of the thirteenth century and, while
the Augustinians did not come in the immediate wake of the
Norman conquerers as did the Friars Preachers and the Friars
Minor, the line of their early foundations synchronizes closely
with 'the extent of English culture and power in the country
up to the middle of the fourteenth century'.[48] The first foundation was made at Dublin about 1280, Cork was founded before
1288, then followed Drogheda around 1295, Tipperary about
1300 and so on until by 1341 an arc of Augustinian friaries could
be traced from Drogheda to Adare.

The Augustinian friary of medieval Cork which stood on the
south bank of the Lee outside the city wall is marked on most
of the old maps as 'the church or Abbey of St Austine'.
Why it should have been called the *Red* Abbey has never been
satisfactorily explained, more especially because its remaining
ruins are quite definitely composed of limestone. Some ancient
maps of Cork indicate the Red Abbey Marsh, the Red Abbey
Island on which the friary was built, and the Red Abbey
Bridge which spanned the river from Lavit's Island (part of
the South Mall) to the Red Abbey Marsh.[49] Opinions vary as
to the date of the Red Abbey's foundation and the name of its
founder. Sir James Ware places it in the reign of Edward I
(1272–1307);[50] Archdall accepts the theory of Lodge[51] that
Patrick de Courcey, lord of Kinsale, who lived in the reigns of

48   F. X. Martin, 'The Augustinian Friaries in pre-Reformation Ireland', *Augustiniana*, vi (1956), 356.

49   The present Parliament Bridge is successor to the Red Abbey Bridge which was a wooden structure.

50   D. O'Sullivan, 'Monastic Establishments of Mediaeval Cork', *Cork Hist. Soc. Jn.*, xlviii (1943), 15, quoting Sir James Ware's *Disquisitiones*, p. 197.

51   John Lodge, *The Peerage of Ireland*, iv, 35.

Henry V and Henry VI was its founder, and Smith who accepts this theory gives 1420 as the date of foundation,[52] but all are contradicted by Father F. X. Martin, O.S.A., who maintains that de Courcey was not founder but benefactor of the Red Abbey. Two references in the Augustinian general archives at Rome caused Lubin in his *Orbis Augustinianus* and Alemand in his *Histoire Monastique d'Irlande* to place the Cork foundation at 1472 and 1475 respectively. Both dates are incorrect. Our first contemporary reference to the Red Abbey comes from the will of John de Wynchedon who in 1306 directed that his body should be buried with the friars of the Blessed Augustine in Cork. The Augustinians were therefore in Cork before 1306, and may have come before 1288 as is suggested by an entry in the *Sarsfield Papers*. The foundation is nowhere mentioned in the papal registers.

Judging from the height of its sixty-four-foot tower (a fifteenth-century addition) and from the dimensions of its east window measuring thirty feet by fifteen (and now blocked up), the Red Abbey must have been an imposing building. The tower which was built in 1420 and is today a valuable landmark of old Cork, is square-built and supported on four equal arches, a solitary but dignified relic of medieval architecture and local skill. The church of the Augustinians contained two chapels, one of which was the gift of the Sarsfield family.[53] Apart from such meagre details, references to the Cork Augustinians of the medieval period are disappointingly scanty. From state sources the first available reference to them is dated 8 July 1348 when Edward III, in return for contributions for the support of some Irish Augustinian students in England, was to share in daily masses at four of the Irish friaries, one of which was Cork.[54] From the general Augustinian archives in Rome come references dated 1472 and 1475, both dealing with the introduction of the Observant reform which will be the subject of a later chapter here.

A letter written on 18 March 1656[55] by the Augustinian provincial James O'Mahony recalled an ancient custom whereby all Cork merchants who engaged in foreign trade were bound to offer some gift to the Augustinians before leaving and on

52   Smith, *History of Cork*, i, 378.

53   Martin, 'The Augustinian Friaries in pre-Reformation Ireland', p. 370.

54   *Cal. pat. rolls, 1348–50*, p. 114 (reign of Edward III).

55   Though strictly speaking outside the ambit of medieval history, the reference in this letter is necessary as a pointer to the extent of Augustinian possessions in medieval Cork.

returning from their business expeditions. While this may have been so, it is difficult, in face of evidence to the contrary, to accept the provincial's statement to Lubin that the Cork friary was richly endowed 'with lands stretching from the port of Cork right up to the priory'.[56] In the first place the bishop's manor of Fayd, as we saw in an earlier chapter, extended from the cathedral eastwards down the river to Douglas and Blackrock (Mahon). Secondly, Father O'Mahony's statement as to the wealth of the friary does not tally with an entry in the *Archivium Generale Augustinianorum* under date January 1494 which ordered that provision be made for the monastery of Cork, the goods of which had been despoiled (*cuius bona dilapidantur*).[57] Finally, a 'new dormitory'[58] mentioned in an inventory taken in 1540 cannot be seriously entertained as incontrovertible evidence of improved fortunes for the Augustinians. The property of the order as listed before dissolution did not amount to anything beyond the monastery, church and precinct, three small gardens and a cemetery, a third part of a mill in Ballybrack, Douglas, and the tithes of Ballybrack which was an area covering roughly about two acres. At best, this inventory is unreliable. It includes as Augustinian property some important items which belonged to the Friars Minor of Shandon, namely, the Friars' Mill, Gowles Weir and certain lands in Teampal-na-mBrathar.[59] Post-Reformation grants and leases of the property of the Augustinian friars of Cork deal exclusively with the lands of Douglas and Ballybrack and lead to the conclusion that a grant made by Edward IV circa 1474 in favour of the eremites never became effective. The grant, according to Archdall, gave the eremites 'a parcel of land in Shandon, near Cork, in breadth between the lands of St. John the Baptist, on the north, and the lands of the said William and John [White] on the south, and in length from the land of the Grey Friars, on the west, to the highway on the east'.[60] In the last analysis the legend which credits the Augustinians with having 'lands stretching from the port of Cork right up to the priory' had its origin in a translation error which misread *portum* for *portam*—a pardonable error indeed considering the

56   Martin, 'The Augustinian Friaries in pre-Reformation Ireland', p. 370.

57   F. X. Martin and A. de Meijer, 'Irish Material in the Augustinian Archives, Rome, 1354–1624', *Archiv. Hib.*, xix (1956), 108.

58   *Extents Ir. mon. possessions*, p. 140.

59   Ibid., pp. 140–1.

60   Mervyn Archdall, *Monasticon Hibernicum*, p. 125 n.

illegibility of the medieval hand. The site of the Red Abbey was not far removed from the South Gate of the city.

Like the Friars Preachers the early Augustinians in Ireland were under supervision from England, and although the animosities caused by the Bruce invasion in other orders seem to have by-passed them, they had their own internal struggles to cope with. By the mid-fourteenth century signs of dissatisfaction in the Irish vicariate led to deprivation of privileges, and this in turn engendered a dispute with the English provincial whose decisions were unacceptable in Ireland. An interesting feature of the dispute was that a deputation sent in 1391 to the general chapter at Würzburg demanding semi-autonomy for the Irish houses was the outcome of proceedings initiated not by native but by Anglo-Irish friars. The general chapter's sympathetic attitude resulted in the restoration of limited local self-government to the Irish friaries in May 1392 and in the confirmation of this privilege by the general chapter of Rimini in 1394.[61] By the first half of the fifteenth century the balance of power in Augustinian houses had passed to the native Irish brethren. The new trend which manifested itself in the west of Ireland in the early decades of the century had asserted itself so successfully that when Hugh O'Malley was appointed vicar of the Irish chapter in 1457 the gaelicization of the Augustinians was assured. Dearth of records makes it difficult to determine the extent to which gaelicization permeated the Red Abbey community. It appears, however, that Cork opted out of the general movement towards reform and/or gaelicization and that in the late fifteenth century the civil authorities exercised considerable control over the affairs of the Red Abbey.

THE MENDICANT CONTROVERSY

Thanks to the influence of the friars, several reforms were inaugurated in the church during the thirteenth century when pluralism and non-residence were rife, when benefice-holders were often only in minor orders, when clerical education left much to be desired and when church services even at best were but carelessly performed. Under the influence of the mendicants the revival of preaching created better relations between priests and people, even though a time was to come when the very success of the friars would evoke acrimonious exchanges between them and the secular clergy. The quarrel between them was threefold, involving the friars' right to

61   Martin, 'The Augustinian Friaries in pre-Reformation Ireland', p. 356.

preach, to hear confessions and to bury the dead in their own churches and cemeteries; the popularity enjoyed by the itinerant friar entailed a certain loss of prestige for the parish clergy, while the right to hear confessions and bury the dead entailed a loss of finance. The chief protagonist of the rights of the secular clergy was Richard FitzRalph, archbishop of Armagh (1346–60), whose campaign against the friars arose from his failure to find any gospel warrant for mendicant poverty.[62] He was also convinced that the friars were courting favour with the well-to-do by offering them absolution on easy terms, and he insisted that they exceeded their powers by absolving excommunicates.

How far FitzRalph allowed his zeal to outrun his discretion and how far the friars were justified in their open toleration of existing conditions is not easy to determine, but it is possible that the friars felt some justifiable dissatisfaction with the existing low standards of selection and training of the secular clergy. And it is a fact that the friars as a body were properly trained in a way that the secular priests were not. Modern regulations on seminaries and priestly formation according to the norms of Vatican II are a long step from the haphazard selection and training of the rank and file of the medieval secular clergy. In retrospect, therefore, it is difficult to see how the church could have adequately met the crises of the thirteenth century without the aid of the friars. Of course, reforming bishops of the thirteenth century cannot be overlooked, nor can the contribution of the cathedral schools, but the fact remains that the friars had more to offer. Hence the clash of vested interests between them and the secular clergy.

The controversy waged—furious and bitter—until 1357 when Edward III prohibited further measures against the friars. Nevertheless, on 8 November of that year FitzRalph preached his famous *Defensorium curatorum* before a papal consistory, for he was convinced that the papal privileges conferred on the friars were detrimental to the good order necessary for diocesan government. Formal litigation was initiated at the Curia but FitzRalph was defeated. On 1 October 1358 and on 14 July of the following year two papal bulls confirmed the teaching of *Vas electionis* (1311) which had defined the privileges of the friars in relation to the secular clergy as to preaching, hearing confessions, conducting burials and so forth.[63] Apart from the FitzRalph

62   Aubrey Gwynn, 'Archbishop FitzRalph and the Friars', *Studies*, xxvi, no. 101 (March 1937), p. 53.

63   W. A. Pantin, *The English Church in the Fourteenth Century*, p. 163.

episode, which did not greatly affect Irish friars except the Franciscans in the northern province,[64] this country was generally saved the worst of the prolonged controversy between the mendicants and the seculars. FitzRalphianism was to erupt again in the fifteenth century and its lingering effects were noticeable in certain anti-mendicant decrees issued at the provincial Synod of Cashel in 1453.

---

64 Martin and de Meijer, 'Irish Material in the Augustinian Archives', p. 67, lists a complaint of the Irish Augustinians that their order had been greatly afflicted: *totum ordinem nostrum per dictum Armachanum graviter molestari.*

IX

The Cathedral Chapter

Once the bishop of Cork became independent of the monastery of Saint Finbarr a body of secular clergy attached to the cathedral church became an immediate functional necessity. Although cathedral chapters are known to have been organized in a variety of ways, their objects were everywhere uniform, namely, to act as privy council to the bishop in the administration of the diocese, to advance the cause of clerical education and to maintain the liturgical dignity of the mother-church of the diocese by the perpetuation of the *opus Dei*. The chapter's liturgical function could only be achieved by a body of clerics following some approved rule; such a rule involving community of life and property was called the *vita canonica*, and clerics adhering to it came to be known as canons. The earliest meaning of the term *clericus canonicus* was any clerk living under ecclesiastical law or according to the canons or rules of the church, and a long tradition of such regular common life forms the historical background of the secular cathedrals of medieval Europe. There were chapters of canons regular attached to the churches of religious orders in the diocese of Cork from an early date. The clergy of Saint Catherine's Church were called a chapter (of canons); this church, which was affiliated to the abbey of Saint Thomas, Dublin, followed the rule of the Augustinian Canons of Saint Victor. The monks of Gill Abbey are referred to as 'Canons *de Antro*' in 1306, and later again as canons of the Lateran. Consequently the capitular idea was not unknown in Cork. Bodies of secular canons existed side by side with canons regular in Dublin, but instead of the cohesion and solidarity expected from such mutual contacts, it appears that conflict between both bodies was so notorious that papal intervention alone was able to arrange a *modus vivendi* for them. In time, secular and regular canons filled very different places in the church and in society. With the regular canons the monastic ideal and communal life took precedence over pastoral work, whereas the secular canons found their interests in an ever-widening sphere, at royal and papal courts, in the service of archbishops and bishops and in the schools.[1]

Generally speaking, the type of capitular organization first adopted in Ireland appears to have been tailored to the pattern obtaining in priories of the Austin Arroasian canons who were first introduced into the country by Saint Malachy,[2] and while the extension of Arroasian customs to the monastery of Gill Abbey is doubtful, it is probable that some sort of semi-monastic semi-diocesan chapter functioned in Cork under the monk-bishop Giolla Aedh O Muighin. The arrival of the Normans was followed by the introduction of a more specialized type of cathedral organization based on the prebendal system where each canon in addition to his income from an allotted rectory was also entitled to an allowance from a common fund, the allowance depending on his attendance or non-attendance at the cathedral services.[3] The English secular cathedrals as constituted in post-Norman times adopted a four-square pattern founded on four great dignitaries called the *quatuor personae*, namely dean, precentor, chancellor and treasurer, whose stalls occupied the four corners of the choir. The arch-deacons were normally described as dignitaries but there were instances of archdeacons who, while their archdeaconries 'were reckoned technically as offices or personages in the cathedral, had no seat in chapter owing to the fact that they had no prebends'.[4] In addition to the dignitaries the fully developed chapter of the middle ages included a long list of canons, officers and lesser officials (*ministri inferiores*) in its personnel.

In the absence of documents like the *Black Book of Limerick*, the *Dignitas Decani* and the *Red Book of Ossory* the date of origin of the Cork chapter cannot be ascertained, but it seems to have been functioning during the episcopate of Gregory O hAodha (1172–82) who succeeded Giolla Aedh O Muighin. In 1180 Bishop Gregory 'on the advice of the whole chapter of his church' (*tocius capituli ecclesie sue consilio*), permitted Archdeacon Reginald to grant the church of Saint Nessan to

---

1 Kathleen Edwards, *The English Secular Cathedrals in the Middle Ages*, p. 4; here-after referred to as Edwards, *English Secular Cathedrals*.

2 P. J. Dunning, 'The Arroasian Order in Medieval Ireland', *I.H.S.*, iv (1945), 297–315.

3 G. J. Hand, 'Mediaeval Cathedral Chapters', *Ir. Cath. Hist. Comm. Proc.* (1956), pp. 11–12. See also Edwards, *English Secular Cathedrals*, pp. 33–41, and A. H. Thompson, *The English Clergy and Their Organization in the Later Middle Ages*, p. 76.

4 A. H. Thompson, *The Cathedral Churches of England*, p. 22.

the abbey of Saint Thomas in Dublin.[5] In the same year the bishop confirmed the gift, again with capitular consent, expressed in this case by the phrase *nostro conventu concedente*, which makes it probable that the Cork chapter was still semi-monastic. Nothing further emerges regarding the personnel of the chapter beyond Reginald's status as archdeacon; nor do subsequent grants of churches made to the Dublin abbey carry any references to dignitaries or canons, but it seems likely that the Cork chapter had taken definite shape by the end of Marianus Ua Briain's episcopate, that is, by the year 1224. The diocese of Ross had its chapter by this year also as may be inferred from a mandate issued to the bishops of Emly and Kilfenora, on the petition of the chapter of Ross, to inquire into the election of the dean as bishop and to confirm and consecrate him should the election be proved canonical.[6] The chapter of the diocese of Down dates from the year 1180, that of Limerick from 1205 and that of Cashel from about the year 1224.[7]

From the annates and the papal registers which offer more precise data on the personnel of the Cork cathedral chapter we find that by the end of the fourteenth century there were, in addition to the four principal dignitaries and the archdeacon, seven prebends to which five more were added in the course of the fifteenth century.[8] The total assembly of seventeen would therefore put Cork at least one pace ahead of Limerick in the claim made for that diocese as being, with its sixteen members, 'second only to St. Patrick's, Dublin, which had twenty-eight prebends just before its dissolution in the sixteenth century'.[9] Limited knowledge of other cathedral bodies makes this suggestion nothing more than tentative, but with six more temporary prebends invoiced in the records it is evident that the cathedral chapter of medieval Cork was a body of no mean proportions.

THE DEAN

At the head of the chapter was the dean holding his office originally by election and episcopal confirmation but subsequently by papal provision, the first recorded provision being

---

5   *Reg. St. Thomas, Dublin*, p. 219.

6   *Cal. papal letters, 1198–1304*, p. 97.

7   Otway-Ruthven, *Med. Ire.*, p. 40, n. 14.

8   *Cal. papal letters, 1362–1404, 1396–1404, 1404–15, 1417–31, passim*.

9   G. J. Hand, 'The Medieval Chapter of St. Mary's Cathedral, Limerick', *Med. studies presented to A. Gwynn*, p. 76.

that of George de Rupe in 1359.[10] The dean was *ex officio* chairman of the chapter but only as coequal (*primus inter pares*) with his fellow dignitaries. The deanship was a major elective dignity entailing the cure of souls; because the dean owed his election to the votes of the cathedral canons the tendency was for him to challenge the authority of the bishop and become the independent and separate head of the entire chapter. In choir, as chief priest and representative (*locum tenens*) of the absent bishop, the dean was increasingly accorded the honour and respect due to the head of the church. In spite of this distinction the position of dean was in many ways anomalous. Unless he held a cathedral canonry and prebend he was excluded from discussing chapter business; yet no chapter could be convened unless summoned by the dean. In matters of jurisdiction too there were frequent clashes of opinion as to his right to act independently of the canons who elected him. In fine, his position was such that the canons placed severe limitations on his supervisory and on his corrective powers over the cathedral clergy.

Such restrictions to the contrary, the dean was responsible for the administration of the common lands; he also had the right of visitation save only in respect of prebendaries who enjoyed exemptions in these matters. In the English and contintental chapters the dean and chapter had a varied staff of subordinate officers whose duties were as varied as their titles—officials, proctors, auditors, advocates, registrars, summoners and appointers—but except for the officials (*officiales*) we have no record of such minor functionaries for the diocese of Cork. From the first it would appear that the dean of Cork was a prebendary. The corps of his prebend was constituted by the churches of Cullen, Templebreedy and Templemartin, and in this way he was always assured his due recognition as president and head of the chapter. The first occurring reference to a dean of Cork is found under the year 1237,[11] and from that date until the Reformation it is possible to assemble an almost unbroken succession of appointments to the deanship as indicated in the Appendix.[12]

THE PRECENTOR

The precentorship, a non-major, non-elective dignity with

10   *Cal. papal letters, 1342–62*, p. 311.

11   *Cal. doc. Ire., 1171–1251*, no. 2410.

12   *Cal. papal letters, 1362–1404—1484–92, passim.*

cure of souls[13] was ordinarily filled by collation of the bishop
and in certain cases by the pope in accordance with the provisions of canon law. From the time of Saint Augustine the
church increasingly recognized the importance of song and
music as an aid to worship, and therefore throughout the
Middle Ages when the titles of cathedral personnel showed
considerable variation, the cantor or dignitary in charge of
song was the least variable. By the twelfth century the cantor
or precentor, who ranked among the first four dignitaries,
normally occupied a stall in choir facing that of the dean.
Because his duties were mainly musical and liturgical he was
required to have specialized knowledge in these spheres, and
because little jurisdiction attached to his office, competition
was not to be feared from any of the other dignitaries.[14] The
precentor's main function was choral. He set the pitch for
singing, saw to it that the choir sang together in regular time
and tune, gave the note or key to the celebrant of Mass and was
responsible for the selection of appropriate hymns and chants
for the recurring church feasts. He was required also to correct
faults in singing, control the behaviour of the choristers, and
when the bishop was present at the cathedral services it was
the precentor's duty to give him his cue as to the chants to be
intoned by him. The care, correction and repair of the service
books were also matters for the precentor's attention, and his
word carried great weight in the admission of the lesser cathedral
clergy, more particularly those whose duties would revolve on
song. At first the precentor's duty was confined to the cathedral
clergy, especially to the boy choristers and the young vicars
for whose training he was responsible. Later, as song began
to play an increasingly important part in medieval education,
his sphere of activity was so enlarged that by the fourteenth
century he was responsible for teaching song in all the churches
of the cathedral city. He was assisted by two or three lesser
clerks known as *tabellarii, tabularii* or *exploratores* of faults who
took note of daily misdemeanours, neglect of duty and absences
from choir and duly reported on them.[15]

In Cork, the precentor's prebend in 1302 was derived from
Corbally, to which the rectory of Kinneigh was added in 1487.
Like other members of the chapter the precentor was occasionally cited as papal mandatory; unhappily, these scattered
references offer no real clue as to his importance and dignity

13   *Cal. papal letters, 1417–31*, p. 348.
14   Edwards, *English Secular Cathedrals*, p. 161.
15   Ibid., p. 177.

in the medieval chapter of Cork. With the exception of David de Lang who was precentor in 1265 the names of other pre-fifteenth-century holders of the office have not been preserved, and the fifteenth-century list as such is scanty.

THE CHANCELLOR

The chancellorship was a non-major, non-elective dignity without cure and was originally filled by the bishop and latterly by papal provision. By the middle of the thirteenth century the chancellor ranked third in nearly all English cathedrals (and by application, in Irish cathedrals also), and his duties were more varied and perhaps more exacting than those of his colleagues. He acted as secretary to the chapter, was responsible for drafting its documents and was custodian of the common seal. Over and above these commitments were his educational activities, for he was the medieval counterpart of the ancient *magister scholarum* who occupied a position of immense prestige in the early church. The title *chancellor* was not given to the *magister scholarum* until he had a master or masters under him teaching grammar, while he himself exercised a general supervision over the cathedral schools, granting them licence to teach and confining himself to lecturing in the higher faculties of theology and canon law. As supervisor of education the chancellor combined the offices of *theologus* and *scholasticus*. As *scholasticus* he was master of the cathedral school, as *theologus* he delivered or arranged for the giving of theological lectures. It was his duty to ensure that such lectures were audible and clear and that readings which formed part of the services should be delivered coherently and intelligently. The chancellor was also responsible for the upkeep of the cathedral library in the same way as the precentor was answerable for the maintenance and repair of the service books, and as director of education he administered the endowments of the grammar school and regulated the salaries of those to whom he granted licence to teach. For English cathedral chapters the first mention of a chancellor occurs between 1150 and 1160 at Lincoln and Salisbury. In Cork, where the secular chapter does not seem to have taken full shape until the second decade of the thirteenth century, the term chancellor was probably in use from the beginning. The existence in Cork of a separate *theologus* and grammar master is unascertainable, but it is more than likely that the chancellor filled both posts.

The essential choir duties of the chancellor involved selecting the readers for the cathedral services, determining the lengths of the lessons and supervising their preparation. Here again his duties were complementary to those of the precentor. His secretarial duties so increased with the expansion of the administrative and legal work of the twelfth, thirteenth and fourteenth century cathedral chapters that it became necessary to define his duties more precisely and to give him assistants and subordinates in the chancery. The other dignitaries had their subordinates too, but such under-dignitaries do not appear to have been of importance in any Irish chapter. There are no references to under-dignitaries in Cork, nor is there any reference to a chancellor in the original chapter of Limerick although there is a provocative reference to a sub-treasurer there in the thirteenth century.[16]

In order to ensure free education in the cathedral schools chapters were obliged to provide the chancellor with a benefice sufficiently lucrative to enable him teach without the necessity of charging fees. His financial security was safeguarded by the legislation of the Fourth Lateran Council (1215) which enacted that every cathedral church should support a master of arts and every metropolitan church a theologian. The church of Saint Brigid together with the townlands of Maglin and Curraheen in the parish of Ballincollig constituted the corps of the Cork chancellor's prebend in 1302. Ringrone was added in 1402 for the lifetime of Michael Kenefig.[17]

THE TREASURER

The office of treasurer was a non-major dignity with cure of souls.[18] Like other cathedral dignitaries the treasurer was collated by the bishop but his office too came eventually under papal control. The treasurer's first duty was to preserve the treasures of the church: the gold and silver vessels, ornaments, relics, vestments and altar cloths. He was likewise responsible for providing bread, wine, incense, charcoal, lights and other materials necessary for the church services. His status within the chapter varied considerably but he was most often in the third or fourth place. The medieval treasurer of Cork enjoyed as his prebend the churches of Ballinadee, Kilgobban, Rathdrought and one rectory of Macloneigh.

Every treasurer was expected to keep an exact inventory of the contents of his treasury and he was subject to annual in-

16   *The Black Book of Limerick*, p. 37, no. xxxvii, '. . . dominus Subthesaurarius . . .'
17   *Rot. Pat. Hib.*, no. 208, p. 165.
18   *Cal. papal letters, 1471–84*, pt. 1, p. 127.

spection by the dean and one or two of his canons. In English cathedrals of the post-Norman era—and possibly in Irish cathedrals also—the materials required for services had to be provided at the treasurer's own expense. The provision of lights, e.g., wax and oil, must have been a heavy drain on his finances when it is remembered that cathedral statutes legislated minutely on the exact number and position of all the lamps, candles and tapers which were to be kept burning before altars, shrines and images. The treasurer had to guard the entire church and its furniture while his subordinates were required to maintain silence and order among the laity during services. He had, finally, to see to it that the floors were swept, that the clock was wound, that clock, bells and bell-ropes were kept in repair, and he was responsible for the training and the allocation of the bell-ringers. These multiple duties made residence within the cathedral precinct obligatory for the treasurer.[19]

THE ARCHDEACON

The office of archdeacon, which was in the bishop's appointment, was a non-major, non-elective dignity entailing the cure of souls. And while the position of the medieval archdeacon was anomalous—he might hold every gradation of rank among cathedral dignitaries and *personae*—he was in reality an officer of long standing, whose prestige derived from his earlier position as head of the bishop's *familia*. By the seventh century the archdeacon, as the bishop's right-hand man and chief administrative officer, had established his authority over all possible rivals, but his power began to decline with the rise of the new secular cathedral chapters with their separate endowments and greater independence of the bishop. In England after the Conquest his association with the cathedral church became less and less intimate. He was usually a canon and sometimes a prebendary with a stall in choir and a voice in chapter and he frequently held one or more parish churches appropriated to his office (*personatus*), but his main duty was the supervision of the churches of the diocese.

In Limerick where the archdeacon had a definite prebend he was originally ranked in order next to the dean, but by 1272 he had fallen into line after the *quatour personae*.[20] He was nonetheless an important functionary: the worth of his office in the early fourteenth century was twenty-eight pounds which

19 Edwards, *English Secular Cathedrals*, pp. 223–8.
20 *The Black Book of Limerick*, no. lvii, p. 49; no. lviii, p. 50; no. lxxvii, p. 61.

placed him second only to the dean.[21] In Cork for the same period the archdeacon's valuation was £19 16s 8d,[22] almost three times that of the dean, and if one may thus gauge the prestige of an archdeacon by his grading on a taxation list the archdeacon of Cork would appear to have been every bit as important as his Limerick counterpart. In 1291 the archdeacon of Cork held as benefice the churches of Dunbulloge and Saint Peter's,[23] to which subsequently the churches of Nohoval, Kilmonoge and Dunisky were added. Reginald's claim to being Cork's first-known archdeacon is challenged by Cotton[24] in favour of Giollaphadraig MacCarthy (d. 1158) who is more correctly styled last *airchinnech* of the monastery of Saint Finbarr. As in the case of the deans, the list of pre-Reformation archdeacons of Cork is practically unbroken.

Unlike a cathedral canon the archdeacon was non-resident. His duty, which was extraneous to the cathedral, was more properly diocesan in character, since he was the 'bishop's eye' (*oculus episcopi*) for the diocese. He represented the bishop and by ordinary right was entitled to hold visitations; consequently, the medieval archdeacon was almost universally unpopular. Archdeacons were frequently in receipt of papal indults authorizing them to visit by deputy and receive procurations up to a stated daily maximum the value of which was fixed by papal constitution in 1336.[25] The better to enable him to carry out his diocesan supervision, the archdeacon was given the full status of residentiary for a much shorter period of residence than was obligatory for simple canons. A special stall was usually reserved for the archdeacon near those of the *quatuor personae*, but this did not mean he had *ex officio* the right to the title of cathedral dignitary. He seems to have been always the odd man out.

Apart from visitations, it was the duty of the archdeacon to act as *officialis* in trials for spiritual offences,[26] to examine candidates for orders and to induct incumbents into benefices on receipt of episcopal mandates *ad hoc*. By the fifteenth century however the archdeacon had ceased to be of any great

21   *Cal. doc. Ire., 1302–07*, p. 270.

22   Ibid., p. 280.

23   Brady, *Records*, i, 307.

24   Henry Cotton, *Fasti Ecclesiae Hibernicae*: T.C.D., Cod. Clar. MSS, f. 1, m. 18.

25   W. A. Pantin, *The English Church in the Fourteenth Century*, pp. 98 ff.

26   Webster, *The Diocese of Cork*, p. 83.

spiritual or administrative utility and the few functions remaining to him were mostly connected with either the bishop's duties in the cathedral choir or with those of the parish clergy of the archdeaconry. Many archdeacons regarded their office as a sinecure, and two of those listed for Cork in the fourteenth century would appear to have been more involved in political and secular pursuits than in ecclesiastical affairs. These were Henry de Thrapton, king's clerk and archdeacon of Cork, who in October 1330 was appointed chancellor of the exchequer in Dublin 'during good behaviour and so long as his bodily strength allows',[27] and William Epeworth (1346) who was appointed royal commissioner for collecting a subsidy for the king and whose zeal led to his excommunication by the archbishop of Cashel.

THE BISHOP IN HIS CATHEDRAL CHURCH

Theoretically, the chapter was the bishop's council which assisted him in administering his diocese; in fact, its independent endowment and government often led to friction with him. In the early days of the church when a bishop shared the common life with his cathedral clergy he had been their only head, and this idea continued throughout the Middle Ages, long after the rise of dean or other capitular officials had given the chapters a second head who administered the home government of the cathedral during the bishop's absence on visitation. A division of the common goods (*communia*) of the church in the ninth and tenth centuries made it possible for chapters to control their own affairs and property without regard to the bishop's absence or to the complications of royal control of temporalities in the event of a bishop's death.[28] Increasingly the chapter began to assume the position of an independent corporation, a sort of ecclesiastical republic within the diocesan framework; it became wealthy and privileged and soon resented any form of episcopal interference. One way of minimizing friction was to give the bishop a prebend in chapter as an ordinary member, since in the Middle Ages possession of a prebend generally was the only 'open sesame' to the chapter house. Certain lands belonging to the bishop of Cork corresponded to prebendal parishes, namely, Kilbrogan, Carrigrohane and Inishkenny, but there is no indication as to whether the bishop personally administered these parishes as prebendary or delegated them

27 *Cal. pat. rolls, 1330–34*, 4 Edward III, pt. 2, m. 34, p. 10.

28 Edwards, *English Secular Cathedrals*, p. 99.

to vicars. The incomplete lists of incumbents are unreliable guides.

The principal duty of the chapter, *sede plena*, was to give or withhold consent to the acts of the bishop. Such consent was necessary for any alienations of ecclesiastical property, changes in the state of benefices or the grant of important privileges. There is specific evidence of such capitular consent in the grants made to Saint Thomas's Abbey in Dublin. Though the bishop was the *judex ordinarius* or normal judicial authority within his own diocese, the chapter claimed that its court had undisputed right to judge causes in the lands and churches of vacant prebends and dignities. By the thirteenth century chapters everywhere had established their right to the *jus ordinarium* in the churches appropriated to their common fund, while in those appropriated to prebends, it was the normal thing for individual prebendaries to have their own courts and to legislate accordingly. Each diocese had also a consistorial court or common bench of the diocese, presided over by the bishop's official (*officialis*) and from which there was no appeal to the bishop even though the official's court did not, in theory, supersede the episcopal court.[29]

In other ways too the medieval bishop's liberty of action was shackled by capitular control. Special honour was accorded him whenever he was present in choir, though there were occasions when he had no legal right to celebrate out of his turn or preach without permission from precentor or chancellor. The bishop's voice in selecting the clergy of his cathedral church was limited to the immediate members of the chapter. Vicars choral and other *ministri inferiores* were nominated by individual canons and only by the bishop through devolution or lapse. Episcopal visitations were strongly objected to and avoided whenever possible, and relations between bishops and chapters grew so notoriously difficult that it was not unusual for bishops before election to make certain 'capitulations' to their chapters promising to observe and defend the customs and liberties of the cathedral church. In Cork there are no extant records of any such pre-election compacts nor of arrangements like those entered into in Limerick which resulted in the occupation of the see by a succession of chapter members between 1257 and 1336. For the entire pre-Reformation period only two archdeacons and four deans of Cork were raised to

29 Thompson, *The Cathedral Churches of England*, pp. 51–4.

Canons

episcopal rank,[30] but this in no way proves that the capitular climate in Cork was less stormy than in Limerick, Dublin and elsewhere.

It was in time of vacancy that the medieval chapter was seen at its greatest strength when its most important function, namely that of electing to the bishopric, was invoked. Generally speaking, the normal procedure was followed in Cork: the announcement of the death of the bishop and the petition for licence to elect; and while deviations occurred from time to time, it is clear that the overall attitude of the chapter was one of compliance with the electoral decrees of the Fourth Lateran Council, of King John's charter of 1214 (later confirmed in Magna Carta) and of the letters of Honorious III which exhorted that the rights of kings should be respected. By the middle of the thirteenth century, however, the medieval chapters had mostly reached the peak of their independence. From then on a decline set in and by the early fourteenth century, although the theory of episcopal election by chapter continued to be quoted, it had ceased to have any practical value or application. The age of papal provisions had come.

Like Limerick, the medieval chapter of Cork was well within the borders of Anglo-Ireland, and in Cork as in Limerick papal provision was much more important than royal influence from, roughly, 1320 onwards. Prebendal vacancies in the Cork chapter do not appear to have been greatly raided for the benefit of royal nominees, though on the other hand, Irish names are not particularly in evidence in either episcopal, dignitarial or prebendal lists until well into the fifteenth century. From then until the Reformation the proportion of Irish clergy in the chapter shows a visible increase.

CANONS

After the *quatuor personae* the canons were a most important and necessary group of cathedral clergy whose numbers became fixed before those of vicars choral and other functionaries of lesser grade (*ministri inferiores*). By analogy with Limerick the original number of canons in Cork must have been small, but the quota was eventually finalized at twelve. The papal registers distinguish between canons with and without prebends and those with expectation of prebends. Canons without prebends were probably the *canonici vocales* as distinct from the *canonici*

30   Archdeacons Reginald (1182–87) and Gilbert (1225–38). Deans John McCarroll (1302–21), John Roche (1347–58), Gerald Barry (1358–93) and Milo FitzJohn (1409–31).

reales who are mentioned in the *Black Book of Limerick*.[31] In 1453 by decree of a council held at Limerick the number of *canonici vocales* in each cathedral of the province of Cashel was limited to six.[32] Expectant canons were probably super-numeraries, provided to cathedrals by pope or king, who had to wait until prebends fell vacant for them. As canons they might be allocated a stall in choir but lacking prebends they were excluded from chapter meetings.

Three main sources of income were open to canons: (a) their prebends which were lands donated by the bishop from his manor or else the gift of pious lay benefactors; (b) their share in distributions from the common fund; (c) a share in dis-tributions made at funerals or at the anniversary services of pious benefactors. However as canons fell into the categories of resident and non-resident, and as residence carried with it extra obligations and expenses, the custom developed of confining payment from the common fund to resident canons only. Residentiaries enjoyed other casual revenues as well. A canon might be elected as keeper of the common fund, he might be appointed commissary to visit or administer the common estates, he might be appointed financial officer of the chapter, etc.; to all of these appointments small salaries accrued.

Prebendal valuations varied, the richest ones being usually reserved for non-residents. Papal registers distinguish between sacerdotal and non-sacerdotal prebends, and in England prebends appear to have been graded for priests, deacons and subdeacons, but the distinction upon which these several prebends were graded is not at all clear.[33] Finally, prebends were erected for the lifetime of some individual or until such time as he should secure another permanent prebend. The following list of *prebendae pristinae* represents the pre-Refor-mation prebendal parishes of the diocese of Cork.[34]

Saint Michael's, Shanbally. Erected into a prebend in 1326 by Bishop Philip of Slane,[35] Saint Michael's was taxed at three shillings in the procuration list of 1437 and was not then mentioned as prebendal, but it was definitely a prebend in

31   *The Black Book of Limerick*, pp. lxv–lxvi and no. clxvii, p. 137.

32   David Wilkins, *Concilia Magnae Britanniae et Hiberniae*, iii, 568.

33   Thompson, *The Cathedral Churches of England*, p. 20.

34   Diocesan Archives, Cork. The permanent prebends of this list were retained in the reconstruction of the chapter in 1858 by Bishop William Delany.

35   Smith, *History of Cork*, i, 39.

1615. Anciently a parish, the income of which was derived from the rectory, Saint Michael's is now part of the modern parish of Glanmire in the barony of Barrymore. The original church stood beside the narrow road leading from Dunbulloge to Templemichael Bridge, about five miles from Cork via White's Cross. The names of its prebendaries are missing.

Liscleary became a prebend during the episcopate of John de Ballyconingham in 1332. It was apparently in the donation of the Meades, of whom Smith relates that 'one Meagh or O'Mide presented anciently to this prebend'.[36] Liscleary was rated at six shillings in 1437 and the rectory was the source of income. Liscleary today forms part of the parish of Ballinhassig, while small portions of it are found in the modern parishes of Carrigaline and Monkstown. The greater part of the ancient parish lies to the south of the Owenaboy River, save for the three townlands of Ballyhemikan, Carrigaline and Rafeen which lie to the north-east. The site of the old church lies some two-and-a-half miles west of Carrigaline. William Wynchedon was prebendary of Liscleary in 1392 and John Corre in 1406.

Caherlag which was erected into a prebend in 1349 by Bishop John Roche was apparently a donation of the MacCottyr family who presented to it in ancient times.[37] Caherlag is now in the modern parish of Glounthane and no vestige of its ancient church remains. Its prebendares were John Walsh, 1441; John Butler who was deprived in the same year; John Terry, 1462, and John Barry, 1481.

Holy Trinity. The first explicit reference to Holy Trinity as a prebend occurs in 1392 when Thomas Morgan is mentioned as chaplain of the prebend.[38] It was presumably a prebend in 1295 when William de Muenes was presented, although Webster's interpretation of a fifteenth-century papal taxation mentions Holy Trinity as 'a newly created prebend for sustaining a vicar for the Cathedral Church of Cork'.[39] Various medieval documents refer to Holy Trinity as a free royal chapel in the gift of the king. Its rectory was its principal source of revenue, and its prebendaries were Henry Kyng, 1439; David Meade, 1483; David Creagh, 1483, and Philip Gould, 1488.

36 Ibid.

37 Ibid.

38 *Cal. papal letters, 1362–1404*, p. 203.

39 Webster, *The Diocese of Cork*, p. 96 n.

Killaspugmullane was an ancient parish, a portion of which is now in the modern parish of Glounthane and a portion in Watergrasshill. The site of the church lies three miles from Rathcooney, two from Templeusque and one from Kilquane. Killaspugmullane is the first Cork canonry and prebend mentioned in the papal registers. In 1364 David Gower of the diocese of Limerick was appointed by the pope to this prebend, which was described as 'void by the death of William Epeworthe, so long ago that it has lapsed to the apostolic See'.[40] It was then valued at thirty-two gold florins but was taxed at only one shilling in 1437. The source of revenue was the rectory of Killaspugmullane with half the tithes of the four-and-a-half ploughlands of Cannaway Island and two acres of glebe there.[41] Prebendaries were Gilbert O'Herlihy who died in 1458; John Purcell, 1458; Donal O'Carroll who was appointed in 1458 on the promotion of John Purcell by papal provision to Ferns;[42] Maurice O'Kiely who was deprived in 1466; Maurice Stanton, 1466; Edmund Barry, 1481; Gerald Barry, 1481.

Kilbrogan was designated as a prebend in 1393 when the bishop of Cloyne received a mandate to assign Vincent Whyt to the canonry and prebend of Kilbrogan. In 1437 the prebend was valued at two shillings, while in 1591 the prebendary held only part of the rectorial tithes, the other part being held by the preceptory of Mourne and the abbey of Grange. One rectory of Aglish also formed part of the prebendal revenue. Kilbrogan is now included in the modern parish of Bandon, north of the river and in the barony of Kinalmeaky. No trace of the old church remains and there is a division of opinion as to its exact location. Prebendaries of Kilbrogan were Walter Galle, 1400; Donald O'Mangan, 1418; Thady Murphy, 1493 (no title); Dermot O'Mahony, 1493; Cormac McTadhg (Makaich), 1500; Donal Murphy, 1503.

Kilbrittain was a prebend in 1393[43] but was not listed as such in 1437 when it was taxed at four shillings. Anciently known as *Capella de Kylshinthin de Kilbritton,*[44] it had become *Ecclesia*

---

40 *Cal. papal petitions, 1342–1419,* p. 468.

41 Brady, *Records,* i, 59. Though a post-Reformation reference, this is probably relevant to the medieval period also.

42 *Cal. papal letters, 1455–64,* p. 374.

43 *Cal. papal letters, 1362–1404,* p. 475.

44 Smith, *History of Cork,* i, 39.

de Kilbrittain et Kilshinihan, prebenda nata by 1591.[45] The prebendal revenue was derived from the rectory and from the townland of Kilshinahan in the parish of Kilbrittain. The ruins of the old church are situated in the church field just outside the demesne wall of Kilbrittain Castle.

Killanully was a prebend in 1437 and was taxed at five shillings.[46] It was a benefice with cure (*cum cura*) and the rectory was the only source of revenue. The ancient parish of Killanully is presently divided between the modern parishes of Douglas and Ballinhassig. Its church was located some five miles from Cork on the road from Carrigaline to Ballinhassig. Prebendaries of Killanully were Thomas Sheehan, 1447; Thady O'Daly, 1470;[47] William O'Kelly, 1477; Eugene O'Sullivan, 1478; Eneas O'Duffy, 1482.

Dromdaleague was rated as a prebend in the procuration list of 1437 and was taxed at three shillings.[48] Its valuation was twelve marks in 1441 when Dermot Canty (Ouchanty) was provided to the prebend by papal provision.[49] This ancient prebend is easily recognizable in the modern parish of Drimoleague in the barony of west Carbery. The site of the early church is in the old graveyard of Drimoleague on the Castledonovan Road. Prebendaries of Drimoleague were Randal O'Hurley who died in 1441; Dermot Canty, 1441; Matthew O'Mahony, 1456–57, and Macrobius O'Driscoll for the same years; Lachtin O'Cormack, 1469; Donogh O'Donovan, 1469–70;[50] Nicholas Barry, 1481.

Kilnaglory as a prebend was taxed at three shillings in 1437;

45 Brady, *Records*, i, 133.

46 Webster, *The Diocese of Cork*, p. 400.

47 There is great confusion of names here. On 11 October 1469 the annates contain a bond in the name of Eneas O'Daly (Ydalaid) by Thadeus, elect of Down and Connor, for the canonry and prebend of Killanully. On 15 January of the following year O'Daly was provided on the plea that Thomas O'Sannycayn *alias* Oscolan (Sheehan above) had held without title for about ten years: *Cal. papal letters, 1458–71*, p. 821. On 11 February 1471 a bull was issued to Thady O'Daly for a canonry and prebend of Cork which, according to the annates, was Killanully. In 1482/3 Eneas O'dabayg was provided to the canonry and prebend and Matthew O'Daly was ordered to be removed: *Cal. papal letters, 1471–84*, pt. 1, p.'144.

48 Webster, *The Diocese of Cork*, p. 400.

49 *Cal. papal letters, 1447–55*, p. 170.

50 *Cal. papal letters, 1458–71*, p. 821: Donatus Ydonnayn, 10 March 1469/70. From the annates we have a bond for Donal O'Donianayn by death of Macrobius O'Driscoll, 4 July 1470.

its source of revenue was the rectory in the parish of Ballincollig. The ancient parish of Kilnaglory is now incorporated in the parish of Ballincollig with the exception of a small portion which is in the parish of Ballinhassig. The church was situated five miles from Cork on the old road from Ballincollig to Ovens. The names of its prebendaries are missing.

Inishkenny, also called Ballymolmihill, was a prebend in 1469 and was probably prebendal in 1437 when it was taxed at six shillings. The ancient parish of Inishkenny which was near Waterfall is now incorporated in the modern parish of Ballincollig with a small portion in Ballinhassig. The church of Inishkenny stood four miles west of Cork near Waterfall, one mile to the east of Ballymacadane. Its prebendaries were Maurice Cogan who resigned in 1469; Donogh O'Riordan who held without title in 1469; David Hallinan, 1469; Matthew O'Mahony, 1475; Maurice O'Herlihy, 1482; Cornelius O'Sullivan, 1493; Donogh Cormac, 1494.

Desertmore was a prebend before 1471 and may have been prebendal in 1437 when it was taxed at three shillings. It is presently incorporated in the parish of Ovens in the barony of Muskerry, and its ancient church was situated eight miles south-west from Cork. Its prebendaries were Dermot Sheehan who died in 1469; Richard Purcel who was deposed in 1469 and was succeeded by Maurice O'Sullivan; Donogh O'Riordan, 1470; John O'Herlihy, senior, who held without title in 1482, and John O'Herlihy, junior, who was prebendary in 1485.

Over and above the foregoing, references to certain temporary prebends are also met with, but they carry neither dates of origin nor circumstances of decline. These temporary prebends were:

Carrigaline which was a prebend in 1337 and was then in the gift of Peter de Cogan, a minor. Thomas Harbergh was appointed prebendary of Beauver or Carrigaline in 1386,[51] John Tanner was presented in 1415, and it was still referred to as the prebendal church of Carrigaline in 1489. The church is no longer prebendal but the old name is preserved in the modern church and parish of Carrigaline.

51   Brady, *Records*, i, 59. Smith, *History of Cork*, i, 39, cites incorrectly the 'prebend of Kilnaglory, anciently called Beatae Mariae de Beaver', and has apparently confused Cell na gClerioch or Kilnagleary near Carrigaline with Kilnaglory. The taxation list of 1302 carries the correct citation: Church of Beaver and of Kilnagleragh.

Dunbulloge, in the parish of Glanmire, was a prebend until 1615 but when it was first so recognized is uncertain. In medieval times it formed part of the corps of the archdeacon and only two of its prebendaries have been identified: Hugh Cullen or Collins, 1482, and Matthew O'Daly, 1489.[52]

Kilroan was a prebend in 1418 when Donogh Mangan succeeded on the death of Walter Galle. His successor, William Lowillins, died in 1425, and in the same year Donald O'Reilly was provided to a canonry of Cork and the prebend of Kyllone or Kilroan. There are no other records of this prebend.

Kilgobban became a prebend in 1468 when provision was made to David de Courcey until such time as he should secure another prebend in Cork. In 1493 Kilgobban became a prebend *ad vitam* for John de Courcey. In the same way Knockavilly was created prebend for Donogh Mickellachayn in 1492 and in 1493 Rathdrought was made prebendal for Cornelius Murphy.

Prebends were sometimes granted as rewards for scholastic attainments and sometimes as inducements to study, and consequently dispensations for non-residence were freely granted to enable clerics pursue their studies abroad while retaining their benefices and enjoying their revenues. The tendency to pluralism was strengthened by the non-residential character of certain appointments, particularly those to which the cure of souls (*cura animarum*) did not attach and which were therefore listed as 'compatible', that is, they required no papal dispensation on the part of the holder. In theory, canon law forbade or severely restricted pluralism and non-residence as is clearly seen in the constitution *De Multa* of the Fourth Lateran Council and the constitution *Execrabilis* of John XXII in 1317, but by making exceptions for those studying for higher degrees canon law actually pandered to an abuse which it sought to eradicate. Evidences of pluralism are not wanting in Cork: Adam Cradock who was skilled in canon and civil law was dispensed to hold a plurality of benefices in 1363, Richard O'Hart who had studied canon law for several years was in 1411 granted the deanery of Ross and two vicarages in Cork, and so on. It was not until the period immediately before the Reformation that the evils inherent in this system wrought the greatest havoc on the pastoral mission of the church.

Certain inconsistencies existed in the method of election to prebends, and candidates even when armed with paper quali-

---

52 Bolster, 'Obligationes pro Annatis Diocesis Corcagiensis', p. 20.

fications were sometimes obliged to undergo examination
unless otherwise legitimately dispensed.[53] Nicholas O'Grady
who sought a prebend in 1363 was not obliged to sit for examination because of the intervention of the archbishop of Cashel in
his behalf. On the other hand, Geoffrey Galway, canon of Cork
and holder of a degree in canon law, was marked for promotion
from Kilbrittain to the canonry and prebend of Kilbrogan but
could only be transferred if found fit after examination.[54] All
applicants were not so qualified, especially in the later Middle
Ages when royal, episcopal and secular patronage was increasingly invoked and benefices were exploited and ear-marked
for high officials in church and state. For example, in 1295
Edward I invoked his prerogative of royal patronage and
presented William de Muenes to Holy Trinity, thus compensat-
ing de Muenes for duties discharged in procuring provisions
for the king's wars. In this way the church became the pay-
master of the state, since 'every vacancy in a bishopric, putting
benefices in the bishop's gift at the temporary disposal of the
crown, meant an influx of clerks appointed by the chancery,
and other government officials into vacant prebends as a source
of payment for their services to the state'.[55] Time also came when
royal patronage was invoked regardless of vacancy in a bishopric.

VICARS CHORAL

Non-resident cathedral canons were obliged to appoint members
of the lesser clergy to deputize for them at cathedral services.
Such clerics, who were known as vicars choral, were bound
to continual residence within the cathedral precinct. The
number of vicars usually coincided with that of the canons and
each vicar was partly supported by his own canon. The vicars'
main duty was choral, but they could also serve as deacons
and subdeacons at High Mass, and they became more and more
involved in cathedral duties as cathedral services became more
organized and diversified between the eleventh and fourteenth
centuries. The celebration and singing of the chapter Mass fell
to the vicars choral, as did also the Mass of the Blessed Virgin
and the recitation of the little office.[56] Vicars on appointment
swore fidelity to the dean and chapter and to the canons who

53   Cal. doc. Ire., 1293–1301, p. 236.

54   Cal. doc. Ire., 1252–84, no. 1279.

55   Thompson, The Cathedral Churches of England, p. 24.

56   The Black Book of Limerick, p. lxiii, states that Bishop Donatus Ua Briain founded
his chapter 'to recite the Canonical hours, and especially to celebrate a Mass of the
B.V.M. daily'.

appointed them, and each vicar promised to observe all the statutes concerning himself and his vicarage. His fixed stipend from the canon who appointed him was supplemented by an allowance from the common fund. At first vicars choral were linked by close personal bonds with their superiors until the building of common halls and colleges of residence established their right to security of tenure and their acquisition of common property enabled them to assert their autonomy. Smith quotes a manuscript—now lost—which was copied in 1628 by Robert Travers from an ancient roll (also lost), which gave the original number of vicars choral in Cork as two.[57]

The date at which the vicars choral became part of the cathedral personnel is uncertain. It is beyond doubt, however, that the concession granted in 1278 by Bishop Richard (*rectè* Robert Mac Donnchada) enabling prebendaries to have an 'annual priest' to serve their parishioners instead of a vicar whom they (the prebendaries) could not afford to pay,[58] does not refer to vicars choral but to the wider vicarage system by which the absentee pluralist benefice-holder got a substitute who was called a vicar or chaplain to administer the cure of souls in return for a salary, usually referred to as a moiety. Another reference to the 'vicars of the cathedral church of Cork' which occurs in a deed connected with the episcopate of Bishop John McCarroll (1301–21) may again have bearings on the vicarage system rather than on the institution of vicars choral. But the vicars choral were established in Cork by 1328 and appear to have already achieved a measure of autonomy. In that year, as a corporate body, they received from Bishop Walter le Rede (1326–30) a valuable site near the cathedral '204 feet in breadth, and in length, 200, of our lands and tenements near the city of Cork, for building houses and constructing other necessary matters on said land, which land lies in length between the greater Church [the cathedral] on [the] east and our court on the west. In breadth, between the royal road on the south and the way which leads to our court on the north.'[59] Other grants made out to the vicars choral were the vicarage of Corbally in 1348, donated by Bishop John Roche, the parish church of Desert-serges in 1431 by Milo FitzJohn, the church of Saint Mary le Nard in 1441 and the church of Kilroan in 1447 by Bishop Jordan Purcell. Drinagh, *particula de Drumlag*, in Desertserges was

57   Smith, *History of Cork*, i, 40.

58   Ibid., p. 39. The Travers' document is quoted as follows: 'Concessio Ricardi, episcop. Corcagiensis prebendariis ecclesiae cathedralis Corke, ut propter exilitatem nullum habeant vicarium sed presbyterum annualem qui parochianiis suis deserviat.'

59   Richard Caulfield, *The Annals of St. Fin Barre's Cathedral, Cork*, p. 7.

Robert Coggan's gift to them in 1456, and the rectories of
Fanlobbus (Dunmanway) and Kinneigh which Edmund
Riddefort donated to them in 1447 were confirmed and ratified
by Bishop Purcell. Other minor grants included Clasdow *alias*
Clashduff, Boirnecarty, Ynerynbrenig(?), and the entire rectory of Marmullane (Passage West) which was given to the
vicars choral by the Roches.[60]

These extensive grants point to the recognition of the vicars
choral in Cork as a corporate body which was *per se* independent
of the capitular assembly. In time, this independance may have
constituted uneasy relations with the dean and chapter as was
the case in English secular cathedrals, but we have no corrobora-
tory evidence of the fact. Conflict continued until the religious
revolt of the sixteenth century, after which the institution of
vicars choral was discontinued in the Catholic Church. Today
a few placenames, Vicar Street by Saint Fin Barre's Cathedral,
and Vicar's Acre in Togher ('near the royal road to the south')
are all that remain to perpetuate the memory of the vicars choral
of the medieval diocese of Cork.

CHANTRY PRIESTS

Though usually low-listed in the stratified structure of medieval
secular cathedrals, the chantry priests as an institution lay at
the root of all ecclesiastical establishments in the Middle Ages.
The chantry itself grew out of the anniversary service or anniversary Mass for benefactors of the cathedral. When benefactions
became more numerous and more liberal, the necessity of a
larger staff of *ministri inferiores* became obvious, and from the
twelfth century onwards the establishment of chantries became
increasingly popular, usually taking the form of permanent
endowments of land and rent sufficient to maintain a priest or
priests to say Mass daily in perpetuity for the souls of the founder,
his family and his friends. The foundations of chantries appear
also to have had some connection with a growing devotion to
the Mass which becomes apparent in the thirteenth century.

Chantry priests (*cantaristae* or *capellani cantariarum*) were
also known as stipendiary priests, a term indicating that theirs
was a temporary status with no fixity of tenure such as the
vicars choral enjoyed. At the same time it was not unusual for
a vicar choral to be appointed to a chantry as a means of implementing his normal revenue. Because of such overlappings
it is impossible to estimate the extent to which chantry priests

60   Smith, *History of Cork*, i, 40.

swelled the personnel of the cathedral clergy. As a group the chantry priests, who could be appointed by their patrons, by collation of the bishop, or by dean and chapter, were, like the rest of the *ministri inferiores*, subject in disciplinary matters to the dean and chapter who could deprive, suspend or otherwise penalize them for neglect of duty—for instance, for defrauding the souls of their benefactors of their Masses. Specific times were laid down for these Masses; they were known as *Missae currentes* and were celebrated usually from dawn until ten or eleven in the morning. The chantry priests also helped the vicars with singing and with the chanting of the canonical hours.

Because they had no other specific duties attached to the cathedral, the chantry priests were originally non-resident, but in the fifteenth century colleges on the style of those already in use by the vicars choral were founded for them.[61] For the diocese of Cork there is specific reference to the chantry chapel of Saint Clement in the medieval cathedral of Saint Finbarr, but there is no mention of any associated college of chantry priests. The chapel was on the north side of the cathedral nave, it measured twelve feet by sixteen and is believed to have enclosed the tomb of the chapel's benefactor.[62] Chantries were likewise a feature of Christ Church and Saint Peter's in the sixteenth century and probably existed long before that time. The only indication we have of a chantry college in Cork is the existence of a College of Stone and a Chapel of Saint Laurence; the former was built in 1482 for the support of eight priests to say Mass daily in Christ Church.[63]

ALTARISTS

Clerks in minor orders, never priests, formed the lowest stratum of the staff of the medieval secular cathedral. The altarist was assigned the custody of a particular altar which he served as assistant to an appointed chantry priest. Side by side with the altarists were the choristers, young boys admitted to the cathedral for education and especially for training in psalmody; these were under the care of the precentor, and when their voices broke they were usually incorporated as *ministri inferiores* in one branch or other of the cathedral organization. Altarists, while they were important on the continent and in England, do not appear to have been a feature of Irish secular cathedrals.

61 Thompson, *The Cathedral Churches of England*, p. 164.

62. Webster, *The Diocese of Cork*, pp. 125 and 202.

63 Ibid., p. 138.

THE COMMON FUND

The chapter, as a corporation, could hold and administer property for the common good. Such community of property consisted of a common fund which was originally formed out of that part of the chapter's revenues and estates which remained after the individual canons had been accorded their separate prebends. In churches where a semblance of common life was retained, some of the food of the community was provided from the common fund; elsewhere, distributions of money, known as commons, were made from it in weekly or quarterly payments. By the end of the twelfth century payments from the common fund were made dependent on residence, and in this way the *communia* helped to maintain the large clerical proletariat of the medieval cathedrals. It also paid the salaries of officers and employees of the chapter and formed a treasury from which extraordinary chapter expenses could be met. Revenue forming this common fund came from many sources: rents and fee-farms of the chapter estates and property, tithes from appropriated churches, fines levied on non-resident canons, chapter taxes on prebends and duties payable on entry into residence. There were also such feudal payments as escheats, heriots, reliefs, supplemented by profits from the chapter seal.[64] These latter profits were a valuable source of revenue since many people were willing to pay very high fees for sealed confirmation of their rights and privileges from the chapter.

The official in charge of the common fund was known as the *communar*. He was elected annually, he superintended the collection of the revenue, he distributed the commons to the cathedral clergy and was obliged to submit his accounts regularly to be audited by the chapter. By this twin system of quarterly audit and annual election the chapter could exercise constant control over the management of its income, and although the same communar might be successively returned for a number of years, his re-election did not increase his control over the administration of the fund which retained its 'common' character all through. The *communia* or common fund of the Cork chapter was valued at six marks in 1302, but

64 The seals of the bishops of Cork which have been published by Caulfield date only from 1689 to the present day. One seal, which could be a relic of the pre-Reformation chapter of Cork, is that affixed to a dispensation granted by Dominic Roche, vicar-general of Cork, to James Ronan (*ingenuus adolescens*) and Anastacia Thyrry (*ingenua puella*) in June 1641. The seal represents an angel holding a label on which the original device is no longer decipherable. The neighbouring dioceses of Cloyne and Ross are more fortunate in this respect. Cloyne has the seal of Nicholas Effingham (1284–1320), and Ross that of the Carmelite Stephen Brown who became bishop in 1402.

there is no indication anywhere as to whence it was derived, how it was disbursed or whether it was ever increased.

Apart from the common fund from which salaries and normal common expenses were met, there was a second fund called the fabric fund which was set aside for the building and repair of the cathedral fabric. Its management was entrusted to two residentiary canons known as masters of the fabric, and they, like the communar, were elected annually and enjoyed a fixed salary. Under them they had a clerk of the fabric—he was usually a vicar choral or a chantry priest—and a staff of craftsmen and workmen appointed by dean and chapter and accountable to them for all building projects and for necessary repairs. A document dated 1306 carries a reference to the fabric fund of the church of Saint Mary Shandon,[65] and it is probable that such a fund was part of the cathedral organization as well.

The medieval chapter fulfilled an important role in the life of the medieval diocese in matters liturgical, jurisdictional, administrative and educational. The degree of autonomy won by the chapter members made for frequent clashes with the bishops; but for all that the medieval bishop through his diocesan visitation, his exercise of the *jus ordinarium* and his practice of the right of collation to vacant benefices was enabled to wield certain influence within the chapter body. There is no reason for supposing that relations between the bishops of Cork and their chapters were any different from those obtaining in Saint Mary's, Limerick, and Saint Patrick's, Dublin. In the last analysis, however, and despite inevitable jurisdictional clashes, the cathedral church of a diocese was the one enjoying the greatest prestige, not because its precincts housed the chapter officials and their subordinates, but because it contained the bishop's *cathedra* or chair. In other words, the cathedral church continued to be regarded as the mother-church of the diocese, its seat of administration; and the occupant of that seat was and would always be the bishop.

65   See Chapter XI.

APPENDIX A

*Dignitarial Members of the Medieval Chapter of Cork,
culled from the Calendars of Papal Letters, the
Annates and from the printed Irish and English
Public Records.* Papal providees are indicated with
an asterisk (*); king's clerks with a dagger (†).

DEANS OF CORK

1286 Philip
1302 John McCarroll (MacCarwell) who later became
      bishop.
1323 Dionysius; he was dean for three years.
1328 Philip White
1337 G...
1346 John Roche or de Rupe was dean for a year; he became
      bishop in 1347.
1348 Gerald Barry; he succeeded Roche as bishop in 1358.
* 1359 George de Rupe. He also held canonries without
      prebends in Lismore and Ardfert and the rectory of
      Garothe in the diocese of Emly.
* 1363 William Bula; he became bishop of Ardfert.
* 1404 Milo FitzJohn who became bishop in 1409.
* 1427 Richard Pellyn
* 1441 John Walsh
* 1469 Thomas Cornis
1481 Maurice Standon, canon of Cloyne, was *de facto* dean
      of Cork.
* 1482 Matthew O'Mahony
* 1496 John O'Herlihy
* 1500 Thadeus McCarthy (Tadeus Mackarig)

PRECENTORS

1265 David de Lang
* 1444 William Skiddy; provided on the resignation of James
      Lowe, for whom neither appointment nor provision
      is indicated.
1471 Thomas Healy was deprived.
* 1471 Donogh O'Riordan

1475 John Roche, rector of Saint Mary's, Shandon, and in minor orders only, became precentor.

1481 Maurice Stanton

* 1487 Cornelius Murphy disputed the precentorship with John de Geraldinis: a papal ruling in Murphy's favour permitted him to enjoy the precentorship together with his vicarage of Rathdrought. Later, the rectory of Kinneigh was added.

* 1492 John O'Herlihy

* 1493 Donogh McCarthy (Makarrygh)

CHANCELLORS

1370 Philip Gall

1402 Michael Kenefig

1427 Miles Roche

1467 William MacGibon

* 1474 Matthew O'Mahony

* 1481 Cornelius O'Flynn, abbot of Gill Abbey

* 1483 David Hallinan

* 1488 Philip Gould

TREASURERS

1267 Geoffrey O'Brennan

1370 William Galle

1390 Richard Went

1474 Patrick Lawles; he held the treasureship for twelve or thirteen years without canonical title.

* 1482 Donogh Murphy

* 1483 Eugene O'Sullivan

* 1485 John O'Herlihy

ARCHDEACONS

1180 Reginald

c.1182 Gilbert

1236 Reginald O'Fin

1323 John...

† 1330 Henry de Thrapton

1337 D...

† 1346 William Epeworth

1365 Nicholas de Barry

1385 Robert Roche

1396 John Rede who had been litigating about the archdeaconry since 1391 got possession this year.

1407 Walter Galle

* 1408   John Rede was reappointed.
* 1414   Geoffrey Pellyn
  1430   Richard Scurlag
* 1459   David Meade. In 1469 he was defending his arch-
         deaconry against David Lecurcy, the bull of whose
         provision was lost.
* 1462   John O'Kelly, who was provided 'by deprivation of
         David Meade'.
  1471   Dionysius Hurley or Herlihy
* 1481   Nicholas Barry, treasurer of Cloyne, became arch-
         deacon of Cork.
  1485   William Meade, clerk of the diocese of Limerick
* 1487   Donogh O'Herlihy
* 1489   Donogh Oberlan
* 1498   James [?David] Barry
* 1502   Donogh McCarthy (Macharyg)

APPENDIX B

Townlands of the Prebends

SAINT MICHAEL'S

Ballyamaddree
Ballyskerdane
Ballythomas
Templemichael
Ballinvriskig

LISCLEARY

Ballinphelic
Meadstown
Shanagraigue
Ballea
Ballyginnane
Coolsallagh

Ballyhemiken
Carrigaline (Liscleary)
Raffeen

CAHERLAG

Ballinglanna
Ballyhenick
Ballynagarbragh
Ballynaroon
Dunkettle
Kilcoolishal
Lakenroe
Rowgarrane
Killacloyne
Killahora

HOLY TRINITY

An ancient city parish

KILLASPUGMULLANE

Watergrasshill
Trantstown
Ballingohig
Ballinvinny, N. and S.

Coolnacaha
Kilrussane

KILBROGAN

Callatrim
Caroon, E. and W.

Coolfada
Curryclogh
Derrycool
Gurteen
Kilbeg N. and S.
Kilbrogan, pt.
Knockbrogan, pt.
Laragh
Lisnabauree (Lisbanree)
Littlesilver
Mallowgatton
Mishells
Shinagh
Tullyglass
Roughgrove, E. and W.

KILBRITTAIN

Ballybeg
Ballymore
Baltinakin
Baurleigh
Coolshinagh
Cripplehill
Kilbrittain
Kilanamaul
Kilshinahan
Knockbrown
Knoppoge
Maulmane
Maulshinlahane

KILLANULLY

Ballinreeshig
Killanully
Kilnahone
Ballinvuskig
Rathmacullig, E. and W.

DRIMOLEAGUE

Acres
Aughram
Barnagowlane, E. and W.
Bauragarriff

Barnhulla
Bawnahow, N, and S.
Bohernabredagh
Castledonovan
Ceancullig
Clashduff
Clodagh
Cummeen
Derreenacrinnig, E. and W.
Derryduff
Deelish
Derrynagree, E. and W.
Dromasta
Dromdaleague
Dromduvane
Garranes, N. and S.
Glanaclogha
Glandert
Gurteeniher
Killahane
Kilmore
Kilnahera, E. and W.
Kilscohanagh
Knockane
Knockeenbwee, L. and U.
Leitry, L. and U.
Loughcrot
Maulnaskea
Moyny, E., L., M., U.
Mullaghmesha
Rearahinagh
Reenroe
Seehanes
Shronacarton
Tonafora
Toneagh
Toughraheen

KILNAGLORY

Ballincollig
Ballingully
Ballyburden, Beg and More
Greenfield
Kilnaglory

Knockburden
Lisheens
Ravakeel
Windsor
Ballynore
Ballyank
Knockpogue

Kilmurriheen
Knockalisheen
Knockanmallav'ge
Rochfordstown
Ballyleigh
Oldabbey
Sraleigh

INISHKENNY

Ardarostig
Ballinveltig
Ballinvoultig
Ballinvrinsig
Ballymah
Curraheen
Inishkenny

DESERTMORE

Ballygroman, L. and U.
Clashanaffrin
Garryhesty
Kilbane
Knockanemealgulla
Knocknatreenane
Kilcrea

X

The Deaneries and Parishes

THE DEANERIES

The territorial delimitation of early Irish deaneries which is said to have been introduced at Kells corresponded originally with the territorial subdivisions allotted to the vassal tribes or sub-septs of the dominant tribe in any given area. By analogy with the diocesan organization which equates the diocese with the overkingdom or *mór-thuath*, the deanery, which is a subdivision of the diocese, is said to represent the *Tricha Ced* which was a subdivision of the overkingdom.[1] As a unit of territorial administration the deanery may likewise be regarded as the forerunner of the later civil barony with which it was sometimes coterminous. Thus, while the deaneries were in a sense partly political in origin (and this may explain their fluctuations), as expressions of ecclesiastical organization and administration they represent an important functional development in the medieval church. We have seen that before the Normans came, the church in Ireland had been reorganized on the basis of the territorial diocese; this in turn led to the creation of parishes to the extent that by the fourteenth century when printed records become plentiful, the country was 'covered by a network of parishes . . . [and] . . . in some parts . . . there was already something near the final total of parishes'.[2] It was a natural development that the rural parishes, those farthest removed from the episcopal *cathedra*, should be grouped together under the surveillance of a resident cleric known as a dean, upon whom devolved the duty of visitation and of investigating cases of dilapidation, neglect, abuse and other misdemeanours on the part of clerics and benefice-holders

1 James Hogan, 'The Tricha Cet and Related Land Measures', *R.I.A. Proc.*, xxxvii, sect. c (1929), p. 190.

2 Otway-Ruthven, *Med. Ire.*, pp. 126–7.

within the rural deanery.[3] These rural deaneries succeeded in some cases to ancient bishoprics, in others to the *chorepiscopi* for whom the Synod of Kells (1152) made provision,[4] and in others again to the archdeaconries, but there are no evidences of the last type in Ireland where archdeaconries did not form diocesan subdivisions.[5] We are on surer ground as to the succession of deaneries to older bishoprics and have three examples of the development in the diocese of Cork. The deanery of Ocurblethan embraced the ancient bishopric of Killaspugmullane, the deanery of Kerrycurrihy contained the ancient bishopric of Rosbeg,[6] and the ancient bishopric of Kinneigh lay within the confines of the deanery of Glansalvy.

Two fourteenth-century taxation lists show that there were originally five rural deaneries in the diocese of Cork, namely, Ocurblethan, Kery, Kenalethe *ultra*, Kenalethe *citra* and Corkolwyn. These incomplete taxation lists do not include that part of the diocese extending from Enniskeane and Murragh to Mizen Head where according to later sources two more deaneries, Glansalvy and Foneragh or *Fonn Iartharach*, were established. City parishes were included in the deaneries nearest the city; there was no central deanery as such and there is no indication anywhere of inter-relational activities between the bishop and his rural representatives. Visitation records which would furnish this necessary information are unavailable and while we assume that visitations were carried out when necessary we must deplore the scribal carelessness which neglected to transmit the visitation records to posterity. State records, even when supplemented by the researches of modern scholars and local historians, can never hope to fill this gap occasioned by diocesan indifference.

The Deanery of Ocurblethan

The territory of Ucurp as mentioned in the Innocentian decretal of 1199 was obviously the nucleus of this rural deanery. The tribe of Ui Cuirb Liathain traced descent from Corb, son

---

3 Thompson, *The English Clergy and their Organization in the Later Middle Ages*, p. 67.

4 William Reeves, *The Ecclesiastical Antiquities of Down, Connor and Dromore*, p. 127, quotes the following enactment of the Synod of Kells: 'Ut decedentibus chorepiscopis et exiliorum sedium episcopis in Hibernia, in eorum locum eligerentur et succederent archipresbyteri a dioecesanis constituendi, qui cleri et plebis solicitudinem gerant infra suos limites, et ut eorum sedes in totidem capita decanatum ruralium erigerentur.'

5 Geoffrey J. Hand, 'The Church in the English Lordship, 1216–1307', in Corish, ed., *Ir. catholicism*, ii, pt. 3, p. 17.

6 Plummer, *Vitae SS Hib.*, i, 184.

of Liathan, the tribes descended from Liathan were found scattered over the entire eastern part of county Cork as far as Youghal. They also colonized that part of the barony of Barrymore which is now in the diocese of Cloyne, and they extended westwards over the northern suburbs of Cork as far as Currykippane. By reference to the diocese of Cork we have seen that the territory of Ui Cuirb (Cuirp) Liathain comprised all the parishes lying east and north-east of the city. After the Anglo-Norman takeover this area was erected into the cantred of Ocurblethan, and by the fourteenth century, for ecclesiastical purposes, it was constituted with some modifications into the deanery of Ocurblethan or Ocurbliethan.[7] In terms of contemporary extents this deanery included the ancient parishes of Kilcully, Dunbulloge, Rathcooney, Templemichael, Ardnageehy (Watergrasshill), Ballinaltig, Kilquane, Killaspugmullane, Glanmire, Ballydeloher, Caherlag, Little Island, Shandon (including Saint Catherine's), Saint Peter, Holy Trinity and Saint Nicholas (which was never, strictly speaking, a parish church). The deanery had also within its limits the manors and castles of Shandon and Rathanisky which belonged to the Barrys. Ocurblethan in the time of the first Elizabeth was known as Ogormliehan or Gormlehan and as such is perpetuated in the townland of Gormley in Dunbulloge. Schenbally, now Templemichael, enjoyed a long survival of the deanery tradition. Bishop Downes, who toured the diocese in 1700, noted that 'tis said by the country people, this church was never made use of for divine service, and that it was a place for the clergy to meet in'.[8] All the parishes of this medieval deanery have become incorporated in the present city deanery, as Saint Mary's (North Parish), Gurranebraher, Glanmire, Glounthane and Watergrasshill.[9]

The Deanery of Kery or Kyrricurith

The name Kery or Ciarrigi as given in the decretal of 1199 represents the sept of the Ciarraige Cuirche, most of whose territory, as we have seen, fell to de Cogan in the parcelling out of the kingdom of Cork to the Norman grantees. It is most probable that the deanery of Kery grew up around the Norman cantred of Kerrycurrihy and the de Cogan manor of Carrigaline.[10]

7   Liam Ó Buachalla, 'The Ancient See-lands of the Bishop of Cork in the Northern Suburbs', *Cork Hist. Soc. Jn.*, lxx (1965), 131.

8   Brady, *Records*, i, 290.

9   This area would include as well the ancient parishes of Glenville and Carrignavar.

10   In 1439 this district came into the hands of the earl of Desmond and was later a scene of conflict during the Desmond Wars.

In 1302 the deanery extended westwards to Inishkenny and Kilnaglory, southwards to Templebreedy and embraced the area extending from Rosbeg in Ringaskiddy to Cullen, Bally-martle and Crosshaven. It included the medieval parishes of Liscleary, Ballinaboy, Killanully, Carrigaline, Kilnagleary, Douglas, Corbally, Ballymolmihill or Inishkenny, Kilnaglory, Ringaskiddy, Templebreedy and Carrigrohane. In modern parochial equivalents it included Saint Finbarr's (South and West), Douglas, Passage, Monkstown, Carrigaline, Ballincollig and Ballinhassig. As a civil unit the barony of Kerrycurrihy is now confined to the district between Passage and Templebreedy. It has not been preserved as an ecclesiastical unit, its parishes having been divided between the city deanery and that of Kinsale. The only nominal survival of the ancient sept and deanery is Drumgurrihy (Dromgurrihih) in the parish of Monkstown.

The Deanery of Kenalethe ultra

We have seen that Kenalethe (Kinalea, *Cinel Aedha*) was one of the main subdivisions of the tribal lands of the Ui Eachach Mumhan, and that the sept claimed descent from Aedh, son of Criomthan, who was ancestor of the O'Mahony clan. At some date before the beginning of the fourteenth century the tribeland of Kinalea was adopted by the church as the territorial basis for the two rural deaneries of Kenalethe which were to be distinguished according to their positions astride the river Bandon. Hence the qualifications Kenalethe *ultra* and Kenalethe *citra*. Towards the middle of the thirteenth century the civil district of Kenalethe *ultra* became known as Kinalmeaky or *Cinel mBeice*, from Bec, a seventh-century descendant of Eochaidh, father of the Ui Eachach tribe. The ancient tribal name is preserved only in the list of rural deaneries, the modern barony is still called Kinalmeaky, but except for parts of Bally-modan and Brinny the barony does not otherwise approximate the ancient deanery. As a deanery Kenalethe *ultra* embraced the modern parishes of Courceys or Ballinspittal, Kilbrittain, Bandon and Innishannon, which by fourteenth-century reckoning included Ringrone, Killoney (at Courtaparteen), Temple-trine, Currarane, Rathclarin, Burren, Kilshinahan, Kilbrittain, Kilgobban, Rathdrought, Bandon (Ballymodan), Innishannon, Brinny, Templemichael (de Dowagh) and portion of Cloghan and Kildarra. The fourteenth-century taxation returns give this deanery as Kenalethe *ultra* and Lynnalethe *ultra*, while later records render it as Kinalay *ultra*,[11] Kinnalegh *ultra*[12] and Kinaley *ultra*.[13] The deanery encompassed the birthplace of Saint Finbarr and Rath Raithleann, the governing centre from which the Ui Eachach Mumhan ruled.

The Deanery of *Kenalethe* citra

This deanery, which is also known as Bambech *citra*, lay to the south of the deanery of Kery and extended along the coast from Dunderrow to the mouth of the river Bandon through the ancient parish of Kilpatrick on the tidal estuary of Ringabella Bay and thence on to Kinsale. Within its ambit were the ancient parishes of Ballyfeard, Ballyfoyle, Kinure, Clontead, Rincurran (Charles' Fort), Kinsale, Tisaxon, Leighmoney, Dunderrow, Kilmeedy or Ballymartle, Nohoval, Kilmonoge and Cullen, which today are incorporated in the modern parishes of Belgooly, Tracton, Kinsale and Clontead. It seems likely that Kinalea or Kenalethe was originally a single deanery but that it was divided following the establishment of the Norman baronies of Barry Oge and de Courcey. According to present-day arrangement the medieval deaneries of Kenalethe *ultra* and *citra* are distributed, with some modifications and additions, between the deaneries of Bandon and Kinsale.

The Deanery of *Corkolwyn* or *Corknuwyn*

The deanery of Corkolwyn derives its name from Corca Ifflanloe, the territory of Ui Floinn Lua who extended their sway into the area north of the river Lee and between it and the Blackwater. Here certain interfluvial parishes which belonged to the diocese of Cork at the time of Rathbreasail were erected into the Cloyne deanery of Musgrylin. The deanery of Corkolwyn lay south of the Lee and extended from Ovens to Inchigeela, and except for the townlands of Fergus East and Cronody and part of the parish of Inchigeela, the river formed the boundary of the deanery to the north. Its southern boundary hugged the ridge of hills south of Ballincollig and Kilmurry and proceeded thence to the Shehy mountain south of Gougane Barra.

According to the fourteenth-century taxations the churches of Aglish, Kilbonane, Kilmurry, Cannaway, Desertmore, Ovens and Moviddy (Dundrinan) all lay within the ambit of the

11   Taxation List, 1588. T.C.D., MS E.3. 14.

12   Michael A. Murphy, 'The Royal Visitation of Cork, Cloyne, Ross and the College of Youghal', *Archiv. Hib.*, ii (1913), 173–215.

13   Webster, *The Diocese of Cork*, p. 120, quoting Reeves MS 1067, p. 374.

deanery of Corkolwyn. The parish of Macloneigh lying south
of the river must also have belonged; likewise the parishes of
Kilmichael and Inchigeela which do not appear on the records
until the fifteenth century (1437). The area encompassed by
these two parishes would have belonged either to the parish
of Kilmurry or to that of Macloneigh in earlier times. In terms
of existing parochial arrangements the deanery of Corkolwyn
comprised the parishes of Iveleary, Kilmichael, Kilmurry and
Ovens. A visitation record of 1591 lists the deanery as Corcomoone, that of 1615 calls it Kilmughan-Ifflanloe, and an
inquisition carrying the same date refers to it as Kilmoan
Ifflanloe. As happened in Templemichael, the deanery tradition
appears to have survived in this district down to the year 1731;
a record for that year tells that 'in this parish of [Kilmurry]
Kilmorragh . . . there have met upon solemn occasions, within
these two or three years, many priests to officiate in a body,
sometimes seven, sometimes more, sometimes twenty'.[14] In
both cases however the suggestion must be accepted with
reservation, as there is no direct corroboration forthcoming.

Deaneries for the more westerly parts of the diocese are not
encountered until 1591 and 1615 when two more deaneries
emerge, namely, Glansalvy or Glansalny and Foneragh or
Fonn Iartharach, the establishment of which most probably
synchronized with the erection of the other deaneries.

The Deanery of Glansalny

This deanery, under its more correct form Clansalvy, derives
from the Clann Sealbaigh, the family which gave numerous
abbots and *airchinnechs* to Cork. The Ua Sealbaigh were of the
Cinel Laeghaire[15] sept which in turn was a branch of the Ui
Eachach Mumhan; their territories were coterminous with the
ancient see of Kinneigh, and it is significant that from an early
date the see of Cork held territory at Nedineach which lay
within the confines of the septland of Clann Sealbaigh. The
deanery of Glansalvy therefore was coextensive with the
bishopric of Kinneigh and contained the parishes of Kinneigh,
Fanlobbus or Dunmanway, Murragh or Newcestown, Desertserges, Ballymoney, Drinagh, Drimoleague and Enniskeane.

---

14 'Report on the State of Popery in Ireland, 1731 (Munster)', *Archiv. Hib.*, ii (1913),
138.

15 It is less likely that the name of the deanery originated from the Clann Sealbaigh
of the Corca Laighdhe sept whose headquarters lay between Kilcoe and Inchidony.
See J. T. Collins, 'Some Recent Contributions to Cork Diocesan History', *I.E.R.*, lxxv
(1951), 50–1.

The modern townlands of Kilshallow or Killtallwoge (as rendered in Elizabethan times) and Ballyhalwick (*Baile Ui Shelbhaigh* as pronounced by native speakers) are remnants of the ancient tribeland upon which the deanery of Glansalvy was constituted.

The Deanery of Foneragh (Fonyeragh)

Foneragh, Fonyeragh, *Fonn Iartharach* was the western land of the O'Mahony's of Kinalmeaky stretching from Drimoleague to Mizen Head. It contained the peninsula of Ivagh lying between Dunmanus and Roaring-Water Bay, consequently the word Ivagha, which is a derivation of Ui Eachach, is some-times posed as an alternative for Fonyeragh.[16] The deanery corresponding to Foneragh encompassed the six parishes of Kilmoe, Schull, Kilcrohane, Durrus, Kilmocomoge or Bantry and Caheragh. Politically and ecclesiastically there appears to have been an annexation here, for the parishes belonged originally to the diocese of Ross and the *Fonn Iartharach* itself was wrested from the Corca Laighdhe by the Ui Eachach. There were anciently many septs in this area; the most impor-tant were the Beanntraighe and the O Bairres from whom, respectively, the parishes of Bantry and Muintervara (*Muintir Bhairre*) or Durrus got their names. The fact that the deanery did not retain any of these western tribal names is regarded as token of some form of conquest or annexation.

In the period between the fourteenth century and the present day the rural deaneries of the diocese of Cork underwent many numerical and territorial fluctuations from which there finally emerged four deaneries, namely, the city and suburbs, Bandon, Kinsale and Bantry, the parochial distribution of which will be found in the appendix to this chapter.

THE PARISHES

The parish is the smallest unit in the adminstrative structure of the church, and its origins like those of deanery and diocese were partly civil and partly ecclesiastical. As diocese was coterminous with *mor-thuath* and deanery with *Tricha Ced*, the parish in its turn represented the ultimate administrative division, namely the smaller *tuath* and even the *baile biataigh*. In a more general sense of the word 'parish' has a threefold connotation. It signifies firstly a specific area and population under the jurisdiction of a single cleric who is called a parish

16   Residents of Goleen are referred to as Ivahaghs to this day.

priest. It connotes in the second place the civil parish or division, the origin of which goes back to the fifth or sixth centuries and which was characteristic of countries under the rule of imperial Rome. Outlying districts of the Roman Empire were known as parishes (*parochiae*) and they were administered by a *Presbyter plebanus* or a *Parochianus*. These scattered divisions became the parish proper of pre-Reformation times. There is, finally, the modern parish which is usually a union of two or more civil parishes. According to Brady's *Records* there were some eighty-four parishes in the pre-Reformation diocese of Cork, and Brady, who wrote in 1863, frequently refers to these parishes as units of civil administration when more correctly they represent ancient Catholic ecclesiastical divisions which were adopted by the civil authorities as convenient units of administration. Civil parishes properly so called, that is, parishes created by acts of parliament, are comparatively few in number. At present, parishes of the Church of Ireland correspond closely to the Catholic medieval parishes, whereas modern Catholic parishes, because of the disruption caused in Reformation and post-Reformation times, had to be reorganized in the eighteenth century and the reorganization did not take medieval reckoning into account.

No deep or serious study of the evolution of the parochial system in this country has so far been undertaken, with the result that many questions remain dangling in mid-air with no immediate prospect of reaching ground level. All that can be stated with any certainty is that some beginnings of parochial organization were attempted very early in the twelfth century by Sitric, Norse king of Dublin, grandson to that Sitric who was son-in-law to Brian Boru. On his return from a pilgrimage to Rome Sitric, we are told, set about modelling the church in Dublin on the Roman style. Evidence becomes more clear-cut in the period between 1111 and 1152 when territorial dioceses were set up, but the properly defined and organized parish was unknown until 1171–72 when an important decree of the Synod of Cashel effected a significant breakthrough. The synod decreed that every man should pay tithe to his own parish church. Commenting on this Professor Otway-Ruthven draws some very important conclusions: 'It seems reasonably clear', she says, 'that this marks the real starting point of parochial organization, for tithes are of cardinal importance in the formation of the territorial parish: arising out of the produce of the land, and forming the inalienable property of the rector of the parish, they ensure that the land in question cannot be detached from one parish and attached to another, for this would be to deprive the rector of his property. Thus, once the tithe-supported parish had been formed, its outline became a permanent feature of ecclesiastical geography.'[17]

At an early stage in the history of the church, bishops provided for the spiritual needs of people living at great distances from the episcopal or mother-churches by sending non-resident priests to minister among them. After performing all necessary services these priests reported back to their bishops. In time, as churches and population groups grew more numerous, it was found necessary to allocate resident priests to these outlying areas where the churches were gradually raised to parochial status. Areas chosen for parochial organization were usually large enough to maintain a church and support a priest or rector, sometimes even a vicar as well. This development cannot be traced for the diocese of Cork but the practice of sending priests to outlying churches is known to have prevailed there, and it was still observed by the monks of Gill Abbey and Tracton in medieval times. From the nature of early Irish society it would appear that parishes were first set up in rural rather than in urban areas, and on the whole the parochial boundaries as originally laid down have remained stable through-out the centuries. As the late Canon Power observed, 'the civil parish of the modern Map is the identical parish of the 16th century Visitations, of the Papal Taxations and of the Annates of the intermediate centuries.'[18] This, as we have seen, is also the opinion of Professor Otway-Ruthven.

Three main origins are postulated as starting-points for the delineation of Irish parishes and all three refer to already existing areas of ecclesiastical and secular administration. Such areas were the monastic *termon* lands, the ancient *tuatha* and the grants made by Irish and Anglo-Norman lords to monastic houses in the period after Kells.[19] Applying the test of *termon* lands to the diocese of Cork we find that the only parish which falls into this category was the cathedral parish of Saint Finbarr. The parish of Tracton which grew up around the Cistercian monastery of the same name would not fall into this category. The principal coarbial family in the diocese was that of Ua Sealbaigh, besides whom the only other known family of coarbs in Cork was that of O Longaigh (Long) of Ceannmhuighe or Cannaway. A list of Muskerry lands drawn up by Sir George

17 Otway-Ruthven, *Med. Ire.*, p. 118.

18 Patrick Power, 'The Bounds and Extents of Irish Parishes', *Féilscríbhinn Tórna*, p. 219.

19 Dermot F. Gleeson, *A History of the Diocese of Killaloe*, p. 309.

Carew mentions the O'Longs of Cannaboy in the diocese of
Cork, the O'Herlihys of Ballyvourney, the O'Healihys of
Donoghmore and the O'Cremins of Aghabulloge as the church
families of Muskerry territory. All of these families were freeholders in hereditary occupation of church lands for which
they paid small chief-rents to the bishop of Cork or to the
bishop of Cloyne.[20] Remembering that Saint Brendan was
patron saint of Cannaway church, it is possible that the O'Longs,
if they were not actually coarbs of Saint Brendan, were at least
erenaghs of the monastic *termon* lands which formed the
nucleus of the later parish of Cannaway and the O'Keeffes were
erenaghs of Cullen.

It may yet be possible to prove the existence of other coarbial
families in the diocese, perhaps around Kinneigh where some
sept of the Cinel Laoghaire other than the Ua Sealbaigh may
have flourished. As it stands the whole question is unavoidably
vague and unsatisfactory, for even in the case of Cannaway we
cannot know whether the entire area encompassed by the
parish belonged originally to the church or to the O'Longs.
Carew's list of 1600 mentions four ploughlands of Cannaway
as belonging to the church, and the *Civil Survey* of 1654–56, in
that section dealing with Muskerry, gives the church's holding
as four-and-a-half ploughlands, whereas the entire parish of
Cannaway covered ten ploughlands. We are no nearer a solution
with the knowledge that the remaining ploughlands belonged
to the O'Mahony sept of Clan Finin.

Cork parishes originating in ancient *tuath* lands are more
easily discernible. A map given in *Pacata Hibernia* shows that
in the sixteenth century the barony of Muskerry was parcelled
out into divisions which are seen to correspond more or less to
the modern parishes of the same area. Iveleary, the country of
the Cineal Laoghaire or O'Learys which lay around Loch
Allua, embracing the river Lee at its source and stretching to
a point half-way between Inchigeela and the town of Macroom,
corresponds to the present parish of Iveleary or Inchigeela.
Three districts of Ifflanloe which were *tuath* lands held by the
O'Mahonys correspond to the parishes of Kilmichael, Kilmurry
and part of the ancient parish of Moviddy. It is seldom, however,
that the early *tuath* parishes survived intact down to modern
times, but the parishes of Iveleary and Bantry present good
examples of such continuity. Bantry evolved from the *tuath* of
the Beanntraighe into the barony of Bantry, which in turn
became the basis for the ancient parish of Bantry or Kilmo-

20   W. F. T. Butler, *Gleanings from Irish History*, pp. 125, 253, 389.

comoge. The Beanntraighe were a sub-sept of the Ui Eachach, and their genealogy as traced in the *Yellow Book of Lecan* gives Saint Coman as their patron; hence the ecclesiastical name of Kilmocomoge for the ancient parish. Close to the parish of Iveleary and on its northern boundary is the *tuath*-parish of Kilnamartyra or *Tuath-na-Droman* in the diocese of Cloyne which is still coterminous with the *tuath* from which it originated. The majority of Cork parishes would appear to have been based on *tuatha*, but we are on less sure ground when it comes to parishes originating from the *baile biataigh*. Perhaps Burren, now a townland in Rathclarin, belongs to this category: likely as it seems, there is no direct evidence that it was so.

The Anglo-Norman contribution towards establishing the parochial system in this country was that of 'accelerating a development which would have occurred in any case as part of the process of bringing the church in Ireland into line with the general pattern of western Christendom'.[21] The Anglo-Norman unit of administration was the manor, apropos of which modern scholarship has shown that the creation of parishes kept pace generally with the creation of manors in all areas of Norman settlement. Thus in Cork we have the parish of Beaver or Carrigaline based upon the de Cogan manor of the same name. Similarly the parishes and manors of Shandon, Douglas, Rincurran, Carrigrohane, and so on. Kilbrogan would appear to have evolved from the episcopal sub-manor established there. The growth of parishes from Anglo-Norman grants to monastic houses is likewise relevant to the diocese of Cork even though the number of Norman-sponsored foundations were fewer in Cork than elsewhere. Grants to Tracton Abbey, from which evolved the parish of Tracton, provide an outstanding example of Anglo-Norman liberality which blossomed into parochial status. The origins of the parishes of Clontead, Nohoval and Ballyfeard are probably traceable to the same source. Anglo-Norman grants to the mendicant friars never became parochial, and the Anglo-Normans rarely extended their beneficence to bishops whom they regarded as feudal lords like themselves and as such rival landowners. From the diocese of Cloyne we find that the pre-Reformation parishes of Bridgetown (*de Villa Pontis*) near Fermoy and Ballybeg near Buttevant (*juxta Butoniam*) fit into the category of parishes which grew out of Anglo-Norman grants to religious houses. As to grants received from Irish chiefs, Gill Abbey was constantly at the receiving end of

21 Otway-Ruthven, *Med. Ire.*, p. 126. See also Gleeson, 'The Coarbs of Killaloe', *R.S.A.I. Jn.*, lxxix (1949), 160–9.

MacCarthy liberality but, unlike Tracton and the Benedictine monastery of Saint John the Evangelist in Douglas Street, Gill Abbey never became a parochial centre. Some of the rectories which were later described as impropriate to Gill Abbey, e.g., Killeens, Ballinboy and Barnehely, may have developed from grants made to the Cork monastery, but here again direct corroborative evidence is lacking.

A small number of parishes would seem to have originated in certain notable churches or church sites of the ancient diocese. Aglish (*Eaglais*) is a foremost consideration here. Other probabilities are Killaspugmullane, Kilmoe, Kilgobban (from Saint Abban or Gobban) and Kilnaglory where the relics of Saint Finbarr are believed to have been deposited. Templemichael, Templetrine and Templebreedy would seem to belong to this category also; likewise Rincurran which is said to have been formerly called *Teampull na Trionóide* though there is no verification of the fact. A smaller number of parishes have names descriptive of local topography, namely, Ardnageehy (*Ard na Gaoithe*), Glanmire (*Gleann Meidhir*), Little Island and Knockavilly (*Cnoc Bile*). Some student of philology may yet discover clues offering possible origins for the now obsolete parishes of Rathcooney, Rathclarin, Dunderrow, Ballydeloher, Ballymolmihill, Ballymodan and others. Finally, in the parish of Desertserges (now joined to Enniskeane) we have a parochial arrangement which clearly developed around a hermitage, *Díseart Saorghusa*.

Parishes which are known to have paid chief- or head-rents to the bishop are among the most ancient parishes in the diocese of Cork. These head-rents were levied on monastic lands which fell to the bishop's lot when the conventional diocesan system was set up in the twelfth century. Examples of such head-rent paying parishes were Carrigrohane,[22] Maglin, Ballymolmihill, Ballymacadane and Liskillea. Parishes which became prebendal are similarly stamped with antiquity. Cork parishes belonging to this category are Killaspugmullane, Liscleary, Caherlag, Kilbrittain. Parishes which were allotted to prebends are sometimes referable to early monastic sites, as for example, Cullen which became part of the dean's prebend and which is associated with Saint Fland Find whom the *Martyrology of Tallaght* commemorates on 14 January.

Parishes once established fell into many gradings. First there was the mensal parish, the income of which went to the bishop in addition to whatever revenue his cathedral parish yielded.

22 Norman influence was also a consideration here.

The spiritual responsibilities or *cura animarum* of the mensal parish were entrusted to a vicar, the forerunner of the modern administrator, who was given a special maintenance allowance by the bishop. At this distance and with only marginal references to go on, it is difficult to say which parishes of the medieval diocese of Cork were mensal parishes. Our earliest reference post-dates the Reformation by more than a century and a half, but since Catholic ecclesiastical divisions continued to be maintained in the Protestant economy, it follows that the mensal parishes quoted below must have been analogous to a pre-sixteenth-century arrangement. The earliest available reference to mensal lands as distinct from mensal parishes is contained in a rental dated 1699 which has the following entry: 'Mensal tythes in the parish of Templebrian worth £3 per annum, not set. Half the tythes of a plowland called Skavenise in the parish of Innishonane are mensal tythes, not set. Besides the gardens and yards of Bishop's Court, the marsh land that lies over against the house to the north is reckoned mensal land.'[23] The lands and gardens in question were near the site of the present Protestant episcopal residence west of the cathedral of Saint Fin Barre; the Innishannon ploughland represents the modern townland of Skevanish. A second significant reference comes from the Journal of Dean Davies (1700) from which Brady quotes that 'all these tithes of Ringskiddy and Ballibricken were formerly enjoyed as mensal tithes . . . Ballibricken 'tis supposed is the same with Templebracknany in the Visitation Books'.[24] It seems reasonable to conclude from the foregoing that the episcopal *mensa* in the seventeenth century included—in addition to the parish of Saint Finbarr—the parishes of Templebrian, Innishannon and Templebrackeny or Rosbeg (subsequently Ringaskiddy), and that this arrangement represented a medieval economy which was carried over into post-Reformation times.

A parish might form part of the corps of a prebend, the prebendary was usually a member of the cathedral chapter and he lived within or near the cathedral precincts. A prebendal parish might entail the cure of souls or it might be a prebend *sine cura*, and if the latter the cure of souls was entrusted (as in the case of the mensal parish) to a resident vicar appointed by the bishop or prebendary, and he enjoyed the vicarial tithes or *decimae minores*. The parish priest, when he was a direct appointee of the bishop, had charge of what was termed an

23 Smith, *History of Cork*, i, 131.
24 Brady, *Records*, i, 16.

entire rectory where he had the cure of souls and enjoyed full rectorial tithes or *decimae majores*,[25] and his status was something akin to that of his modern counterpart. There were rectories as well as prebends 'without cure', that is, where the spiritual duties did not devolve on the appointee but were exercised again through vicars or, as we now call them, curates. These vicars could be, and often were, *perpetual* vicars; that is, they enjoyed security of office for life unless they incurred the penalty of removal for some canonical offence or irregularity. The arrangement was open to grave abuse and reached the low-water mark in the period leading up to the sixteenth-century religious revolt. Perpetual vicarages were erected in Dunmanway, Ringrone, Desertserges, Kilcully, Kinneigh, Drinagh, Inchigeela, etc., as is clear from the papal registers and the annate returns. Kinsale, which today is a deanery, was at one time a perpetual vicarage; the rector was the Benedictine prior of Bath in England. The term 'perpetual' was not an absolute. Its extenuations are seen in Kinsale where the 'perpetual' vicarage set up was in time treated as a separate benefice for purposes of papal taxation as the returns for the early fourteenth century demonstrate.

A rectory or parish might be impropriate to some religious institute. The term 'impropriate' derives from the phrase *in proprios usus* which was used in the conveyance of such parishes to the surveillance of some abbot or community. Normally, the abbot of the monastery was rector of the parish and the parish revenue was appropriated to the benefit of his order or community. It was not uncommon for members of an impropriating community to become vicars of impropriate parishes, but more frequently they employed stipendiary priests who were removable at will. The chief impropriators in the diocese of Cork were the monasteries of Gill Abbey and Tracton, the preceptory of Mora (Mourne), the college of Youghal, the abbey of Grany or Grange, the priories of Saint Catherine's, Waterford, and Saint Peter's, Bath, and for a time the abbey of Saint Thomas, Dublin. Except for Gill Abbey and Tracton, these institutions were all extraneous to the diocese, and when we realize that impropriating monasteries had up to fifty parishes between them, the detriment to the church's pastoral mission is incalculable. To cite a few examples: the parishes of Inchigeela, Kilmichael, Kilmurry, Dundrinan were impropriate to Gill Abbey; Ballyfoyle, Ballyfeard, Clontead, Nohoval to Tracton Abbey; Kilcrohane and Monkstown, the one to the

---

25   Tithes will be treated in detail in Chapter XII.

cathedral, the other to Saint Catherine's, Waterford; Caheragh, Schull and Kilmoe to the college of Youghal, and so on. There were overlappings of impropriatorship in places but there are no evidences of administrative conflict. In Aglish the master of Mourne preceptory shared the rectory with the prebendary of Kilbrogan, while in Ovens the master of Mourne and the abbess of Grange were joint impropriators.[26]

Instances of chapels, *capellae*, are also encountered in medieval taxation rolls and while these *capellae* are at times assumed to be the equivalent of modern chapels-of-ease, the interpretation is not viable in all cases. There were six *capellae* in the diocese of Cork at the beginning of the fourteenth century, namely, Kilcully, Templetrine, Currarane, Kilgobban, Rathdrought and Brinny. They may be explained in part by reference to England where the rights of a mother-church (*matrix ecclesia*) were safeguarded by the expedient of ordering those who normally attended the *capellae* to participate at the ceremonies of the mother-church on feast days and on days of special devotion. The six *capellae* of Cork may have belonged to this category. Alternatively, they may have been the chapels of some prominent family in each given locality; or again they may have been votive chapels, mortuary chapels or even chantry chapels on the style of those found in the city parishes of Holy Trinity and Saint Peter's. The fourteenth-century taxation returns and the annates of the late fifteenth and early sixteenth centuries also refer to a church or chapel as a particle, *particula*, by which is meant part of an older church or parish which became absorbed in a newer and enlarged parish. Thus we have *particula Gortnegrosse*, now represented by Gortnacrusha in Templetrine.

Finally we come to parishes which were subject to a system of lay patronage, for patronage whether ecclesiastical or secular

26 These impropriators are found in Murphy, 'The Royal Visitation of Cork, Cloyne, Ross and the College of Youghal', pp. 173–89, and may be taken as continuations of an earlier practice.

The abbey or nunnery of Grange (Grany) was situated, according to Archdall, about one and a half miles from Castledermot in the baronies of Kilkee and Moon, county Kildare (*Monasticon Hibernicum*, ii, 258). Its foundation dates from the year 1200, its founder was Walter de Riddlesford and, while its original dedication is claimed by some to have been in honour of Saint Brigid, it has come down in history as the nunnery of Saint Mary for Augustinian canonesses. The date of Grany's acquisitions in the diocese of Cork cannot be ascertained, but the question as to *how* Grany came to have possessions in Cork is answered in part by a reference to the abbey of Ballymacadane, the original inhabitants of which are said to have been 'Austine Nuns'. There is some confusion too between Grange or Grany in Kildare and Grange in the parish of Ovens, diocese of Cork, which is believed to have been the site of an ancient abbey which ceased to function soon after the establishment of the Franciscan friary of Kilcrea in 1465.

permeated the medieval church at every level. When parishes subject to lay patronage became vacant it was the privilege of the local lord or baron or landowner whose family had donated the land on which the church stood, to exercise the right of advow- son; that is, he presented a new incumbent to the bishop who usually accepted the nomination. Clerics so appointed tended to regard themselves as employees of the local lords whose domestic chapels they served; the duties of the ministry were far from being their primary concern. In Cork where de Courcey presented to Ringrone, Barry Oge to Rincurran, Meade to Liscleary and MacCottyr to Caherlag, we find that the churches in these districts were built quite close to the patrons' residences. The church of Ringrone which stood near de Courcey's castle was designated Courtmaher, which probably denotes mother church, *matrix ecclesia*, in contrast to the smaller church of Kilroan (Killone, Killowney) which lay to the south of Ringrone. Kilroan became a temporary prebend in 1425 and was donated by Bishop Jordan Purcell to the vicars choral in 1447,[27] but it was usually referred to as Courtaparteen (taking its name from the townland upon which it stood) and may have been little more than a chapel-of-ease to the larger church of Ringrone.

The decretal of 1199 with its list of churches extending to the furthest western limits of the diocese suggests that the pre-Reformation parochial divisions were already in process of delimitation. Technically speaking, the fourteenth-century taxations offer the first list of parishes, but data culled from these lists and from the procuration list of 1437 show, however, that parochial geography was not yet static and that re-shuffles entailing the institution of new parishes and the amalgamation of older and smaller ones were a recurring feature of the medieval period. It is not always easy to discover why such amalgamations became necessary, whether they were the outcome of economic, demographic or political conditions. The annates and the papal registers carry occasional references to the effect that adjoining parishes of insufficient revenue could be more conveniently served by a single priest. Thus, for instance, in 1463 a particle of Belgooly (then unoccupied) was joined to Tracton. Similar alignments were achieved between Murragh and an unnamed rectory in 1488 (the former valued at five marks, the latter at one mark), and in 1500 a petitioner asked that the vicarage of Corsruhara or Ballymoney might be united with another unspecified benefice.[28] Political strife

27 *Cal. papal letters, 1417–31*, p. 373.

28 Bolster, 'Obligationes pro Annatis Diocesis Corcagiensis', pp. 3, 18, 28.

and the demands of public convenience dictated the following readjustments in the parish of Innishannon and in the parochial area of Macloneigh-Kilmichael:

In 1475 Cormac MacCarthy, lord of the four carucates (*quatuor carucatae*) of Ballymountain, Curranure, Dromkeen and Knockroe which lay west of the Bandon River in the parish of Innishannon, complained of the great river 'called the Banda which in winter makes great floods. . . . Beyond the said river the Irish rule, but on this side . . . where the said church [of Innishannon] is [situated] the English have dominion and . . . wars often prevail between the two races'. Because of these wars, so the complaint runs, walls, ramparts and great ditches have been made which obstruct the highway and 'it often happens that the said inhabitants are deprived of the Divine Offices.'[29] The petition states that the erection of a separate parish church would cause all such perils and inconveniences to cease and that Cormac would endow the new church with four acres of fertile land 'as it is measured locally'. MacCarthy gave as his opinion that the remaining portion of the parish of Innishannon (which is described as of lay patronage) would provide sufficient maintenance for both rector and vicar. In acceding to this request, Pope Sixtus IV decreed that Cormac MacCarthy (Mekarryg) should be given license to erect a church dedicated to Saint Mary the Virgin, to assign to it a fit endowment and to subject the inhabitants to its rule. After its erection and endowment the rectory was to be collated to Cornelius Murphy (Ymurchu), precentor of Cork. John T. Collins recognizes in this arrangement a foreshadowing of the partition of the parish of Innishannon into Irish and English districts. The town of Innishannon lay at the Cork side of the river Bandon; its church on the river-bank was under the patronage of Barry Oge who held the old tribeland of the Cinel Aedh. West of the river were the still unconquered Irish of west Cork led by MacCarthy Reagh of Carbery.[30]

We get a speculative suggestion along the same lines for the parish of Ballymodan from the late Seán P. Ó Ríordáin in an article published in the *Journal of the Cork Historical and Archaeological Society* in which he recalled a conversation he had in the late 1930s with the then parish priest of Bandon, Canon J. Cohalan, who later became bishop of Waterford and Lismore. Dr. Cohalan pointed out that during the period

29   *Cal. papal letters, 1471–84*, pt. 1, p. 429.

30   John T. Collins, 'Church Government in the South of Ireland, A.D. 1471 to 1484', *Cork Hist. Soc. Jn.*, lxii (1957), 15.

immediately following the Norman invasion the colonists were settled at Innishannon while the O'Mahonys were settled in their lately-built castle west of Bandon and south of the river. 'In these circumstances the rival parties would not be likely to unite for worship at one church and gradually there grew up between their territories the new parish of Ballymodan, endowed in all probability by the Barrys of Innishannon and only gradually spreading its jurisdiction westward.'[31] In view of the limited information then available (the final volumes of the papal registers were not yet published) this surmise of Dr. Cohalan and Seán Ó Ríordáin was uncannily near the point since the parish of Ballymodan (with Kilbrogan it forms the modern parish of Bandon) included the greater part of the town of Bandon which lies south of the river.

Circumstances attendant upon the canonical erection of the parish of Kilmichael belong to the as yet uncalendared period following 1492 which is the terminal date for the fourteenth volume of published papal registers. References given here are taken from a photo-copy of the relevant information as found in the registered *acta* of the first year of the pontificate of Pope Alexander VI. In 1493 a papal mandate directed to the abbot of Tracton and two canons of Cork ordered the investigation of a petition addressed to the Holy See on behalf of Matthew O'Mahony, dean of Cork and perpetual vicar of Macloneigh. O'Mahony was stated to have erected at his own expense and with the consent of the bishop of Cork (Gerald FitzGerald) a church dedicated to Saint Michael the Archangel in the townland of Lackmalloe (Leachwlua), east of Moneycuskar in Macloneigh. The petition asked that the church be elevated to parochial status, that certain townlands should be incorporated in the parish and that the church, the townlands and the inhabitants should be granted to Matthew O'Mahony for his lifetime (*quandiu ipse Matheus vixerit*). The reasons given for the favour sought were (a) the distance to be traversed by the inhabitants of the townlands in question to get to the churches of Macloneigh and Inchigeela, and (b) the enmity then existing between the people of Kilmichael and the parishioners of Macloneigh and Inchigeela. The townlands to be annexed from Macloneigh were Ballina and Lackmalloe (now collectively known as Lackmalloe), Terelton, Ardaneneen,

---

31 Seán P. Ó Ríordáin, 'The Placenames and Antiquities of Kinalmeaky Barony, County Cork', *Cork Hist. Soc. Jn.*, xxxvi (1931), 2.

Dunkynayge,[32] Kilcummer, Greenville, Kilnarovanagh, Mount-music, Cooldaniel, and an ancient townland called Kylmokeallog which is believed to have become absorbed in Cooldaniel. The parish of Inchigeela was to surrender the townlands of Deshure, Cooldorragha (Cooldorrihy), Shanacashel, Mamucky, Cusduff, Kileanna (Johnstown) and Clonmoyle. The petition entered on behalf of Matthew O'Mahony was granted and all the town-lands requisitioned were transferred to Kilmichael with the exception of Kilnarovanagh which remained attached to Macloneigh, although in the present arrangement Kilna-rovanagh is incorporated in Kilmichael. The transfer was arranged with the mutual consent of Bishop Gerald FitzGerald and the vicar of Inchigeela, and on 24 May 1493 Matthew O'Mahony became first parish priest of Kilmichael.[33]

Three lists are here presented as a visual aid towards apprehending the changing parochial pattern of the medieval diocese of Cork. The inclusion of the 1615 list is justifiable on three main counts: the parishes it enumerates were based on an existing pre-Reformation arrangement, its compiler was apparently more painstaking than the fourteenth-century papal proctors and it is chronologically nearer the great divide of 1536-40 than any other medieval reference. To make for greater clarification modern identifications are substituted for the inaccurate taxation renderings and the better to check on parishes which have become obsolete, a certain liberty has been taken with the order of all three lists.

TAXATION A	TAXATION B	ROYAL VISITATION
	Deanery of Ocurblethan	
	Currykippane	Currykippane
Kilcully	Kilcully	Kilcully
Dunbulloge	Dunbulloge	Dunbulloge (Prebend)
Rathcooney	Rathcooney	Rathcooney
Shanbally	Shanbally	Shanbally (Prebend)
Ardnageehy	Ardnageehy	Ardnageehy
Ballinaltig	Ballinaltig	

32 Dunkynayge is now absorbed in Ardaneneen. Its position as given in the survey, 1854–56, was south of Kilnarovanagh. It is evidently the same place as Gearhynegown of the *Books of Distribution*.

33 The traditional account of the origin of Kilmichael is more fanciful. Of a number of friars believed to have been at one time studying in Rome, one, contrary to rule, had his hair cut on a Friday. All the bells of Rome rang out as if in protest, and the pope imposed as penance on the offending friar that he should build a church in the place where he found a goat grazing in a *lios*. On his road of penance the friar came to the present district of Kilmichael and sought refreshment in a local house. He was told that a goat would be milked for his benefit, but the young lad who was sent to milk the goat returned saying she was grazing in a *lios*. The friar decided that this was the 'place of his resurrection' and accordingly built the church of Kilmichael at *Lios a' Chlúbháin*.

Kilquane	Kilquane	Kilquane
Killaspugmullane	Killaspugmullane	Killaspugmullane (Prebend)
Glanmire	Glanmire	Glanmire (Templeusque)
Ballydeloher	Ballydeloher	Ballydeloher
Caherlag	Caherlag	Caherlag (Prebend)
Little Island	Little Island	Little Island
Shandon	Shandon	Shandon
St. Catherine		
Holy Trinity	Holy Trinity	Holy Trinity (Prebend)
St. Nicholas		St. Nicholas
	St. Peter	St. Peter
		St. Mary le Nard
		St. John the Evangelist

Deanery of Kery (Kerrycurrihy)

St. John the Evangelist		
Liscleary	Liscleary	Liscleary (Prebend)
Ballinaboy	Ballinaboy	Ballinaboy
Killanully	Killanully	Killanully (Prebend)
Carrigaline (Beaver)	Carrigaline	Carrigaline
Kilnagleary	Kilnagleary	
Douglas	Douglas	Douglas, *particle*
Corbally	Corbally	Corbally
Kilnaglory	Kilnaglory	Kilnaglory (Prebend)
Ringaskiddy (Rosbeg)		Ringaskiddy
Templebreedy	Templebreedy	Templebreedy
	Inishkenny	Inishkenny (Prebend)
	Carrigrohane	Carrigrohane
		Marmullane (Passage West)

Deanery of Kenalethe ULTRA

Ringrone	Ringrone	Ringrone
Killoney	Killoney	Killoney
Templetrine	Templetrine	Templetrine
Currarane (chapel)	Currarane	
Rathclarin	Rathclarin	Rathclarin
Burren	Burren	Burren
Kilshinahan	Kilshinahan	Kilshinahan
Kilbrittain	Kilbrittain	Kilbrittain (Prebend)
Kilgobban	Kilgobban	Kilgobban
		Gortnacrusha (particle)
Kildarra & Cloghan (part.)		
Rathdrought	Rathdrought	Rathdrought
Bandon (Ballymodan)	Bandon	Bandon
Innishannon	Innishannon	Innishannon
Knockavilly	Knockavilly	Knockavilly
Templemichael (de Duagh)		Templemichael
Brinny	Brinny	Brinny
		Templemartin
		Ballinadee
		Kilbrogan (Prebend)

Deanery of Kenalethe CITRA

Ballyfeard	Ballyfeard	Ballyfeard
Ballyfoyle	Ballyfoyle	Ballyfoyle
Kinure	Kinure	Kinure
Clontead	Clontead	Clontead
Rincurran	Rincurran	Rincurran
Kinsale	Kinsale	Kinsale
Tisaxon	Tisaxon	Tisaxon
Leighmoney	Leighmoney	Leighmoney
Dunderrow	Dunderrow	Dunderrow
Ballymartle	Ballymartle	Ballymartle
Nohoval	Nohoval	
Kilmonoge	Kilmonoge	Kilmonoge
Cullen (Riverstick)	Cullen	Cullen
	Dunagh (? de Duagh)	

Deanery of Corkolwyn

Aglish	Aglish	Aglish
Kilbonane	Kilbonane	Kilbonane
Kilmurry	Kilmurry	Kilmurry
Cannaway		Cannaway
Desertmore	Desertmore	Desertmore (Prebend)
	Dundrinan	Dundrinan
	Ovens	Ovens
		Moviddy
		Dunisky
		Macloneigh
		Inchigeela
		Kilmichael

Deanery of Glansalny

Kinneigh
Dunmanway (Fanlobbus)
Desertserges
Murragh
Drinagh
Drimoleague (Prebend)
Ballymoney (Enniskeane)

Deanery of Foneragh

Kilmoe
Schull
Kilcrohane
Durrus
Bantry (Kilmocomoge)
Caheragh

The anomalies presented by many of these pre-Reformation parishes and their modern counterparts have been invoiced at the beginning of this book, with the suggestion that they may have been the outcome of tribal usage or of friendly compromise; but such common denominators can scarcely apply in all cases and consequently a host of partially answered questions remains. History maintains an inexorable silence on the entire subject, and the historian is in consequence forced to accept each standing arrangement as a *fait accompli* of some ancient unfathomable economy.

Many of the parishes enumerated in the foregoing lists are now no more. Burren and Rathclarin, which were parishes in the deanery of Kenalethe *ultra* in the fourteenth century, were described as rectories in 1478 and were then joined to the prebend of Kilbrittain.[34] Today Burren is absorbed in Rathclarin and Rathclarin is a townland in the parish of Kilbrittain. Smith's *History of Cork* gives a list of the parish churches of the diocese, to which he appends the names of some earlier churches which he claims to have taken from the manuscript of Robert Travers.[35] One such reference is to 'Sanct. Eldridae de Dwaghe, particula de Cloghare and Kildorrery. Anciently belonging to the treasury.'[36] Under the year 1488 the annate returns refer to the unoccupied particles (*particulae nuncupatae*) of Dochan (*rectè* Cloghan) and Kildara, the combined valuations of which were set at three marks.[37] The particles would now correspond to the townlands of Cloghane and Kildarra in the parish of Ballinadee, barony of Carbery East. Kilgobban, which was once a parish in this barony, is today part of the union of Courceys. Brinny was at one time a parish in three moieties, two of which were in the baronies of Kinalea and Carbery East and the third and largest within the barony of Kinalmeaky. It is now in the union of Innishannon but its graveyard is still in use. Here is buried Seán Dearg Nash, the priest hunter, whose house is still pointed out at Brinny Bridge, and to whose memory a tombstone was erected in the cemetery of Kilbrogan. To take one final example: Shortly after 1615 Rossebegg *alias* Bracknan, also called Templebrackmany, disappeared as a parish and became part of Barnehely, which in

34   *Cal. papal letters, 1471–84*, pt. 1, p. 70.

35   Robert Travers was register in 1628; he transcribed his manuscript from an ancient roll. The Travers document was extant when Smith wrote his history, but the 'ancient roll' was missing. Travers's document is now no longer extant.

36   Smith, *History of Cork*, i, 44.

37   Bolster, 'Obligationes pro Annatis Diocesis Corcagiensis', p. 17.

turn was absorbed in the modern parish of Monkstown. Other and similar instances might be multiplied.

The bounds of our ancient parishes constitute the oldest topographical divisions we possess. We get a highly valuable contemporary description of these parishes in that part of the *Civil Survey* of 1654–56 which deals with the barony of Muskerry. The parish bounds are also delineated in the Down Survey and their denominations are listed in the Books of Survey and Distribution of Charles II. After 1690 the history of Irish parishes was diverted into channels which were either predominantly Catholic or predominantly Protestant. To the Protestant rector a parish represented a steady source of income from tithes, and it was important that these sources should be preserved intact. That this was accomplished is seen from the long series or Ordnance Survey sheets which were published at regular intervals until 1907. The fact that these Ordnance Survey sheets present the parishes incorrectly as civic divisions does not in any way take from their importance as preservers of our earliest parochial units of administration.

On the Catholic side, of necessity, the history of parishes followed a completely different course. Amalgamations and unions which have not really affected Protestant parishes until comparatively modern times were an early feature of the Catholic economy. The penal era was predominantly the era of parish amalgamation, for as the supply of clergy decreased it often happened that five or even six parishes were grouped together under a single priest. It could and often did occur that this priest was a graduate of some continental college who was not conversant with either the topography or the boundaries of his outsize parish. Intercourse with Rome was difficult and hazardous and at times impossible; therefore the finer points of canon law were either forgotten or ignored, and many parish amalgamations must have taken place without the necessary canonical approval. After emancipation when the supply of priests became less limited, the amalgamated parishes were subdivided, but in the new subdivision there was 'a sharp reorientation and broadening of regional consciousness with towns as the new foci . . . [and in this way] Downpatrick yielded to Belfast, Cashel to Thurles, Ferns to Enniscorthy and Trim to Mullingar'.[38] Ancient diocesan centres became forlorn and desolate—Clonfert, Kilmore, Killala, to mention but a few. In Cork city the diocesan centre was transferred from

38.   T. Jones Hughes, 'Administrative Divisions and the Development of Settlement in Nineteenth Century Ireland', *University Review*, iii, no. 6 (1964), pp. 14–15.

its traditional site on *Raithín mac nAeda* on the south channel
of the Lee to its present location overlooking the city from the
north; and this, while not as far-reaching as the changes wrought
in the dioceses just mentioned, told its own story of parochial
and diocesan reorientation. And it is a fact that of all the
parishes of the present diocese of Cork, that of Caheragh—
allowing for its two marooned townlands of Upper and Lower
Lissane and Rearhinagh which are cut off by Drimoleague—is
the only one which can be said to be coterminous with the
medieval parish of the same name. The remaining parishes
represent amalgamations of from two to five older parishes,
but the aggregate variation has not appreciably disrupted the
ancient parochial delineation since the peripheral outlines of
the modern divisions still show traces of the original boundaries.
The reason for this is that 'sentiment and historic sense protest
against interference with ancient landmarks; hard utility has
much to say on the other side, but nearly all will agree that only
stern necessity or something akin can justify severance of
ties so venerable and sanctified'.[39]

The erection of new parishes, however, is not always a
severance of venerable and sacred ties; hard utility has opinion
on its side also, especially today when demographic concentration in built-up suburban areas creates demands far in
excess of those made on the medieval parish. Thus in Cork
we have the parish of Douglas which is a detached part of the
ancient parish of Carrigaline; Blackrock, Saint Finbarr's
West and Christ the King, Turner's Cross, which began as
chapels-of-ease to Saint Finbarr's South; Ballinlough, which
was originally a chapel-of-ease to Blackrock; Saint Patrick's,
which was meant to serve the cathedral. And so on, down to
the greatest modern parochial re-arrangement by which the
present bishop, Dr. Cornelius Lucey, has encircled the city of
Finbarr with a 'rosary of churches', one of which—the church
of the Assumption, Ballyphehane—achieved parochial status
on 1 September 1957, eighteen months after its erection as a
chapel-of-ease to Saint Finbarr's South.[40]

---

39.   Power, 'The Bounds and Extents of Irish Parishes', *Féilscríbhinn Tórna*, p. 222.

40   This history was already in process of publication when the Church of the Ascension, Gurranebraher, was accorded parochial status in July 1969, and the parish of
Ballineaspaig was created in January 1970. For this reason the new parishes are not
indicated on the diocesan map.

APPENDIX A
The Modern Deaneries

CITY AND SUBURBS

Cathedral
St. Finbarr's South
St. Patrick's
SS. Peter and Paul's
St. Finbarr's West
Christ the King, Turner's Cross
Ballyphehane
Ballinlough
Blackrock
Gurranebraher
Ballineaspaig
Ballincollig
Glanmire
Glounthane
Watergrasshill

BANDON DEANERY

Bandon
Kilbrittain
Enniskeane
Murragh
Kilmichael
Iveleary
Kilmurry
Ovens
Innishannon

KINSALE DEANERY

Kinsale
Douglas
Passage West
Monkstown
Carrigaline
Tracton
Clontead
Courceys
Ballinhassig

BANTRY DEANERY

Bantry
Muintervara (Durrus)
Goleen
Schull
Caheragh
Drimoleague
Dunmanway

APPENDIX B
Canonical Erection of Kilmichael into a Parish Church
(Reg. Alex. VI, Anno 1, Lib. 7, f. 26, C.A. Lat.)

Alexander etc. Dilectis filiis Abbati Monasterii Beate Marie de Albotractu, Corcagensis dioc., et Cornelio OMurchu ac Thome Omahuna, Canonicis ecce Corcagensis, salutem etc.

Ex commisso nobis. . . . Exhibita siquidem nobis nuper pro parte dilecti filii Mathei YMathuma, perpetui vicarii parrochialis ecclesiae de Maghculaneythe, Corcagiensi dioc., petitio continebat, quod cum olim ipse Matheus, fervore devotionis accensus, unam ecclesiam sine cura sub invocatione Sancti Michaelis Archangeli in villa Leachwlua, dicte dioc., infra limites dicte parrochialis ecclesiae, de suis propriis bonis de licentia Ordinarii loci, construi et edificari fecerit, et de Tyrelleyn et Ardnanygyn, Dunkynayge, Kylltemyn ac Kyllnaromanach et Cnockowrayn, ac de Beatwlua et de Conurdraynach et Kyllmokeallog, ville eiusdem dioc., predicte ecce Sancti Michaelis propinque existunt, et a dicta parrochiali ecclesia distant, et tum propter huiusmodi distantiam, quam etiam quia inter incolas et habitatores dictarum villarum et homines prope dictam parrochialem ecclesiam habitantes vigent inimicitie capitales, incole et habitatores prefati ad dictam parrochialem ecclesiam pro Missis et aliis divinis officiis audiendis, ac ecclesiasticis sacramentis recipiendis accedere commode non possunt, si dicta ecclesia Sancti Michaelis in parrochialem ecclesiam perpetuo erigeretur, ac predicte ab ipsa de Machelnaneythe [*sic*] necnon de Deyssiwir et de Cuylldorcha, Scananyssyl, Rossmogwayn ac Cossnanibh ac Teanua [?] necnon Cluoyn Mayll ville etiam infra limites parrochialis ecce de Insygemeleagh dicte dioc., consistentes inter quarum incolas et habitatores et homines prope dicta, ecclesiam de Insygemeleagh habitatores inimicitie capitales etiam vigent: quique habitatores et incole propterea, ac etiam ob distantian ab ipsa ecclesia de Insygemeleagh ad illam etiam pro Missis et aliis divinis officiis audiendis commode accedere non possunt ab Insygemeleagh parrochialibus eclesiis hujusmodi separeantur et segregarentur, ac ville predicte et illarum incole, habitatores et homines pro parrochia et parrochianis dicte erigende ecclesie assignarentur, ipsaque erigenda ecclesia vicarie dicte ecce de Magheluaneythe, quam dictus Matheus, et asserit, inter alia obtinet, quamdiu ipsi illam obtinuerit uniretur, annecteretur et incorporaretur profecto ex hoc eorundem habitatorum et hominum predictorum commoditatibus consuleretur, divinusque cultus in ipsa erigenda ecclesia susciperet incrementum. Quare pro parte dicti Mathei etiam asserentis vicarie octo, ac erigende ecclesie hujusmodi duodecim marcharum sterlingorum fructus, redditus et proventus se(cundum) co(mmunem) ex(timationem) valorem annuum ut [*sic*] non excedere nobis fuit humiliter supplicatum ut dictam ecclesiam Sancti Michaelis in parrochialem ecclesiam erigere, ac dictas villas ab eisdem matricibus ecclesiis respective separare et segregare, et dictas villas ac illarum incolas et habitatores eidem erigende perpetuo applicare et assignare, illamque postquam in parrochialem ut prefertur erecta fuerit eidem vicarie quamdiu ipse Matheus vixerit; et illam obtinuerit dumtaxat unire, annectere, et incorporare, aliasque in praemissis opportune providere, de benignitate Apca dignaremur. Nos igitur ipsum Matheum cum

quo dudum, ut etiam asserit, ut Decanatum ecc^e Corkagensis,
qui inibi dignitas post pontificalem major existet, ac dictam
vicariam, de quibus, nunc certis modis vacantibus, valeret
eadem auctoritate dispensatum fuit; quique etiam dictum
Decanatum inter alia obtinet, a quibuscunque excommunica-
tionis, suspensionis et interdicti, aliisque ecclesiasticis sententiis,
censuris et penis [*sic*] . . . . si quibus quomodolibet innodatus
existit, ad effectum presentium dumtaxat consequendum harum
serie absolventes, et absolutum fore censentes. . . ac dicti
Decanatus fructuum, reddituum, et proventuum veras annuas
valores presentibus pro expressis habentes, hujusmodi sup-
plicationibus inclinati, descretione vestre per Ap^{ca} scripta
mandamus; quatenus vos, vel duo aut unus vestrum, vocatis
dilectis filiis dictarum parrochialium eccl^{arum} rectoribus, et
aliis etiam quoad hujusmodi unionem evocandi, de premissis
vos diligenter informatis; et si per informationem hujusmodi
ita esse reppereritis et ad hoc Ordinarii loci de etiam dicte ecc^e
Insygemeleagh vicarii expressus accesserit assensus, dictam
ecclesiam Sancti Michaelis in parrochialem ecclesiam, cum
fonte baptismali et aliis insignibus parrochialibus alias [?] sine
rectorum dictarum matricum ecclesiarum prejudicio, auc^{te}
nostra, erigatis, ac dictas villas ab ejusdem [*sic*] Matricibus
ecclesiis respective, dicta auc^{te} separetis et segregetis, ac illas
ipsarumque villarum incolas et habitatores predictos eidem
erigende ecc^e pro illius parrochianis et parrochia perpetuo
applicetis, approprietis et assignetis, necnon dictam erigendam
ecclesiam sic a primeva ejus erectione vacantem, cum omnibus
juribus et pertinentiis suis eidem vicarie quamdiu ipse Matheus
vixerit, et illam obtinuerit, eadem auc^{te} uniatis, annectatis et
incorporetis. Ita quod liceat eidem Matheo, per se, vel per alium
seu alios, corporalem possessionem erigende ecc^e juriumque et
pertinentium predictorum propria auc^{te} apprehendere, et quoad
vixerit et dictam vicariam obtinuerit ut preferetur retinere, ac
illius fructus, redditus, et proventus in suos et uniende ecc^e ac
vicarie predictarum usus et utilitatem convertere, diocesani vel
cujusvis alterius licentia super hoc minime requisita. Non
obstantibus constitutionibus et ordinationibus apostolicis,
necnon quibuslibet privilegiis, indulgentiis et litteris Ap^{cis}
generalibus vel specialibus quorumcunque tenore existent per
que presentibus non expressa, vel totaliter non inserta effectus
earum impediri valeat quomodo libet vel differri . . . . Volumus
autem quod dicta unienda ecclesia propter hujusmodi unionem
debitis non fraudetur obsequiis, et animarum cura in ea nulla-
tenus negligatur, sed eius congrue supportentur onera consueta,
quodque dicto Matheo cedente vel decedente, seu alias dictam

vicariam quomodolibet dimittente, unio, annexio et incorporatio hujusmodi dissolute sint, et esse censeantur, ipsaque unienda ecclesia in pristinum statum revertetur eo ipse . . . .

Datum Romae apud Sanctum Petrum, anno Incarnationis Dominice milesimo quadringentesimo nonagesimo tertio, octavo Kal. Junii, anno primo.

APPENDIX C

The Modern Parishes
(Synopsized from the Cahalane Papers)

1. *City and Suburbs*

SAINT MARY'S or the CATHEDRAL PARISH is a union of the medieval parishes of Saint Mary, Saint Catherine and Curry-kippane. Until 1848 it extended from Healy's Bridge on the west to Lota on the east, from Blarney Lane on the north to the Lee on the south, and for a time it included that part of the north-east marsh which extends as far as the north channel of the Lee. Saint Mary's in medieval times was listed as Schendon; Saint Catherine's was situated on or near the present North Abbey Square, and Currykippane was an ancient parish bounded on the south by the Lee, on the west by the Awbeg, on the north by the park lane of Blarney and the highway towards Blarney, and so to the bog of Curraghcomain, and on the east by Killeens, Knocknahailly, Lisgillea and Shanakiel. The Cathedral parish contains one of Cork's 'rosary of churches', namely, that of the Resurrection, Farranree.* Until July 1969 it contained the church of the Ascension, Gurranebraher, which is now a parish in its own right.

SAINT FINBARR'S SOUTH is a union of the pre-Reformation parishes of Saint Finbarr, Holy Trinity (Christ Church), Ringmahon, Saint Mary le Nard and part of the civil parish of Saint Nicholas. The medieval parish of Saint Finbarr extended from Blackrock to Carrigrohane (exclusive) and included Holy Trinity which originally extended to the north channel of the Lee to the west of Saint Peter's church. In 1750 and in 1810 certain sections of Holy Trinity were ceded to Saints Peter and Paul's, while the churches of Blackrock and Saint Finbarr's West became parochial in the later nineteenth century.

SAINT PATRICK'S, built in 1836 as a chapel-of-ease to the cathedral, was raised to parochial status in July 1848. The original site chosen by Father Prout (Francis Sylvester Mahony)

*In 1971 Farranree was also erected into a parish.

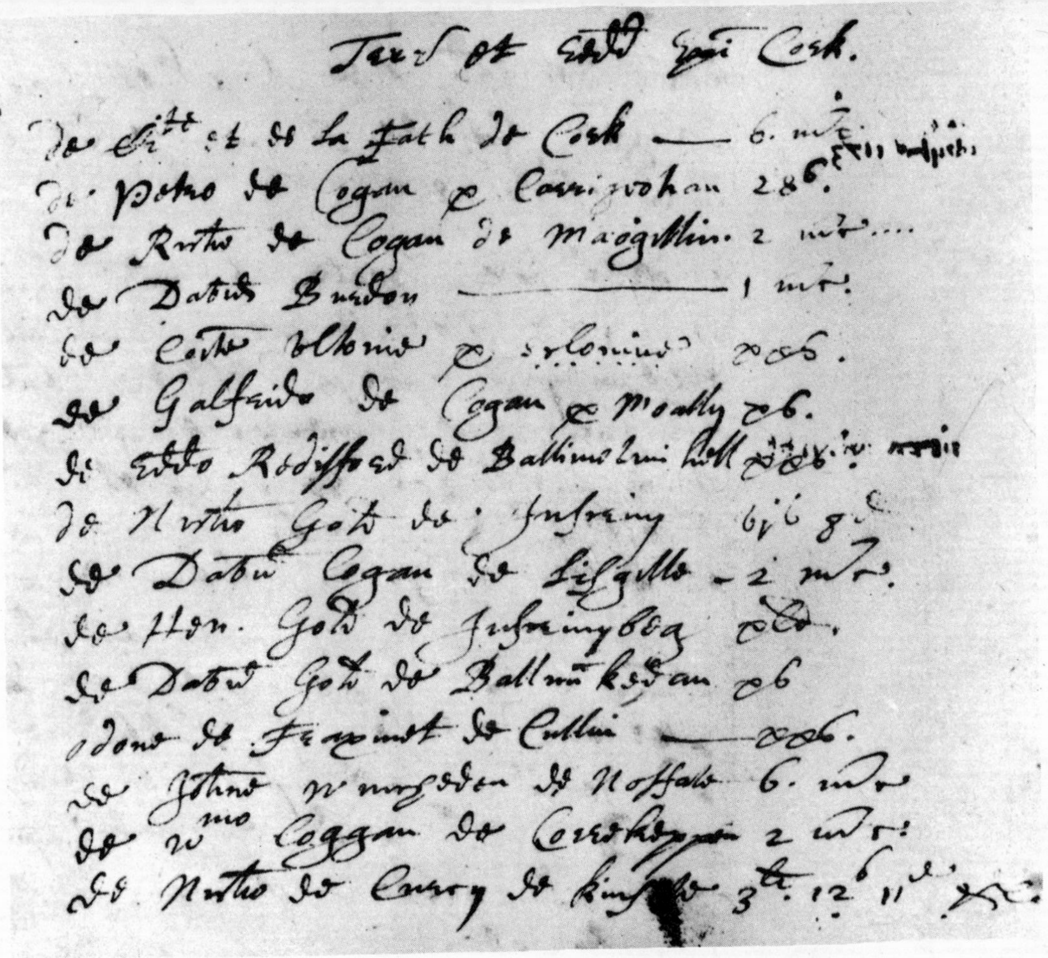

Rental of the Diocese of Cork

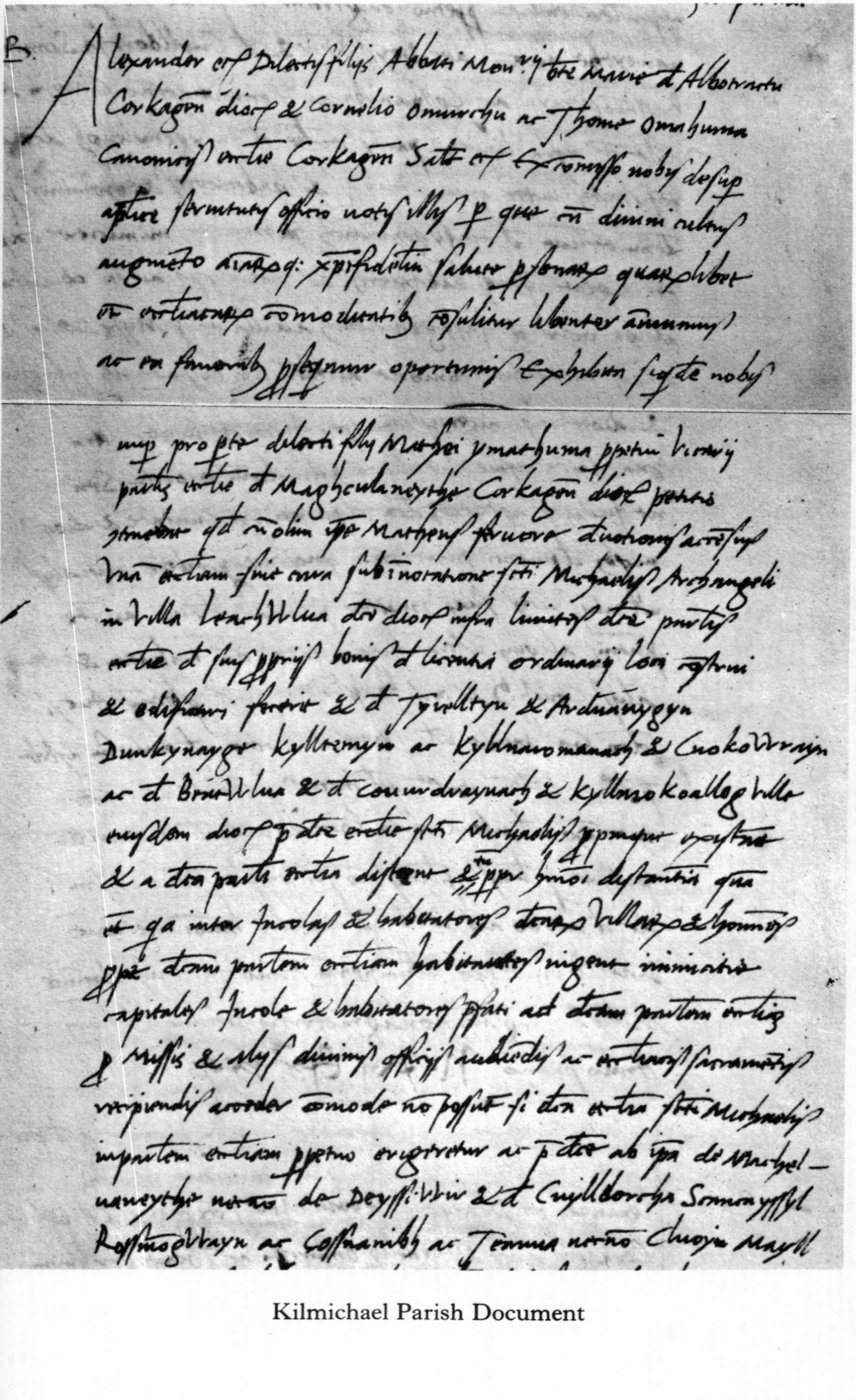

Kilmichael Parish Document

was that now occupied by Saint Luke's Protestant church, but the site appointed by the reigning bishop, John Murphy, was on the lower Glanmire Road. The new chapel, because of its proximity to a nearby brick factory, became known as the Brickfield chapel.

SAINTS PETER AND PAUL'S is a union of the ancient parish of Saint Peter and the civil parish of Saint Paul, with part of the ancient parish of Holy Trinity. Saint Peter's, on the west of the North Main Street, was a parish of small dimensions; Saint Paul's was not at any period a Catholic church. It included the east marsh (north side of Patrick Street–Cornmarket Street–North Channel) and that part of Dunscombe's Marsh between North Main Street, Castle Street and Cornmarket Street which belonged originally to Christ Church. The strip was ceded to Saints Peter and Paul's early in the eighteenth century; the east marsh was added during the episcopate of Richard Walsh (1748–63). In 1810, to quote the church register, 'a portion of the south parish bounded on the north by Lumley's Lane, Tuckey Street and George's Street (Oliver Plunkett Street) to Lapp's Island, including the entire island, was added to the church of Saints Peter and Paul's'. In 1752 the Catholic parish was known as Saint Peter's; in 1766 it was named Saints Peter and Paul's.

SAINT FINBARR'S WEST. This parish, which holds within its ambit some of the most ancient ecclesiastical sites of the diocese, is of comparatively recent erection. In December 1881 the church of the Immaculate Conception was blessed and opened as a chapel-of-ease to the church of Saint Finbarr's South, and in April 1890 this new chapel was raised to the status of parish, to be henceforth known as Saint Finbarr's West. Increasing population in the built-up areas which form the periphery of the parish to the west necessitated another church as adjunct to Saint Finbarr's. Consequently, on 25 September 1960 the church of the Descent of the Holy Ghost was blessed and opened by Most Reverend Dr. Lucey. It became the parish of Ballineaspaig in January 1970.

CHRIST THE KING, TURNER'S CROSS. Originally a chapel-of-ease to Saint Finbarr's South, this church, which was blessed and opened on 25 October 1931 by Bishop Daniel Cohalan, was raised to parochial status on 1 September 1957 by Dr. Lucey. Territorially, the new parish necessitated certain modifications on the then existing boundaries of Saint Finbarr's South.

BALLYPHEHANE. The church of the Assumption, another of Cork's 'rosary of churches', became a parish on 1 September 1957, having originated as a chapel-of-ease to Saint Finbarr's South. The ambit of the new parish encompasses districts originally belonging to the parish of Saint Finbarr.

BLACKROCK. Saint Michael's was opened in 1821 as yet another chapel-of-ease to Saint Finbarr's South; its main function was to supply the spiritual needs of what was then a thriving fishing village. It became parochial in 1848 under Bishop William Delany, but its original parochial boundary was modified on 1 May 1955 on the erection of a new parish at Ballinlough.

BALLINLOUGH. The church of Our Lady of Lourdes was blessed and opened for public worship on 11 September 1938, and was accorded parochial status under Bishop Lucey on 1 May 1955.

BALLINCOLLIG is a union of the medieval parishes of Corbally, Kilnaglory, Carrigrohane, Inishkenny, and a particle called Maglin which belonged to the church of Saint Nicholas.

GLANMIRE is a union of the ancient parishes of Templeusque, Rathcooney, Dunbulloge (Carrignavar), Kilcully and Temple-michael. Recent changes in parish boundaries (3 July 1962) have 'incorporated in Saint Patrick's parish certain territory hitherto in Glanmire parish. This is the territory adjacent to the new Church of Our Lady Crowned.'

GLOUNTHANE is a union embracing the ancient parishes of Caherlag, Little Island*, Ballydeloher, Killaspugmullane and Kilquane. The union was originally called the union of Caherlag and Kilquane; later it was called Lower Glanmire, New Glanmire and Knockraha. In 1838 it was the union of Gloun-thane and Knockraha and since 1840 the name Glouthane has persisted.

WATERGRASSHILL is a union of the ancient parishes of Ardna-geehy and Kilshanahan with some townlands from Dunbulloge, Kilquane and Killaspugmullane. At some date before the end of the eighteenth century Trantstown (Killaspugmullane) and

* Little Island, so called in contradistinction to the Great Island or the Cobh of Cork. Names by which Little Island has appeared in the various records are: *Cellescop Lappan* (from Saint Lappan whose feast occurs on 26 March); *De Insula; Ecclesia Sancti Lappani de Insula Parva; Ecclesia Sancti Lappani de Inysmemele; Sancti Lappani de insula parva als inish vic Neyl.* Mac Neill was a chieftain of the Ui Tassaigh who inhabited this district.

Bishop Island (Kilquane) were added to Watergrasshill. Later, the townlands of Coom, Doonpeter East and West and Knocknacaheragh were transferred permanently from Dunbulloge, while Mitchellsfort, Barnetstown and Rupperagh were detached from that part of Kilquane which lay within the parish of Glounthane.

2. *Deanery of Kinsale*

KINSALE is a union of the ancient parishes of Kinsale, Rincurran, Tisaxon and Dunderrow. In 1740 Dunderrow, Ballymartle, Cullen, Templemichael and probably Tisaxon formed a separate union from that of Kinsale and Rincurran. The present union dates from the year 1766.

BALLINHASSIG is a union of the ancient parishes of Ballinaboy, Liscleary and Templemichael, together with certain townlands from Killanully, Dunderrow, Inishkenny, Ballymartle and Carrigaline. In 1704 Liscleary was in the union of Carrigaline, and Templemichael was in that of Ballymartle. The present union was formed towards the end of the eighteenth century. Ballinhassig is a placename, not a townland, and it does not represent any ancient parish. The three townlands—Ballyhemiken, Raffeen and Carrigaline (84 acres)—which were severed from Liscleary by the civil union of Carrigaline are now in the parish of Monkstown.

CARRIGALINE is a union of the ancient parishes of Carrigaline and Templebreedy. The union was more extensive in 1704 and then included the parishes of Liscleary, Monkstown and Kilmoney. Before the end of the eighteenth century Passage West, Monkstown and Douglas were erected into separate parishes: Liscleary was divided between the union of Passage West and Monkstown and the parish of Ballinhassig.

CLONTEAD (BELGOOLY) is a union of the ancient parishes of Kilmonoge, Ballyfeard, Clontead, Cullen and Ballymartle. The process by which the union was forged was extremely tortuous and was not finalized until 1860.

COURCEYS (BALLINSPITTAL) is a union of the ancient parishes of Ringrone, Kilroan, Templetrine and Ballinadee, and is believed to have been effected in 1752 when the church at Ballinspittal was erected. Previous to this, there was a temporary union of Ringrone, Ballinadee, Templetrine and Kilbrittain. The parish was first called Courceys in the official list of 1814: the Courcey family owned the manor of Ringrone and the barony of Kinsale. In ancient times Courceys country was more extensive than at present; certain townlands were detached from the parish in 1859 and were added to Kilbrittain, e.g., Currarane, Killeens, Clashreagh, Rochestown, Hackettstown, Ballydonas, Glouna-virane, Carrigcannon, Glounavaad and Gurraneasig.

DOUGLAS is a modern parish detached from the ancient parish of Carrigaline. As part of the union of Carrigaline, Douglas had no church until the middle of the eighteenth century, and it attained parochial status between 1753 and 1760.

MONKSTOWN, also a modern parish, dates from 1875. In addition to the civil parish of Monkstown, it incorporated Shanbally, Barnehely, Spike Island, Haulbowline and a number of town-lands from Carrigaline and Liscleary.

PASSAGE WEST represents the ancient parish of Marmullane with part of the civil union of Carrigaline. Up to 1875 Passage included Monkstown, Shanbally and the islands in Cork harbour. Hop Island, which is now part of the parish of Passage West, is believed to have belonged in ancient times to Dunderrow near Kinsale.

TRACTON is a union of the ancient parishes of Tracton, Bally-foyle, Kilpatrick, Nohoval and Kinure. In 1704 the union in-cluded the parishes of Kilmonoge, Ballyfeard and Clontead, but these were detached before 1763 when the Rev. John Mc-Sweeney was appointed to the union of Tracton and the Rev. Daniel Hurley to that of Clontead.

3. *The Deanery of Bandon*
BANDON is a union of the ancient parishes of Ballymodan, Kilbrogan, and the following townlands from the ancient parish of Desertserges: Cappaknockane, Cashel Beg, Dangan More, Knocknagallagh and Moneens. Between 1700 and 1704 Bally-modan and Desertserges formed a separate union; Kilbrogan, Templemartin and Murragh were also distinct. In 1793 Kil-brogan was attached to the Ballymodan–Desertserges union, but in 1817 Desertserges became a distinct parish and in 1858 became part of Enniskeane. The deanery of Bandon is co-extensive with the baronies of Kinalmeaky and Carbery.

ENNISKEANE is a union of the ancient parishes of Kinneigh, Ballymoney and Desertserges, exclusive of certain townlands in each case, namely, *Kinneigh*: Belrose, Laravolta, Lissarourke, Rushfield, Farranmareen, Moneygaff East, Teadies Lower and Kilnacarnagh East which were ceded to Murragh in 1858. *Ballymoney*: twelve townlands in the district of Ballynacarriga which were ceded to Dunmanway after the Reformation. *Desertserges*: certain townlands in Ibawne and Barryroe which were ceded to Bandon in 1817. In the year 1766 Enniskeane was known as the parish of Kinneigh; in 1807 it was called Enniskeane and Kinneigh, and after 1836 the name Kinneigh was dropped.

INNISHANNON is a union of the ancient parishes of Innishannon, Leighmoney, Knockavilly and Brinny. In 1731 Knockavilly and Brinny appear to have formed a separate union from that of Innishannon and Leighmoney; the same arrangement obtained in 1743–44. It seems likely that the union of the four medieval parishes was effected with the appointment of James Roche as parish priest of Innishannon about 1760.

IVELEARY (INCHIGEELA) embraces the basin of the river Lee from its source at Gougane Barra to half-way between the village of Inchigeela and the town of Macroom. In 1493 the parish extended as far as Deshure in Kilmichael, but at that date certain townlands were ceded to Kilmichael.

KILBRITTAIN is a union of the pre-Reformation parishes of Kilbrittain and Rathclarin, with portions of Ringrone, Templetrine, Raharoon (Ballinadee) and Cripple-hill (particle of Ballymodan). The union of Kilbrittain and Rathclarin took place before 1731; the annexation of Raharoon and Cripple-hill was effected later.

KILMICHAEL is a union of the medieval parishes of Kilmichael and Macloneigh. The union extends from *Ath an Teampuill* on the Lee north of Macloneigh to the bridge south of Aultagh Wood, and from Drohinfeerulagh near Duniskey to Dromlough on the west. The churches of Johnstown and Cooldorrihy correspond roughly to the ancient Kilmichael; the church of Toames coincides with the ancient Macloneigh.

KILMURRY is a union of the ancient parishes of Kilmurry, Moviddy, Kilbonane, Duniskey, Cannaway and Dundrinan. The parish of Dundrinan had become absorbed in Moviddy before the Reformation; the remaining parishes were not formed into a union until comparatively recent times. In 1700 Canna-

way was united with Macroom and became united with Kilmurry in 1748 when the union of the dioceses of Cork and
Cloyne was severed.

MURRAGH (NEWCESTOWN) is a union of the ancient parishes of
Murragh, Templemartin and part of Kinneigh. In 1700 the
union included Murragh, Templemartin, Killowen and Kilbrogan, but this union disintegrated in 1793 when Kilbrogan
was united with Ballymodan. For a short period in the eighteenth
century Kilbonane was united with Templemartin. From 1807
onwards Templemartin and Murragh formed a distinct union,
and after 1836 Murragh was accepted as the official name of the
parish.

OVENS is a union of the ancient parishes of Athnowen, Desertmore and Aglish. Prior to 1700 Aglish was united with Magourney, but in 1714 Aghina, Aglish and Ovens formed a union
which continued until 1731 when the present union of Aglish,
Desertmore and Athnowen was formed. The union has persisted
except for the years 1812–25, during which Aglish was united
with Cannaway. The ancient prebend of Desertmore was never
given precedence in the modern union.

4. *The Deanery of Bantry*
BANTRY is a union of the ancient parishes of Inniscuinge and
Kilmocomoge. Inniscuinge (*Inniscuingi*) is believed to have
comprised some islands in Bantry Bay, notably Chapel Island
and Coney Island. As a parish, Inniscuinge disappeared at an
early date and is believed to have become absorbed by Durrus
and Kilmocomoge in early medieval times.

CAHERAGH is coterminous with the ancient parish of the same
name. During the greater part of the eighteenth century
Caheragh was united with Drimoleague from which it became
detached again in 1860. Two townlands of Caheragh—Lissane
Upper and Lower and Rearahinagh—are cut off by Drimoleague
from the main body of the parish: this may be consequential
upon the ancient union or may have had its origin in some early
tribal arrangement.

DRIMOLEAGUE is a union of the ancient parishes of Dromdaleague and Drinagh. In 1704 part of Drinagh was united with
Dunmanway, while Drimoleague, Caheragh and the remnant
of Drinagh formed a distinct union. The separation of Caheragh
was effected in 1760 when Father Florence O'Driscoll was

appointed parish priest of Caheragh and Father Cornelius Deasy became parish priest of Drimoleague-Drinagh.

DUNMANWAY is a union of the ancient parish of Fanlobbus and the following townlands of Ballymoney: Ardea, Ballinacarriga, Buddrimeen, Bunanumera, Carrigeen, Currabeg, Edencurra, Garranure, Glan, Grillagh, Inchfume, Kilcaskan, Kilvinane and Kilvurra. The union appears to have taken place in early post-Reformation times. Brady places it before the year 1700 and states that it was an accomplished fact in the Catholic arrangement by that date.

GOLEEN (KILMOE) includes the ancient parish of Kilmoe and part of the ancient parish of Schull, whence it is sometimes referred to as West Schull. The parish includes the Fastnet Lighthouse and Mizen Head, which was fixed as the western boundary of the diocese at Rathbreasail in 1111. In medieval times the parishes of Durrus, Kilcrohane, Kilmoe, Schull, Caheragh and Bantry were known collectively as *Ivagha*; this name was eventually applied exclusively to the inhabitants of Goleen.

MUINTERVARA (DURRUS) comprises the ancient parishes of Durrus and Kilcrohane. In early times the parish of Durrus extended to the western end of Bantry and appears to have included the present abbey site. Some townlands in this district, formerly in Durrus, are now included in the parish of Bantry.

SCHULL represents the ancient parish of the same name less a small number of townlands on the west which are in the parish of Goleen and the townland of Greenmount which belongs to Kilcoe in the diocese of Ross. Of the neighbouring islands, East Calf and Skeam East and West belong to Aghadown in Ross, while Mid and West Calf, Castle Island, Long Island, Horse Island and Goat Island belong to Schull. In ancient times Schull belonged to the diocese of Ross; when it became part of Cork, nineteen ploughlands in the area became possessions of the see of Cork.

XI

Catholic Cork
in the Fourteenth Century

A comprehensive, if incomplete account of the churches and religious practices of medieval Cork is enshrined in two important documents of the early fourteenth century, namely the papal taxation lists of 1302–06[1] and the testament of John de Wynchedon, 1306. The taxations give a list of the churches and parishes of the diocese; the Wynchedon will furnishes a valuable description of medieval Cork in its religious and social aspects. John de Wynchedon was a citizen of some standing, a member of the wealthy burgher class. The family, later known as the Nugents of Aghamarta near Crosshaven, was of Norman origin, and a Wynchedon was provost of Cork in 1254. John de Wynchedon lived, apparently, in the parish of Holy Trinity (Christ Church) where he had two stone houses. He also had tenements in Dungarvan near the North Gate, in John Street and on the Douglas Road, and he owned landed property in Kilnagleary near Carrigaline.[2] From the acreage under crops and the stock of cattle mentioned in the inventory attached to his will, Wynchedon's lands were extensive, but little is known of the tenure under which these lands were held. It seems likely that most of the land was entailed when John de Wynchedon made his will: his eldest son Richard who inherited ten acres of land in Kilnagleary 'entered [his holding] by hereditary succession after the death of John de Wynchedon, his father . . . who died seised'.[3]

In 1327 this Richard Wynchedon was appointed by King Edward II 'to dispose of, for the King's advantage, one thousand

1 For argument on the dating of these taxations, see Chapter XII.

2 Windele, *Cork*, p. 41, described Dungarvan as 'a principal street lying north and east, having walls to the east and west; always stated to be in the suburbs and in Shandon parish'.

3 *Cal. justic. rolls, Ire., 1305–07*, pp. 374–5.

288

cows which he was to receive . . . as fines for different seditions'.[4]
The Roll of Landgable Rents in the city gives many prominent
Wynchedon names; the Roche and Sarsfield Papers indicate
the extent of Wynchedon property; the papal registers carry
entries relative to beneficed Wynchedon ecclesiastics; consequently, although the family suffered in the confiscations
following the rebellion of 1641 and although the Wynchedons
were not listed among the prominent citizens of Cork in 1652,
their status in the medieval period is sufficient guarantee for
regarding the will of John de Wynchedon as something in the
nature of a directory of Catholic Cork in the opening years of
the fourteenth century.[5] Taken in broad outline, the will
reveals the deep piety of the testator. John de Wynchedon was
a family man, the father of ten children, two of whose sons were
members of religious orders in the city: Adam, a Friar Minor,
and John, a Friar Preacher. The reality of Wynchedon's faith
is evident in his liberality to the churches of Cork, in his benevol-
ence and charity, his concern for the clergy and for his own soul
after death, in the devotional practices which he enumerates
and in his provision of material support for the hospitals and
institutions then functioning in Cork. Signed at his home in
Cork on the octave day of Saints Peter and Paul, 1306, this
will is more conveniently treated under separate headings than
in the order laid out by the testator.

CHURCHES AND CLERGY

In all, fifteen churches are enumerated, four of which are
designated as parish churches, namely, Saint Mary, Shandon,
Saint Catherine's, Saint Peter's and Holy Trinity or Christ
Church. The churches of Saint Nicholas, Saint Mary le Nard
and Saint Brendan are omitted and the church of Saint Finbarr
is not accorded parochial status. In a diocesan history however,
the cathedral church of the diocese claims priority of treatment,
even though, as in the case of Cork, the exigencies of history
have necessitated the erection of a new cathedral church in a
district other than that occupied by the original.

Church of Saint Finbarr

While the date at which the first church of Saint Finbarr was
built cannot be ascertained it stands to reason that when the

---

4 Windele, *Historical and Descriptive Notices of the City of Cork and its Vicinity:
Gougaun-Barra, Glengarriff and Killarney*, p. 253; hereafter referred to as Windele,
South of Ireland.

5 The manuscript of the Wynchedon will and its *vera copia* are catalogued in the
British Museum as Add. MS 19868, ff. 5a–5b and 7b–8b.

monastic bishop became a diocesan in the twelfth century a
cathedral church became a *sine qua non* of ecclesiastical organization. The first explicit reference to the church of Saint
Finbarr is contained in the decretal of 1199, but there can be
no doubt as to its existence during the episcopate of Bishop
Gregory (1172–82) when we find explicit evidence of a cathedral
chapter. During the medieval period, while there are references
to the personnel of the chapter, there is no suggestion as to
the erection of another cathedral, but it is scarcely likely that
the original church of the decretal lasted, even with repairs,
down to the Reformation. It would appear that the church
taken over at the Reformation was at least the second church
constructed to the south of the river on the site now occupied
by the cathedral of Saint Fin Barre. When taken over by the
Protestants this church contained at least one chantry, the
chapel of Saint Clement, beyond which little else is known
concerning the medieval cathedral. An interesting discovery
by Dr. Caulfield has established that the present site of Saint
Fin Barre's contains evidences of three distinct cemeteries,
the remains of each presenting distinct ethnological peculiarities.
He also maintains that the first or lowest of these cemeteries
was 'the original Cemetery of St. Finbarre and may be coeval
with the age of the Saint'.[6]

Saint Mary, Shandon

This was a parish church before 1306 and it stood on Shandon
Hill on the site presently occupied by the church of Saint Anne
(Church of Ireland). Little is known of the medieval church of
Saint Mary, Shandon (it was burned in 1690), but there are
scattered references to it in documents like papal taxations,
procurations and papal mandates. John de Wynchedon made
a bequest to the fabric of the church of Saint Mary—evidence
here that cathedral churches were not the only ones having a
special fund for repairs and incidental expenses. Similar
donations are found in Wynchedon's provisions for other city
churches.

    In Shandon, as in other parishes, the terms 'parish priest'
and 'rector' are apparently used synonymously to indicate the
priest of the parish who was charged with the care of souls.
Both terms are ancient, but the term 'rector' developed a wider
application in course of time, and the scheme of rectories was
a development from a custom whereby patrons who had founded

6   Richard Caulfield, *The Annals of St. Fin Barre's Cathedral, Cork*, pp. xii, 106.

and endowed churches attached the revenues of these foundations to religious orders who for their part undertook to provide
chaplains to serve the parishes. These chaplains were usually
but not necessarily chosen from the secular clergy. By this
system of appropriations monasteries or other clerical corporate
bodies acquired a determined portion of the parochial fruits
(estimated at about two-thirds). The remaining fraction went
to pay the resident priest or vicar who performed the parochial
duties. With all its disadvantages and abuses the system of
appropriations had at least this to recommend it: it gave
bishops an opportunity of ensuring that a parish should be
properly and continuously served by the ordination of a
vicarage, since in 1306 it was enacted that 'if a church belonged
to a monastery the rector ought to present to the bishop within
six months a perpetual vicar; otherwise he (the vicar) shall be
appointed by the bishop.'[7] Over the centuries the whole system
had come to be governed by canon law. Firstly, the diocesan
bishop by formal deed granted a certain parish (*rectoria*) to a
monastery for its own use (*in proprios usus*). The impropriator
(appropriator)—in this case the religious community—was
instituted as rector, but from the circumstances of the case,
personal residence was not demanded. The bishop by formal
document then established or ordained the vicarage in the
parish, setting aside a suitable portion (*congrua portio*) of its
revenue for the vicar. In this way the vicarage became 'perpetual',
the incumbent was given security of tenure, and after the
Lateran Council of 1215 his position became 'analogous to an
irremovable parochus of modern Canon Law'.[8] Before the end
of the thirteenth century, owing to the incorporation of parishes
with prebends and episcopal *mensae*, the general dispensation
for purposes of studies permitted and even encouraged by the
Cum ex eo of Boniface VIII, and other causes and customs, the
rectors of many parishes had ceased to be bound by residence
and the actual parochial work was done by the vicar employed
and salaried by the rector. This permanent or perpetual vicar
was sometimes referred to as *persona*, and he had specific
canonical rights.

In Saint Mary, Shandon, the cleric presented by the patron
(Coppingers) and approved by the bishop was known as the
rector and the parish was his rectory. It is confusing to find the

---

7 Moorman, *Church Life in England in the Thirteenth Century*, quoting K. J. von
Hefele, *Histoire des Conciles*, ix, 517.

8 J. O'Connell, 'Obligationes pro Annatis Diocesis Ardfertensis', *Archiv. Hib.*, xxi
(1958), 2.

term vicarage also applied to Saint Mary's, sometimes in union with the rectory and on other occasions independently. Available records throw no light on the circumstances under which this development took place.

Saint Catherine

This church is believed to have been originally a parish church before its incorporation in the cathedral of Saint Mary in post-Reformation times (1666). In the twelfth century the tithes of the church were granted to the abbey of Saint Thomas in Dublin and in the taxations of 1302 it was valued at ten shillings. The Wynchedon will makes a bequest to the chapter of Saint Catherine, the reference here being not to a cathedral chapter properly so called but to the chapter of canons of Saint Victor. Although much of the later history of Saint Catherine's is obscure, the grant to the Dublin abbey was not permanent and the parochial status of the church was still recognized in 1523 when William O'Fin was named as its parish priest. The church was later appropriated to the Midleton abbey of Chore (*De Choro Benedicti*) and was listed among the possessions of that abbey in 1544.[9]

Today the boundaries of Saint Catherine's parish are no longer traceable but extant references place the church on the north side of the city, outside the walls, between the North Abbey Square and the modern Churchfield. Under date 1520 there is reference to 'the Church of St. Catherine on the west, the King's road on the south and west, and from thence to the *great rock* on the north'. An entry for 1595 mentions 'the lane or way to St. Katherine's churchyard to the west, the Queen's highway leading to Currykippane on the north and east' and for the year 1629 Windele cites 'a plot of ground without the north gate, extending from the *Hospitale* on the east to St. Katherine's Church on the west'.[10]

Saint Peter

Situated within the city walls at the western side of the North Main Street, Saint Peter's was one of the oldest parish churches of Cork. Architecturally it was a church of the pointed Norman style and is first mentioned in the decretal letter of 1199. Under date May 1269 Prince Edward (later Edward I) gave confirmation to the bishop of Cork and his successors of the

9   Webster, *The Diocese of Cork*, p. 155.
10   Windele, *South of Ireland*, pp. 57, 64.

patronage and advowson of certain churches, among them 'the chapel of St Peter at Cork' (*capelle Sci. Petri Corcag*).[11] The grant was made for 'the health of his own and his ancestors' souls and for the relief of the estate of the church of Cork'. Frequent references to Saint Peter's after this date are pointers to its importance in the civic life of the diocese. Thus, in 1380 an Irish 'parliament' met in Saint Peter's to nominate a governor for Ireland in place of Edmund Mortimer who had died in the Dominican abbey of Saint Mary of the Island.

The parish of Saint Peter's included the district of Dungarvan which lay outside the North Gate of the city; hence the church is sometimes styled the church of Saint Peter in Dungarvan in the suburbs of Cork.[12] Saint Peter's was rated at twelve marks in 1302; shortly afterwards it was designated a rectory, but there was no question of lay presentation as Saint Peter's became the prebend of the archdeacon. There are no references to a vicarage in Saint Peter's, and it is likely that the archdeacon, whose position did not preclude the care of souls, functioned *per se* without the services of a *locum tenens*. He could, and probably did, employ a stipendiary priest when necessary. References in the Wynchedon will to the clergy of Saint Peter's enumerate Master Robert, the parish priest; John Arnold's son who was 'priest of the said church', and there are two bequests to 'any other priest'. As the term 'priest' is used indiscriminately in the will, Wynchedon's references could be to chantry priests or stipendiary priests—we have no way of deciding. A significant feature of this will is its complete lack of reference to dignitaries even though the contemporary papal taxations mention the *quatuor personae* and the archdeacon.

Within, Saint Peter's Church contained two chapels: the Lady chapel which is mentioned in the Wynchedon will and in the Landgable Roll of Edward I (*chapelle de Marie Eccles. Petri*), and the chapel of Saint Catherine which was endowed by the Galway family. Saint Peter's was the burial place of many of Cork's oldest families—Roches, Walshes, Myaghs (Meades), Tirrys and Galways—while an interesting will proved in the prerogative court of Canterbury in 1581 directed that the body of John Hawker of Challock, Kent, should be buried 'in St Peter's Church in the Cittie of Cork in Ireland, so neere as maie be unto the place where Arthur Carter, late Provost of Munster, lyeth'.

11 Ibid., p. 57.

12 Webster, *The Diocese of Cork*, p. 150.

Christ Church

Holy Trinity or Christ Church stood on the site presently occupied by the Protestant church of the same name on the eastern side of the South Main Street and was complementary to Saint Peter's in being one of the earliest parishes established within the walls of Cork. Throughout the pre-Reformation period and up to the end of the sixteenth century Holy Trinity maintained a status of paramount importance in the religious life of the citizens. On all public festivals the mayor and corporation of Cork attended Holy Trinity as did also the judges of the assizes before each session's commencement. Notwithstanding some uncertainty as to its earlier parochial history, Holy Trinity was mentioned in the decretal of 1199 and in the taxation list of 1302. As early as 1295 the benefice was in the gift of the crown and in that year was conferred by Edward I on William de Muenes.[13] In the following century Holy Trinity was a free royal chapel, reserved one would imagine for royal clerks, as the following excerpts show.

In 1382 John Kingston was appointed to the chapel of Holy Trinity from which the former chaplain had resigned. Four years later Thomas de Everdon, clerk, was appointed to the free chapel of Holy Trinity and a mandate for his admission was directed to Gerald (Barry), bishop of Cork. Within the next two years Thomas Barton was presented and was designated 'keeper of the free chapel or parson (*persona*) of the Church of Holy Trinity'.[14] In 1439 Henry Kyng became prebendary of Holy Trinity and was inducted by Bishop Jordan Purcell, but he was dispossessed about four years later by David Meade whose father was mayor of Cork and who 'by a sinister information' got possession of Holy Trinity.[15] Even though Meade failed to secure acceptance, admission or induction, his family maintained a constant interest in Holy Trinity, and we find that in 1502 one James Myagh (Meade) granted 'two acres of land is the parish of St. Nicholas, Liscleary, together with the advowson of that parish to the Church of the Holy Trinity,' '*in augmentacionem divini cultus in eadem ecclesia Sanctae Trinitatis.*'[16]

References to Holy Trinity in the Wynchedon will are of two kinds and may be tabulated as follows:

13   *Cal. doc. Ire., 1302–07*, p. 236.

14   Patents 10 and 12 Richard II.

15   *Statute Rolls of the Parliament of Ireland, Reign of Henry VI*, ed. H. F. Berry, pp. 541–2.

16   Webster, *The Diocese of Cork*, p. 134 n.

parish priest or rector	priest in charge
vicar	fabric revenue
other priests	recluse
clerk	

In the first column we see the set-up of a parish church; the second shows an arrangement similar to that of Saint Philip's, Saint Stephen's and Saint Brigid's as will be shown below. The only viable explanation of the anomaly is the existence of two churches with the same titular in 1306, even though direct information on the matter is completely lacking. The clerk here mentioned was either an altarist or a chorister, one of the *ministri inferiores* of the medieval chapter and in minor orders only. It was not unusual in medieval times to appoint such clerks to parishes, and some of them after studying ecclesiastical subjects under the parish priest subsequently took orders.[17] Many of them, however, had no intention of proceeding to major orders, and in the thirteenth century the connived 'marriages' of these clerks were quite common. John de Wynchedon made bequests to the son of the clerk of Holy Trinity.

Holy Trinity in the sixteenth century and probably also at an earlier date contained two chantry chapels, namely, the chapel of Saint James which was endowed by the Whites and the equally well-endowed Lady chapel (*capella Beatae Mariae infra ecclesiam Sanctae Trinitatis*). Here in the Lady chapel and in Christ Church generally many leading Cork families were interred; their monumental headstones and flagstones within and around the present church are a directory of now-extinct names, the bearers of which once regulated the affairs of the city. In addition to the site occupied by Holy Trinity and its adjacent cemetery, two neighbouring sites were granted to the prebendary for the support of the chantry. These were the College of Stone and the chapel of Saint Laurence. The former, which was also called the *Fause House* or College of Christ Church, was situated on the south side of the present Christ Church lane, extending from the South Main Street to the Grand Parade. There is no evidence to show that Holy Trinity was at any time a collegiate church, although the eight massing priests for whose support Philip Gould granted the college in 1482 are identical with the number in the College of Youghal which was founded in 1464. The chapel of Saint Laurence

17 This medieval custom is recalled in the case of Father Laurence Callanan, O.F.M., who studied for a time under Father Colman Sarsfield, P.P., Saint Finbarr's South (1704–51).

occupied the site of the brewery near the South Gate. There is no official record of its ever being a parochial church notwithstanding that the will of Andrew Galway in 1581 mentions the parish of Saint Laurence. This church or chapel measured one hundred feet by forty-five, and up to the time of renovations in the early 1960s some remains of the old building were still visible on the brewery premises.

John de Wynchedon's provision for Holy Trinity directed that his son William should be given 'my stone house nearer the church of Holy Trinity' on condition that each year he should provide 'a waxen light weighing five pounds [to be placed] before the image of the Blessed Virgin in the same church'. Wynchedon provided also for the fabric fund of Holy Trinity, for the rector, the vicar, any other priest and the clerk. He bequeathed two altar cloths for the high altar of the church and directed that five pounds of waxen paper should be burned annually before the crucifix in the church.

Saint Mary Magdalen

The will of John de Wynchedon is the only extant reference to the church of Saint Mary Magdalen and its adjoining leper hospital to which he bequeathed forty pence. Its putative site was outside the North Gate of the city, probably to the west of the medieval church of Saint Mary, Shandon, but as it is not indicated on any of the old maps of Cork it must have ceased as a place of worship at an early date.

Saint John the Baptist

Immediately after the Magdalen Church the Wynchedon will mentions the church of Saint John the Baptist 'to the east' (*Sancti Johannis oriental* [*rectè, orientali*]) which suggests another site in the Shandon area near the Kiln river, at or near Saint John's Street.[18] Windele, on the other hand, tells that 'to the rear of the North Main Street between it and the Queen's Old Castle . . . stood in the middle ages a Benedictine nunnery dedicated to St. John the Baptist'.[19] Evidence otherwise forthcoming strengthens the theory that the nunnery of Saint John the Baptist was located in the northern suburbs and that it was the only convent then existing (in the fourteenth century) where the daughters of wealthier citizens could be maintained

18   *Cal. justic. rolls Ire., 1295–1303*, p. 154.
19   Windele, *Cork*, p. 22.

and educated.[20] Apart from the plea entered on behalf of Agnes de Hareford, further references to Saint John's are scanty. By an inquisition taken in 1326 it was found that Henry de Cogan granted to Prior William FitzRoger of Kilmainham three houses and their appurtenances in Shandon. That these included or were contiguous to Saint John's church may be assumed from the fact that in 1320 the same prior had sued one Richard Ryther for a mill and three acres of land in *Saint John's Town* near Cork, while in 1348 another prior of Kilmainham recovered from John Rych a tenement in John's Street, Cork.[21] With reference to Windele's statement, however, there appears to have been a Benedictine convent dedicated to Saint John the Baptist within the city walls, on or near the present Cornmarket. Beyond that this convent was founded by William de Barry no record of its history or activities has been preserved. It is believed that materials from this ancient building were used in the erection of the Cornmarket, the Bridewell and the Custom House which in former times were located in that neighbourhood.

Saint Philip

Here again John de Wynchedon mentions a church whose existence is not endorsed in either the Innocentian Decretal or in the fourteenth-century taxation lists. Judging from the geographical route followed by Wynchedon, Saint Philip's stood in the south of the city.[22] The mention of a church of Saint James in a document bearing the same date as the Wynchedon will may be a pointer to the location and identification of Saint Philip's. The relevant passage in this document states that in 1302 'Friar Parlip (Philip), prior of the Dominicans, sued Matthew de Cantilon for a messuage and its appurtenances in St. Nicholas Street, which he claimed in right of his church of St. James in Cork, and which Gilbert Planck, the late prior, had unjustly alienated to Thomas Sarsfield'.[23] The church of Saint James appears to have been near that of Saint Nicholas and may have been identical with that of Saint Philip, seeing that Saints Philip and James are traditionally coupled and share a common feast day on 11 May. Relative to this church, John

20 *Cal. doc. Ire., 1293–1301*, no. 801.

21 N.L.I., King MSS; labelled 'King's *Collectanea* for the Ecclesiastical History of Ireland' and transcribed by Walter Harris (1686–1761).

22 Denis O'Sullivan, 'The Testament of John de Wynchedon of Cork, *anno* 1306', *Cork Hist. Soc. Jn.*, lxi (1956), 86, suggests 'the little ruined church near the entrance gates to Lehenagh House', but this seems too far out to be viable.

23 Windele, *Cork*, p. 49.

de Wynchedon bequeathed forty pence to the fabric, six pence to the clerk and half-a-mark to the recluse (*inclusa*). The final reference may indicate that Saint Philip's was solely an anchoretic foundation.

Saint Brigid

The church of Saint Brigid stood within the ambit of an ancient fort at the top of Tower Street, on or near Lyscotekyn, the later Cat Fort.[24] It was mentioned in 1199 but not in the taxation list of 1302. John de Wynchedon's bequests were to the fabric of the church, to the female recluse (*inclusa*) and to the priest attached to the church. It appears that Saint Brigid's was a nunnery of sorts, but its independence was early absorbed as part of the *spiritualia* of the cathedral chancellor. There is no evidence to prove that Saint Brigid's ever achieved parochial status, and it does not appear to have had any particular individual history. The ruins of the church had disappeared by 1700 and in the meantime the Cat Fort had been erected on the site. Today all traces of this fort have been removed.

Saint Stephen

This church was associated with the leper hospital of the same name which stood on Stephen Street just outside the south wall of medieval Cork and within the present constitutional parish of Saint Nicholas. The church of Saint Stephen, which was of later erection than the hospital, had no parochial status; the officiating priest there was appointed and paid by the hospital trustees after presentation by the bishop. As this priest was neither rector nor vicar, and as his main duty was confined priest with the status of a modern chaplain. John de Wynchedon to celebrating Mass in the church, he was probably a stipendiary bequeathed twelve pence to him.

Wynchedon's arrangements for the Regulars of Cork are interesting. To the Augustinian Eremites he left eight marks for the repair of the choir stalls, twenty shillings for the sustenance of the brethren attending their chapter in Ireland and three marks 'so that a friar may celebrate Mass for my soul every day for the first year after my death'. He wished to be buried with the Augustinians and provided two hundred pounds of wax for lights to be placed around his body (*pro lumina circa corpus meum*). Bequests to the Friars Preachers and the Friars Minor were almost identical. Each community was allotted two marks for the necessities of the chapter, three for the testator's soul and three without any stipulation attached. To his sons, John, a Dominican, and Adam, a Franciscan, he bequeated five pounds each. Philip Michis, prior of Saint Mary of the Island, was to receive ten shillings and Friar William FitzAdam a half-mark, and an additional grant of two pounds was made to the Franciscan Geoffrey Lumley. Finally, John de Wynchedon bequeathed forty pence to the canons regular *de Antro* and a similar sum to the recluse attached to the monastic church.

Three other city churches not enumerated by John de Wynchedon—Saint Mary le Nard, Saint Nicholas and Saint Brendan—next claim attention.

Saint Mary le Nard

The Innocentian Decretal of 1199 contains the earliest extant reference to the controversial church of *Sancta Maria in Monte*, better known as the church of Saint Mary le Nard. Some authorities claim 'Nard' to be a derivation from if not an abbreviation of spikenard, the ointment with which Mary Magdalen anointed the feet of Jesus. Others regard the word as a corruption of the original Irish title, *Cill Mhuire an Aird*, which is so aptly rendered by the *Sancta Maria in Monte* of the decretal. But there is no difference of opinion as to the location of this church which stood in the southern suburbs on or near the site later occupied by Elizabeth Fort. The existence of a district called *Nard* in this sector of the city is borne out by documents of the fourteenth, sixteenth and seventeenth centuries. In 1307 we find reference to 'Seynte bridestrete in the Narde'.[25] For the year 1588 there is mention of two beds of a garden situated in the Nard extending from Saint Stephen's Leper Hospital. In 1616 a lease was granted of 'a garden in Leonard Street near holy roodes church without the South Gate'.[26] There are possibilities of connection too between le Nard and Leonard Street which abuts Barrack Street and may contain the relevant clue as to the church's title. The church of le Nard, which was dedicated to Saint Mary Magdalen, was also known as the church of Holy Rood and Holy Cross.

Saint Mary le Nard was originally a possession of Gill Abbey, according to Brady.[27] In 1270 the (so-called) parish of le Narde was granted to Bishop Reginald by Prince Edward who was lord of Ireland, but we have seen that this grant was subsequently a matter of dispute between King Edward I and Bishop Robert Mac Donnchada. In a taxation list of the fifteenth century the church of Saint Mary le Nard, which was not mentioned in the fourteenth-century list, was described as paying a pension to Saint Finbarr's, probably to the vicars choral. The church was in ruins before 1615, but the district lived on as a distinct entity, its boundaries being fixed at Barrack Street, French's Quay and Kayser's Hill. Such a constricted area would scarcely justify parochial status for Saint Mary le Nard (rectors and vicars are nowhere mentioned), and consequently it is probable that it served as chapel of the leper hospital on French's Quay. After the decay of the hospital the revenues of Saint Mary le Nard were claimed by the cathedral church of Saint Finbarr. Not a single trace remained of the church of le Nard after the erection of the great stone fort in the reign of the first Elizabeth.

Saint Nicholas

The omission of this chapel from the Innocentian Decretal is due to its having been granted by Roger of Oxford to the abbey of Saint Thomas during the episcopate of Bishop Gregory O hAodha, 1172–82. In the ratification of this grant made by Bishop Reginald the chapel of Saint Nicholas was said to have been situated in the court (*curia*) of Gilbert, son of Turgerius, who was mayor of Cork under Dermot MacCarthy.[28] Saint Nicholas was the official chapel of the Danish mayor of Cork and the place of assembly for the city's Danish population. It was a distinct entity as regards tithes, but there is no evidence that it achieved parochial status in the post-Norman period, and some form of authority over the chapel and its property was asserted by the bishop of Cork by the stipulation that a sum of English money and a pound of wax should be given each year to the church of Saint Finbarr on the feast of Saint Nicholas. We find no names of perpetual vicars appointed by the Dublin abbey although such appointments were the normal procedure in the case of impropriate churches or chapels. Saint Nicholas was apparently an establishment of minor importance by comparison with Holy Trinity and Saint Peter's; but for all that, it had its patrons, as documents of the sixteenth century prove.

28   *Reg. St. Thomas, Dublin*, p. 209.

The non-inclusion of Saint Nicholas in the decretal of 1199 and the inclusion of the church of Saint Nessan has led to the inference that they were one and the same, but this view is untenable in the light of the register of Saint Thomas's Abbey, which contains a ratification by Bishop Reginald of the grant of the chapel of Saint Nicholas and an earlier grant of the church of Saint Nessan. This church was located on the south of Barrack Street near the site of Saint Stephen's Priory or on the site later occupied by the Mendicity Asylum (1832).

Saint Brendan

The church of Saint Brendan was situated to the north of the river Lee near the road topping the Glanmire heights and leading to Youghal. The principal quays and docks lay almost beneath Saint Brendan's, and to this church came sailors after their voyages to make their thank-offerings to the navigator saint. At one time the tithes of Saint Brendan's and a considerable part of its adjoining lands were appropriated for the upkeep of the neighbouring leper hospital of Glenmaggyr. No other records of the church remain, but its burial-ground at Ballina-mought continued in use long after the church itself had fallen into decay.

HOSPITALS

The will of John de Wynchedon mentions four hospitals then functioning within the medieval city of Cork. The hospital of Saint John the Evangelist to which he donated a feather bed with its habiliments (*lectum de plumis cum pertinenciis*) has been treated in an earlier chapter. The other three were leper hospitals, namely, Saint Stephen's Hospital in the southern suburbs just outside the city walls and within the present constitutional parish of Saint Nicholas, Saint Mary Magdalen's outside the North Gate and, finally, an unnamed hospital, that of the 'lepers near the bridge' (*leprosis residentibus iuxta pontem versus fratres Praedicatores*). This hospital was located somewhere along French's Quay between the South Gate Bridge and the Abbey of the Isle, or else at one of the arches over the mill stream near the abbey. Outside the city, leper houses were to be found in Glenmaggyr (Glen-Maiur), Dilbey, Longum Vadum, Kinsale and Synssonerian. The multiplication of lazar-houses at this period suggests that some form of dermatitis or cutaneous disorder must have been endemic. France alone had 2,000 leper hospitals in the thirteenth century and England had lazar-houses before the First Crusade. But in those days of imperfect medical knowledge the term 'leprosy' seems to have been applied generically to every form of skin ailment, and leprosy as such can never have been prevalent even in mild form in Ireland.[29] Absence of segration and the location of leper hospitals within or near medieval cities bear out this point, and it would appear that the so-called leper hospitals of Cork city and county were therefore founded for the treatment of certain grievous and virulent forms of dermatitis rather than for the care of lepers.

Saint Stephen's Hospital

This best-known of all the medieval institutions of Cork city was founded between 1250 and 1277 as a leper hospital under the patronage of Saint Lazarus. Its administration was in the hands of a religious society or brotherhood known as Lazarists; this society did not form an order strictly so called but belonged to the category of nursing congregations founded for specific social and charitable purposes. The Lazarists (Knights of Saint Lazarus) made relief work for lepers their principal concern, and until an edict of Pope Innocent IV (1243–54) put an end to the practice, the grand master of the Lazarists was always a leper.

Saint Stephen's church, as we have seen, stood in Stephen Street. The priory and the hospital occupied the entire area stretching from Stephen Street to Hospital Lane and its southern boundary was Cat Lane, the present Tower Street. The hospital cemetery, which in later years became an Anabaptist burial-ground, was also in Stephen Street not far from the church. Other lands accredited to the Lazarists were widely scattered over the city and suburbs from Ballinamought and Cahergal in Mayfield to Croghtamore and Ballinlough. The 'spittal lands' which were once part of the manor of Fayd were apparently donated by the bishop to the leper hospital; these lands included part of the Curragh district near Turner's Cross. It is probable that the English king and the corporation of Cork made original endowments to the hospital, and to it John de Wynchedon bequeathed forty pence for the lepers, the same sum for the fabric fund of the church and twelve pence for the chaplain.

---

29   D. O'Sullivan, 'Monastic Establishments of Mediaeval Cork', *Cork Hist. Soc. Jn.*, xlviii (1943), 13. There was segregation of a sort imposed. Lepers from Glenmaggyr were forbidden to advance beyond *Bóthar na Lobhar* leading from Glanmire to Mayfield. By a strange process of devolution, *Bóthar na Lobhar* is today known as Lovers' Walk.

Hospitals

303

The chief functionary of Saint Stephen's was known as the prior, guardian, warden or master. A dispute relative to lands belonging to Saint Stephen's Hospital was successfully resolved in 1296 when 'the *custos* of the House of Lepers of St Stephen recovered for his house the two carucates of land of Lisneynam and Ballymacgoun', that is Ballinamought and Cahergal. Under date 1307 the 'master of the Lepers of St Stephen's' is mentioned in another deed.[30] On 22 November 1408 Henry IV granted the custody of Saint Stephen's, then vacant and in his gift, to Henry Fygham, chaplain, for life. In 1419 and again on 22 November the chaplaincy was either confirmed for Henry Fygham or else conferred for life on another cleric of the same name.[31] The *custos* in post-Reformation times was as often a layman as a cleric, and from the date of its erection the hospital had a governing body composed of priests, prominent laymen and appointees of the corporation.

The last pre-dissolution reference to Saint Stephen's recalls the reception of a brother into the nursing congregation. Our source is a notarial instrument witnessing that on 14 January 1511 in the church of Holy Trinity at Cork, Father William Roche, provincial of the Dominicans in Ireland, appeared before Philip Gull (Gould), official general of Cork, showing a letter of the prior and convent of the leper hospital of Saint Stephen to the effect that George Roche, sometime bailiff of the city had been 'received as a brother of the said house'.[32]

A quaint practice relative to Saint Stephen's is recorded during the reign of James I. Cormac MacCarthy of Blarney claimed as by immemorial custom the right to entertainment for twenty-four hours for himself and his entourage whenever he or they rode into Cork. The hospitality was expected in exchange for firebote and housebote, which meant that timber for fuelling purposes and for repairs to the hospital could be obtained gratis on MacCarthy's estate. At the dissolution Saint Stephen's, possibly because of its social importance, was not among the early institutions marked out for spoliation. Its subsequent history is easily traceable in the records of the hospital and priory which happily have escaped destruction.

Glen Maiur

The identification of this hospital offers no difficulty—its

30   Windele, *South of Ireland*, p. 80.

31   Archdall, *Monasticon Hibernicum*, p. 126.

32   *Calendar of Letters and Papers, Foreign and Domestic . . . Henry VIII, 1509–14,* pt. I, no. 1026, p. 505.

location, however, is problematic. Two feasible theories are suggested: (a) The hospital was at *Cnocán na Lobhar* otherwise Knocknalour or Lepers' Hill at Glenville about six miles north of Glanmire. This is mountainous land containing about 545 acres. (b) The fourteenth-century taxation rolls refer to Glenmaggyr, later called Templeuskey or Templeusque, a townland north of Sarsfield's Court and which was the original Glanmire. Directly across the glen to the south-west is the village of Upper Glanmire in the townland of Ballinvriskig. The leper hospital of the Wynchedon will may have been located at the old church and graveyard on this townland of Templeusque.

Dilbey

The reading of the will at this juncture may very well be 'the lepers of Kilbeg', in which case Killbeg near Garrettstown or Ballinspittal seems probable.[33] Ballinaboy near Ballinhassig is also suggested.[34]

Kinsale

The known existence of a *domus leprosorum* in Spittleland between Kinsale and Brown's Mills suggests that the *contracto* (*tecto*) of Kinsale referred to by John de Wynchedon was a leper hospital of sorts.[35] The boundaries of Spittleland were determined by the grand jury of Kinsale in 1661 in a survey which disclosed that a small shoulder of land called the *bóithrín comhgar* or short cut, extended from Kinsale to Lepers' Well and originally belonged to Spittleland. Beyond this, however, it is not possible to give an exact location for the leper site of Kinsale.

De Longo Vado

This is probably *Atha Mhaide* or Riverstick where topographical evidence is particularly relevant. A stream called the Sliugga, rising at Dubhsliabh, flows through Riverstick and passes via Cullen to Mount Long or *Longum Vadum*, and a site significantly called *Tobar na Lobhar* or Lepers' Well is found in Piercetown,

33 R.I.A., Cork Inquisitions, ii, 127: Garrettstown *als* Kielbegge.

34 D. O'Sullivan, 'The Testament of John de Wynchedon', p. 87.

35 In the will, the usual form of bequest to lazar-hospitals is 'to the lepers of . . .' An exception appears to have been made for Kinsale. The translation of *contracto* as a bequest to 'the paralysed man' is not without its merits, but scribal expediency cannot be overlooked, and the contracted Latin at this point could have meant a house or shelter: *tectum—tecto*.

Cullen. There are no topographical endorsements of the theory that *De Longo Vado* had connections with Aghada.[36]

Synssonerian

This could mean one of the Sovereign Islands off the south coast near Kinsale.[37] Tradition maintains that in Preghane, Rincurran, on the mainland overlooking the islands, a special site known as *Cumar a' Dúna* was allocated to persons suffering from contagious diseases. Special windows known as 'leper squints' were cut in the walls of Kinsale church and in several of Cork city churches to accommodate the lepers who were otherwise debarred from participation in religious ceremonies.

RELIGIOUS PRACTICES

The Mass, the central act of Catholic worship, is written large on the will of John de Wynchedon. Bequests for Masses are left to all the religious orders of the city and to the clergy of other churches and chapels, one outstanding entry being the provision of 'a fit friar (*integrum fratrem*) to celebrate Mass every day for a year' for the repose of the testator's soul. Intimately connected with the celebration of Mass is the Catholic sense of respect for the altar, and consequently John de Wynchedon donated two altar cloths (*duo linthiamina*) for the principal altar in the church of Holy Trinity.

The Wynchedon will bears witness likewise to the Catholic devotion to the Virgin Mary and mentions shrines and Lady chapels in the churches of Saint Mary, Shandon, Saint Peter's and Saint John the Evangelist's where votive lights were to be burned at the request of the testator. The Lady chapel in Holy Trinity, which was Wynchedon's own parish church, and the Lady chapel in Saint Peter's were accorded more generous bequests than were the shrines of other churches. Such outward expressions of devotion were somehow natural in the case of this citizen who prefaced his will by consigning his soul to God, to the Blessed Virgin and to the whole company of the blessed.

A crucifix in Holy Trinity is also mentioned with a request to William Wynchedon to provide annually a wax candle or

36 D. O'Sullivan, 'The Testament of John de Wynchedon', p. 87.

37 The Sovereign or Sovern Islands, so-called after the district *Inis Soverna* south of the Lee. The name Sabhrona was applied by the Danes to the river, and in the *Annals of the Four Masters* under date 1163 is a notice that 'Muirchertach Ua Mailseachlainn, son of Domhnall, royal heir of Teamhair, fell off the bridge of Corcach and was drowned in the Sabhrann.' D. O'Sullivan, 'The Testament of John de Wynchedon', p. 87, suggests Innishannon for Synssonerian.

taper weighing five pounds in honour of this great object of devotion. Veneration for crucifixes was not confined to strictly 'church devotions'; wayside shrines were a peculiar feature of medieval piety. Cross Street is said to have been named from 'one of those market crosses raised in old Roman Catholic times in the public ways to keep alive in the people the spirit of religion'.[38] Such a market cross occupied a prominent position on the main street of medieval Cork. Crosses were likewise erected to guide and guard the way to a church, and tradition tells of the Cross of Saint Brigid which stood on Crosshaven Hill as a guide to mariners. The Cross of Cameleire on the south channel of the Lee is another example.

The Wynchedon will has a reference and a bequest to John, son of Walter Reich, 'whom I sponsored at baptism'. The expression used, *quem levavi de sacro fonte,* corresponds with that still in use in the Roman ritual. In medieval times a baptismal font was the sign and privilege of a parochial church as distinct from a chapel-of-ease. One finds also a reference to a *portiforium* or breviary. For many centuries recitation of the divine office in community or choir was customary; the introduction of private recitation necessitated the provision of a book that could be conveniently taken out of doors. Hence *porto foras* and *portiforium* from which the Irish *portús* can be easily recognized.

The recluses mentioned in connection with Holy Trinity, Gill Abbey, Saint Brigid's and Saint Philip's were a unique feature of the religious life of medieval Cork. Even more unusual was the fact that except for the recluse of Gill Abbey who was a monk, the others were female *inclusae*. As an expression of religious life the recluse differed essentially from either the anchorite or the hermit. Anchorites were a regular feature of early Irish asceticism; townlands like Rathanker in Monkstown point to their existence in Cork. Saint Finbarr's hermitage at Gougane Barra puts the diocesan patron temporarily in this category also—a category which included most Irish saints at one stage or other of their spiritual development. Anchorites and hermits sought out wild and lonely places, far away from human contacts and distraction. For the recluse, a walled-in enclosure attached to a church or monastery was his or her habitation. Such enclosures were common in continental countries and seem to have conformed to a set pattern, namely, a stone building of dimensions twelve feet by twelve, having

38　Windele, *Cork*, p. 14.

three apertures: one facing the choir of the church through which the recluse received Holy Communion; another directly opposite through which food was passed in, and a window of glass or other such substance to admit light. In Ireland cells of this kind were attached to the cathedral of Waterford, to Saint Canice's in Kilkenny, to Saint Dulough's in Dublin and to Inis Cealtra, Lough Derg, where there is still a magnificent example of one to be seen. The recluse idea was also common in England, and this, coupled with the fact that Cork was a very English city, may explain the establishment of recluse enclosures there in the fourteenth century.

In course of time certain modifications were introduced into the lives of both hermits and recluses. Anchorites who had been living in scattered sites or in small brotherhoods were amalgamated by Pope Alexander IV (1254–61) into one order under the Rule of Saint Augustine and were henceforward known as the Hermits of Saint Augustine or the Augustinian eremites, some of whom established themselves in the Red Abbey of Cork before the year 1288. The recluses (*inclusi*) resisted the group system and other reforms of the thirteenth century and continued to live their own existence as solitaries attached to churches and monasteries. Besides their personal dedication as ascetics, these recluses may have also looked after vestments and church linen, and the fact that they were able to accept bequests points to a more active apostolate than would be generally expected. The foundation of nunneries and schools was an important development for the recluses, as may be judged from the case of Agnes de Hareford. It may be that in addition to her establishment at Saint John the Baptist she founded another school or nunnery near Saint Brigid's. Saint Brigid's was the prebend of the chancellor, and it is probable that part of its revenue may have been diverted towards this project. As the fourteenth century advanced a more active apostolate began to supersede the ascetic life, recluses became less numerous and by 1330 it was decreed that 'without the express permission of the Bishop no one ought to live as an *inclusus* or *inclusa* (ascetics, nuns or religious) who for motives of devotion shut themselves up in a single cell.'[39]

Apart from its importance as an ecclesiastical directory, the will of John de Wynchedon ,with its appended inventory portrays the social conditions obtaining in medieval Cork. Merchants in

39 Von Hefele, *Histoire des Conciles*, vi, 816.

the early medieval period engaged in the lucrative export of provisions for the French and Scottish wars; fish ranked high in the list of exports, and as we have seen, hides and skins, wheat, oatmeal, malt and meat were also exported. Agricultural economy was based on tillage, living conditions appear to have been average, food was good and the standard of living compared favourably with that of other countries. Land continued to attract city merchants, many of whom invested their capital in holdings by purchase or by mortgage. But this was not altogether a blessing for the landowners, since documentary evidence shows that many of them were encumbered with the mortgages of the city merchants.

Mills and fisheries were numerous. Mills referred to are the Bishop's Mill, Saint Augustine's Mill, the Gill Abbey Mill, and so on. Ownership of certain of these mills was on a co-operative basis; for example, the Augustinians had one-third of a mill at Douglas and others had an eighth part of a mill in Shandon. Fishing weirs in which religious communities and leading families had ownership or interest were to be found at frequent intervals along both channels of the Lee. Mills and fisheries gave employment, but because of the seasonable nature of fishing, unemployment or at least under-employment cannot have been unknown. Those engaged in trades appear to have been relatively independent; at least this is the inference to be drawn from the Roche and Sarsfield Papers which show that butchers, cobblers, smiths, carpenters and the like had houses and gardens of importance. Those enjoying such luxuries were probably master-craftsmen, for this was a time when trade was organized on the guild system.

Housing conditions for the poorer classes were less favourable. They lived in mud-walled cabins with thatched roofs and no chimneys, badly lighted and worsely ventilated and heated with turf from the Monarea bog. John de Wynchedon's specific stress on his two *stone* houses suggests that such houses were the exception rather than the rule. Yet the poor were not unprovided for. John de Wynchedon left specific bequests in their favour, and the spirit of his fourteenth-century testament is reproduced in other wills which, like his, have been preserved. What is recorded in 1700 of Mr. Terry of Watergrasshill who gave one-seventh of the milk of his stock to the poor must have been traditional and handed down from a time when charity was recognized as a Christian duty and a Christian bond between wealthy and needy.

Thus, in retrospect one can visualise medieval Cork as a city well provided with churches with clergy and with hospitals;

a city with a vigorous religious life and with ample provision for the sick, the infirm and the needy; a city where the great thirteenth-century monastic renaissance had already taken root and where saintly recluses were enriching by the asceticism of their lives that tradition of piety and learning which Saint Finbarr prophesied would never be lacking in Cork.[40]

40 Plummer, *Bethada náem nÉrenn*, i, 17.

XII

The Diocesan Economy

Having thus far outlined the origins of the diocese, the establishment of the cathedral chapter and the erection of its prebends, the delineation of the deaneries and the organization of the parochial divisions, our next consideration is the diocesan economy. By diocesan economy is meant the valuation of the bishopric and of the various prebends, benefices and minor ecclesiastical offices throughout the diocese, the sources from which the diocesan revenues were derived and the corresponding outlay which devolved upon all clerics in descending scale from the bishop to the frequently under-salaried priest or vicar administering one of the smallest chapels in the diocese. In approaching a study of diocesan economy the historian is severely handicapped by a total lack of sources such as might lawfully be expected in parish registers and the like. Fortunately, this lack is more than compensated for by information culled in a wider context and under an interesting variety of headings.

In the first instance the ecclesiastical taxation lists for Cork in the early fourteenth century, catalogued in the fifth volume of Sweetman's *Calendar of Documents relating to Ireland*, are of paramount importance. Sweetman copied these lists from contemporary exchequer rolls, but because of his defective eyesight the entries, including twelve pages of corrections, abound with errors. Nevertheless these inadequacies are no bar to identification, and consequently Sweetman's lists may be taken as basic guides to diocesan evaluations.

Secondly comes the *Calendar of Papal Letters* now available in fourteen volumes covering the years 1198–1492. A few explanatory comments on the papal archives may not be amiss. The *Dataria Apostolica* in the Vatican archives are divided into three main sections: *Registra Supplicationum*, *Registra Lateranensis* and *Brevia Lateranensia*. The Lateran Register (together with the Avignon Register from the Avignon Archives) was incorporated in the *Calendar of Papal Letters*. The register of petitions was not included in this calendar but a start was made when the *Calendar of the Register of Petitions* covering the years 1342–1419 *only* was published. The principal interest of this register as distinct from the register of bulls lies in the fact that the petitions it records often contain details of more or less value which are not recited in the bulls issued to answer them. The register of petitions is regarded as basic source material for diocesan histories and its entries are considered to be more important than material found in the *Calendar of Papal Letters*. Entries for Cork are more numerous in the latter volume and it is here that more precise information on the diocesan economy is to be found. As a complementary source, Theiner's *Vetera Monumenta Hibernorum et Scotorum* which was published in Latin in 1864 may also be consulted. But Theiner must be handled with caution: his facts are not always correct, and he was obviously more concerned with calendaring items of English and Scottish interest than with matter bearing on Ireland.

Our third source are the annates[1] or bonds for first-fruits which contain well over a hundred entries for the diocese of Cork for the years 1421–1526. When combined with the entries of the *Calendar of Papal Letters* we have at hand an enormous collection of material which if calendared and annotated would constitute a highly valuable source history of the diocese.

Fourthly we have a taxation of the diocese made in 1588 (31 Elizabeth) and officially calendared as MS T.C.D. E. 3. 14. Even though it is a post-Reformation compilation, this taxation list is important as a guide to the diocesan economy. The same is true of the visitation conducted in 1615 by William Lyon, Protestant bishop of Cork, Cloyne and Ross. Officially documented as Reeves MS 1066 T.C.D., this source supplies us with the western deaneries of Glansalny and *Fonn Iartharach* together with several extra parishes not listed in Sweetman's calendar.

Incidental data on the episcopal revenue may also be culled from rent rolls and escheatry accounts dealing with the official channelling of temporalities during vacancies of the see. These accounts, which have been already treated at length in Chapter VI, require but a passing reference in the present context. Finally, for assessing the medieval valuation of the diocese of Cork there exists a sixteenth-century rental of Cork—*Additional Charter 13600* British Museum*—which is a lengthy document,

---

1 Edited and annotated by Sr. M. Angela [Evelyn] Bolster, *Archiv. Hib.*, xxix (1970), 1–32.

beginning and ending abruptly and showing no date. This lack of precision must not be regarded as minimizing in any way the value and importance of this document. A composite application of the data uncovered in all the foregoing areas of documentation will give a viable exposition of the Cork diocesan economy in its pre-Reformation form, while the inclusion of Protestant compilations covering the opening years of the seventeenth century must be accepted as a *sine qua non* of any comparative survey.

THE EPISCOPAL MENSA

On his elevation to the episcopacy the medieval bishop became *ipso facto* a landlord on a considerable scale with the profits—*temporalia*—accruing from the ownership of manors forming the greater part of his income. We have already estimated the income of the bishop of Cork in the form of rents from the manor of Fayd, part of which was levied on the city of Cork. We have likewise noted that the bishop was in receipt of money from the cathedral parish proper, from the mensal parishes of Templebrian, Innishannon and Templebrackeny or Rossbeg, and from parishes like Carrigrohane, Maglin, Innishkenny, Aglish, etc., which paid head-rents to him. Also noted has been the division of the tithes of Kinsale between the bishop and Nicholas de Courcey.

A second source of episcopal revenue, known as *spiritualia*, connoted the income due to the bishop in virtue of his office as spiritual head of the diocese. The *spiritualia*, which were variable sums, came mainly from synodals or cathedratics and from procurations. Synodals arose out of a bishop's right to demand a sum of money, usually about two shillings, from every person cited to attend the synod. The sum varied according to the parish. Synods were held with a view to church order and discipline and were an outcome of the reforming programme drafted at the Fourth Lateran Council (1215); while we have no direct evidence of the fact except for Dublin and Ferns, it is beyond question that Irish bishops in general invoked synodal enactments within their dioceses.[2] Procurations were visitation fees exacted from all parishes and religious houses within the diocese, prebendaries alone excepted. At first the term 'procurations' was applied to the hospitality accorded the bishop and his entourage during the visitation; later a sum of money

2 Aubrey Gwynn, 'Provincial and Diocesan Decrees of the Diocese of Dublin during the Anglo-Norman Period', *Archiv. Hib.*, xi (1944), 31–117. See also C. R. Cheney, 'A Group of Related Synodal Statutes of the Thirteenth Century', in *Med. Studies presented to A. Gwynn*, pp. 114–32.

was accepted in lieu of hospitality and its maximum was fixed by the constitution *Vas electionis* of Pope Benedict XII in 1336. A third payment known as 'quadragesimal' or *Laetare Jerusalem* was paid by the clergy on the fourth Sunday in Lent to defray the costs of the chrism which was supplied by the bishop for the Easter ceremonies.[3] The quadragesimal, which was a normal levy in English cathedrals, was probably a feature of the medieval Irish church as well.

The fourteenth-century taxation list of papal tenths for the year 1302 gives the combined value of the *spiritualia* and *temporalia* of the bishop of Cork as forty pounds, but gives no indication as to its division. The later list of 1306 (*rectius* 1316) values the *spiritualia* as 40 marks (£26 13s 4d) and the *temporalia* (rents, lands and all things arising from temporalities) as 64 marks (£42 13s 4d). Incomplete and defective as these taxation returns may be, their importance is such that an understanding of the circumstances under which they were levied is at once desirable and necessary.

In 1288 King Edward I obtained from the pope a grant for six years of the tenths or tithes of England, Ireland, Scotland and Wales on condition that he would go on crusade to the Holy Land. The returns of this levy became a national record which served as a standard for all taxes paid to the pope and king right down to the year 1537 (28 Henry VIII). In 1291 Pope Nicholas IV sent letters to his collectors in Ireland, Thomas St. Leger, bishop of Meath, and Thomas de Chaddesworth, dean of Dublin, instructing them on matters of procedure. The value of the taxation was to be *juxta veram extimationem*, and the tax was to be levied for six years in certain specified areas. In February of the following year (1292) the king commanded his bailiffs, sheriffs and other officials to facilitate the collectors by every means in their power. But the church in Ireland was greatly impoverished when Pope Nicholas imposed this tax: the king had recently called upon the clergy for a tenth of their spiritualities in order to defray his personal expenses, so the archbishops of Cashel and Tuam and the bishop of Kildare replied that they and their clergy were so poverty-stricken that they could not meet the demands placed upon them by the pope. Consequently, the 1291 taxation of Pope Nicholas IV was not levied in Ireland although the valuation returns for the dioceses of Limerick, Cork, Cloyne, Ross, Emly, Cashel and Waterford have been printed in the *Eighth Report* of the Irish Record Commissioners which was

3 · Moorman, *Church Life in England in the Thirteenth Century*, p. 125.

found among the records at Westminster by one of the English sub-commissioners of records.[4]

Notwithstanding the remonstrance of 1291 a fresh assessment for three years was placed on the Irish clergy in 1302. The pope was in urgent need of subsidies to support war against the king of Aragon, and the more expeditiously to receive this money he promised the English king a share in the proceeds.[5] Then in 1306 King Edward I obtained from Pope Clement V a grant for two years of all the ecclesiastical tithes or *decimae papalis* in his dominions. The time factor was extended to four and finally to seven years, with the proviso that Queen Margaret should receive £2,000 for five years and the Prince of Wales half that amount for a specified term. One-fourth of the proceeds of the last four years was designated as appropriated for the necessities of the Roman church (*pro necessitatibus Ecclesiae Romae*). Richard de Beresford and William de Ryvere were appointed sub-collectors for the tax of 1302–06; their agents were usually the rural deans and each deanery recorded its own returns. In the preface of Sweetman's *Calendar of Documents relating to Ireland* (1302–07) we find that for the dioceses of Meath, Limerick, Cloyne, Emly, Cashel, Ross, Waterford and Cork there are two sets of returns bearing different dates in which the amount of valuation and taxation varies while churches taxed in one list are entered in the other as 'destroyed during the war'.

In a recent study of these early fourteenth-century ecclesiastical valuations of Ireland, Geoffrey J. Hand[6] has opened a door to further investigation of the subject, more especially when he questions the suggestion of Reeves that where there are two sets of valuations for the same diocese one may be dated 1302 and the other 1306.[7] Dr. Hand shows that in 1316 a single tenth was granted to Edward II by Pope John XXII, in pursuance of which the bishop of Winchester as principal collector was mandated to re-evaluate all benefices and taxable temporalities in Ireland which had been withered, wasted or destroyed during the Bruce invasion. At the same time Dr. Hand cautions that 'it would be unwise to assume too much

4 Irish Record Commissioners, *Supplement to the Eighth Report: Extract from Certain Rolls* (forming part of Pope Nicholas's Taxation, A.D. 1291), app. 5.

5 William Prynne, *Records*, pp. 998–9.

6 G. J. Hand, 'The Dating of the Early Fourteenth-Century Ecclesiastical Valuations of Ireland', *Irish Theological Quarterly*, xxiv (1957), 271–4.

7 Reeves, *Ecclesiastical Antiquities of Down, Connor and Dromore*, pp. x–xii.

about the Record Office rolls until a painstaking analysis of the returns for each diocese has done all that can be done to date them from internal evidence. . . . None the less there is . . . a strong case for dividing the rolls into two groups. Rolls 1, 2, 4 and 6 . . . were apparently compiled about the last years of Edward I; some of them at least were used in the collection of the biennial tenth of 1306.'[8] Roll 1 contains all northern and western dioceses; roll 2 deals with Dublin, Kildare and Meath; roll 4 with Limerick, Cloyne, Ross and Emly, and roll 6 with Waterford, Cashel and Cork. Dr. Hand's final premise is that rolls 3 (Meath alone) and 5 (Cloyne, Limerick, Ross, Ardfert, Kilfenora, Killaloe, Waterford, Lismore, Cork, Cashel and Emly) together with a *nova taxatio* of Dublin and a later taxation of Ossory were evidently made in or after 1316 in response to the order to re-evaluate after the Bruce campaign. All the rolls were entered at Westminster on 1 October 1322; and as a comparison of taxation rolls for England for the years before and after the Scottish wars shows a considerable drop in revenue, the same in a sense holds true for Ireland. In other words, the valuations of Irish dioceses give an idea of the economic aftermath of the Bruce invasion.

For the diocese of Cork the two taxation lists available are referred to as 'Taxations 1302–06' with the supposition that perhaps they represent one and the same survey. A notable difference in the arrangement and content of the lists makes this supposition untenable, and consequently the possibility that the second list could be more correctly dated 1316 cannot be ruled out. And if, while admitting this possibility, we remember that the fourteenth-century valuations are an index to the economic impact of the Bruce invasion, we shall find that the invasion scarcely ruffled the economies of Cork. Even allowing for some small depreciations here and there, the overall valuations in the second list show an increase of £12 19s 8d over the earlier returns. The two lists now follow in their entirety.

List A	List B
Revenue of the Bishop of Cork in spirituals and temporals, £40; spirituals of the dean, 10 marks; spirituals of the archdeacon, 29 m. spirituals of the precentor, 5½ m.	Taxation of the temporalities of the Lord Bishop of Cork in rents, 40 marks; in lands and all things arising from temporalities, 24 marks; in all things arising from spirituals,

8 Hand, 'The Dating of the Fourteenth-Century Valuations', p. 274.

List A

spirituals of the chancellor, 3½m. spirituals of the treasurer, 3 m. temporalities of the Abbot *de Albo Tractu*, £10; temporalities of the Abbot *de Antro*, 10 marks; the priory of Legan, county Cork, 10 marks. For these nine entries the total valuation given was £97.6s.8d. of which a tenth valued at £9.14s.8d. was proved.

List B

40 marks. (The bishop's total is quoted at £69.9s.8d. of which £6.18s.8d. was proved as a tenth); the jurisdiction of the dean of Cork, 30s. of the archdeacon, 100s. and the *Communia* of Cork, 6 marks. The total valuation of the six entries was given as £79.6s.8d.

THE DEANERY OF OCURBLETHAN

List A

Chapel of Kilcully, 30s.
church of Dunbulloge, 5 marks, 30d.
Rathcooney, £4.
Shanbally, 30s.
Ardnageehy, 30s.
Ballinaltig, 30s.
Kilquane, 3 marks;
Killaspugmullane, 3 marks;
Glanmire, 3 marks, 10s.
Ballydeloher, 20s.
Caherlag, 3 marks, 10s.
Little Island, 20s.
Shandon, 6 marks;
Church of St Catherine, 10s.
Holy Trinity, 7½ marks;
St Nicholas 10s.
Total valuation for sixteen entries, £34.10s.0d., of which £3.9s.0d. was proved as tenth.

List B

Church of Currykippane 3 marks; 'of which the vicar takes a moiety'.
Kilcully, 3 marks;
Dunbulloge, 7 marks;
Rathcooney, £8.
Ardnageehy, 8 marks, with a moiety to the vicar.
Shanbally, 3 marks, with a moiety to the vicar.
Ballinaltig, 4 marks, of which the vicar takes a third.
Kilquane, 5 marks;
Killaspugmullane, 4 m. with a moiety to the vicar.
Ballydeloher, 6 marks, of which the vicar takes a third part.
Caherlag, 7 marks.
Shandon, 7 marks of which the vicar takes a moiety;
St Peter, 12 marks;
Holy Trinity, 15 marks, with a moiety to the vicar.
Church of Little Island, 40s. of which the vicar takes a moiety. Total valuation given as £64.13s.4d. with a tenth proved at £6.9s.4d.

THE DEANERY OF KERY (KYRRICURITH)

List A

St John the Evangelist, 40s.
Liscleary, 6 marks, 10s.
Ballinaboy, 13½ marks;
Killanully, 4½ marks;
Carrigaline } 13½ marks;
Kilnagleary }
Douglas, 6 marks, 10s.
Corbally (described as
'formerly attached to the
Precentorship of Cork'),
4 marks;
Ballymolmichill (Inishkenny),
4 m, 'excepting the portion
of the Precentorship in the
church of Corbaly'.
Kilnaglory, 30s.
Ringaskiddy, 15s.
Templebreedy, 3 marks, 10s.
Sum of taxation for eleven
entries, £42.10s.8d.; tenth
proved, £4.4s.4d.

List B

Ballinaboy, 12 marks;
Liscleary, 8 marks;
Killanully, 8 marks;
Church of Carrigaline with
its appurtenances, namely
Kilnagleary and Douglas,
£33.9s.8d.;
Corbally, 9 marks;
Inishkenny, 6 marks;
Carrigrohane, 4 marks
(described as having no vicar)
Kilnaglory, 3 marks;
Templebreedy, 10 marks;
Priory of Legan in tem-
poralities and spiritualities,
10 marks;
Temporalities of the Abbot
de Antro, 10 marks;
The sum of taxation for
eleven entries is given as
£86.16.4d. and the tenth is
given as £8.13s.7½d.
The upcurve of valuation is
very evident here.

THE DEANERY OF KENALETHE *ultra* (LYNNALETHE *ultra*)

List A

Ringrone, 18 marks
Kilroan (Killoney), 15s.
Templetrine, 4½ marks
Currarane, 4½ marks
Rathclarin, 3 marks
Burren, 3½ marks
Kilshinahan, 30s.
Kilbrittain, 30s.
Chapel of Kilgobban,
4½ marks
Particle of Kildarra and
Cloghan (Ballinadee), 1 mark
Rathdrought, 30s.
Ballymodan, 5 marks, 40s.
Innishannon, 18 marks

List B

Ringrone, 10 marks
Killoney, 20s.
Kilgobban, 6 marks
Templetrine, 6½ marks
Currarane, 5 marks
Rathclarin, 4 marks
Burren, 8 marks
Kilshinahan, 3 marks
Kilbrittain, 3 marks
Rathdrought, 4 marks
Donaghucharry (? Ballinadee),
5 marks
Ballymodan, 7 marks
Innishannon, 15 marks
Brinny, 5 marks

Vicarage of Innishannon, £10
Chapel of Brinny, 3 marks, 10s
Knockavilly, 7½ marks   Knockavilly, 10 marks
Templemichael, 4½ marks   The total valuation was £62,
The sum of taxation for seven-   and the tenth proved at
teen entries was £65.5s.0d.,   £6.4s.0d.
and the tenth amounted to
£6.14s.6d.

Note Kenalethe *ultra* in 1302 was of all Cork deaneries the most solvent, containing the two richest benefices in the diocese, namely Ringrone and the rectory of Innishannon, both valued at 18 marks or £12 each. The deanery also contained the particle (*particula*) of Kildarra and Cloghan which carried the lowest valuation of the entire diocese and entitled its holder to one solitary mark. By the later returns Ringrone had fallen from 18 marks to 10, while Innishannon, the rectory and vicarage of which had returned 18 marks and £10 respectively in 1302 was valued as a single entity at 15 marks, and the particle of Kildarra and Cloghan had disappeared. These two places are again mentioned in an Annate entry for 1488 which describes them as 'unoccupied particles' or *particulae nuncupatae*, valued at 3 marks and vacant by devolution (*per devolutionem*).

THE DEANERY OF KENALETHE *citra* (BAMBECH *citra*)

Ballyfeard, 9 marks   Leighmoney, 5 marks
Ballyfoyle, 4½ marks   Dunagh (Templemichael),
Kinure, 30s.   8 marks
Clontead, 4½ marks   Kilmeedy, 8 marks
Rincurran, 7½ marks   Cullen, 5 marks
Kinsale, 30s.   Ballyfeard, 10 marks
Tisaxon, 3 marks, 10s.   Ballyfoyle, 6 marks
Leighmoney, 3 marks   Nohoval
Dunderrow, 3 marks   Kinure, 3 marks
Kilmeedy, 6 marks   Kilmonoge, 4 marks
Nohoval, 3½ marks   Clontead, 7 marks
Kilmonoge, 3½ marks   Rincurran, 10 marks
Cullen, 5 marks   Kinsale, 3 marks
For thirteen entries the   Tisaxon, 6 marks
valuation registered was   Dunderrow, 4 marks
£38.10s.0d., and the tenth   The total valuation for
proved was £3.17s.0d.   fourteen entries was
     £55.6s.8d., and the tenth
     proved was £5.10s.8d.

THE DEANERY OF CORKOLWYN (CORKNUWYN)

Aglish, 20s.
Kilbonane, 20s.
Kilmurry, 10s.
Cannaway, 10s.
Desertmore, 20s.
The five entries returned a valuation of £4, of which 8s. was proved as the requisite tenth.

Dundrinan (Moviddy), 30s., 'excepting a portion to the Hospital', that is the Preceptory of Mourne.
Kilmurry, 2 marks, of which the vicar takes a moiety.
Aglish, 2 marks
Kilbonane, 2 marks, of which the vicar takes a moiety.
Desertmore, 2 marks
Ovens, 3 marks, 'excepting a portion to the Hospital.'
The temporalities of the Abbot *de Albo Tractu*, £10
The sum of taxation is given as £17.16s.8d., with the tenth proved at £1.17s.8d.

On examining all returns more minutely we find that the only entries which remained static in the period between the two valuations were the church of Cullen and the revenues of Tracton, Gill Abbey and Legan. Taking the taxations as a whole, the incomes of all benefice-holders were more or less evenly balanced, exclusive only of the high-income rectors of Ringrone and Innishannon and the subsalaried cleric to whose lot fell the particle of Kildarra and Cloghan. For places registering an annual value below the seven-and-one-half mark level (and they were numerous), papal and royal taxations must have constituted a grievous imposition. The total valuation of the province of Cashel according to the findings of 1302–06 amounted to £3671 2s 0d, to which the diocese of Cork contributed £283 13s 4d. Comparable figures for the other dioceses of the province were as follows: Cashel, £660 5s 4d; Emly, £313 6s 8d; Limerick, £391 14s 2d; Killaloe, £317 18s 4d; Ross, £45 5s 0d; Ardfert, £178 16s 6d; Waterford, £125 17s 8d; Lismore £711 8s 2d; Cloyne, £582 13s 4d, and Kilfenora, £60 3s 4d.[9]

The valuations for the remaining two deaneries of Glansalny and *Fonn Iartharach* can only be accepted as tentative and as probably indicative of an earlier economy. By 1615 territorial additions and valuations to the existing deaneries were as follows:

9 *Cal. doc. Ire., 1302–07*, pp. 280–323.

Marmullane in the deanery of Kery is valued at four pounds; Kenalethe *ultra* included Templemartin which was part of the prebend of the dean and is not valued, and Kilbrogan which is rated at four pounds. Finally Corkolwyn or Kilmoan-Fflanloe is seen to include the vicarage of Kilbonane, fifty shillings; the vicarage of Moviddy, three pounds; Macloneigh for which no valuation is given because the master of Mora and the treasurer of Cork were joint rectors; Inchigeela which for a similar reason is likewise not valued, and the vicarage of Kilmichael which is rated at £6 13s 4d.

THE DEANERY OF GLANSALNY

In this deanery the vicarage of Kinneigh is valued at nine pounds; the vicarage of Fanlobbus or Dunmanway at six shillings; the vicarage of Desertserges at twenty-five pounds; the rectory of Murragh at four pounds; the vicarage of Drinagh at seven pounds; the rectory of Drimoleague at five pounds and for the rectory of Ballymoney eleven pounds is suggested.

THE DEANERY OF FONN IARTHARACH

Here the vicarage of Kilmoe was rated at eight pounds; no valuation was returned for Schull; the vicarage of Kilcrohane showed a return of three pounds, that of Durrus six pounds, of Kilmocomoge or Bantry, six pounds, and the vicarage of Caheragh showed eight pounds.[10]

EPISCOPAL EXPENDITURE

So much for the general valuations of the diocese. We now turn to episcopal expenditure and find that a bishop's main expense lay in the maintenance of his own household with its legal officers, its ecclesiastical attendants, chaplains and clerks, with those entrusted with the management of the bishop's estates and with his household staff properly so called. And while the entourage of an Irish bishop cannot have been as overwhelming as that of his English and continental counterparts, it goes without saying that most Irish bishops of the thirteenth and

10   An explanation of the exclusion of this section of the diocese from earlier lists may be the fact that four of the seven benefices in Glansalny, namely, Kinneigh, Fanlobbus, Desertserges and Drinagh, belonged to the vicars choral; while in *Fonn Iartharach* the entire six rectories of the 1615 visitation were impropriate to various religious houses. Kilmoe, Caheragh and Schull were impropriate to the College of Youghal; Kilcrohane and Durrus to the cathedral of Waterford; Kilmocomoge to the church of Saint Catherine in Waterford. See Murphy, 'The Royal Visitation of ,Cork, Cloyne, Ross and the College of Youghal', pp. 188–9.

later centuries could not have functioned without the aid of some personal staff (as distinct from the chapter) to attend to matters of routine administration. Small wonder then that the medieval bishop invoked whenever possible his right of procuration which was the cheapest way of provisioning his household. Another way of reducing personal expenses was the bishop's exercise of the right of collating members of his household to cathedral prebends; and this carried the extra advantage of increasing his control over the chapter. Apart from his essentially household expenses, the bishop was expected to support worthy causes like crusades, church building funds and the like, and he was expected to aid any of his clergy who might find themselves in financial difficulties.

Oppressive as such incidental demands might be, they were as nothing compared with the accumulating burden of papal taxation which during the Avignon period (1305–78) was part of the conscious development of a deliberately centralized and specialized form of papal government. On the positive side, the Avignon period witnessed the emergence of what were later to become traditional administrators, financiers and judges, and during this period too the *Corpus Juris Canonici* burgeoned to produce the most competent and centralized system of government which the Middle Ages knew and which actually grew out of the reforms initiated by the great Pope Innocent III and the Lateran Council of 1215. In Avignon was established a chancery, a secretariat and a system of law courts, alongside of which functioned the consistory or body of cardinals *in curia*, and the Rota which heard and decided suits arising out of presentation to benefices. It was during the Avignon period that the practice of reservation to the Holy See of all benefices throughout the church was extended and developed to a point where the thirteenth-century compromise between canon and civil law could no longer hold. Because of this diffusion of papal provisions the *camerarius* or cardinal finance minister became the most important of papal officials; his collectors (*collectores in partibus*) were to develop into the nuncios, who with the Secretariat of State make up the papal diplomatic service as it is known today.

Direct Curial Taxations

The system of taxation evolved at Avignon was twofold, involving direct taxes to be paid *ad Curiam* and indirect or diocesan taxes which were levied on the spot.[11] Taxes paid directly to the curia were many and varied:

11 G. Mollat, *The Popes at Avignon, 1305–1378*, pp. 319–20.

1. *Servitia communia* or common services to be paid by bishops and abbots immediately on nomination, on confirmation, on consecration and even on translation to another see or abbey by the pope. Originally confined to sees and abbeys with an income exceeding 100 gold florins, the *servitia communia* were ultimately levied in practically all areas where papal reservation obtained. It has been estimated that from the time of Boniface VIII (1296–1303) the returns from the *servitia communia* comprised one-third of the papacy's gross annual income from taxes on the revenues of bishops and abbots.

2. *Minuta Servitia* were petty services which also fell on newly-appointed bishops and abbots who had to pay five small payments varying from one-twelfth to one-twenty-fourth of their annual income to subsidize the curial staff and members of the cardinals' household.

3. *Sacra, subdiaconum and quittance fees.* The first of these, paid by bishops and abbots on consecration to the *camerarius*, the clerks of the *camera* and the sergeant-at-arms, amounted to one-twentieth of the total paid in common services. The *subdiaconum*, which was payable to the papal subdeacon, was equal to one-third of the *sacra*. The quittance fees were paid to the apostolic *camera* and to the cardinals' *camera* and were variable sums.

4. *Chancery fees* were levied to defray expenses entailed in the dispatch, sealing and registering of letters of grace and justice.

5. *Visitationes ad limina apostolorum* were dues originally payable on occasions of pilgrimage to the tombs of the apostles Peter and Paul in Rome. Later, the *ad limina* taxes were levied when bishops and abbots, either personally or through delegates, reported at specified intervals on the state of their sees and abbeys.

6. *The cense* was a tax levied on kingdoms subject to the Roman Church. For Ireland this tax amounted to 300 marks to which each bishop had to subscribe a sum proportionate to the size of his diocese.

Finally, the Avignon popes benefited by *pallium* dues from archbishops, by legacies, by the reversion of the possessions of those who died intestate *apud Curiam*, by the imposition of fees on clergy and laity for various offences, by fees for commutation of vows and penances, by coinage fees and by a host of other incidental levies.

Indirect Taxations[12]

Oppressive as were the direct curial taxes they were as nothing by comparison with the more numerous local levies entrusted at first to special envoys and later to the *collectores in partibus*. Collectors were nominated for an indefinite period and their powers were such that they could supersede episcopal authority and even excommunicate bishops. Their function was mainly supervisory, the practical work being done by sub-collectors who in turn were assisted by clerks. The taxes levied in this manner fall into five main categories:

1. *Tenths (decimae papalis)* were extraordinary levies exacted by the Avignon popes to enable them meet the demands made on their finances by the exigencies of warfare. In principle, all ranks of the clergy, exclusive only of cardinals and Hospitallers, were subject to the tenth or tithe, any delay in payment of which was punishable by excommunication.

2. *Annates (annatae, fructus primi anni, annualia, annalia)* were revenues derived from a benefice during the first year's tenure of a new incumbent. The annates were first introduced by Pope Clement V in 1306 for England only and for benefices falling vacant by the death of an incumbent 'at the Roman Curia' (*apud Curiam Romanam*). The sum could be paid immediately or in three annual instalments, and was levied not merely on bishoprics but on all diocesan benefices subject to direct provision by the Holy See. The tax was levied on a more extensive scale by Pope John XXII (1316–34),[13] and within twenty years the annates were extended to the whole church for benefices to which the Holy See had nominated. By 1376 there was scarcely a single benefice in any diocese outside the net of papal reservation. Still the tax was not paid regularly, and the better to facilitate its collection Pope Boniface IX (1389–94) reduced the amount to be paid by the appointee to half the first year's revenue, but he stipulated that the person collated should pay before receiving his bull of appointment. Remissness in payment continued until 1464 when Pope Innocent VIII issued a bull threatening non-paying bene-ficiaries with deprivation.[14] Poor benefices with an annual revenue not in excess of six English marks or about twenty-four gold florins were exempted from the annate tax. The application

12   Ibid., p. 321.

13   The annate tax was not levied in Ireland until after 1400.

14   *De Annatis Hiberniae*, i, Ulster, p. xxvi.

of this exemption in the diocese of Cork will be dealt with hereafter.

3. *Procurations*. These were visitation fees, affecting bishop and clergy alike, the nature and scope of which are best seen in a mandate of Gregory XI in 1377 in which the bishop of Emly was appointed papal nuncio and collector with unusual powers in the dioceses of Cashel, Lismore, Waterford, Cloyne, Limerick, Emly, Killaloe, Ardfert, Cork, Ross and Kilfenora. The bishop was to exact, with faculty to give acquittances, fruits and rents due by virtue of the reservation made by the pope of the first year's fruits and rents of priories, dignities, *personatus*, administrations, offices, canonries and prebends and all other benefices, secular and regular, exempt and non-exempt, with or without cure of souls, the only exceptions allowed being confined to certain minor benefices. The bishop was simultaneously mandated to execute a recent reservation made by the pope of (1) moveables and other personal property of archbishops, bishops and abbots at the time of their death; (2) rents and rights pertaining to the archiepiscopal, episcopal and abbatial *mensa* during voidance, and (3) fruits and rents during voidance of all benefices whatsoever which were already void at the beginning of the pontificate (of Gregory XI) or which since then had become void at the Apostolic See.

By a third mandate the bishop of Emly was to exact and receive for three years a tenth of the fruits and rents in the cities and dioceses to which he was deputed collector, the benefices of cardinals alone excepted. One half of the first year's tenth was to be paid at Michaelmas of the year in which the mandate was issued (1377). The remainder was to be collected at the following Easter and the same system was to be invoked for the remaining two years. Finally, the bishop of Emly was to exact, receive and transmit to the *camera* the money due from archbishops, bishops and abbots by virtue of their promotion to their prelacies. He was to compel the contumacious by papal authority and to invoke, if necessary, the assistance of the secular arm.[15] Whether or not the bishop of Emly appropriated some of the proceeds of these procurations, his fiscal abilities were not again requisitioned for papal service. In 1380 he was compelled to give an account of the money received[16] and from that date until 1489 the levying of papal taxes in Ireland, England and Scotland was entrusted to the *collectores in partibus*.

15 *Cal. papal letters, 1362–1404*, p. 156.

16 The outbreak of the Great Schism served to exacerbate relations between collectors and their victims.

4. *Caritative subsidies (subsidia caritativa)* were a development of a practice whereby bishops and abbots from the twelfth century onwards begged free gifts from their subordinates in times of financial stress. By the fourteenth century the popes were exacting this subsidy, the charitable or caritative nature of which was completely gone since any remissness in payment carried with it the risk of excommunication.

5. *The lesser cense*, as distinct from that levied directly, was paid in order to obtain and retain papal protection. It was an irregular payment at best and added as little to the papal coffers as it deducted from episcopal ones.

The papacy finally levied the 'Peter's pence' collection in certain specified areas, it enjoyed the revenues of vacant benefices in the pope's conferment (*vacantes in curia*) and it also enjoyed the rights of spoil, that is, the right to seize the house and goods of any deceased bishop. The application of the right of spoil (*jus spolii*) provided the fourteenth-century papacy with one of its most substantial sources of income, for the sale of the furniture of deceased prelates realized enormous sums and the papal library at Avignon was enriched by the addition of rare and valuable books. In respect of all the foregoing taxes, the papacy granted delays, respites and postponements, but 'it was generally uncompromising in its insistence on the principle that payment must be made. The structure of taxation was such that it was virtually impossible for the taxpayers to escape from its stranglehold.'[17]

Valuations of the Major Dignitaries

We next turn to the *quatuor personae* and the archdeacon who functioned so conspicuously in the medieval chapter and whose incomes are invoiced at some length in the papal registers and in the annates.

The Dean. In 1291, that is, in the taxation of Pope Nicholas IV which was not levied in Ireland, the jurisdiction of the dean of Cork was estimated at thirty shillings, and the church of Cullen which formed part of his prebend was valued at five marks.[18] We have seen that in 1302 his *spiritualia* were valued at ten marks and that by 1306/16 his valuation had dropped to thirty shillings. (A mark was the equivalent of 13s 4d.) In 1359 the deanship was valued at nine marks, in 1363 it was worth ten pounds[19]

17 Mollat, *The Popes at Avignon*, p. 334.

18 Brady, *Records*, i, 326.

19 *Cal. papal petitions*, p. 337, 425.

and in 1427 it was valued at five marks.[20] In 1441 it was rated at twelve marks[21] and in 1481 at twenty-four marks.[22] When Thaddeus MacCarthy was provided in 1500 the deanship was still valued at twenty-four marks.[23]

The Precentor. In 1302 the precentor's prebend of Corbally yielded five and one-half marks.[24] In 1444 the precentorship was valued at ten marks sterling,[25] by 1470 it had risen to twenty-six marks[26] and in 1475 to thirty marks, although the rector of Shandon who wished to unite the precentorship with his rectory informed the pope that its valuation was only twenty marks.[27] When Cornelius Murphy was appointed in 1487 the precentorship was then valued at twenty-four marks.[28]

The Chancellor. The chancellor's prebend was valued at three and one-half marks in 1302. In 1474 the chancellorship was valued at eight marks,[29] and in 1482 when Cornelius O'Flynn, abbot of Gill Abbey, was provided it carried the same valuation.[30] As mentioned earlier, the chancellor's income came from Saint Brigid's church and from the townlands of Maglin and Curraheen in Ballincollig parish, to which Ringrone was added in 1402 for the lifetime of Michael Kenefig.

The Treasurer. The income of the treasurer was given as three marks in 1302. In 1474 it was worth twelve marks, in 1482 it had dropped to eight marks[31] and in 1485 when John O'Herlihy was provided its valuation was given as ten marks.[32]

The Archdeacon. In 1291 the archdeacon of Cork held as benefice 'the church of Dunbollogge, seven marks, and the church of Saint Peter, twelve marks'.[33] In 1302 his *spiritualia* were valued

20 *Cal. papal letters, 1417–31*, p. 560.

21 *Cal. papal letters, 1431–47*, p. 173.

22 *Cal. papal letters, 1471–84*, pt. 2, p. 140.

23 Bolster, 'Obligationes pro Annatis Diocesis Corcagiensis', p. 28.

24 *Cal. doc. Ire., 1302–07*, p. 307.

25 *Cal. papal letters, 1431–47*, p. 438.

26 *Cal. papal letters, 1458–71*, p. 360.

27 *Cal. papal letters, 1471–84*, pt. 2, p. 418.

28 *Cal. papal letters, 1484–92*, p. 220.

29 *Cal. papal letters, 1471–84*, pt. 1, p. 422.

30 Bolster, 'Obligationes pro Annatis Diocesis Corcagiensis', p. 12.

31 *Cal. papal letters, 1471–84*, pt. 1, pp. 393, 127.

32 Bolster, 'Obligationes pro Annatis Diocesis Corcagiensis', p. 16.

33 Brady, *Records*, i, 307.

at twenty-nine marks, and in the later taxation his jurisdiction was valued at a hundred shillings. In 1396 the archdeaconry was valued at ten marks,[34] it had risen to fifteen marks in 1378[35] and to twenty marks in 1414.[36] It dropped to sixteen marks in 1418,[37] rose to twenty marks in 1459 and had soared to thirty marks in 1462.[38] It carried the same valuation of thirty marks in 1485 when William Myagh (Meade) was provided, but in 1486 its valuation had reverted to twenty marks.[39] In 1487 and 1489 it was once more rated at thirty marks, and in 1502 the archdeaconry united with the rectory of Innishannon netted a return of thirty-seven marks.[40] By all accounts the archdeacon was the most highly-salaried official of the medieval diocesan chapter of Cork.

CLERICAL INCOMES

The medieval church presented each of its incumbents with a benefice or living and a *cura animarum*. In virtue of the first a cleric gained possession of a certain area of land called a glebe with the accompanying right of collecting a tithe or tenth part from each of his parishioners, rich and poor alike. The *cura animarum*, which gave him spiritual jurisdiction, entitled him to collect whatever he could by way of voluntary fees or offerings from the people entrusted to his care. Clerical incomes, therefore, derived mainly from land and from the offerings of the people.

Land

The glebe was a plot of church land utilized by the rector and the vicar as grazing ground for a cow or two and as a market garden for provisioning their own household. Glebe-lands varied greatly: those mentioned in Brady's *Records of Cork* would appear to be survivals of the economic organization of the pre-Reformation diocese of Cork, although the acreage given is probably more extensive than that allotted in earlier

---

34 *Cal. papal letters, 1362–1404*, p. 542.

35 *Cal. papal letters, 1396–1404*, p. 170.

36 *Cal. papal letters, 1404–15*, p. 476.

37 *Cal. papal letters, 1417–31*, p. 89.

38 *Cal. papal letters, 1455–64*, pp. 395, 476.

39 *Cal. papal letters, 1484–92*, pp. 105, 124.

40 Bolster, 'Obligationes pro Annatis Diocesis Corcagiensis', p. 29.

times.[41] Also connected with land was the levying of tithes
which were an important and highly lucrative source of income
for the medieval church. Tithes, which were taken as originating
and having sanction in Genesis 28:22, were normally divided into
two classes: the greater or garb tithes which were levied on corn
of every variety, and the lesser tithes which covered practically
every other kind of natural production. Theoretically, the
rector of a parish enjoyed the garb tithes, the vicar enjoyed the
lesser tithes; in actual practice the rector was able to channel
much of the proceeds of the lesser tithes to his own advantage.
The greater tithes varied according to the size of the parish,
the nature of the land, the extent to which agriculture was
pursued and the amount of land under monastic control within
the parish. Chief among the lesser tithes was the tithe on hay
which was levied at every cutting. Next came tithes on all other
crops, wild and cultivated—flax, timber, fruit, market produce—
while the issue of animals and their natural products were also
subject to tithe. The rector could also claim 'his share of . . .
wool, milk, honey, bees-wax and even the down of geese'.[42]

While we have no definite information as to the levying of the
foregoing multiple tithes in the diocese of Cork (some of them
must have been common), we find that tithes on fish were
levied in maritime parishes like Schull where 'the Minister
generally agrees with them [the parishioners] for so much a
boat'.[43] This tithe on fish, which was carried over into post-
Reformation times, was common in the fourteenth century and
was a levy which often gave rise to difficulties when fishermen
anchored in the port of another parish where the local rector
demanded the tithe for himself as a prescriptive right. To
clarify the situation, Richard Went, perpetual vicar of Kinsale,
in 1398 petitioned and secured the issue of a mandate to the
dean of Cloyne 'to forbid his [Went's] parishioners who gain
their living by sea-fishing to pay tithe of their catch to rectors and
vicars of churches near the shore, or other places without
Kynsale whither they repair for refreshment . . . or are driven
by stress of weather or other causes, but with the intention of
returning home.'[44] From then on, according to the terms of
this mandate, rectors and vicars were forbidden to exact tithe

41   Brady, *Records*, i, *passim.*: 1693, Inishkenny, 6 acres; 1687, Aglish, 5 acres; 1700,
Dunmanway, 12 acres; 1704, Murragh, about 40 acres of glebe around the church.

42   Moorman, *Church Life in England in the Thirteenth Century*, p. 117 ff.

43   Brady, *Records*, i, 171.

44   *Cal. papal letters, 1396–1404*, p. 263.

on fish on the basis of prescriptive custom. For post-Reformation times there are also references to tithes on turf and potatoes which, according to the report of Bishop Downes in 1700, the people of Ringmahon paid in kind. Finally, an *agistment* or tithe levied on the rent of a mill was paid by the inhabitants of Ballymoney.[45] It seems probable that the levying of tithes in Cork and in other dioceses was geared mainly to the type of occupation generally prevailing.

Offerings of the People

These were as interesting as they were varied and must have contributed a considerable addition to what a pastor gained from his own glebe-land and from the returns of other people's lands. On certain feasts of the church—Christmas, Easter, titular and the like—the faithful were expected to mark the occasion by a special offering quite distinct from the Mass-pennies they were encouraged to contribute each time they attended Mass. The Mass-pennies were also collected at anniversaries and were augmented by 'book money' which was the general name given to fees collected at marriages, churchings, baptisms (occasionally) and funerals. Thus, for instance, William Robinson, vicar of Ballinaboy, received fifty shillings annually for his services and the same amount in 'boke-money'.[46] The visitation of the sick was likewise regarded as an occasion when some money gift might be expected, while mortuary fees and sums exacted for witnessing wills were still another addition to rectorial and vicarial revenues. Over and above the money offerings, certain gifts in kind were also donated, such as bread, wax or candles for use in the church and in the priest's house. The custom obtaining in England of giving the clergy eggs at Easter, cheese at Pentecost and fowl at Christmas was probably practised in Ireland as well.

All things considered, the beneficed clergy of the thirteenth and fourteenth centuries must have been relatively wealthy. Beneath them, however, the existence of the ordinary parish clergy, a heterogeneous and stratified group, as numerous as they were poor, brings to light the grave inconsistencies of the medieval church. Among this clerical proletariat perhaps the worst off were the vicars of impropriate parishes, the revenues of which were enjoyed almost in their entirety by some religious

45 Brady, *Records*, i, 39, 16.

46 Ibid., p. 14.

community who paid a miserable pittance to an overworked vicar and expected him to discharge all the duties of residence and cure of souls.

CLERICAL EXPENDITURE

For expenditure, the clergy were liable to tithes, to episcopal visitation, to papal and archiepiscopal procurations and to incidental taxes imposed by the English king. Of these the most immediate and dreaded was the episcopal visitation, for the bishop, as well as bringing an entourage who had to be provisioned, came also to inspect the property of the church, the efficiency of the clergy and the conduct of the parishioners in general. As this was the bishop's principal way of keeping in touch with his clergy, personal or archidiaconal visitation or procuration must have been pursued fairly regularly, but here again we are at a loss for concrete evidence. There are no extant records of episcopal visitations in Cork, and for an archiepiscopal levy our only source is the defective procuration list of 1437 which was compiled on the occasion of the triennial visitation of the archbishop of Cashel. Although nowhere stated, the impost would appear to be one-tenth of the assessed income in each case.

Vicar de Drinagh	3s.od.	Rec. & Vic. de	
Praebend Kilbrogan	2s.od.	Kilmichael	8s.od.
Rector ibm.	2s.od.	Rec. & Vic. de	
Rec. de Aglish	2s.od.	Perinshigulagh	4s.od.
Vic. de	2s.od.	Praebend de	4s.od.
Vicar. de Murragh	6s.od.	Vic de Durrus	4s.od.
Rincurran	9s.od.	Vic. de Kilcrohane	4s.od.
Tisaxon	5s.od.	Vic. de Kilmocomoge	2s.od.
Kinsale	3s.od.	Praeb. de	
Ecc. de Dunderrow	3s.od.	Killaspugmullane	1s.od.
Ecc.. de Ringrone	4s.od.	Rec. de Cannaway	1s.od.
Ecc. de Sanct. Brigid	5s.od.	Rec. & Vic. de	
Rec. & Vic. de Schull	4s.od.	Macloneigh	4s.od.
Rec. & Vic. de Kilmoe	4s.od.	Praeb. de Killanully	6s.od.
Rec. & Vic. de		Ecc. de Knockavilly	10s.od.
Christ Church	9s.od.	Ecc. de Brinny	2s.6d.
Ecc. de Carrigaline	6s.od.	Ecc. Sanct. Peter	9s.od.
Vic. de Templebreedy	3s.od.	Nohoval	6s.od.
Ecc. de Templemartin	4s.od.	Kilmonoge	4s.od.
Ecc. de Cullen	6s.od.	Vic. de Aglish	2s.od.
Vic. de Ballymodan	4s.od.	Rec. & Vic. de Moviddy	3s.od.

Rec. & Vic. de Carrowey 4s.od.

Ecc. de Ardnageehy 4s.od.

Vic. de Rathclarin 4s.od.

Praeb. de Kilnaglory 3s.od.

Praeb. de . . . . 3s.od.

Praeb. de Caherlag 5s.od.

Ecc. de Rathclarin 7s.4d.

Rec. de Corbally 1s.1od.

Carrigrohane 3s.od.

Rec. & Vic. Ovens 4s.od.

Rec. de Kinneigh 1s.od.

Praeb. de
Drimoleague 3s.od.

Ecc. de Shanbally 3s.od.

Ecc. de Kilquane 3s.od.

Templeusque 5s.od.

Rec. & Vic. Little
Island 6s.od.

Ecc. de Ballydeloher 6s.od.

Ecc. de Caheragh 3s.od.

Vic. de Dunmanway 3s.od.

Vic. de Kinneigh 1s.6d.

Ecc. de Ballymoney 4s.od.

Ecc. de Leighmoney 4s.od.

Vic. de Bally . . . 5s.od.

Ecc. de Ballymartle 5s.od.

Templemichael 9s.od.

Ecc. de Innishannon £1.os.od.

Kilbrittain 4s.od.

Praeb. de Liscleary 6s.9d.

Vic. de Liscleary 4s.od.

Vic. de Kilbonane 1s.od.

Duniskey 1s.od.

Kilcully 3s.od.

Dunbulloge 7s.od.

St. Catherine 1s.od.

Macloneigh 1s.od.

Templetrine 6s.od.

Cloghan *als* Kildareny 4s.od.

Kilgobbin 6s.od.

Rathdrought 4s.od.

Ballinadee 6s.od.

Rathcooney 3s.od.

Rec. & Vic. de Shandon 8s.od.

LAICORUM PROCURATIONES

Rec. de Durrus 4s.od.

Ecc. de Kilmurry 1os.od.

Rec. de Kilmichael 2s.od.

Rec. de Inchigeela 2s.od.

Rec. de Ballymodan 3s.od.

Rec. de Kilmocomoge 2s.od.

Ecc. de Ballinaboy 3s.od.

Kilpatrick 4s.od.

Rec. de Ballyfeard 5s.od.

Ecc. de Ballyfoyle 6s.od.

Ecc. de Kinure 3s.od.

Ecc. de Clontead 6s.od.

Rec. de Templebreedy 6s.od.

Rec. de Brinny 2s.6d.

Rec. una de Ovens 3s.od.

Rec. de Kilbonane 1s.od.

Rec. de Kilmoney 3s.od.

Rec. de Kilcrohane 4s.od.

Rec. de Barnahely 1s.od.

Rec. de Kinsale 3s.od.

Una Rec. de Aglish 2s.od.[47]

To take a few random comparative surveys of this procuration list and the taxations of 1302–06 we get a rather interesting picture of a fluctuating diocesan economy. Places which maintained an undisturbed valuation were Kilcully, Kinsale, Caherlag and Templetrine. Those showing an appreciation in value (and in taxability) were Ardnageehy which went from thirty shillings to two pounds, and places like Liscleary in two parts, Templemichael, Nohoval and Kilbrittain.[48] In the devalued section, Innishannon and Ringrone, the two wealthiest benefices in 1302, had each dropped from twelve pounds to ten pounds and two pounds respectively. Ballyfeard had fallen from nine marks or six pounds to two pounds, ten shillings. Cullen from five marks (£3 6s 8d) to two pounds, and the prebend of Killaspugmullane had dropped in value from two pounds to ten shillings. For the student interested in comparative statistics these lists constitute a challenge which is suggested as a fruitful area of research for the future historian.

The value of annate bonds as a source for evaluating the diocesan economy cannot be over-emphasized. Their importance is that they represent this economy for the century immediately preceding the Reformation. However, a detailed treatment of the 105 entries for the diocese of Cork would be as undesirable as it would be unnecessary in the present context; consequently, a few quotations will suffice as a basis for a comparative estimate, and for this purpose a simple chart is offered as a visual aid. For further simplification all valuations are given in terms of pounds, shillings and pence rather than in marks, and as quotations in each case connote actual valuations, the excerpts from the procuration list of 1437 have been multiplied by ten to bring them into line with the other sources quoted.

TAXATIONS, 1302-06		PROCURATIONS, 1437	ANNATES	
Ringrone	£12	£2	£9 6s.8d.	(1471)
			£4 13s.4d.	(1505)
Drimoleague		£1 10s.0d.	£8	(1441)
Fanlobbus		£1 10s.0d.	£8	(1464)
Killaspugmullane	£2	10s.0d.	£8	(1466)
			£9 6s.8d.	(1481)
Kilcully	£1 10s.0d.	£1 10s.0d.	£2 13s.4d.	(1469)
			£9 6s.8d.	(1484)
Kinneigh		£1 2s.6d.	£5 6s.8d.	(1470)
Kilmoe		£2	£10 13s.4d.	(1472)
			£13 6s.8d.	(1492)
			£6	(1510)
Kinsale	£1 10s.0d.	£1 10s.0d.	£20	(1474)
			£24	(1500)
Rathcooney	£4	£1 10s.0d.	£10 13s.4d.	(1481)
Kilbrogan		£2	£13 6s.8d.	(1481)

48 Templemichael increased from 4½ marks to £4 10s 0d; Nohoval from 3½ marks to £3; Liscleary (in two parts) from 6 marks, 10s, to £5; Kilbrittain from 30s to £2.

Inishkenny	£2 13s.4d.		£8	(1482)
Glanmire }	£2 10s.0d.	£2 10s.0d	£8	(1485)
Templeusque }				
Macloneigh		£2	£8	(1488)
			£4	(1492)
Drinagh		£1 10s.0d.	£4 13s.4d.	(1492)
Kilmichael		£2	£8	(1493)

Owing to the practical impossibility of giving modern equivalents for the quotations cited, the lists must be taken at their face value. An obvious deduction is that the annate entries show a decided increase in valuation as against the taxation and procuration returns. Factors contributing to this appreciation in value have not come to light; neither can it be ascertained why places like Ringrone, Kilmoe and Macloneigh dropped so suddenly in the annate list after a spectacular increase in each case. But not all the annate returns offer the same suggestion of wealth, for there are instances where the stated revenue was at or below the six-mark level, in which cases the bulls were restored *sine obligatione* or *propter paupertatem*. A more detailed résumé of the annates for the diocese of Cork will be given in a later chapter. For present purposes the fluctuations they represent towards the turn of the century may have been a direct outcome of the Wars of the Roses and of the local strife which characterized the abortive efforts of Lambert Simnel and Perkin Warbeck, both of whom used Cork as a base for operations against England.

There remain the two sixteenth-century documents as sources for information on the diocesan economy. The first is an 'Old Rental of County Cork' which though undated appears to have some connection with an assessment for some subsidy mentioned in one of its entries.[49] Whether the assessment was a tithe or other fractional division is not clear, and for this reason it is not possible to prove or disprove a depreciation in the parochial valuations. What is important, however, is that this assessment as applied to churches in the diocese represents a royal levy on the parishes in question.

Par. de Kinalmeaky,	8s.	Par. de Kilmichael,	4s.
Par. de Ballyfoyle	10s.	Par. de Carrigaline	6s.8d.
Par. de Kilpatrick	4s.	Par. de Templebreedy	4s.
Par. de Cannaway	9s.	Par. de Ringrone	13s.4d.

49   The entry reads: 'Walter Prindirgast quia cessatur in parochia de Templebridy, iiijs. per certificacionem Richardi Ailward militis et Andree Barrett, Commissionariorum subsidii predicti patet.'

Par. de Kinsale	20s.	Par. de Kilmonoge	6s.8d.
Par. de Ardnageehy	6s.8d.	Par. de Kilmurry	4s.
Par. de Moviddy	4s.	Par. de Desertmore	4s.
Par. de Duniskey	4s.	Par. de Knockavilly	3s.
Par. de Macloneigh	4s.	Par. de Inchigeela	5s.4d.[50]

We do not know if this impost was ever collected, but assuming that it came at a time when Protestantism was being introduced into Ireland, all the evidence goes to suggest that few of the returns enumerated above ever found their way into the state treasury. But because of this and other similar incidental levies, coupled with papal, archiepiscopal and episcopal taxations and procurations, the pre-Reformation clergy of the diocese of Cork were particularly tax-ridden. With the exception of the bishop, the *quatuor personae* and the benefice-holders of Ringrone and Innishannon, the remainder of the clergy fell into a fairly normal income group, while not a few fell into the undersalaried category, i.e., those who served in the 'particles' and those mentioned in the annates as having had their bonds restored *sine obligatione*.

Our second sixteenth-century document is a taxation of the diocese undertaken in 1588 and officially calendared as MS T.C.D. E.3.14. It deals with part of the diocese only, but for that part it shows the same fluctuations that are noticeable in previous returns. Of thirty-five entries on this list, nineteen (including the bishop, dean, archdeacon, chancellor and treasurer) show a devaluation; twelve, including precentor register, an increase; two places are mentioned which do not appear on the earlier taxations (Kinneigh[51] and Fanlobbus) and two have remained static (Cannaway and Killaspugmullane). The devalued entries on the following list are indicated with an asterisk.

	£	s.	d.		£	s.	d.
The Bishop of Cork	25	0	0*	Prebend of Inishkenny	2	6	0*
The Archdeacon	7	1	8*	,, ,, Kilnaglory	2	5	0
Prebend of Liscleary	3	0	0*	Vicarage of Kinsale	3	0	0
,, ,, Killanully	4	0	0	,, ,, Ringrone	3	0	0*
,, ,, Kilbrittain	1	13	4	,, ,, Kinneigh	1	10	0
Rectory of Rynouran	4	0	0	,, ,, Fanlobbus	1	10	0
(probably Rincurran)				,, ,, Shandon	3	10	0*
Rectory of Leighmoney	4	0	0	,, ,, Ovens	1	10	0
,, ,, Ringrone	6	0	0	,, ,, Little Island	2	0	0

50   B.M., Add. Charter 13600*.

51   Kinneigh and Fanlobbus were mentioned in the procuration list of 1437.

,, ,, Kilgobban	3	16	0	
,, ,, Templetrine	4	0	0	
,, ,, Rathclarin	3	16	0	
,, ,, Innishannon	5	6	8*	
,, ,, Knockavilly	4	0	0*	
The Dean of Cork	3	0	0*	
The Precentor	8	0	0	
The Chancellor	2	0	0*	
The Treasurer	1	0	0*	
Prebend of Desertmore	3	0	0*	

,, ,, Ballymodan	2	0	0*
,, ,, Cannaway		10	0
,, ,, Rincorran	4	0	0*
Church of Moylumerynebollan	2	0	0
,, ,, Rathcooney	1	10	0*
,, ,, Holy Trinity	1	16	8*
,, ,, St. Michael's	1	0	0*
(Shanbally)			
Church and Chapel of			
Kilshinahan		10	0*[52]

On the subject of clerical income, we have seen that the revenue of priests was derived customarily from tithes and that such tithes were the equivalent of one-tenth of the gross produce of certain crops. Socially, therefore, the tithe system as practised in medieval times meant that the church encouraged tillage and cultivation. It is on record that about the year 1240 root crops were practically unknown, but wheat, oats, barley and rye, as well as beans, peas and onions were grown extensively. Rotation of crops was practised on a two- or three-year system; cows, sheep and fowl were plentiful, and in general the standard of living in Ireland could compare favourably with that of other countries.[53] Historians are adamant in maintaining that taxes on the clergy, procurations and first-fruits made heavy inroads on clerical incomes and must have led to impoverishment and dissatisfaction among them. With the removal of these so-called foreign imposts at the Reformation, one would have expected a lowering of the supposed burdens on the clergy and correspondingly on the laity. But such was not the case. The royal visitation conducted by Bishop William Lyon is our first available indication of the workings of the 'reformed' system in 1615, that is, about seventy years after its inauguration.[54] From this we get the following figures for the principal churches in the deanery of Kenalethe *ultra*. Once again we take the fourteenth-century taxation list as our basis of comparison.

---

52   Brady, *Records,* i, xvii.

53   M. J. McEnery, 'The State of Agriculture and the Standard of Living in Ireland in the Years 1240–1350', *R.S.A.I. Jn.*, 1 (1920), 1–18.

54   Michael A. Murphy, 'The Royal Visitation of Cork, Cloyne, Ross and the College of Youghal', *Archiv. Hib.*, ii (1913), 173–215.

	1302–06			1615		
	£	s	d	£	s	d
Ringrone	12	0	0	30	0	0
Templetrine	3	0	0	16	0	0
Kilbrittain	1	10	0	4	0	0
Ballymodan	2	17	0	7	0	0
Innishannon	12	0	0	14	0	0
Knockavilly	5	0	0	10	0	0

Taken at their face value, the figures of the royal visitation cer-tainly show an increase—and in many instances a considerable one—on the medieval rating. One must, however, guard against forming hasty conclusions; the great inflation of the sixteenth century must be borne in mind in assessing the relative values of the above list. But even with this cautionary attitude, it remains nonetheless true that ecclesiastical taxation under the 'reformed' system fell heavily on the Catholics who felt keenly the injustice of being forced to contribute to the ministerial salaries of an alien church which they did not recognize, from which they accepted no service and which was officered and endowed beyond all proportion to its duties. The tithe question as such, with its attendant disturbances and outrages, belongs more properly to the history of the modern diocese of Cork.

APPENDIX

Rental of Certain Places in County Cork : Sixteenth Century

(Additional Charter 13600*)

Pierce Gould fitz Adam in Templebodane iiijs. et in Disart ijs. John' Mathewes ijs. Jacob' Gould ijs. Jacob' Waters ijs. Georg' Tirry in Downgorne ijs. et in Agglish iiijs. qui omnes et singuli eorum Cessantur in moioribus (*maioribus*) summis in Comitatu Civitatis Corck prout per seperales certificaciones sub manibus Par Lane militis Edmundi Tirrey et Davidi Tirry fitz Stephen patet Attingentibus inter se ad . . .

Patricio Cleere quia Cessatur et soluit in Civitatem Dublin tantitum ubi habitat. Ideo hic allocatur . . . iiijs.

Jacob' Jyodnett quia Cessatur in parochia de Lislige in xjs., in parochia de Kinalmeky viijs., prout per Certificacionem Episcopi Corcagensis et Henrici Beecher patet. Ideo hic allocatur . . . viijs.

Thoma' Daunt quia sol' in parochia de Belafoile xs. et Cessatur in parochia de Kilpatrick iiijs., prout per Certificacionem Andree Barret et Henrici Beecher patet. Ideo his allocatur . . . iiijs.

John fitz Gerrald de Clone quia soluit in parochia de Cloyne vj.li. Ideo hic allocatur in Kilbrine iiijs. Clonmyne iiijs. Farrihie iiijs. Kilsanie iiijs. in Tolleglass iiijs. et Kilbolone iiijs. attingentes in toto ad . . . xxiiijs.

Eddm. Coppinger et Johannem Forrest quia bis Cessatur ad vjs. le peece videlicet ut Comiss' et in villa de Youghall attingentes ad . . . xijs.

Katherine Sarsfield ijs. Edm. Martle iiijs. et Christofer Gould ijs. qui tres Cessantur in Civitate Corck in maioribus summis prout per debit. exam' inde patet . . . viijs.

Connogher Cronine quia ter Cessatur in parochia de Cannaway videlicet in iiijs., ijs. et iiijs. (Ideo hic allocatur et hic) (ultra iiijs. per ipsum solutis) prout per Certificaciones Andree Barett et Caroli McCarty Commissionariorum ibidem patet hic allocatur . . . vjs.

Gully O Leachy quia cessatur in Civitate Corck ad viijs. prout per Certificacionem Edmundi Tirry et Davidi Tirrey fitz Stephen Commissionariorum ibidem patet. Ideo hic allocatur ... ijs.

John Rapley quia Cessatur in parochia de Kilwyne in eadem summa ubi sol' prout per Certificacionem Richardi Ailward et Andree Barret Commissionariorum ibidem—patet. Ideo allocatur in baronia de Morne Abbey . . . iiijs.

John O Mony quia Cessatur in Civitate Corck ad vjs. viijd. ubi sol' prout per Certificacionem Par. Lane militis et Edmundi Tirry patet. Ideo hic allocatur . . . iiijs.

John Meade quia bis Cessatur videlicet in Manvawraghe ijs. et in parochia de Mogeally ad xiijs. iiijd. ubi sol'. Ideo hic allocatur . . . ijs.

Teig Mc Shane quia bis Cessatur videlicet in parochia de Lesson ad iiijs. et in parochia de Ballinedehie ad iiijs. prout per Certificacionem Dermot McCarty et Jaccobi Roche Commissionariorum ibidem patet. Ideo hic allocatur . . . iiijs.

Cahir O Callaghane quia Cessatur in parochia de Kilsany xxs. prout per Certificacionem Dermot Mc Carty et Andree Barrett. Ideo hic allocatur in Kilbrine iiijs. et Malloe iiijs. In toto . . . viijs.

John Mc Donnell quia Cessatur in Civitate Corcke ad vjs. viijd. prout per Certificacionem Par Lane et Eddmundi Tirry Commissionariorum ibidem patet. Ideo hic allocatur . . . vs.iiijd.

Donnell O Dowgan quia bis Cessatur videlicet in parochia de Kilwine vs.iiijd. et in parochia de Kilbrine iiijs. Ideo hic allocatur . . . iiijs.

Cahill O Garry quia Cessatur in Civitate Corck ad ixs.iiijd. prout per Certificacionem Parlane militis et Eddmundi Tirry patet. Ideo hic allocatur . . . viijs.

John Barry quia soluit in parochia de Rathbarry xxs. Ideo hic allocatur in parochia de Liscarrell xxijs.iiijd.

Philip O Callock alias Barry quia Cessatur in parochia de Carigline in Comitatu Civitate (*sic*) Corck ad vjs.viijd. prout per Certificacionem Eddmundi Tirry et Patricii Tirry patet. Ideo hic allocatur . . . . vs.iiijd.

Thomas Stephens quia bis Cessatur videlicet in parochia de Rathgoggan xs. et in parochia de Shandrome iijs. Ideo hic allocatur . . . ijs.

William O Murcho quia Cessatur in Civitate Corck ad vjs. viijd. prout per Certificacionem Eddmundi Tirry, Davidi Tirry et Patricii Tirry. Ideo hic allocatur . . . iiijs.

John Connell quia Cessatur in Comitatu Civitatis Corck ad vjs.viijd. prout per Certificacionem Eddmundi Tirry et Parlane militis Commissionariorum ibidem patet. Ideo hic allocatur . . . vs.iiijd.

John Mc Gibbone quia bis Cessatur in eadem summa videlicet in parochia de Rathgoggane iiijs, et in parochia de Collyne iiijs. Ideo hic allocatur iiijs.

Walter Prindirgast quia Cessatur in parochia de Templebredy iiijs, prout per Certificacionem Richardi Ailward militis et Andree Barrett *Commissionariorum subsidii predicti patet*. Ideo allocatur in parochia de Kilnecoule . . . iiijs. (This entry suggests that the rental was taken because of some royal subsidy being levied in Cork).

David Goggan quia Cessatur in Civitate Corck ad viijs. Ideo hic allocatur virtute Certificacionis inde sub manibus Eddmundi Tirry et Davidi Tirry fitz Stephen, patet . . . vs.iiijd.

Peirce Power quia bis Cessatur in eadem summa videlicet in parochia de Fermoy iiijs. et in parochia de Downeraile iiijs. Ideo hic allocatur . . . iiijs.

Donogh de Castletresses quia soluit in Civitate Corck vjs.viijd. Ideo hic allocatur virtute Certificacionis inde sub manibus Eddmundi Tirry et Patricii Tirry Commissionariorum ibidem . . . vs.iiijd.

John Growe quia Cessatur in Civitate Corck ad xvjs. prout per Certificacionem Par: Lane et Eddmundi Tirry Commissionariorum ibidem patet. Ideo hic allocatur . . . xs.viijd.

Edmund Roch quia Cessatur in parochia de Rinrone in xiijs.iiijd. prout per Certificacionem Andree Barrett et Jacobi Roch Commissionariorum ibidem patet. Ideo hic allocatur in parochia de Kinsale . . . viijs.

Cormac Mc Donagh Mc Carty quia Cessatur in parochia de Kilmohonoge in vjs. viijd. prout per Certificacionem Dermot Mac Carty et Andree Barrett Commissionariorum ibidem patet. Ideo allocatur in parochia de Naghovally iiijs.

Randall Clayton quia Cessatur in Civitate Corck ad xxiiijs. Ideo hic allocatur iiijs.

. . . fitz Richard vjs. Robert Mead viijs. William . . . ck vjs.viijd. Edward Ashton vs.iiijd. Thomas Holmes viijs. John Stephens viijs. Richardo Nixon iiijs. Patricio Betoe iiijs. Richardo Hunt iiijs. John Martine iiijs. Teig Oge iiijs. Jacobo Ford iiijs. Radulpho Day iiijs. William Rushell iiijs. quia omnes dupliciter taxantur videlicet in parochia de Ballelogh et Ballehayses solvend' in parochia de Ballehay ubi resident prout per Certificacionem Richardi Boyle militis et Richardi Aldworth militis, Commissionariorum subsidii predicti patet. Attingent' inter se ad . . . lxxiiijs. (The manuscript is torn at the beginning of this entry).

Donogho Leary quia Cessatur in Comitatu Civitatis Corck in vjs.viijd. prout per Certificacionem Par. Lane et Eddmundi Tirry Commissionariorum ibidem patet. Ideo hic allocatur . . . . vjs.

William Gould quia Cessatur in Civitate Corck ad xs.viijd. Ideo hic allocatur . . . ijs.

Daniell Mc Conn ne booley quia bis Cessatur videlicet in parochia de Killanahan xiijs.iiijd. et in parochia de Arnegee vjs.viijd. Ideo hic allocatur vjs.viijd.

Morish Brenadh alias Walsh quia bis Cessatur videlicet in Clonie xiijs.iiijd. et in Cahirultane iiijs. Ideo hic allocatur . . . iiijs.

William Coch quia bis Cessatur videlicet in Youghall viijs. et in Castlelions iiijs. Ideo hic allocatur . . . iiijs.

Gerrott Russell quia Cessatur in Comitatu Civitatis Corck ad vjs.viijd. prout per Certificacionem Eddmundi Tirry et Davidi Tirry. patet. Ideo hic allocatur . . . vs.iiijd.

Teig O Hogane quia Cessatur in Comitatu Civitatis Corck ad vjs.viijd. prout per Certificacionem Eddmundi Tirry et Davidi Tirry Commissionariorum patet. Ideo hic allocatur . . . vs . . . (*torn*).

Conner Mc Donogh quia bis Cessatur videlicet in Disert xs. viijd. et Gortroe xiijs.iiijd. Ideo hic allocatur . . . xs.viijd.

Thomas Barry quia bis Cessatur in iiijs. videlicet in Lisgoole et Templenecarrigy . . . iiijs.

Owen O Downeley quia bis Cessatur in Eastchurch in eadem summa . . . ijs.

Donogh O Lanchy quia bis Cessatur videlicet in parochia de Ballinegarra ad iiijs. et in parochia de Castlelions iiijs. Ideo hic allocatur . . . iiijs.

William Mead quia Cessatur in Civitate Corcke ad xs.yr (*sic*) prout per Certificacionem Thome Gould et Eddmundi Tirry Commissionariorum ibidem patet. Ideo hic allocatur . . . iiijs.

David fitz Robert Sisk quia bis Cessatur videlicet in Corckbeg iiijs. et in Aghaddy iiijs. . . . iiijs.

John Conogh quia bis Cessatur in eadem summa videlicet in Corckbegg et Aghady . . . iiijs.

John Galwane quia bis Cessatur videlicet in Youghall ijs. et in Aghady vs.iiijd. Ideo hic allocatur . . . ijs.

John Mc Donnell O Riordan quia Cessatur in parochia de Macromp in vs.iiijd. prout per Certificacionem Char. Mc Carty et Andree Barrett patet in parochia de Clondrohed iiijs. Ideo hic allocatur . . . iiijs.

Owen Mc Egan bis Cessatur in ijs. in parochia de Aghenagh prout per Certificacionem Andree Barrett et Henrici Beecher patet. Ideo hic allocatur . . . ijs.

Donogh Mc Shane bis in parochia de Moviddy ad iiijs. Donogh Mc Barnane bis in Downesky ad iiijs. Shane O Rin bis in Macloneghy ad iiijs. Teig O Leighan bis ad iiijs in Kilmichill. Donogh Mc Donell bis ad iiijs. in Kilmurry. John O Leyne bis in Disartmore ad iiijs. prout per seperales Certificaciones sub manibus Caroli Carty et Andree Barrett Commissionariorum ibidem patet. Attingent' in toto ad . . . xxiiijs.

John Mc Conn' buy in parochia de Kannowy vs.iiijd. et in parochia de Killmwr . . y iiijs. . . . iiijs.

(Torn) . . . O Dannohie in Drishane Cessatur bis
. . . Donnell O Colmane bis in Drishane
. . . Dermot buy O Callaghane bis ad iiijs.
. . . prout per tres Certificaciones
Caroli . . . Andree Barrett patet. Attingent' ad . . . xijs.
. . . quia Cessatur in Kinagh . . . de Aghinagh ad vjs. pro . . .
Commissionariorum patet. Ideo hic allocatur vjs.

Thome Roe O Shinghane in Mocremp (*sic*) iiijs. et in Aghbollug iiijs. prout per Certificacionem inde patet . . . iiijs.

Donogh Oge Carty in Aghbullog iiijs. et in Drishane ijs. prout per Certificacionem inde patet . . . ijs.

Teig Mc Melaghlin in Ballivorny viijs. et in Clonedroghed vs.iiijd. prout per Certificacionem inde patet . . . vs.iiijd.

John Duff alias Merigagh bis in Macromp iiijs. Teig O Linsy in Kilmerty bis ad iiijs. Dermot Mc Donell in Disertmore bis ad iiijs. Philip O Longy bis in Keilbonane ad iiijs. Teig Roe O

Healy in Donoghmore bis ad iiijs. Donogh Mc Edmund bis in Kilmichell ad iiijs. Melaghlin Mc Teig bis in Ballivorny iiijs. Conn Mc Donagh bis in Kinnewy ad iiijs. Morrogh Mc Donogh alias Tullihan bis in Aghebulog ad iiijs. prout per Certificaciones sub manibus Andree Barrett et Edwardi Beecher Commission-ariorum ibidem patet. Attingent' inter se ad . . . xxxvjs.

Davido Domino Barry xiijs.et Johanne Domino Coursy xijs. qui duo Cessantur inter nobiles et Consiliarios recipiend' a Willelmo Usher milite Collectore inde. Ideo hic allocatur . . . xxvjs.

Teig O Lonsy quia bis Cessatur in baronum de Bellavorny ad vs.iiijd. et iiijs. prout per Certificacionem Andree Barrett et Edward Beecher patet . . . iiijs.

Donnell Mc Teig O Foron quia bis Cessatur in Clondroghed ad vs.iiijd. at iiijs. prout per Certificacionem Andree Barrett et Edwardi Beecher patet . . . iiijs.

Awly Mc Moriertagh quia bis Cessatur in Knockivilly videlicet ad vs.iiijd. et iiijs. prout per Certificacionem Amdree Barret et Edwardi Beecher Commissionariorum subsidii predicti patet. Ideo hic allocatur . . . iiijs.

Teig Mc Donnell alias Teig Meriragh O Hingirdle quia bis Cessatur in Kilmichell ad vs.iiijd. et iiijs. prout per Certificac-ionem Andree Barret et Edwardi Beecher patet . . . iiijs.

Teig Mc Dermody Carty quia bis Cessatur videlicet in Inshigil-lagh vs.iiijd. et Kilmichell prout per Certificacionem Andree Barret et Edwardi Beecher Commissionariorum ibidem patet . . . (*The rest of the Roll is torn away*).

XIII

The Fourteenth-Century Gaelic Resurgence

No history of fourteenth-century Ireland would be complete without reference to the Gaelic resurgence which was symptomatic of a general ecclesiastical, political and social awakening throughout every part of the country. Contributory factors to the resurgence were (a) the Bruce invasion (1315–18) which in Munster and more particularly in Thomond was marked by the battle of Dysert O'Dea, 10 May, 1318; (b) the Black Death of 1348 which exacted a heavy toll from among the Anglo-Irish urban population to the extent of weighting the balance in favour of the native race and which made impossible any re-covery of the thirteenth-century position; (c) the constant absorption of England's personal and material resources in the Hundred Years' War which redounded to the advantage of the native Irish and to that of the semi-hibernicized Anglo-Irish who were as great a threat to the 'obedient English' as were the Irish themselves.[1]

Ireland at the end of the reign of Edward II was a land of absentees, English by birth, who drew money out of the country but never visited it, and whose lands became the basis on which a race of new baronial lords built their fortunes. Growth of local lordship and immunity became a prominent feature of society, both English and Irish, from the accession of Edward III (1327) to the end of the Wars of the Roses (1485). Coupled with this was the steady gaelicization of the Anglo-Irish, some of whom were beginning to form patriarchal septs after the Gaelic fashion. Border-lands everywhere were under attack and native victories of individual chiefs or confederacies were counted in hundreds, though no conscious all-Ireland aim is anywhere recorded. The more effectively to bring the Irish under law, either peacefully or by coercive means, Sir Anthony

---

1   Edmund Curtis, *A History of Medieval Ireland*, p. 219.

Lucy, justiciar, drew up several important ordinances for Ireland in 1331. One proclaimed that the Irish and the English were to be under the same law 'excepting the service of betaghs'.[2] Whether or not this edict was generally enforced is doubtful, but its emancipatory grant of English law was definitely conferred on Donal MacCarthy of Carbery.

Less pacific was Sir Anthony Lucy's Act of Resumption which revoked all grants made during the king's minority and was aimed directly at the earls of Ormond and Desmond. The justiciar ordered an inquisition to be made into the descent of the kingdom of Cork, and because FitzStephen, according to this inquisition, left no legal heirs of his moiety in that kingdom, half the land of Desmond was ordered to be restored to the king.[3] Almost immediately an Anglo-Irish patriot party was formed, and by a tacit and local, but universally practised understanding with the native race, this party became so increasingly invincible that by 1341 under the leadership of Desmond, the land of Ireland, according to the annals, stood at the point of breaking forever from the hands of the English king. From now on the problem of the apparent loyalty and secret disloyalty of the colonists was to prove a constant headache to the administration. To halt the defection, the earl of Desmond, Sir William Birmingham, his son Walter and many other prominent Anglo-Irish lords were arrested early in 1331. Sir William was hanged in June, but his arbitrary execution, far from having the desired effect, created such consternation that Sir Anthony Lucy was recalled to England, Desmond was released and the Act of Resumption was temporarily shelved.

King Edward's own absenteeism must be regarded as contributory to the breakdown of English power in Ireland. As events proved, his decision to concentrate on the rebellious Scots and on the French was fatal to his interests in Ireland. English influence in the north collapsed with the murder of the young earl of Ulster in June 1333; half a century later the greater part of the province had reverted to the Irish order. In Connacht the gaelicized de Burgos became so entrenched in local support and sympathy that by 1375 the race of Mac-William Iochtarach had come into being. In Desmond the exploits of Maurice FitzThomas entitled him to recognition as first of the Anglo-Irish patriot leaders, 'the first English lord that imposed coign and livery upon the king's subjects; the first that raised his estate to immoderate greatness by that wicked

2   *Stat. Ire., John–Hen. V*, p. 325.

3   Orpen, *Normans*, iv, 236, states that the findings were unjust.

extortion; the first that rejected the English laws and government and drew others away by his example to do the like; the first peer of parliament that refused to come to the parliament when summoned by the king's authority; the first that made a division and distinction between the English of blood and the English by birth'.[4]

Similarly with the native Irish. Even in places where enfeoffment had been extensive the English colony was recoiling at such a rate that in 1351 Edward III saw fit to confirm the grant of Magna Carta issued by his father for Ireland in 1320. The enactment papered over the cracks between the king and his Anglo-Irish barons, it protected Desmond, Ormond and others against arbitrary dispossession, but it failed to halt the trend of gaelicization or the native resurgence. The most significant signs of the decay of English power in Ireland by the 1360s were the decline in revenue, the reduction of the parliamentary subsidy and the remission to earls, prelates, barons, magistrates and commons of Ireland, both lay and cleric, of all their debts, accounts, escheats and fines. There were instances also of desperation and impatience among 'loyal' colonists especially in Leinster, and it was in an effort to revive the lagging fortunes of these loyal anti-Gaelic and anti-feudal residents that Edward III resolved to send his third son, Lionel of Clarence, to Ireland: 'Because our land of Ireland . . . is now subjected to such devastation and destruction that, unless God avert and succour the same it will be plunged soon into total ruin, we have for the salvation of the said land ordained that our dear son Lionel shall proceed thither with all dispatch and with a great army.'[5] Lionel's extensive campaigns in Desmond and against the clans of Leinster had no lasting effect, and while the treasury reports for the period of his lieutenancy showed an increase on former periods, he did not recover any land for the colonists. He returned to England in April 1364 but was back in Cork exactly a year later, whence by a devious circuit which took in Kilmallock, Carlow, Castledermot, Trim, Mullingar and Drogheda, he convened his celebrated parliament at Kilkenny in February 1366.

The Statutes of Kilkenny failed of their purpose to loosen the grip of gaelicization, and subsequent efforts to re-enact them were given their quietus at Poynings' parliament in 1494 which pronounced them obsolete. Church support for the statutes was

4 John Davies, *A Discovery of the True Causes why Ireland was never entirely Subdued . . .*, p. 307.

5 Otway-Ruthven, *Med. Ire.*, p. 285.

anomalous; it could scarcely have been otherwise in view of the prohibition against the admission of any Irishman 'of the nations of the Irish' to any cathedral or collegiate church or to any ecclesiastical benefice or religious house among 'the English of the land'. It is true that the archbishops of Dublin, Cashel and Tuam fulminated excommunication against all who dared to contravene the regulations made at Kilkenny, but it did not automatically follow that their suffragans were like-minded. In fact, only five bishops—Waterford, Lismore, Killaloe, Leighlin and Cloyne—endorsed the action of the archbishops. Gerald Barry, bishop of Cork, made no commitment.

After Lionel's departure in 1367 the deputyship was held for two years by Gerald FitzMaurice, earl of Desmond. He was succeeded in June 1369 by Sir William de Windsor whose duty it was to cope with the Irish enemies, to restore governmental efficiency and to improve relations between the Anglo-Irish and the mother country to the extent of making them pay for their own defence and, if possible, of subsidizing England's war with France. His task was not easy of accomplishment since the situation in Ireland showed a steady deterioration following Lionel's departure. In 1375, for instance, a jury swore that because of 'divers tribulations and the risks of the roads' the citizens of Cork could not come to the exchequer at Carlow without 'a great posse of armed men'.[6] De Windsor's overall programme was unsuccessful, but his viceroyalty is significant in that it provoked a clash over taxation which exacerbated relations between the king and the Irish church.

De Windsor's failure to halt the native resurgence and re-establish English power in Ireland was acknowledged in December 1376 when Edward III on the petition of the mayor, bailiffs and citizens of Cork remitted the sum of £34 13s 4d exacted from them by summons of the exchequer in Ireland. They complained that for two years the suburbs of their city and neighbouring parts had been burned by the assault of certain Irish enemies and English rebels and that thirty-six of the king's lieges in the city had been treacherously killed or apprehended. A survey of civic history for the fourteenth century is revelatory of a general situation. Cork was among the few Irish cities spared to the English, but it was now under constant attack from Irish enemies and was unable to discharge the fee-farm of the city or the rent of the Fayth. For the first three decades of the century the payment was sporadic at best. By 1340 the attacks of the Irish had assumed such enormous

6   *Cal. pat. rolls, 1374–77*, p. 207.

proportions 'in Cork and in places adjacent' that in 1342 neither fee-farm nor rent could be collected.[7] The next appeal for commutation came as a result of the Black Death: on 12 July 1351 the mayor, bailiffs and commonality of Cork sent a supplication to the king to the effect that 'on account of the last pestilence (1348) in these parts, as well as by destruction and waste done by the king's enemies, and various other causes' they were brought to such great need and poverty as to be unable 'without depression of their state' to pay the farm of eighty marks for their city and six marks for le Faythe.[8] The king granted respite pending investigation, but in May 1354 the mayor was again seeking mitigation for arrears incurred and which exceeded fifty pounds.[9] In July of the same year 'a fourth part of the city [was] burnt by mischance',[10] and by 1382 the situation became such that the mayor was given license to treat with Irish rebels until further orders.[11] Thus right through the fourteenth century the citizens of Cork paid heavily for the privilege of royal patronage which their city enjoyed. It was little satisfaction to them that on occasion permission was granted to spend the rent-money in repairing the city walls: they were actually paying for their own defence.

James Butler, second earl of Ormond, who succeeded de Windsor in 1376, yielded place in 1380 to Edmund Mortimer to whom the loyal English in Ireland looked for leadership in their effort to regain control. After some successes in the north and in the midlands Mortimer died in Cork on 26 December 1381, and in 1385 his infant son Roger was declared heir to the throne of England then occupied by Richard II, who was so harassed by internal upheavals and foreign commitments that the early years of his reign were devoted to matters more immediate than the Gaelic resurgence. By 1392 English affairs had improved, there was internal calm and external dangers were temporarily warded off by a truce with France and a nominal peace with the Scots. Richard II was convinced that a personal campaign in Ireland would recoup the losses sustained through abstenteeism. But Irish successes continued to increase, and in Munster communications had become so chaotic that in 1393 it was decreed that because the way between the city of Cork and the county of

7   *Cal. pat. rolls, 1340–45*, p. 567.

8   *Cal. pat. rolls, 1350–54*, p. 118.

9   *Cal. close rolls, 1354–60*, p. 76.

10   *Cal. pat. rolls, 1354–60*, p. 87.

11   *Cal. pat. rolls, 1381–85*, p. 116.

Limerick was most difficult and perilous, John of Desmond should provide a convoy 'for all hawkers and carriers of victuals, corn and merchandise, in going and returning between the said city and county during the king's will'.[12] Furthermore, because the country around Cork 'was destroyed and ruined by enemies of the king and by English rebels', the earl was to receive reasonable fees and customs from the carriers in remuneration for the labour and expense incurred on their behalf in the king's service.

The two visits of Richard II in 1394 and 1399 were an appropriate denouement to England's experiments and failures with the renascent Irish nation. Richard found himself confronted with three types of people, namely, 'the wild Irish, our enemies, the Irish rebels (degenerate English) and the obedient English'. His plan for the recovery of the English lordship was to admit Irish kings and chiefs to full legal status under the crown. On the surface the scheme was successful. Led by O'Neill of Tyrone, the Irish chiefs, exclusive of O'Donnell, did homage to the king or to his representative, swearing to obey him and to attend at parliament when summoned by him or by his deputies. The submissions, which were made in Irish, were translated into English by special interpreters and were then recorded in Latin. On 13 February 1395 Taig MacCarthy Mór wrote to the king from Ballaghath, that is, Ballea near Carrigaline: 'I humbly recommend myself and all mine . . . to your Lordship, signifying . . . that my ancestors from the time of the Conquest . . . and I also all my life, have been the men of you and your ancestors, attempting nothing ever against your royal Majesty . . . nor do I obtain [i.e. hold] any possessions save those which from of old I have obtained under your dominion and that of my lord, the Earl of Desmond.'[13] MacCarthy Mór did homage to the king at Kilkenny on 6 April, and in the same month MacCarthy of Carbery, MacCarthy of Muskerry and others 'in the parts of Cork' submitted to the duke of Rutland who had been despatched to Munster to accept the submissions. The wording of these and other submissions and the many protestations of loyalty addressed to the English king suggest indeed that the great fourteenth-century resurgence was not *per se* antagonistic to the monarchy. It was chiefly a movement motivated by the greatest of all motivating causes in Irish history, namely, the reconquest of land. Each chieftain strove to be

---

12   J. Graves, ed., *A Roll of the Proceedings of the King's Council in Ireland, 1392–93*, pp. 120–1.

13   Edmund Curtis, *Richard II in Ireland, 1394–95, and Submissions of the Irish Chiefs*, p. 158.

supreme in his own territory. Given that security, it mattered little to a MacCarthy, an O'Mahony or an O'Sullivan who was the nominal king of Ireland. The fourteenth-century resurgence therefore, as already stated, was not the outcome of concerted campaigning, but the ultimate result of the individual efforts of Irish chieftains to secure each his own lordship of his ancestral lands. Time was to show how far the submissions made to Richard II fell short of that monarch's hopes and intentions.

The direct involvement of the Irish church in the political turmoil of the fourteenth century is somewhat difficult to assess, but it seems too great a generalization to hold that 'church lands were, in theory at least, secure from Irish and Norman alike. Like the lay chieftains, the diocesan bishops of the century were ready, as far as prudence and necessity required, to acknowledge the royal power of the English king. There is no evidence that they played any active part in the local warfare, either as contestants or as instigators. Neither is there much evidence that the laity of either side attacked church lands or seized church property.'[14] It goes without saying that involvement expresses itself in many forms.

We have seen that Edward I (1272–1307) achieved a *modus vivendi* with the Irish church on three main issues: episcopal appointments, the delineation of the respective competencies of royal and ecclesiastical courts, and taxation.[15] We have also seen that during the zenithal period of English domination in Ireland the royal power was confined, for ecclesiastical purposes, almost exclusively to the provinces of Dublin and Cashel and to the diocese of Meath. Local peculiarities abounded, but clashes between the Irish church and the crown were not frequent and it is only fair to add that bishops in purely Irish districts were at the mercy of native chieftains in a manner no less aggravating than that which obtained within the common law area.[16] As yet however the Irish church was not actively participant in the political arena although racialism within the church was not unknown. It was imputed to the Franciscans and the Dominicans that they 'made much of' the Irish race,[17] and in 1310 the Irish parliament vetoed the admission of any Irishman into a religious house 'in a territory at peace, or in English land'.[18] The repeal of

14   Gleeson, *A History of the Diocese of Killaloe*, p. 332–3.

15   J. A. Watt, 'English Law and the Irish Church: The Reign of Edward I', in *Med. studies presented to A. Gwynn*, p. 137.

16   Powicke and Fryde, *Handbook of British Chronology*, pp. 305 ff.

17   *Cal. doc. Ire.*, 1285–92, p. 10.

18   *Stat. Ire., John–Hen. V*, p. 272.

this law, under pressure from Archbishop Walter Jorz of Armagh, does not take from its significance. Laws similar to it were to appear again and again in the statute books throughout the fourteenth century.

During the Bruce invasion the clergy became actively participant both for and against the Scots, and while not entirely impelled by racialism there can be no doubt that racial distinctions already existing were now greatly exacerbated. For these years there are numerous plunderings and sackings of churches and religious houses on record, mostly in the north-east, but none, so far as we know, in Cork where the impact of the invasion was negligible. Conversely, however, the invasion shows to what extent Edward II (1307–27) enjoyed papal support during these years. Within a year of his election in 1316 Pope John XXII was informed by the king that 'the fraudulent machinations and the malicious and false collusion' of some Irish prelates against the royal power had been a paramount consideration in the risings connected with Bruce's campaign.[19] The complaint also stated that 'the prelates of the Irish race do not cease to provoke against us the spirit of the people'.[20] A simultaneous letter to the superior general of the Franciscans accused the friars of inciting the Irish to rebellion. The king therefore filed an appeal asking the pope that for the present no native Irishman should be appointed bishop or archbishop without the king's previous consent. King Edward was so far successful that vacancies in Cashel, Dublin and Ossory were filled to his satisfaction with churchmen whose first concern was to restrain the clergy, both secular and regular, from inciting the people to rebellion. A general excommunication of the king's enemies was issued, to be followed shortly by an excommunication of the followers of Robert and Edward Bruce and of those mendicants, *daemonum adjutores*, who were said to be publicly preaching rebellion.[21] The liaison between the English king and the pope was mutually advantageous. As a corollary to Edward's need for securing papal approval for his Irish policy, there was the critical condition of the papal treasury, the desirability of an English alliance to counterbalance the encroachments of the French monarchy on the Avignon papacy, and the fact that John XXII 'was disposed to take seriously the papal function as feudal lord of

19   Rymer, *Foedera*, iii, 615–16, under date 25 March 1317.
20   Curtis, *Med. Ire.*, p. 185.
21   Rymer, *Foedera*, iii, 630–1.

England'.[22] Pope John's tepid response to the remonstrance of the Irish chieftains is therefore self-explanatory.

The remonstrance, presented in 1317, was an indictment of the lordship of Ireland and of the policy of the Anglo-Irish settlers. In it, the Irish chiefs with Donal O'Neill at their head charged the English kings with violating the spirit of Adrian's grant, especially in matters touching the native church. The ancient Irish kings, they said, had 'eminently endowed the Irish Church with lands, ample liberties and many possessions' and added that 'at the present time she [the church] is for the most part sadly despoiled of those lands and liberties by the English'.[23] Having failed to secure redress from the reigning king, the chiefs were now appealing to his suzerain the pope, pointing out the cruelties inflicted upon the native race by the colonists who declared that 'to kill an Irishman was no more than to kill a dog'. Because they despaired of justice from the king, the Irish had decided to repudiate his authority and therefore Donal O'Neill, 'by hereditary right King of Ireland', surrendered his rule to Edward Bruce, earl of Carrick, 'sprung from the most illustrious of our ancestors'.[24] But the days of the great popes were over, and John XXII was soon to send personal congratulations to Edward II on the defeat of Bruce at Foghairt in 1318.[25] Yet the remonstrance did not go altogether unheeded. The pope reminded the king of the necessity of dispensing justice to the Irish, and he charged his legates to keep the Irish claim before the king. He even implied the application of a sanction against royal mismanagement in Ireland. A second papal translation of the lordship of Ireland was apparently not outside consideration and is implicit in the pope's words to the king: 'You should scrupulously refrain from all such courses as may justly provoke against you the wrath of that God, the Lord to whom vengeance belongeth . . . who is described as having rejected His own peculiar people, and made a transfer of their kingdom to others, on account of the unrighteous acts of which they had been guilty.'[26] King Edward undertook to investigate the situation obtaining in Ireland and to be just and lenient towards the Irish. In pursuance of the king's promise the Irish were admitted to

22 J. A. Watt, 'Negotiations between Edward II and John XXII concerning Ireland', *I.H.S.*, x (1956–57), 4.

23 Edmund Curtis and R. B. McDowell, eds., *Irish Historical Documents, 1172–1922*, p. 39.

24 Edmund Curtis, *History of Ireland*, p. 98.

25 *Cal. papal letters, 1305–42*, p. 422.

26 Theiner, *Vetera Mon.*, nos. 422, 423.

English law in 1321, 'as well within liberties as without', and legislation was set in motion to check on various aspects of maladministration by royal officials.[27]

But for all that, the Irish parochial clergy *qua* Irish suffered the same deprivations as the regulars under Edward II and Edward III. In 1350 an insidious venom was injected into the church in the form of Richard FitzRalph's denunciation of the mendicants, and for the next ten years this controversy re-dounded to the detriment of ecclesiastical prestige generally— but from it the friars emerged triumphant. Meanwhile new legislation was being forged, and in 1366 came the veto enacted at Kilkenny that no Irishman 'of the nations of the Irish' should be admitted to any cathedral or collegiate church by provision, collation or presentation *of any person* whatever, or to any benefice of holy church among the English of the land, and that no house of religion situated among the English, exempt or non-exempt, should in future receive Irishmen to profession, and 'any that shall do otherwise and thereof be attaint[ed], the temporalities [shall] be seized into the hand of our Lord the king, to remain at his will'.[28]

It was also decreed that beneficed clergy living among the English were to learn English. As subsequent events proved, the statutes were not absolute norms and time and again the king exercised his royal prerogative to the extent of permitting Irish-men to hold benefices even though this was contrary to the spirit of the statutes. Thus it may be said that the *modus vivendi* achieved by Edward I was, within limits, connived at by his successors. Under Richard II (1377–99) a knowledge of English was again considered desirable among benefice-holders, and in 1381 the pope was asked not to make provision to anyone who could not speak and understand English 'since experience teaches that of the diversity of tongues in that land wars and divers tribulations have arisen'.[29] But by 1381 the English power in Ireland had reached its nadir and the strangle-hold of the English kings over the Irish church was in consequence greatly relaxed. The emancipation of the church from royal control revolved upon the vexed question of taxation and on the introduction on a large scale of the system of papal provisions which had become the normal process of appointment to

---

27   Curtis and McDowell, *Irish Historical Documents*, p. 47.

28   *Stat. Ire., John–Hen. V*, p. 445.

29   Otway-Ruthven, *Med. Ire.*, p. 139, quoting *Stat. Ire., John–Hen. V*, pp. 434, 444–6, 466–8.

bishoprics by the mid-fourteenth century, even though out-lying dioceses like Raphoe, Kilmore and Kilfenora seem to have continued to elect bishops without papal provisions up to the end of the century.[30]

The question of taxation falls into two main sections, namely, the efforts made on the one hand by the English kings to tax the Irish church in an endeavour to subsidize their wars against Scotland and France, and on the other, the attempt to arrest the flow of money from the king's realms to the papacy, more especially during the years of the papal residence at Avignon. Money thus diverted was regarded as an indirect contribution to enemy coffers. In respect of taxing the Irish church we find that in January 1347 the archbishop of Cashel with his suffragans of Limerick, Emly and Lismore decreed the excommunication of beneficed clergy who contributed to a war subsidy which had been granted by the parliament at Kilkenny in October 1346, but to which none of the bishops of the province had assented. Any cleric who paid the subsidy was to be deprived *ipso facto* and rendered incapable of holding any benefice in the province. Lay tenants of church lands who contributed were likewise to be excommunicated, and they and their sons to the third generation were to be hindered from holding benefices.[31] At Clonmel in February the archbishop, 'wearing his pontificals in the middle of the town', excommunicated all who were in any way connected with levying the subsidy. Among those men-tioned was William of Epeworth, archdeacon of Cork, king's clerk and principal collector for Munster, who when the bishops refused to grant the subsidy, sought to levy it off the church tenants. Because of the archbishop's determination, many who had agreed to the subsidy now refused to pay it and the king was deprived of an estimated 100 marks.

Another example of local taxation difficulties is afforded by an action taken in 1375 by the viceroy, Sir William de Windsor. At a parliament held in Kilkenny the viceroy's appeal for a 'willing subsidy' from the prelates, peers and commons in parliament was opposed by Milo Sweetman, archbishop of Armagh. De Windsor countered the archbishop's objection by royal letters issued under privy seal commanding sixty repre-sentatives of the Irish parliament to meet and debate on Irish affairs before the council of England in February 1376. The sixty were to be selected on a basis of two from each county

30   Powicke and Fryde, *Handbook of British Chronology*, p. 305.

31   Walter Harris, 'Collectanea de Rebus Hibernicis', ed. C. McNeill, *Anal. Hib.*, no. 6 (1934), p. 348.

representing nobles and commons, two clerics from each diocese and two members from each corporate town. Replying on behalf of the clergy, Archbishop Sweetman declared that 'we are not bound, according to the liberties, rights, laws and customs of the church and land of Ireland, to elect any of our clergy and send them to England for the purposes of holding parliaments and councils there.' The attitude of the hierarchy towards taxation was soon to undergo a change, and it was a complaisant body of proctors and bishops who attended a later parliament of 1380 and voted certain specified sums of money for the king.

PAPAL PROVISIONS

Although Edward I and Clement V had reached a state of harmony regarding Anglo-papal relations, the English barons looked with disfavour on papal interference in their country's affairs. Attempts to stem the outflow of English money to the papal coffers was signified by legislation of the type embodied in a statute of 1307 (25 Edward I) which enacted that 'no Abbot, Prior, Master, Warden or any other Religious person of what-soever condition or state he be, . . . shall [send] out of [the country] any tax imposed . . . under the name of rent, tallage [or] tribute'.[32] Heavy penalties were threatened for contravention of this statute. Edward I, who needed papal support, was able to manoeuvre between local malcontents and the pope, and under Edward II, apart from an abortive effort to lessen papal control at the parliament of Carlisle which condemned the practice of flooding English benefices with foreign clerics, Anglo-papal relations were, on the whole, maintained. John XXII supported the king against the Scots, and meanwhile the scope of papal provisions was being consistently extended. In the reign of Edward III (1327–77) differences began to arise, for the king had no intention of surrendering the right of the crown to the revenues of vacant bishoprics. With the accession of Clement VI in 1342 the conflict became overt and bitter, and a parliament of 1343 forbade the introduction into England of 'letters, briefs, suits, reservations, provisions, instruments or other documents contrary to the rights of the king or his subjects'.[33] The next year, in a famous letter dated 11 July 1344, Clement VI declared the

32   *Stat. Ire., John–Hen. V*, p. 242.

33   Mollat, *The Popes at Avignon*, p. 263.

God-given primacy of the Roman pontiff over all churches in the world and announced that by virtue of this right, he possessed 'full authority to dispose of all churches and all ecclesiastical dignities, offices and benefices'.[34] Subsequent Anglo-papal legislation is best understood from an investigation of the origin, scope and implications of the system so loudly denounced in the parliament of 1343.

In an effort to attain greater centralization within the church the Avignon popes began to lay claim to an ever-increasing share in the collation of benefices and to exercise their right of reservation (the right claimed by the pope in virtue of his *plenitudo potestatis* to confer a benefice vacant or about to fall vacant) without reference to the ordinary collators. Reservation was of two kinds, special and general, the latter more comprehensive in scope and applicable to all benefices of a certain category in the church as a whole, while the former was concerned with one benefice only 'by reason either of its location, or its status, or its persons, and lasted either for a specified time or for ever'.[35] As regards the general reservation, Clement IV's decretal *Licet ecclesiarum* of 27 August 1265 gave the pope full authority to dispose of the benefices of people dying *apud Curiam*. The phrase *apud Curiam* was extended by Boniface VIII to include those dying within a radius of two days' march (*dietae*) of the papal court. Clement V extended the papal power of reservation by every species of pretext: vacancies occurring by the resignation made by an incumbent to the pope or to some member of the curia, by the death of any member of the curia, by promotion. Finally John XXII laid down by the constitution *Ex debito* that in future papal reservation extended to all benefices where vacancies occurred through deposition or privation, by disallowance of an election, by refusal to allow a request to elect, by provision or translation to another benefice. From now on, at the hands of John XXII's successors, special and general reservations were constantly increased, and in this way the decay of the traditional elective system reached its nadir during the last years of the Avignon papacy. Concentration of power in the Holy See, while it may have had overtones of autocracy, was at the same time a partial remedy for the evils arising from elections. Cathedral chapters suffered great losses in prestige, but Mollat insists that they 'were the agents of their own downfall for discord was endemic in their midst, diverse

34 Ibid., p. 264.
35 Ibid., p. 336.

abuses all too frequently vitiated their elections, and the authority of metropolitan bishops no longer provided a remedy prompt enough or sufficiently effective to deal with the misfortunes of the churches'.[36]

Centralization was a key factor in the implementation of papal provisions, but papal reservations had also their political and financial aspects and, in view of the monetary returns accruing to kings and nobles from the exercise of ecclesiastical patronage and advowsons, the extension of papal provisions was bound to provoke conflict. But the Avignon popes were nothing if not diplomats, and generally speaking there seems to have been a mutually advantageous if tacit agreement between the papacy and the ordinary collators. In England the legislation of John XXII was at first welcomed by the clergy who were anxious to free themselves from royal bondage; but their attitude stiffened when they saw that the pope was flooding England with foreign prelates, and they felt that the papal coffers were sieves through which English money flowed into enemy hands. The denunciations uttered by the parliament of 1343 were only the first blast of an opposition which became climactic in the Statute of Provisors, 9 February 1351, and in the Statute of Praemunire, 23 September 1353. The former denied the pope's right to provide to vacant bishoprics and other elective dignities and benefices and stated that if patrons and bishops failed to exercise their rights within a period of six months the collation was to revert to the king or to those in whose gift the benefices had originally belonged. Imprisonment and liability to fines hung over the head of anyone who contravened this statute which, however, was not given effective implementation until during the sixteenth-century Henrician schism. The Statute of Praemunire forbade anyone 'to arraign the king's subjects in a foreign court in matters whose cognizance belongs to the king's court'.[37] Already in January 1353 apostolic collectors had been forbidden to collect annates in cases where incumbents appointed in defiance of papal reservations had not taken possession. On top of this, the prohibition of appeals to Rome as embodied in Praemunire could have proved highly prejudicial to the papacy, but as events proved, this statute remained as theoretical as did that of Provisors and for a similar length of time. Neither statute was extended to Ireland (an attempt to extend Provisors failed in 1411), nor indeed was Ireland immediately affected by subsequent Anglo-papal

36   Ibid., p. 338.
37   Rymer, *Foedera,* iii, pt. 1, p. 8.

legislation which continued to mark the English scene down to the year 1377, by which time although certain agreements had been arrived at, the main problem of conflicting royal and papal jurisdictions had not by any means been solved.

Open conflict was reserved for a later date in Ireland, and as far as can be judged from the papal letters, papal intervention was used either in co-operation with the king or more directly in filling disputed vacancies. In the latter instances papal diplomacy tended to fall in with local preferences and prejudices rather than with the kings, and it was in this way that papal provisions played an important role in hastening the decline of English power in Ireland. From the first introduction of papal provisions into Ireland a certain inconsistency in the method of filling vacant bishoprics and benefices is noticeable; this arose from the fact that the appointment of a papal providee to a particular diocese or benefice did not mean that papal provision was henceforth the only viable method of filling future vacancies in the diocese or benefice in question. The contrary was often seen to have been the case, and until papal provisions became fully operative and accepted in the fifteenth century a certain elasticity continued. So we find that the pope with the king's approval provided Philip of Slane (1321) and Walter le Rede (1327) to Cork, Edmond Kermedin to Ardfert and John, abbot of Combe, to Cloyne,[38] while for the same period appointments were made by the king to Killaloe, Cashel and Ardfert, and there is no date of provision given for Bishop John Roche who was appointed to Cork before December 1347. With such duality of procedure overlapping and friction were practically unavoidable. Then too, Irish chapters were as antagonistic as those in England to the loss of prestige entailed in their deprivation of the right to elect a successor to a vacant bishopric. Open friction between chapters, kings and popes was, however, generally avoided by the simple expedient of translation and by the obvious willingness of successive popes to co-operate as far as possible with the royal will. When friction did occur, it was the papal candidate who usually carried the day; and while there are definite instances of royal restrictions on papal provisions in the fourteenth century, it is also noticeable that as the century advanced the royal officials were finding themselves less and less able to exclude papal providees. The distinction between bishops *inter Hibernicos* and bishops *inter Anglos* was becoming as outdated as the *congé d'élire* itself.

The system of papal provisions which compromised capitular

38 *Cal. papal letters, 1305–42,* p. 212.

prestige and royal control of vacant bishoprics proved highly advantageous to suffragan bishops in that it gave them opportunity of appealing to the pope in matters of disputed elections, of which there are examples in Armagh and Tuam, and against the encroachments of the metropolitans, of which there is an outstanding example in the province of Cashel. This problem, for the investigation of which the bishops of Cork, Ross and Lismore were cited by papal mandate, was not without its political overtones. Its immediate aftermath was an attempt made by Edward II to unite the diocese of Cloyne with that of Cork[39] and the diocese of Lismore with that of Waterford, thereby putting the ecclesiastical jurisdiction of the two lesser dioceses into safer hands, according to English reckoning. The case raised in Cashel is indicative of abuses which in the fourteenth century were flourishing in the Irish church.

Briefly, the trouble was this. An unwilling candidate refused to take office when elected by the chapter of Cashel in 1317. In the following year the postulation of the chapter for John Mc-Carroll, bishop of Cork, was rejected and the vacancy was filled by the translation of William FitzJohn of Ossory.[40] The new archbishop antagonized his suffragans by extortionate procurations, more especially in Cloyne where he took £40 from the dean, 100 marks from the archdeacon and 150 marks from clergy and people. On the death of the bishop of Cloyne the archbishop usurped the episcopal jurisdiction, again levied heavy procurations, ordered the archdeacon (who had been coadjutor) to deliver the bishop's insignia to him and had him imprisoned and excommunicated for refusing. Meantime, the dean had been appointed to the see by papal provision: the archbishop had him also imprisoned together with the chancellor, precentor and treasurer and certain canons of Cloyne. In the appeal lodged by the chapter of Cloyne to the pope, William FitzJohn was charged with having dispensed benefices in Cloyne to his own supporters, some of them laymen 'to whom he relaxed forty days of enjoined penance'. Though under excommunication for not paying the tax on his bull of provision to the archbishopric, he had confirmed and consecrated the bishops-elect of Killaloe and Kilmacduagh and had confirmed an excommunicate monk as prior of Bridgetown (*de Villa Pontis*). Grave charges against the character and integrity of the archbishop were then invoiced; whether these charges were true or fabricated is not clear, but the complaints were so far successful that the pope accepted the candidate proposed by the chapter and provided him to the see of Cloyne.[41]

An extraordinary chain of events may have justified the foregoing appeal, but the precedent established was a dangerous one on which subsequent 'Rome-runners' capitalized, for one of the greatest abuses connected with the system of papal provisions in the fifteenth century was that many provisions were secured at Rome through denunciation of the occupants of coveted benefices. Temporary residence at Rome was the surest way to preferment; thus clerics by subterfuge, canvassing and other questionable methods secured provision to vacancies for which they were totally unfit. In retrospect, therefore, the non-involvement of the Irish hierarchy in the political resurgence of the fourteenth century may be explained in terms of preoccupation with the internal affairs of the church which was simultaneously undergoing its own resurgence. We now turn to an investigation of how the diocese of Cork fared under the duality of royal appointments and papal provisions.

41 Ibid.

XIV

The Diocesan Episcopacy, 1302–1393

POPES		BISHOPS OF CORK		KINGS OF ENGLAND	
Boniface VIII	1296–1303	John McCarroll	1302–1321	Edward I	1272–1307
Clement V	1305–1314			Edward II	1307–1327
John XXII	1316–1334	Philip of Slane	1321–1327	Edward III	1327–1377
		Walter le Rede	1327–1330		
		John de Bally-			
Benedict XII	1334–1342	coningham	1330–1347		
Clement VI	1342–1352	John Roche	1347–1358		
Innocent VI	1352–1362	Gerald Barry	1359–1393	Richard II	1377–1399
Urban V	1362–1370				
Gregory XI	1370–1378				

In contrast to the dioceses of Ardagh, Clogher, Raphoe, Killaloe, Ross, Tuam, Elphin and many others where as a result of the Gaelic resurgence a succession of Irish-born prelates ruled during the greater part of the fourteenth century, the diocese of Cork had a racially mixed and predominantly Anglo-Irish run of bishops for almost the same period. With the exception of John McCarroll (and possibly of John de Ballyconingham who may have had connections with the townland of Ballycunningham in Donoughmore) the fourteenth-century bishops of Cork are seen to have been representatives of the Anglo-Norman element in the diocese and country. Deans of Cork for the fourteenth century, with the notable exception of John Mc-Carroll who later became bishop, were English or Anglo-Irish.[1] The archdeacons were certainly non-native, two of them were king's clerks: Henry de Thrapton, who became chancellor of the exchequer, and William of Epeworth who was principal collector in Munster for a royal subsidy by Edward III in 1347. There are no extant records of fourteenth-century precentors, there is only one known chancellor whose name, Philip Gall, does not ring native, and two non-Irish treasurers, William

1   See Chapter IX, Appendix A.

Galle and Richard Went. If, therefore, the loyalties of a diocese may be gauged from the personnel of its chapter, the loyalties of Cork are clear. The same racial imbalance is seen in the filling of diocesan canonries and prebends where names like Lawles and Went, Codyngton, Cradok, Bolton, Barton and Pellyn predominate and do not give way to Ossyghan (Sheehan), Oceallaid (O'Kelly) and Ocronyn (Cronin) until well into the fifteenth century. Clearly then, English influence was still a power to be reckoned with in ecclesiastical affairs, for the colonial interest had been long established in Cork and the ferocity of the race war was apparently not yet felt within the church here. The location in Cork of the English Council under Roger Mortimer from November 1315 to January 1318 is a pointer to Cork's continued loyalty to King Edward II. At the same time, an ecclesiastical resurgence was beginning to germinate everywhere, and the decrees of the Council of Vienne in 1311–12 will be seen to have had a definite bearing on the vicissitudes of the church in Ireland. The principal decrees of the council (after those ordering the suppression of the Templars) dealt with the duties of bishops, with lay usurpation of ecclesiastical property and with outlining principles for the settlement of disputes over the rights of presentation to benefices. In Cork, as elsewhere, the fourteenth century was the century of increasing lay interference with diocesan appointments; it was also a period of escalating irregularities. Pope Clement V who summoned the Council of Vienne is remembered not because of the council but as the first of the Avignon popes. In 1309 he took up formal residence in the house of the Friars Preachers at Avignon, thereby inaugurating the so-called Babylonish captivity of the church.[2]

JOHN MCCARROLL, 1302–1321

John McCarroll (Mac Carwell, MacKerwyl), dean of Cork, was elected bishop by vote of the chapter on 30 April 1302. All the normal pre- and post-election formalities were observed, and in due course King Edward I notified Stephen, archbishop of Cashel, that the proceedings had the royal assent. The archbishop confirmed the election and the temporalities were restored on 12 June.[3] A writ relative to the restoration commissioned John Wogan the justiciar to deliver the temporalities to 'John McKerwil, receiving first from him letters under his and the

2 Mollat, *The Popes at Avignon*, chap. 1, *passim.*

3 *Cal. doc. Ire., 1302–07*, pp. 64, 74, 80.

chapter's seals that this grant shall not prejudice the royal rights or be held as precedent for the future'. It would appear that on this occasion at least, the earlier injunction to Geoffrey de Morisco[4] regarding vacant sees was applied to Cork; from this it may be inferred that the finances of the diocese were then somewhat precarious. This is borne out by the escheatry account of Walter de la Haye in 1302 which shows a depreciation on the returns for an earlier vacancy in 1277. The difference registered was £35 13s 0d for a four-month vacancy in 1302 as against £23 15s 11d for a two-month voidance in 1277.[5] A letter written by Edward I to Bishop McCarroll on 10 August 1302 throws light on a custom which was sometimes, though not generally, observed on the appointment of a bishop: 'Whereas the latter [the bishop], by reason of his new creation, is bound to give an annual pension to a clerk to be named by the K[ing], until the clerk be provided by the Bishop with a competent ecclesiastical benefice; and whereas the K[ing] names William de Langeton for that purpose; the K[ing] directs and prays the Bishop to grant to William, out of the Bishop's chamber such a pension as may become the giver and receiver, until William be duly provided with a competent ecclesiastical benefice.'[6]

In the first year of John McCarroll's episcopate a royal charter granted murage tolls to the citizens of Cork for six years. The money was to be spent on the maintenance and repair of the city walls but the king was to be kept informed of the amounts realized by the tolls.[7] By 1317 the citizens were released from accounting for the toll and from fees attached to wine-gauging, and in the following year one of Cork's most important and detailed charters was issued. It confirmed previous privileges, allowed a newly-elected mayor to be sworn in by his predecessor in presence of the citizens without having to go to Dublin, released the citizens from murage and other tolls throughout the royal dominions, granted them the assize of bread, weights and measures and empowered them to punish all malefactors except those convicted under crimes specifically reserved to the justiciar's court.[8]

Details of John McCarroll's activities as bishop of Cork are scanty. In 1307 he was involved in law proceedings over land at

4   *Cal. doc. Ire., 1171–1251*, no. 1519.

5   See Chapter VI on the feudal bishop.

6   *Cal. doc. Ire., 1302–07*, no. 102.

7   *Rot. pat. Hib.*, p. 6, no. 80.

8   *Chart. privil. immun.*, pp. 48, 49.

an unidentified place called Corrothir. At an assize of novel
disseisin John Martel, Adam Odoly and the bishop were
accused of having disseised David le Fleming of part of his
freehold at Corrothir. The freehold amounted to twenty-four
acres of land and one of moor, of which the bishop alienated ten
acres of land and the acre of moor. The lands were confiscated
by the king, but Bishop McCarroll maintained his claim and
upon investigation of the charter on which his claim was based,
'the fine (confiscation) imposed on him was pardoned by the
justiciar . . . [because] the tenements [were] given to the bishop
and his heirs and not to his church'.[9] From this rather ambiguous
statement it would appear that a distinction was made between
a personal grant to a bishop and a grant made to the church.
Bishop McCarroll next sought to improve the status of the
vicars attached to his cathedral and was so far successful that
the king ordered his justiciar to inquire whether it would be to
the detriment of the king or others to permit the bishop of Cork
to purchase an unnamed church and the church of Kilgobban
in his diocese and to appropriate them to the cathedral church
of Cork and to its vicars forever.

The Gill Abbey economy fared badly by comparison and was
unable even to support its personnel. The pipe rolls of the Irish
exchequer for the reign of Edward II contain an entry under
the heading, 'Abbey of Weym, county Cork', to the effect that
the king's Irish escheator 'answered nothing for the rents and
issues of the Abbey of Weym, Order of St. Augustine, in the
king's hands from May 14 to September 18, 1318, because the
temporalities of the abbey were not sufficient for the support of
the monks there; and were delivered to David de Driga, the
abbot-elect, by writ of September 1318'. A similar account,
headed 'Weeme Abbey, county Cork', is found among the lists
of wards and escheats for 1323–25, when the reigning bishop of
Cork (Philip of Slane) was apparently too preoccupied with
affairs of state to interest himself in the monastery's lack of
funds. Poverty continued to stalk Gill Abbey for the greater
part of the fourteenth century, but it did not deter aspirants to
the monastic life. That this was so is clear from a papal mandate
issued authorizing the 'transfer to the Augustinian monastery of
St. Mary, Kells . . . in the diocese of Meath, . . . William O'Michian, Augustinian canon of Gill Abbey (*de Antro Sancti Finbarri*)
in the diocese of Cork, which latter monastery is so much impoverished by wars etc. that its inmates, especially on account

9 *Cal. justic. rolls Ire., 1305–07*, p. 439.

of the multitude of them, cannot well be maintained'.[10] The restored territorial fortunes of Gill Abbey were clearly invoiced at the dissolution, but there is no indication as to the manner (impropriation or donation) in which these possessions were acquired.[11]

Bishop McCarroll was postulated for the archbishopric of Cashel in 1318 but the postulation was rejected and William FitzJohn of Ossory was appointed by papal provision. On 20 February 1321 John McCarroll was provided to Meath and was translated to Cashel in 1327.[12] He died in London in 1329 on his return from a visit to Rome.[13] Friar Clyn records his death as follows: '1329. *Circa festum Sti. Petri ad Vincula, obiit Londoniis Johannis McCarwyll, primo Episcopus Corkagiensis, postea Midensis, postremo factus Archiepiscopus Casselensis, de Curia Romana rediens.*' John McCarroll's elevation to the episcopal chair of Cork was the last occasion on which all customary formalities were observed, and even though the Cork chapter endeavoured to reassert its electoral rights, its members soon realized that a new era of ecclesiastical appointments had dawned with the elevation of John XXII to the papacy. Bishop McCarroll therefore stands Janus-like at the point of time when the medieval electoral custom receded before the more centralized system of provision which in our own day is again being adjusted and adapted to suit the requirements of the twentieth-century church.

PHILIP OF SLANE, O.P., 1321–27

Following the translation of John McCarroll to Meath, Philip of Slane, a member of the Dominican community of Saint Mary of the Island, was appointed bishop of Cork. This Friar Preacher may be regarded as the first bishop of Cork to be appointed by papal provision, although opinions vary as to the circumstances of his appointment. Rymer, following Harris-Ware, states that the pope, *at the request of the king*, promoted Philip of Slane to Cork.[14] Theiner gives 20 February 1321 as the date of provision; the *Calendar of Papal Letters* details a provision for 25 March and shows that on the same day concurrent

---

10   *Cal. papal letters, 1404–15*, p. 280.

11   *Extents Ir. mon. possessions*, pp. 141–3.

12   *Cal. papal letters, 1305–42*, pp. 162, 216.

13   Robin Flower, 'Manuscripts of Irish Interest in the British Museum', *Anal. Hib.*, no. 2 (1931), p. 339, quoting Cotton MS Vespasian, B. xi, f. 136.

14   Rymer, *Foedera*, iv, 54.

letters were issued to the dean and chapter of Cork, to the clergy and people of the diocese and to the king.[15] The royal mandate issued on 16 July leaves no room for ambiguity. It ordered the restoration of the temporalities of Cork to Philip, a Friar Preacher, *'whom the pope has preferred to the said bishopric'*.[16] It is not inconceivable that Philip of Slane as a cleric acceptable to the English king was preferred by the pope as a matter of policy. Compromise arrangements of this nature were a common feature of politico-papal arrangements at this period, and in the filling of key vacancies the king usually got the man he wanted.[17] Philip of Slane, who had attended the final trial of the Templars in 1307, belongs to the category of thirteenth- and fourteenth-century clerics and bishops who by training and inclination were civil servants and diplomats rather than churchmen. He was a king's clerk; the greater part of his career was spent as royal emissary to the court of Avignon, and in August 1321, shortly after his appointment as bishop of Cork, he departed on one of his many visits to England. John de Pembrok and John le Blound were appointed as his attorneys during his absence.[18] During the bishop's sojourn in England King Edward II asked and obtained reinforcements against the Scots and requested money or other gifts from the mayor and bishop of Cork.[19]

King Edward's parliamentary efforts at pacification in Ireland were part of a greater scheme which envisaged a far-reaching programme of ecclesiastical reform. For such a venture, the co-operation of the papacy was vital, and the better to ensure it he announced on 21 May 1324 that Philip of Slane, bishop of Cork, was on his way to the curia *pro quibusdam negotiis reformationem status terrae nostrae contingentibus*.[20] Bishop Philip was also seeking the rectification of certain defective papal letters touching a foundation of Dominican nuns.[21] In a letter to Cardinal Gaucelino the king requested the emendation of the letters and sought to enlist the cardinal's support in promoting the mission of Philip of Slane. King Edward wrote in similar vein to Archdeacon John de Lascapan of Nantes.[22] Pope John

15 *Cal. papal letters, 1305–42*, p. 212.

16 *Cal. pat. rolls, 1321–24*, p. 5.

17 Mollat, *The Popes at Avignon*, pp. 264–6.

18 *Cal. pat. rolls, 1321–24*, p. 10.

19 *Cal. close rolls, 1318–23*, p. 530.

20 Watt, 'Negotiations between Edward II and John XXII concerning Ireland', p. 6.

21 Rymer, *Foedera*, iv, 53: 'de quodam defectu in Litteris Papae corrigendo . . .'

22 Ibid., pp. 53–4: 'Rex, dilecto clerico suo, Johanni de Lescapon, Archidiacono Nannanetsi . . .'

XXII encouraged King Edward's project-scheme for a reformation of the state of Ireland but referred it back for consideration to the archbishops of Dublin and Cashel and to Philip, bishop of Cork. The archbishops of Armagh and Tuam are inexplicably excluded from the discussion notwithstanding that disturbances were widespread in the provinces of Ulster and Connacht and that the archbishop of Tuam was directly concerned in the second article of the revised proposals for reform. Before leaving Avignon Philip of Slane presented the pope with an abridged version of the *Topographia Hibernica* of Giraldus Cambrensis under the title *Libellus de descriptione Hiberniae* which he dedicated to John XXII and which he had translated into Provençal for the benefit of Avignon clerics not conversant with the Latin of Giraldus.[23]

On arrival at the court of Edward II, the committee nominated by the pope consulted with magnates and ministers of state and reconsidered the king's proposals. By 28 May 1325 Philip of Slane was again *en route* for Avignon with three amended proposals relative to Irish church affairs. The tenor of the articles was as follows:

1.   That sentence of excommunication should be publicly and solemnly promulgated on apostolical authority by the archbishops and other prelates in Ireland against disturbers of the peace and ministers who preached against the position of the king in Ireland. In other words, the clergy were to preach loyalty, and with this in view, special instructions were ordered to be delivered in cathedrals and parish churches at least four times a year.

2.   That small and poor bishoprics, the revenue of which did not exceed twenty, forty, or sixty pounds sterling, and which were ruled over by the mere Irish, should be united with archbishoprics and bishoprics of cities or other important centres.[24]

3.   That abbots and priors of monasteries and priories and all regular convents of whatever kind should admit English equally

---

23   This relic of Philip of Slane's mission is catalogued as B.M., Add. MS 17920, concerning which Robin Flower has the following reference in *Anal. Hib.*, no. 2 (1931), p. 317: 'In Add. MS British Museum, a MS written in the 14th century in Italy (or more probably in southern France) is a curious abbreviation of the Topographia under the title *Libellus de descriptione Hiberniae* (ff. 164–188b). In a prologue addressed to Pope John XXII, the writer describes himself as a certain Philip of the Dominican house of Cork. The Latin abbreviation is most interesting as the basis of a Provençal version in Add. MS xvii, 920, ff. 20–29, a manuscript of the 14th century which has been edited (indifferently, according to the review of Paul Meyer in *Romania*, xxi, 451) by J. Ulrich.'

24   The implications of this proposal for the diocese of Cork will be discussed in Chapter XVI.

with the mere Irish, a policy observed in monasteries ruled over
by the English. By such means it was hoped to break the national
exclusiveness of religious houses where racial disunion was a
miniscule reflection of the general attitude then prevailing
throughout the country.[25]

Notwithstanding their obvious ecclesiastical bearing, the
articles were not without definite political overtones in their
endeavour to enlist church support for promoting Anglo-Irish
interest in the country. But John XXII, while apparently agreeing
with the three-point suggestion, took no immediate steps towards
implementing the scheme. His only definite reaction was his effort to unite the sees of Cork and Cloyne on the grounds, as
expressed in a petition of Edward II, that the revenues of Cork
barely realized sixty pounds and those of Cloyne were not sufficient to support a bishop. The real excuse for amalgamation was
to bring the diocese of Cloyne, the major part of which lay *inter
Hibernicos*, under control of Cork where colonial interest was of
long standing. In response to the king's appeal John XXII
issued a mandate of amalgamation on 30 July 1326, the mandate
to take effect on the voidance of either see and without prejudice
to the metropolitan. Beyond this, the clergy were not instructed
to preach loyalty, nor were the regulars obliged to reorganize
their personnel by the admission of mixed nationalities into their
communities. A possible explanation of the pope's inactivity
may be found in the simultaneous removal from the sphere of
Irish affairs of the three sturdiest Anglo-papal churchmen of
the time. Archbishop Alexander Bicknor of Dublin fell from
royal favour, William FitzJohn of Cashel died in 1326 and
Philip of Slane early in March of the following year. Before
suitable replacements could be found for the vacancies Edward
II was deposed and the projected scheme for reformation was
allowed to lapse. The third article was revived in 1337 when
Edward III ordered that Irishmen faithful to him should be
admitted to religious houses of the English,[26] although in 1360
the same monarch commanded that 'mere Irishmen should be
excluded from civil posts and that all benefices should be conferred on English clerks'.

One important charter was issued for Cork during Philip of
Slane's episcopate. Charter 17 Edward II in 1323 confirmed all
former privileges and safeguarded the citizens' rights by the

---

25   In 1291 a general chapter of Friars Minor in Cork ended in a riot. In 1297 the
prelates of Armagh and Down were indicted for refusing to receive clerks of English
blood. In 1299 the English bishop of Kildare fulminated against friars who in the
Irish language spread the seeds of rebellion, etc.

26   Fitzmaurice and Little, *Franciscan province Ire.*, pp. 110–12, 127–8, 137.

clause that no representative of the king should take for the king's use against the will of the owners any victuals from citizens or merchants frequenting the city. Such provisions could only be purchased by authority of letters patent issued under the Great Seal of England.[27] The remaining charters for the fourteenth century were mostly confirmatory and contained little by the way of new privileges for the citizens.[28]

WALTER LE REDE, 1327–1330

The bull of John XXII ordering the amalgamation of the dioceses of Cork and Cloyne was not invoked on the death of Philip of Slane. Instead, the Cork chapter made an unsuccessful bid to circumvent a papal providee by the election of a bishop according to the traditional custom of the *congé d'élire*. Their nominee was John le Blound, dean of Cloyne, who had been appointed attorney during the first absence of Philip of Slane in 1321. The mandate for restoration of the temporalities was issued on 22 March 1327 in answer to the petition of John Went, canon of Cork, and William Netilton, vicar of Little Island: *Rex (recitans quod concesserat Johanni le Blound, decano ecclesiae Clonensis et electo ecclesiae Corcagensis, temporalia episcopatus predicti) mandavit, quod, facta extenta, acceptaque a prefato electo securitate ad respondendum Regi de ea, ipsi temporalia predicta liberari faciantur.*[29] The proceedings were pronounced irregular because the mandate was issued in the name of the deposed King Edward II, and it is doubtful if John le Blound was ever consecrated. A *congé d'élire*—issued according to Brady on 12 May 1327—directed the chapter to proceed to the election of a bishop, and the following statement from Ware's list of bishops would seem to endorse Brady's premise: 'If he [John le Blound] was consecrated, he sate not long, for licence of election was granted to the dean and chapter on 12 May 1327.' This is also quoted by Lynch.[30] John le Blound is mentioned in the annals of the Cork Dominicans as prior of Saint Mary of the Island in 1340, but there is no indication in the annals to the effect that he was ever bishop of Cork.

Pope John XXII ignored the independence bid of the Cork

---

27   *Cal. charter rolls, 1300–26*, p. 460.

28   *Chart. privil. immun.*, p. 79.

29   *Rot. pat. Hib.*, p. 37.

30   Lynch, *De praesulibus Hib.*, ii, 142: 'Si consecratus fuerit, non diu supervixit, compertum enim successoris eligendi facultatem 12 Maii 1327 a rege decano et capitulo concessum fuisse.'

chapter and in April appointed Canon Walter le Rede to the bishopric, which was described as 'void by the death of Philip'.[31] Concurrent letters were issued to the dean and chapter, to the clergy and people of the diocese, to the vassals of the church in Cork, to John, archbishop-elect of Cashel, and to the king. After his consecration by Bishop Peter of Palestrina on 12 July, Walter le Rede was bidden to betake himself at once to his diocese.[32] Theiner's account of the provision is less abrupt: he records that in 1327 Walter le Rede was preferred to the bishopric of Cork and was given permission to go there: *licentia ad suam ecclesiam eundi datur*.[33] On 18 October the temporalities were restored by the justiciar Thomas FitzJohn, earl of Kildare,[34] and Walter le Rede's canonry of Cork and prebend of Lismore were given to John le Preston, a pluralist who held canonries in Cashel, Cork and Waterford and the rectory of Kilcede in the diocese of Limerick.[35]

Our only record of the episcopate of Walter le Rede in Cork is his grant of land to the vicars choral of his cathedral church.[36] He was translated to Cashel in November 1329[37] and for the second time in two years the bull of John XXII was ignored. A new bishop was provided to Cork and the amalgamation of the dioceses was put back for another century.

JOHN DE BALLYCONINGHAM, 1330–1347

The provision of John de Ballyconingham on 5 January 1330 resulted in an ecclesiastical complication, an instance of overlapping between capitular election and papal provision. John, who had been rector of Ardwyn in the diocese of Down, had been appointed bishop of Down by the dean and chapter and with the king's approval, *rege assentiente*. He was confirmed and consecrated by the archbishop of Armagh who was apparently unaware that the appointment was reserved to the pope, who had meanwhile provided Ralph de Kilmessan, O.F.M., to the vacancy. A tactical solution was found by translating John de Ballyconingham to Cork with the suggestion that he could be

31   *Cal. papal letters 1305–42*, p. 256.

32   Ibid., p. 259.

33   Theiner, *Vetera mon.*, no. 466, p. 236.

34   *Cal. pat. rolls, 1327–33*, no. 185.

35   *Cal. papal letters, 1305–42*, p. 290.

36   Smith, *History of Cork*, i, 40.

37   *Cal. papal letters, 1305–42*, p. 307.

recalled again to Down if an amicable transfer could be arranged.[38] Theiner comes up with the statement that 'John of Cork and Ralph of Down would better serve God and their own souls if John were transferred to Down and Ralph to Cork',[39] while Lynch is incorrect in stating that John de Ballyconingham's election as bishop of Down was repudiated by John XXII.[40] Situations such as this were not unusual, and the case in question gives ample proof that the papacy endeavoured to settle such entanglements in the manner most acceptable to local preferences and prejudices. The filling of vacancies in Down, Connor and Ardagh in the second decade of the fourteenth century produced a confused series of elections, provisions and translations which paralleled the case of John de Ballyconingham. These overlappings were caused by 'Rome-runners' who infested the curia when vacancies were announced and whose position on the spot gave them advantage to secure appointments ahead of the local candidates. An instance of this nature occurred in Cork in the second half of the fourteenth century when Gerald FitzGerald, by means of forged letters and false representation, had himself appointed successor to the ailing Bishop Jordan Purcell.

The temporalities of Cork were restored to John de Ballyconingham on 30 May 1330 and a simultaneous document to the archbishop of Cashel contained an oath to be taken by both Ralph and John.[41] Luke Wadding in a reference to this procedure inclines to the opinion that 'some change in the form of the oath of consecration was then introduced . . . else why send over the form of a known and usually practised oath?'[42] For the remainder of his episcopate the records contain few references to John de Ballyconingham. In the year of his consecration he was nominated by John XXII to appoint to the office of public notary, and the papal mandate shows that the office was conferred on Thomas Johannis Bouer of the diocese of Ross, on two persons chosen by Bishop Henry of Saint David's, on two chosen by the bishop of Cork and on three selected by Stephen, archbishop of Armagh.[43] In 1330 Archdeacon Henry de

38   Ibid., pp. 315, 320.

39   Theiner, *Vetera mon.*, no. 492, p. 249.

40   Lynch, *De praesulibus Hib.*, ii, 143: 'Verum a pontifice Joanni XXII illa electio rejecta est, unde sperato episcopatu Joannis excidit.'

41   Theiner, *Vetera mon.*, pp. 249–50.

42   Luke Wadding, *Hibernia Primatialis et Episcopalis*, ii, 96, g. 13.

43   *Cal. papal letters, 1305–42*, p. 324.

Thrapton became chancellor of the exchequer and in 1345 Archdeacon William of Epeworth was excommunicated; in neither case have we any inkling of subsequent episcopal reaction. During the years of these archidiaconal undertakings John de Ballyconingham and his chaplain, Adam Mansell, were involved in a tortuous case concerning the theft of a cow from Adam Coppinger. The cow was taken from Corragh and carried to the bishop's manor of Fayd, and notwithstanding Coppinger's evidence the bishop insisted on his claims to the lands of Corragh 'as in right of his church of St. Fynbarry'. The case dragged on until 1340 when the bishop emerged victorious and Coppinger lost his cow.[44] The final entry for John de Ballyconingham's episcopacy is dated 1345 when, as a result of a petition filed by him, by the archbishop of Cashel and the bishops of Lismore, Cloyne and Emly, the pope commissioned the bishop of Limerick to grant dispensation to Earl Maurice of Kildare to marry Joan, daughter of Earl Maurice of Desmond; the couple were related to the third and fourth degrees of kindred.[45] Bishop John de Ballyconingham died on 29 May 1347.

JOHN ROCHE, 1347–1358

John Roche or de Rupe was elected to the bishopric—there is no record of his provision—and was consecrated in December 1347. His only recorded function is his appropriation of the vicarage of Corbally to the vicars choral in 1348, but for all that the years of his episcopacy left their mark on the civic history of Cork and were a period during which attention was once again focused on the prevailing lack of educational facilities—a lack which affected all ranks of the clergy from the episcopate through the high benefice-holders and prebendaries down to the not-infrequently unlettered country cleric who lived in a predominantly oral society. A second feature of these years was the virulent epidemic of bubonic plague, commonly known as the Black Death, which struck Ireland in August 1348, making its first appearance in Howth and Drogheda and probably also in Cork which was then engaged in a brisk trade with Bristol from where the epidemic is said to have come to Ireland. The plague, which travelled by way of the thronged trade routes, spread with vicious speed and may be regarded as a negative indication of the degree to which commerce had unified Europe and penetrated into the most remote areas on the periphery of

44 Webster, *The Diocese of Cork*, p. 405.

45 *Cal. papal letters, 1342–62*, p. 164.

the continent.[46] The Black Death left its mark particularly on Irish cities and towns. Dublin and Drogheda 'were almost destroyed and wasted of men.' In Dublin alone some fourteen thousand are said to have died, and by Lent 1349 the plague reached Kilkenny. Here eight Friars Preachers died in one day; twenty-five Friars Minor had already died in Drogheda and twenty-three in Dublin, and from the Franciscan Friar Clyn comes the most graphic eye-witness account of the ravages of the pestilence:

> Hardly in any one house did one only die, but commonly man and wife with their children and household went one way, that of death. And I, Friar John Clyn, of the order of Minors and the convent of Kilkenny, have written those notable facts which happened in my time in this book, as I have learned them as an eye-witness, or from trustworthy accounts, and lest notable deeds should perish with time and recede from the memory of those to come, seeing so many evils and the whole world as it were in evil plight, I, awaiting death among the dead, have set them down in writing . . . and lest the writing should perish with the writer . . . I leave parchment to continue the work, if perchance any man survive, or any of the race of Adam may escape this pestilence and continue the work so begun.[47]

Friar Clyn succumbed to the Black Death soon afterwards. An inquisition taken in Cork in 1451 returned that 'in the time of the said pestilence the greater part of the citizens of Cork and other faithful men of the king dwelling there went the way of all flesh'.[48] It was also returned that because of the pestilence and of the destruction and waste done daily by the king's Irish enemies dwelling near the city, 'as also by fires occurring there by mischance and various other disturbances', the people of Cork were so impoverished that they were unable to pay the required fee-farm of eighty marks for their city and six marks for 'le Faygh'. The king granted them respite till the morrow of the following Michaelmas and one year afterwards to make good the deficit and in order that he might by inquiry satisfy himself as to the causes of their inability to pay. Dublin, New Ross and Clonmel were similarly successful in a petition for assistance to redeem them from impoverishment resultant upon the plague.

46 Denys Hay, *The Medieval Centuries*, p. 124.
47 *The Annals of Ireland . . . by Friar John Clyn and Thady Dowling*, pp. 35–8.
48 Otway-Ruthven, *Med. Ire.*, p. 268, quoting Genealogical Office MS 192.

Mortality figures for the secular clergy were perhaps less high than those registered for the friars, but their depleted ranks seem to have been filled at random and without reckoning the character or quality of would-be aspirants. Ill-considered investments of this nature were to pay unwholesome dividends within the next century and a half. The depleted ranks of the clergy offered untold scope for the exercise of royal prerogative, for despite the extension of papal provisions and the decline of English power and prestige, royal presentation was repeatedly invoked during the fourteenth century. Royal influence over vacancies in Cork is seen especially in regard to the church of Beaver or Carrigaline and to the free royal chapel of Holy Trinity. Royal appointments may be followed from 1350 to 1392, and in no case is there evidence of friction between the king and the reigning bishop.[49]

The great dearth of educational centres in fourteenth-century Ireland came into prominence in 1348 through a petition addressed by the Augustinians to Edward III, in which they pointed out that since 'there was and is no study of the liberal arts and Holy Writ in Ireland' it was their custom to send six Irish friars to England to study that they might be able to preach the word of God more effectively. On their return to Ireland, four of these friars would celebrate divine service daily in the four Augustinian churches of Dublin, Drogheda, Cork and Rosspoint, 'for the souls of the king's progenitors and their heirs'. The students selected for English schools (*studia*) were normally subsidized by their Irish brethren who now, because of wars and various adversities and because the charitable contributions of the people had fallen off, found themselves unable to honour their commitments. The friars appealed to the king for help, and while Edward III made alternative provision for the students his settlement was far from measuring up to the educational needs of the time.[50] It is not easy to be definitive on the subject of clerical education in Ireland at this period, but it seems certain that following the destruction of the school of Armagh between 1184 and 1186 no effort was made to repair the educational deficit until the opening years of the fourteenth century.

In 1311 Archbishop John Lech of Dublin sought papal permission to establish a university in Dublin on the plea that while there were some doctors and bachelors of theology in Ireland and others who lectured as masters in arts, there was no school for higher learning (*scholarium universitas vel generale*

49 See final Appendix: Priests of Cork.

50 *Cal. pat. rolls, 1348–50*, p. 114.

studium) in Ireland, in Scotland or in the Isle of Man. The disadvantage under which Irish students laboured was aggravated,
he said, by the hazards and expense of overseas travel. Pope
Clement V in a bull dated 13 July 1312 authorized the setting
up of an Irish university, but the project was halted by the
death of John Lech in 1313, following which the see of Dublin
remained vacant for four years. The scheme was revived under
the more dynamic Alexander Bicknor in 1320–21; the organization of the new university followed the lines of English
universities and its legislation suggests the prior existence of
schools of theology run by the Irish Franciscan and Dominican
friars. Courses in the university were to be mainly in theology
and canon law, a faculty of divinity was established and three
doctors of divinity were appointed by Edward III. The first
appointees were William Hardite (de Hardits), O.P., Henry
Cogry, O.F.M., and Edmund Karnardin (de Kermerdyn or
Caermarthen), O.P., who later became bishop of Ardfert. The
archbishop reserved to himself and his successors the appointment of a secular or regular priest to the university personnel,
and first choice fell on William Rodiart (de Rodyard), dean of
Saint Patrick's, who was appointed doctor and teacher of canon
law and first chancellor of the university.[51] The university lacked
the support of both English government and Irish people and it
quickly languished, even though Lionel, duke of Clarence, tried
to revive it in 1364 by granting land to the dean and chapter of
Saint Patrick's on condition that they should offer mass for the
king's welfare and employ an Augustinian friar 'to teach theology
in a house of scholars, for whose maintenance the grant was
made'.[52] This also proved abortive, but Professor Curtis quotes
the university as maintaining an uneasy and vague existence
down to the sixteenth century, and he cites an entry in Archbishop Alen's register which tells that at a synod convened by
Archbishop Walter FitzSimons in 1494 sums were voted by the
suffragan sees of Dublin for the upkeep of lecturers in the
university for a period of seven years. The annual total netted
from five sees amounted to about twenty-seven pounds.[53]

How then were clerics educated for the ministry? Clerics in
pre-Carolingian times had been trained in bishops' households;
clerics since Trent have received specific seminary training, but
the problem of mass education for the clergy was never properly

51   Fitzmaurice and Little, *Franciscan province Ire.*, p. 108.

52   Aubrey Gwynn, 'Anglo-Irish Church Life in the Fourteenth and Fifteenth
Centuries', in Corish, ed., *Irish Catholicism*, ii, no. 4, p. 31.

53   Curtis, *Med. Ire.*, p. 366.

solved in the Middle Ages. The universities represented a possible and partial solution to the problem, but here again the
number of clerics who could secure university education was
marginal and presented its own crop of problems. Generally
speaking, the monastic orders, particularly the mendicants, had
their own schools or *studia particularia*, though when it came to
higher education the Irish friars had no other option but to go
abroad for degrees. The petition of the Augustinians (1348)
shows that they had not yet established their own house of
studies. Medieval Ireland does not seem to have had any
organized system of grammar and chantry schools;[54] Irish
records are silent on this subject. Still an argument from silence
is an unreliable hypothesis and it is probable that some form of
collegiate or chantry education was provided, and that students
showing promise were sent for higher studies to Oxford and
Cambridge. Their expenses were defrayed through the conferment of certain benefices, prebends or 'livings' upon them.
Benefices of this nature were in the gift of the bishop or in that
of the king or lay magnate who had the right of presentation to
certain churches. The king's nominees for benefices were known
as king's clerks (*clerici regis*), and even in an age when pluralism
was a byword the amassed benefices of other pluralists were
dwarfed by those held by the king's favourites. Papal policy
approved and even encouraged the retention of benefices by
clerics pursuing advanced studies even though this principle of
promoting clerical education cut right across another important
principle of church reform, namely, the drive against pluralism
and non-residence. A solution was found in dispensing beneficed
clerics for seven years or so from assuming priest's orders on
condition that they became subdeacons and provided a deputy
or vicar to see after the needs of their parishes. This system left
much to be desired, it was limited in scope, it was of advantage
only to those lucky enough to have benefices and did nothing to
help the vast clerical proletariat of unbeneficed stipendiary
priests who did most of the church's pastoral work and who were
apparently as uneducated as they were poor.

The will of John de Wynchedon in 1306 mentions clerks in
connection with the churches of Holy Trinity, Saint Peter's,
Saint Catherine's, Saint Mary, Shandon, Saint John's and Saint
Philip's. If these were student clerks, to whom was their

---

54 Gwynn, 'Anglo-Irish Church Life', p. 31, cites an inquisition of Edward III
which shows that the canons of Saint Thomas's Abbey in Dublin were charged with
the duty of providing for the support and education of twenty-four young clerks
(*clericulos*) who lived in the abbey for as long as they wished to remain there to pursue
their studies.

education entrusted? To the chancellor of the diocese? If so, where did he get his own degrees, if he had degrees? What was the scope of his instructions? How did the cathedral school of Cork compare with those of other dioceses? How far ahead, or behind, was a cleric educated here as compared with those he met at Oxford? The papal registers leave the reader in no doubt as to the large number of Cork clerics who attended Oxford, and while this points to a reasonable standard of local education the actual situation can never go beyond the realm of surmise and speculation.

In 1348—the year of the Black Death and of the Augustinian petition—the cause of education was championed by Richard FitzRalph of Armagh who showed his concern in a sermon preached on 25 March. Taking as his text the occurring feast of the Blessed Virgin he enumerated three instances in which Marian intercession should be sought, namely, 'because of the pestilence which is flooding the land, because of the abounding malice of men, and because of the ignorance that is due to the lack of all higher education' (*propter nostram insipienciam qui remoti sumus ab omni studio generali*).[55] Another effort was made to establish a university in Dublin in 1358 when the king promised special protection to scholars travelling thither,[56] but the plaint of Irish clerics in 1363 tells its own story. This was a joint petition which some eighteen Irish and Anglo-Irish clerks presented to Pope Urban V in November 1363, in which they informed the pope that 'by reason of pestilence and wars in these parts there is a great lack of clerks and the value of benefices is small'. Each petitioner asks for some benefice in Ireland, and 'since the churches of Ireland were not otherwise burdened by papal provisions' they prayed the pope 'to expedite the said petitions especially as the petitioners come from the ends of the earth, and this is the first roll he has received from them'. The pope 'must not be surprised that the petitioners have no scholastic degrees, inasmuch as in all Ireland there is no university or *studium*'. Nevertheless these same petitioners are not afraid of being rejected on examination.[57] The dioceses represented on this roll of petitions are Meath, Dublin, Kilfenora, Limerick, Down, Cork, Cashel, Ardfert and Cloyne. Relative to Cork, Thomas Mychyan petitioned for a benefice in the gift of the bishop of Cork, valued at sixty gold florins with cure of souls (*cum cura*) or twenty without, and Richard de Valle,

55   Gwynn, 'Richard FitzRalph, Archbishop of Armagh', *Studies*, xxii (1933), 399.

56   Fitzmaurice and Little, *Franciscan province Ire.*, p. 109.

57   *Cal. papal petitions, 1342–1419*, p. 467.

'skilled in law, of Cork', asked for the treasurership of Limerick valued at sixty gold florins, 'especially as it has been long void, and by reason of its small value has not been given to anyone by the pope or by the ordinary'. Pope Urban V granted to each petitioner the benefice for which he asked, and in this way David Gower of the diocese of Limerick, scholar of canon law, was given the canonry and prebend of Killaspugmullane (Kyllaspowk Molane) in Cork. The plea for an Irish university was to be voiced again in 1465 in words repetitive of the appeal of the Irish clerks, but this effort too was destined to go into the limbo of unachieved aspirations. Meantime the barometer of clerical education, discipline and prestige continued to drop.

GERALD BARRY, 1359–1393

Gerald, who was dean of Cork, was provided to the see before 14 February 1359,[58] and although Eubel credits him with a second provision on 8 November 1362 his statement is not endorsed in any other source.[59] Nor does Eubel give any explanation as to why the second provision was issued. Notwithstanding this initial vagueness, Gerald Barry is a gratifying subject for investigation in that, unlike his immediate predecessors, he managed to get into the official records where he is depicted as a person of some importance in the contemporary social and political milieu. In 1360 he was nominated to a council specially convened in Waterford to discuss problems attendant on the settlement of wages for the servant and labouring classes.[60] These later years of the reign of the third Edward saw the unsuccessful attempt to halt the gaelicization of the Anglo-Norman colonists and the shaping of the Irish parliament into a mould it was to preserve until the summoning of the Reformation parliament in Dublin in 1536. An epoch-making parliament convened in 1372 added to the commons two clerical proctors from each diocese: Gerald Barry was summoned to attend this parliament by mandate of King Edward III.[61] Here we have one of the earliest instances of a bishop of Cork, as distinct from an abbot *de Antro*, attending parliament. Even more epochal was the parliament of 1380 which was held in Dublin on

58 Ibid., pp. 311, 377.

59 Eubel, *Hierarchia Catholica Medii Aevi*, p. 211.

60 Smith, *History of Cork*, ii, 137.

61 *Rot. pat. Hib.*, i, pt. 1, p. 83: 'Rex, G. Episcopo Corkagensis mandavit quod in propria persona apud Balahath die Martis intersit una cum procuratoribus pro clero sui diocesis ad tractandum super his quae custode Hibernie et consilio ordinari contigeret.'

Saturday in the morrow of All Saints' Day. Clerical attendance
at this parliament included the archbishops of Cashel and Tuam,
the guardian of the spiritualities of the archbishop of Armagh
and of the bishop of Meath, and the bishops of Kildare, Leighlin,
Ossory, Ferns, Lismore and Waterford, Cork, Limerick, Cloyne.
Clogher, Ardfert, Emly, Elphin, Down, Killala, Clonfert, Ross
Connor, Clonmacnoise, Raphoe, Breffny and Derry. Gone now
was the episcopal opposition which voiced strenuous resistance
to the proposed taxation of clerical proctors at de Windsor's
parliament in 1375. This assembly of 1380 voted certain new
customs which were enumerated as 43 Edward III and which
were to be levied and collected for three years at the ports of the
land. The assessment was on herrings, salmon and other fish,
on every hin or pipe of wine, on dead meat, wheat, barley, wool,
salt, etc.[62]

Bishop Gerald Barry was among the prelates and nobles who
assembled in Saint Peter's church in 1381 to elect a successor to
Edmund Mortimer, earl of March and Ulster, who had died in
the house of the Friars Preachers. Early in the following year he
was dispensed because of infirmity from attendance at parliament.[63] On 8 February 1387 and on 27 November 1392 he was
ordered by royal mandate to present Thomas Barton[64] and
Maurice Morgan[65] to the prebend of Holy Trinity, and on 18
April 1390 he was mandated to grant the prebend of Beaver to
John Pelyn.[66] Both benefices were in the gift of the king, and the
appointments were made without friction although there is a
suggestion of a clash of sorts in January 1383 when the king,
exercising the royal prerogative, admitted John Horsington to
custody of the rectories of the churches of Kinsale and of Saint
John the Evangelist in 'le Fairgh' near Cork.[67] The exercise of
the royal prerogative was not confined solely to providing incumbents to vacant benefices; cognizance was also taken of
church lands, as is clear from the following *Inspeximus* of the
assignment of the dower of Johanna Rocheford in 1372. Grants
of land in Cork made to her by Edward III included 'the
advowson of the vicarage of Beaver (Carrigaline), a third part of

62   Curtis and McDowell, *Irish Historical Documents*, p. 62.

63   *Rot. pat. Hib.*, i, pt. 1, p. 14b: 'Rex ad peticionem Geraldi episcopi Corkagensis et
racione infirmitatis eius, concessit ei quod ad parliamentum aut concilium minime
compellatur.'

64   Ibid., p. 132.

65   *Cal. pat. Rolls, 1391–96*, p. 203.

66   *Cal. pat. rolls, 1388–92*, p. 241.

67   *Rot. pat. Hib.*, i, pt. 1, p. 58.

the burgage of Beaver, valued at £4. 8s. od. per annum, of Douglas, valued at £4. 12s. od. per annum, and a third part of the fishery there; a third part of the mill of Kilnagleragh; one mark revenue from Ballibetagh; a third part of a carucate of land in Shandon with one-third of all tenements therein, and a third part of the profits of Beaver and Shandon'.[68]

Cork during the two final decades of Gerald Barry's episcopate was a city greatly impoverished and 'much weakened . . . by the King's Irish enemies'.[69] A record dated 1376 (and already quoted) shows that at an inquisition taken before Gerald, bishop of Cork, it was proved that the citizens 'on account of divers tribulations and risks of the roads' could not come to the exchequer at Carlow (Catherlagh) without a great posse of soldiers.[70] At that date they owed £45 13s 4d fee-farm for their city and had nothing with which to pay. By 1389 all mention of le Fayth had disappeared, and in this year the citizens were pardoned eighty marks for the city. The final entry for the fourteenth century is dated October 1392 and is again a petition from the mayor for pardon and remission of 'arrears of the farm of their city for four years past, . . . for the defence and fortification of the city and the repair of its walls and bridges in consideration of [the] damage thereto by reason of the invasion and proximity of the king's enemies'.[71] In the midst of these appeals we find evidence too that the citizens refused to pay twenty pounds out of the fee-farm to the earl of Desmond in lieu of expenses allowed him by the king for his services in providing escort for merchants plying between Cork and Limerick.[72] Other pointers to Cork's impoverishment at this date were the many permissions granted for importing corn because of the devastation of the neighbouring countryside,[73] and the prohibitions issued to the city merchants in respect of trading with Irish enemies without special license. The provision trade of the city was cramped in 1394 when Richard II forbade the export of provisions from all corporate towns.[74] These and other similar enactments were grievously detrimental to the city's economy, and although Cork had become a staple

68   *The Red Book of the Earls of Kildare*, ed. G. Mac Niocaill, entry no. 151.

69   *Cal. pat. rolls, 1388–92*, p. 152.

70   *Cal. pat. rolls, 1374–77*, p. 207.

71   *Cal. pat. rolls, 1391–96*, p. 203.

72   Graves, *Roll of the Proceedings of the King's Council in Ireland*, pp. 120, 127.

73   *Rot. pat. Hib.*, i, pt. 1, pp. 136, 142.

74   *Cal. close rolls, 1392–96*, p. 219.

town early in the fourteenth century, she soon lost her monopoly, and the time was not far distant when for a brief moment she was to break away from her traditional loyalty and rally to the support of two Yorkist pretenders.

Bishop Gerald Barry died on 4 January 1393 after one of the longest episcopates of the medieval diocese of Cork. He was buried, according to Caulfield, in his own cathedral.[75] The see remained vacant for the next two years, and in the wider sphere of church affairs a disputed election in 1378 had resulted in the geographical division of Christendom into two bitterly hostile and rival obediences.

75   Caulfield, *Annals of St. Fin Barre's Cathedral, Cork*, p. 8.

XV

The Diocese of Cork
and the Great Western Schism

ROMAN POPES		AVIGNON POPES		PISAN ANTI-POPES	
Urban VI	1378–1389	Clement VII	1378–1394		
Boniface IX	1389–1404	Benedict XIII	1394–1417		
Innocent VII	1404–1406				
Gregory XII	1406–1415			Alexander V	1409–1410
				John XXIII	1410–1415

BISHOPS OF CORK			KINGS OF ENGLAND	
Gerald Barry	1358–1393	(Roman Obedience)	Richard II	1377–1399
Roger Ellesmere	1396–1406	(Roman Obedience)	Henry IV	1399–1413
Richard Kynmoure	1406–1409	(Roman Obedience)		
Milo FitzJohn	1409–1431	(Roman Obedience)	Henry V	1413–1422
Patrick Foxe	1409–1417	(Pisan Obedience)		

The seventy-three years of the 'Babylonish captivity' at Avignon
(1305–78) caused the papacy to be looked upon with disfavour
and suspicion by all who distrusted France and her kings and
who resented the rich harvest of favours and concessions which
that country reaped as a result of papal residence on French
territory.[1] This period saw especially the emergence of strong
anti-papal tendencies in England which were given expression
in the statutes of Provisors (1351) and Praemunire (1353), the
one abolishing the pope's right to nominate to ecclesiastical
vacancies in England, the other forbidding appeals to Rome.
During this period too John Wycliffe developed his politico-
ecclesiastical campaign against papal authority. The Avignon
popes cannot have been unaware of the disadvantages of their
position, but they allowed opportunity after opportunity to slip
by until eventually it required all the persuasiveness of Catherine
of Siena to urge Gregory XI back to Rome in 1376. The elation
caused by this achievement was short-lived. Pope Gregory's
death on 27 March 1378 precipitated a crisis in church history in

1 C. M. D. Crowder, 'Henry V, Sigismund and the Council of Constance: A
Re-examination', *Historical Studies*, iv (1963), 93.

which new and unwelcome theories on papal authority and church government were mooted by thinkers who exploited the occasion to capitalize on the embarrassment of the papacy by the inauguration of the movement known as the conciliar movement. The implications of this new trend, which aimed at instituting an ecclesiastical equivalent of parliamentary government, were far-reaching and revolutionary. From an early date in the history of the church the primacy of the pope had been an acknowledged principle; the councils of the Middle Ages had been summoned and presided over by successive popes and their chief function had been to register the papal will. Now it was stated that supreme power did not reside in the pope but in a general council representing the entire church. Originally held by John of Jandun and Marsiglio of Padua, the prolongation of the schism caused these theories to be adopted and elaborated on by Pierre D'Ailly, Gerson and others who declared that since Christ had accepted the authority of the Blessed Virgin and Saint Joseph, so must the pope submit to the judgement of his mother the church. By 1408 even the cardinals were ready to fall in with conciliarist ideas, not because they believed a general council was superior to the pope but because in the situation then obtaining only a general council could decide who was pope.

The circumstances leading up to the schism revolved upon the papal election held twelve days after the death of Pope Gregory XI. The cardinals' choice was Bartholomew Prignani, archbishop of Bari, who took the name of Urban VI. He was an Italian who would not be likely to remove the papacy again to Avignon, and consequently the turmoil which had accompanied the conclave subsided. As archbishop of Bari, Urban VI had been unpretentious and kindly; as pope he proved so unbearable that one by one the non-Italian cardinals left Rome for Fondi in the kingdom of Naples. They were shortly joined by the Italian members of the sacred college, and at Fondi on 24 September they elected a French cardinal, Robert of Geneva, who called himself Clement VII. Pope Urban excommunicated the assembly at Fondi and created a new college of cardinals, but the die was cast. Two popes were now claiming the allegiance of Christendom and each had been elected by the same body of cardinals. After an unsuccessful attempt to drive Urban VI from Rome, Clement VII sailed for Avignon on 20 June 1379.

Europe was henceforth divided between adherence to a Roman or a French obedience. The decisions ultimately reached reflect the extension of political considerations into the field of ecclesiastical concern to such an extent that the church found her domestic problems judged in the light of external political problems rather than on their own merits.[2] The adherence of saints, mystics and leading theologians to both obediences further aggravated a situation which produced doubt and confusion in men of good will everywhere. England, from a traditional policy of opposition to France, sponsored Urban VI; so did Germany and most of Italy. Spain, Scotland and France declared for Clement VII. The situation in Ireland reflected that obtaining on the continent. Areas where English or Anglo-Norman power was strongest adhered to the Roman obedience; political expediency suggested the Avignon obedience in places where English power had recently lost prestige through the Gaelic resurgence of the fourteenth century. Hatred of England rather than conviction of the righteousness of the Clementine cause was what set the pace; but while Clement VII and his successors had some supporters in Armagh and Tuam, Ireland's sympathies lay mainly with the Roman claimants, even allowing for subsequent re-shufflings when the two obediences became three after 1409.[3]

English influence was more pronounced in the province of Cashel than in those of Armagh and Tuam, yet even here local peculiarities abounded. At the commencement of the schism the archbishop of Cashel was the Franciscan Philip of Torrington who is believed to have been English or at least Anglo-Irish. Torrington, who was a graduate in theology from Oxford and Cambridge, was provided to Cashel in 1373 by Gregory XI, and in the first year of the schism he was sent as representative of England to treat with Urban VI on certain affairs of urgency. Under such an ardent Urbanist the province of Cashel might have been expected to support the Roman claimants all through, but this was not so. On Torrington's death Clement VII appointed an Irish Franciscan, Michael, provincial minister of Ireland, to the vacancy on 22 October 1382. Friar Michael does not appear to have received either royal assent or general recognition[4] and there followed a four-year vacancy during which the temporalities of the see were absorbed by the exchequer. In the end the Urbanist cause prevailed and an Anglo-Irish prelate, Peter Hackett, was confirmed by Pope Urban VI in 1384. Hackett was succeeded in 1406 by an Irishman, Richard O Hedian, at the time of whose appointment the Avignon cause

2   Ibid.

3   Aubrey Gwynn, 'Ireland and the English Nation at the Council of Constance', *R.I.A. Proc.*, xlv, sect. c (1940), pp. 203–4.

4   Fitzmaurice and Little, *Franciscan province Ire.*, p. 162.

had suffered many defections. It seems probable that Archbishop
O Hedian recognized the jurisdiction of the later Roman claimants, but the general situation in the archdiocese was extremely
complicated.

Of the ten suffragan sees of the province, Waterford and
Lismore—which had been united in 1363—were to be in
English hands for the next hundred years. Cork and Cloyne,
which were to be united after the schism, had been already in
English control for over a century. Limerick, having suffered
English rule for the greater part of the thirteenth and fourteenth
centuries, entered the new century under an Irish prelate,
Cornelius O'Dea, who was ruling in 1400. The position in Emly
appears to have been in dispute, and the dioceses of Ross,
Ardfert, Killaloe and Kilfenora were under native control.[5] Lack
of records makes it impossible to give an accurate estimate of the
number of Irish bishops who favoured the Avignon obedience,
for the Avignon registers covering the years of the schism are
no longer extant. Such lacunae to the contrary, there can be no
doubt that except for a disputed succession in the last decade of
the schism, the diocese of Cork favoured the Roman claimants
all through. Two extracts from the *acta* of Boniface IX (successor to Urban VI) confirm Cork's Romanist loyalties for the
last years of Bishop Gerald Barry's episcopate. The first is dated
1391 and states that 'John Rede, bachelor of canon law . . . is
litigating in the apostolic palace about the archdeaconry of
Cork'.[6] The second, under date 1393, reads, 'To the archdeacon
of Limerick, William Wynchidon, canon of Cork and a foreign
bishop named: mandate to collate and assign to Richard Went,
treasurer of Cork, student at Oxford for seven years in canon
and civil law, the perpetual vicarage of Kynsale in the diocese of
Cork, valued fifty marks, void by the death of Remund de
Garri.'[7]

The death of Urban VI on 15 October 1389 and the election
of Boniface IX on 2 November ended all hopes of an early
settlement of the schism, then in its eleventh year. A second
effort at conciliation proved equally abortive on the death of
Clement VII in 1394. The last months of Pope Clement's life
were darkened by the development of conciliarist theories in
the University of Paris; these theories were adopted by the
university to justify its determination to end the schism even

5   Gwynn, 'Ireland and the English Nation', pp. 203–4.

6   *Cal. papal letters, 1362–1404*, p. 402.

7   Ibid., p. 413.

at the expense of abruptly terminating the careers of both rival popes.[8] Under Pope Clement's successor, the Spaniard Pedro de Luna who called himself Benedict XIII, there emerged a dramatic struggle between the Avignon pope and the French which ultimately led to the councils of Pisa and Constance, to the full development of the conciliar theory and to the building up of the theory concerning the liberties of the Gallican church. Benedict XIII may be truly said to have played all his rivals off the stage. He was a scholar, a diplomat, a jurist, who after his formal deposition retired to his family fortress at Peñiscola in Spain where he continued till the end of his days to regard himself as the lawfully-elected pope. He died in September 1424. Of the Roman popes, Boniface IX died in 1404; his successor Innocent VII, after a brief pontificate of two years, was succeeded by Gregory XII who governed the church of the 'Roman obedience' from 1406 until his formal abdication at Constance in 1415.

ROGER ELLESMERE, 1396–1406

On 3 December 1395 Roger Ellesmere was provided to the see of Cork by Pope Boniface IX[9] and in the following March the justiciary was ordered by Richard II 'to deliver the temporalities of the bishopric of Cork to Roger Ellesmere, provided thereto by the pope, whose fealty the king has taken and to whom he has restored the said temporalities'.[10] The records do not usually give evidence of the repayment to newly-elected bishops of the income derived from episcopal temporalities *during vacancy*.[11] In Roger Ellesmere's case we have explicit evidence that the revenue of the see was granted to him 'from the death of Gerard [*sic*], the late bishop, until 31 March last when the king caused the temporalities to be delivered to him, and licence for him to receive the same whether absent from Ireland or present, by his proctors . . . and to bring away to England the monies arising therefrom for one year and to enjoy them'.[12] Roger Ellesmere was apparently a king's clerk, one of those who formed an essential part of the organized government of both England and Ireland, and even though there is no extant record of his

8   Philip Hughes, *A History of the Church*, ii, 243.

9   Eubel, *Hierarchia Catholica Medii Aevi*, ii, 211.

10   *Cal. pat. rolls, 1391–96*, p. 722, under date 1396.

11   It will be recalled that a similar arrangement was made in the case of Robert MacDonnchada.

12   *Cal. pat. rolls, 1391–96*, p. 723.

activities in Cork there is a curious reference in the papal registers to a union of Cork and Ardfert in the year 1400. This reference is contained in a mandate directing the prior of Bridgetown (*de Villa Pontis*), Fermoy, to collate and assign to Nicholas Oconyll, canon of Cloyne, the perpetual vicarages of the churches of Clonmyn and Ruskyn in the diocese of Cloyne, notwithstanding that the appointee already held the canonry and prebend of Inskarech (Inniscarra) in Cloyne and the annexed perpetual vicarage of Addirpon (Macroom), and that the pope had 'lately ordered provision to be made to him of canonries with expectation of prebends of the churches canonically united [*sic*] of Cork and Ardfert'.[13] In the absence of other entries which might explain or qualify the foregoing, it may be taken as simply conveying that Nicholas Oconyll was to be given prebends constituted from a number of small adjoining parishes, some prebends being in Cork and others in Ardfert.

Within a year of Roger Ellesmere's provision a deadlock involving the archdeaconry of Cork was solved in a manner indicative of the decline and the abuses then prevalent in the church. John Rede, a canon of Limerick, had been provided to the archdeaconry by Pope Urban VI, but the provision was impeded in consequence of a quarrel with a certain Robert Roche who eventually took possession. Pope Urban had committed the case to an auditor, but Roche died still in possession and Pope Boniface IX appointed a second auditor to surrogate Robert Roche's right (if he had such) to John Rede, and to admit him to the archdeaconry which was to be collated and assigned to him. By this time (1397/8) it was found necessary to remove William Gulton of Dublin who had meantime seized upon the vacancy. Gulton duly resigned and the pope again ordered that John Rede should be restored to the archdeaconry, notwithstanding that he was a pluralist holding 'the canonry and prebend of Donoghmore in Limerick, . . . [that he was] litigating in the apostolic palace about the canonry and prebend of Regale in Cashel, . . . [that he had] recently had provision made to him of the deanery of Waterford, . . . [and] had [secured] canonries [and prebends] in Ferns and Lismore, with expectation of prebends . . . in the diocese of Lincoln'.[14] From an entry dated 1401 we learn that John Rede was only a deacon and that he was dispensed 'during five years not to be bound to have himself ordained priest on account of his deanery . . . or of any

---

13   *Cal. papal letters, 1396–1404*, p. 451.
14   *Cal. papal letters, 1362–1404*, p. 542.

other benefices, with or without cure, which he holds or may obtain'.[15] To his already long list of benefices John Rede was also provided to the parish church of Crisselow in the diocese of Limerick. Bishop Roger Ellesmere died in 1406.

RICHARD KYNMOURE (?CLONMORE), 1406–1409

Richard Kynmoure, a priest of the diocese of Dublin, was dispensed in March 1399 to hold for seven years in addition to the benefice of Clinnure or Clumore in the diocese of Armagh, 'one other benefice with cure or otherwise compatible, even an elective dignity, major or principal, and united respectively, *personatus* or office in a metropolitan, cathedral or collegiate church, and to exchange both as often as he pleases for two similar or dissimilar incompatible benefices'.[16] Eventually the rectory of Clinnure became void by the provision and the approaching consecration of 'Richard, elect of Cork' and was reserved to one John Possewyk.[17] The Roman Pope Innocent VII provided Richard Kynmoure to the see of Cork before 6 October 1406[18] but the temporalities had not yet been restored by the following February. The non-restoration was probably due to a weakening of English influence in Cork at the time. A report to the king's council in Ireland in 1399 had stated that Irish enemies were strong and arrogant and of great power, that there was 'neither power nor rule to resist them' and that 'the county of Cork with everything is given to others along with the Liberties of an Earl palatine'.[19] The report, coming so shortly on the submission of the Irish chiefs to Richard II in 1394–95, shows that the submissions in Desmond were as transient as those in other parts of the country.[20]

No records remain to show if and when the temporalities were restored to Richard Kynmoure. The suggestion that he was *persona non grata* cannot be dismissed. On 14 February 1406 King Henry IV ordered that the temporalities of Cork should be given to Bishop Gerald Condon of Cloyne who was apparently a more reliable ecclesiastic than Kynmoure: 'The king grants Gerald, Bishop of Cloyne, the temporals of the

15   *Cal. papal letters, 1396–1404*, p. 411.

16   Ibid., p. 246.

17   *Cal. papal letters, 1404–15*, pp. 87, 88.

18   Powicke and Fryde, *Handbook of British Chronology*, p. 325. Eubel gives 13 November 1406 as the date of provision.

19   Curtis and McDowell, *Irish Historical Documents*, p. 69.

20   Curtis, *Richard II in Ireland*, p. 45.

bishopric of Cork which came into his hands by the death of the bishop there.'[21] Considering the date given, the deceased bishop was Roger Ellesmere. Gerald Condon died in 1409 and from the bull of provision of the next bishop of Cork it is clear that Richard Kynmoure had died before July of the same year: *'Rex, ad peticionem, licentiam dat decano et capitulo ecclesiae cathedralis Corkagensis alium episcopum eligendi loco Ricardi nuper episcopi defuncti. Data periit.'*[22] We shall see that the provision of Milo FitzJohn supplies the answer.

Meantime the schism deadlock continued with no appearance of yielding on either side even though Pope Gregory XII had agreed in 1406 to resign if the Avignon pope, Benedict XIII, did likewise. Their mutual unwillingness to co-operate and their inability to understand that 'politics, even spiritual politics, is the art of the possible',[23] began to bring nations together and led to the councils which eventually restored unity. The schism could have been healed in one of three ways: (1) Both popes could be persuaded to resign; this was the *via cessionis*. (2) There could be a withdrawal of obedience from one or other pope: this was called *subtractio obedientiae*. (3) A general council could decide the issue: this was the *via concilii*. Failure of the first and second alternatives led the cardinals and the University of Paris to convene the Council of Pisa on 29 March 1409, but by this time there were too many political motives involved in upholding existing rival claimants to make it possible that the council's pope should receive that general acceptance which alone could bring the schism to an end.[24] So the Council of Pisa, despite the unanimity with which its members deposed Popes Gregory XII and Benedict XIII as schismatics, heretics and perjurers, was doomed to failure. Its appointment of Alexander V was both irregular and revolutionary, and the unwillingness of Gregory XII and Benedict XIII to accept sentence of deposition served only to add further complications to an already labrynthine problem. During the next six years three 'popes' claimed the allegiance of Christendom, for while the Pisan anti-pope enjoyed the widest obedience, Gregory XII

21 *Rot. pat. Hib.*, pt. 1, p. 185, no. 41: 'Rex commisit Geraldo episcopo Clonensis custodiam temporalium episcopatus Corkagensis, in manu sua per mortem ultimi episcopi ibidem.'

22 Ibid., p. 189, no. 7.

23 F. R. H. du Boulay, 'The Fifteenth Century', in *The English Church and the Papacy in the Middle Ages*, ed. C. H. Laurence, p. 207.

24 Mandell Creighton, *A History of the Papacy from the Great Schism to the Sack of Rome*, i, 256.

and Benedict XIII still had their supporters. When Alexander V died after a pontificate of less than a year, the Council of Pisa brought utter discredit on its cause by the election on 17 May 1410 of Baltassare Cossa, cardinal-legate of Bologna, who took the name of John XXIII. Despite the irregularities of the Pisan proceedings, England and France were by now hostile to Roman and Avignon popes alike. England's transfer of allegiance to Alexander V had immediate repercussions in the diocese of Cork in a disputed succession, the first of many to disturb the see of Finbarr for the greater part of the fifteenth century. The situation had a curious parallel in the diocese of Killaloe.[25]

MILO FITZJOHN 1409–1431

In July 1409 Milo FitzJohn, dean of Cork, was provided to the bishopric and was consecrated by mandate of the Roman pontiff Gregory XII.[26] Eubel is incorrect in placing his appointment in 1418 in succession to Patrick Foxe. His qualifying statement is more to the point: *Jam 1409, July 18 et 26 tunc decanus ipsius ecclesiae a Greg. XII in epum. Corcag. (non Carthagen) provisus, se obligaverat pro se et praedec. Ricardo* [Kynmoure], *Rogerio* [Ellesmere], *Geraldo* [Barry]. Milo FitzJohn's stormy episcopate saw the extension to Cork of the stalemate obtaining in the church following the Council of Pisa, for the three 'popes' of the post-Pisan era had their counterparts in three rival claimants to the see of Cork. Two of the claimants, Milo FitzJohn and Patrick Foxe, fought out their claims during the final years of the schism. The third claimant, John Paston, was provided to the bishopric in May 1425 on the fraudulent representation of the death of Milo FitzJohn.[27] Taken all in all, the years 1409 to 1431 present in the diocese of Cork a situation of unusual complexity which seems to have been thoroughly exploited in the general confusion engendered by the ramifications of the Great Schism. Rival appointments to vacant bishoprics and benefices are met with previous to the schism and continued long after the schism had passed into history. In this respect, therefore, Cork was no exception, but it would be difficult to find a more complex set of circumstances elsewhere.

PATRICK FOXE, 1409–1417

Milo FitzJohn's appointment in July 1409 by mandate of Gregory XII does not appear to have been followed up by

25 Gleeson, *A History of the Diocese of Killaloe*, p. 389.

26 *Cal. papal letters, 1417–31*, p. 48.

27 Ibid., p. 405.

restoration of temporalities. England had by this time gone over
to the Pisan allegiance, and English kings were usually glad of
any excuse to retain episcopal revenues in royal hands for as
long as possible. Three months after FitzJohn's provision Patrick
Foxe *alias* Raghat, Ragged or Ragget, was provided to Cork by
the Pisan anti-pope Alexander V.[28] Foxe, who was apparently of
Anglo-Irish extraction, is believed to have been born at Ballyragget in County Kilkenny; hence his surname as given in the
sixth and seventh volumes of the *Calendar of Papal Letters*. His
status as king's clerk is clear from an extract from Smith to the
effect that 'on the 11th June, 1400, the Earl of Kildare, Patrick
Fox and Walter Fitz-Gerald were appointed *custodes pacis et
supervisores custod*[i] *um pacis* in the counties of Cork, Limerick
and Kerry . . .'.[29] A king's clerk (or *clericus regis*, to give him his
official title) was already on the road to promotion, and it was
possibly because of service in this quality that Patrick Foxe
secured several of his previous appointments. He appears for the
first time in the *Calendar of Papal Letters* in 1406 as a clerk of
the diocese of Ossory, a member of the household of Henry,
bishop of Tusculum, a student well versed in canon and civil
law and a graduate of Oxford and Cambridge. In 1407 he was
provided by Gregory XII to the deanery of Ossory and was
simultaneously assigned to the canonry and prebend of Culeueny
in Cloyne.[30] Finally, in October 1409 Pope Alexander V, with
the strength of England's allegiance at his back, provided Patrick
Foxe to the see of Cork. Pope Gregory's previous provision of
Milo FitzJohn was ignored; FitzJohn, while he enjoyed some
local support, was unacceptable to the English because of his
Irish sympathies and outlook. Even when the present impasse
had been resolved FitzJohn was still under suspicion and was
accused in 1421 by the bishops of Lismore and Cloyne of having
an Irish heart.[31] The provision made by Alexander V in October
1409 was confirmed in May 1410 by Pope John XXIII: 'To
Patrick, elect of Cork. Decree that these presents shall be
sufficient proof of the provision made to him by Alexander V,
who, learning at the beginning of his pontificate that before his
accession the see of Cork had become void by the death of
Richard [Kynmoure] specially reserved it . . . and [made]
provision of it to Patrick, then dean of Ossory and in minor

28   *Cal. papal letters, 1404–15*, p. 197.

29   Smith, *History of Cork*, ii, 10, quoting Rot. Turr. Bermingh., 1 Henry IV.

30   *Cal. papal letters, 1404–15*, pp. 114, 124.

31   Curtis, *Med. Ire.*, p. 296.

orders only.' Proof of Foxe's consecration is found in a papal mandate of 1412 by which John XXIII provided Nicholas Broune, B.C.L., to the deanery of Ossory which became void and reserved to the pope by the promotion 'made by Alexander V . . . of Patrick [Foxe], Bishop of Cork, and by his consecration performed by mandate of the present pope'.[32]

Foxe's appointment as bishop of Cork was one thing; his administration of the see was quite another matter, and there is no proof that he ever gained possession. Custody of the temporalities had been granted in 1409 to Richard O Hedian, archbishop of Cashel, and evidence of their restoration to Foxe is lacking.[33] In 1411 the see was regarded as vacant or at least in dispute, since the *spiritualia* were also in the hands of the archbishop.[34] Even the chapter of Cork admitted the vacancy when in August 1414 Richard O Hedian was deputed to act as administrator-general in spirituals during the voidance of the see.[35] It is a fair assumption, therefore, that neither Milo FitzJohn nor Patrick Foxe enjoyed the temporalities of Cork between 1409 and 1414. Foxe continued to enjoy English support, and royal control was consistently invoked during these years in appointments to the church of Holy Trinity. For instance, a royal mandate of 1414 ordered all mayors and others in Ireland to arrest and imprison all rebels who schemed to impugn the royal right which had been exercised in collating the free chapel of Holy Trinity in Cork to John Martell in succession to Maurice Omorgain. Patrick Foxe, who was styled bishop of Cork in this mandate, was ordered to admit and institute Martell, and all archbishops and others in Ireland were prohibited 'from doing anything in derogation of the king's royal right or [in any way] weakening the said collation'.[36]

By 1414 the political involvements of John XXIII had driven him to seek assistance from the Emperor Sigismund who exacted as the price of his support that a general council would be summoned on German territory. Sigismund's desire to end

---

32 *Cal. papal letters, 1404–15*, pp. 197, 242.

33 *Rot. pat. Hib.*, p. 194b, no. 4b, which in the original contracted Latin reads: 'Rex ob cust' et labor' circa reformacionem pacis in Momon' et Lagen' concessit Rico. aepo. Cassel' custod' tempium epatus Cork' quamdiu in man' Regis fuerit.'

34 Ibid., p. 198b, no. 27: 'Ricardus Pellyn, clericus, habet litteras Regis de presentatione ad vicariam de Kinsale, Cork. dioc. vacantem racione privacionis Johannis filii gerot' *alias* Johannis Corre. Et dirigunter letterae illae Ricardo archiepiscopo Cassel' custod' spirit' Cork', sede vacante.'

35 *Cal. papal letters, 1417–31*, p. 428.

36 *Cal. pat. rolls, 1413–16*, p. 293.

the scandal of the schism was not without ulterior motives: a general council held under imperial auspices would show the emperor off to best advantage. Under such circumstances the forthcoming council was to mark an epoch in the history of the church. Hitherto, as we have noted, church councils had been summoned and presided over by the popes, with the reigning emperor or his delegate in attendance. Now, a general council under Sigismund's auspices was convened at Constance in November 1414, and because princes as well as prelates attended, this great assembly was as much a diet of the empire as a council of the church. It continued until April 1418 and, in the words of a modern writer, the council 'spanned the renewal of the weary war between England and France in the summers of 1415 and 1417, and it witnessed at a distance, Agincourt, the occupation and siege of Harfleur, the treaty of Canterbury between Henry V and Sigismund, king of the Romans, and the beginning of the campaign to seize Normandy and the French crown'.[37] The political issues of the Hundred Years' War were as potent as the schism in splitting Christendom into rival camps during these years.

The threefold programme of the Council of Constance included the restoration of unity in the church, the eradication of heresy and the introduction of reform. The numerical superiority of the Italians who would be sure to oppose the deposition of John XXIII was neutralized by the division of the council into four *nations*, a system then customary in the more important European universities. The countries having most claim to representation were Italy, Germany, France and Spain, but Spain out of loyalty to Benedict XIII sent no representatives to Constance, and thus England was admitted into partnership with the other three nations. In this way, writes Aubrey Gwynn, 'it was possible for the small group of prelates nominated by Henry V to act and vote as representing one fourth of the whole Catholic Church'.[38] The subsequent disputes concerning Spain's recognition as a fifth nation and the questioning of England's right to be accounted as one of the four nations of western Christendom need not be dwelt upon. It suffices to stress that Gregory XII formally abdicated, through his envoys, in July 1415. John XXIII, who had fled to Schaffhausen, was deposed. Benedict XIII, who refused to abdicate, retired to Peñiscola where he maintained himself in papal splendour until his death in 1424. His deposition by the council fathers at

37 Crowder, 'Henry V, Sigismund and the Council of Constance', p. 94.

38 Gwynn, 'Ireland and the English Nation', p. 191.

Constance paved the way for the election of Odo Colonna as Pope Martin V on 11 November 1417. Once the formalities of his election were over Martin V issued a formal denial of the conciliar theory and claimed sole initiative for the papacy in questions of church reform. Unfortunately, Pope Martin abandoned reform, mainly because of its association with conciliarist ideas; but by closing the door on reform he opened it on revolution, and it was through this open door that Martin Luther was to march in 1517 bringing large sections of the medieval church with him.

The Council of Constance was therefore epochal in the history of the medieval church. It healed the schism by receiving the abdication of the Roman pope and by deposing the other two claimants. With the election of Odo Colonna it inaugurated a reinvigorated papal monarchy, and by its division into separate nationalities it showed that within the structure of the universal church national churches were already acquiring a special significance. The activities of the 'English nation' at Constance had immediate bearings on the history of the diocese of Cork.

Patrick Foxe's qualifications in theology and canon law together with the prestige attaching to his position as *clericus regis* secured his appointment as leading canonist on the English delegation to Constance in 1414. He has the added distinction of being the only Irish prelate who attended the council. In January 1415 he was given leave of absence for two years from Henry V; and while his departure must have gone far towards relaxing the tensions prevailing in the diocese of Cork since 1409, the case of Milo FitzJohn was not to be settled for another three years. When Foxe reached Constance in the spring of 1415 John XXIII had already taken flight to Schaffhausen, and on the *acta* of the council Foxe's name first appears on 29 May when he was one of five judges appointed to pass sentence on the fugitive pope to whom he owed his confirmation and consecration as bishop of Cork. All through 1415 Foxe occupied a prominent place on commissions dealing with such problems as communion under two species for the Bohemian dissidents, reconciliation of the rival obediences of John XXIII and Gregory XII, examination of the privileges of the Franciscan Third Order. In July 1415 he was one of those who passed sentence on John Huss—a rather anomalous distinction in view of the safe-conduct granted to the Bohemian reformer. On 13 December 1415 the signing of the Concordat of Norbonne marked the final secession of cardinals from Benedict XIII. Patrick Foxe endorsed this document as bishop of Cork and representative of the province of Cashel.

In February 1416 Foxe was member of a commission appointed to deal with the Hussites of Bohemia and the Teutonic Knights; he spent the next two months investigating problems relative to the bishopric of Salzburg, and in May he was among those responsible for passing sentence of death on Jerome of Prague, friend and disciple of Huss. The problems of Spanish representation at Constance which provoked disputes between English, Spanish and French delegates were about to claim Foxe's attention when in September 1415 a second English delegation arrived at Constance. From now on Foxe was eclipsed by the English theologian, John Polton, dean of York, but he continued to be a person of some consequence in the assembly. He was one of the judges who issued the citation which on 22 July 1417 formally deposed Pedro de Luna (no longer called Benedict XIII), and in September of that year he was appointed to consider the rival claims of the kingdoms of Aragon and Castile. This marks the last occurrence of his name on the official files of Constance.[39]

Shortly after the election of Martin V on 11 November 1417, Patrick Foxe returned to Ireland, but there is no evidence to show that he made any attempt to reinstate himself as bishop of Cork. The nine-year-old deadlock was resolved in January 1418 when Pope Martin V by special mandate to the bishop of Teramo, the abbot of Tracton (*de Albo Tractu*) and the dean of Cork, confirmed the appointment of Milo FitzJohn as bishop of Cork and ordered that he should be restored to possession. By the same instrument Patrick Foxe was translated to Ossory in succession to Thomas Snell, and Pope Martin validated the translation 'as though there had been no litigation in the Roman Court about the provision made to him of the see of Cork, between him and Milo'.[40] Ossory then ranked second in importance among the suffragan sees of the province of Dublin; it was Foxe's native diocese and, as it was rated higher than Cork in the Anglo-Irish economy of the time, Foxe was amply rewarded for his services at Constance. By providing him to so important a diocese Martin V was probably acknowledging his indebtedness to the support of the English vote which was a weighty consideration in the conclave which elevated him to the papal throne. Patrick Foxe, bishop of Ossory, died before July 1421,[41] having, in the words of the Four Masters, 'governed his

39   Ibid., pp. 213–17.

40   *Cal. papal letters, 1417–31*, pp. 46, 48.

41   Ibid., p. 190.

flock with justice and equity and fed them both by his example and instruction'.

Pope Martin's indebtedness to England was further discharged by a concordat of 1418 in which he gave certain specific guarantees. He agreed that he would only appoint a moderate number of cardinals and that he would select them from the various provinces of Christendom. Diocesan bishops were given the right to examine indulgences and to deal with cases of suspension and the like. The pope was not to appropriate parish churches to monasteries he wished to favour, but appropriations made during the schism were allowed to stand—subject to the approval of local bishops who were to have a greater say in such matters for the future. Englishmen were to be considered eligible for appointment to some of the offices in the papal administration, and henceforth clergy were not to be dispensed to hold a plurality of benefices 'except noble persons and men of very good birth'. Finally, the cure of souls was safeguarded by the annulment of dispensations granting exemption from holy orders to benefice-holders, monks were not to be dispensed to hold benefices and archdeacons were ordered to carry out their visitations in person.[42] This concordat, inasmuch as it contained the seeds of reform, was overlooked and lost sight of in the maelstrom of politics which colour the next century of Anglo-papal relations.

Foxe's translation to Ossory and Milo FitzJohn's confirmation as bishop of Cork did not restore any measure of tranquillity to the diocese. The date at which the temporalities were restored to Bishop FitzJohn is not known, but it is beyond question that diocesan affairs were now grievously aggravated through several irresponsible collations and provisions made during the pontificate of Innocent VII and more particularly during that of John XXIII. In 1404 a papal mandate collated and assigned the vicarage of Kinsale to John Corre, a pluralist whose incumbencies included the rectory of Kylmid, the benefices (without cure) of Rosmunli, Ballymodan and Kilmoe and the prebend and canory of Liscleary, in addition to which he was collector to the *camera* in the cities and dioceses of Cork and Ross.[43] Here we have an example of an abuse peculiarly though not exclusively characteristic of the Avignon regime; an abuse which, as we have seen, was permitted and even encouraged by some popes and which wrought havoc on the spiritual welfare of the faithful in the period leading up to the Reformation. Pluralities were the

42   du Boulay, 'The Fifteenth Century', p. 212.

43   *Cal. papal letters, 1404–15*, p. 87.

rule rather than the exception of all Irish dioceses during the Great Schism, and while the majority of Cork appointments for this period belong to the pluralist category the selection of John Corre's collation is justified by the intricacies caused by several overlapping mandates of John XXIII and Martin V.

The legislation of Pope John XXIII reveals a papacy reduced to the low-water mark of corruption and abuse. Provision was by that time the invariable method of appointment, 'Rome-runners' were common and the astonishing number of irresponsible provisions to Irish dioceses suggests the absence of any adequate check for the prevention of abuses. Provisions were made on the false news of a bishop's death, rival bishops were a common feature of many dioceses and cases of forgery were not unknown. In illustration of the provisions typical of John XXIII we find that in 1414 he collated and assigned the archdeaconry of Cork to Geoffrey Pellyn, a clerk of the diocese of Emly, 'who lately received Papal dispensation as the son of a bishop and an unmarried woman, to be promoted to all, even holy orders'.[44] The overwhelming number of such collations in the papal registers is sufficient indication of the general character of the Irish clergy in the period under consideration. From Killaloe comes an instance—which cannot have been isolated—of the provision to the chancellorship of a ten-year-old youth, the son of a deacon (who was also a religious) and an unmarried woman.[45] Even in 1469 when the schism could no longer be cited as an excuse for corruption, Thomas Cornis, dean of Cork, was involved in a collation of this nature in the diocese of Lismore where he had unlawfully retained possession of a canonry and prebend. The pope (Paul II) in removing Thomas Cornis ratified the provision of Theobald de Botiller, clerk of the diocese of Cashel and in his twelfth year, 'notwithstanding [the pope's] late constitution against the making of provision of cathedral canonries and prebends to persons unless they have completed their fourteenth year'.[46]

In Cork, Geoffrey Pellyn for reasons unknown had resigned from the archdeaconry before 1418, but later entries in the papal records for the years 1418–27 show that the admission of the Pellyn family into Cork did not redound to the peaceful functioning of the diocesan administration. John Pellyn, presumably a relative, succeeded Geoffrey in the archdeaconry, and Richard Pellyn who for some obscure reason had been

44 Ibid., p. 476. The archdeaconry was declared 'void by the death of Walter Galle'.

45 Gleeson, *A History of the Diocese of Killaloe*, p. 387.

46 *Cal. papal letters, 1458–71*, p. 688.

removed from the deanship was reinstated by Pope Martin V in August 1418. Pellyn, who held canonries and prebends in Lismore and Emly, managed to acquire the perpetual vicarage of Kinsale from which through representation to John XXIII he had secured the expulsion of John Corre who had been the nominee of Innocent VII.[47] There is no papal mandate to prove Richard Pellyn's removal from Kinsale, but a state of disturbance there is indicated by Pope Martin's collation and provision of Robert Holhgan *alias* de Cork, an abbreviator of papal letters and bachelor of canon law to the perpetual vicarage of Kinsale 'of which he has not got possession'.[48] The multiplicity of local conflicts of this nature show Martin V's utter inability to stem the tide of abuse; in fact, his over-cautious policy towards conciliarist ideas was the least appropriate answer to the needs of the time.

Abuses other than those arising out of pluralism and rivalry were equally prevalent. A record dated 1417 shows that Donald Omongayn, a deacon of the diocese of Cloyne, had for more than a year retained the rectory of Bruhenny (Bruchundi) in Cork without either dispensation or ordination. Nevertheless, Omongayn, the illegitimate son of a cleric and an unmarried woman, was permitted to keep the rectory and was collated to the canonry of Kilbrogan in 1418. Similar instances could be multiplied for every other diocese in Ireland. The over-all picture was far from edifying. On the other hand, when one considers that the interplay of personal rivalries between Milo FitzJohn and Patrick Foxe left them with little time for anything but self-determination, the growth of irregularities in Cork seems to have been almost inevitable. Some irregularities were offset to a degree by the frequent issues of papal mandates of pardon and rehabilitation to clerics who wished to have their collations canonically approved and clarified. Thus in 1435 Donald O'Reilly (Orealich) was rehabilitated 'on account of having obtained the vicarage of Ballymodan and subsequently without dispensation the rectories of the parish churches of Murragh and Templetrine and parcels of the parish churches of Ballymountain and Kildara, all of which he had held for several years'. O'Reilly had to resign from the vicarages, rectories and parcels, but he was collated to the canonry and prebend of Kilroan and was appointed rector of Ringrone, the combined value of which amounted to fourteen marks.[49]

47 *Cal. papal letters, 1417–31*, pp. 89, 90.

48 Ibid., p. 189.

49 Ibid., pp. 44, 382.

To make diocesan confusion worse confounded, Pope Martin V followed up his rehabilitation of Milo FitzJohn[50] by a confirmation of the union of the dioceses of Cork and Cloyne as requested by Bishop Adam Payn of Cloyne. Milo FitzJohn resisted the arrangement but it was advocated by Adam Payn in the parliament of 1421 and was eventually referred to Rome. Meantime, while Milo FitzJohn's canonical title was unassailable, he appears not to have gained control of the temporalities of the see. Peter Copener and John Kelly of the city of Cork (*de civitate Corcagie*) held them in 1422, and in that year they were transferred by order of Henry VI to William, son of Thomas Copener, at forty shillings per annum.[51] It is not known when or how Milo FitzJohn regained the temporalities, but he seems to have enjoyed them at least from 1425 until his death when by order of Henry VI they were granted to Nicholas, bishop of Ardfert, and Richard Scurlag, archdeacon of Cork.

JOHN PASTON, 1425

John Paston *alias* Wortes of Norwich was the final claimant to the see of Cork during the later years of Milo FitzJohn's turbulent episcopate. The sixth volume of the *Calendar of Papal Letters* describes Paston as an Augustinian friar who left the order in 1415 and became a secular priest.[52] The seventh volume of the same series represents him as a monk of Cluny in the diocese of Macon who was provided by Pope Martin V to the priory of the Cluniac monastery of Bromholm in the diocese of Norwich in November 1420. Paston was duly installed and, in spite of the opposition headed by Nicholas Luddon, monk of Bromholm, he ruled there as prior until 1425. By then his ambitions had soared higher than the priorship to place him among the ranks of those English and Irish monks and friars who took advantage of the confusion of the early post-schism era to attain to episcopal status in vacant Irish dioceses. On 23 May 1425 Paston was provided to the see of Cork, then declared 'void by the death of Milus'.[53] But Milo FitzJohn was not dead, and even if he were, it is difficult to reconcile Paston's provision with Pope Martin's confirmation of the diocesan amalgamation of Cork and Cloyne. For all his scheming, John

---

50　FitzJohn was confirmed in January 1418; the decision regarding the amalgamation of the dioceses was announced in September.

51　*Rot. pat. Hib.*, p. 226, no. 6, and p. 228b, no. 83.

52　*Cal. papal letters, 1404–15*, p. 465.

53　*Cal. papal letters, 1417–31*, pp. 180, 405.

Paston, though consecrated, did not secure possession in Cork, nor did his incursion into episcopal politics make him any more acceptable in the monastery of Bromholm to which he returned in 1426. Opposition against him had gained momentum during his absence, and in November 1425 a letter written by William Paston throws doubt on the very identity of this pseudo prior-bishop. William Paston's plaint was that 'Johne Wortes that namythe hym self Paston, and affermith hym untrewely to be my cousyn. . . . It is told me sithen that the seyd John Wortes is in the cite of Rome, sacred a bysshop of Ireland, *videlicet episcopus Corcagensis*, wherby it is seyd here that his pretense of his title to the priourie of Bromholme is adnulled and voide'.[54] A second letter from William Paston, dated 1 March 1426, states that 'Myn adversarie is become Bysshop of Cork in Irland, and there are two other persones provided to the same bysshopriche yet lyvying, before my seyd adversarie; and by his acceptacion of this bysshopriche he hath pryved hym self of the title that he claymed in Bromholm'.[55]

John Paston *alias* Wortes had also a civil offence to his charge; a writ was issued to the sheriff of Norwich 'to attach and bring before the council John Paston *alias* Wortes and others for violation of the Statutes of Provisors, 25 Edward III and 16 Richard II'.[56] The complaint lodged before John Brundale, former prior of Bromholm, was that Paston had crossed the sea without royal license, had secured provision to the priory in the court of Rome and had achieved installation through the expulsion of Brundale. Having eluded capture for over twelve months, Paston surrendered on 24 May 1427; he was imprisoned at Fleet but was shortly liberated on renouncing his claim to the priory of Bromholm.

His after career is interesting. In 1433 he was appointed vicar-general to Bishop Rudolph Deiphilt of Utrecht (1433–55) with permission to perform episcopal functions within that diocese.[57] He is accorded a passing reference in *Bataviae Sacra Prologomena* for the year 1449 when an address is recorded from 'John, Bishop of Cork, to Rudolph, Bishop of Utrecht'. Lastly, the eleventh volume of the *Calendar of Papal Letters* contains a mandate from Pope Callistus III, dated 7 May 1457, relative to the collation of a canonry and prebend in Saint

54 J. Gairdner, ed., *The Paston Letters*, i, 19, letter no. 5, dated 5 November 1425.
55 Ibid., p. 25, letter no. 7, dated 1 March 1426.
56 Ibid., iii, app.
57 Eubel, *Hierarchia Catholica Medii Aevi*, i, 208; ii, 137.

Mary's, Utrecht. This mandate is addressed to 'John, Bishop of Cork, residing in the city of Utrecht'.[58] John Paston died at Utrecht in 1459 and, like the lonely Benedict XIII at Peñiscola, he insisted to the end of his days on the righteousness of his canonical election as bishop of Cork. His signature to a letter written in 1427 summarizes the attitude he maintained through life: '*Johannes Paston, en temps passé Priour de Bromholm, et pour le present, evesquels de Corkagen.*'[59]

When did Milo FitzJohn die? The fraudulent representation by means of which John Paston secured provision to the diocese of Cork has been uncritically accepted, namely, that Milo FitzJohn died in 1425. Against this assumption it is beyond question that Milo FitzJohn was still alive in 1431 and that he officiated as bishop of Cork in that year. An important document, quoted in Smith's *History of Cork* describes various concessions made by successive bishops of Cork to the vicars choral of the cathedral.[60] To these vicars choral Milo FitzJohn collated the parish church of Desertserges on 3 June 1431. The entry in its original Latin reads as follows: '*Collatio iisdem fact. per Milonem episcop. Corcagiens, eccles. parrochialis de Desertserges, 3 Junii, 1431.*'[61]

A second document, dated Dublin, 28 June, 10 Henry VI, or 1431 and already quoted, announces the granting of the temporalities of Cork to Nicholas, bishop of Ardfert, and Richard Scurlag, archdeacon of Cork. The temporalities are said to have come into the king's hands *per mortem Milonis nuper episcopi.*[62] The conclusion to be drawn from a comparison of both documents is that Milo FitzJohn died sometime between 3 June and 28 June 1431. It seems likely from the evidence of the later document that he enjoyed the temporalities of the see at least from the date of John Paston's unsuccessful intrusion until the time of his death.[63] The omission of his name from the papal registers for the years 1425–31 is consequently as baffling and inexplicable as the provision of Jordan Purcell to the united sees of Cork and Cloyne on the resignation of Adam Payn in 1429.

58 *Cal. papal letters, 1455–64*, p. 325.

59 Gairdner, The Paston Letters, i, 24, letter no. 6.

60 Smith, *History of Cork*, i, 40. For re-affirmation of these grants see Chapter IX.

61 Ibid.

62 *Rot. pat. Hib.*, p. 255b, no. 115.

63 Webster, *The Diocese of Cork*, p. 81, makes the unlikely suggestion that the temporalities were in the king's hands from 23 March 1423 until after 28 June 1432.

XVI

The United Dioceses of Cork and Cloyne

In Chapter III it was shown that the first scheme for an Irish hierarchy as envisaged at Rathbreasail in 1111 was based on the provinces of Armagh and Cashel each containing twelve suffragans. The failure of the Rathbreasail settlement led to the wider legislation of Kells in 1152 by which the Irish church was organized into four provinces, the number of suffragans was fixed at thirty-four and the two small bishoprics of Ardmore and Mungret in the province of Cashel were given doubtful temporary recognition. The four archbishops were retained throughout the medieval period but a series of amalgamations and absorptions, notwithstanding the emergence of the diocese of Annadown in Tuam and of the diocese of Dromore in Armagh, reduced the suffragan episcopate from thirty-four to thirty-two. This hierarchy of four archbishops and thirty-two suffragans prevailed until the fourteenth century.

The development of a great number of Irish bishoprics from pre-existing monastic churches led inevitably to friction between bishops and coarbs on the vexed question of the allocation of property. There must have been a considerable imbalance in the method of division in places (the coarbial families cannot have been easy to dislodge), and in view of the fluctuating fortunes of medieval Ireland it is not surprising that by the beginning of the fourteenth century many Irish dioceses were too poor to support episcopal administration. This being so, a scheme envisaging a radical reorganization of Irish diocesan geography was part of the reform plan submitted in 1325 to Pope John XXII by Bishop Philip of Slane in the name of King Edward II. At this period the English king still exercised extensive control over episcopal elections and over the delivery or restoration of temporalities, and although the common law area declined during the fourteenth century, royal power continued to be effective throughout Leinster and in wide areas of Munster.

Edward II's proposal was that the thirty-two Irish bishoprics should be reduced to ten, inclusive of the four archbishoprics, and that the administrative centre of each diocese should be a royal city (*civitas regia*). Inherent in the proposal was the subjection of the diocesan structure more directly to royal control; this was all the more desirable since the remonstrance of 1317 had shown the extent to which Irish princes were backed by their bishops. Native episcopal hostility had been complained of by Edward I who left on record his inability to exercise his rights over temporalities during times of vacancy because his officials dared not venture into certain dioceses.[1] The specious tenor of Edward II's representations was that papal, rather than royal, control over the Irish church needed tightening up. But the pope was cautious: Irish representatives at the Council of Vienne (1311–12) had brought forward charges amounting to an indictment of King Edward's policy of ecclesiastical encroachment. Their complaints, which complemented those listed in the remonstrance of the princes, dictated to the pope the inadvisability of increasing the king's opportunities for controlling the Irish episcopate. Not that the suggestions of King Edward were entirely shelved. Pope John XXII, for whom ecclesiastical centralization was a major consideration, appreciated the necessity for some diocesan amalgamation and he legislated accordingly. The outcome must have been disappointing. Attempts at union in the province of Tuam had only a partial success; Annadown was united with Tuam but the dioceses of Achonry and Kilmacduagh resisted. Lismore did not become permanently united to Waterford until 1362/63, a union of Cork and Cloyne was effected between 1429 and 1432, and Down and Connor were amalgamated in 1441.[2]

The threefold efforts towards amalgamating the dioceses of Cork and Cloyne cover the period 1326–1418. In pursuance of King Edward's proposal John XXII issued a decree for union on 30 July 1326, the union to become effective on the voidance of either see and without prejudice to the metropolitan. We saw in the previous chapter that the voidance which occurred in Cork in November 1329 with the translation of Walter le Rede to Cashel was filled, not by the pre-arranged amalgamation but by the provision of John de Ballyconingham. The records are non-committal as to why the dioceses were not united. A second attempt at amalgamation was made on 13 September

1 J. A. Watt, 'Negotiations between Edward II and John XXII concerning Ireland', pp. 5 ff.

2 Powicke and Fryde, *Handbook of British Chronology*, pp. 303–05.

1376 when Gregory XI at the request of Bishop Richard Wye of Cloyne exemplified the bull of John XXII. Again the undertaking proved abortive. Finally on 21 September 1418 Bishop Adam Payn of Cloyne secured from the newly-elected Martin V a confirmation of the union as decreed in 1326/27.[3] Martin V was not immediately successful; the union of Cork and Cloyne did not become effective until the resignation of Adam Payn in 1429 and the provision of Jordan Purcell to the united dioceses in 1429/32. The union was fostered in the English interest, for apart from a few places like Cork, Kinsale, Mallow and Buttevant the country of Desmond was 'beset by Irish rebels, many of the smaller towns had been wiped out', no borough survived west of Buttevant and Mallow, and west of that was MacCarthy's country until Dingle was reached.[4]

JORDAN PURCELL, 1429–C.1477

The circumstances of the provision of Jordan Purcell, chancellor of Limerick, to the united dioceses of Cork and Cloyne are given as follows in the papal registers: 'To Jordan, elect of Cork and Cloyne. Provision to him, chancellor of Limerick, priest, of the said united sees, void by the resignation, made *extra curiam* and admitted by the pope, of Adam, bishop in the universal church, during whose administration the pope specially reserved them.'[5] The provision was dated 15 June 1429 and carried the usual faculty of consecration by any Catholic bishop assisted by two or three others. The consecrating prelate was to convey Jordan Purcell's oath of fealty to the pope without prejudice to the archbishop of Cashel. No account was taken of Milo FitzJohn who was vehemently opposed to the union. We have seen that he officiated as bishop of Cork on 3 June 1431, that is, two years after Jordan Purcell's provision. Nothing is known of the relative positions or of the inevitable conflicts between the rival claimants during the interim, but Jordan Purcell had not secured possession by mid-year 1431. The death of Milo FitzJohn gave him opportunity to petition for a new provision to be based, not on a vacancy caused by the resignation of Adam Payn but by the death of Payn or of Milo FitzJohn. The plea was successful. On 6 January 1432 Pope Eugenius IV confirmed Jordan Purcell as bishop of the

---

3   *Cal. papal letters, 1417–31*, p. 65.

4   Curtis, *Med. Ire.*, pp. 361–2, 414.

5   Cal. papal letters, 1427–47, p. 109. The title 'bishop in the universal church' was usually applied, as in this case, to a bishop who had resigned his see.

united dioceses of Cork and Cloyne and validated his appointment as from the date of the original provision.[6] The retrospective clause would validate any jurisdictional acts of the bishop (there are none on record) but it can scarcely be said to have consummated the union of the two dioceses. Properly speaking, the date of amalgamation is January 1432 when the second provision was issued to Jordan Purcell.

Difficulties next arose regarding the temporalities, an order for the restoration of which was not issued until 25 September 1432 and then with the proviso that the bishop should renounce whatever was prejudicial to the royal dignity in his letters of appointment. Even granted that Jordan Purcell made this renunciation it appears that Nicholas, bishop of Ardfert, and Archdeacon Richard Scurlag of Cork still held the temporalities with a strong hand and conspired to keep the bishop from enjoying them. On 15 December 1432, in answer to an appeal from the bishop, King Henry VI revoked the letters patent which had been granted to Nicholas and Richard.

As bishop of the united dioceses of Cork and Cloyne, Jordan Purcell had a long and chequered episcopate. His position cannot have been an enviable one, for he had two diocesan chapters to deal with, each of which looked upon him not in his dual capacity as bishop of Cork and Cloyne but as bishop of Cork or bishop of Cloyne according to the area in which he discharged his official functions. Thus we find Jordan, bishop of Cloyne, dealing with collations, deprivations and institutions in Dungourney, Britway and Castlemagner, and as bishop of Cork dealing with the same matters in Drimoleague and Desertserges.[7] He is referred to as bishop of Cork and Cloyne in 1459 in a collation involving the perpetual vicarages of Aghabulloge (Achadbolog) and Clondrohid (Gluoyndiothead) in Cloyne and of Aglish (Eglasmughitiala) in Cork.[8] He is similarly accorded his full title in 1464 on the foundation of the collegiate church of Youghal. In view, therefore, of his rather tenuous position as bishop of Cork and Cloyne it is not surprising that a great part of the Purcell episcopate was disturbed by rival claimants to the see, and that one of these claimants enjoyed extensive support over large areas in Cloyne.

In sympathy and outlook Jordan Purcell was more colonial than native and as such must have fitted in easily to the milieu of fifteenth-century Cork. The continuing loyalty of Cork, its

6   Ibid., pp. 141, 380.

7   *Cal. papal letters, 1458–71*, pp. 158, 164, 214, 344, 467.

8   Ibid., p. 43.

bishopric and its citizens is seen in the Carew Manuscripts which under date 1445 contain a testimonial from Jordan, bishop of Cork and Cloyne, the deans and chapters of the united dioceses, the mayor and bailiffs of Cork, William, Lord Barry, sheriff of county Cork, Maurice, Lord Roche, and the sovereigns and commons of Youghal to James, earl of Ormond, recently appointed lieutenant to the king in Ireland. Cork's support was an expression of gratitude to the new lieutenant because recently Ormond 'hath laboured with great hosts to the said city and county [of Cork] and the parts thereabout, whereas he hath chastised and warred the king's enemies and rebels and put them in dread, and comforted greatly the liege people without any extortion or oppression done to any true liege men.'[9]

A review of some of Jordan Purcell's duties as papal mandatory will furnish an idea of the variety of tasks which fell to his lot as bishop of Cork. In January 1435 he was commissioned by mandate of Pope Eugenius IV to legislate with the bishops of Ardfert and Kilfenora on a confused situation then obtaining in the diocese of Killaloe where a disputed succession presaged future and similar troubles in Cork.[10] Later in the same year he was active in a Limerick diocesan dispute. An appeal of Thomas O'Mahony (Macimochana), archdeacon of Limerick, to Pope Eugenius IV contained that although he had canonically obtained the archdeaconry, Philip de Geraldinis, clerk of the diocese of Limerick who claimed the archdeaconry as his own, caused O'Mahony to be summoned before Jordan, bishop of Cork and Cloyne, whom Thomas, bishop of Emly, had appointed executor of papal letters in the case. O'Mahony complained that Bishop Purcell had given an unjust definitive sentence against him and had imposed perpetual silence on him; but O'Mahony thought better to appeal to the Apostolic See even though it was hard for him to litigate in the Roman court from such remote parts 'on account of divers costs usual in such cases'. The pope, 'seeing that Thomas on account of his fear of Philip's power' had no hope of justice in Limerick, ordered the archbishop of Cashel and the bishop of Ardfert as mandatories to investigate the matter and to restore Thomas O'Mahony should his complaint be substantiated.[11]

Bishop Jordan Purcell was twice mandated in 1439 to rectify certain marriages contracted in the diocese of Cork and Cloyne.

9   *Cal. Carew MSS*, v, 461.

10   Gleeson, *A History of the Diocese of Killaloe*, p. 407.

11   *Cal. papal letters, 1427–47*, p. 525.

The first mandate authorized him to absolve Cornelius, son of Dermot O'Mahony (yMachu[n]a), prince, and Aulina, daughter of Ronald MacCarthy (Leccarrych), also a prince, from excommunication incurred by the marriage they had consummated 'not in ignorance that they were related' within the forbidden degrees of kindred. The bishop was to dispense Cornelius and Aulina and, after temporary separation, to permit them 'to contract anew and remain in the marriage which they had formerly contracted'. Their present and future offspring were to be considered legitimate. A similar mandate was issued in the same month (June 1439) in favour of Magonius Omolcron and Margaret Sullivan (Yhullevant) of Cork, and in favour of Raymond Cantton and Evelyn Roche of Cloyne in March 1440.[12]

In 1441 an action of the Cork chapter which cut right across the papal reservation of all major cathedral dignities could have led to serious trouble between Cork and the Holy See. Bishop Jordan resolved a dispute over the deanship in which Miles Roche was an intruder by removing Roche and conferring on him the rectory of Kilgobban (Kyllgobbayn). The chapter invoked ancient custom, elected John Walsche, canon of Cork, to the deanship, and 'had the election confirmed by the ordinary'. Bishop and chapter appear to have been ignorant of or to have overlooked the decree of papal reservation, and consequently Walsche's appointment and confirmation were invalid. The deadlock was obviated in what had now become the traditional method of resolving problems of this nature and which shows that in the fifteenth century as in the fourteenth the papal power was used with scrupulous care to satisfy local requirements and to meet local demands. Pope Eugenius IV confirmed John Walsche's appointment and permitted him to retain his canonry of Caherlag to which a subsequent mandate added the rectory of Little Island (*S. Lappani de Inysmemele alias parvae insulae*).[13]

Of far greater importance and interest for the student of ecclesiastical history was Jordan Purcell's compilation of a rent roll showing the extent of the bishop's estates in the Anglo-Norman parts of the diocese. The document, which we have considered in an earlier chapter[14] and which furnishes information similar to that contained in the fourteenth-century *Pipe Roll of Cloyne*, might justifiably be styled the 'Pipe Roll of Cork'; it seems probable that Jordan Purcell so appreciated

12   *Cal. papal letters, 1431–47*, pp. 65, 70.
13   Ibid., pp. 173, 197.
14   B.M., Add. MS Ascough 4787, f. 78v, in Chapter VI.

the Cloyne roll that he issued special orders for the compilation of its counterpart for Cork. If for no other reason, therefore, his episcopate made an important contribution to the history of the diocese of Cork which for the medieval period is characterized by a frustrating lack of documentation.

The Purcell episcopate was the period of the great earls and of aristocratic home rule and was marked by an attempt to assert a complete separation from England except for the personal link of the crown. Success attended these efforts and by a gradual process the Anglo-Irish built up a strong rampart of native rule which, until 1534, no English government was able to break.[15] Under James, sixth earl of Desmond, most of Munster formed a small kingdom in which the MacCarthys, O'Sullivans and others owed military service and paid head-rents to the earl, and families like the Barrys, Roches and Barretts were forced to give him some of their lands. In 1421 Robert, son of Geoffrey Cogan, granted to Earl James 'all his possessions in county Cork'; these comprised, among other areas, fifteen manors in the barony of Kerrycurrihy with the manor of Shandon included. The Cogan castle of Carrigaline commanded Cork harbour, so that Desmond now controlled Limerick, Tralee, Youghal and Cork, the chief ports of Munster. The Decies country in Waterford was also his, together with the counties of Limerick, Kerry and Cork. The original *Regnum Corcagiense*, for so long connected with the MacCarthys, had become his, and while it could be argued that his earldom was merely nominal, James of Desmond was the first of the Old English to combine a power derived from feudal grants, brehon custom and the acquisition of crown rights, to rule a whole province as a palatine earl, to reign over an Irish population like a Gaelic king and to take his place in Dublin among the peers of the state. He fostered all things native and had marriage connections with Clanricardes and O'Briens, but he was so dexterous in adjusting his sails to the winds of politics that no open accusation could be brought against him. To all appearances he was the king's strong man, he attended or was represented at parliament, he preserved Munster for the Englishry, and openly, his nationalism went no further than to sympathize with the home rule party.

An admirer and supporter of Richard, duke of York, who ruled as viceroy from 1447 to 1460, James of Desmond with James of Ormond stood sponsor for Richard's son George, the future duke of Clarence. In 1450 Richard of York departed for England

---

15   Curtis, *Med. Ire.*, p. 303.

where events were moving relentlessly in the direction of war, and he left behind him as deputy Sir James Butler, a Lancastrian advocate whose house and county were firm supporters of the red rose right up to the Tudor era even though James himself perished in the Wars of the Roses and his brothers became absentees. Richard, duke of York, returned to Ireland in November 1459 and gave such generous hand-outs to the Anglo-Irish at a parliament in Drogheda in February 1460 that Anglo-Ireland became almost predominantly Yorkist. Richard's son Edmund, duke of Rutland and earl of Cork, became chancellor, and even though Richard's death in December 1460 was followed by the murder of Rutland, Ireland's loyalty to the white rose remained steadfast.

The attainder of the Ormond Butlers was the sequel to the Yorkist triumph at Towton Field in March 1461, following which Edward IV continued to govern Ireland through Anglo-Irish deputies. An Ormond-sponsored Lancastrian rising was crushed at Pilltown near Carrick-on-Suir in 1462; its importance as an extension of the York–Lancaster dispute was over-shadowed by its being a native feud between the Butlers and the Geraldines. Worth noting too is the reversal of the attainder on the Butlers in parliaments held in 1465 and 1468, even though the earls of Ormond did not again reach pre-eminence until Anne Boleyn readmitted them to favour under Henry VIII.

Earl James of Ormond was succeeded by his son Thomas in 1463 and he and the earl of Kildare became joint leaders of the home rule party. Desmond was appointed deputy for the duke of Clarence in April 1463, and in January 1464 Kildare became chancellor. In this way the Yorkists wooed allegiance at the cost of further strengthening the home rule aristocracy. As deputy, Earl Thomas of Desmond held two parliaments. The first, convened during the winter 1463–64, passed a statute in direct contravention of those of Kilkenny to the effect that since 'the profit of every city and town in the land depends principally on the resort of Irish people bringing merchandise thereinto, the people of Cork, Waterford, Limerick and Youghal may trade with the Irish in spite of all statutes [to the] contrary'.[16] In his next parliament in 1465 Desmond enacted that the Irish inhabitants of Meath, Louth, Dublin and Kildare were to assume English surnames, to dress as English and to swear allegiance to the king within a year.

It is perhaps in the domain of culture and religion that Earl Thomas FitzGerald deserves best of posterity. His parliament

16   Ibid., p. 329.

of 1465 deplored the lack of an Irish university (*studium generale*) and enacted that 'inasmuch as the land of Ireland has no university within it, which if it had it would promote as much the increase of knowledge and good governance as avoidance of riot and misgovernance, it is ordered that there shall be a university at Drogheda where may be made bachelors, masters and doctors in all sciences and faculties as at Oxford.'[17] This project like its predecessors also proved abortive even though lack of higher education in Ireland was at this time aggravated by the exclusion of Irishmen from Oxford. Earl Thomas would not be denied; he directed all his energies towards the advancement of the collegiate church of the Blessed Virgin at Youghal which he had founded in December 1464. Letters patent from Edward IV empowered Robert Miles and Philip Christopher, chaplains of the college, to purchase lands to the annual value of twenty marks for the upkeep of the collegiate church.[18] Papal bulls of protection and confirmation were subsequently issued, and the endowments of the church included certain parsonages and vicarages adjacent to the town of Youghal together with parishes in the dioceses of Cork, Cloyne, Ross and Ardfert. Smith gives the churches as follows: the churches of Youghal, Clonpriest, Kilcredan, Ardagh, Ichtermurragh, Garrivoe and the vicarage of Kilmacdonough, all adjacent to Youghal; the parish churches of Ballynoe *alias* Newtown, Aghern, Moyallow (Mallow) in the diocese of Cloyne; Carrigaline in the diocese of Cork; the parishes of Miros and Caharah in Ross [*sic*] and four other parishes in Ardfert.[19] The foundation charter and the appropriation of the specified tithes to the church were confirmed by Bishop Jordan Purcell under his own seal and that of his coadjutor, William Roche, archdeacon of Cloyne. Earl Thomas fell from favour in 1467 and was captured and beheaded at Drogheda on 14 February 1468, but his foundation was ratified by his son James in 1472 and by Maurice FitzGerald in 1496. This collegiate church of Youghal was the first Irish university to get off the ground, so to speak— the forerunner by 130 years of Trinity College—but since its history belongs more directly to the diocese of Cloyne it calls for treatment at the hands of a Cloyne historian. After a life-span

17 Ibid. pp. 329–30.

18 Smith, *History of Cork*, i, 55, quoting Rot. Canc. N. 29 , anno 3 Edward IV.

19 Ibid. 'In the charter of the foundation there is only mention made of the parishes of Newtown, Olehan, Aghern and Moyallow, but the others were granted afterwards by the Earls of Desmond and Popes.' It is clear from the royal visitation that the collegiate church had claims on Kilmoe and Schull in the diocese of Cork.

of little over a century the collegiate church, following the
liquidation of the Desmond Geraldines in 1583, went the way
of other Irish ecclesiastical foundations and suffered many
changes of ownership until under James I it became the property
of Richard Boyle, earl of Cork.[20]

The year of the foundation of the college of Youghal (1464)
marks the thirty-second year of Jordan Purcell's administration
of the united sees of Cork and Cloyne, and from the foundation
charter of the collegiate church it is clear that a coadjutor had
been appointed by that date. The appointment which gave
the right of succession to the appointee was made in response
to representations made to Rome that the bishop of Cork and
Cloyne was an octogenarian who, because of old age and
impotence, was no longer able to discharge his pastoral office,
in consequence of which grave abuses remained unchecked while
the clergy of the city and diocese of Cork and Cloyne were
grievously harassed by lay encroachments.[21] The following
cases exemplify the types of abuse then common. Nicholas
O'Kelly (Oceallaid), a canon of Cork and prebendary of
Kilbrittain, was reported as having dilapidated the goods of his
canonry and prebend; he 'publicly kept a concubine and for
many years neglected to reside in the church of Cork or in the
said prebend and celebrate and serve therein'. When John
Cronin (Ocronyn), a student in canon law, wished to succeed
to O'Kelly's prebend he was prevented because of the favours
O'Kelly enjoyed in the city and diocese of Cork.[22] This occurred
in 1447. In 1459 during the pontificate of Pius II John
Omongayn, rector of Kinneigh (Cenneith), obtained the perpetual vicarage of Ringrone (Rynnroyn) by presentation of
the patron and institution of the ordinary and detained it with
his rectory for more than a month without dispensation; the
vicarage had remained vacant because Omongayn dilapidated
its goods, committed simony and neglected to reside and serve
there. David Miach (Meade), archdeacon of Cork in 1459 was
'an open and notorious fornicator' who committed simony and

---

20   Ibid.

21   Theiner, *Vetera mon.*, p. 430–1. The papal letters give the following account:
'Jordan, bishop of Cork and Cloyne, is an octogenarian and is so old and without
bodily strength and sight that he cannot exercise the pastoral office in person, whereof
many excesses and crimes of his subjects remain unpunished and many goods of the
said churches and of the episcopal *mense* are in the hands of laymen, and the vassals
thereof and the clergy of the city and diocese are burdened with exactions by the
said laymen'.

22   *Cal. papal letters, 1447–55*, p. 293.

dilapidated the goods of his archdeaconry.[23] The papal effort
to halt these abuses was not of a kind likely to prove effective.
O'Kelly was replaced in Kilbrittain by John Cronin, rector of
Templetrine, who claimed that his rectory was not more than
a mile distant from the prebend; it seemingly counted for little
that he was now holding incompatible benefices. In the case
of Ringrone the abbots of Gill Abbey (*de Antro*) and Tracton
(*de Albotractu*) were ordered to deprive Omongayn and collate
and assign the vicarage to Dermit Canty (Ouchante), 'who was
lately dispensed by papal authority on account of illegitimacy as
the son of unmarried parents (i) to be promoted to all even
holy orders and hold a benefice even with cure (ii) to receive and
retain a canonry of Cork and the prebend of Drumdaliag
[Drimoleague] and to resign them as often as he pleased'.[24]
The papal rectification of the archdeaconry was an order that
John Okeallayd *alias* Macgillaruag, a priest of the diocese of
Clonfert, 'the son of a priest, professed of the Cistercian order
and an unmarried woman' should be provided in place of
Meade. For the present, Meade's power was such that O'Kelly
could not safely meet him in the city or diocese of Cork,[25] but
O'Kelly succeeded to the archdeaconry in 1463.

At episcopal level papal intervention threw the united dioceses
into over thirty years of turmoil and confusion during which
the activities and counter-activities of 'Rome-runners' added a
chaotic element to an already overcharged situation. The
'Rome-runners' were William Roche, whose family held extensive territories in north and north-east Cork, and Gerald
FitzGerald (de Geraldinis), third son of Richard FitzMaurice
FitzGerald, who 'was by the Erle of Desmond made capten of
his kerne and his seneshall in Imokellye, of whome the seneshall
of Imokellye and Sir John FitzEdmond of Clone do descend'.[26]
Roche and FitzGerald were clerics of Cloyne; their efforts can
only be interpreted as an endeavour to weight the balance of
power in favour of their own diocese where the decree of
amalgamation had been ill received.

William Roche, archdeacon of Cloyne and in minor orders
only, was appointed coadjutor to Jordan Purcell on 27 May

23 *Cal. papal letters, 1455–64*, pp. 392–3, 475.

24 Ibid., pp. 392–3.

25 Ibid., p. 475.

26 A curious old manuscript pedigree of the FitzGeralds of Imokilly, the original
of which was formerly preserved in the registry of Cloyne, gives some interesting data
on the FitzGeralds of Cloyne and Ballymartyr. See *Cork Hist. Soc. Jn.*, iii (1894),
213 ff.

1461 by mandate of Pope Pius II, who ordered the bishops of Emly and Ross and the abbot of Fermoy *alias de Castrodey* in the diocese of Cloyne, 'to appoint, provided that the chapter of Cloyne or the greater part thereof consents, William Roche, archdeacon of Cloyne, of a race of earls, to be coadjutor to the said bishop [Jordan Purcell], and moreover as soon as the said churches [of Cork and Cloyne] are no longer ruled by the said bishop and until provision is made of them, to commit to the said William the rule and administration of the said churches in spirituals and temporals'. Bishop Purcell, who does not seem to have been consulted and who did not apply for a coadjutor, made no demur until the counter-claims of Gerald FitzGerald brought matters to a head. FitzGerald, a canon of Cloyne and, like Roche, in minor orders only, secured provision to the united sees of Cork and Cloyne, 'void recently at the apostolic See and therefore reserved to the pope, by the resignation of Jordan (now) a bishop in the universal church, then Bishop of Cork and Cloyne, made to the pope by John, elect of Ardagh, substituted as proctor by Jordan's proctor, John OHedian, archdeacon of Cashel and Ossory'.[27] FitzGerald, who was only twenty-nine, was dispensed to exercise the rule, cure and administration of the united churches of Cork and Cloyne, and on 3 February 1462 he was granted faculty of consecration by any Catholic bishop assisted by two or three others.[28] The issue of this provision within six months of William Roche's appointment is just one in a long series of counter-provisions which bedevilled Cork diocesan affairs for the next thirty years.

FitzGerald was at Rome during the foregoing proceedings, but he did not follow up his appointment. He was still in Rome in 1463 when he was given a papal letter of safe-conduct for the transaction of certain business in which the pope was said to have been interested. The letter, which was undated but which was issued after 25 March 1463, requested 'a safe-conduct for Gerald, . . . elect of Cork and Cloyne, papal nuncio and commissary, and Thady, Clerk, a Friar Preacher and a scholar in theology (whom the pope has joined to the said Gerald, elect, for the easier execution of the matters committed to him), who have to go in person to divers parts of the world, especially to Ireland, for the prosecution of certain business of the pope concerning the catholic faith and the rest of the faithful'.[29] The

27 *Cal. papal letters, 1455–64*, pp. 425, 469.

28 Ibid., p. 473.

29 Ibid., p. 694.

exact nature of the pope's business has not come to light, but
it is beyond doubt that the papal commission was not executed,
for at this juncture Jordan Purcell made a joint appeal to Pope
Pius II and to Edward IV against both Roche and FitzGerald.
Roche was charged with the commission of many grave crimes
to the prejudice and grief of Bishop Jordan and with unlawful
occupation of the united sees. The charge against Gerald
FitzGerald was that he had forged certain instruments through
which he had secured provision to the united sees and had
striven to expel the rightful bishop.[30] It is nowhere on record
that William Roche was then in actual occupation or that Gerald
FitzGerald had expelled Jordan Purcell from the united sees,
but the bishop appears to have won the ear of the king at whose
request the pope on 14 April 1463 commissioned the archbishop
of Cashel and the bishops of Exeter and Limerick to investigate
the charges brought against the intruders. Should they be
legally satisfied that Roche had secured his appoinment as
coadjutor by false statements and had, in consequence, taken
wrongful possession of the revenues of the united sees, they
were to deprive him of the coadjutorship, compel him to
submit an account of his administration and restore the revenues,
fruits, etc., to Bishop Jordan Purcell. Should the charge of
forgery against Gerald FitzGerald be substantiated he was to
be debarred from consecration 'until the pope has otherwise
disposed', and both he and Roche were to be prohibited 'under
pain of *ipso facto* excommunication' from meddling with the
affairs of Cork and Cloyne.[31]

The papal mandate was followed on 22 June by a royal writ
from Edward IV to his lieutenant and deputy in Ireland, to
William de la Barre, David Roche, Edmund Baret, the mayors
of Cork and Youghal and the sub-prior of Kinsale, ordering
them to ensure that the archbishop and other bishops nominated
should 'carry out the pope's mandate with regard to the dispute
in the bishopric of Cork and Cloyne'.[32] A gap in both papal and
state records prevents a follow-up of this ecclesiastical inquiry,
but from subsequent events its findings—if compromising—
would appear to have been negatived by Gerald FitzGerald
who either by intrigue or diplomacy, had himself consecrated
in Rome during the pontificate of Pius II who died on 14
August 1464. Assuming that the consecration took place after
the findings of the commission, the favour which FitzGerald

---

30 Theiner, *Vetera mon.*, pp. 448–9.

31 *Cal. papal letters, 1455–64*, p. 472.

32 *Cal. pat. rolls, 1461–67*, p. 273; 3 Edward IV, m. 5.

enjoyed in papal circles is obvious. But consecration was not the 'open Sesame' to Cork and Cloyne: Gerald FitzGerald was still referred to as an *electus* in 1466. An entry from the Roman transcripts in the Public Record Office, London, tells that on 30 April 1466, a certain Maurice Stanton promised to pay the annate on a canonry and prebend of Kahirultayn in Cloyne which became vacant *per promotionem Reverendi Patris Domini Geraldi electi ecclesiarum Clonensis et Corkagensis.*[33] That these vacancies were at least of two years standing and reflect a general inattention to the *cura animarum*, the pastoral mission, is detailed in the following mandate issued on 10 April 1466 by Pope Paul II to the abbot of Fermoy (*de Castro Dei*), to the treasurer and to Rory Macconmara, a canon of Cloyne: 'A canonry of Cloyne and the prebend of Kahirultayn therein having become void and *ipso facto* reserved to the gift of Pius II by that pope's promotion of Gerald (now) Bishop of Cork and Cloyne, to those united churches, and by his consecration carried out at the apostolic See by order of the said pope; and the said pope having died without having disposed thereof, remaining still void and reserved to the present pope, he hereby orders the above three to collate and assign them . . . to Maurice Stantun.' Stanton was to be provided also to the precentorship of Cloyne and to the prebend of Killaspugmullane (Kylasbuyc-mellayn) in Cork, both of which were about to become void by the privation of Cornelius Oteye, priest of the diocese of Limerick, who, 'by his own temerity and without any collation or provision detained possession of them for between two and three years'.[34]

By 1464 then the dioceses of Cork and Cloyne had a bishop who was an octogenarian, a coadjutor who was still in minor orders and a third claimant, Gerald FitzGerald, who had the advantage of consecration over his opponent William Roche. Episcopal and coadjutorial relations during the next few years were anything but harmonious and cannot but have had disturbing effects on the clergy and people of the united dioceses. William Roche's name appended to that of Jordan Purcell on the foundation charter of the collegiate church of Youghal would seem to warrant that the bishop then favoured his coadjutor, but the climate had changed by 1468 when, at the suggestion of Jordan Purcell, the erection, institution and union of the various parsonages, vicarages and parishes to the collegiate church were given papal confirmation in a document which

33   P.R.O., Roman transcripts, series 31/1, vol. xxix, f. 7.

34   *Cal. papal letters, 1458–71*, p. 481.

contained no reference to Roche, but which was issued 'in authentic letters of the bishop [Jordan Purcell] sealed with his seal and with public instruments'.[35] Roche was equally capable of independent action, for we find that in 1468 'William Roste, archdeacon of Cloyne, coadjutor to Bishop Jordan, in virtue of an alleged power from the Apostolic See' conferred the perpetual vicarage of Clonfert in the diocese of Cloyne on Donatus Sheehan (Oscyn). Like many other benefice-holders in Cork and Cloyne the appointee entertained grave doubts as to the validity of his appointment and petitioned the Holy See for confirmation. The papal reply, in which Jordan Purcell and William Roche were ignored, took the form of a mandate to the prior of Saint Catherine's, Waterford, and the archdeacon and chancellor of that diocese to assign the vicarage to Sheehan.[36]

Meantime Gerald FitzGerald was indefatigable in urging his case against that of William Roche. Success attended his efforts. In 1470 the archbishop of Cashel, a known supporter of Roche, was ordered to put an end to Roche's pretensions and was commanded under severe sanctions to desist from favouring him. He was further commanded, for the sake of peace and the interest of religion, to assist Gerald FitzGerald in his endeavours to secure the rule and administration of the united sees. In 1462 Gerald FitzGerald had been promoted on the alleged resignation of Jordan Purcell; in 1470 he was confirmed as his successor, and the papal mandate of confirmation carried a sentence of suspension against William Roche.[37] Jordan Purcell was henceforth relegated to retirement. One of his last official functions, as calendared in the papal registers, is dated 18 April 1469 when he received the resignation of Maurice Gogan from the prebend of Inishkenny (Instrim [*sic*] *alias* Baleymalmihill) and deprived Thady Sheehan (Osychayn) of the perpetual vicarage of the parish church of the same place.[38] The resignation and privation were apparently of some years standing; the mandate recounts that Donogh O'Riordan (Orywardain), clerk of the diocese of Cloyne, held the prebend

35   Ibid., p. 624.

36   Ibid., p. 654.

37   Theiner, *Vetera mon.*, p. 464: ' . . . ipsum vero Willelmum . . . suspensum decernimus'. Jordan Purcell has the distinction of having had the longest episcopate in the entire history of the diocese of Cork. Its span of thirty-eight years (1432–70) has the advantage of two years on that of Bishop Daniel Cohalan who was provided as coadjutor to Dr. Thomas Alphonsus O'Callaghan on 25 May 1914; he was consecrated on 7 June, but did not succeed to the bishopric until 29 August 1916. He died on 24 August 1952.

38   *Cal. papal letters, 1458–71*, p. 689.

for between one and two years and that Robert Sheehan
(Osyhyhayn) of the same diocese had 'unduly detained the
possession of the vicarage for between four and five years, by
his own temerity and without any title or tittle of right'.

The accession of Sixtus IV (1471–84) to the papal throne
was William Roche's opportunity. Proceeding on the lines of
FitzGerald he filed his application for succession to Cork and
Cloyne by fraudulently announcing the death of Jordan Purcell.
The forgery worked, and on 26 October 1472 William Roche
was provided to the united churches of Cork and Cloyne,
'void by the death of Jordan *extra curiam*', during whose lifetime
they were specially reserved to the pope. Concurrent letters
were issued to the chapters of Cork and Cloyne, to the clergy
and people of the cities and dioceses, to the vassals of the
churches, to the archbishop of Cashel and to Edward, king of
England.[39] Roche, though still in minor orders, was given
faculty on 28 October to be consecrated by any Catholic bishop
of his choice in communion with the Apostolic See, assisted by
two or three others and without prejudice to the archbishop of
Cashel. Eubel quotes from the *Schede di Garampi* to the effect
that Roche neglected to pay the customary tax on his provisions.[40]
Because of this omission it seems probable that he was not
consecrated in 1472, but it is beyond doubt that he had achieved
canonical episcopal status by the year 1475.

Roche's provision was contested by Gerald FitzGerald whose
sphere of jurisdiction would seem to have been coterminous
with the Cork and Cloyne possessions of the earl of Desmond.
Similarly Roche's area of jurisdiction was apparently in the
Roche country of north and north-east Cork. Neither claimant
can have enjoyed the full temporalities of the united sees, and
it is not known where they fixed their respective ecclesiastical
headquarters. Therefore, Cork, like the dioceses of Killaloe,
Clogher and Kilmore, affords an example of a split diocese,
differing from the other three in that the struggle for supremacy
in Cork was one between representatives of the Norman families
of the diocese whereas those in Killaloe, Clogher and Kilmore
revolved upon the rival claims of native clerics and Norman
intruders. Roche's position was generally weaker than that of
FitzGerald, and even among clerics who supported him there
was a prevailing lack of confidence in the validity of his official
acts, more especially with regard to provision to benefices.

39 *Cal. papal letters, 1471–84*, pt. 1, p. 351.

40 Coleman in *Annats, Ulster*, pp. xxv–xxvi, states that non-paying appointees
were threatened with privation.

Witness, for example, the petition of Donough Cronin (Ocionyn) in 1472 who was provided to the perpetual vicarage of Aghinagh (Achadfinach) but doubted the validity of his appointment because William Roche who instituted him 'was litigating about the possession of the see against a certain adversary'.[41] There was also the petition of Donatus Oseyn who had been provided to the perpetual vicarage of Clonfert by Roche. Oseyn had held the vicarage for three years but in 1479 began to doubt the validity of his provision and sought papal confirmation for reassurance. It would appear too that at the time of Donough Cronin's petition in 1472 Roche had not been consecrated. The steps by which he secured consecration are not known, and the fact of his consecration can only be arrived at by deduction. On 17 April 1475 William, bishop of Cork and Cloyne, and Louis Macray, O.P., petitioned Pope Sixtus IV for confirmation of the gift of John de Geraldinis, knight of Kerry, to the Dominican order. The gift was 'a certain abandoned stone wall with certain lands adjacent thereto in the town of Gleannuyr [Glanworth], in the diocese of Cloyne, in order that there should be built there a house for the perpetual use and habitation of the said friars'. The petition mentions the consecration of a *cemetery and oratory* by William Roche, thus affording conclusive evidence that he had achieved episcopal orders by that date.[42]

Jordan Purcell, whose reported death was catalogued in the papal registers under date 1472, died in his nineties in or about the year 1477. Our authority for this statement (as in the case of Milo FitzJohn) is again the Travers' document quoted by Smith which records that the rectories of Fanlobbus (Dunmanway) and Kinneigh, which were conferred on the vicars choral by Edmund Riddefort, were confirmed by Jordan, bishop of Cork and Cloyne in 1477: *confirmata per Jordanum episcopum Corcag. et Clonensis, an.1477*.[43] Did this mean that Jordan Purcell still continued to officiate as bishop of Cork and Cloyne? If so, what of relations between him and Gerald FitzGerald? What measure of support did he enjoy, and what were his activities between 1470 and 1477? These and other related questions must remain unanswered. The printed records offer no solution, but a statement from Gerald FitzGerald (to be quoted subsequently) will at least verify the contention that the aged bishop was still alive in 1477. His death, while it may

41   *Cal. papal letters, 1471–84*, pt. 1, p. 108.

42   Ibid., pt. 2, p. 433.

43   Smith, *History of Cork*, i, 40.

have eased the situation somewhat, did not add up to any strengthening of William Roche's position either in the united dioceses or at Rome. In fact, a papal reply to an appeal made in 1478 contained a rebuttal of Roche. Thady Mac Carthy (Macarryg), canon of Cork, petitioned the Holy See for confirmation of the union of the rectories of Burren and Rathclarin to his canonry and prebend of Buelly (probably Killanully). The union thus constituted had been in the joint gift of Bishop William Roche and his chapter, but the papal reply was addressed to the dean, the archdeacon and the precentor, to the exclusion of the bishop, and directed that 'for greater precaution they [were] to make the appropriation anew'.[44] As bishop of Cloyne William Roche made his visitation of the church of Bruhenny (Bruchane) in 1481, but there is no further ecclesiastical function attributed to him after that date even though he still continued to press his claim against Gerald FitzGerald.

The ferocity of this protracted conflict may be gauged from the list of charges invoiced against Roche by Gerald FitzGerald in 1484. It is significant that on this occasion FitzGerald claimed to have exercised the rule and administration of the united churches of Cork and Cloyne for seven years, that is, since 1477. His statement therefore synchronizes with the suggestion inherent in the Travers' document that Jordan Purcell did not die until that year. FitzGerald's indictment of Roche—even allowing for a certain amount of exaggeration and for the fact that Gerald FitzGerald had originally secured his provision by forgery—shows to what extent partisan feelings went in Cork and Cloyne during the disturbed years of the succession dispute. The tenor of FitzGerald's complaint was that Roche had in many ways disturbed him in the rule and administration of the united dioceses, had caused his followers in Cork and Cloyne to be despoiled of their goods, had caused the city of Cloyne and especially the *mensa* of the vicars there to be burned, had perpetrated many homicides and had caused many goods to be violently removed from the church and cemetery of Cloyne. Roche was also charged with having twice imprisoned Gerald FitzGerald and in consequence—so the complaint runs—he (Roche) and his followers had been excommunicated by the then archbishop of Cashel and his suffragans, notwithstanding which, 'and aided and abetted by divers rectors, vicars and abbots', he had violently appropriated the fruits of the churches of Cork and Cloyne.[45] Rome's reply was swift and decisive;

44 · *Cal. papal letters, 1471–84*, pt. 1, p. 70.

45   Ibid., p. 187.

one might almost say that Rome was impetuous in accepting at their face value the charges adduced by a man whose forgery cannot but have been known in curial circles. The pope admonished William Roche and his abettors, under pain of *ipso facto* excommunication, to desist from interference with Bishop Gerald and to make satisfaction to him. Executory mandate was simultaneously issued to the abbot of Saint Mary's, Midleton (*de Choro Benedicti*), to John Barri, a canon of Cork, and to the official of Cork who were directed to invoke the aid of the secular power against Roche. The archbishop of Cashel was exhorted to help Gerald FitzGerald recover his possessions, as were all other archbishops, bishops, prelates, princes, knights and other temporal rulers, especially Earl James of Desmond, John Barri, Maurice Roche, Donough MacCarthy, prince of Carbery, and Donough Mor O'Mahony of Dunmanus.[46]

William Roche's episcopate, in the canonical sense, terminated with the issue of the foregoing papal directive, but he did not resign officially until 1490 when his resignation was cited in a bull providing Thaddeus MacCarthy to the bishopric. Nothing is known of Roche's subsequent activities, but Webster is incorrect in placing his death as occurring in 1484. Webster's tenet is an erroneous application of an inscription discovered by Westropp on a grave in the priory church of Brinkburn in Northumberland. The legend on this grave reads: *Hic jacet Willelmus, Quondam Clunensis Episcopus, ac Dunelmensis Suffraganeus et Prior istius monasterii, cuius animae propiciatur Deus; qui obiit anno Domini cccclxxxiiij.*[47] *Clunensis* was one of the Latin variants for Clonmacnoise, and in the later fifteenth century one William, bishop of Clonmacnoise, happened also to be prior of Brinkburn and suffragan of Durham.[48] William Roche died in 1498 or 1499.

It was only to be expected that the protracted succession dispute should prove detrimental to the exercise of the ministry, should foster dissensions within the dioceses and should encourage a series of those irresponsible provisions and collations which were part of the legacy of the Great Schism. In 1475 a dispute over the precentorship led to 'an exchange of insults, blows and bloodshed' between Cornelius Murphy (Ymurchu) and an unnamed opponent. Murphy, who was excommunicated

---

46 There seems to be some confusion of names here. Donough MacCarthy, prince of Carbery and mentioned above, died in 1452, leaving a son Cormac, but there was no Donough in 1484.

47 Webster, *The Diocese of Cork*, p. 165.

48 Michael Kiely, 'Episcopal Succession in Cork and Cloyne in the Fifteenth Century', *I.E.R.*, xl (1932), 123.

for his part in the brawl, still officiated 'at Mass and other divine services', but was nevertheless absolved by papal mandate and provided to the precentorship in June 1475.[49] It counted for little at Rome that John Roche, rector of Saint Mary, Shandon, and in minor orders only, had been provided to the precentorship in the previous April. An earlier abuse arising out of collations to the precentorship involved Gerald FitzGerald, who was still practising forgery and who sought by surreptitious letters of provision to have John de Geraldinis appointed to the precentorship in 1470.[50] Thus a three-fold rivalry developed between John de Geraldinis, Cornelius Murphy and John Roche. Pope Innocent VIII decided in favour of Murphy and permitted him to enjoy the precentorship together with his vicarage of Rathdrought, to which by a later mandate the pope permitted the rectory of Kinneigh to be joined.

Similar disturbances arose over the chancellorship. In 1482 Matthew O'Mahony (Omathuna) who was 'behaving as chancellor' was persuaded by Abbot Cornelius O'Flynn (Offlayn) of Gill Abbey to resign. Negotiations followed between Cornelius and Abbot Raymond Barry of Tracton and resulted in a charge of simony and a sentence of excommunication against Cornelius O'Flynn who by bargaining had secured the chancellorship for himself. David Hallinan (Ohalynayn), a canon of Cork, presented these facts to the pope (Sixtus IV) and was himself provided to the chancellorship; but his intrusion was resented, and feelings ran so high that Ohalynayn was afraid to meet either of the two abbots in the city and diocese of Cork.[51] Eventually Ohalynayn secured possession and ruled as chancellor until 1488.

Then there was the instance of two clerks charged in 1482 with having held for several years without canonical title the perpetual vicarage of Agalasmaschala or Aglish and the treasureship of Cork—this was but one of countless other parallel abuses. Nor can the situation in Kinsale have been unique considering the prevailing confusion. In 1484 the rector of Kinsale was an English Benedictine monk who because of the language barrier could neither hear confessions nor administer the sacraments, and who refused to appoint a vicar who could do so.[52] His refusal led to his removal and replacement by Maurice Martel, whose family gave its name to the town of

49   *Cal. papal letters, 1471–84*, pt. 1, p. 418.

50   *Cal. papal letters, 1458–71*, p. 360.

51   *Cal. papal letters, 1471–84*, pt. 1, p. 124.

52   Ibid., p. 176.

Ballymartle. An inverse situation to that obtaining in Kinsale had previously arisen in Waterford. Nicholas Hennessy, who was appointed bishop of Waterford and Lismore in 1482, was *persona non grata* to the dean of Waterford and to certain influential citizens because he could neither understand English nor speak it intelligently. Thus while the people of Waterford desired their clergy to be well-versed in the king's English, those of Kinsale opted for a native speaker.

Consequences of the succession dispute were also noticeable in the diocese of Cloyne. Of these the most extreme case is that found in a mandate of 1480 ordering the dean of Lismore to collate a vacant canonry and prebend in Cloyne to John de Geraldinis, *then aged eleven.*[53] The benefice had been detained unjustly for over four years by Edmund (Egimundus) Roche. Those responsible for appointments of this nature had but little time for the souls of Christian people; their preoccupation was with ecclesiastical revenues which they siphoned off for purposes other than ecclesiastical. For this reason the provision of minors was not uncommon; its continuance was assured by a sort of connived papal approval, as happened in 1469 when the archdeacon of Ossory was mandated to assign and collate a canonry of Lismore with the prebend of Donachmore *alias* Kyltahan in the same diocese to twelve-year-old Theobald de Botiller, clerk of the diocese of Cashel. Thomas Cornis, dean of Cork, who had detained possession for over two years without title, was to be removed and by special indult Theobald de Botiller was to receive and retain the benefices 'notwithstanding the pope's late constitution against making provision of cathedral canonries and prebends to persons unless they have completed their fourteenth year'.[54]

Clearly, then, the abuses prevalent in Cork and Cloyne were not all offshoots of the succession dispute, for of all centuries the fifteenth was that in which diocesan organization everywhere was most in jeopardy, mainly because of pluralism and non-residence which, from the nature of things, had now become erected into a system. The typical pluralist would hold one prebend in a cathedral or collegiate church together with one parish church with cure of souls. Such benefices were 'compatible', needing no papal dispensation, which was required only for the holding of two or more benefices with cure of souls. The extent to which pluralism could go is exemplified in John

53 Not to be confused with John de Geraldinis who was a claimant for the precentorship of Cork in 1470.

54 *Cal. papal letters, 1458–71*, p. 688.

Stack, canon of Limerick, who was dispensed to hold a canonry of Cloyne and the prebend of Cuyllcolling and Brechmuy (value three marks), the prebend of Effyng in Limerick (fifteen marks), the deanery of Ardfert (twenty marks), the archdeaconry of Limerick (sixty marks), the rectory of the parish church of Dungarvan in the diocese of Lismore (one hundred marks), a canonry of Tuam and the prebend of the small churches of Conmacniculy and Conmacnimara (ten marks). Compared with these appointments and with those of *clerici regis* the provisions made to Thomas Oseancan, B.C.L., holder of a canonry of Cork and the prebend of Killanully, were only a mild form of pluralism. In addition to his canonry and prebend Oseancan was dispensed to hold the deanery of Limerick (forty marks), a canonry of Cloyne and the prebend of Kilcredan (four marks), the vicarage of Ardmore (eight marks) and the deanery of Lismore. Canons holding benefices outside of Ireland are likewise encountered, and while their number was not large, we find a Cork cleric in their midst. John Purcell, canon of Cork and bachelor in canon law, was rector of Brant Broughton in the diocese of Lincoln (twenty marks), he was archdeacon of Lismore (twelve marks), was litigating at the Roman court about a canonry and prebend of Ossory (ten marks) and he crowned his achievements by becoming bishop of Ferns, collector to the papal *camera* and apostolic nuncio.[55] The lucrative returns from these accumulated benefices (even though some pluralists were comparatively poor men) were completely out of keeping with the meagre salaries paid to vicars and other stipendiary priests upon whom the *cura animarum* devolved. Overworked and under-salaried, these clerics have been aptly termed an impoverished clerical proletariat.

The extent to which pluralism was permitted, practised and even encouraged (e.g., for purposes of study) by papal dispensation shows an appalling disregard for the care of souls among those who sought preferment in the church during the fourteenth and fifteenth centuries. Pluralism begot non-residence, for the more livings a man had the less time he could spend in each. Various efforts were made to force incumbents to reside but, as already noted, the flow of dispensations from Rome negatived the efforts of the reformers, and even though incidental papal legislation helped to rationalize and control pluralism, it was perhaps asking too much that the papacy should abolish the system altogether. In the long run the spiritual

55   *Cal. papal letters, 1447–55*, pp. 453, 369, 361.

vacuum created by non-residence became a fertile seed-bed for the neglect, the indifference and the countless other faults and misdemeanours invoiced against the clergy in the later volumes of the papal letters. Here we get instances of benefices left so long vacant that their collation had lapsed to the Apostolic See. There were fourteen of these in Cloyne in the fifteenth century and about ten in Cork: Desertmore, Macloneigh, Ringrone, Kilnaglory, Aglish, Killanully, Leighmoney, Kilbrogan, Inishkenny and Holy Trinity.[56] Clerics are charged with having usurped and detained benefices for many years without canonical title—in some cases without ordination.[57] Others, though deprived, have continued to celebrate Mass in defiance of the power of the keys, for which they have been excommunicated. Others again have dilapidated the goods of their prebends, have disposed of all moveables and by their refusal to dwell within their prebends have deprived their people of divine service and of the sacraments. In 1447 Nicholas O'Kelly (Ocealayd) of Kilbrittain allowed a child to die without baptism.[58] In 1484 the perpetual vicar of Aghabulloge in Cloyne left one of his parishioners die without the sacraments.[59] Father Ambrose Coleman in his introduction to *De Annatis Hiberniae* gives similar instances for the northern province; the remaining provinces of Dublin and Tuam conformed to the same pattern. Confronted with such a general decline in discipline and morals, it is a fair assumption that even had Cork and Cloyne been spared the debacle of the succession dispute the history of the united dioceses would still have followed the lines detailed above.

Only two of Gerald FitzGerald's official acts—following his victory over William Roche in 1484—have been committed to record. The first is a charge of simony which was brought against him in 1486 for advancing a follower of the FitzGeralds to the prebend of Ballayath (probably Ballea, Carrigaline) to which John Roche, baron of Fermoy, had the right of presentation. There is no indication that the charge was proved. In the same year a letter of Innocent VIII, preserved in the Costelloe Collection and addressed to Gerald FitzGerald, bishop of Cork and Cloyne, refers to his application for one vicar general for the two dioceses. Gerald FitzGerald's arguments for reducing

56 Bolster, 'Obligationes pro Annatis Diocesis Corcagiensis', and *Cal. papal letters, 1458–71, 1471–84, 1484–92, passim.*

57 *Cal. papal letters, 1458–71, passim.*

58 *Cal. papal letters, 1447–55*, p. 293.

59 Denis Buckley, 'Diocesan Organization: Cloyne', *Ir. Cath. Hist. Comm. Proc.* (1954), p. 10.

the vicars general were in line with those advanced by Edward II in 1326, namely, an insufficiency of funds and the conviction that the spiritual interests of both dioceses could best be promoted under one vicar general.[60] The proposition may also have envisaged an increase of control for Gerald FitzGerald in Cloyne where there must still have been pockets if not larger areas of support for William Roche. The request was not granted.

During the final years of the Roche-FitzGerald conflict both became involved in the political upheavals attendant upon the Wars of the Roses. The battle of Bosworth, 21 August 1485, was a triumph for the red rose, but though Henry Tudor became king of England at that date, half a century was to pass before the new monarchy really operated in Ireland. So strong were the claims of the white rose that Ireland, or more precisely Anglo-Ireland, became the stage for two successive attempts to overthrow the Tudor dynasty. First was the attempt of Lambert Simnel whose sponsors declared him to be Edward, earl of Warwick, and whose cause was espoused by the archbishops of Armagh and Dublin, the bishops of Meath and Kildare, William Roche, bishop of Cloyne [sic], the earl of Kildare and James FitzGerald, earl of Desmond. Simnel was crowned as Edward VI in Dublin on 24 May 1487, but on 16 June, at a battle fought at Stoke near Newark, his supporters were vanquished and the pretender became a scullion in King Henry's kitchen. He was later promoted to the position of royal falconer and is believed to have ultimately become a servant in the household of Sir Thomas Lovell. William Roche as bishop of Cloyne was included in the pardon issued in 1488 to all participants in the Simnel affair. The pardon, which was enshrined in statute 3 Henry VII, conceded general pardon for crimes, with remission of forfeiture of lands to Octavian, archbishop of Armagh, and concurrent pardons to Walter, archbishop of Dublin, to William, bishop of Cloyne, to John, bishop of Meath, and to Edmund, bishop of Derry. The abbot of Saint Thomas' Abbey, Dublin, and the Cistercian abbots of Baltinglass, Mellifont, Bective, etc., were likewise pardoned.[61] Later in the same year (1488) the treasurer and chamber of the exchequer were directed to pay the sum of twenty marks to the bishop of Cloyne 'by way of rewarde for his costes and expenses, to be borne into and from oure land of Ireland by

---

60   Kiely, 'Episcopal Succession in Cork and Cloyne in the Fifteenth Century', p. 121.

61   W. Campbell, ed., *Materials for a History of the Reign of Henry VII*, ii, 315.

oure commaundment'.[62] William Roche resigned shortly afterwards, and a pension of one-third of the revenues of the sees of
Cork and Cloyne was assigned to him by papal bull dated
Rome, 11 Kal. Maii, 1490.[63] Brady incorrectly cites William
Roche as the bishop of Cork mentioned in a pardon granted in
1496 to supporters of Perkin Warbeck, the second Yorkist
pretender. As will be shown presently, the bishop in question
was Gerald FitzGerald. Brady supports his statement by saying
that 'is it not very unusual to give the title of Bishop to a person
after his resignation', which while true does not apply in the
present instance.[64] Roche's resignation was made in favour of
Thaddeus MacCarthy—he would still not concede an inch to
Gerald FitzGerald—and this entry of a MacCarthy into the
ecclesiastical sphere was to spark off another of those racial
conflicts which were then dangerously simmering in an
atmosphere of mounting political tensions.

In a situation in which the maintenance of a dignified *status
quo* was becoming increasingly difficult, the position in Munster
contained its own inherent problems. We have noted that the
Desmond Geraldines had become rulers of the ancient *Regnum
Corcagiense*; at the same time the MacCarthy lordship had been
gradually rebuilding until under MacCarthy Mór it extended
from the lakes of Killarney southwards to Bantry Bay and thence
eastwards to Macroom. A junior branch, MacCarthy Reagh,
were lords of Carbery, a district lying between Bantry and
Innishannon, and when James, the sixth earl of Desmond, came
to power in 1400 none had resented the Geraldine intrusion
more than MacCarthy Reagh. The hostility thus engendered,
though temporarily dormant, erupted with the provision of
Thaddeus MacCarthy and further complicated the ecclesiastical
administration of the dioceses of Cork, Cloyne and Ross.

In the sphere of civic development it appears that conditions
obtaining in Cork in the fourteenth century were continued
well into the fifteenth. The accumulating arrears of the fee-farm
and frequent grants of the *cocket* (this was a custom valued at
twenty marks a year to be spent in repairing the city walls) to
enable the citizens become solvent suggests a steadily deteriorat-
ing economy. The royal policy which in 1394 forbade the export
of provisions from the corporate towns had by 1463 so shackled
commercial intercourse that by special edict the citizens of

62 Ibid., p. 320; entry dated 1 June 1488.

63 Cork Diocesan Archives.

64 Brady, *Records*, ii, 44.

Cork, Limerick, Waterford and Youghal were permitted to exchange all manner of merchandise, except guns and provisions in time of war, with the native Irish.[65] By 1489/90 Cork merchants were again exporting hides to Bristol, but by then Waterford had outstepped Cork in the volume and value of its trade. The final grant of concessions was contained in charter 2 Edward IV, 1462, which was a confirmation of former charters but which mentions that eleven parish churches in the city and suburbs within a radius of one mile were burnt and destroyed by reason of the war stirred up by Irish enemies and English rebels. The opening round of the conflict between William Roche and Gerald FitzGerald must have contributed in great measure to this destruction. The names of the plundered churches cannot be ascertained, but assuming that the statement is correct, parochial organization in the city and suburbs shows a marked development upon that outlined in the Wynchedon will of 1306.

A charter dated 8 July (or 1 August) 1482 gives the geographical limitations within which the confirmatory privileges and grants of Cork were to be enjoyed: 'And in order that there may be no doubt touching the metes and bounds of the said city [of Cork] the King [Edward IV] hereby grants that the mayor and citizens of Cork and their heirs and successors shall enjoy the said liberties and franchises in the city and suburb, and in all the port, to wit, as far as the shore or point called Renrawre on the west side of the port, and as far as the shore or point called Renowdran on the east side of the port, and to the castle of Cargrongha on the west side of the city, and in all the towns [*oppidis*], pills [*pilis*], creeks [*crecis*], burghs [*burgis*] and strands [*strondis*] to which the flow of the tide reaches between the said two points.'[66] Renrawre and Renowdran represent the twin forts of Camden (*Dún Uí Mheachair*) and Carlisle (*Dún an Dáibhsigh*) which guard the entrance to Cork harbour. The castle of Cargrongha is easily recognizable as Carrigrohane.

On the question of currency some interesting snippets concerning Cork occur in the state records up to the fifteenth century. Cork had a short-lived mint operated by the city bailiffs as early as 1295.[67] Silver and copper pieces of small denomination and stamped *Civitas Corcaciae* were coined in

65   *Statute Rolls of the Parliament of Ireland, 1st to the 12th Years of the Reign of Edward IV*, ed. H. F. Berry, p. 139.

66   William O'Sullivan, *The Economic History of Cork City*, p. 290.

67   *P.R.I. rep. D.K. 38*, p. 51.

Cork in 1304, but as they were subject to frequent clippings they were easily devalued. Fifteenth-century minting enterprises of native Irish and English colonists were halted by statutes of Henry VI in 1447 and 1456, while Edward IV established the principle that money in Ireland should always be kept at a lower value than English currency. This struck a blow at Ireland's foreign commerce since foreign merchants would not bring their merchandise to a country where money was light and bad.[68] A new national coinage was struck in 1459 and the old coins were condemned, but the new mintage was damned by Edward IV who passed a new issue of cheap coins in 1467–68 and devalued them by half within two years. However, local mints were at work and in 1472 we find King Edward invoking sanctions against 'divers coiners' in the city of Cork and in the neighbouring towns of Youghal, Kinsale and Kilmehalok (between Douglas and Crosshaven). The threat was ignored, the money-makers remained in business and Cork was given royal sanction for a mint in 1474.[69] The royal bounty was short-lived. In 1475 the king ordered the closure of all mints in Ireland save only those in Dublin, Drogheda and Waterford, and in 1476 statute 16 Edward IV enacted that 'the silver and coin lately made in Cork, Limerick, Youghal and other places in Munster, except Waterford, being neither lawful in itself, nor of lawful weight or alloy' should be 'utterly damned and taken in no payment'. Irish currency became so devalued that by the close of the fifteenth century it was excluded from England, Wales and Calais, and the men of Waterford were imprisoned for bringing it into Bristol in 1477. It was not until the closing years of the reign of the first Elizabeth that definite steps were taken to stabilize the currency 'for the good of the realm'. How Cork fared under the Elizabethan and later fiscal systems is outside the ambit of the present volume.

In common with other Irish chartered cities and towns and after many fluctuations of fortune and status Cork had attained a large measure of municipal independence by the close of the fifteenth century. Like other towns too its democratic origins had yielded to an oligarchic set-up in which families like Wynchedon, Coppinger, Gould, Skiddy and others held the balance of wealth and power. But there was also perceptible a constant growth of a more native element in the ecclesiastic, civic and industrial life of the city. The growth was marked by

68   W. O'Sullivan, *The Economic History of Cork City*, pp. 55–7.

69   *Cal. pat. rolls, 1467–77*, p. 468.

the emergence of families like the Meades and the Ronaynes and by the increasing number of canons and prebendaries of Irish extraction who begin to predominate among the benefice-holders. Right through the fifteenth century these Irish names are conspicuous in the papal letters and in the annate entries for Cork. Among them we find, among others, names like Murphy (Ymurchu), MacCarthy (Mekarrygh), O'Reilly (Orealich), Coughlan (Ocochlain), O'Mahony (Ymathuna) and O'Callaghan (Okeallakayn).[70]

70   Bolster, 'Obligationes pro Annatis Diocesis Corcagiensis', and *Cal. papal letters, 1458–71, 1471–84, 1484–92, passim.*

XVII

The Observant Reform in the Diocese of Cork

During the course of the fourteenth and fifteenth centuries when political upheavals and episcopal succession disputes were rife in the county and diocese of Cork, the germination of a second spring began to revitalize the mendicant orders in what came to be known as the Observantine reform or the Observant movement which affected Augustinians, Dominicans and Franciscans but had no impact on the Carmelites, at least in the period under discussion. The term 'Observant' is self-explanatory, and the Observant movement in all three orders advocated, as Vatican II has advocated in our own times, a return to sources, to a rekindling of the spark which animated the original founders. And while, according to Father Canice Mooney, 'different aspects of reform were stressed in different countries and in different decades, . . . in general an appeal went out for a greater spirit of prayer, devotion and recollection; for withdrawal from unnecessary and harmful worldly distractions; for greater moderation in the use of things, for the abolition of fixed revenues and for the alienation of superfluous lands and property'.[1] The great Observant movement spread to Ireland from the continent where its development may be seen as an effort to extricate the mendicant orders from the stagnancy of tepidity and decline into which, when their first flush of enthusiasm and fervour had abated, they seem to have inevitably drifted. Contributory factors to the decline were numerous. The Black Death which ravaged Europe between 1347 and 1349 exacted a heavy toll from monastic communities; their depleted ranks were filled by a non-differential process of hasty recruiting which admitted many who in normal times would never have been accepted. Shortly afterwards, the Avignon captivity followed by the debacle of the Great Schism

---

1   Canice Mooney, 'The Franciscans in Ireland', *Terminus* (November 1954), p. 245.

produced serious cleavages in the ranks of the friars. The complications of maintaining regular observance in the face of tempting dispensations held out by rival popes in return for support for their respective causes are too obvious to be delayed upon. As we have seen, the Council of Constance ended the schism without effecting any serious movement for reform.[2] The Observant movement therefore—to quote the Augustinian historian, Father F. X. Martin—was one aspect of 'a clamant desire for reform within the church', and Father Martin further maintains that 'because the Mendicant Orders were tightly-knit international bodies it was natural that their brethren in Ireland adopted the reform before the other sections of the Irish Church'.[3]

The extension of the Observant movement into Ireland was spearheaded by the Augustinians in 1423; after them the Dominicans ran a close second in 1425 or 1426, with the Franciscans bringing up the rear in 1433. In the long run, however, the Franciscans were the most important of the three groups. When the movement got under way Observant friars of all three orders were to be found in each of the provinces, but gradually a definite pattern emerged showing the Augustinians and Dominicans strongest in Connacht and the Franciscans predominating in Munster. The drive of higher religious motives behind this great triple Observant movement cannot for one moment be questioned, but neither can it be denied that the movement derived an essential part of its driving force from the conscious or semi-conscious desire of the native Irish personnel of the three orders to wrest the hegemony of their respective provinces from the hands of the Anglo-Irish. Therefore the Observant movement was not without its political overtones. In each of the orders the reform had its own distinctive characteristics, and while each was independent of the others the reform movements took root within the same decade (1423–33) and there were incidental features common to all three.

As regards direction, the early friars came to this country from England; the fifteenth-century Observants came from

---

2 An ambitious programme for reform included proposals for the reorganization of the Curia and College of Cardinals, regulations regarding grants of dispensations and indulgences, the abolition of annates and papal provisions. A far-reaching constitutional change was introduced in 1417 by the decree *Frequens* which provided that another council should meet in five years' time, a second seven years later and others thereafter at regular ten-yearly intervals. We have seen that Pope Martin V was not partial to reforms which had conciliar implications.

3 F. X. Martin, 'The Irish Friars and the Observant Movement in the Fifteenth Century', *Ir. Cath. Hist. Comm. Proc.* (1960; published 1961), p. 11.

the continent. The Augustinians had no Observant house in
pre-Reformation England, the English Dominicans rejected
the reform and it was only with difficulty that the Franciscan
Observants established themselves there. Later, a group of
these Observants was to suffer martyrdom for their uncompromising resistance to the sixteenth-century Reformation. It
was mainly from Italy that the impetus towards Observant
reform came: from Lecceto near Siena in the case of the
Augustinians, from Milan in that of the Dominicans and from
Rimini for the Franciscans. In Ireland the Gaelic parts of the
country became the natural habitat of the Observant movement,
for the friars were not unaware of the growing potentialities
of the territories under native sway, and consequently the
toning-up of religious life in Ireland kept pace, one might say,
with the decline of English authority in the country. The
fruitless expeditions of Richard II and his rather ignominious
departure in 1399 highlighted England's failure to halt the
emergent Gaelic race in the fourteenth century, while growing
liaisons between Anglo-Irish and Gael went far towards
eliminating the tensions inherent in the struggle for existence
which for over two centuries had been the native Irishman's
lot in life. During these centuries interim contacts with Rome
had been a powerful expedient in counterbalancing the flooding
of church vacancies with English clerics, and it is therefore
not surprising that a movement emanating from Italy should
make its Irish headquarters in those parts which were predominantly native. Coupled with this preference for the
native-held districts, the Observant friars of the fifteenth
century were in one particular aspect in direct contrast to their
brethren of the thirteenth. The mendicant movement in its
origins was typically urban, its pastoral apostolate was directed
towards the spiritual needs of the town-dwellers and the early
friaries were built within or close to the walls of medieval cities
and towns. The Observant movement, on the other hand, was
a rural development, its friaries were established in remote
and lonely places and, in the beginning at any rate, the pastoral
apostolate does not seem to have been accorded any priority
by the advocates of reform. What Father Canice Mooney says
of the Franciscan Observants may be taken as applicable likewise to the Augustinians and Dominicans: 'In the beginning,
stressing the contemplative aspect of the Franciscan vocation,
they favoured houses in remote sites removed from the bustle
and distraction of the towns.'[4]

4 Mooney, 'The Franciscans in Ireland', *Terminus* (November 1954), p. 246.

The spread of the Observant movement in the diocese of Cork did not altogether conform to the general trend. The reform was fully implemented by the Dominicans of Saint Mary of the Island, but no rural friary made its appearance. The nearest one was at Glanworth, county Cork, in the diocese of Cloyne which was established in 1475. Similarly with the Augustinians from whom the reform received only a very qualified acceptance. Munster being the area where Franciscanism was strongest it is not surprising to find three new friaries established in the diocese of Cork during the years of the Observant reform. These new friaries were an elusive foundation at Gahannyh in 1442, Ballymacadane in 1450 and Kilcrea in 1465; in addition there was a community of Observants on Sherkin Island off the coast of Cork in the diocese of Ross.[5] By 1461 the Conventual houses of Youghal (diocese of Cloyne) and Timoleague (Ross) were taken over by the Observants. A detailed account of this great Observant movement would be out of place in a diocesan history such as this; consequently, a skeletal outline of background developments in each of the three orders will serve as a prologue to its introduction into Cork. For such an outline difficulties abound, sources are meagre and the distinction between Conventuals and Observants, particularly among the Augustinians and Dominicans, not always as clear-cut as might be desired.

We have seen that from the time of their arrival in the thirteenth century the Dominicans and Augustinians were subject to English provincials but that the Franciscans were more fortunate in having an independent Irish province from the beginning. Racial strife culminating in the uproarious chapter of 1291 in Cork led to the papal bull of 1312 which denied the Franciscans the right to elect their own provincial. This was a restriction under which they chafed until 1469 when Father William O'Reilly was elected. The Dominicans, who showed an equal dislike for English supervision, were given independence in 1378 in a decree promulgated at the general chapter of Florence in 1374 and confirmed in that of Carcassonne in 1378.[6] In the year 1397 Pope Boniface IX at the instigation of King Richard II revoked the proceedings of the Carcassonne chapter and left the Irish Dominicans as circumscribed as before. By a second bull issued in 1397 the pope confirmed the right of the English provincial to appoint a vicar provincial for Ireland. In 1484 a plea for the erection of an Irish

5 Fitzmaurice and Little, *Franciscan Province Ire.*, p. 196.

6 Pochin Mould, *The Irish Dominicans*, p. 60.

province was again rejected, and it was not until 1536 when
the English Dominicans were dispersed that Pope Paul III
formally established the Dominican province of Ireland.
Likewise with the Augustinians: by 1394, as result of representations to their prior general they secured a palliative measure of
autonomy guaranteeing the restoration of their early privileges
and protection from undue interference from England. But
they were not granted independence.

To friars thus bridling under English control the implications
of the Observant movement on the continent were nothing if
not provocative. By papal decree continental Observants were
permitted to live independently of local Conventual provincials,
though for the time being they were still subject to the Conventual superiors general in Rome. However, as the reform
gained momentum, distinctions began to be made between
Observants and Conventuals—distinctions which in turn bred
dissensions within the orders, particularly among the Franciscans
who finally split on these headings in 1517. Because of this
cleavage it is somewhat easier to follow the course of the
Franciscan Observant movement than it is to plot the graph of
Augustinian and Dominican reform. Even with this, a certain
confusion is unavoidable in the period working up to 1517, and
here a good deal of unjustifiable inaccuracy has been allowed to
creep in.[7] There can be no inaccuracy, however, in stressing the
obvious: Irish friars saw that the transference of any house
from Conventual to Observant jurisdiction entailed the right
to independence of the English Conventual provincial and of
his vicar in Ireland. This was a natural extension of the right
accorded by the papacy to the European Observants.

AUGUSTINIANS

The first Augustinian house of the regular Observance to be
established in Ireland was at Banada, county Sligo; its establishment dates from September or October 1423. Friars from other
houses of the order in Ireland could be accepted at Banada subject to the consent of the prior and his community, and even
though this house was liable to visitation from the Irish vicar
provincial or his representative in Connacht, it was ultimately
under the immediate jurisdiction of the prior general of the
order.[8] Other Augustinian Observant foundations were made
at Dunmore, county Galway, in 1427, Ballyhaunis, county

7   Mooney, 'The Franciscans in Ireland', *Terminus* (November 1954), p. 245.

8   F. X. Martin, 'The Irish Augustinian Reform Movement in the Fifteenth Century',
in *Med. studies presented to A. Gwynn*, p. 239.

Mayo, in 1430, Scurmore, county Sligo, in 1454 and at Murrisk in Mayo in 1457. Like the foundation at Banada these houses were semi-autonomous, and the movement they represented was strengthened in 1458 when Hugh O'Malley of Banada was elected president of a chapter of the Irish province which was held in June of that year at Tullow, county Carlow. During these years the rift between Irish and Anglo-Irish friars and the English administration was widening. An Observant house was founded at Callan, county Kilkenny, in 1461 which, more than any of the earlier establishments, enjoyed a greater measure of independence from the English provincial and his Irish representative, and with the establishment of this house at Callan the Observant movement began to emerge for the first time into Anglo-Irish territory. For present purposes the most important record of this period is found in an entry in the Augustinian registers for May 1472 which authorized the extension of the reform to the already existing friaries of Adare and Cork. The reform was not to be introduced without the approval of the communities concerned: *si maior pars fratrum illorum conventuum et sanior fuerit contenta et praebuerit assensum.*[9]

The Red Abbey community in Cork did not take kindly to the projected reform. Opposition was such that in 1475 Giacomo d'Aquila, the prior general, released the friars from association with the Observants: *Absolvimus conventum Corkagie a societate observantionorum [sic] . . . et reduximus dictum conventum sicut antea erat scilicet sub obedientia vicarii districtus.*[10] Two theories are advanced in explanation of this hard core of opposition manifested to those Observants who apparently became members of the Red Abbey community from 1472 to 1475. In the first place, local feeling may have objected to a jurisdiction exercised from Kilkenny. There is also the possibility that this attitude may have been acerbated by the fluctuating fortunes of the Wars of the Roses. There is likewise a charge of mal-administration which the magistrates of Cork city brought against the 'foreign Observants'. The complaint is calendared in the general Augustinian archives in Rome under date 4 January 1494 and concludes by asking that provision be made for the Cork monastery, *cuius bona dilapidantur a fratribus dictis de observantia alienigenis, ut a magistratibus terre illius*

9   F. X. Martin and A. de Meier, 'Irish Material in the Augustinian Archives, Rome, 1354–1624', *Archiv. Hib.*, xix (1956), no. 68, p. 94.

10   Ibid., no. 82, p. 97.

informati sumus.[11] The archives divulge only one other reference to the Red Abbey of pre-Reformation times. An entry in the register of the prior general Anselmo de Montefalco (1485–95) instructed the Irish vicar provincial to prohibit the admission of lay persons into the abbey, from which it appears that an abuse which had gained ground even in Banada was equally prevalent in Cork. Whether or not the situation within and the atmosphere pervading the Cork Augustinian community underwent a change for the better before the year 1541, we have no means of knowing. For the fifteenth century, however, evidence to hand suggests that the Red Abbey can scarcely be numbered among the Irish Augustinian houses of the regular Observance.

DOMINICANS

The Dominican Observant movement is practically synonymous with the name of Raymund of Capua who became master general of the Urbanist or Roman section of the order in 1380 and who pushed forward a highly-developed programme of reform from then until his death in 1390. His plan was to set up a house of strict observance in each province of the order in the hope that these small beginnings would act as leaven in the lump of the entire Dominican family. With the spread of the reform, it was intended that reformed houses would undergo a transfer of control from their local provincials to that of vicars general for each group. The vicars general would be subject directly to the master general. A somewhat similar reform had been attempted by Raymund's immediate predecessor, Elias Raymond of Toulouse, but his French nationality was not acceptable to either the English king or the English friars, and to add complexity to the situation Elias Raymond opted for the Clementine or Avignon obedience while England adhered to the Urbanist cause. The Dominicans split on the obedience issue in 1380: the Urbanists elected Raymund of Capua as master general and the Clementine section retained Elias Raymond in office.[12] Under these circumstances the efforts of Raymund of Capua to extend the Observant reform to England were foredoomed to failure. Matters were different in the west of Ireland where already existing houses, following the example of Athenry, adopted the Raymundine reform although new houses did not begin to be established until after Raymund's death.

11 Ibid., no. 122, p. 108.

12 Pouchin Mould, *The Irish Dominicans*, p. 60.

The first Irish Dominican Observant foundation was made in 1425 at Portumna on a site which boasted a ready-made chapel belonging to the Cistercians of Dunbrody in Wexford. The Cistercians had called this the chapel of the Annunciation of Saint Mary, but when the Dominicans had safeguarded their own rights there the titular was changed and the Portumna foundation became known as the church and priory of Saint Mary and Saint Peter and Saint Paul.[13] Papal concern for the move towards regular observance saw to the needs of the friars by granting an indulgence of ten years to the faithful who contributed in alms or in kind to the upkeep of the friary. The second Observant house, that of Longford, dates from 1429 when a new friary was erected on the ruins of an earlier building which had been razed to the ground during a local conflict. Contemporaneously there occurred the growth of the Dominican Third Order which indicates a quickening of reform among the laity, but there is little evidence from Dominican sources to support the idea of Third Order regulars which were an outstanding feature of the Franciscan Observant movement. A foundation made at Urlar in 1434 and another at Burrishoole in 1469 and 1486 flourished once initial difficulties connected with their being established without the necessary papal approval were overcome.

Like the Augustinians, the Dominican friars of the Observance began to drift from the jurisdiction of the English province, and their desire for independence was given formal expression in 1484 when Irish delegates to the general chapter at Milan filed a petition for the setting up of an Irish province. Their petition succeeded; Maurice O'Mochain Moralis was appointed first provincial and on 10 November he was authorized to reform the houses of Coleraine, Drogheda and Cork. The records, which tell that by 1505 the reform was in full swing in the abbey of Saint Mary of the Island, give no details as to how this was achieved. Father O'Mochain is credited with having introduced the reform into Youghal, Cork and Limerick, and his success in these areas is regarded as an indication of how the friars in the Anglo-Irish towns were joining up with the native Irish Dominicans. The same trend was noticeable in the other orders of friars as well. Drogheda refused to accept the Raymundine reform: it was later to throw its gates open to the Franciscan Observants. O'Mochain's tenure as Irish provincial was terminated in 1491 by the re-exemplification of the papal bull of Boniface IX in 1397, and from 1491 until

13   Ibid., p. 66.

1536 the course of Irish Dominican history became progressively more complex and confused. By 1505 there were three distinct Dominican superiors in Ireland, namely, the vicar of the English provincial, the vicar general of the reformed houses in the English parts of the country, and the vicar general of the 'Irish nation'. By 1518 the groupings were reduced to two, the reform group and those still adhering to the English province.

For these years one final reference to the Dominican house in Cork emerges from the records to the effect that Cork, Limerick and Youghal initiated a move for a link-up of the Irish Dominican houses in Anglo-Irish towns with the Dominicans of the reform in Holland. The project did not materialize even though John de Bauffremes, vicar general of the reformed congregation of the Netherlands, came to Ireland to explore the possibilities of the situation.[14] Cork's role in these negotiations is perhaps the most vital clue to the active participation of the Dominicans of Saint Mary of the Island in the great reform movement of Blessed Raymund of Capua.

FRANCISCANS

From about the middle of the fourteenth century, when Englishry was receding and Irishry extending, the mutual relationships between the native Irish and the Anglo-Irish sections of the Franciscan family in Ireland are obscure, but it is probable that in the second half of the century the English and Irish friars drew closer together for support against the attacks of Richard FitzRalph of Armagh. Notwithstanding this violent controversy a remarkable revival, punctuated by the foundation of a number of houses in the west and south-west, but principally by the growth of the Third Order regular and by the introduction of the Strict Observance was taking place within the order in Ireland.[15] By 1385 there were four Irish congregations of the Third Order in existence. In 1426 when Pope Martin V granted a special indult to the brethren and sisters of the Third Order in Ireland, the movement had already become institutionalized. After that date the Third Order regular consisted of groups of men (sisters are no longer mentioned) who lived in community and who had their own churches. The first community of regular Tertiaries to receive papal recognition was Killeenbrenan in county Mayo, not far

14   Ibid., p. 72.
15   A bull of Pope Callistus III to Irish Tertiaries in 1457 referred to Killeenbrenan as the first and most notable of all their houses in Ireland.

from Ballinrobe. This foundation dates from the year 1428.[16]
Then came similar developments in the dioceses of Tuam,
Killala, Achonry and Connor. The extension was phenomenal,
yet when Father Donogh Mooney (d.1624) was listing these
Third Order friaries he could find only two in Munster—
Killeennagallive in county Tipperary and Ballymacadane in
the county and diocese of Cork.[17]

Ballymacadane Abbey

The ruins of the friary of Ballymacadane stand some nine
miles from Cork city and about two miles to the west of Old
Abbey or Waterfall. The origins of the abbey are obscure and
continue to vex historians, but there is no difficulty in recog-
nizing the abbey under the following etymological variations:
Ballyvacadane, Ballimackedan, Ballymagadain, Bally mac
Edan, Ballymacduan, Ballyvaggaddan, Ballimacidane, Monais-
tirvicadane, etc. The theories as to its origin are many and
varied and in the long run inconclusive.

Smith maintains that Ballyvacadane was founded by Cormac
MacCarthy Mac Teige, surnamed *Láidir*, for 'Austine Nuns'
about the year 1450.[18] Archdall is doubtful as to whether it
was a friary or a nunnery. Sir James Ware brackets Ballymacadane with Cloggagh in Timoleague but is non-committal in
respect of the order of friars in question. He points out that an
inquisition taken in 1584 mentions nothing of the order, its
founder or its patron. As against this argument, the presence
of Franciscans in Ballymacadane is corroborated by another
inquisition taken on 1 June 1588 in which it was stated that
'Felemy Mac Owen and other friars of the Order of St Francis
were in possession thereof' and that the tithes of the said (abbey)
lands belonged to the rectory of Inishkenny.[19] Father Mooney,
as mentioned, listed Ballymacadane (Ballymagadain) as a house
of the Franciscan Third Order.[20] J. P. Hayes in one of the
earliest volumes of the *Journal of the Cork Historical and
Archaeological Society* reverts to the idea of a nunnery. He
gives 1472 as the date of the foundation and, quoting from a

16 Mooney, 'The Franciscans in Ireland, *Terminus* (July-August 1956), p. 88.

17 Ibid., p. 89. Tertiaries were to be found at Clonkeen, east Galway, between
1428–41, at Rosserk near Ballina in 1441, and so on throughout the west, north-west
and north-east until 1487. By 1488 there was a house of the Third Order at Kilshane
near Ballingarry, county Tipperary.

18 Smith, *History of Cork*, i, 154.

19 Webster, *The Diocese of Cork*, p. 385.

20 Brendan Jennings, 'Brussels MS. 3947: Donatus Moneyus, De Provincia Hiberniae
S. Francisci', *Anal. Hib.*, no. 6 (1934), p. 104.

patent roll in the British Museum, lists Honor ní Carthaigh as first abbess of Ballymacadane.[21] Smith's date, 1450, is accepted rather than that set out in the patent roll, but there is an argument in favour of both. A short-lived nunnery founded in 1450 may have given place to a Franciscan foundation later in the century.

The tradition that Ballymacadane was built originally for Austine nuns is strengthened by reference to its MacCarthy founder and benefactor, Cormac *Láidir*, ninth lord Muskerry, whom the Four Masters extolled as 'an exalter and reverer of the Church'. Patronage of the Franciscans was a MacCarthy characteristic, but it was not exclusive, since it was also a MacCarthy who re-established the monastery of Gill Abbey for Augustinian canons regular in 1134. Further corroboration of an Augustinian heritage for Ballymacadane is found in the *Fiants of Elizabeth* which show that Gill Abbey owned considerable property in the surrounding district. Nothing is known of Ballymacadane during the first century of its existence, but if we accept Father Donogh Mooney's ruling that it belonged to Franciscan Tertiaries, we must see it as spearheading the Franciscan Observant movement in the diocese of Cork. 'There were a great number of men belonging to the Third Order in Ireland who lived in community and devoted themselves to a religious life,' wrote Father Mooney in 1617. 'They were principally engaged in assisting the local clergy in their pastoral duties and in conducting schools for the education of the boys of the district. A portion of their monasteries was invariably set apart for the latter purpose . . .'.[22] The words may well apply to the Franciscan abbey of Ballymacadane.

The origins of the Irish Franciscan Observant movement may be traced to the late fourteenth century when friars agitating for a revival of religious observance were found in scattered and unorganized groups endeavouring by their own example to counteract the general inertia which surrounded them. With the increase of their numbers, particularly in the Irish-speaking districts, they sought permission from their Conventual provincial to come together in certain houses where they could put their ideals into practice while still remaining under his jurisdiction.[23] It was an easy step from this arrangement to the foundation of the first house of Strict Observance at Quin in the territory of Sioda Cam Mac Namara. This was actually a

21   J. P. Hayes, 'Ballymacadane Abbey, County Cork', *Cork Hist. Soc. Jn.*, iii (1894), 141-3.

22   Fitzmaurice and Little, *Franciscan Province Ire.*, p. xxxii.

23   Mooney, 'The Franciscans in Ireland', *Terminus* (November 1954), p. 246.

re-founding of the earlier abbey of Quin which Father Francis Mahony in his *Brevis Synopsis Provinciae Hiberniae Fratrum Minorum* states to have been founded in 1402 and which Wadding says was older than the fifteenth century.[24] At all events, on 12 October 1433 Pope Eugenius gave papal approval for a new foundation (*de novo fundare*) in the town of Quin for the use and dwelling-place of Friars Minor who would there serve God under regular observance: *inibi sub regulari observantia Altissimo servituram*. This final phrase of the papal letter has led scholars to hold that Quin was the first house of Franciscan Strict Observance in Ireland, but A. G. Little in his introduction to Father E. B. FitzMaurice's *Materials for the History of the Franciscan Province of Ireland* qualifies this opinion: 'The first house of the Strict Observance established in Ireland is said to have been Quin (?1402 ?1433),' he wrote. 'This was founded by the Macnamaras as a burial place for their family instead of Ennis. It is thus connected with their long struggle for independence against the O'Briens of Thomond. The new friary was built with a magnificence and apparently endowed with a generosity more in harmony with family pride than with the ideals of the Observant friars. The papal licence for the foundation of Quin should perhaps be taken in connection with Martin V's abortive attempt to reform the whole order by the "Constitutiones Martinianae" in 1430 rather than with any exclusive Observantine Movement. There is nothing to show that the convent differed in practice or in constitutional position from the other houses of the province. At any rate it was an isolated phenomenon . . .'[25] Despite Professor Little's insistence, modern Franciscan historians continue to regard Quin as the starting-point of the Franciscan Observant movement. Between 1440 and 1448 Donald, son of Thady MacCarthy of Desmond, granted the friars another secluded spot at Muckross on the shores of Loch Lein. A document dated 1468 mentions that for the past twenty years Father Richard Chilvart and a community of friars had been living a life of strict penance and regular observance there.[26] For the year 1442 comes reference to the Cork foundation at Gahannyh which is believed to have been at Goleen,[27] but lack of further details makes it impossible to connect this foundation with the Observant reform movement.

24 Gleeson, *A History of the Diocese of Killaloe*, p. 491.
25 Fitzmaurice and Little, *Franciscan Province Ire.*, p. xxxii.
26 Mooney, 'The Franciscans in Ireland', *Terminus* (November 1954), p. 246.
27 Fitzmaurice and Little, *Franciscan Province Ire.*, p. 196.

In 1449 Pope Nicholas V in a mandate to Bishop Jordan Purcell, to the dean of Cork (probably John Walsche) and to David Ogillagymain, canon of Ross, gave permission to Fineen O'Driscoll of Ross 'to found and build in his territory, to the honour of God, St. John [the] Baptist and St. Francis, a house for Friars Minor of the Observance'. By the same instrument Donogh O'Mahony (Omabba, Omawa) of Cork was permitted to build, within the diocese of Cork, another Observant house, 'to the honour of God, St. Mary the Virgin and St. Francis'.[28] The site offered by O'Driscoll was on Sherkin Island, but there is no reference to any building on Sherkin until 1460 or 1462, by which time the Observance in Ireland had become firmly established on an organized basis. The papal go-ahead does not seem to have been availed of in O'Mahony's case; the suggestion that the MacCarthy foundation of Kilcrea in 1465 was the outcome of the permission of 1449 is untenable.

The turning-point in the Franciscan Observant movement was reached in 1456 with the foundation at Moyne on the west shore of Killala Bay. Moyne, to quote Father Canice Mooney, was the first friary that could fully lay claim to the title 'Observant' because it adhered to the Observant rites and practices and was subject, not to the Irish Conventual provincial but to the ultramontane vicar-general.[29] In this way Moyne was an advance on Quin which remained under Conventual jurisdiction until the general suppression of the monasteries under Henry VIII. After the foundation at Moyne there was no halting the drive towards emancipation from England, and events began to move more rapidly than had been anticipated. In May 1460 Pope Pius II gave permission to the Observants to take over four houses from the Conventuals (subject to a majority vote of the communities concerned) and to elect one of the Observant friars as vicar provincial to whom they would owe allegiance and who, in turn, would be subject to the ultramontane vicar general. The Observants elected Father Malachy O'Clune as their first vicar provincial, and since they were already under the ultramontane vicar general, they now became independent in practice of the Irish Conventual provincials. The rapidity of recurring papal enactments relative to Observant-Conventual relations was such that the Observants discovered too late that the election of O'Clune and subsequent legislation enacted by him was probably invalid. The position was clarified by August 1460 and O'Clune's position was

28 *Cal. papal letters, 1447–55*, p. 202.
29 Mooney, 'The Franciscans in Ireland', *Terminus* (November 1954), p. 247.

confirmed and legalized by papal decree.[30] The permission to take over some of the Conventual houses was speedily availed of, and before the end of 1461 the friaries of Youghal, Timoleague and Kilconnell had changed hands. Conventual appeals to Rome were ineffectual. Papal favour towards the Observants was confirmed, perpetual silence was imposed upon the Conventuals and they were shortly to see Multyfarnham go over to the Observants. Offers of sites for new foundations became so numerous that the Observants were not able to keep up with the demand. For this reason a favourable opening in Donegal which presented itself in 1464 had to be postponed until 1473 or 1474 in view of already existing commitments at Adare, which was founded in 1464, and at Kilcrea, which dates from 1465 even though the *Annals of Ulster* place its foundation at 1478.

Kilcrea Friary

Cormac *Láidir* MacCarthy, founder and patron of Ballymacadane was likewise founder and benefactor to the friary of Kilcrea. He also built the castles of Kilcrea, Blarney and Carrignamuck. Kilcrea Castle, situated in Shanacloyne to the west of the friary, became the favourite residence of the Muskerry branch of the MacCarthy family and the baronial centre for Lord Clancarty's tenants in the parishes of Ovens, Kilmurry and Kilmichael. The name Kilcrea, which has been subjected to many interpretations, is commonly taken as connoting the church of Saint Cera (Cyra, Chier, Creda), a female saint of the seventh century on whose identity historians are far from unanimous. Lanigan states that 'she is said to have been the daughter of one Duibhre and of the illustrious family of Muskerry in the now county of Cork,' and he gives her feasts at 5 January and 16 October.[31] The *Félire of Oengus* under 5 January commemorates 'Ciar in Muscraige Tire . . . of Conaire's race . . . in Mag Escat', while Ciar, an African martyr, is cited in the same source under 16 October. The *Martyrology of Donegal* honours 'Cera of Magh Ascadh' on 16 October, and under the same date the *Martyrology of Gorman* commemorates 'Cera, mother of Dub's children of Mag Ascad'. It is not in any way essential to the present history to decide whence Saint Cera originated—in Muskerry, in Upper Ormond or in Donegal, for she is acclaimed in all three places—but it is significant that those who have written at length on the saint have not really

30 Ibid., p. 248.

31 J. Lanigan, *An Ecclesiastical History of Ireland*, iii, 129.

succeeded in establishing her at Kilcrea. According to Westropp, Saint Cera is said to have founded a hermitage at Desertmore, while Colgan places an abbey of Austin nuns at Kilcrea and maintains that it was founded in the sixth century by Saint Cera.[32] This Augustinian foundation, according to Smith, was not at Kilcrea but 'at a place called Grany, now Grange, which is a mile E[ast] of the abbey of Kilcrea in the parish of St Owen's called the Ovens'.[33] The absence of either cill-site or hermitage remains leads to the conclusion that the name Kilcrea, as such, had no early ecclesiastical roots. The place was known in olden times as Gearhy (Geary), a name still surviving in the *Gaorthadh* near Macroom, and it was referred to in the seventeenth century as the Great Bog of Muskerry consisting of 560 acres of land interspersed with island woods.[34]

The fifteenth-century Franciscan friary of Kilcrea was situated in picturesque surroundings on the bank of the river Bride. It was dedicated to Saint Brigid and is said to have been liberally endowed—a statement which, however, is not borne out by the inventory of its possessions made at the dissolution in 1542. The property of Kilcrea at that time comprised the abbey and its precincts, the half-ploughland of Ballinvollin (130 acres, 3 roods, 8 perches), an eel weir and a grist mill, the total annual value of which was set at £15 sterling. There may have been other unspecified lands connected with the abbey: this is the conclusion suggested by the reference to 'Knock-anewoolin and ye rest of ye lands belonging to ye Abbey of Kilcrea' which occurs in that part of the *Civil Survey* of 1654–56 dealing with the barony of Muskerry. There is also the probability that the myth concerning the legendary possessions of Kilcrea may have originated through confusion with the lands owned by Sir Cormac MacCarthy in 1619. Sir Cormac's possessions lay in the vicinity of Kilcrea and comprised the manor, castles, townlands and hereditaments of Kilcrea, Shanacloyne and Ferrygowne, containing half a ploughland worth sixpence sterling; the lands of Knockeygowgie, of equal value and extent; Ballinvollen or Knockwollyn, with the mill and a weir, together with the abbey of Kilcrea containing half a ploughland.[35]

Kilcrea's lack of territorial possessions was offset by the abbey itself. Its buildings, judging from the ground plan, were of

32 Colgan, *Acta SS Hib.*, p. 391. 5.

33 Smith, *History of Cork*, i, 173 n.

34 *Civil Survey*, barony of Muskerry.

35 *Cork Inquisitions, R.I.A.*, vii, 198 ' . . . ac in precinct' monaster' de Kilcrea cum dimid' carucat' terr' vocat' Knockanvillin cont' 130 ac. ¾ terr' . . .'

massive proportions, with the present ruins testifying to the
solid nature of the early construction. In accordance with
prevailing custom, the founder's family enjoyed the right of
burial within the abbey precincts. The founder, who was done
to death by his own kinsmen near Carrignamuck in 1494, was
laid to rest in the north-east chancel near the high altar. His
tomb bore the legend: *Hic jacet Cormacus filius Thadei. fil.
Cormaci. fil. Dermitii magni MacCarthy, Dns. de Muscraigh
Flayn, ac istius conventus primus fundator. A.D. 1494.* From
then until 1616 successive members of the MacCarthy family
were interred at Kilcrea. The last MacCarthy burial which
took place there was that of Sir Cormac Mac Diarmaid in 1616.[36]

Little is known of the internal history of the pre-Reformation
friary of Kilcrea beyond the claim made by authorities who
postulate a high level of cultural and intellectual activity within
the community. If this is so, then Kilcrea represented a breakthrough for the Observants whose leaders in these early days
of the reform showed little interest in the development of higher
learning or in providing university education for their friars.
Their sights were directed at what for them were more important fields of endeavour. With the Conventuals, on the
other hand, the cultural tradition was already well established
and, while the Observants were not yet anywhere near the
vanguard of cultural development, Conventual friars were
pursuing higher studies in arts, philosophy and theology in
continental universities. In the unsuccessful negotiations for a
university at Dublin in 1475 the Conventuals claimed that
'within their ranks they had many learned lectors to fill the
different chairs and plenty of keen students to fill the benches'.[37]
One important survival of the cultural activity of Kilcrea is an
Irish translation of the *Travels of Sir John Maundeville* which
is now a treasured possession the Bibliothèque Municipale of
Rennes. The writer was Finghin O Mathuna, scholar and
linguist from Rosbrin in the parish of Schull, and he wrote his
manuscript in 'Cillcreide Abbey' on Maundy Thursday 1472.
A homily on poverty is believed to have been transcribed at
Kilcrea about the same period.[38] Kilcrea was among the houses
visited by Brother Mícheál Ó Cléirigh in 1629 when he was
collecting data for his monumental work of historical compilation.

36 Thomas O'Herlihy, bishop of Ross, was buried in Kilcrea in 1579.

37 Mooney, 'The Franciscans in Ireland', *Terminus* (July-August 1955), p. 85.

38 Athanáis Ó Gibealláin, 'The Franciscan Friary of Kilcrea', in *Kilcrea Friary,
1465–1965*, p. 12.

When the Observant movement eventually widened its horizons its record for scholarship far outshone the achievements of the Conventual section of the order. 'The glory of being the spearhead of Irish Catholic resistance to the Protestant Reformation; of having founded St. Anthony's College, Louvain, and St. Isidore's College, Rome; of having given to Ireland the *Annals of the Four Masters* . . . and to the Franciscan Order its own great annals; all this', writes Father Canice Mooney, 'rightly belongs to the Friars Minor of the Observance'.[39]

Circumstances attendant upon the final reference to the pre-Reformation friary of Kilcrea are a sinister prologue to what was in store for Irish religious houses during and after the Henrician schism. In 1514 covetous lay lords were cautioned by Maurus, abbot of Cashel, to respect the privileges of the Franciscans in Kilcrea, Shandon and Timoleague. The hammer-stroke came in August 1542 when Henry VIII ordered his deputy and council in Dublin to ensure that the earl of Desmond and others should take inventories 'for the king's use, of all the religious houses in the counties of Limerick, Cork, Kerry and Desmond', and that they should dissolve those houses and put them into safe custody.[40] The execution of the royal will which carried with it the defection of Sir Cormac Mac Teige MacCarthy belongs to the next volume of the history of the diocese.

The election of Father William O'Reilly as Irish provincial in 1469, which was such a signal victory for the native Irish members of the Franciscan order, tended to put a new complexion on matters within the Irish province. O'Reilly was a Conventual friar, and while he favoured the Observant movement as such, he disapproved of the trend which was amputating Observant houses from the Conventual family. Before his appointment as provincial he had secured permission (1456) for the Observants of the custody of Nenagh to establish a house in north Connacht, an area into which the Franciscans had never successfully penetrated. In 1459 he was given the old parish church of Saint Patrick at Elphin, and this church, like Quin and Muckross, remained in the hands of the Conventuals till the suppression. After Father O'Reilly's appointment many of those who had gone over to the Observants sought papal permission to return to the Conventual houses, place themselves again under the jurisdiction of their Conventual provincial and continue to live the life of regular observance.

39   Mooney, 'The Franciscans in Ireland', *Terminus* (January-February 1955), p. 6.

40   Ó Gibealláin, 'The Franciscan Friary of Kilcrea', p. 13.

They complained of the large number of Conventual houses left abandoned and derelict, of others operating on skeleton communities and unable, through sheer lack of personnel, to minister to the spiritual needs of the people, while at the same time the few Observant houses in existence were all bursting at the seams and were established in the country.[41] The Conventual friars of the Dublin custody, in an endeavour to fill their empty houses, were obliged to secure permission to receive and retain friars from other Irish custodies, provided they were worthy and obedient religious. The effort at re-conventualisation was already marked by the erection of Conventual friaries in Irish-speaking rural areas like Clonkeen (1453), Stradbally (1453), Elphin (1456) and Monaghan (1462), but it seemed as if nothing could halt the transfer of houses from the Conventuals to the Observants.

The transfers were effected in a variety of ways, sometimes with the consent of communities, sometimes through pressure of outside influences (this happened at Carrickfergus), some-times through agreement between Conventual and Observant superiors (as in Ennis), and there were cases where entire communities, after a dogged resistance to reform, made final and unconditional capitulation. This happened in Galway, Armagh, Athlone, Downpatrick, Dundalk and Monaghan. The Observant movement had not taken over in Buttevant, Dublin, Galbally, Kilkenny, Nenagh, New Ross and Roscrea before the general suppression, but the Observants of the seventeenth century took advantage of favourable opportunities to establish themselves in as many of these places as was possible.[42] The dates at which other Conventual houses passed over to the Observants are mainly conjectural: the following provisional list affords a good cross-section of the extent and phenomenal diffusion of the great urge to reform which characterized Franciscanism in fifteenth-century Ireland: Meelick, 1479; Wexford, 1486–87; Bantry, 1482, 1522 or 1532; Askeaton, 1497; Cork, 1500; Cavan, 1502; Trim, Drogheda and Monas-teroris, not later than 1506; Ardfert, 1517–18; Kildare, 1520; Waterford, 1521; Limerick, 1534; Clonmel, 1536, and Cashel, 1538.

A seemingly impenetrable veil of silence shrouds the extension of the Observant movement to the Grey Friary of Shandon. Franciscan historians are of opinion that Wadding's description of the friary as the 'mirror of all Ireland', *speculum*

---

41   Mooney, 'The Franciscans in Ireland', *Terminus* (January-February 1955) p. 8.

42   Ibid., (November 1954), p. 249.

totius Hiberniae, refers to the period between acceptance of the Observant reform and the suppression, though Wadding himself had an earlier period in mind. The issue of letters patent to the citizens of Cork on the authority of the Observantine vicars provincial in 1501 places Cork's acceptance of the reform at the turn of the century.[43] The reform seems to have been well under way before 1518 when Wadding cites a document recording a decision of the earl of Kildare in the unravelling of a dispute between the friars and the Goolde (Gould) family. The community of the Grey Friary of Shandon are referred to in this document as the 'Observantines of Corck'.

Fifteenth and early sixteenth-century statistics of the order provide interesting details of development. Conventual houses in Ireland numbered between thirty-five and thirty-seven in the year 1420. By 1506 the Observants had fifteen or sixteen friaries and their personnel numbered four hundred friars. On the eve of the general suppression of the monasteries the Observants had about thirty houses, the Conventuals some two dozen and there were thirty-two houses of the Third Order regular in existence. Taken as a whole, the mendicant Observant movement put a mighty treasury of spirituality and zeal at the service of the pre-Reformation Irish church in the form of about nine houses of Observant Augustinians, eleven of Dominicans, and, as we have just noted, thirty Franciscan Observant friaries and thirty-two centres of a flourishing Third Order regular. The church was to benefit from this great spiritual reservoir when suppression and confiscation struck in the sixteenth and later centuries.

---

43 Wadding, *Annales Minorum,* ii, 311.

XVIII

Blessed Thaddeus MacCarthy

We have seen that the Desmond Geraldines succeeded to the ancient *Regnum Corcagiense*; they had endowed the convents of Friars Minor and Friars Preachers at Youghal, had founded and endowed the collegiate church of Youghal and had secured possession of the united dioceses of Cork and Cloyne in the person of Gerald FitzGerald. The slumbering antagonism between the FitzGeralds who were colonists and the MacCarthy native chiefs erupted with the appointment of Thaddeus MacCarthy to the sees of Cork and Cloyne in 1490. In an age of controversial bishops, Thaddeus was perhaps the most controversial in that the dispute surrounding him deals not alone with his claim to the see of Ross or to those of Cork and Cloyne, but with his birthplace, his parentage and his genealogy. The disturbed period in which he lived, the dearth of more minute documentation and the existing ecclesiastical confusion in Cork, Cloyne and Ross make him a difficult subject for study. Historians, because of his proven sanctity, have dealt kindly with him to the detriment of his FitzGerald and O'Driscoll opponents. Dispassionate analysis however shows that Odo O'Driscoll was not altogether the black sheep of the diocese of Ross, and that the ambitions of the MacCarthy sept were a major factor in aggravating an already explosive situation in the diocese of Cork and Cloyne and in drawing the diocese of Ross into the same maelstrom.

Thaddeus MacCarthy was born in the county of Cork sometime during the year 1456. His mother was reputedly a daughter of Edmund FitzMaurice, ninth lord of Kerry. His father's name is nowhere given. By the mid-fifteenth century the MacCarthy sept had divided into four main branches, namely, the senior branch of MacCarthy Mór of Kerry whose family were princes of Desmond, MacCarthy Reagh of Carbery, MacCarthy of Muskerry and MacCarthy of Duhallow. All claimed descent from Heber, second son of Milesius. By a less

448

fanciful but more credible pedigree they were descended from Cormac MacCarthy, bishop-king of Munster, whose name is associated with Saint Malachy, with the monastery of Gill Abbey and with Cormac's Chapel at Cashel. The MacCarthy tradition of benefaction to church and monastery is seen in the Cistercian abbey of Maur (*de Fonte Vivo*) in Ross and in the Franciscan abbeys of Cork, Timoleague, Ballymacadane and Kilcrea. At the period of which we speak the power of the MacCarthys was very great in Muskerry where the sept of Cormac *Láidir* so dominated local history that Canon Soroglio, an Italian biographer of Thaddeus, assumed that this was the sept from which Thaddeus came.[1]

Contemporary to Cormac *Láidir* was another MacCarthy chief, Cormac of Carbery or Cormac MacCarthy Reagh, son of Donogh, successor to Donal MacCarthy Reagh. Donogh MacCarthy died in 1452 and evidence proving that Cormac MacCarthy of Carbery was the MacCarthy Reagh in 1475 (and by inference, before that date) is twofold. Firstly, a papal mandate under date 4 July 1475 and quoted in a previous chapter shows that Cormac MacCarthy (Mekarryg), lord of the places of Ballymountain, Curranure, Dromkeen and Knock-roe situated on the west of the Bandon River in the parish of Innishannon, sought permission of the Holy See to erect a parish church for these townlands, commonly called the *quatuor carucatae*, to which he promised to give as endowment four acres of fertile land.[2] Cormac must have been lord of the entire district at that time. Secondly, a Rennes manuscript of 1475 shows that Cormac, son of Donchad (Donogh), son of Donal Rua, was MacCarthy Cairbreach, which by some is interpreted as tanist.[3] Cormac was ousted from the chieftaincy after 1478; from him are descended the MacCarthy Reaghs or Rabaghs, and it is probable that when he and his sept were deprived of the chieftaincy of Carbery in 1478 they secured some lands as private gentlemen. Their lands are said to have centred around Monteen Castle near Rosscarbery and Coolmaine Castle in Kilbrittain. Tradition connects Thaddeus MacCarthy with the Kilbrittain branch of MacCarthy Reagh, and it is interesting to note that the last bishop of the united sees of Cork and Cloyne was also a MacCarthy Rabagh (Reagh).

The birthplace of Thaddeus presents its own problems. Assuming that he was a MacCarthy Reagh, one might suggest

1 Cork Diocesan Archives, 'Acts for the Process of the Beatification of Thaddeus Machar', p. 20. Published Rome 1896, for private circulation only.

2 *Cal. papal letters, 1471–84*, pt. 1, p. 428.

3 O'Mahony, *A History of the O'Mahony Septs,* p. 127, n. 51.

Kilbrittain were it not that Kilbrittain was a frontier post subject to violent clashes and changes of ownership between the MacCarthys and the de Courceys. Kilbrittain Castle had been built by Patrick de Courcey, eleventh baron of Kinsale, on what was originally MacCarthy territory and from which the MacCarthys eventually ousted the de Courceys and made it a MacCarthy stronghold. It is more likely that Thaddeus Mac-Carthy was born in the castle of Carriganass which was contiguous to the townlands of Ballymountain, Curranure, Dromkeen and Knockroe, and which may have been then and for some time previously the residence of Cormac MacCarthy Reagh. A confirmatory clue is found in a reference made to Thaddeus's birthplace by the Italian Father Benvenuti of the Congregation of Christian Doctrine who wrote in 1800 that 'Blessed Thaddeus was born in *Castello Clavinense* in Hibernia or Ireland, of the royal blood of Macher, and was probably an archbishop in the county of Clarch or Clariense, the village of Joan in the said county being found in the maps to be the seat of an archbishop . . .'[4] Reading *Clarinense* for *Clavinense* the obvious identification is Rathclarin. The village of Joan or John could be Innishannon which is said to have been the Inch of John (*Iniseoganan* of the 1199 decretal). The reference to the seat of an archbishop may be interpreted as that of a mother-church. Innishannon was such a mother-church (*matrix ecclesia*) and like Carriganass it lay within easy reach of the townlands mentioned in Cormac's petition of 1475.[5]

The first certain reference to Thaddeus MacCarthy occurs on the occasion of his appointment to the see of Ross on 29 March 1482. He was then in his twenty-seventh year and was described as 'a cleric of the diocese of Cork . . . *de nobile genere ex utroque parente procreatus ac morum honeste decoratus*'.[6] It has been suggested, but without basic proof, that he was educated in either the Franciscan friary of Timoleague or in that of Kilcrea which was founded and endowed by Cormac *Láidir* in 1465. Another tentative suggestion is that he received his education in the monastery of Ballymacadane which was also a MacCarthy foundation. More than likely, Thaddeus followed the procedure of earlier medieval times when aspirants to the priesthood were placed in the care of rectors proficient in the training of youth and under whose tuition they imbibed

4   Cork Diocesan Archives, 'Acts for the Process', p. 32.

5   A vague tradition maintains that Thaddeus was born at Aha Lisheen near Carrigroe to the west of Clonakilty; it seems likely that the Carrigroe of tradition became confused with Knockroe, the townland on the borders of which Carriganass was situated.

6   Cork Diocesan Archives, 'Acta Apostolicae Sedis', xxviii, 187.

some elements of ecclesiastical and secular knowledge. In this way Thaddeus may have been indentured to his near relative and namesake, Canon Thady MacCarthy, rector of the union of Rathclarin and Burren in the MacCarthy Reagh territory around Coolmaine.[7] Thaddeus is believed to have pursued further studies under another relative, Don Raymond, professor in the University of Paris, and he seems to have completed his studies in Rome. He was in Rome on 29 March 1482 when his appointment as bishop of Ross was announced. He was dispensed because of his youth and was consecrated (erroneously as events proved) bishop of Ross on 3 May 1482 in the church of Saint Stephen de Caeco. The consecrating prelate was Archbishop Stephen of Antivari who was assisted by Bishop Daniel, Bishop Rhosus of Cilicia and Bishop Julian of Bertinoro, Italy.[8] Thaddeus MacCarthy's consecration was solemnized on the feast of the Finding of the True Cross.

The appointment of Thaddeus MacCarthy to the see of Ross was made on the erroneous assumption of an existing vacancy there. His bull of provision declared the bishopric to be vacant by the death of Donald: failure to investigate the circumstances warrants the conclusion that the papacy had quickly forgotten the recent forgeries and false representations made by claimants to the sees of Cork and Cloyne. Donald; bishop of Ross, had died in or about 1473. Since that time Odo O'Driscoll—who had been provided by Pope Sixtus IV and consecrated by the archbishop of Cashel assisted by his suffragans of Killaloe, Limerick and Emly—had exercised the office of bishop 'in peace' for about nine years, had been accepted by the dean and chapter and had received the fruits of the episcopal *mensa*. O'Driscoll's succession, which should have taken effect on the resignation of Bishop Donald, was compromised by the bishop's death and although the matter was purely technical, Odo O'Driscoll sought and obtained validation of his position as bishop of Ross. Pope Sixtus IV decreed that 'Odo's letters of provision should hold good from the [death of Bishop Donald] . . ., and that the provision itself and also Odo's consecration and his administration as bishop should also be valid, as if provision had been made to him of the said church [of Ross] as being void by Donald's death'.[9] A similar validation had been sought in 1432 by Jordan Purcell *vis-à-vis* Adam Payn

7 We are nowhere given any indication as to his qualifications.

8 W. M. Brady, *Episcopal Succession in England, Scotland and Ireland* . . ., ii, 107.

9 *Cal. papal letters, 1471–84*, pt. 1, p. 142.

and Milo FitzJohn and his own succession to the sees of Cork and Cloyne.

Thaddeus MacCarthy, with his long absence from Ireland, can scarcely have known anything of the background of intrigue underlying his appointment as bishop of Ross, nor can he have been prepared for the deluge of opposition which was released against him in Ross. The root of the trouble was that Sixtus IV provided Thaddeus to Ross 'upon being falsely informed that the said church . . . was still void' by the death of Bishop Donald.[10] The principal opponents to the provision of Thaddeus were the powerful Corca Laighdhe sept of O'Driscoll who resisted him as the usurper of a bishopric which was based on their own septlands. The ecclesiastical deadlock was aggravated by current political turmoil, civil discontent and internecine strife. Muskerry was divided against itself, family solidarity having been undermined by partisanship engendered during the Wars of the Roses. Patronage of Yorkist and Lancastrian claimants, coupled with the fluctuating fortunes of the war, saw at one time the Geraldines, at another time the Butlers in the ascendant. The time came when party patronage intruded upon ecclesiastical interests, and churchmen willing to ally themselves with the supporters of the rival English houses were not wanting. Thus it happened that Thaddeus MacCarthy returned to take possession of a bishopric the territory of which was constantly menaced. Sectarian feeling favoured O'Driscoll from the start: the Wars of the Roses had brought FitzGeralds and MacCarthys into frequent combat and the post-war attitude of the former was bitterly unrelenting. The appearance of a MacCarthy claimant to the bishopric of Ross was a reopening of old wounds.

Backed by the support of the archbishop of Cashel and his suffragans of Killaloe, Limerick and Emly and of the dean and chapter of Ross, Odo O'Driscoll made a personal appeal to Pope Sixtus IV in August 1483. Thaddeus MacCarthy had meantime returned to Ireland and—so the complaint runs— had 'with the help of lay power . . . despoiled Odo . . . of the rule and administration and of the goods of the [episcopal] *mensa*, and intruded himself, as he still does, to the grave hurt of the said Odo, who has therefore with great labour and expense and peril of the roads, come in person to the apostolic see'. The pope ordered Thaddeus MacCarthy to desist from his intrusion; his abettors, ecclesiastical and lay, under pain of excommunication, deprivation and interdict were to withdraw

10   Ibid.

their support from him, and Odo O'Driscoll or his proctor was to be readmitted to 'corporal possession' of the rule and administration of the church of Ross. He was to exercise the cure and administration in spirituals and temporals as formerly, and the church and its goods were to be restored to him. Should it prove impossible for Odo and the canons obedient to him to remain in the cathedral church of Ross, the pope provided for the transfer of the chapter 'to such other church in the diocese as shall seem good to Odo or his proctor'.[11]

Thaddeus MacCarthy continued to press his claim in defiance of the papal warning. Repeated excommunications by the council of Munster bishops were equally unavailing, and the dispute in Ross continued to fester until 21 July 1488 when Pope Innocent VIII confirmed the action of Sixtus IV against Thaddeus MacCarthy, 'son of iniquity', and pronounced the sentence of excommunication upon him and on certain named accomplices. Furthermore, the pope invoked the aid of the secular arm against them, annulled all the acts of Thaddeus 'and all letters which should be impetrated by him from, or granted to him, by the apostolic see'.[12] Odo O'Driscoll was named bishop of Ross in this decree, and the pope ensured that previous apostolic letters should not mislead simple people by pronouncing all such letters null and void. Odo O'Driscoll then laid the city and diocese of Ross under interdict.[13]

Thaddeus appears to have been in residence with the Franciscans of Timoleague when news of the papal decision reached him, but he would still not yield. On the advice of Edmund de Courcey, a former member of the Timoleague community and at that time bishop of Clogher (to be later transferred to Ross), he appealed his case because 'having been proclaimed unheard, he desired an inquiry to be made to whom the church [of Ross] lawfully belonged', but he insisted that he was ready to obey justice.[14] The pope commissioned Oliver, bishop of Sabina and cardinal of Naples, to hold a judicial inquiry to which Odo O'Driscoll and Thaddeus MacCarthy were to be summoned. Bishop Oliver was empowered to remove the censures from Thaddeus and from other essential witnesses so as to enable them to participate in the trial at which a charge of simony against Odo O'Driscoll was also to be investigated. If proved, this charge, which according to the

11 Ibid., pp. 142–3.
12 *Cal. papal letters, 1484–92*, p. 31.
13 Cork Diocesan Archives, 'Acts for the Process', p. 5.
14 *Cal. papal letters, 1484–92*, p. 310.

supporters of Thaddeus belonged to O'Driscoll's pre-episcopal
career, would have constituted an irregularity which would
have militated against his provision. The charge was that before
his appointment to Ross Odo O'Driscoll had entered the order
of Friars Minor of the Strict Observance from which he again
opted out before completing his year of probation. Before
entering he had held a perpetual vicarage (probably Aghadown)
which the then bishop of Ross conferred upon another cleric,
and in order that this cleric might resign it to him Odo O'Driscoll
was said to have given valuable consideration—'a certain sum
of money or other goods'.[15] This indictment of O'Driscoll in
1490, that is, seventeen years after his appointment as bishop and
eight years after the provision of Thaddeus, introduced a new
element into a situation which had been partially solved on
29 December 1489 when the abbey of Maur (*de Fonte Vivo*)
which had been held *in commendam* by Edmund de Courcey
was conferred *in commendam* on Thaddeus MacCarthy for life.
The revenues of the abbey would appear to have been then
Thaddeus's only source of revenue. While the papal commission
of investigation was in session news reached Rome of the
resignation of William Roche in 1490 from the united dioceses
of Cork and Cloyne. With Roche's resignation, curial irrespon-
sibility towards the diocese of Cork, Cloyne and Ross reached
epic proportions.

Three papal decrees came from the hand of Pope Innocent
VIII on 21 April 1490. The first, which dealt with the Ross
succession, solemnly pronounced Odo O'Driscoll as the legitimate bishop of that diocese and absolved him from any
irregularities that may have existed in his provision, both in the
case of simony, as was asserted, and of succession to Donald, as
was admitted. The papal document which absolved O'Driscoll
ad cautelam suggests that the charge of simony had not been
substantiated. It was solemnly declared that Thaddeus Mac-
Carthy never had any legitimate claim to Ross, and in respect
of his supposed claim, perpetual silence was imposed upon
him and on his adherents.[16] 'The pope . . . hereby declares . . .
that the said Thady never had any right and has no right in the
rule and administration [of the church of Ross], and imposes
perpetual silence upon him . . .'[17] Quite clearly, therefore,
Thaddeus MacCarthy had never been bishop of Ross. Of the

15   Ibid., p. 261.
16   Cork Diocesan Archives, folio entitled *Reg. Bull. Secret., Tomus*, 5, f. 18.
17   *Cal. papal letters, 1484–92*, p. 260.

remaining decrees of Innocent VIII, one provided Thaddeus to the sees of Cork and Cloyne on the resignation of William Roche, the other by a special *motu proprio* provided him to the same sees in the event of William's death.[18] The double provision may have safeguarded Thaddeus MacCarthy against the possibility of invalidity, but it ignored the occupancy of the united dioceses of Cork and Cloyne by Bishop Gerald Fitz-Gerald. Having settled the succession dispute in Ross at the expense of the neighbouring dioceses of Cork and Cloyne, Innocent VIII confirmed the interest of Thaddeus MacCarthy in the abbey of Maur and allowed him 'to hold the same during his life, with such other bishopric or diocese to which he might hereafter be appointed'.[19]

On 4 June 1490 Thaddeus MacCarthy, who after his recent experiences in Ross cannot have been unaware of the complexities of succession in the dioceses of Cork and Cloyne, bound himself to pay the customary tax on his bulls of provision,[20] he redeemed the bulls of William Roche on 1 December (Roche was a non-payee) and on 20 May 1491 he was granted a respite of eight months in which to discharge the debts thus contracted. The date of his arrival in Cork is not known but it must have been before 18 July 1492. On that date he was furnished with a papal bull from Innocent VIII denouncing all who opposed him in Cork and Cloyne and calling upon all subjects to support him in the government of the united sees. The leaders of the opposition were mentioned by name in a roll-call, the extent of which shows an intense and concerted resistance to Thaddeus MacCarthy: Maurice, earl of Desmond, William Barry (Barrymore), Edmund Maurice de Geraldine, the corporation of the city of Cork, the corporate body of the University of Youghal, the brothers of the earl of Desmond, of William Barry, of Edmund Maurice, and finally, Philip Ronan, cleric of the diocese of Cork, who was *officialis* or judge of the ecclesiastical court of Cork.[21] The only great family, apart from the MacCarthys, not in opposition to Thaddeus were the Roches, but even they were compromised by the fact that Earl Maurice of Desmond was married to Ellen Roche,

---

18   Cork Diocesan Archives, '*Summarium Addionale* to the Process for Beatification', pp. 10–12.

19   F. P. Carey, *Blessed Thaddeus MacCarthy*, p. 5.

20   Michael Kiely, 'Episcopal Succession in Cork and Cloyne in the Fifteenth Century', *I.E.R.*, xl (1932), 124–5.

21   Cork Diocesan Archives, Arch. Vat. Reg., vol. 690, fols. 178b–182.

daughter of Maurice, Lord Roche of Fermoy.[22] From a numerical point of view Thaddeus was fighting a lost cause. Armed men took possession of the cathedral and all remonstrances of the MacCarthy faction that the property of the church should be restored to its lawful pastor (Thaddeus) were met with refusal and derision. Geraldine supporters were quick to notice that the papal bull contained no condemnation of Gerald FitzGerald, whom the MacCarthys regarded as the head and source of opposition to Thaddeus and who still insisted on the validity of his own title to the united sees of Cork and Cloyne.

A special mandate attached to Pope Innocent's bull of 18 July 1492 counselled the Irish archbishops, bishops and prelates and his beloved sons Gerald, earl of Kildare, Florence Mac-Carthy (Reagh), prince of Carbery, Thaddeus, prince of Desmond, Donogh Oge MacCarthy, Maurice Roche and the brothers, sons and subjects of Gerald, earl of Kildare, to assist Thaddeus in regaining possession of the united sees.[23] But the dioceses of Cork and Cloyne were not to know the blessings of the saintly rule of Thaddeus MacCarthy. Armed with his twofold vindication Thaddeus left Rome after 18 July 1492 and either from inclination or through sheer necessity assumed the guise of a pilgrim, travelling unaccompanied and incognito. His journey took him through the Piedmontese city of Ivrea with which his name was destined forever to be linked. Ivrea lay some thirty miles north of Turin; it was formerly an important city on the main highway to the north of Europe via the Great Saint Bernard, and history records the names of many

22   Maurice, earl of Desmond, 1487–1520: his brothers were Thomas, Gerald and John. He was married to Ellen, daughter of Maurice, Lord Roche.

William Barry (Barrymore) was first son of John Barry by his second wife who was the daughter of MacCarthy Reagh. William Barry himself was married to a daughter of Cormac *Láidir*.

Edmund Maurice de Geraldine was either brother or nephew to Gerald FitzGerald who claimed to be bishop of Cork and Cloyne. It seems probable that he was Gerald's nephew, the son of Maurice FitzGerald of Ballymartyr (Castlemartyr).

23   Identifications of these nominees are as follows:
Gearóid Mór, Great Earl of Kildare.

Florence (Finghin), prince of Carbery, was third son of Diarmaid an Dúna, and was married to Catherine, daughter of Thomas, eighth earl of Desmond. His brothers were Donal and Dermot.

Thaddeus, prince of Desmond, was MacCarthy Mór, son of Donnell Oge who died in 1468 and who was son of Tadhg na Mainistreach. This Tadhg or Thaddeus was MacCarthy Mór in 1489 according to the *Annals of Ulster*.

Cormac, son of Thaddeus, was probably Cormac *Láidir* or a son of Thaddeus of the previous entry.

Donogh Oge MacCarthy is said to have been lord of Duhallow.

illustrious persons who halted there on their journeys to and
from Rome. It was at Ivrea, according to the Bollandists, that
Saint Patrick was consecrated bishop when news of the death
of Palladius reached him. Saint Bernard's *Life of St Malachy*
mentions that the great Irish reformer-saint passed through
Ivrea on his way to Rome and worked a miracle in favour of the
ailing son of the man with whom he lodged. Another archbishop
of Armagh, Blessed Concord, likewise tarried at Ivrea and
died there while on a journey from Rome to Chamberry in
Savoy.

Close to Ivrea lay the little hamlet of Aosta in the shadow of
an Alpine spur which ran eastwards from Mount Iseran to the
Dora-Baltea, a tributary of the river Po. Aosta's chief feature
was a pilgrim hospice called the Hospital of the Twenty-one
which was founded in 1005 by the lords of Chalont and Solerio.
In 1310 Bishop Alberto Gonzaga of Ivrea united it to the
chapter of the collegiate church of Saint Orso so that pilgrim
canons might always have a place of lodging. He stipulated that
the rector of the hostel should always be a canon of Saint Orso,
that he should be presented by the chapter of Saint Orso and that
one-third of the revenues of the hospital should be spent in
hospitality and in the care of the sick.[24] Thaddeus MacCarthy
died in this hospital on 24 October 1492. The circumstances
surrounding his death are calendared in a manuscript history
of the ancient city of Ivrea which was compiled in 1763 by
Canon Robesti of Ivrea. He tells that 'in the year 1492 there
died in the Hospice of St Anthony, of the 'Twenty-one',
Thaddeus of the royal family of Macher, Bishop in Ireland of
a diocese unknown (to the writer). According to tradition,
this prelate, in returning from Rome, having passed through
Ivrea *incognito*, entered the public Hospice of Pilgrims . . . There,
worn out by fatigue and consumed by the love of God which
irradiated his inner soul, he died unknown to anybody, at a
certain time during the night. At the same time there appeared
to the Bishop of Ivrea, Nicholas Garigliatti, a great light
within which he saw a prelate. At the same time also in the
Hospice, the bed in which he lay appeared, as it were, all aflame
and on fire without being consumed or injured in any way.
Being astonished at this, the attendants informed the Bishop
who himself having been made aware of the sanctity of the dead
prelate by the vision, went to the Hospice in wonder at these
great happenings. There he saw the dead prelate clad in the

24 Patrick Hurley, 'Blessed Thaddeus MacCarthy', *Cork Hist. Soc. Jn.*, ii (1896),
506. The hospital was destroyed during the Franco-Spanish war of 1544, but the
church was reconstructed and enlarged under Saint Anthony, Abbot, as titular.

humble clothes of a poor pilgrim. And having examined his papers, he saw that he was a bishop, and in fact, the very person he had seen in the vision, surrounded by light at the moment of his death. God having worked so many miracles to glorify His servant Thaddeus, Bishop Garigliatti commanded that the body be vested in pontificals and buried in the cathedral church. There it was placed beneath the table of the altar of St Andreas the Apostle, in a marble urn. In this urn there had already been placed the body of St Eusebius, a former Bishop of Ivrea, the precise date of whose reign is unknown.'[25]

The announcement of Thaddeus's death reached Ireland in 1493 in a brief of Pope Alexander VI conferring the abbey of Maur (*de Fonte Vivo*) on Dermot O'Huallachain. The brief declared that the abbacy had become vacant *per obitum bonae memoriae Episcopi Corkagensis et Clonensis commendatarii.* Thaddeus, it will be remembered, obtained the monastery *in commendam* in 1489. Alexander VI's brief admitted a vacancy in the united sees of Cork and Cloyne; nevertheless, no move was made towards appointing a successor to Thaddeus, nor were any steps taken in Ivrea to secure more precise information concerning the saintly pilgrim around whom an aura of mystery was thickening. It is possible that the ecclesiastical authorities in Ivrea feared a claim for the repatriation of Thaddeus's remains and made as little commotion as possible about his death. The unrest then prevailing in the united sees, coupled with recurring clashes between the MacCarthys and the FitzGeralds make such a claim unlikely. For the time being the FitzGeralds were in the ascendant and Gerald FitzGerald, bishop of Cork and Cloyne, was not the person to surmount family jealousies when it came to honouring a MacCarthy. Even the MacCarthys themselves were indifferent; an estrangement between them and Thaddeus had developed out of his disapproval of their efforts towards establishing him in the diocese of Ross.

But though neglected by his own kindred and forgotten in his own country, Thaddeus MacCarthy found his niche in Ivrea as one whose intercession was the source of many miracles for the inhabitants of this Alpine city. Details of miracles accredited to him were unfortunately lost in a fire which destroyed the Ivrea episcopal archives in 1620. Documents surviving in other collections however (these were carefully scrutinized at the beatification process in 1893) show that his remains reposed with those of other saints in the cathedral at

25   Cork Diocesan Archives, 'Process for the Beatification', pp. 29 ff.

Ivrea and that he enjoyed a popular *cultus* there. Evidence to this effect comes from three main sources. Firstly, a partly injured manuscript preserved in the episcopal library at Ivrea and dating from 1492 or from the early years of the sixteenth century tells that many bodies of saints and martyrs lie in the cathedral. 'There also lies Thaddeus, of royal lineage, of the ancient stock of Macher.'[26] The second source is a calendar of saints and *beati* compiled on 20 October 1488 by a priest named Roland and placed at the beginning of the manuscript breviary then in use in the diocese of Ivrea. An interpolation occurs in this calendar under the month of October. It states that many miracles were worked by Thaddeus, and that one miracle favoured 'Lergerius, the writer, who suffered much from fevers'. The interpolation, which was written in 1492 or shortly afterwards, reads: *Anno Domini millesimo quatercentesimo nonagesimo secundo, die vigesima quarta Octobris migravit de hoc saeculo in pace R.D.D. Thaddeus, Episcopus Yberniensis, qui post paucos dies cepit multa miracula facere: et pro Magistro Lergerio, scriptore, qui multum vexabatur febribus.*[27] Our third source, which comes from the library of the king of Turin, is an early sixteenth-century manuscript which contains miscellaneous information on the city of Ivrea, including data similar to that already outlined on Thaddeus MacCarthy.[28]

Apostolic visitation files of the cathedral of Ivrea show that the public veneration authorized by Bishop Garigliatti in 1492 continued to be paid 'to the body of Saint Thaddeus, bishop in Ireland and confessor' (*Il Corpo di S. Taddeo, Vescovo d'Hibernia e Confessore*). An old manuscript catalogue of the relics of the cathedral church of Ivrea tells of a custom according to which the cathedral canons on each recurring second Sunday after Easter announced to the faithful that 'the body of Saint Thaddeus, bishop in Ireland and Confessor' lay amongst these precious and highly-venerated relics. To this Monsignor Angelo Perusio, whom Pope Gregory XIII sent as apostolic visitator to Piedmont in 1585, adds his testimony that the remains of Blessed Thaddeus rested under the table of the altar of Saint Eusebius (to which the title of Saint Andrew had been given) and that 'God had adorned the body itself with many miracles performed since 1492.'[29] Monsignor Octavius

26 Ibid., p. 16.

27 Ibid., p. 17.

28 Ibid.

29 Ibid., pp. 21, 19.

Asinari in his visitation of 22 March 1647 confirmed the preservation of the remains and mentioned in particular the figure of a bishop painted on the wall at the epistle side of the chapel, beneath which was the following inscription: *In hoc altare dictum fuit requiescere sacras reliquias Beati Thaddaei Epi. Hyberniae; qua de causa credunt in facie altaris scripta fuisse ista verba; sepulchrum Beati Thaddaei Epi. Hyberniae. Et in pariete laterali ipsius capellae ad cornu Epistolae sub insignibus cujusdam Epi. in muro depictis leguntur ista verba ; Tenet lapis hic ossa Thaddaei Presulis Hyberniae, geniti de stirpe Hialar.*[30]

Between 1650 and 1742 when the next visitation took place the inscription on the reliquary had been changed and Thaddeus given the title of martyr: *Sepulchrum Sancti Eusebii, Ep. et Sancti Thaddaei, Episcopi Hyberniae et Martyris.* The new title would appear to have been based on the opposition Thaddeus encountered and of which the papal letters on his person gave ample proof. These multiple titles of bishop, confessor and martyr conferred on Thaddeus occasioned a solemn visitation of Ivrea on 22 August 1742 by Monsignor Michael de Villa, bishop of Ivrea. Canon Robesti related that Monsignor de Villa 'caused to be opened the tomb in which were the two holy bodies (Saint Eusebius and Thaddeus). And first, having lifted up the marble cover, there were seen within two bodies so placed that the head of each lay at the feet of the other. There was also found an inscription written upon parchment which is still preserved in the Capitular Archives of the city. Above St Eusebius was found the body of the blessed Bishop Thaddeus completely preserved, the intact skeleton of whom was clothed in a purple soutane and rochet. A white beard fell upon the breast, and on the right hand was seen an episcopal ring. The skeleton of Saint Eusebius, also completely intact, was similarly observed. These facts were solemnly witnessed and the bodies from the tomb were sealed and deposited in the sacrarium of relics in the Cathedral Church. The ring was taken by the Bishop, and its green stone was set in gold. This ring is in daily use. Of all these facts I myself was a witness and spectator.'[31]

Assisted by many dignitaries and aided by three surgeons Monsignor de Villa identified the body of Thaddeus, bishop

30 Hurley, 'Blessed Thaddeus MacCarthy', *Cork Hist. Soc. Jn.*, iii (1897), 95, explains *de stirpe Hialar*, 'the race of eagles', by a rather incongruous declension from the Irish word *fiolar*. He maintains that when the MacCarthys adopted armorial bearings, the motto selected by MacCarthy Reagh (the Kilbrittain branch to which Thaddeus belonged) was *Fortis, Ferox et Celer*, which, according to Father Hurley, was 'evidently referring to the eagle'.

31 Cork Diocesan Archives, 'Process for the Beatification', pp. 29 ff.

in Ireland, who died in 1492 and who had been uninterruptedly venerated since that date. The body was removed to a new sarcophagus bearing the inscription: *Corpus Sti. Thadaei, Epi. Hyberniae, recognitum prout ex testimonialibus diei 22 Augusti in visitatione Illmi. et Rmi. D.D. Michaelis de Villa, Epi. Ipporegien.*[32] Father Benvenuti of the Congregation of the Christian Doctrine in a work entitled *A History of the Ancient City of Ivrea* (1800) makes particular reference to this visitation.

Native interest in Thaddeus MacCarthy dates from as late as 23 June 1847 when Archbishop Daniel Murray of Dublin received a gift of 1,000 francs from the bishop of Ivrea for the relief of the Irish famine-stricken poor. The subscription was accompanied by a request for information *de Beato Thaddeo Episcopo Hiberniae*, concerning whom the bishop sent the following details: *Anno Domini millesimo quadringentesimo nonagesimo secundo, die vigesima quarta Octobris, Eporodiae (antiqua urbis Transalpinae in Pedemontio) postremum obiit diem in hospitio peregrinorum sub titulo Sancti Antonii, quidam viator incognitus; atque eadem instante lux mira prope lectum in quo jacebat effulsit, et Episcopo Eporediensi apparuit homo venerandus Pontificalibus indumentis vestitus. Thaddeum Macher Hiberniae Episcopum illum esse innotuit et chartis quas deferebat; et in Cathedrali ejus corpus solemni pompa depositum est sub altari, et in tumulo sancti Eusebii Episcopi Eporediensis, atque post paucos dies cepit multa miracula facere.*[33] The bishop of Ivrea mentioned that the papers indicating the country, family, episcopal character, etc., of Thaddeus had been destroyed by fire in the sixteenth century and concluded his inquires by asking if there had been any persecution of bishops in Ireland in his time.

Dr. L. F. Renehan, president of Maynooth, was commissioned to investigate the case and went to Ivrea in 1850 to collect all surviving traditions of Thaddeus MacCarthy. Certain points from his findings cannot be corroborated, for example, details concerning the *monastic* life of Thaddeus for which there is not a shred of evidence in the papal registers. The tenuous connections of his early life with the monasteries of Timoleague, Kilcrea and Ballymacadane cannot be accepted in justification of Dr. Renehan's suppositions. Other tenets of Dr. Renehan are patently incorrect. Thaddeus MacCarthy was born in Cork, not Kerry; his family was MacCarthy Reagh, not MacCarthy Mór, and his consecration was the act not of Innocent VIII but of Sixtus IV. The bishop of Ivrea's final question posed no

32   Ibid., p. 26.

33   Hurley, 'Blessed Thaddeus MacCarthy', *Cork Hist. Soc. Jn.*, ii (1896), 508.

problem. There was no persecution of bishops in Ireland in 1492, whatever Thaddeus's papers with their details of opposition to him in Cork and Cloyne may have suggested to the contrary.

Subsequent correspondence between the bishop of Ivrea and Dr. Renehan aroused a new interest in the pilgrim bishop for whose beatification Monsignor Richelmy of Ivrea, Bishop Thomas Alphonus O'Callaghan of Cork, and the clergy and laity of Cork and Cloyne petitioned the Holy See in the early 1890s. Canon Soroglio, vicar general of Ivrea, undertook all investigations relative to the beatification, and Monsignor Michael Antonino of the Sacred Congregation of Rites was charged with the conduct of the proceedings which lasted from 19 August 1893 to 26 August 1895. The decree of beatification was confirmed on the latter date by Pope Leo XIII. Its promulgation was fixed for 12, 13 and 14 September 1896, and was effected in presence of the reigning bishops of the three dioceses associated with the chequered career of Thaddeus MacCarthy: Bishop Thomas Alphonsus O'Callaghan of Cork, Bishop Robert Browne of Cloyne and Bishop William FitzGerald of Ross. Thaddeus MacCarthy, the fifteenth-century rejected bishop of all three dioceses, had at last come into his own. The beatification decree confirmed the centuries-old reverence which attached to him in Ivrea and authorized the extension of his cult to the dioceses of Cork, Cloyne and Ross.

The claim of Thaddeus MacCarthy to beatification did not rest on the validity of his claim to be bishop of Cork and Cloyne or of any other see. It lay rather in his heroic life and in his proven sanctity which was sealed by the testimony of the miracles worked through his intercession. He has been honoured with the title of 'White Martyr of Munster' even though the title of martyr in its generic sense cannot be said to apply to him. His persecution as such was the outcome of political pressure and, while he was sincere in his attachment to the church, his supporters and sponsors were far from sharing his lofty ideals. On the other hand, the title of 'confessor' under which he was beatified must be accepted with certain reservations. He was above all else a bishop defending his rights against adversaries; his pastoral apostolate was minimal. But as applied to him the term 'confessor' signifies one who by excelling in the practice of Christian virtue was a living witness to Christ, one whose every action confessed Christ before men. In an age when the exploitation of benefices for political purposes had developed into a fine art, the provision of Thaddeus MacCarthy to the dioceses of Cork and Cloyne could have obviated the shameful happenings of the final decade of the fifteenth and the opening years of the sixteenth centuries. Thaddeus MacCarthy was a man of God, absolutely without rancour, a man whose holy life and heroic fortitude placed him far ahead of contemporary Irish ecclesiastics. With clean hands he restrained the animosity and unchristian attitudes of his followers, he submitted patiently to the calumnies and denunciations of his enemies and bore in silence the heavy burden of physical and mental suffering. In 1483 'having been proclaimed unheard' all he asked was that a lawful inquiry should be held and he professed himself 'ready to obey justice'.[34] By rising above his times, this silent and holy man gave example not only to the age in which he lived but to posterity. As a modern writer puts it: 'If he were not blessed with red martyrdom, he assuredly was blessed with white martyrdom, bearing his endless trials and troubles with heroic fortitude, and manifesting holy prudence in the most difficult situations.'[35]

Following the death of Thaddeus MacCarthy in 1492 the succession dispute in the dioceses of Cork and Cloyne entered its final and perhaps most complicated phase. Gerald Fitz-Gerald ruled unopposed as the acknowledged bishop of the united dioceses from 1492 to 1499. His resignation in 1499 was accompanied by a statement to the effect that he had been in *peaceful* possession of the sees for thirty years. Even Rome was sceptical, for the last years of the FitzGerald administration were of a pattern with the turmoil which arose out of the forgeries and falsities of the mid-century. Politically and ecclesiastically, the final decade of the fifteenth century was a time of extreme confusion.

On the political side was the effort to prove a case for Perkin Warbeck in his claim to be Richard of York, King Edward's second son, who had escaped from the Tower of London. Warbeck arrived in Cork in the autumn of 1491 and was immediately supported by John Waters, mayor of Cork, by Maurice, earl of Desmond, by Lords Roche, Barry and de Courcey, the White Knight and the knights of Glin and Kerry who represented junior banches of the Munster Geraldines. To these were joined Archbishop David Creagh of Cashel, the bishop of Waterford and Lismore, and Bishop Gerald Fitz-Gerald of Cork and Cloyne. Warbeck, having rallied practically the whole of Munster to his cause, left Ireland for Flanders and did not return again until 1495. In the meantime the Irish

---

34 *Cal. papal letters, 1484–92*, p. 310.

35 Carey, *Blessed Thaddeus MacCarthy*, p. 20.

policy of Henry VII had stiffened, and re-shuffles in the administration showed a determination to work up the Tudor cause by all means practicable. Outstanding incidents in the purge of over-mighty officials were the temporary deposition of the Great Earl of Kildare and the Poynings' interlude, which while not immediately successful had ultimately far-reaching effects in that it annulled the home rule triumph of the century and wiped out fifty years of colonialism in which Dublin had become the capital of an Anglo-Irish state.[36] A new era in Anglo-Irish relations had dawned with the advent of the Tudors who were no respectors of persons, and notwithstanding that the Great Earl was astute enough to ride the current, the overmighty Geraldines were to be ruthlessly liquidated before the end of the sixteenth century.

Warbeck returned to Cork in July 1495 and with eleven ships laid siege to Waterford on the twenty-third of that month. The city was simultaneously blockaded on land by Maurice *Bacach*, ninth earl of Desmond, but the siege failed and Waterford was relieved by Poynings on 4 August. Warbeck then sailed for Scotland where he married Lady Catherine Gordon, cousin to King James. In August of the following year (1496) Gearóid Mór was reinstated, and on 26 August Gerald FitzGerald, bishop of Cork and Cloyne, was specifically mentioned in the general pardon issued to all supporters of Warbeck.[37] Thereafter the Warbeck episode petered out to an inglorious conclusion. Accompanied by his wife and two young children the imposter effected a third landing at Cork in July 1497, there to find that his cause had outlived itself. He returned to England, surrendered to the authorities and was executed at Tyburn in November 1499. With him was executed Mayor John Waters who was not included in the general pardon of 1496. For the moment Irish affairs were tolerably quiescent, but the support given to Simnel and Warbeck attracted the notice of the foreign and domestic enemies of the new Tudor dynasty and within a few decades the earl of Desmond would be negotiating with the emperor and the king of France for help against the encroachments of Henry VIII.

36 Curtis, *Med. Ire.*, p. 349.

37 Rymer, *Foedera*, xii, 634: 'Sciatis quod de Gratia Nostra Speciali, ac ex certa Scientia et mero motu Nostris, pardonamus, remissimus ac relaxamus . . . David, Archiepiscopo de Kassel; Thomas, Episcopo de Lysmore ac Waterford; Geraldo, Episcopo de Corke & Clone; Mauricio, Comiti de Dessemond; Edmundo FitzMorys, Baroni de Clannor; Magistro Thomae de Dessemond; Magistro Johanni de Dessemond; Mauricio Geralti et Thomae FitzGerot de Dessemond; Mauricio Domino Roche; Jacobo Domino Coursy; Jacobo Domino Barete; Domino Mauritio le White Knight; Domino Mauritio Milite de Kerye, etc.'

Two final contestants for the bishopric of Cork and Cloyne entered the stage of history in the year 1499. The claimants were Patrick Cant or Condon, abbot of the Cistercian monastery of Fermoy (*de Castro Dei*), and John FitzEdmund FitzGerald, nephew to the reigning bishop. By a strange paradox both claimants were sponsored by the earl of Desmond, *Comes Desimoniae*. The facile expedient of naming MacCarthy of Desmond as Cant's sponsor and Maurice FitzGerald, earl of Desmond, as supporter to his own kinsman cannot be seriously entertained.[38] The subtleties of the situation went far deeper: MacCarthy was the prince of Desmond, *Princeps Desimoniae*, but the title of *Comes Desimoniae* was reserved exclusively to the FitzGerald earls of Desmond. The date of Cant's provision as given in Eubel and confirmed by the *Codex Consistorialis* is 15 February 1499, and the bishopric was then valued at 300 florins. The bull of provision stated that the united sees were vacant *per obitum Jordani*, conveying no doubt, that the vacancy was caused by death rather than by resignation, privation, translation or the like, and the *Codex* describes the dioceses as *in dominio Comitis Desimoniae qui non recognoscit nisi Sanctum Petrum et Sedem Apostolicam*.[39] Maurice of Desmond had supported Warbeck but had been restored to favour in 1496; consequently the foregoing can only refer to the years immediately before 1496 when as a Yorkist sympathizer the earl might well have styled himself as one answerable to no other authority save that of the Apostolic See. If we assume this to have been the case, Desmond's support for Cant, who was an outsider and member of an influential east Cork family, must be interpreted in terms of a desire to end a situation which for so long had produced chaotic conditions in Cork and Cloyne. The *per obitum Jordani* had its own significance: by going back to a bishop whose provision was uncontestably valid, the deadlock which had developed from the provisions of William Roche and Thaddeus MacCarthy would be obviated.

The earl reckoned without Gerald FitzGerald who decided (in 1499) to resign not in favour of Cant but of his own nephew, John FitzEdmund FitzGerald who was in his twenty-seventh year. King Henry VII favoured FitzEdmund and on 8 April 1499 asked the pope to confer the bishopric on him, adding that the reigning bishop had resigned in his favour: '*Die 8 Aprilis, 1499, Lectae literae Ser^mi Regis Angliae ad S^mum*,

---

38 Kiely, 'Episcopal Succession in Cork and Cloyne in the Fifteenth Century', pp. 3 ff.

39 Brady, *Episcopal Succession*, ii, 81.

quod cum commendasset D. Joannum Edmundi de Geraldinis ad ecclesias Corkagen. et Clonen. in dominio suo Hiberniae unitas, in cujus favorem a moderno [? *moderante*] *Episcopo resignacio facienda erat . . .*'[40] The king condemned the papal attitude which prohibited Gerald FitzGerald's resignation on the 'assertion of Irish subjects that the Earl of Desmond had recommended a certain abbot of Fermoy' to the vacant sees. He protested that letters from his subjects were given more consideration than his own and touched a sore spot on Anglo-papal relations by referring to his right to nominate candidates to vacant sees.[41]

Whatever the cause, the earl of Desmond withdrew his recommendation of Patrick Cant on 25 April and on the same day Edmund de Courcey, bishop of Ross, apostolic nuncio and collector of taxes in Ireland,[42] added his support to the proposal of Gerald FitzGerald. On 27 April letters from the bishops and from the dean and chapter of Ross were issued to the effect that Gerald FitzGerald had been validly appointed and consecrated bishop of the churches of Cork and Cloyne by authority of Pope Pius II (in 1464) and had enjoyed peaceful possession of the united sees for thirty years, *ac jam 30 anno et ultra in pacifice possessione, summa cum benevolentia et obedientia totius cleri et Capituli ipsarum ecclesiarum fuisse.*[43] A very confused consistory assembled on 19 June 1499 to sift this overwhelming bulk of contradictory evidence and to consider the proposed appointment of John FitzEdmund FitzGerald. His provision was objected to on the plea that since Patrick Cant had been provided on the death of Jordan Purcell, and Thaddeus MacCarthy on the resignation of William Roche, it was not possible for anyone, in the face of so many bishops, to have enjoyed *peaceful* possession of the dioceses for thirty years:

40   Ibid., quoting *Acta Consistorialia.*

41   Ibid., p. 82: 'Qua ex re vehementer mirari majorem subditis suis et infimis hominibus, quam literarum suarum testimonio fidem adhiberi, plurisque valere apud Suam Beatitudinem unius privati Domicelli ac subditi sui, quam suam ipsius commendationem, cum praesertim eadem ipsa diu jam antea cognitis suis legitimis causis, et rationibus promotiones ipsas Hibernicas et earum nominationes sibi concesserit, ac saepius repititis brevibus libere promisit. Demum eandem ipsam instantissime rogabat quod sibi semel concesserat ac toties suis brevibus confirmarat, id nunc inviolabiliter praestare vellet. *Barberini.*'

42   Edmund de Courcey, a Franciscan of Timoleague Abbey and professor of divinity, was appointed to Clogher in 1484 and to Ross in 1494. On his appointment to Clogher, the abbey of Maur which he held *in commendam* was conferred on Thaddeus MacCarthy. Edmund de Courcey resigned the see of Ross in 1517 and retired to Timoleague which he reconstructed with aid from his nephew, James, Lord Kinsale. He died on 15 March 1518.

43   Brady, *Episcopal Succession*, ii, 83.

quonammodo fieri posset ut in possessione 30 annos fuerit, cum interea et tot Episcopi extiterint. . .[44]

A later consistory of 26 June reconsidered the whole position, admitted the resignation of Gerald FitzGerald, annulled the provision of Patrick Cant and provided John FitzEdmund FitzGerald to the united sees of Cork and Cloyne by papal decree of Pope Alexander VI.[45] Gerald FitzGerald, whose protagonist William Roche had died within the previous year, now made his final bow on the stage of diocesan history, and John FitzEdmund FitzGerald, suitably armed with papal provision and dispensation because of youth, became bishop of the sees of Finbarr and Colman. The thirty years war was over.

---

44 Ibid.

45 Brady, *Episcopal Succession*, ii, 83: Alexander VI 'admisit resignationem D. Geraldi de Geraldinis, de ecclesiis Corkagen et Clonen. invicem unitis in Hibernia, sub archiepiscopatu et provincia Casselen, in dominio Comitis Desimoniae subditi Regis Angliae et de eis providit in titulum D[no] Joanni Edmundi de Geraldinis, cum dispensatione super defectu aetatis cum esset xxvii annorum, et cum retentione beneficiorum suorum.'

XIX

The Eve of the Reformation

POPES		BISHOPS OF CORK	KINGS OF ENGLAND
Alexander VI	1492–1503	John FitzEdmund	Henry VII 1485–1509
Pius III	1503	Fitzgerald 1499–1520	Henry VIII 1509–1547
Julius II	1503–1513	John Benet 1523–1536	
Leo X	1513–1521		
Adrian VI	1521–1523		
Clement VIII	1523–1534		
Paul III	1534–1549		

The sixteenth century opened on a sinister note with a charge of murder invoiced against David (?James) Barry, archdeacon of Cork and Cloyne. The *Annals of the Four Masters* record under date 1500 that the archdeacon slew the Barrymore, his own kinsman, and subsequently suffered a like fate himself at the hands of another Barry. Twenty days after the perpetration of the crime the earl of Desmond had the archdeacon's body disinterred and 'he made it into dust and ashes' (*min agus luaith do dhenum de*), according to an entry in the *Annals of Ulster*. Two years later the earl, who still sought vengeance and 'not having the fear of God before his eyes', robbed and spoiled the bishop's estates on the assumption that John FitzEdmund FitzGerald was privy to Barrymore's death. Only one other record of John FitzEdmund's episcopate remains in the form of 'a sentence pronounced by John, Lord Bishop of Cork and Cloyne, in Christ Church in Corcke, 25 May, a.d. 1514, to confirm Gerott (Garrett) in the principalitie of the Rotchfords'.[1] The entry has a twofold significance. From it we learn that in 1514 the Rotchfords were still tenants-in-fee of the

---

1 Smith, *History of Cork*, i, 363. Witnesses to this record were Patrick Cant, abbot of Fermoy and one-time appointee to the see of Cork; Master Philip Gull (Gould), official of Cork; Edmund Tyrry, mayor of Cork; John Galwey and William Tyrrey, former mayors.

bishop—or, to quote Smith's commentary sentence, they were vassals of the bishop (*vassali Episcopi Corcagen[sis]*). By inference, therefore, the bishop of Cork continued to enjoy head-rents from the Manor of Fayd up to the eve of the Reformation. A more important feature of the record is its appended seal, the oldest known seal of a bishop of Cork. Caulfield describes this seal as follows: 'In the centre is represented a Bishop in his pontificals on a horse, walking on what resembles waves (probably an allusion to a certain legend in the life of St Fin Barre). *In chief*, a demi figure of a Bishop giving the benediction. *In base*, a dragon.'[2] The legend enshrined in the seal recalls Saint Finbarr's visit to Saint David of Minevia who is said to have presented him with a horse, 'and he rode the animal straight over the sea to the west.'[3]

John FitzEdmund FitzGerald died before 27 August 1520.[4] The Earl of Surrey conveyed news of his death to Cardinal Wolsey with the suggestion that the vacancy should be filled by some Englishman, for Cork was an important port and city, its episcopal revenues were tempting, the prestige attached to the bishopric was high and it was of supreme urgency that the vacancy should be filled by a compliant cleric. 'The Busshop off Cork is ded', wrote Surrey, 'and grete [*sute is made*] to me to wright for men off this contre; some say it is worth 200 markes by yere, some say [*more*]. My poure advyse shuld be that it shuld be bestowed upon som Inglish man. The Busshop of Leyghlin . . . myght do gode service here. I besech Your Grace let none off this contre have it, nor none other, but such as woll dwell theropon, and such as dare, and woll speke, and roffle, when nede shalbe.'[5] With singular disregard for his plea for a residential prelate, Surrey's nominee, Thomas Halsey, was the most notorious absentee of the time. Halsey, bishop of Leighlin, was an Englishman who never once set foot in the diocese of his appointment. He served at the Fifth Council of the Lateran, 1512–17, and died at Westminster some time after the date of Surrey's letter.

---

2   Caulfield, *The Annals of St. Fin Barre's Cathedral, Cork*, p. 10.

3   Plummer, *Vitae SS Hib.*, i, 69.

4   Lynch, *De praesulibus Hib.*, ii, 144–5, has the following incorrect entry listed under the diocese of Cork: 'E Romanis tabulis discimus quod Cluanensis episcopatus per obitum ultimi episcopi donatus fuerit, 10 Novembris 1517, D. Quintino, fratri Ordinis Minorum'. The reference is to the diocese of Clonmacnoise, *Cluanmacnosensis* or *Cluanensis*; in the first volume of *De praesulibus Hib.*, Lynch gives the correct entry under its correct heading: 'Quintinus quidam Ordinis Minorum hunc episcopatum obtinuit provisione pontificia, 10 Novembris 1516; post autem sedem annos viginti duos possessam, obiit, 1538.'

5   *Cal. S. P. Ire., 1509–73*, ii, pt. 3, p. 42.

Other letters from Surrey to Wolsey during this period revolve upon the vexed question of Wolsey's pretended legatine powers in Ireland. He had been appointed *Legatus a latere* for England in 1520 and had regarded his appointment as equally applicable to Ireland; but Surrey had his own mind on the matter. A second letter dated 6 September 1520 from Surrey and his council again announced the death of the 'Bishop of Cork and Clone' and stated that 'many of great alliance in the land have made suit for the bishopric, which we have forborne, having respect for their abilities, learning and virtuous consecration, which by examination perceived in them slender and feeble.' Surrey now proposed Walter Wellesley, prior of Conal, 'a famous clerk, noted the best in the land, a man of gravity and virtuous conversation and a singular mind'. Wellesley excused himself as 'not apt . . . [for the bishopric] as well because he was situate among his friends and kinsmen and in the other parts [i.e., in Cork] but a stranger'.[6] He would accept the bishopric however (it was now valued at 100 marks) if he could retain his priory *in commendam*. His petition was rejected, but he was luckier in 1531 when he became bishop of Kildare and was permitted to retain his priory together with the bishopric. He administered both until his death in 1539.

The vacancy in Cork was filled on 28 January 1523 by the provision of John Benet, priest of the diocese of Cloyne.[7] Brady's *Records*, Cotton's *Fasti* and the *State Papers* postulate a case for a bishop named Patrick who is said to have ruled the diocese for one year, 1521–22. The Sarsfield and Tirry Papers mention the same bishop as witness to the will of Patrick Hygyn in 1521. This pseudo-bishop was probably Patrick Cant, abbot of Fermoy (*de Castro Dei*), whose appointment was annulled in 1499 and who apparently repudiated the annulment; but he was never consecrated, nor did he ever rule as bishop of Cork and Cloyne.[8] John Benet occupies a unique position as the last Catholic bishop to rule the united sees of Cork and Cloyne before the introduction of the Reformation. As with the majority of his predecessors we have few records of his episcopate as such but contemporary evidence of political and religious ferment is not wanting. And because a review of current trends in policy and thought is essential as a prologue to any discussion

---

6 *Letters and Papers, Foreign and Domestic, Henry VIII, 1519–23*, pt. i, no. 971.

7 Lynch, *De praesulibus Hib.*, ii, 145.

8 Ibid., p. 144: 'Tabulae Romanae docent quod Corcagiensis episcopatus 15 February 1499 per obitum Jordani collatus fuerit D. Patricio: ut puto, debebat dicere per obitum D. Thadaei. Timeo etiam errorem . . .'

of the Reformation, Bishop Benet may be temporarily relegated to the background.

At the beginning of the sixteenth century the power of the English king in Ireland bade fair to be exterminated. The native resurgence of the fourteenth and fifteenth centuries had proved so successful that when Henry VIII ascended the throne in 1509 the native chiefs held almost all of Ulster, three-quarters of Connacht, north and west Munster, the midlands of Meath and Leinster and that portion of the east coast lying between Dublin and Wexford. The demographic structure of the country also registered major changes. By the sixteenth century the O'Briens, one-time kings of Munster and high kings of Ireland, reigned only in Thomond, having lost their lands on the left bank of the Shannon. In Cork and Kerry the MacCarthy and O'Sullivan territories bounded those of the Desmond Geraldines, a circumstance which led to intermittent warfare. Munster was racially divided between the Butlers of Ormond and the Geraldines, and royal power was so negligible that the majority of colonists were subjects of one or other of the three great earls of Kildare, Ormond and Desmond. The towns too had attained a great measure of prosperity and civilization. Protected by walls from the attacks of the native Irish, sufficiently distant from Dublin to be free from undue interference, these towns—Cork, Limerick, Waterford, Galway and others—were to all purposes self-governing republics in the sixteenth century with little more than nominal connection with England. It was only in times of attack from the native Irish that their dependence on England was invoked. The net result, therefore, of the long Kildare viceroyalty had been the reversion to Irish habits and Irish customs of the greater part of Ireland outside the Pale. The early years of Henry VIII saw the decline of the great house of Kildare and the reinstatement of the Butlers of Ormond through their kinship with Anne Boleyn. Less has been recorded of Desmond history during this period despite the fact that Desmond lands were more extensive than were those of Kildare and the earls of Desmond had become independent rulers in Munster. Since the execution of Earl Thomas FitzGerald in Drogheda in 1468 the Desmonds had grown suspicious of English power and were, in turn, suspect themselves. James, tenth earl of Desmond, was master of great resources. He commanded 400 horse, 3 battalions of galloglasses, a battalion of crossbowmen and gunners and 300 kerne, to which his sub-chiefs all supplied

9 B.M., Lansdowne MS 159, f. 3.

their quota. MacCarthy Mór commanded 40 horse, 2 battalions of galloglasses and 2,000 kerne.[9]

A report sent to the king in 1515 was far from encouraging. Ten English counties were paying annual tribute in trade for the goodwill of the Irish chiefs. MacMurrough was getting black rent from Wexford, O'Carroll from Kilkenny and Tipperary, Limerick was doubly taxed by O'Brien of Ara and O'Brien of Thomond, and the citizens of Cork were purchasing immunity from attack by an annual tribute of forty pounds to MacCarthy, lord of Muskerry. The further English were practising Irish law 'and had fallen from English ways'. The roll-call of these lapsed colonists included the earl of Desmond and his Geraldine kinsmen, the Barrys, Roches, de Courceys and Barretts of Cork and the Powers of Waterford. Even Sir Piers Butler and his captains were accused of following the Irish order and of making peace and war without license from the king.[10] The report concluded with a request that the king would take the reformation of Ireland in hand, would deprive the native lords of the power of governing and would appoint an English deputy. By 1517 Irish forces in Thomond were reported to have increased, but Henry VIII made no move until 1520 when a series of new charges against Gearóid Óg led to his dismissal in favour of the earl of Surrey whose letter of appointment carried details of a new and experimental policy of conciliation. The king insisted that circumspect and politic ways should be used to bring the independent Irish captains into obedience and he advocated 'sober ways, politic drifts and amiable persuasions founded in law and reason, [rather] than by rigorous dealing'.[11] He had already come to the conclusion that 'to spend so much money for the reduction of that land, to bring the Irish in appearance only of obeisance, were a thing of little policy, less advantage and least effect' and even proposed to extend to the Irish the protection of English law which had been denied them by the Plantagenets.[12]

Surrey, however, pursued a more belligerent course.[13] 'After my poor opinion', he wrote, 'this land shall never be brought to good order and due subjection but only by conquest.'[14]

10   Constantia Maxwell, ed., *Irish History from Contemporary Sources, 1509–1610*, p. 79.

11   *Cal. S. P. Ire., 1509–73*, pt. 2, pp. 51–4.

12   Ibid.

13   Henry's conciliation policy of 'Surrender and Re-grant' was subsequently inaugurated by Lord Leonard Grey.

14   *Cal. S. P. Ire., 1509–73*, pt. 2, pp. 73–5.

During 1520–21 he marched from one end of Ireland to the other. Chieftain after chieftain was defeated, submitted and revolted again; while Surrey was convinced that this island would need to be thoroughly subdued before it could be properly governed he soon learned that it was easier to devastate a country than to subdue it. Surrey may have derived some satisfaction from the developing anarchy in Munster through feuds between Ormond, Desmond and MacCarthy, but otherwise his own campaign was so utterly disappointing that he begged to be recalled in 1521. He was replaced by Ormond, but in 1523 Ormond was superseded by Gearóid Óg. Before resigning Surrey received the submission of Cormac Oge MacCarthy whom he described as 'a sadd wise man' desirous of becoming the king's subject as an Englishman, offering to hold his lands of the king and anxious to become a baron and to attend parliament and councils.[15] In this way Cormac Oge sought to protect himself against the encroachments of the earl of Desmond and to shake off all allegiance to MacCarthy Mór. His expedient was ultimately successful insofar as it enabled the MacCarthys of Muskerry to escape the fate that overtook the rival house of Desmond.

Irish diocesan history for the immediate pre-Reformation years is almost completely atrophied for want of source materials. The *Calendar of Papal Letters*—fourteen volumes dealing with 'regulars', 'provisions', 'vacant dignities', 'vacant prebends', 'benefices about to become vacant' and 'concerning different forms' (*de diversis formis*), stop short at the year 1492. The annates, to a degree, help to fill the hiatus between 1492 and 1536, but even here the supply of available evidence merely scratches the surface of demand. Calendared state papers and miscellaneous incidental sources give occasional snippets of information, but in the long run the historian can only proceed from analogy and deduction. Here Pandarus, author of a tract entitled *Salus Populi* (1515), offers a challenging lead in the charges he levels at the clergy: 'Some sayeth that the prelates of the church and the clergy is much the cause of all the misorder of the land; for there is no archbishop ne bishop, abbot ne prior, parson ne vicar, nor any other person of the church, high or low, great or small, English or Irish, that useth to preach the word of God, saving the poor friars beggars; and when the Word of God do cease, there can be no grace . . . persons of ye Church covet more to live by ye plough rusticall than by law of

15 Ibid., p. 47.
16 T.C.D., MS E.3.16.

ye plough apostiall.'[16] A glance at the contemporary church will show the extent to which these indictments of Pandarus were justified.

The general need for reform in church organization and discipline was a constant theme throughout the fourteenth and fifteenth centuries; but reform measures never got off the ground and the abuses at which they were aimed continued to flourish with impunity, even with the connivance of the papacy through the grant of dispensations which sanctioned pluralism, absenteeism and other like abuses which were inconsistent with the church's pastoral ministry and the care of souls. Reform was among the priorities on the agenda at Constance (1414–18) but we have seen that it was shelved in favour of unity and a desire to end the schism. Once the schism was healed the new nationalism which was burgeoning in church as well as state diverted ecclesiastical attention into channels other than those of reform. The final effort to halt abuses was made at the Fifth General Council of the Lateran which was summoned in 1515 and ended its sessions in March 1517, a few months before Luther published his ninety-five theses at Wittenburg. The decrees of the Fifth Lateran Council touched upon current problems, but as before, these decrees were not enforced and the question of reform was not to receive papal attention for another thirty years.

Authorities differ on the extent to which abuses had undermined the pre-Reformation Irish church. At one extreme one finds Father Ambrose Coleman in his introduction to *De Annatis Hiberniae* considering it 'painful to come across several disastrous instances of the ruin and desolation which befell various churches and districts as the effect of rapacity, lawless and petty warfare' as also of the neglect and indifference of the clergy.[17] At the other extreme Father M. V. Ronan tends to minimize the extent of religious decay and is quite forthright in disagreeing with a report sent by Archbishop Inge of Dublin to Wolsey in February 1528 attributing 'the sorrowful decay of this land' to the lack of good prelates and curates in the church.[18] The church, as we saw in Chapter XII, took a good deal from the people by way of tithes and other incidental offerings in money and in kind. She had certain spiritual benefits to confer on them in return, namely, regular services, preaching, sacramental facilities, education and at times medical help as well. By the fifteenth century the church as

17   *Annats, Ulster*, pp. xvii ff.
18   M. V. Ronan, *The Reformation in Dublin*, p. xxiv.

organized in Ireland did not measure up to this standard. The 121 decrees of the Synod of Cashel which was held at Limerick in 1453 throw much light on contemporary church usage; they show too the extent to which the synod tried to halt the activities of the mendicant friars whom Pandarus credits with being the only ones then preaching the word of God.

Every church was to have three images or statues—the Blessed Virgin, the crucifixion and the titular saint—as well as a vessel duly consecrated for holding the Body of Christ. Priests were to be responsible for repairs in the chancel, the laity for repairs in the body of the church and for the upkeep of the cemeteries. Churches were to be properly built, in nave and chancel, according to the people's means. No threshing was to be allowed within the church and churches were to be kept free of property or animals belonging to the laity. Directives were issued for the administration of the Blessed Sacrament to the sick. The divine office was to be recited on Sundays and holy-days and on three other days of the week, and no non-singing cleric was to be appointed to a church where the divine office was customarily chanted. The clergy were to be suitably clad and were to be distinguished from the laity by the *gascomarcon* (soutane) and biretta. A later provincial synod held in Dublin in 1512 forbade the clergy to wear long hair or allow it to conceal their ears. Clerics were also forbidden to play football under penalty of a fine of forty pence to the bishop and twenty more to the church of the place in which they engaged in that exercise (*ubi talis ludus exercetur*).[19] The Synod of Cashel ordered every parish priest to provide at his own expense a missal, a silver or silver-gilt chalice, an amice, cincture, alb, maniple, stole, chasuble, surplice, a wooden baptistry and the holy oils for his church. On every Sunday and holy-day a list of excommunicates was to be read aloud in church: this must have been a formidable addition to the normal notices considering the variety of crimes to which the penalty of excommunication attached. Where churches or chapels annexed to parish churches were found to have become ruinous, the bishop was empowered to set aside the fruits of the parish church for necessary repairs. Transgressors of this rule were to be punished by order of the provincial council. Decree number eight of the Synod of Cashel stipulated that emoluments deriving from 'chapels recently erected by laymen' were to be handed over

19 *Annats, Ulster*, p. xv.

to the parish church of the parish in which these chapels had been built.[20]

Decree number twelve ordained that no questors were to be admitted into the province of Cashel without special episcopal permission. Questors from the primatial see alone were excepted (*exceptis B. Patricii nuntiis et questoribus*), and this concession, it has been pointed out, provided for the continuance of a custom introduced by Brian Boru as a means of securing support for the archbishop of Armagh from the clergy and laity of Munster.[21] In its reference to the mendicants the Synod of Cashel laid down categorically that their permission to quest did not entail any right to preach, and it passed a law forbidding the faithful *under pain of mortal sin* to attend the sermons of any friar who had not received the necessary episcopal permission to preach. This strange enactment was probably an offshoot of the anti-mendicant campaign of Philip Norris, a secular priest of Armagh, who in the vociferous FitzRalph tradition denounced the friars as 'worse than heretics . . . thieves and robbers . . . ravening wolves . . . worse than the traitor Judas, anti-Christs and disciples of Mahomet'.[22] Norris, like FitzRalph, was cited to appear before the Holy See and like FitzRalph was condemned. Having pursued the friars for years he finally submitted but did not live to see that the friars he condemned were to prove the strongest bulwark of the Irish church when persecution struck in the sixteenth century.

If we leave the Synod of Cashel and turn to the papal registers and the annates, we shall find that the annals of the diocese of Cork as there presented make painful and disedifying reading. So too with other dioceses. For this reason the diocese of Cork must be examined in the light of the general features of ecclesiastical administration and organization which come in for the most vehement censures, namely, the monastic system, pluralism and absenteeism, impropriation and lay patronage, papal provisions and the lack of an educated clergy. Most of these factors have been considered already relative to earlier centuries; their continuance and proliferation during the fifteenth and early sixteenth centuries is sufficient justification for their inclusion in this final summary.

---

20   The full text of the decrees of the Synod of Cashel was first printed in the third volume of Wilkins's *Concilia Magnae Britanniae et Hiberniae*, pp. 565–71. The manuscript from which he printed his copy is now catalogued as MS F.3.16, T.C.D. Father John Begley printed the text of the decrees from Wilkins in his *Diocese of Limerick, Ancient and Medieval*, where they are listed on pp. 431–41.

21   Gleeson, *A History of the Diocese of Killaloe*, pp. 92, 512.

22   *Annats, Ulster*, p. xvi.

THE MONASTERIES

Here we are presented with a study of contrasts. Thanks to the Observantine reform movement the Franciscans, Dominicans and to a lesser extent the Augustinians (of Cork)[23] had emerged from their own internal renewal spiritually well equipped for encountering the onslaught of the sixteenth-century religious revolt. The work of the Friars Minor generally during this period has won for them the encomium of Father Ambrose Coleman, O.P., who says, 'it is due to the Franciscans (who must have almost outnumbered the three other mendicant orders taken together) to say that to their strenuous preaching and opposition to heresy during the sixteenth century, to which there are several references in the State Papers, is mainly due under God the preservation of the Catholic Faith in Ireland'.[24] Intellectually, the friars with their *studia particularia* had a cultural advantage over the contemporary diocesan clergy. Against these orders we find none of the crimes invoiced against the monks of Mellifont, Dunbrody, Baltinglass, etc., and it is with pardonable pride in his own order that the late Father Canice Mooney boasted that 'even the hostile historian will search in vain for evidence of degeneracy or serious scandal— with the single exception of the unfortunate and understandable racial strife [which permeated every stratum of life in medieval Ireland]'.[25] Sources to hand divulge neither good nor ill of the Benedictine monks of Saint John the Evangelist in Douglas Street; they are equally non-committal in the case of the Knights Hospitallers. Both orders seem to have had 'floating' communities with frequent transfers of members, and this may account, partly, for the silence of the records.

On the reverse of the picture, however, stand the monasteries of Gill Abbey and Tracton, untinctured by reform and very much a prey to prevalent abuses. In 1467 Miles Roche, abbot of Tracton, was excommunicated at the instance of a certain creditor residing at the Roman court. Roche continued 'wittingly, openly and publicly' to celebrate Mass and other divine services; it is an eloquent reflection on the discipline of the time that he was later provided to the see of Leighlin. In 1482 the abbots of Tracton and Gill Abbey were simoniacs, bargaining over the chancellorship. At other times we find one or other abbot accused of dilapidating the goods of his monastery, converting them to evil uses and neglecting his spiritual commitments, but

23 The situation in the Red Abbey defies proper analysis, but conditions obtaining there are not to be applied to the Augustinian Order as a whole.

24 *Annats, Ulster*, p. xvi.

25 Mooney, 'The Franciscans in Ireland', *Terminus* (September 1954), p. 194.

there are no charges of immorality invoiced against either the abbots or the communities of Tracton and Gill Abbey. The situation was the same in Cloyne. To take one example, Rory Olathnan, Cistercian abbot of Saint Mary's, Midleton (*de Choro Benedicti*), had dilapidated and converted to evil use the goods of his monastery, had committed simony and perjury and 'was greatly defamed of the said and divers other crimes'.[26]

PLURALISM AND ABSENTEEISM

So much has already been said under this heading that it seems almost unnecessary to labour the point again, yet of all evils underlying the pre-Reformation church that of pluralism was the most pernicious. Pluralism was an old vice which was known at the Council of Chalcedon in 451 and though condemned in 1215 by the decree *De Multa* and in 1317 by the bull *Execrabilis* it continued to flourish throughout the fifteenth century as extracts already quoted from the papal registers have shown. The palliative institution of medieval vicarages was no answer to the problem: an underpaid, overworked vicar was no substitute for a resident pastor committed to the duties of the ministry. Poverty in the vicarage and stipendiary priest category did not necessarily connote incompetence; there must have been many efficient and devoted men among them, but there is no getting away from the fact that spiritual malnutrition was endemic, and there seems to have been no regularized system of visitation whereby abuses might be checked and a proper standard of spiritual services maintained. How successful was episcopal visitation in the diocese of Cork? What of archidiaconal visitation? Did these visitations even take cognizance of pluralists? What sanctions did they invoke against pluralism and non-residence? These are questions which may never be answered, and here the lack of sources is most felt. Signs are, however, that the church in Cork as in other dioceses attracted a large number of pluralists, men with little or no sense of vocation who managed to accumulate the highest and most lucrative livings, sometimes without ever assuming the responsibilities of the priesthood.[27]

Episcopal absenteeism and long inter-regnal vacancies were common features of the Irish church in the fifteenth century and in the early decades of the sixteenth. Thomas Halsey of Leighlin and Richard Wilson of Meath were both absentees.[28]

26　*Cal. papal letters, 1458–71*, pp. 559, 124, 179.

27　*Cal. papal letters, 1458–71, 1471–84, 1484–92, passim.*

28　Philip Wilson, *The Beginnings of Modern Ireland*, p. 133.

The diocese of Clogher was vacant from 1511 to 1519, Kildare was without a bishop from 1513 to 1526, Raphoe from 1517 to 1534[29] and Dromore seems to have had no resident bishop during the greater part of the fifteenth century. By 1467 this diocese had become so impoverished owing to the absenteeism of five bishops that no one was willing to accept it and it remained vacant for the next twenty years. George Braun who was provided in 1487 resided for some years in his diocese, but any good he achieved was negatived by a succession of three more absentees.[30] These years saw protracted succession disputes in the diocese of Cork. In Kilmore a disputed succession was ended by a gentleman's agreement between the rival candidates by which they shared the profits of the see between them. The arrangement seems to have worked amicably; both prelates attended a provincial synod in 1494 and signed their names in the official record as Thomas and Cormac, by the grace of God, 'bishops of Kilmore'.[31]

Even where bishops were resident within their dioceses the conduct of many was not calculated to advance the interests of the church. Annalistic records allege serious crimes against Cormac Mac Coghlan, bishop of Clonmacnoise, who raised his illegitimate son to the archdeaconry;[32] against William O'Farrel, bishop of Ardagh, who still comported himself as captain of his nation 'even after he had put on the mitre',[33] and against the bishops of Ferns, Ossory, Leighlin and Waterford who became involved in local feuds and conflicts.[34] It is also on record that Edmund Butler, archbishop of Cashel and illegitimate son of the eighth earl of Ormond, waged war against his father in the course of which most of the churches in Kilkenny and Tipperary were destroyed, while the citizens of Waterford complained loudly against the depradations of Finnin O'Driscoll whom they branded as the archbishop's pirate.[35]

Apart from these belligerent ecclesiastics, local princes and chieftains had lost respect for the rights and privileges of the church. The eighth earl of Kildare (1478–1513) burned the cathedral of Cashel; James, ninth earl of Desmond, 'and other

29   Brady, *Episcopal Succession*, ii, 307, 350.

30   Henry Cotton, *Fasti Ecclesiae Hiberniae*, iii, 278–80.

31   Ibid., p. 156.

32   *The Annals of Ireland : Mac Firbisigh*, p. 204.

33   James Ware, *A Commentary of the Prelates of Ireland from the First Conversion of the Irish Nation to the Christian Faith down to Our Times*, p. 254.

34   Ferns: John Purcell; Ossory: Milo Barron; Leighlin: Matthew Saunders; Waterford: Nicholas Comyn.

35   Wilson, *The Beginnings of Modern Ireland*, p. 136.

sons and daughters of iniquity' plundered the lands of the
bishop of Ardfert in 1488, and in 1502 his brother Maurice
ravaged the estates of John FitzEdmund FitzGerald, bishop
of Cork and Cloyne.[36] The Butlers waged intermittent warfare
with the archbishops of Cashel, Armagh suffered periodically
from O'Neill incursions and the O'Donnells were not above
confiscating the temporalities of Raphoe. Cathedrals seem to
have been everywhere in ruins; an inquiry instituted in 1515
by Pope Leo X regarding the dioceses of Clonmacnoise, Ardagh
and Ross showed this to have been true in Clonmacnoise and
Ardagh but not in Ross, but the impoverished condition of
Ross caused the pope to unite it in 1519 (for the lifetime of
Thady Irril) with the equally impoverished distant diocese of
Dromore, *propter tenuitatem utriusque ecclesiae*.[37] Reports from
Anglicized and semi-Anglicized districts reflect as unfavourably
on the church in these areas as do reports from areas under
native administration. The complete absence of references to
the united dioceses of Cork and Cloyne in records to hand cannot
be taken as exonerating the united dioceses from the charges
attaching to the Irish church in general—all the more so as the
unrest and turmoil which fermented in Cork and Cloyne were
only imperfectly remedied by the appointment of John
FitzEdmund FitzGerald in 1499.

IMPROPRIATION AND LAY PATRONAGE

The jurisdiction of a fifteenth-century bishop over the clergy
and churches of his diocese was far from being as clearly defined
and understood as it is at present. Between the bishop and a
great section of his clergy stood a formidable number of
monastic impropriators and lay patrons. Impropriating monasteries controlled seventy churches in the diocese of Cloyne and
about fifty in the diocese of Cork. Some of these impropriators
were diocesan, others were extra-diocesan; these extra-diocesan
bodies controlled about nineteen churches or rectories in Cork.
They administered them through the custom of leasing their
possessions on farm or on yearly pension to secular clerks.
Under an arrangement of this nature abuse was inevitable: the
grantees made light of the pension, neglected the ministry and
allowed the churches to fall into decay. Several examples of
peculation could be cited for the diocese of Cloyne during this
period, but the evil was equally endemic in Cork. A general
reference to the dioceses of Cloyne, Ardfert, Cork and Killaloe

36   Theiner, *Vetera mon.*, pp. 484, 506.

37   Brady, *Episcopal Succession*, ii, 109.

for the year 1469 states that in these dioceses certain tithes and possessions belonging to the priory of Saint Catherine in the diocese of Waterford were 'wont to be granted to farm to secular clerks, . . . who [did] not make full payment to the prior of such farm or yearly pensions'.[38] An instance bearing directly on Cork is found under date 1487, and is in the form of a complaint from David de Courcey (Cursi), archdeacon of Cork, and Cornelius O'Mahony, clerk, who represented that 'the fruits of the rectories of Brine, Kylbrogayn, Kylmaneayn, Bouys and Achmartan [were united] to the abbatial *mensa* of the nuns' monastery of Tane [Grany, Grange], O.S.A., in the diocese of Leighlin.' From 'time immemorial' these fruits were granted to farm to ecclesiastical persons (? clerks) through whose neglect, so the petition states, 'the said churches [were] not properly kept, . . . that of Bryne [Brinny] having its roof and walls in ruin'.[39] We have stated in an earlier chapter that where the impropriators were diocesan the danger of neglecting outlying parishes cannot have been so imminent as in that attaching to impropriators who were domiciled in Waterford, Dublin and Bath. Where the rectory and monastery shared the same locality—as, for instance, in Tracton where the abbot was rector of the parish—the likelihood of abuse was considerably lessened. Unfortunately the later records of Tracton make this view untenable for the diocese of Cork notwithstanding all the canonical safeguards that had developed from the legislation of the Fourth Lateran Council of 1215.

Abuses also attached to the practice whereby benefice-holders and prebendaries secured monasteries and abbeys *in commendam*. The methods by which these collations were secured were not always above board—with consequent detriment to the church's spiritual mission. Thus, for instance, in the second half of the fifteenth century we find Richard Walche, canon of Cork, 'meddling *de facto*' with the rule and administration of the monastery of Gill Abbey (*de Antro Fymbarri*) under pretext of certain surreptitious papal letters. The abbot complained that Walche, 'without any canonical title or tittle of right', had detained the monastery *in commendam* for about a year.[40] It is not unlikely that Walche, following a practice that had become common, attributed neglect to the monks of Gill Abbey in order to channel the monastic revenues in his own direction.

Even more pernicious than impropriation was the evil of

38 *Cal. papal letters, 1458–71*, p. 331.

39 *Cal. papal letters, 1484–92*, p. 32.

40 *Cal. papal letters, 1458–71*, p. 303, under date 1468/9.

lay patronage with its accompanying right of advowson. Lay patronage was multi-sided, ranging from the crown through the lay magnates down to the country gentry. Right up to the Reformation the crown by its own right, *pleno jure*, continued to enjoy the advowsons of crown livings and to appoint to the royal free chapels, one of which was Holy Trinity or Christ Church in Cork. Thus on 22 March 1515 by letters patent of King Henry VIII issued from Richmond, George Roche was presented 'to the church of Holy Trinity in the diocese of Cork and Cloyne *vice* Philip Gowles'.[41] That the king should have such control over one of the most important city parishes was indeed a sign of the times, and the day was not far off when the fourteenth-century statutes of Provisors and Praemunire were to be invoked in such a manner as to give Henry VIII 'canonical' control over the priests of his realm.

The ramifications of lay patronage were more far-reaching than those of royal patronage, for in Ireland, as elsewhere, lay magnates exercised very extensive rights of patronage and advowson. Churches under lay patronage were usually those mentioned in the annates and papal letters as being so long vacant that their collation had lapsed to the Holy See. The practice of lay patronage bred simony on a large scale: anyone seeking preferment or promotion in the church need only attach himself to some master and he was on the right road. The resultant damage to the *cura animarum* may be gauged from the case of Nicholas Nutin' [*sic*], rector of the parish church of Little Island (Inchemaknell) who promised Cardiffe, a layman (*dilecto filio Cardiffe laico*) and patron of the church, that if Cardiffe presented him to the rectory 'he would give him a certain sum of money, thereby incurring simony and the sentence of excommunication'. After the bargain and part payment, Cardiffe presented Nutin' to the then bishop of Cork (Jordan Purcell), 'who, perhaps in ignorance of the bargain instituted him' to the rectory which he managed to retain for about nine years.[42] Entries for Cork in the papal registers for the fifteenth century and in the annates which carry over into the opening decades of the sixteenth century, bear the stamp of wide-spread lay patronage throughout the diocese. A random selection from both sources will indicate the overall situation. The canonry and prebend of Liscleary was 'of the patronage of laymen' in 1406 and the rectory of Kilmedy (Kylmid) was 'in lay fee'. In 1411 the vicarages of Kilcrohane and Kilmo-

41 Patent 9 Henry VIII, pt. 1, m. 14.
42 *Cal. papal letters, 1458–71*, p. 327, under date 1469.

comoge (Bantry) were 'in lay fee'; so was the rectory of Murragh (Madracha) in 1413, while in the following year the bishop and treasurer of Cork were mandated to assign to Dominic O'Reilly (O'Reilig) the perpetual vicarage of Bally-modan which was 'of the patronage of laymen'.[43] From the annates it emerges that lay patronage was exercised in Ringrone in 1465 and 1471, in Rathcooney in 1481, in Ballymartle in 1492 and in Innishannon in 1502.[44]

PAPAL PROVISIONS

There is much conflict of opinion as to the merits and demerits of the system of papal appointments to vacant benefices. On the credit side is to be noted the fact that the introduction of the system brought about a constant correspondence between the Irish church and the papacy for more than a century before the religious cleavage of the sixteenth century. In this way the pope was kept conversant with diocesan and parochial affairs. This contact with Rome through papal provision and through pilgrimages undertaken by Irish bishops made for the general independence of the church and tended to lessen the area of state interference in spiritual concerns which was taking on national dimensions in England. Secondly, the statute decreeing that collation to benefices left too long vacant lapsed legiti-mately to the apostolic see was a safeguard against the trafficking with the temporalities of such vacant benefices in which patrons both lay and ecclesiastical were deeply involved. Thirdly, papal provisions were particularly beneficial to Ireland as a counterpoise to the recurring enactments forbidding the admission of native clergy to benefices within their own church. Even a cursory glance through the annates for the diocese of Cork shows that the most prominent appointees were those bearing the Irish names of O Murchú, O'Herlihy, O'Cronin, O'Daly, MacCarthy, O'Mahony and the like.

On the debit side the extension of papal provisions to minor benefices was fraught with evil consequences. Appointments were secured through subterfuge, canvassing and downright fraud. Almost everyone who filed a petition was successful, and it must be squarely faced that many petitioners were little better than rogues and opportunists who wanted at all costs to safeguard the lawful enjoyment of church livings.[45] The papal records make no reservations in their character sketches

43 *Cal. papal letters, 1404–15*, pp. 88, 256, 425, 428.

44 Bolster, 'Obligationes pro Annatis Diocesis Corcagiensis' *passim*.

45 du Boulay, 'The Fifteenth Century', p. 228.

of these papal appointees. Matthew O'Mahony, canon of Cork and prebendary of Drimoleague (Drummydaliag), is presented to the reader as a person 'much defamed in those parts, to the shame of the clerical order'.[46] John Buler was an usurer who had dilapidated the goods of his prebend of Caherlag.[47] Maurice Kelleher (OKyelliri), canon of Cork and precentor of Cloyne, is depicted as 'an open fornicator [who] has dilapidated and converted to his profane and evil uses the goods of the said precentorship and of the prebend of Kylasbuicmellayn [Kill-aspugmullane] in Cork, and committed perjury and is defamed in those parts of many other excesses and crimes'.[48] Another feature of the records for this immediate pre-Reformation period is the enormously high illegitimacy rate among the clergy, and we encounter therefore a steady flow of dispensations from Rome for the benefit of illegitimates who sought ordination and benefices. A recent survey (1965) of this subject shows that illegitimates were classified according to whether they were children of unmarried parents, of adulterous parents or of clergy, and it points out that in the second half of the fifteenth century the number of dispensations for children of clergy doubled.[49] Appointments to vacant benefices in Cork, in common with appointments to other dioceses, are weighted with these dispensations and present a dismal picture of a pastoral mission going dangerously to seed.

A second disadvantage of the system of papal provisions was the restriction it placed on episcopal jurisdiction, more parti-cularly in matters of legislation where a bishop could find himself overridden by a cleric who claimed to act *per breve Domini Papae*. Papal provisions also cut across the right of episcopal patronage; while it is true that bishops as well as kings, abbots and lay magnates were known to be exploiters of benefices, a bishop would normally be more selective in his choice of candidate than would a distant pope. As it happened very little patronage was left in the hands of the bishops. It was not unusual either for a bishop to be cited before the officials of another diocese, or for an archbishop to be cited before his suffragans. The system which catered for such happenings was pernicious, yet the procedure was more or less taken for granted, and thanks to the centralization effected by the

---

46   *Cal. papal letters, 1455–64*, p. 265, under date 1456.

47   *Cal. papal letters, 1458–71*, p. 124, under date 1461.

48   Ibid., p. 542, under date 1466.

49   du Boulay, 'The Fifteenth Century', p. 229.

popes of the thirteenth and fourteenth centuries 'the position of the pope was so assured that it does not appear to have excited any animosity among clergy or people and only a fitful opposition at intervals from the civil power'.[50] The real blast did not come until 1536, but a royal decree of 1524 was a minatory forecast of what was already in the mind of Henry VIII: 'As bishops and clergy give much help to rebels, let none but English be appointed . . . That churches be built and repayred and ministers reformed, and no temporal man have any spiritual benefice, *and no provision from Rome be allowed*' (italics mine).[51]

Taxations connected with papal provisions were heavy and at times exorbitant,[52] but the medieval papacy can scarcely be blamed for holding on to this source of revenue at a time when popes were confronted with pressing commitments in the nature of crusades against the Turks and the necessity of defending the temporal rights of the Holy See against the pretensions of powerful European rulers. Popes John XXII and Sixtus IV may well have earned notoriety as benefice-mongers; nevertheless, the abuse of a right does not render that right indefensible, and it cannot be gainsaid that determined efforts were made from time to time to obviate abuse in the sphere of ecclesiastical finance. A decree of the Council of Pisa in 1409 laid down that the annate tax was not to be exacted before an appointee took possession of his benefice; all that was required on collation was a promise or guarantee (*obligavit se Camerae*) to pay the tax within a specified time, six months or so from the date of taking possession (*et promisit solvere annatam . . . infra sex menses a die habitae possessionis computandos*). Benefices with a valuation of less than twenty-four gold florins or valuing six English marks were *ipso facto* exempt from the annate tax. These were listed as *infra taxam*, or it was stated of them that they did not make the grade, *non ascendunt summam*. In such cases the providee got his bull of provision *sine obligatione*. The phrase *Restituta fuit (bulla) quia narratur intrusus, et est pro Ibernico (Hibernico)* is even more frequently met with, and in respect of the latter clause Irish appointees as such received their collations gratis. There are 105 annate entries for the diocese of Cork from which some interesting details of the immediate pre-Reformation church in Cork emerge.

1. Only five benefices fell into the *infra taxam* category. These were the deanship, which was valued at five marks in 1427;

50 *Annats, Ulster*, p. xxi.

51 *Letters and Papers, Foreign and Domestic, Henry VIII, 1524–30*, pt. 1, p. 80.

52 Mollat, *The Popes at Avignon*, pp. 319–20.

Little Island, valued at six marks in 1441; a canonry and an unnamed prebend, valued at six marks in 1471; Murragh and an unnamed rectory, valued at six marks in 1488, and Glanmire, carrying the same valuation in 1492.

2.   As against current usage we find that in 1464 Raynald (Randal) Hurley, appointee to Ballymoney (Corsruhara), promised to pay the tax on his bull of appointment even though his benefice was rated at only four marks. In 1493 when a bull was issued for the erection of a canonry and prebend from the rectory of the parish church of Kilgobban (Kilgohagin), John de Courcey (Cursy) was similarly required to pay the tax on these combined benefices which again realized only four marks.

3.   An entry for the year 1471 goes to the opposite extreme. David de Courcey (le Currey) was provided to the rectory of Ringrone; it carried a valuation of twenty-four pounds and yet de Courcey was granted remission of one-third of his tax (*dimissa tertia parte*).

4.   There were thirty-one cases of intruders (*intrusi*) in the annates and seven instances of bulls being restored *pro Ibernico* (*Hibernico*).

5.   The annates show only one reported case of simony contained in a bull issued in 1474 providing Philip Coppinger (Copener) to the perpetual vicarage of Kinsale which he had previously acquired through simony (*per simoniam assecutus est*).[53] The papal registers furnish countless instances of simoniacal benefice-holders in the diocese for the period under consideration.

LACK OF CLERICAL EDUCATION

We have traced the great dearth of scholastic centres in medieval Ireland up to the foundation of the College of Youghal in 1464. Less has been said on the subject of clerical education for the simple reason that so far no satisfactory study has appeared showing how education was provided for the parish clergy. Available sources are vague, but it seems almost certain that medieval Ireland had no organized system of grammar and chantry schools such as England had,[54] and it is a commonplace of Irish history that Irishmen were traditionally forced to seek their education in exile. Alexander Bicknor's proposed university of 1321 languished for want of funds and the same is true of the second University of Dublin founded by bull of Sixtus IV

---

53   Bolster, 'Obligationes pro Annatis Diocesis Corcagiensis', p. 8.

54   Gwynn, 'Anglo-Irish Church Life in the Fourteenth and Fifteenth Centuries', p. 30.

in 1475 at the petition of the mendicant friars. For the friars themselves, particularly the Franciscans and Dominicans, several scholastic institutions are met with in the immediate pre-Reformation period. Flourishing schools (*studia particularia*) at Nenagh, Armagh, Galway, Ennis, Drogheda and Dublin were centres of Franciscan education, with Dominican houses of study (*studia solemnia*) at Dublin, Limerick and Athenry. How far the secular clergy were able to take advantage of these facilities is not known, but it would seem that by contrast with English and continental custom whereby monastic cathedrals contributed towards the extension of higher studies, the friars did not make all that much of a contribution in Ireland. A great amount of research is still required on this important subject.

Where then were the clergy educated in these pre-seminary days? How many of them studied canon law as a preparation for the pastoral mission? Recent investigation of extant records has indicated that many of the English-born bishops who administered Irish dioceses in the thirteenth and fourteenth centuries were graduates of Oxford,[55] but there are also indications that the bulk of those who equipped themselves scholastically did so as a means towards aiding their chosen careers as pluralists, for most of the medieval pluralists happen also to be canonists. But even allowing for such ulterior motives the number of clerics who went to Oxford or Cambridge was marginal. From relevant entries in the annates and papal registers we find that in the entire diocese of Cloyne only two of the beneficed clergy had degrees in canon law.[56] The diocese of Ardfert boasted a small sprinkling of canonists, and three canonists were provided to that see during the fifteenth century.[57] No canonist was provided to the see of Cork for the same period, whereas several canonists were appointed to the vacant benefices of the diocese. Beginning at the year 1390 we find Richard Went, one-time treasurer of Cork and later perpetual vicar of Kinsale, described as a 'student at Oxford for seven years in canon and civil law'.[58] For the fifteenth century proper there were Richard Pellyn, dean of Cork, 1418; Robert Holhgan *alias* de Cork, B.C.L. and abbreviator of papal letters, who was

55   Ibid., p. 23.

56   D. Buckley, 'Diocesan Organization: Cloyne', *Ir. Cath. Hist. Comm. Proc.* (1956), p. 11.

57   J. O'Connell, 'Diocesan Organization: Kerry', *Ir. Cath. Hist. Comm. Proc.* (1956), p. 2.

58   *Cal. papal letters, 1362–1404*, p. 413.

perpetual vicar of Kinsale in 1421;[59] John Walsche, B.C.L., dean of Cork in 1441;[60] John O Cronin, B.C.L., of Kilbrittain, 1447; Thomas Oseancan (Sheehan), B.C.L., canon and prebendary of Killanully, 1447; John Purcell, B.C.L., canon of Cork, 1447,[61] and Lachtin O Cormick who was prebend of Drimoleague[62] and perpetual vicar of Fanlobbus (Dunmanway) in 1464.[63] An entry for the year 1464 tells that Randal Hurley, rector of Ballymoney, had lectured in canon law for more than a year and a half at the University of Oxford.[64]

There must also have been clerics who were educated in places other than Oxford and Cambridge. In 1426 John Walshe of Cloyne was dispensed from proceeding to any holy order while studying at a university or in a *studium particulare*, and in 1455 Edmund Canton was given a similar dispensation for seven years.[65] In Cork, Lachtin O Cormick of Drimoleague and Fanlobbus (1463/4) is described as having 'studied canon and civil law for several years',[66] and in 1485 Pope Innocent VIII dispensed John O'Herlihy 'who intends to engage in the study of letters' to receive the treasureship of Cork, a canonry and the prebend of Desertmore and 'to retain them together for life under one and the same roof, and not to be bound for five years to be promoted to deacon's and priest's orders', provided that within a year he would be promoted to the order of subdeacon.[67] Clearly, therefore, there must have been some *studia* or centres of higher learning in Ireland for the ordinary cleric who could not go abroad, but no solution has so far been formulated as to whether these *studia* were attached to monasteries, to collegiate churches or to chantries. There is evidence, however, of a *studium particulare* in Limerick in 1463.[68]

Relatively speaking, the diocese of Cork with seven or eight canonists fared somewhat better than the neighbouring dioceses of Cloyne and Ardfert; but, on the other hand, possession of a university degree—while it was a sign of specialized education—

59   *Cal. papal letters, 1417–31*, pp. 90, 189.

60   *Cal. papal letters, 1431–47*, p. 173.

61   *Cal. papal letters, 1447–55*, pp. 293, 368, 369.

62   *Cal. papal letters, 1458–71*, p. 215.

63   Bolster, 'Obligationes pro Annatis Diocesis Corcagiensis', p. 3.

64   *Cal. papal letters, 1458–71*, p. 215.

65   Buckley, 'Diocesan Organization: Cloyne', p. 11.

66   *Cal. papal letters, 1458–71*, p. 215.

67   *Cal. papal letters, 1484–92*, p. 89.

68   Gleeson, *A History of the Diocese of Killaloe*, pp. 510–11.

did not always guarantee any training in religious knowledge. Whatever else its benefits, the structure of the medieval university was not geared to that strictly vocational training which is the goal of the seminary. Certain clerics were educated, but they were not theologians and could even be classed as 'monstrously ignorant' (*enormiter illiterati*) in matters pertaining to the sacred sciences. William Bula who was dean of Cork in 1363 and who was skilled in medicine is a standard example of this type of cleric.[69] As against this minority of university graduates and alumni of native centres of study there stood a large number of defectively educated benefice-holders and a proletariat of unbeneficed stipendiary priests, 'pedlars of God's word' in the Pauline sense, upon whom the bulk of the pastoral ministry devolved and at whose hands it inevitably suffered. The case of Donough Coughlan (Ocochlayn) cannot have been an isolated one. Donough Coughlan was perpetual vicar of Kilmoe (*alias* Kilmochot) in 1458 and was charged with having 'neglected the cure of the parishioners on account of his ignorance of letters'.[70]

The decrees of the Synod of Cashel, 1453, show a marked pre-occupation with the provision of education and with the maintenance of a proper standard among aspirants to the priesthood. They point also to the existence of qualified teachers (*magistri*) in Ireland at that time, but as the decrees do not elaborate on the matter the only reasonable conclusion is that these *magistri* were probably priests who were lectors in canon law and who operated from their own residences. There is a suggestion that they may also have been canons regular, but for Cork there is no evidence to show that the monks of Gill Abbey made any contribution to the educational projects of the medieval diocese. Decree number fifty-three of the Synod of Cashel forbade *magistri* under pain of excommunication to admit to their lectures noblemen or others whom they considered unsuitable for advancing the work of God, *de quibus non est spes quod in ecclesia Dei profecerint*. This decree was apparently aimed at prohibiting influential and ambitious laymen who had no intention of proceeding to major orders from acquiring that minimum of ecclesiastical learning which would enable them to secure coveted benefices, the revenues of which would keep them in security for the remainder of their lives. The tenor of decree number seventy-one was on the same lines. It forbade clerks under pain of a forty-shilling fine to

69   *Cal. papal petitions, 1342–1419*, p. 425.

70   *Cal. papal letters, 1455–64*, p. 352.

accept the sons of noblemen (*filios nobilium*) into their houses for fostering (*ad nutriendum*) without special licence from the ordinary.

Broadly speaking, therefore, the work of clerical education was not altogether neglected during the fifteenth century. Irish students were not unknown on the continent during this period. One of the most outstanding native Irish theologians on the continent at the end of the fifteenth century was the Franciscan Maurice O'Fihilly (Mauritius de Portu), who was given the title *flos mundi* in tribute both to his learning and his gentle character. O'Fihilly was a native of county Cork; after studying at Oxford he became regent of the Franciscan School of Studies at Milan and regent doctor in theology at Padua. He was known also as *Maurice de Hibernia*, and according to Holinshed's *Chronicle*, he was profoundly learned in the logics, philosophy, metaphysics and divinity.[71] Maurice O'Fihilly was provided to the see of Tuam by Pope Julius II in 1506; he died as archbishop of Tuam in 1513.[72]

Lay education in medieval Ireland seems to have been in better condition than clerical education generally. Alice Stopford Green showed that in the fifteenth century there was some study of English among cultivated Irishmen whose preference was for travel literature and stories rather than for homilies and the like. Fingin O'Mahony's castle at Rosbrin overlooking the island-dotted expanse of Roaring-Water Bay was a noted intellectual centre. O'Mahony, who was proficient in Latin and in English, was, say the Four Masters, 'the general supporter of the humanity and hospitality of west Munster'. Among those who were welcomed at Rosbrin was Donal O'Fihely of Cork, a student at Oxford (circa 1480) and a tireless and industrious compiler of the treasures of history and antiquity. He dedicated his annals of Ireland to O'Mahony; these annals afterwards passed into the library of Florence MacCarthy.[73] O'Mahony himself made a translation from the English of the travels of Maundeville and there must have been several other scholars of like calibre in the Ireland of this period. Most of the literati of the country were laymen, professors of the native language, experts in the brehon laws, preservers of ancient culture and tradition who did outstanding work as torch-bearers but whose dedication to what was native

---

71 Alice Stopford Green, *The Making of Ireland and Its Undoing*, p. 246.

72 Gwynn, 'Anglo-Irish Church Life in the Fourteenth and Fifteenth Centuries', p. 37.

73 Green, *The Making of Ireland and Its Undoing*, p. 238.

kept this country almost completely outside the sphere of the classical Renaissance of the fifteenth century. While her scholars graced the intellectual courts of Europe and her literati at home were masters of Greek and Latin, Ireland herself remained aloof and in isolation while this new spirit of inquiry was quickening the intellectual pulse of Europe. From what we have mentioned of political history we know that Ireland's non-involvement was not altogether a result of her insularity. The English policy of excluding Irish clerics from preferment in their own church was forwarded by the non-encouragement of a native faculty for higher studies (three attempts at which had been blighted), since proficiency in theology and canon law would lend weight to the claims of the Irish clerics. But for all that, Ireland's aloofness from the fifteenth-century Renaissance may well be seen to have been her safeguard and a contributory factor to her steadfastness in the faith in face of tremendous difficulties in the centuries ahead. Her insularity shielded her against that breath of searing criticism which was a feature of the literary revival and the rock on which so many of the revivalists perished. The Irish people, therefore, on both the intellectual and ideological levels, were not prepared to accept any change in their religious beliefs. And while there were obvious similarities between church government in England and in Ireland in the centuries leading up to the Reformation, there were likewise marked differences which constituted a serious obstacle to the ambitions of the English king in his bid for the headship of the church in Ireland. We now return to the bishop during whose episcopate were heard the first rumblings of England's final breakaway from Rome.

JOHN BENET, 1523–1536

John Benet (Bennet, called by some Ferret)[74] is believed to have been descended from Richard Bennet and his wife Alice who were co-founders of Saint Mary's Church, Youghal, which was founded after the erection of the collegiate church by Earl Thomas of Desmond in 1464. Benet was a priest of the diocese of Cloyne, he selected the collegiate church of Youghal as his episcopal residence and in his will he endowed its chantry with lands and houses in and around Youghal. His episcopate is shrouded in anonymity—no state records have preserved any details concerning him and only three of the annate entries for the diocese cover the years of his administration. All three entries complain of *intrusi*. An entry of 1525 cites certain un-

74 Lynch, *De praesulibus Hib.*, ii, 147.

named and unoccupied benefices (*beneficii nuncupati*) and
mentions an *intrusus* in each case. An *intrusus* was cited for
Dunderrow in 1526 and for certain parts of Liscleary, Inishkenny, Templemichael and Tisaxon (*annata unius . . . et alterius
. . . et reliqui . . .*).[75] From the fact that there were only four
instances of this nature recorded for the twenty-one years of
John FitzEdmund's episcopate and three for the first two years
of John Benet's, diocesan affairs would appear to have been
getting progressively chaotic. The situation cannot be fully
assessed, but the pastoral ministry must have been gravely
neglected and the need for reform imminent. But diocese and
city were alike prosperous, and this prosperity was given high
priority by the earl of Surrey in 1520 when his announcement
of the death of John FitzEdmund was accompanied by the
information that the bishopric was 'worth two hundred marks
a yere'. The bishopric was probably equally lucrative at the
end of the Benet episcopate.

Bishop Benet stocked the library of the collegiate church of
Youghal with many valuable volumes from his own personal
collection. A catalogue of these books drawn up in 1490 shows
some rare literary treasures: tracts of canon law; decretals;
eight missals, five of which were entered as *missalia pulchra
pergamena*; the *Life of Christ* by Ludolph of Saxony; the letters
of Jerome and the works of Gregory the Great, Saint Thomas
Aquinas, Saint Bonaventure, Saint Antoninus and others.
Books of Sacred Scripture included five for use in choir and
twelve copies of the Bible, one of which was entitled *Una Biblia
Tripartita et alia parvae quantitatis*. Another treasure was a
five-volume copy of the Old and New Testaments with the gloss
of Nicholas de Lyra. There were also *Quattour Evangelistae in
quattuor voluminibus*; a volume containing the Books of Wisdom,
Canticles, Ecclesiastes and Ecclesiasticus, and a volume
entitled *Petrus de Aurora*. Another small volume was enriched
cum quibusdam historiis provinciae Hiberniae. In 1523 other
acquisitions from Bishop Benet's collection were added to
the Youghal library. Among them were *Liber meditationum
Sancti Bonaventurae cum aliis meditationibus et chronicis Gerald-
inorum* and *Biblia de impressione, in rotunda forma, in manu
Johannis Cornelii*.

The steps by which Henry VIII began in 1527 to solve his
family problem through divorcing Catherine of Aragon did not
immediately affect the Irish church although sycophantic clerics
were already established in major benefices throughout the

75   Bolster, 'Obligationes pro Annatis Diocesis Corcagiensis', p. 32.

country. The Act of Supremacy of 1534 which transformed Mary's Dowry into an Anglican realm and the suppression of the monasteries which created a new landed gentry were sinister auguries of what awaited Ireland. The blow was dealt in 1536, the year in which John Benet, last pre-Reformation bishop of Cork and Cloyne died, and Cork would seem to have been the first Irish diocese filled by Henry VIII in his self-appointed role as supreme head of the church in his own dominions. Brady tells of the existence 'in the office at Dublin (of) a licence of 27 Henry VIII to the Deans and Chapters permitting them to elect a bishop in the room of the late John Benet, and recommending Dominic Terry (Tirrey) to succeed him. The *congé d'elire* was then used in Ireland, now better changed to a king's letter, nominating the successor.'[76]

The story which recounts the efforts made to enforce the 'reformed' doctrines in the diocese of Cork belongs to a later volume of our history. It is a mottled story of light and shade, of persecution and banishment, of heroic courage and constancy, penetrating deep into the darkness of the penal night but ultimately revealing a Catholicism purged and purified by suffering emerging once more into the full noontide of vigour, vitality and apostolic effectiveness. Today, the diocese of Finbarr has extended its apostolate far beyond the tribeland of the ancient Uí Eachach, beyond the territories outlined in the decretal of 1199 and beyond the limits set at Rathbreasail and Kells, to include the Peruvian parishes of El Porvenir, Florencia de Mora and Esperenza. This twentieth-century apostolic enterprise bids fair to outshine any other achievement in the long annals of Finbarr's diocese of Cork.

76   Brady, *Records*, ii, 45.

APPENDIX

PRIESTS OF CORK

	Place of appointment (if specified)	*Source*
1180	Reginald, archdeacon of Cork, the first priest of whom there is mention in the written sources.	*Reg. St. Thomas, Dublin,* pp. 202, 211.
	Stephen, parson of Holy Trinity.	
	Aggir, William, Henry, priests.	Ibid., pp. 214, 216.
1263	Geoffrey O'Brennan, treasurer;	
	David de Lang, precentor.	*Cal. doc. Ire.,* ii, no. 767.
1276	Richard le Blund is appointed to the church of Fersketh in the diocese of Cork.	4 Edward I, m. 10.
1290	David O'Currey, canon of the church of Cork, studying in England.	*Cal. doc. Ire.,* iii, no. 719.
1295	Geoffrey, vicar of Holy Trinity.	*Cal. justic. rolls, Ire.,* ii, no. 33.
1295	William de Muenes has letters of presentation to the church of Holy Trinity.	*Cal. doc. Ire.,* iv, no. 327.
1302	Peter Mathei, canon of Cork;	
	Robert, rector of Innishannon.	*Cal. doc. Ire.,* v, no. 74.
1306	John Ruffus, parochial priest of Holy Trinity;	
	Robert, parochial priest of Saint Peter's.	Wynchedon Will.
1324	Nicholas de Lager, canon of Cork (gets canonry, prebend and archdeaconry of Cloyne and is to resign canonry and prebend of Cork).	*Cal. papal letters,* ii, 241.
1327	Walter le Rede, canon of Cork;	*Cal. papal letters,* ii, 256.
	John Went, canon of Cork;	
	William de Netilton, vicar of Little Island.	*Cal. pat. rolls 1330–34,* p. 33.
1330	Henry de Thrapton, clerk, archdeacon of Cork, appointed Chancellor of the Exchequer.	*Cal. pat. rolls 1330–34,* p. 10.
1332	William Obrodir, canon of Cork.	*Cal. papal letters,* ii, 372.
1337	Adam Mansell, chaplain.	Webster, *Diocese of Cork,* p. 405.
1341	Adam Miagh (Meade), chaplain.	*Roche & Sarsfield MSS.*
1343	Nicholas O'Grady, canon of Cork.	*Cal. papal petitions,* p. 23.

	Place of Appointment (if specified)	*Source*
1350	John de Bolton, king's clerk, is granted the prebend of Beaver (Carrigaline); John de Codyngton is granted the prebend of Beaver and Douglas.	*Cal. pat. rolls, 1348–50, pp.* 503, 548.
1352	Maurice de Rochford is ratified as parson of Beaver.	Ibid., p. 544.
1357	George de Rupe, canon of Cork, is appointed dean.	*Cal. papal petitions,* p. 311.
1363	Adam Cradock·has canonry and prebend of Cork.	Ibid., p. 416.
1364	Thomas Mychyan of the diocese of Cork petitions for a benefice. David Gower, scholar, of the diocese of Limerick, is recommended for canonry and prebend of Killaspugmullane. Richard de Vall (Wall), of the diocese of Cork, petitions for treasureship of Limerick.	Ibid., p. 468. Ibid., p. 468. Ibid., p. 468.
1367	William de Karell, king's clerk, is ratified in the prebend of Beaver.	*Cal. pat rolls 1367–70,* p. 25.
1375	Thomas Rys, Thomas Whyte, canons of Cork.	*Caulfield MSS.*
1377	John Walsh, rector of Little Island.	*Cal. rot. pat. Hib, passim.*
1387	Thomas Harbergh to be prebendary of Beaver. Thomas Barton appointed to the free chapel of Holy Trinity.	*Pat. 10 Richard II,* No. 44. *Pat. 10 Richard II,* No. 45.
1390	John Pelyn, prebendary of Beaver.	*Cal. pat. rolls 1388–92,* p. 241.
1391	Richard de Garri, perpetual vicar of Kinsale.	*Cal. papal letters,* iv, 413.
1392	William Wynchedon, canon of Liscleary. Maurice Morgan, chaplain of the prebend of Holy Trinity. Richard Went, treasurer of Cork, to be perpetual vicar of Kinsale.	*Cal. papal letters,* iv, 413. *Cal. pat. rolls 1391–96,* p. 203. *Cal. papal letters,* iv, 413.
1393	Vincent Whyt, canon of Cork, prebendary of Kilbrogan. Geoffrey Galwey to get prebend on death of Whyt and to resign canonry and prebend of Kilbrittain. Philip Lowe, rector of Holy Trinity.	*Cal. papal letters,* iv, 475. *Cal. papal letters,* iv, 445. *Cal. papal letters,* iv, 542.
1396	Robert Roche, perpetual vicar of Kinsale.	
1400	Walter Galle, perpetual vicar of Beaver, to be promoted to canonry and prebend of Kilbrogan.	*Cal. papal letters,* v, 295.
1404	Richard Went, Ringrone.	*Pat. 5 Henry IV,* No. 48.
1406	John Corre, perpetual vicar of Kinsale; deprived in 1411.	*Cal. papal letters,* vi, 87.
1411	Randal Hurley (Omurchayli), canon of Cork, papal mandatory.	*Cal. papal letters,* vi, 253, 256, 427.

Place of Appointment (if specified)	*Source*
Reginald O'Hart, of diocese of Ross, provided to the perpetual benefices without cure, called rectories, one in the parish of Kilcrohane, the other in that of Kilmocomoge, in lay fee. O'Hart had been already appointed to the deanery of Ross by John XXIII.	*Cal. papal letters*, vi, 256.

1413   Donald O'Reilly (Orealig), perpetual vicar of Ballymodan (Ballimudayn).
William Looney (Lini), rector of Murragh (Madratha) to get perpetual vicarage of Rincurran (Rindcorrayn); Murragh to be given to Donald O'Reilly of previous entry.   *Cal. papal letters*, vi, 425.

1414   John Martel received grant from king of the free chapel of Holy Trinity.   *Cal. pat. rolls 1413–16*, p. 20.

1415   Richard Pellyne, perpetual vicar of Kinsale; John Corre deprived.   *Cal. papal letters*, vi, 154.
Richard O'Hedyian appointed to free chapel of Holy Trinity. Mayor and bailiffs ordered to put him in possession.   *Pat. 2 Henry IV*, No. 60.

1417   Gilbert O'Herlihy (Ohiarley), canon of Cork, papal mandatory.   *Cal. papal letters*, vii, 88.

1418   Robert Barry, canon of Cork, to be archdeacon of Cloyne.   *Cal. papal letters*, vii, 89.
Donald Mangan (Omongayn), deacon [*sic*] of Cloyne, to get canonry and prebend of Kilbrogan (Kyll Brogayn).   *Cal. papal letters*, vii, 50.

1420   Robert Myles, chaplain.   *Roche & Sarsfield MSS.*

1421   John Hurley (Omurchile), perpetual vicar of Fanlobbus (Dunmanway); bond entered on his behalf by a relative, Donal Hurley of Killaloe.   *Cal. papal letters*, vii, 215, and *Annates*.
Robert Holhgan *alias* de Cork, perpetual vicar of Kinsale.   *Cal. papal letters*, vii, 166, 189.

1425   William Lowillins, canon and prebendary of Kilroan.   *Cal. papal letters*, vii, 382.
Richard Went, rector of parish church of Ringrone. The rectory had been held by Donogh O'Dea for more than ten years without title.   *Cal. papal letters*, vii, 383.
Donald O'Reilly, appointed to the prebend of Kilroan and the rectory of Ringrone, had to resign the vicarage of Ballymodan, the rectories of Murragh and Templetrine and the parcels of the parish churches of Ballymountain and Kildara. He was given his bond *sine obligatione*.   *Cal. papal letters*, vii, 383. *Annates*.

1427   Miles Roche, chancellor of Cork, to be perpetual vicar of Kinsale and dean of Cork. He was permitted to hold the deanery and the perpetual vicarage for seven years (*ad septennium*), but had to resign the chancellorship.   *Cal. papal letters*, vii, 560. *Annates*.

1432   Edmund FitzAdam, chaplain of Beaver.   *10 Henry V*, pt. 1ª, No. 1.

	Place of Appointment (if specified)	*Source*
1437	Nicholas Cotterell was inducted into the church of St. Mary, Glanmire.	*Roche & Sarsfield MSS.*
1440	David Meade was granted the free chapel of Holy Trinity, void by the death of Thomas Glene. In 1422 he had been expelled by Richard O'Hedyan, John Morrogh and Henry Kyng.	*Cal. pat. rolls 1436–44*, p. 467.
1441	Dermot Canty (Ouchanty) provided to the prebend of Drimoleague of which Hugh O'Mahony is to be deprived. Appointed to canonry also; both benefices had been held by Randal Hurley without title for more than a year.	*Cal. papal letters*, ix, 170.
	John Walsche, dean of Cork, appointed to parish church of Little Island. Thomas Terry to be deprived.	*Cal. papal letters*, ix, 173 and *Annates.*
	The dean was notified that 'for the performance of his burdens he is bound to keep two priests.'	*Cal. papal letters*, ix, 197.
1446	Henry Gleeson (Glassane), vicar of Kinsale	*Roche & Sarsfield MSS.*
	John Purcell, canon and prebendary of Cork.	*Cal. papal letters*, x, 368.
1447	Thomas Sheehan (Oseancan) *alias* Scolan, canon and prebendary of Killanully (Kylhynly).	*Cal. papal letters*, x, 369.
1447/8	John Cronin (Ocronyn), rector of Templetrine (Treyne), to be given canonry and prebend of Kilbrittain of which Nicholas Kelly is to be deprived.	*Cal. papal letters*, x, 293.
1448	John O'Leary (Olaegere), rector of Kilmoe in the diocese of Cork, to be given chancellorship of Ross.	*Cal. papal letters*, x, 380.
1450	Donald Mangan (Omonghan), canon of Cork, to be given rectory of Ballymoney (Currsruhura) on deprivation or death of Patrick O'Donovan or by resignation of Dermot Kiely (?Mackelchy).	*Cal. papal letters*, x, 512.
1453	Maurice O'Herlihy and Donald Mangan, canons of Cork, papal mandatories.	*Cal. papal letters*, x, 640.
	John Mulchrone to be provided to rectory of Ballymartle (Kyllimidh) on deprivation of Thomas Mulchrone.	Ibid.
1456	Macrobius O'Driscoll, Drimoleague.	*Cal. papal letters*, xi, 265.
	Henry Kyng appointed to free chapel of Holy Trinity; deprived after four years by David Myagh (Meade).	*Cal. statute rolls, Henry VI*, p. 541.
1456/7	Matthew O'Mahony (Omaythmagmna) holds canonry and prebend of Drimoleague.	*Cal. papal letters*, xi, 265.
1457/8	Donald Coughlan (Ocochlayn) to be appointed perpetual vicar of St. Brandon's, Kilmoe (Kylmo *alias* Killmochot). John Coughlan was late holder of the vicarage.	*Cal. papal letters*, xi, 352.

Place of Appointment (if specified)	*Source*
1458 Donald O'Carroll (Okearwyll), canon, for prebend of Killaspugmullane.	*Cal. papal letters*, xi, 374.
Donald O'Mongayn becomes rector of Kilmoe after litigation in which Donald Coughlan was deprived.	*Cal. papal letters*, xi, 352.
1459 John Terry has bond for rectory of Templeroan *als* Templetrine.	*Cal. papal letters*, xii, 125 and *Annates*.
Thadeas Donegan (Odonnagayn) obtains parish church of Tisaxon (Teadhsaghsan).	*Cal. papal letters*, xi, 392.
Gilbert Long (Ylongaygh), priest of Cork, for vicarage of Aglish (Aglasmughitiala) and Clondrohid.	*Cal. papal letters*, xii, 42.
John Mangan (Omongayn), rector of Kinneigh, obtains perpetual vicarage of Ringrone without title.	*Cal. papal letters*, xi, 392.
Dermot Canty, priest, who holds a canonry and prebend of Drimoleague, to get perpetual vicarage of Ringrone.	*Cal. papal letters*, xi, 392.
1461 John Terry to have canonry of Cork and prebend of Caherlag and rectory of Ballintubrid if John Buler is deprived from Caherlag and Thomas Cotter (de Cotyr) from Ballintubrid (Cloyne).	*Cal. papal letters*, xi, 392.
1463 John Herlihy (Omurhyle), perpetual vicar of Fanlobbus.	*Cal. papal letters*, xii, 215.
Lachtin Cormack to be given perpetual vicarage of Fanlobbus on death of John Herlihy. Lachtin entered his bond for the vicarage.	*Annates*.
1464 Randal Hurley to be given rectory of Ballymoney, vacant by death of Dermot Kiely.	*Cal. papal letters*, xii, 215 and *Annates*.
1465 John Houlihan, perpetual vicar of the parish church of Kilkeran, Ross, to have perpetual vicarage of Ringrone which James Courcey held for more than one year without being ordained.	*Cal. papal letters*, xii, 417, and *Annates*.
1466 John Cronin and Macrobius O'Driscoll, canons of Cork, papal mandatories.	*Cal. papal letters*, xii, 467.
Denis Cummins (Ocumyn), clerk of diocese of Ross, to get perpetual vicarage of Desertserges on death of Donal Mangan.	*Cal. papal letters*, xii, 467.
Maurice Stanton to have canonry and prebend of Killaspugmullane, of which Maurice O'Kelly (or Kelleher), canon of Cork and precentor of Cloyne is deprived.	*Cal. papal letters*, xii, 542.
1467 Donald O'Herlihy and Richard Walsh, canons of Cork, papal mandatories.	*Cal. papal letters*, xii, 559.
1468 John White (Fwyt), canon of Cork, papal mandatory.	*Cal. papal letters*, xii, 289.
David de Courcey to have rectory of	

Place of Appointment (if specified) Source

Kilgobban which is to be erected into a
prebend of Cork. *Cal. papal letters*, xii, 289.
Dermot O'Keeffe and Donogh Mangan,
canons of Cork, papal mandatories. *Cal. papal letters*, xii, 302.
Richard Walshe, canon of Cork. Ibid.

1469 Maurice O'Sullivan of Ardfert, who held
vicarage of Kilnaglory, is dispensed and
given prebend of Desertmore on privation of
Richard Purcell. *Cal. papal letters*, xii, 658.
Edmund Mandeville, canon and papal
mandatory. *Cal. papal letters*, xii, 327.
David Meade, archdeacon of Cork, to get
rectory of Little Island on death of Thomas
Finn; Nicholas Nutin' to be deprived. *Cal. papal letters*, xii, 327.
Maurice Gogan resigned prebend of
Inishkenny;
Thadeus Sheehan was deprived of perpetual
vicarage of same which Robert Sheehan [*sic*]
had pretended to hold without title;
David Hallinan to be given a prebend,
canonry and vicarage. *Cal. papal letters*, xii, 689.
Macrobius O'Driscoll died. *Cal. papal letters*, xii, 325.
Eneas O'Daly (Ydalaid), cleric of Cloyne,
gets rectory of Kilcully and prebend of
Killanully; a bond on his behalf was entered *Cal. papal letters*, xii, 821.
by Thadeus, bishop-elect of Down and Connor. *Annates.*

1469/70 Randal Hurley, canon and papal mandatory. *Cal. papal letters*, xii, 341.

1470 Philip Roche is granted a canonry and
prebend of Cork. *Cal. papal letters*, xii, 778.
Donough Mangan, priest of Cork, enters
bond for perpetual vicarage of parish church
of Kinneigh which he held for thirteen years
without title. *Annates.*
Donough O'Riordan, precentor, canon and
prebendary of Desertmore, to be prebendary
of Inishkenny. *Cal. papal letters*, xii, 360.
Donough O'Donovan, archdeacon of Ross,
to have a canonry of Cork and prebend of
Drimoleague; bond on his behalf was entered
by Donal O'Driscoll, rector of Castlehaven
(Glanberdhan). *Annates.*

1470/1 Thadeus O'Daly, clerk, to have canonry and
prebend of Killaspugmullane. *Cal. papal letters*, xii, 821.

1471 Thadeus Donegan to get the rectories of
Tisaxon and Leighmoney. *Cal. papal letters*, xii, 372.
Donough O'Riordan, cleric of Cloyne, enters
bond for canonry and prebend of Desertmore
and for precentorship of Cork. *Annates.*
David de Courcey is granted the rectory of
the parish church of Ringrone, in patronage
of laymen. *Annates.*

1472/3 Donald Coughlan, priest of Cork, enters
bond for perpetual vicarage of parish church

Place of Appointment (if specified)	*Source*

of Kilmoe (Kyllino *alias* Killnoch Sancti
Brandani), vacant by privation of Dermot
Canty.   *Annates*.

1474   Philip Coppinger enters bond for perpetual   *Cal. papal letters*, xiii, pt. 1,
        vicarage of the parish church of Kinsale.   p. 176, and *Annates*.

1474/5 John Roche, rector of St. Mary's,   *Cal. papal letters*, xiii, pt. 1,
        Shandon.   p. 418.

1475   Matthew O'Mahony to have canonry of Cork
        and prebend of Desertmore, void by death of   *Cal. papal letters*, xiii, pt. 1,
        Donough O'Riordan.   p. 422.
        Donough O'Donovan and Thaddeus Daly,
        canons of Cork, papal mandatories with
        reference to the erection of a parish church
        for four townlands west of the Bandon river.   *Cal. papal letters*, xiii, pt. 2,
        Cornelius Murphy to be rector of the new   p. 428.
        church.

1477   William O'Keeffe is granted the canonry and
        prebend of Killanully and Kilnahone.   *Annates*.

1478   Eugene O'Sullivan enters bond for canonry
        and prebend of Killanully, unoccupied and
        vacant by privation of John Burdon. Eugene
        O'Sullivan also got the perpetual vicarage of
        the parish church of Drishane in the diocese   *Annates and Cal. papal letters*,
        of Ardfert.   xiii, pt. 1, p. 127.
        Thaddeus MacCarthy, canon of Cork, enters
        bond for rectories of parish churches of
        Rathclarin and Burren, to be united with his
        canonry and prebend of Cork.
        William White is presented to rectory of
        Holy Trinity, void by privation of David   *Cal. pat. rolls Ire.*, *1477–85*,
        Meade.   p. 103.

1479   Donough Mangan enters bond for perpetual
        vicarage of parish church of Inchigeela.   *Annates*.

1480   Randal Hurley, canon and papal   *Cal. papal letters*, xiii, pt. 2,
        mandatory.   p. 684.

1481   Gerald Barry, cleric of Cloyne for canonry
        and prebend of Killaspugmullane, vacant by
        death of Edmund Barry.   *Annates*.
        Donald Phelan, perpetual vicar of Caherlag.   *Annates*.
        Maurice Stanton, dean of Cork, is granted
        the parish church of Rathcooney.   *Annates*.
        Gerald Barry, John Barry, canons of Cork.   *Annates*.
        John Barry, perpetual vicar of St. Mary's,
        Clonmel on Great Island, for canonry and
        prebend of Caherlag, for perpetual vicarage
        of St. Mary's on the Great Island, for
        Templerobin and for St. Mary's Shandon
        (Cendun).   *Annates*.
        Thomas Quill (Ocuyll), priest of Ross, for
        perpetual vicarage of parish church of
        Kilcrohane, vacant by privation of Dermot   *Annates and Cal. papal letters*, xiii,
        O'Sullivan.   pt. 2, p. 761.

1482   David Creagh is presented to free chapel of   *Cal. pat. rolls Ire., 1477–85,*
Holy Trinity.   p. 309.
Philip Gould is presented to Christ Church.   Ibid., p. 311.
In 1483 the archbishop of Cashel received a
papal mandate to assign a canonry in Cork
and the prebend of the free chapel of Holy
Trinity to David Creagh . . . 'Philip Gould,
under pretext of a presentation by Edward,
King of England, has without any other title
detained possession for between two and   *Cal. papal letters,* xiii, pt. 1,
three years.'   p. 144.
Cornelius O'Flyn, abbot of St. Finbarr's
monastery, *de Antro,* for chancellorship and   *Cal. papal letters,* xiii, pt. 1,
for perpetual vicarage of Liscleary.   p. 124.
John O'Herlihy, priest of Cork diocese;
Donough Murphy, priest of Cork diocese.
John O'Herlihy, cleric of Cloyne, enters
bond for canonry of Cork and prebend of
Inishkenny.   *Annates.*
Odo Collins or Cullen for Rathcooney.
David Hallihan, canon of Cork, is granted
the chancellorship and perpetual vicarage of   *Annates.*
Kilnaglory.   *Annates.*

1482/3 David Hallinan and John Cronin, canons and
papal mandatories, appointed to assign to   *Annates.*
Eugene O'Sullivan of Ardfert the perpetual
vicarage of Aglish in Cork and the   *Cal. papal letters,* xiii, pt. 1,
treasureship of Cork.   p. 127.
Hugh Collins (Odo Cullen) enters bond for
canonry of Cork and prebend of Dunbulloge
and for parish church of St. George of
Dunbulloge.   *Annates.*

1483   Philip Gould is cited as intruder in Holy   *Cal. papal letters,* xiii, pt. 1,
Trinity.   p. 144.

1483/4 Maurice Sheehan of Ardfert is granted the
perpetual vicarage of Leighmoney which   *Cal. papal letters,* xiii, pt. 1,
Donald O'Connor held without title.   p. 164.

1484   Thaddeus Coughlan, priest of Cork, for
perpetual vicarage of parish church of
Kinneigh, vacant by resignation of Thaddeus
Mangan.   *Annates.*
Dermot Long, clerk of Cork: reservation to
him, *motu proprio,* of a benefice in the gift of   *Cal. papal letters,* xiii, pt. 1,
the bishop and chapter of Cork.   p. 165.
John Cronin and Philip Coppinger, canons;
Maurice Mortel, clerk of diocese of Cork, is
appointed to perpetual vicarage of parish   *Cal. papal letters,* xiii, pt. 1,
church of Kinsale.   p. 176.
John Barry, canon and papal   *Cal. papal letters,* xiii, pt. 1,
mandatory.   p. 187.

1485   John O'Herlihy, junior, cleric of Cloyne,
enters bond for treasureship of Cork and
for canonry and prebend of Desertmore
which Donough Murphy and John O'Herlihy,

Place of Appointment (if specified)	*Source*

senior, held for some years without title. *Annates.*
Maurice Stanton, dean of Cork, enters bond
for rectory of parish church of Glanmire
which Thaddeus Quinn (Okyun) held
without title. *Annates.*

1487 Donough O'Herlihy, canon of Cork. *Annates.*

1488 Thaddeus Murphy, canon of Cork, for
prebend of Cork (not specified) and for the
particles of Cloghan and Kildarra in
Ballinadee. *Annates.*
Cornelius Murphy, precentor of Cork, to get
perpetual vicarage of church of Kinneigh,
vacant by privation of Eugene Fehilly. *Cal. papal letters,* xiv, 219.
Matthew O'Mahony, dean of Cork, for the
perpetual vicarage of Macloneigh. *Annates.*

1489 Philip Gould for canonry of Cork and
prebend of free royal chapel of Holy Trinity. *Annates.*
Donough Macauley is given a bull for the
union of the vicarage of the parish church
of Murragh with another ecclesiastical
benefice. *Annates.*
Raymond Barry, abbot of Tracton, gets
parish churches of Innishannon and
Dunderrow, vacant by privation. *Annates.*
Edmund Murphy, clerk, binds himself for a
canonry of Cork and prebend of Killanully,
and for the perpetual vicarage of the
prebendal church of Carrigaline, to be united
to the prebend during his lifetime (*ad vitam*). *Annates.*
Matthew O'Daly, cleric of Cloyne, for a
canonry of Cork and prebend of Dunbulloge. *Annates.*

1490 Dominus Butler, chaplain, was attorney for
the transfer of Ronan property in Cork. *Roche & Sarsfield MSS.*
Thaddeus Murphy and Donough O'Herlihy,
canons and papal mandatories. *Cal. papal letters,* xiv, 264.

1492 John Coughlan, cleric of Cork, perpetual
vicar of Kilmoe. *Annates.*
Cornelius O'Riordan, priest of Cloyne, for
perpetual vicarage of the parish church of
Macloneigh to be united with the vicarage of
Twosist and the perpetual vicarage of
Drishane (both in Kerry), during his
lifetime. *Annates.*
Thaddeus Collins, cleric of Ross, vicar of the
parish church of Drinagh. Later in the year
he entered a bond for the perpetual
vicarages of Kilgobban in Cork and Kilmeen
in Ross. *Annates.*
Donough O'Callaghan, cleric of Cloyne,
appointed to parish church of Knockavilly
which was to be erected into a prebend for
his benefit. *Annates.*
Edmund Murphy, perpetual vicar of
Ballymartle and Ballymodan. *Annates.*
Philip Ronayne, official (*officialis*) of Cork. *Cal. papal letters,* xiv, 44.

Place of Appointment (if specified)	*Source*

Thaddeus Mangan, priest of Cork, appointed
to the perpetual vicarages of Inchigeela and
Kinneigh, vacant by privation of Donough
Mangan and Cornelius Murphy. — *Annates.*
Maurice Sheehan, priest of Cork, perpetual
vicar of Leighmoney. — *Annates.*

1493   Philip Gould, canon of Cork, is attorney for
the transfer of de Cogan property. — *Roche & Sarsfield MSS.*
Matthew O'Mahony, dean of Cork, for
perpetual vicarage of Macloneigh. Later in
the year he was appointed to the newly-
erected parish of Kilmichael. — *Annates.*
Donough O'Callaghan, vicar of the parish
church of Desertserges. — *Annates.*
Dermot O'Mahony, junior, clerk of Cork, for
the canonry and prebend of Kilbrogan which
Thady Murphy held for many years without
title. — *Annates.*
Cornelius O'Sullivan, cleric of Cork,
appointed to a canonry of Cork and prebend
of Inishkenny. — *Annates.*
John Courcey receives bull for erection of
a canonry and prebend in Cork from the
rectory of Kilgobban, for life (*ad vitam*). — *Annates.*

1494   Thomas Mehigan or Meehan, vicar and
rector of Schull. — *Annates.*
Donough Cormack, cleric of Cork, gets
canonry of Cork and prebend of Inishkenny. — *Annates.*
Randal Hurley, perpetual vicar of Fanlobbus,
to get the prish churches of Caheragh and
Ballymoney, vacant by devolution. — *Annates.*

1498   John Hegarty to have, for life, the united
vicarages of the parish church of Ringrone,
diocese of Cork, and of 'Raln *vel* Kaln'
(unidentified) in the diocese of Ross. — *Annates.*
Dermot Houlihan, cleric of Ross, to be
appointed to a canonry and prebend to be
newly-erected in the church of Cork from
parish churches vacant there. — *Annates.*

1499   Nicholas Kiely, appointed to the rectory of
Rincurran and to the perpetual vicarage of
Innishannon, vacant by privation. — *Annates.*
John Barry, cleric of Cork, for vicarage of
the parish church of Brinny, vacant by
privation of Dermot O'Leary. — *Annates.*

1500   David Cronin, priest of Cork, perpetual
vicar of Desertserges. — *Annates.*
William Cronin for churches of Currarane
and Ballyvolane in Ballinadee. — *Annates.*
Cormac MacHugh (Makaich), for canonry
and prebend of Kilbrogan. — *Annates.*
Thady McCarthy, dean of Cork, go get
parish churches of Rathclarin and Burren. — *Annates.*
Edmund Courcey, perpetual vicar of Kinsale. — *Annates.*

Place of Appointment (if specified)	*Source*

1502   Donough McCarthy, canon and archdeacon of Cork, is appointed to the rectory of Innishannon which is to be united with the canonry and prebend of Inishkenny during his lifetime.   *Annates.*

1503   Donal Murphy, cleric of Cloyne, to get canonry and prebend of Kilbrogan and vicarage of Kilbonane.   *Annates.*

1505   Thady McCarthy, archdeacon of Ross, enters bond for union of the archdeaconship with the perpetual vicarage of the parish church of Ringrone.   *Annates.*

1510   David O'Mahony, cleric of Cork, to get the rectory of Kilmoe and a part (*particula*) of the rectory of Schull.   *Annates.*
    Randal Hurley, junior, canon of Cork, to be vicar of the parish churches of Templetrine and Kinsale.   *Annates.*
    John Hurley, canon of Cork, vicar of Myross in diocese of Ross and of Brinny in the diocese of Cork.   *Annates.*
    Dermot McCarthy, cleric of Cork, vicar and rector of Drinagh and vicar of Inchigeela.   *Annates.*

1511   Donald Hurley, cleric of Cork, enters bond for the parish churches of Kilgobban, Rathdrought and Ballinadee.   *Annates.*

1513   Randal Hurley, cleric of Cork, canon and prebendary of Drimoleague.   *Annates.*

1517   James Courcey, cleric of Cork, for the parish churches of Ringrone and Templetrine.   *Annates.*
    Goerge Roche is presented to the church of Holy Trinity in place of Philip Gould.   *Pat. 8 Henry VIII*, pt. 1, m. 14.

1525   Eugene McCarthy, cleric of Cork or Cloyne, enters bond for a simple perpetual benefice called an Office, vacant by the death of Donough McCarthy (see entry under date 1502).   *Annates.*

1526   Donal McCarthy, cleric of Cork, for the rectory of Dunderrow and a canonry and prebend of Cork.   *Annates.*
    Thomas Shea (Shyo), O.S.A., Cork, to get the vicarages of Liscleary and Inishkenny and the parish churches of Inishkenny and Tisaxon.   *Annates.*

1531   Dominick Coppinger, cleric of Cork.   *Roche & Sarsfield MSS.*

BIBLIOGRAPHY

PRIMARY SOURCES

British Museum

Add. Charter 8674. An account of the reception of George Roche, former bailiff of Cork, into the House of Saint Stephen without the walls of Cork. It is dated January 1511/12 and is the oldest account of religious ceremonies of this nature in Cork.

Add. Charter 13600*. A rental of certain places in Cork—a long roll, beginning and ending abruptly and showing no date. Believed to be a sixteenth-century document.

Add. MSS Ascough 4784, f. 77v. Revenue account of the see of Cork.

Add. MSS Ascough 4787, f. 78. A compendious document containing a list of bishops and deans of Cork between 1288 and 1447, a grant made by Bishop Walter le Rede (1327–30) to the vicars choral in 1328, entries regarding Cloyne.

Add. MSS Ascough 4787, f. 78v. A rental of the possessions of the bishop of Cork. The folio also contains part of a papal taxation, *Tax Papae Civit' Corcag et Suburb.*, for which no date is shown.

Add. MSS 4793, f. 70. Dermot's Charter.

Add. Roll 8671: *Rotulus Landigabilis Civitatis Corke*. At the back of the roll is given *Redditus Civitatis Corck*. The roll is endorsed in a modern hand and is dated 'about the reign of Richard II (1377–99) or Henry IV (1399–1413)'.

Clarendon MS 4783.

Egerton MS 205. Containing a catalogue of inquisitions post mortem from the Rolls Office, Dublin.

Harleian MS 35. Dealing mainly with Anglo-Irish political and ecclesiastical relations, beginning with the Tudor period.

Lansdowne MS 159, f. 3. Dealing with the affairs of Desmond.

MS Rawlinson B. 479, f. 114. Containing *Episcopi Corcagensis post Anglorum ingressum* from *Collectanea Varia Jacobi Waraei, equitis aurati.* Sir James Ware had a list of the sees of Ireland as they were divided among the four provinces by Cardinal Paparo. He stated that it was preserved in the *Codex Censuum* of Cencius the chamberlain, afterwards Pope Honorius III. On this is based the greater part of Ware's *De Hibernia et Antiquitatibus Eius.*

MS Rawlinson B. 485, Bodleian. Lives of the saints in Latin.

Miscellanea of the Chancery, bundle 87, file 2, no. 23. Placita apud Tylagh at Dublin, 25 and 26 Edward I (Rex *versus* Bishop of Cork), relative to the churches of Kaylmahanok, Saint Mary del Nard, Nothynnal and Saint Peter, Dungarvan, in the suburbs of Cork.

Rentals and Surveys Roll 936. This roll has been edited by Newport B. White under the title, *Extents of Irish Monastic Possessions, 1540–1541.*

Roche and Sarsfield Manuscripts (abstracts).

Wynchedon Will and its *vera copia* : Add. MS 19868, ff. 5a–5b, 7b–8b.

Cork Diocesan Archives

Acta Apostolicae Sedis, xxviii.

Acta for the Process of the Beatification of Thaddeus Machar. Rome 1896.

Arch. Vat. Reg. vol. 690, fols. 178b–182.

Eporedien: Confirmationes Cultus ab Immemorabili Tempore Praestiti Servo Dei Thaddaeo Machar, Episcopo Hibernensi. Rome 1897.

Registrum Bull. Secret. Tomus 5.

Summarium Originale to Acta Apostolicae Sedis, xxviii.

Marsh's Library, Dublin

Codex Kilkenniensis. A manuscript of the Lives of the Irish saints, in Latin.

MS C.1.27, from Webster's collection of the Caulfield Manuscripts.

National Library of Ireland

King Manuscripts. Archbishop William King's *Collectanea* for an ecclesiastical history of Ireland.

Public Record Office of England

MS M.P.F. 94. Caulfield's sketch of the abbey of Bantry.

Roman Transcripts: P.R.O. 31/1, vol. xxix, f. 28.

Public Record Office of Ireland

Lodge Manuscripts.

MS 2N.60.4B. The Procuration List of 1437.

Royal Irish Academy, Dublin

Cork Inquisitions (selected). Including R.I.A. MS no. 12, Hodges and Smith.

Stowe Missal, R.I.A. MS Stowe, D.11.

Windele Manuscripts.

Trinity College, Dublin

MS E.3.11. Lives of Irish saints, in Latin.

MS E.3.14. Taxation list, 1588.

MS E.3.15. Visitation book, 1591.

MS E.3.16. *Salus Populi*, a tract proposing reform in Ireland.

MS F.1.16. Concerning Tracton Abbey.

MS K.6.16 Containing Lynch's *Historia Ecclesiastica*, vol. ii.

Reeves MS 1066. The royal visitation of Cork, Cloyne, Ross and the College of Youghal, 1615.

Reeves MS 1067. Transcript of the regal visitation, 1634.

University College, Cork

Caulfield Manuscripts.

Vatican Archives

Archivium Secretum Apostolicum Vaticanum, 935; Reg. Alex. VI, anno 1, Lib. 7, f. 26. This outlines the canonical erection of the parish of Kilmichael.

Registrum Vaticanum 4, f. 150r-v, Lateran 12 April 1199. Scritture originale riferite nelle Congregazioni Generali, vol. 294.

GENERAL BIBLIOGRAPHY

Analecta Bollandiana, no. 69. Brussels 1951.

Ancient Laws and Institutes of Ireland. 6 vols. Dublin 1865–1901.

Anderson, M. 'Columba and Other Irish Saints in Scotland'. *Historical Studies*, v (1965), 26–36.

Annála Connacht . . . (A.D. 1224–1544). Edited by A. Martin Freeman. Dublin 1944.

Annála Ríoghachta Éireann: Annals of the Kingdom of Ireland by the Four Masters from the Earliest Period to the Year 1616. Edited and translated by John O'Donovan. 7 vols. Dublin 1851. Reprint, New York 1966.

Annála Uladh, Annals of Ulster; otherwise Annála Senait, Annals of Senat: A Chronicle of Irish Affairs, 431–1131, 1155–1541. Edited by W. M. Hennessy and B. MacCarthy. 4 vols. Dublin 1887–1901.

Annals of Clonmacnoise, being Annals of Ireland from the Earliest Period to A.D. 1408, Translated into English, A.D. 1627, by Connell Mageoghagan. Edited by Denis Murphy. Dublin 1896.

Annals of Inisfallen (MS Rawlinson B 503). Edited and translated by Seán Mac Airt. Dublin 1951.

Annals of Ireland [A.D. 571–931]: Three Fragments Copied from Ancient Sources by D[ubhaltach] MacFirbisigh. Edited and translated by John O'Donovan. Dublin 1860.

Annals of Ireland together with the Annals of Ross by Friar John Clyn and Thady Dowling. Edited by Richard Butler. Dublin 1849.

Annals of Loch Cé: A Chronicle of Irish Affairs, 1014–1690. Edited by W. M. Hennessy. 2 vols. London 1871. Reflex facsimile, Dublin 1939.

'The Annals of Tigernach'. Edited by Whitley Stokes. *Revue Celtique*, xvi–xviii (1895–97).

De Annatis Hiberniae : A Calendar of the First-fruits' Fees Levied on Papal Appointments to Benefices in Ireland, A.D. 1400–1535, extracted from the Vatican and Other Roman Archives, vol. i: Ulster. Edited by M. A. Costello and Ambrose Coleman. Maynooth 1912.

Archdall, Mervyn. *Monasticon Hibernicum*. Dublin 1873.

Bagwell, Richard. *Ireland under the Tudors with a Succinct Account of the Earlier History*, 3 vols. 1885–90. Reprint (3 vols.), London 1963.

Barraclough, Geoffrey. 'The Making of a Bishop in the Middle Ages'. *Catholic Historical Review*, xix (1933–34), 275–319.

Barry, Edmund. *The History of Barrymore*. Cork 1902.

Barry, John. 'The Appointment of Coarb and Erenagh'. *Irish Ecclesiastical Record*, xciii (1960), 361–5.

———. 'The Erenagh in the Monastic Irish Church'. *Irish Ecclesiastical Record*, lxxxix (1958), 424–32.

———. 'The Status of Coarbs and Erenaghs'. *Irish Ecclesiastical Record*, xciv (1960), 147–53.

Begley, John. *The Diocese of Limerick, Ancient and Medieval*. Dublin 1906.

Bennett, George. *The History of Bandon*. Cork 1869.

Binchy, D. A. Review of *The Church in Early Irish Society*, by K. Hughes. *Studia Hibernica*, vii (1967), 219–20.

———. *Críth Gablach*. Mediaeval and Modern Irish Series, vol. xi. Dublin 1941.

———. 'The Irish Benedictine Congregation in Mediaeval Germany'. *Studies*, xviii (1929), 194–210.

———. 'Sick-maintenance in Irish Law'. *Ériu*, xii (1938), 78–134.

The Black Book of Limerick. Edited by J. MacCaffrey. Dublin 1907.

Blake, Martin. 'An Old Rental of Cong'. *Journal of the Royal Society of Antiquaries of Ireland*, xxxv (1905), 130–5.

Blanchard, Jean. *The Church in Contemporary Ireland*. Dublin 1963.

Bolster, M. Angela [Evelyn], 'Obligationes pro Annatis Diocesis Corcagiensis'. *Archivium Hibernicum,* xxix (1970), 1–32.

The Book of Leinster, formerly Lebar na Núachongbála. Edited by R. I. Best, Osborn Bergin and M. A. O'Brien. 5 vols. Dublin 1954–67.

Boswell, C. S. *An Irish Precursor of Dante.* London 1908.

Brady, John. 'The Catholic Chapter of Meath'. *Irish Ecclesiastical Record,* lii (1938), 286 ff.; liv (1939) 269 ff.

———. 'The Origin and Growth of the Diocese of Meath'. *Irish Ecclesiastical Record,* lxxii (1949), 1–13, 166–76.

Brady, William Maziere. *Clerical and Parochial Records of Cork, Cloyne and Ross.* 3 vols. Dublin 1863.

———. *The Episcopal Succession in England, Scotland and Ireland, A.D. 1400 to 1875.* 2 vols. in one. Rome 1876–77.

Brenan, M. J. *An Ecclesiastical History of Ireland.* 2nd ed. Dublin 1864.

Brooks, Eric St.J. 'Unpublished Charters Relating to Ireland, 1177–82, from the Archives of the City of Exeter'. *Proceedings of the Royal Irish Academy,* xliii, sect. c (1936), pp. 313–66.

Bruodine, Anthony. *Propugnaculum Catholicae Veritatis.* Prague 1669.

Buckley, Denis. 'Diocesan Organization: Cloyne'. *Proceedings of the Irish Catholic Historical Committee* (1956), pp. 8–11.

Butler, W. F. T. *Gleanings from Irish History.* London 1925.

Byrne, F. J. 'The Ireland of St Columba'. *Historical Studies,* v (1965), 37–58.

Calendar of Documents Relating to Ireland. Edited by H. S. Sweetmen. 5 vols. London 1875–86.

Calendar of Entries in the Papal Registers Relating to Great Britain and Ireland: Papal Letters. Edited by W. H. Bliss, J. A. Twemlow and C. Johnson. 14 vols. London 1893–

Calendar of Entries in the Papal Registers Relating to Great Britain and Ireland: Petitions to the Pope, 1342–1419. Edited by W. H. Bliss. London 1896.

Calendar of Inquisitions Post Mortem and Other Analogous Documents, vol. i: Reign of Henry III. London 1904.

Calendar of Ormond Deeds. Edited by Edmund Curtis. 6 vols. Dublin 1932–43.

Calendar of Patent and Close Rolls of Chancery in Ireland, Henry VIII to 18th Elizabeth. Edited by James Morrin. Dublin 1861.

Calendar of the Carew Manuscripts Preserved in the Archiepis-copal Library at Lambeth. Edited by J. S. Brewer and W. Bullen. 6 vols. London 1867–73.

Calendar of the Charter Rolls. 6 vols. London 1903–27.

Calendar of the Close Rolls. 60 vols. London 1892–1962.

Calendar of the Fine Rolls. 22 vols. London 1911–62.

Calendar of the Justiciary Rolls, or Proceedings in the Court of the Justiciar of Ireland. Vols. i (1295–1303) and ii (1305–07) edited by J. Mills. Dublin 1905–14. Vol. iii (1308–14) edited by M. C. Griffith. Dublin 1956.

Calendar of the Patent Rolls, 1232–47 [etc.]. London 1906–

Calendar of the State Papers Relating to Ireland, 1509–73. Edited by H. C. Hamilton. London 1860.

Campbell, W., ed. *Materials for a History of the Reign of Henry VII, from Original Documents Preserved in the Public Record Office*. 2 vols. London 1877.

Canivez, Joseph. *Statuta Capitulorum Generalium Ordinis Cisterciensis*, vol. ii. Louvain 1934.

Capgrave, John. *The Chronicle of England, 1328–88*. Edited by F. C. Hingeston. London 1858.

Carey, F. P. *Blessed Thaddeus MacCarthy*. Dublin 1937.

Carrigan, William. *The History and Antiquities of the Diocese of Ossory*. 4 vols. Dublin 1905.

Caulfield, Richard. *The Annals of St Fin Barre's Cathedral, Cork*. Cork 1871.

———. *The Council Book of the Corporation of Cork*. Cork 1876.

———. *The Council Book of the Corporation of Kinsale*. Cork 1878.

———. *The Council Book of the Corporation of Youghal*. Cork 1879.

———. *Lecture on the History of the Bishops of Cork and the Cathedral of St Fin Barre*. Cork 1864.

————. *Rotulus Pipae Clonensis ex Originali in Registro Ecclesiáe Cathedralis Clonensis.* Cork 1859.

Chartae, Privilegia et Immunitates, being Transcripts of Charters and Privileges to the Cities, Towns, Abbeys and Other Bodies Corporate; 18 Henry II to 18 Richard II, 1171 to 1395. Dublin 1889.

Chartularies of St Mary's Abbey, Dublin, Preserved in the Bodleian Library and British Museum, with the Register of Its House at Dunbrody; and Annals of Ireland, 1162–1370. Edited by J. T. Gilbert. 2 vols. London 1884–86.

Cheney, C. R. 'A Group of Related Synodal Statutes of the Thirteenth Century'. In *Medieval Studies Presented to Aubrey Gwynn, S.J.* Edited by J. A. Watt, J. B. Morrall and F. X. Martin. Dublin 1961.

Cheney, C. R., and Semple, W. H. *Selected Letters of Pope Innocent III Concerning England.* London 1953.

Chronicon Scotorum: A Chronicle of Irish Affairs . . . to 1135, and Supplement . . . 1141–1150. Edited by W. M. Hennessy. London 1866.

The Civil Survey, A.D. 1654–56. Edited by R. C. Simington. 10 vols. Dublin 1931–61.

Cogadh Gaedhel re Gallaibh: The War of the Gaedhil with the Gaill. Edited by J. H. Todd. London 1867.

Colgan, John. *Acta sanctorum veteris et maioris Scotiae, seu Hiberniae sanctorum insulae . . .* Louvain 1645. Reflex facsimile, Dublin 1948.

Collins, John T. 'Church Government in the South of Ireland, A.D. 1471 to 1484'. *Journal of the Cork Historical and Archaeological Society,* lxii (1957), 14–21.

————. 'The Longs of Muskerry and Kinalea'. *Journal of the Cork Historical and Archaeological Society,* li (1946), 1–9.

————. 'A McCarthy Miscellany'. *Journal of the Cork Historical and Archaeological Society,* liii (1948), 95–103.

————. 'The O'Crowleys of Coill tSealbhaigh'. *Journal of the Cork Historical and Archaeological Society.,* lvi (1951), 91–4; lvii (1952), 1–6, 105–9; lviii (1953), 7–11.

————. 'Some McCarthys of Blarney and Ballea'. *Journal of the Cork Historical and Archaeological Society,* lix (1954), 1–10, 82–8; lx (1955), 1–5, 75–9.

———. 'Some Recent Contributions to Cork Diocesan History'. *Irish Ecclesiastical Record*, lxxv (1951), 50–4.

———. 'The Ui MacCaille: A.D. 1177 to 1700'. *Journal of the Cork Historical and Archaeological Society*, l (1945), 31–9.

———. 'Unpublished Cork Inquisitions in the R.I.A.' *Journal of the Cork Historical and Archaeological Society*, lxv (1960), 76–82, 127–9.

———. 'Where Was the Green of Cork?' *Cork Examiner*, 6 January 1934.

Conway, Colmcille. 'Sources for the History of the Irish Cistercians, 1142–1540'. *Proceedings of the Irish Catholic Historical Committee* (1958), pp. 16–23. Published 1959.

———. *The Story of Mellifont.* Dublin 1958.

Cook, G. H. *The English Mediaeval Parish Church.* London 1953.

———. *Mediaeval Chantries and Chantry Chapels.* London 1947.

Corish, Patrick J., ed. *A History of Irish Catholicism.*

Cotton, Henry. *Fasti Ecclesiae Hibernicae.* 6 vols. Dublin 1848–78.

Cox, Richard. *Hibernia Anglicana or the History of Ireland from the Conquest thereof by England to this Present Time.* London 1869.
———. 'On a Manuscript Description of the City and County of Cork, cir. 1685 . . .' Edited by S. F. Johnson and T. Lunham. *Journal of the Royal Society of Antiquaries of Ireland*, xxxii (1902), 353–76.

———. 'Regnum Corcagiense or a Description of the Kingdom of Cork . . .' Edited by R. Day. *Journal of the Cork Historical and Archaeological Society*, viii (1902), 65–83, 156–79.

Creighton, Mandell. *A History of the Papacy from the Great Schism to the Sack of Rome.* 6 vols. London 1897–1903.

Crowder, C. M. D. 'Henry V, Sigismund and the Council of Constance: A Re-examination'. *Historical Studies*, iv (1963), 93–110.

Curtis, Edmund. 'The Court Book of Esker and Crumlin'. *Journal of the Royal Society of Antiquaries of Ireland*, lx (1930), 38–51 ff.

———. *History of Ireland*. University Paperback, Methuen, London. Reprint 1964.

———. *A History of Medieval Ireland, from 1086 to 1513*. 2nd ed. London 1938.

———. 'Richard, Duke ŏf York, as Viceroy of Ireland, 1447–1460'. *Journal of the Royal Society of Antiquaries of Ireland*, lxii (1932), 158–86.

———. *Richard II in Ireland, 1394–95, and Submissions of the Irish Chiefs*. Oxford 1927.

Curtis, Edmund, and McDowell, R. B., eds. *Irish Historical Documents, 1172–1922*. London 1943.

Cusack, M. F. *The History of Cork*. Cork 1875.

Daniel-Rops, Henri. *Cathedral and Crusade*. New York, Doubleday Image Book, 1964.

Davies, John. *A Discovery of the True Causes why Ireland Was never Entirely Subdued . . .* Dublin 1704.

de Burgo, Thomas. *Hibernia Dominicana*. Dublin 1762.

The 'Dignitas Decani' of St Patrick's Cathedral, Dublin. Edited by Newport B. White. Dublin 1957.

Downes, Dive. 'Visitation of His Diocese (Cork)'. *Journal of the Cork Historical and Archaeological Society*, xiv (1908), 66–74, 141–9; xv (1909), 19–28, 78–90, 126–31, 163–80.

du Boulay, F. R. H. 'The Fifteenth Century'. In *The English Church and the Papacy in the Middle Ages*, edited by C. H. Laurence, pp. 195–242. London 1965.

Dunning, P. J. 'The Arroasian Order in Medieval Ireland'. *Irish Historical Studies*, iv (1945), 297–315.

———. 'Irish Representatives and Irish Ecclesiastical Affairs at the Fourth Lateran Council.' In *Medieval Studies Presented to Aubrey Gwynn, S.J.*, edited by J. A. Watt, J. B. Morrall and F. X. Martin, pp. 90–113. Dublin 1961.

———. 'The Letters of Innocent III as a Source for Irish History'. *Proceedings of the Irish Catholic Historical Committee* (1958), pp. 1–10.

———. 'Letters of Pope Innocent III to Ireland'. *Archivium Hibernicum*, xiii (1947), 27–44.

Dwyer, J. A. *The Dominicans of Cork City and County*. Cork 1896.

Edwards, Kathleen. *The English Secular Cathedrals in the Middle Ages.* Manchester 1949.

Edwards, R. Dudley. 'Papal Provisions in Fifteenth Century Ireland'. In *Medieval Studies Presented to Aubrey Gwynn, S.J.*, edited by J. A. Watt, J. B. Morrall and F. X. Martin, pp. 265–80. Dublin 1961.

Erlington, Charles R., ed. *The Whole Works of Most Rev. James Ussher, D.D.* 4 vols. Dublin 1847.

Eubel, Conrad. *Hierarchia Catholica Medii Aevi.* 3 vols. Münster 1913.

Expugnatio Hibernica : Giraldi Cambrensis Opera, vol v. Edited by J. F. Dimock. London 1867.

Extents of Irish Monastic Possessions, 1540–1541, from Manuscripts in the Public Record Office, London. Edited by Newport B. White. Dublin 1943.

Fahy, E. M. 'Inishleena Abbey and Other Sites in the Lee Valley'. *Journal of the Cork Historical and Archaeological Society*, lxii (1957), 65–76.

Féilire Huí Gormáin ; The Martyrology of Gorman. Edited by Whitley Stokes. London 1895.

Félire Oengussa . . . or the Martyrology of Oengus the Culdee. Edited by Whitley Stokes. 2nd ed. Dublin 1905.

Fitzgerald, D. P. 'The Friary of Shandon'. *Cork Examiner*, 27 June 1925.

————. 'Old Cork Churches'. *Cork Weekly Examiner*, 4 July 1925.

Fitzmaurice, E. B., and Little, A. G. *Materials for the History of the Franciscan Province of Ireland.* Manchester 1920.

Flower, Robin. *The Irish Tradition.* Oxford 1947.

————. 'Manuscripts of Irish Interest in the British Museum'. *Analecta Hibernica*, no. 2 (1931), pp. 292–340.

Friedal, V. H., and Meyer, Kuno. *La Vision de Tondale.* Paris 1907.

Fuller, Thomas. *A Church History of Britain from the Birth of Jesus Christ until the Year 1648.* London 1655.

Gairdner, J., ed. *The Paston Letters, 1422–1509.* 4 vols. Edinburgh 1910.

Gasquet, F. A. *The Eve of the Reformation*. London 1900.

Gauchat, P. *Hierarchia Catholica Medii et Recentioris Aevi*. Münster 1935.

Genealogiae Regum et Sanctorum Hiberniae, by the Four Masters. Edited by Paul Walsh. Maynooth 1918.

The Genealogy of the Corca Laighdhe. Edited by John O'Donovan. Dublin 1849.

Gesta Regis Henrici Secundi Benedicti Abbatis : The Chronicle of the Reigns of Henry II and Richard I, 1169–1192. Edited by W. Stubbs. 2 vols. London 1867.

Gibson, C. B. *The History of the County and City of Cork*. 2 vols. London 1861.

Gleeson, Dermot F. 'The Coarbs of Killaloe'. *Journal of the Royal Society of Antiquaries of Ireland*, lxxix (1949), 160–9.

———. *A History of the Diocese of Killaloe*. Dublin 1962.

Goblet, Y. M. *A Topographical Index of the Parishes and Townlands of Ireland in Sir William Petty's MSS [sic] Barony Maps (c. 1655–9) and Hiberniae Delineatio (c. 1672)*. Dublin 1932.

Goodman, A. J. *Who Are the Augustinians?* Melbourne 1944.

Graves, J., ed. *A Roll of the Proceedings of the King's Council in Ireland, 1392–93*. 1877.

Green, Alice Stopford. *The Making of Ireland and Its Undoing*. London 1909.

Griesser, P. Bruno, ed. *Analecta Sacri Ordinis Cisterciensis*, *Annus 11* (January-December 1946), parts 1–4.

Grosjean, Paul. 'Les Vies de S. Finbarr de Cork'. *Journal of the Cork Historical and Archaeological Society*, lviii (1952), 47–54.

Gwynn, Aubrey. 'Anglo-Irish Church Life in the Fourteenth and Fifteenth Centuries'. In *A History of Irish Catholicism*, ii, no. 4, edited by Patrick J. Corish.

———. 'Archbishop FitzRalph and the Friars'. *Studies*, xxv (1936), 81–96; xxvi (1937), 50–67.

———. 'Bishop Samuel of Dublin'. *Irish Ecclesiastical Record*, lx (1942), 81–8.

———. 'The Bishops of Cork in the Twelfth Century'. *Irish Ecclesiastical Record*, lxxiv (1950), 17–29, 97–109.

————. 'The Black Death in Ireland'. *Studies*, xxiv (1935), 25–42.

————. 'The Centenary of the Synod of Kells, 1152'. *Irish Ecclesiastical Record*, lxxvii (1952), 161–76, 250–64.

————. 'Gregory VII as Modern Scholars See Him'. *Studies*, lxxxix (1950), 40–50.

————. 'Ireland and Rome in the Eleventh Century'. *Irish Ecclesiastical Record*, lvii (1941), 213–32.

————. 'Ireland and the Continent in the Eleventh Century'. *Irish Historical Studies*, viii (1953), 192–216.

————. 'Ireland and the English Nation at the Council of Constance'. *Proceedings of the Royal Irish Academy*, xlv, sect. c (1940), pp. 183–233.

————. 'Ireland and Würzburg in the Middle Ages, 752–1497'. *Irish Ecclesiastical Record*, lxxviii (1952), 401–11.

————. 'Irish Monks and the Cluniac Reform'. *Studies*, xxix (1940), 409–30.

————. 'Lanfranc and the Irish Church'. *Irish Ecclesiastical Record*, lvii (1941), 481–500; lviii (1941), 1–15.

————. 'The Origins of the Diocese of Killaloe'. In *A History of the Diocese of Killaloe*, by Dermot F. Gleeson. Dublin 1962.

————. 'The Origins of the Diocese of Waterford'. *Irish Ecclesiastical Record*, lix (1942), 289–96.

————. 'The Origins of the See of Dublin'. *Irish Ecclesiastical Record*, lvii (1941), 40–5, 97–112.

————. 'Pope Gregory VII and the Irish Church'. *Irish Ecclesiastical Record*, lviii (1941), 97–109.

————. 'Provincial and Diocesan Decrees of the Diocese of Dublin during the Anglo-Norman Period'. *Archivium Hibernicum*, xi (1944), 31–117.

————. 'Richard FitzRalph, Archbishop of Armagh'. *Studies*, xxii (1933), 389–405, 591–607; xxiii (1934), 396–411.

————. 'St. Anselm and the Irish Church'. *Irish Ecclesiastical Record*, lix (1942), 1–14.

————. 'St. Malachy of Armagh'. *Irish Ecclesiastical Record*, lxx (1948), 961–78; lxxi (1949), 134–48, 317–31.

————. 'The Twelfth Century Reform'. In *A History of Irish Catholicism*, ii, pt. 1, edited by Patrick J. Corish.

Hagan, John. 'Miscellanea Vaticano-Hibernica, 1580–1631 (Vatican Library: Borghese Collection)'. *Archivium Hibernicum*, iii (1914), 227–365.

Hand, Geoffrey J. 'The Church and English Law in Medieval Ireland'. *Proceedings of the Irish Catholic Historical Committee* (1959), pp. 10–18.

————. 'The Church in the English Lordship, 1216–1307'. In *A History of Irish Catholicism*, edited by Patrick J. Corish, ii, part 3, pp. 1–43.

————. 'The Dating of the Early Fourteenth-Century Ecclesiastical Valuations of Ireland'. *Irish Theological Quarterly*, xxiv (1957), 271–4.

————. *English Law in Ireland, 1290–1324*. Cambridge 1967.

————. 'Mediaeval Cathedral Chapters'. *Proceedings of the Irish Catholic Historical Committee* (1956), pp. 11–14.

————. 'The Medieval Chapter of St. Mary's Cathedral, Limerick'. In *Medieval Studies Presented to Aubrey Gwynn, S.J.*, edited by J. A. Watt, J. B. Morrall and F. X. Martin. Dublin 1961.

Harris, Walter. '*Collectanea de Rebus Hibernicis*'. Edited by C. McNeill. *Analecta Hibernica*, no. 6 (1934), pp. 248–450.

Hay, Denys. *The Medieval Centuries*. Rev. ed. London, University Paperbacks, 1964.

Hayes, J. P. 'Ballymacadane Abbey, County Cork'. *Journal of the Cork Historical and Archaeological Society*, iii (1894), 141–3.

Healy, John. *Ireland's Ancient Schools and Scholars*. Dublin 1902.

Hefele, K. J. von. *Histoire des Conciles*. New French translation, corrected and augmented by H. Leclercq et al. Vols. iv, v. Paris 1907.

Historic and Municipal Documents of Ireland, 1172–1320. Edited by J. T. Gilbert. London 1870.

Hogan, Edmund. *Onomasticon Goedelicum locorum et tribuum Hiberniae et Scotiae*. Dublin 1910.

Hogan, James. 'The Tricha Cet and Related Land Measures'. *Proceedings of the Royal Irish Academy*, xxxvii, sect. c (1929), pp. 148–235.

Holland, Michael. 'The Monastery of St. Francis at Cork'. *Journal of the Cork Historical and Archaeological Society*, xxiii (1917), 121–5.

Holland, W. R. *A History of West Cork and the Diocese of Ross*. Skibbereen 1949.

Hughes, J. Jones. 'Administrative Divisions and the Development of Settlement in Nineteenth Century Ireland'. *University Review*, iii, no. 6 (1964), pp. 8–15.

Hughes, Kathleen. 'The Celtic Church and the Papacy'. In *The English Church and the Papacy in the Middle Ages*, edited by C. H. Laurence, pp. 1–28. London 1965.

———. 'The Church and the World in Early Christian Ireland'. *Irish Historical Studies*, xiii (1962), 99–116.

———. *The Church in Early Irish Society*. London 1966.

———. *Irish Monks and Learning*. Poblet 1963.

Hughes, Philip. *The Church in Crisis : A History of Twenty Great Councils*. London 1961.

———. *A History of the Church*. 3 vols. London 1935–50.

Hull, Eleanor. *A History of Ireland*. London 1914.

Hurley, Patrick. 'Blessed Thaddeus McCarthy, Bishop of Cork and Cloyne'. *Journal of the Cork Historical and Archaeological Society*, ii (1896), 497–509; iii (1897), 94–100.

Hurse, A. E. 'Monkstown and Passage West, County Cork'. *Journal of the Cork Historical and Archaeological Society*, xxx (1925), 15–20.

Irish Monastic and Episcopal Deeds, A.D. 1200–1600, Transcribed from the Originals Preserved at Kilkenny Castle, with an Appendix of Documents of the Sixteenth and Seventeenth Centuries Relating to Monastic Property after the Dissolution. Edited by Newport B. White. Dublin 1936.

Irish Record Commissioners. *Supplement to the Eighth Report : Extract from Certain Rolls forming Part of Pope Nicholas's Taxation, A.D. 1291, Found among the Records at Westminster . . . containing the Dioceses of Limerick, Emly, Cashel, Cloyne, Cork and Waterford*.

Jennings, Brendan. 'Brevis Synopsis Provinciae Hiberniae FF. Minorum'. *Analecta Hibernica*, no. 6 (1934), pp. 139–91.

————. 'Brussels MS 3947: Donatus Moneyus, De Provincia Hiberniae S. Francisci'. *Analecta Hibernica*, no. 6 (1934), pp. 12–131.

Joyce, P. W. *Irish Names of Places*. Dublin 1913.

————. *A Social History of Ireland*. 2 vols. London 1903.

Kavanagh, D. J. *The Augustinian Order*. New York 1937.

Keating, Geoffrey. *Foras Feasa ar Éirinn : The History of Ireland*. Edited by D. Comyn and P. S. Dineen. 4 vols. London 1902–14.

Kenney, J. F. *The Sources for the Early History of Ireland : An Introduction and Guide*, vol. i: Ecclesiastical. New York 1929.

Kiely, Michael. 'Episcopal Succession in Cork and Cloyne in the Fifteenth Century'. *Irish Ecclesiastical Record*, xl (1932), 113–32.

Knott, Eleanor. 'A Poem of Prophecies'. *Ériu*, xviii (1958), 55 ff.

Knox, H. T. *Notes of the Early History of the Dioceses of Tuam, Killala and Achonry*. Dublin 1914.

Lanigan, J. *An Ecclesiastical History of Ireland, from the First Introduction of Christianity among the Irish to the Beginning of the Thirteenth Century*. 4 vols. Dublin 1829.

Lascelles, Rowley. *Liber Munerum Publicorum Hiberniae*. 2 vols. London 1852.

Laurence, C. H., ed. *The English Church and the Papacy in the Middle Ages*. London 1965.

Lawlor, H. J. *The Fasti of St. Patrick's*. Dundalk 1930.

————. 'A Fresh Authority for the Synod of Kells'. *Proceedings of the Royal Irish Academy*, xxxvi, sect. c (1922), pp. 16–22.

————. *St. Bernard of Clairvaux's Life of St. Malachy of Armagh*. London 1920

Leabhar Gabhála : The Book of Conquests of Ireland ; the Recension of Mícheál Ó Cléirigh, part 1. Edited by R. A. Stewart Macalister and J. MacNeill. Dublin 1916.

Leabhar na g-Ceart or The Book of Rights. Edited by John O'Donovan. Dublin 1847.

————. 'Saint Malachy, the Gill Abbey of Cork and the Rule of Arrouaise'. *Journal of the Cork Historical and Archaeological Society*, liv (1949), 41–60. Prepared in conjunction with T. J. Walsh.

————. 'The Testament of John de Wynchedon of Cork. *anno* 1306'. *Journal of the Cork Historical and Archaeological Society*, lxi (1956), 75–88.

O'Sullivan, Florence. *The History of Kinsale*. Dublin 1916.

O'Sullivan, William. *The Economic History of Cork City, from the Earliest Times to the Act of Union*. Cork 1937.

Otway-Ruthven, A. J. 'Anglo-Irish Shire Government in the Thirteenth Century'. *Irish Historical Studies*, v (1946), 1–28.

————. 'The Character of Norman Settlement in Ireland'. *Historical Studies*, v (1965), 75–84.

————. *A History of Medieval Ireland*. London 1968.

————. 'The Medieval Church Lands of County Dublin'. In *Medieval Studies Presented to Aubrey Gwynn, S.J.*, edited by J. A. Watt, J. B. Morrall and F. X. Martin, pp. 54–73. Dublin 1961.

————. 'The Native Irish and English Law in Medieval Ireland'. *Irish Historical Review*, vii (1950).

————. 'Parochial Development in the Rural Deanery of Skreen'. *Journal of the Royal Society of Antiquaries of Ireland*, xciv (1965), 111–22.

Pacata Hibernia: Ireland Appeased and Reduced, or an Historie of the Late Warres in Ireland, especially within the Province of Mounster under the Government of Sir George Carew. Edited by S. H. O'Grady. 2 vols. London 1896.

Pantin, W. A. *The English Church in the Fourteenth Century*. Cambridge 1955.

Plummer, Charles, ed. *Bethada náem nÉrenn; Lives of Irish Saints . . .* 2 vols. Oxford 1922.

————, ed. *Vitae Sanctorum Hiberniae, partim hactenus ineditae . . .* 2 vols. Oxford 1910.

Power, Patrick. 'The Bounds and Extents of Irish Parishes'. In *Féilscríbhinn Tórna*, pp. 218–23. Cork 1947.

————. *Crichad an Chaoilli*. Cork 1932.

————. *The Diocese of Waterford and Lismore.* Cork 1937.

Powicke, F. M., and Fryde, E. B., eds. *Handbook of British Chronology.* 2nd ed. London 1961.

Prynne, William. *Records: A Compendious Tractate and Chronological Collection of Records in the Tower of London and Court of Exchequer.* London 1668.

Rae, E. C. 'The Sculpture of the Cloister of Jerpoint Abbey'. *Journal of the Royal Society of Antiquaries of Ireland,* xcvi (1966), 59–92.

The Red Book of Ormond. Edited by Newport B. White. Dublin 1932.

The Red Book of the Earls of Kildare. Edited by G. Mac Niocaill. Dublin 1964.

Reeves, William *The Ecclesiastical Antiquities of Down, Connor and Dromore.* Dublin 1847.

Register of the Abbey of St. Thomas the Martyr, Dublin. Edited by J. T. Gilbert. London 1889.

Registrum de Kilmainham, 1326–50. Edited by Charles McNeill. Dublin 1932.

'Report on the State of Popery in Ireland in 1731 (Munster)'. *Archivium Hibernicum,* ii (1913), 108–55.

Reports of the Deputy Keeper of the Public Records in Ireland. Dublin 1869–1918.

Richardson, H. G., and Sayles, G. O., eds. *Parliaments and Councils of Mediaeval Ireland.* Vol. i. Dublin 1947.

Ronan, M. V. 'The Diocese of Dublin'. *Irish Ecclesiastical Record,* xliii (1934), 486–509.

————. *The Reformation in Dublin.* Dublin 1926.

Rotulorum Patentium et Clausorum Cancellariae Hiberniae Calendarium. Edited by E. Tresham. Dublin 1828.

Ryan, John. *Irish Monasticism, Its Origins and Early Development.* London 1931.

Rymer, Thomas, ed. *Foedera, Conventiones, Litterae et Cujuscunque Generis Acta Publica . . .* 4 vols. London 1816–69.

Sheehy, Maurice P. 'The Bull *Laudabiliter*: A Problem in Medieval Diplomatique and History'. *Journal of the Galway Archaeological and Historical Society,* xxix (1961), 45–70.

————, ed. *Pontificia Hibernica: Medieval Papal Chancery Documents Concerning Ireland, 640–1261.* 2 vols. Dublin 1962, 1965.

Smith, Charles. *The Ancient and Present State of the County and City of Cork.* 2 vols. Cork 1893.

Statute Rolls of the Parliament of Ireland, 1st to the 12th Years of the Reign of King Edward IV. Edited by H. F. Berry. Dublin 1914.

Statute Rolls of the Parliament of Ireland, Reign of King Henry VI. Edited by H. F. Berry. Dublin 1910.

Statute Rolls of the Parliament of Ireland, 12th and 13th to the 21st and 22nd Years of the Reign of Edward IV. Edited by James F. Morrissey. Dublin 1939.

Statutes and Ordinances and Acts of the Parliament of Ireland, King John to Henry V. Edited by H. F. Berry. Dublin 1907.

Stokes, G. T. *Ireland and the Anglo-Norman Church.* 2nd ed. Dublin 1892.

Stokes, Whitley. *Lives of Irish Saints from the Book of Lismore.* Oxford 1890.

Theiner, Augustin, ed. *Vetera Monumenta Hibernorum et Scotorum.* Rome 1864.

Thompson, A. H. *The Cathedral Churches of England.* London 1928.

————. *The English Clergy and Their Organization in the Later Middle Ages.* Oxford 1947.

Wadding, Luke. *Annales Minorum.* Quaracchi 1931.

————. *Hibernia Primatialis et Episcopalis.* Rome 1731.

Walsh, Paul. 'The Dating of the Irish Annals'. *Irish Historical Studies,* ii (1940), 355–74.

Walsh, T. J. *In the Tradition of Saint Finbarr.* Cork 1951.

Ware, James. *A Commentary on the Prelates of Ireland from the First Conversion of the Irish Nation to the Christian Faith down to Our Times.* Dublin 1704.

————. *De Hibernia et Antiquitatibus eius.* London 1654.

————. *The Whole Works of Sir James Ware Concerning Ireland.* Edited by Walter Harris. 2 vols. Dublin 1739–45.

Warner, Ferdinando. *The History of Ireland from the Earliest Authentic Accounts to the Year 1171.* 2 vols. Dublin 1770.

Watt, J. A. 'English Law and the Irish Church: The Reign of Edward I'. In *Medieval Studies Presented to Aubrey Gwynn, S.J.*, edited by J. A. Watt, J. B. Morrall and F. X. Martin, pp. 133–67. Dublin 1961.

———. 'Laudabiliter in Medieval Diplomacy and Propaganda'. *Irish Ecclesiastical Record*, lxxxvii (1957), 420–32.

———. 'Negotiations between Edward II and John XXII Concerning Ireland'. *Irish Historical Studies*, x (1956–57), 1–21.

———. 'The Papacy and Episcopal Appointments in Thirteenth-Century Ireland'. *Proceedings of the Irish Catholic Historical Committee* (1959), pp. 1–9.

Webb, J. J. *Municipal Government in Ireland.* Dublin 1918.

Webster, Charles A. *The Diocese of Cork.* Cork 1910.

Went, A. E. 'The Fisheries of the River Lee'. *Journal of the Cork Historical and Archaeological Society*, lxv (1960), 27–35.

Wilkins, David, ed. *Concilia Magnae Brittanniae et Hiberniae.* 4 vols. London 1737.

Wilson, Philip. *The Beginnings of Modern Ireland.* Dublin 1912.

Windele, J. *Historical and Descriptive Notices of the City of Cork and Its Vicinity: Gougaun Barra, Glengarriff and Killarney.* Cork 1844.

———. *Windele's Cork: Historical and Descriptive Notices of the City of Cork from Its Foundation to the Middle of the Nineteenth Century.* Revised, abridged and annotated by J. Coleman. Cork 1910.

The Yellow Book of Lecan . . . Edited by Robert Anderson. Facsimile. Dublin 1896.

Index of Persons

Note: Names carrying the prefixes *de* and *le* (or variations of these) are indexed under the name following. Example: de Barry, *see* Barry.

Abbreviations: abb. = abbot
abp. = archbishop
bp. = bishop
preb. = prebendary

A

Abban (Gobban), xxxvii–xxxviii
Acher (Aggirus), 176
Adrian IV, 102, 351
Adrian VI, 468
Aedh of Kilbrennan, xxxviii
Aedh of Mic Ciair, 16, 17
Aedh Uargarb, xxxi, xxxiv, 1
Aggirus, *see* Acher
Aidan of Lindisfarne, 20
Ailill, abb., 47
Ailly, Pierre d', 382
Alexander III, 110
Alexander IV, 64, 218, 307
Alexander V, 381, 388, 389, 390
Alexander VI, 458, 467, 468
Alphonso of Portugal, 132
Amairgen, 1–6
Amalgaid, coarb of Patrick, 51
Anselm, abp. of Canterbury, 56, 60, 64, 65
Aquis, Nicholas de, O.F.M., 216
Arundel, Andrew de, 193
Asinari, Octavius, 460
Augustine, St, 217
Auters, Thomas des, 107
Auxilius, 35
Axebrugge, John de, 137

B

Bairre (Barre, Finbarr), xxxi, xxxix–xlviii,
    1–24, 36–38, 44, 45, 49, 51, 54, 62, 308
Baithin, *see* Cormac and Baithin
Bakepuz, William de, 188
Ballyconingham, John de, bp. of Cork,
    160, 237, 360, 369–71, 402
Baret, Edmund, 413
Barre (Finbarr), *see* Bairre
Barre (Barri), John, 419
Barre, William de la, 413
Barrfind of Achad Chaillten, xlvii
Barrfind of Inis Doimhle, xlvi, xlvii
Barton, Thomas, 294, 378
Barry, David de, 108
——, David [? James], *Annals of the Four
    Masters*, 468
——, Edmund, 238
——, Gerald, bp. of Cork, 235n, 294, 360,
    377–80, 381, 384
——, Gerald, preb. of Killaspugmullane,
    238

——, James, abb. of Tracton, 146
——, James [? David], archdeacon (papal
    providee), 250
——, Sir John de, 195
——, John, preb. of Caherlag, 237
——, John, abb. of Tracton (1499), 146
——, John, last abb. of Tracton (1540),
    146, 150
——, Nicholas, 239
——, Odo de, 142, 150
——, Philip de, 107, 204
——, Philip FitzWilliam de, 109
——, Philip Mac Owen, 144
——, Raymond, abb. of Tracton, 146, 420
——, William de, 194, 297, 405
Barry, Viscount, of Shandon, 209
Barrymore, William, 405, 455
Bauffremes, John de, 433
Beanntraighe, *see* Bantry (*general index*)
Bearach, 421
Bec, xxxi
Benedict XII, 360
Benedict XIII, 381, 385, 388, 392, 393,
    400
Benedict, bp. of Ross, 81, 89
Benet, John, bp. of Cork and Cloyne,
    470–1, 491–3
Beresford, Richard de, 314
Bernard of Clairvaux, 70, 77, 78, 457
Bernard, John, 165
Bicknor, Alexander, abp. of Dublin, 367,
    374, 486
Birmingham, Walter, 344
——, Sir William, 344
Bloet, Petronilla, 208
Blound, John le, 207, 365, 368
Blund, Richard le, 189
Boleyn, Anne, 408, 471
Boniface VIII, 193, 291, 322, 360
Boniface IX, 323, 381, 384, 385, 386, 432,
    435
Boru, Brian, 48, 51, 54, 260, 476
Botiller, Theobald de, 396, 421
Bouer, Thomas Johannis, 370
Boyle, Richard, 410
Braun, George, 479
Brayghnock, Richard, 146
Brendan of Birr, 6, 7, 20, 21
Brendan the Navigator, xxxvii, xxxix, xl,
    xlvi, 22

529

Bricius, bp. of Limerick, 81
Brisset, Jordan, 132
Broune, Nicholas, 391
Browne, Robert, bp. of Cloyne, 462
Brundale, John, 399
Bula, William, 489
Buler, John, 484
Burden, David, 169
Burgo, Hugo de, bp. of Limerick, 183
Butler, James, 2nd earl of Ormond, 347, 405, 408
——, John, 237
——, Thomas, 408

C

Cainneach, St, 7, 8, 21, 22
Cairbre Crom, 62
Callistus III, 399
Cant, Patrick, 465, 466, 467, 468n, 470
Cantilon, Matthew de, 297
Canty (Ouchanty), Dermot, 239, 411
Carew, family of, 108
——, Maurice, 195
——, Odo de, 108
Carter, Arthur, 293
Carthage (Mochua), St, xxxix, 92
Cathal, martyr, 49
Cathmog, abb. and bp., 38
Cauntiton, Thomas de, 166
Celestine III, 197
Cellach (Celsus), abp. of Armagh, 55, 65, 67, 72
Cera, St. 442, 443
Chaddesworth, Thomas de, 313
Cheeves, Richard, bp. of Leighlin, 115
Chilvart, Richard, 440
Christopher, Philip, 409
Ciaran of Saighir, xxxvi-xxxvii
Clann Sealbaigh, see Ua Sealbaigh
Clann Sinnaich, see Ui Sinnaigh
Clarence, George, duke of, 407
——, Lionel, duke of, 345, 374
Clement IV, 355
Clement V, 214, 314, 354, 355, 360, 361
Clement VI, 354, 360
Clement VII, 381, 382, 383, 384
Clement VIII, 468
Clok, Richard, 165
Cloprote, Robert de, 140
Clyn, John, 372
Codd, Roger, 145
Cogan, David, 169
——, Geoffrey, 169
——, John de, 189
——, Margarita, 106
——, Maurice, 240
——, Milo de, 88, 104, 105, 106, 107, 118, 139, 174, 189
——, Peter, 169, 240

——, Richard de, 109, 169
——, Robert FitzGeoffrey, 110, 407
Coggan, Robert, 244
Cogry, Henry, O.F.M., 374
Colman of Cloyne, xxxiv, xl, 62, 162
Colman of Kinneigh, xl, 71
Colton, John, 206
Columba, 22
Columbanus, 25, 37
Columcille, 20, 22
Coman of Bantry, xl
Compton, John de, 137
Comyn, John, abp. of Dublin, 156, 175
Conaing (Connmhach), abb., 43
Concord, canon of Annadown, 185
Condon, Gerald, bp. of Cloyne, 387, 388
Copener, Peter, 398
——, William, 398
Coppinger, Adam, 160, 371
——, Philip, 486
Corc, king of Cashel, xxx
Cormac, Donogh, 240
Cormac and Baithin, 15, 19
Cormick, Lachtin, see O'Cormack, Lachtin
Cornis, Thomas, 396, 421
Cornwalshe, David de, 147
Corre, John, 237, 395
Coughlan, Donough, 489
Courcey, David de, 241, 481
——, Edmund de, bp. of Clogher and Ross, 454, 466
——, Gerald de, 163, 170
——, John de, 163, 241, 486
——, Nicholas, 170
——, Patrick de, 108, 218, 470
Cradock, Adam, 241
Creagh, David, abp. of Cashel, 463
——, David, preb. of Holy Trinity, 237
Cronin, Donough, 417
——, John, 410, 411, 488
Cullen, Hugh (Odo), 241
Culthan, John, 146
Cummian *Fada*, 25, 37, 39
Cummian of Durrow, 41

D

Dartel, don Pedro, 132
David of Minevia (Cell Muine), xlvi, 5, 17, 21, 469
Deiphilt, Rudolph, bp. of Utrecht, 399
Desmond, Earls of, see FitzGerald
Dominic, St, 201, 202, 204
Domnall, bp. of Cork, 37, 38
Donatus (Donngus), bp. of Dublin, 59
Dosmangen, xxxix
Dubdaleithe, coarb of Patrick, 47
Dubduibne, 1

E

Edward I, 113, 116–18, 167, 180, 189, 190,
192, 205, 292, 294, 300, 313–14, 349,
352, 354, 360, 361, 402
Edward II, 216, 314, 343, 350–1, 358, 360,
361, 363, 365, 366, 367, 378, 401, 402
Edward III, 145, 148, 216, 219, 222, 343,
345, 346, 351, 354, 360, 367, 373, 374,
377, 378
Edward IV, 220, 408, 409, 413, 426, 427
Effingham, Nicholas, bp. of Cloyne, 115,
193
Elias Raymond of Toulouse, 435
Ellesmere, Roger, bp. of Cork, 190, 381,
385–7
Eltin, *see* Multose
Eochaidh, prince of Ui Eachach, xxx, 1,
256
Eolang of Aghabulloge, 17, 19, 21
Epeworth, William, 233, 238, 353, 371
Estdene, William de, 193
Eugene, bp. of Ardmore, 81
Eugenius IV, 93n, 403, 405, 406
Eusebius, St, 458, 459

F

Fachtna of Ros Ailithir, xl, 10, 22
Feidlimid, king of Cashel, 46, 47
Ferdomnach, bp. of Kildare, 60
Fiama, hermit, xliv, 19
Fiannachta, abb. and bp., 38
Finbarr, *see* Bairre
Finnechta, abb., 38
FitzAdam, William, 299
FitzAnthony, Thomas, 136, 167, 181
FitzAudelm (FitzAldelm), William, 119
FitzGeoffrey, John, 144, 186
FitzGerald, earls of Desmond:
——, Gerald, bp. of Cork and Cloyne,
270, 271, 370, 411, 412–19, 420, 423,
424, 425, 455, 456, 458, 463, 466, 467
——, James, 6th earl, 109, 407
——, James, 9th earl, 419, 424, 479
——, John, 348
——, John FitzEdmund, bp. of Cork and
Cloyne, 465, 466, 467, 468, 469, 480,
492
——, Maurice *Bacach,* 371, 455, 456, 463,
464, 465, 480
——, Thomas, 7th earl, 408, 409, 456
FitzGerald, earls of Kildare:
——, Garret Mór (Gerald), 464
——, Gearóid Óg, 472, 473
——, Gerald FitzMaurice, 346, 456
——, Maurice, 344, 371
FitzGerald, Maurice, early Norman gran-
tee, 107
——, Walter, 390

——, William, bp. of Ross, 462
FitzGilbert, John, 195
FitzHugh, Alexander, 105
——, Raymond, 105
FitzJohn, Milo, bp. of Cork, 235n, 243,
381, 388, 389–91, 393, 395, 397, 398,
400, 403, 452
——, Thomas, justiciar, 369
——, William, bp. of Ossory, 358, 364,
367
FitzMartin, Robert, 109, 141
FitzMaurice, Edmund, 448
——, Gerald, 195
FitzRalph, Richard, abp. of Armagh, 222,
223, 352, 376, 437, 476
FitzRobert, Philip, 195
FitzRoger, William, 297
FitzSimons, Walter, abp. of Dublin, 374
FitzStephen, Ralph, 106, 108
——, Robert, 88, 104, 105–107, 118, 174,
189, 344
FitzWalter, John, 81
Flann Find, *see* Cullen *(general index)*
Fleming, David le, 363
Flemyng, John, 146
Florence, bp. of Ross, 89
Forcalquier, Guy de, 132
Foxcote, Thomas de, 137
Foxe, Patrick, bp. of Cork and Ossory,
381, 389, 393, 394, 397
Francis of Assisi, 200, 201, 202, 203
Fulbourn, Stephen, bp. of Waterford, 117
Furlong, David, 146
Fygham, Henry, 303

G

Gall, Philip, 360
Galle, Walter, 238
——, William, 361
Galway, Andrew, 296
——, Geoffrey, 242
——, John, 468n
Garigliatti, Nicholas, bp. of Ivrea, 457,
458
Garri, Remund de, 384
Gelasius (Gilla Mac Liag), abp. of Ar-
magh, 77, 80
Geraldine, Edmund Maurice de, 455
——, John de, 420
Geraldinis, John de, Knight of Kerry, 417
——, Philip, 405
Gerard, Peter, 131, 132
Gervase, abb. of Arrouaise, 196
Gilbert, bp. of Cork, 182, 183, 184, 235n
Gilbert (Giolla Easpoig), bp. of Limerick,
63, 65–67, 73, 77
Gilbert, mayor of Cork, 103, 153, 300
Gilbert of Sempringham, 196

Giraldus Cambrensis, 89, 110, 111, 112, 366
Gobban, *see* Abban
Gobban Corn, *see* Dunmanway *(general index)*
Gobnait, *see* Ballyvourney *(general index)*
Gogan, Maurice, 415
Gonzaga, Alberto, bp. of Ivrea, 457
Gordon, William, 139
Gould (Gold), Nicholas, 169
——, Philip, 237, 295, 303, 468n, 482
Gower, David, 238, 377
Graynell, Richard, 146, 147
Gregory I, 5
Gregory VII, 56, 58
Gregory IX, 114
Gregory XI, 324, 360, 381, 382, 383, 403
Gregory XII, 381, 385, 388, 389, 390, 392, 393
Gregory XIII, 459
Gros, Raymond le, 103, 107, 108
Gulton, William, 386

H

Hackett, Peter, abp. of Cashel, 383
Hallinan, David, 240, 420
Halsey, Thomas, bp. of Leighlin, 469, 478
Harbergh, Thomas, 240
Hardite, William, O.P., 374
Hareford, Agnes de, 194–6, 199, 307
Hawker, John, 293
Haye, Walter de la, 116, 169, 362
Hennessy, Nicholas, bp. of Waterford and Lismore, 421
Henry I, king of England, 132
Henry II, 89, 102–104, 110–12, 119, 120, 173
Henry III, 113–15, 117, 118, 144, 154, 167, 180, 183, 186, 212
Henry IV, 303, 381, 387
Henry V, 219, 381, 382
Henry VI, 219, 398, 400, 403, 427
Henry VII, 112, 424, 464, 465
Henry VIII, 313, 408, 464, 471–2, 482, 485, 492, 493
Herlihy, David, 215
Herlihy (Hurley), Randal, 488
Hodyne, William, 149
Holhgan, Robert, 397, 487
Honorius III, 112, 113, 201, 235
Horsington, John, 137, 138, 378
Hua Mutain, Mugron, 36, 49, 50
Huss, John, 393, 394
Hygyn, Patrick, 470

I

Ilgar, William, 148
Inge, Hugh, abp. of Dublin, 474

Ingewurde (Ingworth), Richard, 207, 208
Innocent II, 77, 78
Innocent III, xxxi, 3, 82, 110, 112, 113, 117, 200, 201, 217, 321
Innocent IV, 113, 115, 217, 302
Innocent VI, 360
Innocent VII, 381, 385, 387, 397
Innocent VIII, 323, 420, 423, 453, 454, 455, 456, 461
Iserninus, 35
Istod, John, 135

J

Jerome of Prague, 394
John XXII, 241, 314, 323, 350, 354–6, 360, 364, 366–9, 401, 402, 485
John XXIII, 381, 389–93, 395, 396
John, king of England, 103, 104, 109, 113, 119, 135, 153, 154, 177, 179, 200
John of Jandun, 382
Jorz, Walter, abp. of Armagh, 350
Julian, bp. of Bertinoro, 451
Julius II, 468, 490

K

Karmardin (Kermedin), Edmund, 357, 374
Kelleher, Maurice, 484
Kelly, John, 398
Kenefig, Michael, 230, 326
Kilmessan, Ralph de, 213, 369, 370
Kyng, Henry, 237, 294
Kynmoure, Richard, bp. of Cork, 381, 387, 390

L

Lachtin, St, 20
Laeghaire, xxxi
Laighin, Laighne, xxxvi
Lambert, John, 137
Lanfranc, abp. of Canterbury, 55, 59, 60
Lang, David de, 187, 188, 229
——, Thomas de, 193
Langeton, William de, 362
Lasair, xliv, 2, 197; and companions, 197–9
Lascapan, John de, 365
Laurence, bp. of Cork, 184, 185, 188
Lawles, Patrick, 93n
Lech, John, abp. of Dublin, 373, 374
Leo IX, 56
Leo X, 468, 480
Leo XIII, 462
Lexington, Stephen, 143, 147, 197
Loan (Lochan), *see* Bairre
Lochan, cleric, 6, 7
Lombard, William, 135

Londres, Henry de, abp. of Dublin, 155, 179

——, Richard de, 104

Lovel (Lovell), John, 192

——, Sir Thomas, 424

Low, Andrew, 149

Lowillins, William, 241

Lucey, Cornelius, bp. of Cork and Ross, 276, 493

Lucy, Sir Anthony, 344

——, Richard de, 137

Luddon, Nicholas, 398

Lughaidh, prince of Ui Eachach, xxxiv

Lumley, Geoffrey, 299

Lynch, Thomas, 134

Lyon, William, Protestant bp. of Cork, Cloyne and Ross, 335

M

Mac Aedha, Cathal, xli, 92

Mac Broic, sept, xxx, xxxi

Mac Cais, sept, xxx, xxxi

McCarroll, John, bp. of Cork, 166, 235n, 243, 358, 360, 361–4

MacCarthy of Carbery (Reagh), 449

——, Cormac, bp.-king, 57, 73–77, 80, 449

——, Cormac, lord of Ballymountain, 269, 449

——, Cormac Lehenagh, 80–82, 103, 174

——, Dermot of Kilbawne, 80, 89, 102–104, 108, 174, 300; charter of, 80, 81, 89

——, Donal, 344, 449

——, Donough, archdeacon and precentor, 73

——, Donough, prince of Carbery, 419

——, Florence, 456

——, Thaddeus, bp. of Cork and Cloyne, 425, 448–67

——, Thaddeus (Thady), dean, 326

MacCarthy of Duhallow, 448

——, Donogh Oge, 456

MacCarthy Mór (Muskerry), 208, 210

——, Cormac *Láidir,* 438, 439, 442, 444, 449

——, Cormac Oge (of Blarney), d. 1536, 303, 473

——, Sir Cormac, c. 1619, 443, 444

MacCarthy, Christian, abb. of Ratisbon, 57

——, Dermot 'the Thin', O.F.M., 217

——, Florence, bp. of Cork, 23, 24

——, Gilla Pádraic, *airchinnech,* 49, 51, 232

——, Thady, canon, 418, 451

——, Don Raymond, 451

Mac Cathain, Oengus, 3, 8, 40

Mac Cathasaigh, Dunlaing, 43, 46

Mac Ciair, *see* Ui Mic Ciair

Mac Ciaruchain, Colum, 49, 54

Mac Clanchy, John, 137

Mac Cluasaigh, Colman, 25

Mac Coghlan, Cormac, 479

Mac Conaid, Saorbreathach, 37, 38, 39

Mac Conglinne, Anier, 23, 44, 45

Macconmara, Rory, 414

Mac Cuilleanain, Cormac, 47, 52

Mac Cuirp [? Cormac], 5, 8, 18, 21

Mac Donnchada, Robert, bp. of Cork, 115, 161, 165, 166, 189–95, 243, 300, 385n

Mac Finguine, Cathal, 44, 45

Mac Firbis, Dubhaltach, 47

Mac Foirceallaigh, Fland, 43

Mac Garbhaith, Aedh, 47

McKenna, Matthew, bp. of Cloyne, 91

Mac Lenine, *see* Colman of Cloyne

Mac Liag, Gilla, *see* Gelasius

Mac Maelumha, Suibhne, 36, 38

Mac Miandach, Aedh, 16, 17, 61

McNamara, Lewis, O.F.M., 214

Mac Namara, Sioda Cam, 439

Mac Owen, Felemy, 438

Macray, Louis, O.P., 417

Mac Robartaigh, Muiredach (Marianus), 57

Mc Tadhg, Cormac, 238

Mac Tigernaigh, Feidlimid, xxxiv–xxxv

Mac Tire, chief of Imokilly, 107, 108

Maedoc of Ferns, 17, 21

Maelgorm, 47

Maelmordha, 47

Magunel, Raymond, 107

Mahon (Mathgamhain), king of Munster, 21, 47, 48, 54

Malachy (Maol Maodhóg), 70, 73, 74, 77–79, 175, 196, 225, 457

Malchus, bp. of Waterford, 60, 73

Manchin, abb., 44

Mangan, Donough, *see* Omongayn, Donald

Mansell, Adam, 160, 371

Maolmuadh, 52, 54

Marianus Scottus, 57

Marsiglio of Padua, 382

Martell (Martel), John, 343, 391

——, Maurice, 420

Martin of Tours, xxxv

Martin V, 211, 393–8, 403, 430n, 437, 440

Mathew, bp. of Cloyne, *see* O Mongagh, Mathew

Mathgamhain, *see* Mahon

Meade (Miagh), David, archdeacon, 410

——, David, preb. of Holy Trinity, 294

——, James, 294

——, William, 328

Michis, Philip, 299

Mickellachayn, Donogh, 241

Midia, Philip de, 146
Miles, Robert, 408
Mochua, St, *see* Carthage, St
Modichu, 2
Montefalco, Anselmo de, 435
Mooney, Canice, O.F.M., 215, 429, 431, 441, 445, 477
——, Donogh, O.F.M., 438, 439
Moralis, Maurice O'Mochain, O.P., 436
Morgan, Maurice, 378
Morisco, Geoffrey de, 116, 183, 362
Mortimer, Edmund, 206, 293, 347
——, Roger, 206, 347, 361
——, Sir Thomas, 206
Muenes, William de, 193, 237, 242, 294
Multose (Eltin), xxxviii-xl
Murphy, Cornelius, 241, 269, 326, 419, 420
——, Donal, 238
——, Donatus, 93n
——, John, bp. of Cork, 211
——, Thady, 238
Murray, Daniel, abp. of Dublin, 461
Muskerry, Lord, 4
Mychyan, Thomas, 376

N

Nash, Seán Dearg, 274
Nessan, St, xlv, 10, 22, 23, 24, 45
Netilton, William, 368
Nicholas IV, 62, 144, 212, 313, 325
Nicholas V, 441
Ninian, *see* Candida Casa *(general index)*
Norris, Philip, 476
Nutin', Nicholas, 482

O

O hAodha, Gregory, bp. of Cork, 81, 119, 133, 173-5, 176, 225, 290, 300
——, Murchad, bp. of Cork, 176, 177, 178
O'Brennan, Geoffrey, 187, 188
O'Brien (Ua Briain), Conor, 73
——, Dermot (Diarmaid), 21, 55, 59, 72
——, Domhnall Mór, 72, 102, 104
——, Muirchertach (Murtough, son of Turlough), 55, 59, 60, 63, 64, 66, 69, 72, 104
——, Turlough (Terdelvachus), 55, 63
O'Callaghan, Thomas A., bp. of Cork, 13n, 415, 462
O'Carroll, Donal, 238
Ó Cléirigh, Mícheál (O'Clery, Michael), xlvi, xlvii, 2, 8, 444
O'Clune, Malachy, O.F.M., 441
O Cochlain, abb. and bp., 38
O Conairche, *see* Ua Conairche
O'Connor, *see* Ua Conchubhair
Oconyll, Nicholas, 386

O'Cormack (Cormick), Lachtin, 239, 488
O'Cremin, erenaghs, 262
O Daly, Matthew, 241
——, Thady, 239
O'Dea, Cornelius, 384
Odoly, Adam, 363
O'Donovan, Donogh, 239
O'Driscoll, Fineen, 441
——, Macrobius, 239
——, Odo, bp. of Ross, 448, 451, 452, 454
O Dubhthaig, Tadhg, 75
O'Duffy, Eneas, 239
O'Fihely, Donal, 490
O'Fihilly, Maurice, 490
O'Fin, William, 292
O'Flynn, Cornelius, 326, 420
Ogillagymain, David, 441
O'Grady, Nicholas, 242
O Haingli, Samuel, bp. of Dublin, 60, 72
O'Hart, Richard, 241
O'Healihy, erenaghs, 70, 262
O'Hedian, John, 412
——, Richard, abp. of Cashel, 383, 391
O'Herlihy, erenaghs, 262
O'Herlihy, Gilbert, 238
——, John, 240, 326, 488
——, Maurice, 240
O'Huallachain, Dermot, 458
Ohuallachayn, Robert, 146
O'Hullachan, Donatus (Dongus), abp. of Cashel, 81, 174
Okeallayd, John, 411
O'Keeffe, erenaghs, 262
O'Kelly, Nicholas, 410, 423
——, William, 239
O'Kiely, Maurice, 238
Olathnan, Rory, 478
O'Long (O Longaigh), erenaghs, 261, 262
O'Magram, William, O.F.M., 209
O'Mahony sept, xxx, xxxi, xxxv, 1, 90, 259
——, Cian, 54
——, Donchadh, son of Cian, 102
O'Mahony, Cornelius, 481
——, Denis (hermit), 13
——, Dermot, 238, 406
——, Donogh, 419, 441
——, Matthew, dean of Cork, 3, 239, 240, 270, 271, 420, 483
——, Thomas, archdeacon of Limerick, 405
O'Malley, Hugh, O.S.A., 221, 434
O Maoldubh, Niall, 38
O Mathúna, Finghin, 444, 490
O'Michian, William, 363
Omolcron, Magonius, 406
O Mongagh, Mathew, bp. of Cloyne, 81
Omongayn, Donald (Donogh), 238, 241, 397

Omorgain, Maurice, 391
O Muighin, Giolla Aedh, 74, 76, 78, 79, 93, 94, 173, 176, 225
O'Neill, Donal, 351
O hOisin, Aodh, 74, 75
O'Reilly, Dominic, 483
——, Donald, 240, 397
——, William, O.F.M., 214, 432, 445
O'Riordan, Donogh, 240, 419
Ormond, Earl of, *see* Butler, James
O Ruaidhri, Gillachrist, 54, 55
O Saolbach, *see* Ua Sealbaigh
Oseancan, Thomas, 422
Oshefeth, Philip, 193
O'Sullivan, Cornelius, 240
——, Eugene, 239
——, Maurice, 240
O'Sullivan Bere, Dermot, 215
Oteye, Cornelius, 414
O'Toole, Laurence, abp. of Dublin, 119, 178
Ouchanty, *see* Canty
Oxford (de Oxeneford), Roger, 119, 176, 300

P

Palladius, xxxvi, 34
Pandarus *(Salus Populi)*, 473–4
Paparo, John, 79, 80
Paschal II, 131
Paston, John, pseudo-bp. of Cork, 389, 398, 399, 400
——, William, 399
Patrick, St, xxxvi, 10, 12, 34, 35
Patrick, bp. of Dublin, 59
Paul II, 396
Paul III, 433, 468
Paul V, 13
Payn, Adam, bp. of Cloyne, 398, 400, 403, 451
Pelagius, xxxvi
Pellyn (Pelyn), Geoffrey, 396
——, John, 378, 396
——, Richard, 396, 397
Pembrok, John de, 365
Penrys, Simon, 165
Perusio, Angelo, 459
Peter, bp. of Palestrina, 369
Philip of Slane, bp. of Cork, 207, 236, 357, 360, 364–8, 401
Piperharewe, Richard de, 190
Pius II, 149, 410, 413, 414, 441, 466
Pius III, 468
Planck, Gilbert, 297
Poer, Simon le, 108
Polton, John, 394
Possewyk, John, 387
Prendergast, Philip de, 109, 136, 139, 142, 182, 209

Preston, John le, 369
Purcel, Richard, 240
Purcell, John, 238, 422, 488
——, Jordan, bp. of Cork and Cloyne, 169, 243, 244, 294, 403–407, 409, 411, 414, 415, 416, 418, 441, 451, 465, 466, 482

R

Rane, Hugh de, 132
Raymond of Provence, 132
Raymund of Capua, 435
Rechtmor, Feidhlimidh, xlvii
Rede, John, 384, 386
——, Walter le, bp. of Cork, 158, 243, 357, 360, 368, 369, 402
Redisford, Edward, 169
Reginald, archdeacon and bp. of Cork (1182–87), 175, 179, 225, 226, 232, 235n
Reginald, bp. of Cork (1267–76), 161, 188, 190, 191
Reich, Walter, 306
Rhosus, bp. of Cilicia, 451
Richard II, 145, 148, 347, 348, 349, 352, 360, 379, 385, 387, 431, 432
Richard of Wexford, 115
Riddefort, Edmund, 244, 417
Robesti, canon of Ivrea, 457, 460
Robinson, William, 329
Roche, John, baron of Fermoy, 423
——, Maurice, Lord, 405, 419, 456
Roche, David, archdeacon, 413
——, Dominic, 246n
——, Edmund, 421
——, George, bailiff, 303
Roche, George, 482
——, John, bp. of Cork, 136, 235n, 237, 243, 256, 360
——, John, precentor, 418
——, Miles, abb. of Tracton, 146, 148, 149, 477
——, Richard, 170
——, Robert, archdeacon, 386
——, William, bp. of Cork and Cloyne, 409, 411, 414–19, 424, 454, 455, 465, 466, 467
Rocheford, Johanna, 378
Rochford (Rotchford) family, 170, 172, 468
Rodiert, William, 374
Ronan, Philip, 455
Ronayne, Maurice, 139
Ruadhan of Lorrha, 15
Ruisine, *see* Inis Pich *(general index)*
Rupe, George de, 227
——, William de, 165
Rutland, Edmund, duke of, 348, 408
Rych, John, 297

Ryther, Richard, 297
Ryvere, William de, 314

S

St. Leger, 313
Samuel, bp. of Dublin, *see* O Haingli, Samuel
Sanford, John de, 112, 161, 163, 164, 169
Saorbreathach, *see* Mac Conaid, Saorbreathach
Sarresfield, Daniel, 81
Sarsfield, Thomas, 297
Scot, Michael, abp. of Cashel, 182
Scurlag, Richard, 398, 400, 404
Seadna, xxxviii
Senan of Iniscathaigh, xxxiv, xxxix, xlv, xlvi
Sheehan, Dermot, 240
——, Donatus, 415, 417
——, Thady, 415
——, Thomas, 239, 488
——, Robert, 416
Sheyne, Matthew, Protestant bp. of Cork, 171
Sigismund, 391, 392
Simnel, Lambert, 333, 424, 464
Sitric, king of Dublin, 260
Sixtus IV, 93n, 269, 416, 417, 420, 451, 452, 453, 461, 485, 486
Snell, Thomas, bp. of Ossory, 394
Soroglio, canon of Ivrea, 462
Stack, John, 422
Stanton, Maurice, 238, 414
Stephen, abp. of Armagh, 370
Stephen, abp. of Cashel, 361
Stephen, bp. of Antivari, 451
Strongbow, 204, 132
Surrey, earl of, 469–70, 472–3, 492
Sweetman, Milo, abp. of Armagh, 354

T

Tanner, John, 240
Terdelvachus, *see* O'Brien, Turlough
Terry, John, 237
Thrapton, Henry de, 233, 360, 371
Tigernach, king of Raithleann, 2
Tirry, William, bp. of Cork and Cloyne, 13
Torrington, Philip, abp. of Cashel, 383
Travers, Robert, 182, 243, 274, 417, 418
Tyler, Wat, 132
Tyrri, Thomas, 93n
Tyrry, Edmund, 109, 468
——, William, 468

U

Ua hAilgenain, Mac Bethad, 54, 55
Ua Baigill, Caincomruc, 65

Ua Briain. *See also* O'Brien
——, Donatus (Donnchad), bp. of Limerick, 175, 177, 181, 242n
——, Marianus, bp. of Cork, 178, 179, 181, 182, 226
Ua (Ui) Ceinneidigh, Finn Mac Ceilleachair, 51, 55
Ua Cinnaedha, Dubdaleithe, 49, 50
Ua Cochlain, bp. of Cork, 37, 55
Ua Conaing, Domnall, 55
Ua Conairche (O Conairche), Christian, bp. of Lismore, 79, 80, 81, 102, 110, 174
Ua Conchubhair (O'Connor), Diarmaid (Dermot), 80, 81, 82
——, Toirdelbach, 72, 73
Ua Dubhthaigh, Muireadach, 74
Ua Dunáin (Dúnáin), Maol Muire, 60, 63, 65, 67
Ua hÉnna, Domhnall, 58, 60
Ua hEnna, Matthew, bp. and legate, 55, 181
Ua Enne, Gilla Patraic, 54
Ua Laithidhe, Domhnall, 46
Ua Meanngorain, Cellach, 49
Ua Muirchertaig (Muirchertaigh), Nehemius, 70, 71, 78
Ua Rebachain, 40
Ua Sealbhaigh (Clann Sealbaigh, O Saolbach), 40, 50, 71, 177, 258, 261, 262
——, Celleach, 37, 40, 58
——, Clereach, 37, 40, 49, 51, 54
——, Domhnall, 40, 49, 51, 78
——, Gilla Pádraic, 38, 40
Ui Briuin Ratha, 1
Ui Criomthann, 15, 19
Ui Cuirb Liathain, *see* Ocurblethan *(general index)*
Ui Eachach, xxx, xxxi, xxxiv-xxxv, 1, 15, 22, 43, 61, 62, 71, 89, 103, 258, 259, 493
Ui Fidgheinte, xxx, 52
Ui Floinn Arda, 49
Ui Floinn Lua, *see* Ifflanloe *(general index)*
Ui Liathain, xxx, 93
Ui Mic Caille, 93, 103, 107
Ui Mic Ciair (Mac Ciair, Umacciair), xxx, xxxi, 16, 19, 22, 61, 93
Ui Sinnaigh (Clann Sinnaich), 40, 65
Ui Toirdhealbaigh, 52, 54
Urban V, 360, 376, 377
Urban VI, 381, 382, 383, 384, 385

V

Valle, Richard de, 376
Villa, Michael de, bp. of Ivrea, 460

W

Wadding, Luke, O.F.M., 207, 208, 209, 213, 370, 446, 447
Walche, Richard, 481
Waleys, Stephen le, 166
Walsh (Walsche), John, dean of Cork, 93n, 406, 441, 488
Warbeck, Perkin, 333, 425, 463, 464, 465
Waters, John, 463, 464
Wellesley, Walter, 470
Went, John, 368
——, Richard, 328, 361, 384
White, Geoffrey, 179
——, George, 170
Whyt, Vincent, 238
William of Jerpoint, bp. of Cork, 187, 188
Wilson, Richard, 478

Windsor, Sir William de, 346, 353
Wogan, John, 192, 193, 361
Wolsey, Thomas, Cardinal, 469–70, 474
Wycliffe, John, 381
Wye, Richard, bp. of Cloyne, 403
Wylton, Thomas de, 137
Wynchedon, Adam, O.F.M., 216, 289, 299
——, John, 138, 219, 288–90, 295–8, 203, 304, 305, 307, 375
——, John, O.P., 289, 299
——, Richard, 139, 288
——, William, 237, 296, 304, 384

Y

York, Richard, duke of, 407, 408

General Index

Abbreviations: archdioc. = archdiocese   bar. = barony   dioc. = diocese

A

Abhainn Mhór, *see* Blackwater
Abhall Ceithernaigh, 74, 75
Achad Durbcon, 2, 3, 8, 12, 13, 15, 197.
  See also Macroom
Achonry, dioc., 402, 438
Act of Resumption, 344
Adare, 218, 434, 442
Agalasmaschala, *see* Aglish
Aghaboe, xliv, 7
Aghabulloge, 5, 17, 262, 404, 423
Aghada, 88, 108, 305
Aghadown, 86, 198, 454
Aghamacart, 11
Aghamarta, 288
Aghinagh, 14, 415
Aglish (Agalasmaschala, Moally), 14, 87,
  90, 160, 170, 171, 257, 264, 273, 319,
  328n, 330, 331, 404, 420, 423
Airthir Cliach, *see* Mac Cuirp *(index of
  persons)*
Alba Landa, 141, 147, 148, 150
Albigenses, 202
Albo Tractu, de, see Tracton Abbey
altarists, 245
Annadown (Enachduan), dioc., 185, 401,
  402
annates, 261, 323
Antrum Bairre *(de Antro), see* Gill Abbey
Aosta, 457
Ardagh, dioc., 68, 360, 370, 479, 480
Ardananeen, 270
Ardfert (Kerry), dioc., xxxvii, 68–71, 79,
  89, 113, 315, 319, 324, 357, 376, 378,
  384, 386, 405, 409, 421, 446, 480, 487,
  488
Ardmore, dioc., 74, 401
Ardnageehy (Watergrasshill), 83, 85, 90,
  238, 255, 264, 271, 308, 316, 331, 334
Argatross, xxx
Armagh, archdioc., 67, 68, 77, 113, 116,
  358, 378, 383, 446, 480, 487
———, monastery of, 39, 40, 49, 51, 65
Arrouaise, canons of, 76, 77, 175, 196, 225
Articuli Cleri, 118
Askeaton, 446
Athenry, 487
Athlone, 208, 212, 446
Athnowen, *see* Ovens
Augustinian Eremites (Austin Friars),
  190, 202, 217, 218, 298, 373, 375, 429,
  430, 431, 433–5, 447, 477
Auxerre, 35
Avignon, 321, 323, 350, 355, 361, 365,
  366, 381, 382, 384, 429

B

Balilanocane, 105
Balimakin, 181
Ballaghath (Ballayath, Ballea), 348, 423
Ballibetagh, 380
Ballinaboy, 256, 263, 272, 317, 331
Ballinacurra (Castlecore, Corth Castle),
  108, 195
Ballinadee, 86, 230, 272, 274, 331
Ballinaltig, 255, 271, 316
Ballinamanaghe, *see* Knocknamanagh
Ballinamought, 301, 302, 303
Ballinaspick (Bishopstown), 160, 171,
  276n
Ballineadig, 15
Ballincollig, 21, 80, 170, 171, 230, 240,
  256
Ballincurrig, *see* Corragh
Ballinhassig, 80, 170, 239, 240, 256
Ballinlough, 276, 302
Ballinrobe, 437
Ballinspittal (Courceys), 15, 164, 256, 304
Ballintemple, 134
Ballinvannegh, *see* Monkstown
Ballinvollin (Knockanewoolin), 443
Ballinvriskig, 304
Ballybeg, 263
Ballybrack, 220
Ballybricken, 92, 171
Ballyburden, 170
Ballydeloher, 90, 255, 264, 272, 316, 331
Ballyfeard, 146, 150, 257, 263, 266, 273,
  318, 331
Ballyfouloo, 135, 136, 183
Ballyfoyle, 146, 150, 257, 266, 273, 318,
  331, 333
Ballyglannagh, 138, 140
Ballyhalwick, 259
Ballyhaunis, 433
Ballyhemikan, 237
Ballyleigh, 82
Ballymacadane, 82, 170, 199, 208, 240,
  264, 432, 438, 439, 449, 450, 451
Ballymacoda, 16
Ballymartle (Kilmeedy, Kylmid), 195,
  256, 257, 273, 318, 331, 395, 421, 482
Ballymodan, *see* Bandon
Ballymolmihill (Castlewhite, Rochfords-
  town), 170, 240, 256, 264, 317
Ballymoney (Corsruhara), 258, 268, 272,
  320, 329, 331, 486, 488
Ballymountain, 269, 397, 449, 450
Ballyphehane, 80, 159, 205, 276
Ballyragget, 390
Ballyspillane, 146, 150

538

Ballyvourney (Boirneach, Oirnidhe), xxxvii, 197, 198, 262
Baltimore, 169
Baltinglass, 424, 477
Banada, 433, 434
Bandon (Ballymodan), xxxi, 86, 90, 109, 146, 150, 238, 256, 269, 272, 317, 330, 331, 335, 336, 395, 397, 483
Bangor, 18, 24, 37, 74, 77
Bantry (Beanntraighe, Kilmocomoge), 84, 87, 169, 171, 259, 262, 273, 330, 331, 482-83
——, friary of, 208, 215, 216, 446
Barnehely, 80, 264, 274, 331
Barretts, bar., 109
Barrymore, bar., xxxvii, 255
Bath, *see* St Peter
Bealach Leachta, battle of, 54
Bealach Mughna, battle of, 47, 52
Bealahaglaskin Bridge, 4
Beanntraighe, *see* Bantry
Bearhaven (Beara, Bere), 6, 75, 84, 90
Beaver, *see* Carrigaline
Bective, 424
Belfast, 275
Belgooly, 146, 148, 149, 150, 257, 268
Benedictines, Irish foundations in Europe, 56-58. *See also* Saint John the Evangelist
Bere, *see* Bearhaven
Birr, 20, 43
Bishopstown, *see* Ballinaspick
Black Death, 172, 343, 347, 371, 372, 376, 429
Blackrock (Mahon), 160, 220, 276
Blackwater (Abhainn Mhór), 6, 70, 93
Blarney, 91, 442
Boirneach, *see* Ballyvourney
Bollandists, 24, 457
Boreenmanna, 133, 134
Bosworth, battle of, 424
Brant Broughton, 422
Brechmuy, *see* Cuylcolling and Brechmuy
Breffny, dioc., 378
Bridgetown *(de Villa Pontis)*, 263, 358, 386
Brigowne, xxxvii
Brinny, 267, 272, 274, 318, 330, 331
Bristol, 186, 371, 427
Britway, 404
Bromholm, 398, 399
Bruce invasion, 214, 315, 343, 350, 351
Bruhenny, 397, 418
Burren, 92, 256, 263, 272, 274, 317, 418
Burrishoole, 436
Buttevant, 214, 216, 403, 446

C

Caheragh, 2, 90, 195, 259, 267, 272, 276, 320n, 331, 409

Cahergal, 302, 303
Caherlag, 15, 90, 91, 195, 237, 255, 264, 268, 272, 316, 331, 484
Cairn Thierna, *see* Fermoy
Caithness, 23
Callan, 434
Cambridge, xliv, 375, 487, 488
Camden Fort, 426
Cameleire, Cross of, 134, 306
cána, 42, 44, 45, 51, 52
Candida Casa, xxxv
Cannaway (Cannaboy), xxxiv, 87, 90, 171, 257, 261, 262, 272, 319, 330, 333, 334, 335
——, island, 238
canons, classification of, 235
Canterbury, 56, 65, 73
——, Treaty of, 392
Cape Clear, xxxvi, xxxvii, 6
Carbery, bar., 11, 239, 274
Carcassonne, 432
caritative subsidies, *see* curial taxes
Carlisle Fort, 426
——, parliament of, 354
Carlow, 345, 346, 379
Carmelites, 203, 217
Carn Ui Néid, *see* Mizen Head
Carrickfergus, 186, 208, 446
Carrigaline (Beaver), 109, 140, 142, 157, 237, 239, 240, 256, 263, 272, 276, 317, 330, 333, 373, 378, 409
Carriganass, castle of, 450
Carrignamuck, castle of, 442, 444
Carrigrohane, xxxi, 83, 169, 171, 233, 256, 263, 264, 272, 312, 331, 425
Carrigtwohill, 89, 91, 107, 158
Carrigyknaveen, 14
Cashel, archdioc., 67, 68, 79, 113, 116, 182, 188, 194, 226, 275, 313, 314, 315, 319, 324, 349, 350, 357, 369, 376, 378, 383, 393, 421, 446, 479, 480
——, synod of (1101), 59, 62-64
——, synod of (1172), 102, 110, 260
——, synod of (1453), 223, 475-76, 489
Cashelean, xxxvi
Castlecomer, 6
Castlecore, *see* Ballinacurra
Castledermot, 345
Castlelyons, 158, 204
Castlemagner, 404
Castleventry, 50
Castlewhite, *see* Ballymolmihill
Castro Dei, de, see Fermoy
Cat Fort (Lyscotekyn), 298
cathedral chapters, 173, 175, 177, 184, 224, 225 ff., 233-5, 247, 355
Cavan, 446
Cell Muine, *see* David of Minevia *(index of persons)*

Cell na Cluaine, 14, 15, 19, 20
Celtic church, 34 ff., 47, 48, 51, 59, 63, 66
cense, *see* curial taxes
Chalcedon, council of, 478
chantry chapels, 134, 290, 293, 295, 305
chantry priests, 244, 245
Charleville, 88
charters, *see* Cork, charters granted to
Choro Benedicti, de, see Midleton
Christ Church (Holy Trinity), 84, 134, 193, 206, 237, 242, 245, 255, 267, 272, 288, 294–6, 305, 316, 330, 335, 373, 375, 378, 391, 423, 468, 482
Ciarraighe Luachra, 103
Cill Manach, *see* Knocknamanagh
Cineal (Cinel) Laoghaire, 71, 158, 262
Cistercians, 131, 141, 142, 150
Clairvaux, 78, 79, 147
Clangibbon, bar., xxxvii
Clare, xxxviii, 214
Clashanure, 15
Clashduff, 244
Clenor, 88
clerical incomes, 327–9
Clerkenwell, 132
Clinnure (Clumore), 387
Cliu, *see* Mac Cuirp *(index of persons)*
Cloggagh, 438
Cloghan (Mardyke), 81
Cloghan and Kildarra, 256, 272, 274, 317, 331, 397
Clogheen, 26
Clogher, dioc., 68, 360, 378, 414, 479
Clonakilty, 195
Clonard (Cluain Ioraird or Irard), 68, 199
Clondalkin, 49
Clondrohid, 404
Clonenagh, 15
Clonfert, dioc., 46, 68, 275, 378, 411
Clonkeen, 446
Clonmacnoise (dioc. and monastery), 18, 37, 39, 43, 69, 117, 378, 419, 479, 480
Clonmede, 144
Clonmel, 353, 372
Clonmel (Great Island), 106, 194, 446
Clonmoyle, 271
Clonmyn, 386
Clonpriest, 62, 88, 409
Clontead, 144, 146, 150, 257, 263, 266, 272, 318, 331
Cloyne (Cluain Uamha), dioc., 15, 62, 70, 72, 78, 79, 83, 89, 91, 113, 263, 313, 314, 315, 319, 324, 357, 358, 359, 376, 378. *See also* Cork and Cloyne
——, manor of, 158
Cloyne, Pipe Roll of, 158, 162, 169
Cluainbeg, xxxix, 198
Cluain Ioraird, *see* Clonard
Cluan Achad, *see* Macloneigh
Clumore, *see* Clinnure

Cluny, 56
Coleraine, 207, 436
College of Stone, 245, 295
common fund, 236, 246
conciliar movement, 382, 385
Cong, abbey of, 74, 75, 80, 175
Congé d'élire, 112, 114, 115, 118, 157, 187, 157, 168, 493
Conmacnicully and Conmacnimara, 422
Connacht, xxxvii, xlvii, 67, 72, 430
Connor, dioc., 68, 370, 378, 438
Constance, council of, 385, 392–4, 430, 474
Conventuals, 432, 433, 439, 441, 442, 444, 445, 446
Coolcashin, 7, 8, 11
Cooldaniel, 271
Cooldorrihy, 271
Coolmaine, 449, 451
Coolmore (Culmore), 135, 136, 183
Corbally, 228, 243, 256, 272, 317, 326, 331, 371
Corca Baiscinn, xxx
Corca Dhuibhne, xxx, 47
Corca Laighdhe (Dairine), xxx, 1, 49, 61, 71, 74, 93, 198, 452
Corco Airchind Droma, *see* Kilmurry
Corcomoone, *see* Corkolwyn
Corincknopoge, *see* Lee fisheries
Cork, charters granted to, 153, 154, 177, 368, 426
——, courts in, 155, 163, 164, 165, 182, 192
——, customs levied in, 167, 168, 186, 378
——, dioc., 115, 116, 117, 120, 156, 183, 313–15, 360, 369, 376, 378, 395
——, diocesan limits, 61, 68, 69, 79, 82 ff.
——, *faithche* (Fayth) of, 158, 159, 167, 346–7, 372, 378
——, fee farm of, 155, 167, 181, 346–7, 378
——, guilds in, 167
——, kingdom of *(Regnum Corcagiense)*, 104, 174, 407, 425, 448
——, liberties of, 426
——, mayor of, 153, 206, 347, 405
——, mint in, 426–7
——, monastery of, xxxi, 17, 18, 24, 37, 38, 39, 43–47, 159, 224, 232
——, school of, 18, 24
——, sheriff and bailiffs of, 155, 181, 206, 303, 347, 405
——, trade of, 167, 168, 371, 379–80, 408, 425–6
Cork and Cloyne, 367–8, 384, 398, 400, 402–404, 409, 413, 416, 418, 423–4, 452, 455–6, 458, 462, 467, 470, 480
Corkbeg, 88
Corkolwyn (Corcomoone), deanery of,

254, 257–8, 320
Corragh (Ballincurrig), 160, 371
Corringrahine, *see* Lee fisheries
Corrothir, 363
Corsruhara, *see* Ballymoney
Corth Castle, *see* Ballinacurra
Coul, manor of, 158
Coulcour and Sleveens, 3, 91
Courceys, *see* Ballinspittal
courts, *see* Cork, courts in
Crimdarin, 107
Croghtamore, 302
Cronody, 6, 91
Crookhaven, 87, 171
Crossbrennan, 6
Crosse's Green, 159, 204
Crosshaven, 109, 256
Crossmolina, 78
Cullen (Riverstick), xl, 83, 86, 170, 171, 227, 257, 264, 272, 305, 318, 319, 325, 330, 365
Culdees, *Celí Dé*, 41, 43, 44
Culeueny, 390
Culmore, *see* Coolmore
curial taxes, 321–5
Curraghconway, 171
Curraheen, 230, 326
Curraheenbrian, 54
Curranure, 269, 449, 450
Currarane, 267, 272, 317
Currykippane, 83, 170, 171, 271, 292
Cusduff, 271
customs, *see* Cork, customs levied in
Cuylcolling and Brechmuy, 422

D

Dairine, *see* Corca Laighdhe
Dalcassians, 50, 54, 55, 72
decimae papalis, see curial taxes, l.15
Decretal letter (1199), xxxiii, 82–89, 110, 177, 268, 299, 300
Derry, dioc., 37, 68, 378, 424
Derva, 150
Desertmore, 15, 19, 88, 240, 257, 266, 273, 319, 334, 335, 423, 443, 488
Desertserges, 87, 243, 258, 264, 273, 320, 400, 403
Deshure, 271
Desmond, Desmumha, xxx, xxxv, xxxvi, 62, 69, 72, 102, 104, 106, 177, 181, 344, 465, 471
Dilbey, 301, 304
Dingle, 403
Dominicans (Friars Preachers), 201, 203, 206, 207, 218, 298, 349, 361, 372, 374, 429–32, 435–7, 448, 477, 487
Donachmore (Kyltahan), 421
Donegal, 345, 442
Donoughmore (Cloyne), 62, 86, 360

Donoughmore (Limerick), 386
Douglas, 80, 83, 109, 157, 160, 162, 181, 184, 220, 239, 256, 263, 272, 276, 317, 379
Down, dioc., 68, 77, 226, 369, 370, 376, 378
Downpatrick, 275, 446
Drimoleague (Dromdaliag), 71, 87, 90, 239, 258, 273, 320, 331, 332, 404, 411, 484, 488
Drinagh, 243, 258, 266, 273, 320, 330, 333
Drogheda, 186, 203, 205, 207, 212, 218, 345, 371, 372, 373, 407, 427, 436, 471, 487
Dromdaliag, *see* Drimoleague
Dromkeen, 279, 449, 450
Dromore, dioc., 401, 479
Dromorkan, *see* Kilmurry
Dublin, 154, 156, 186, 203, 205, 218, 362, 372, 373, 377, 427, 446, 464, 486, 487
——, archdioc., 59, 60, 73, 79, 113, 116, 212, 312, 315, 349, 350, 376, 423
Duleek, 68, 69
Dunboy, 75
Dunbrody, 147, 436, 477
Dunbulloge, 90, 232, 241, 255, 271, 326, 331
Dundalk, 446
Dunderrow, 146, 256, 264, 273, 318, 492
Dundrinan (Moviddy), 85, 109, 133, 257, 262, 266, 273, 320, 330, 334
Dungarvan (Cork), 136, 140, 189, 192, 288, 293
—— (Lismore), 422
Dungourney, 404
Dunisky, 87, 273, 331, 334
Dunkynayge, 270
Dunmanway (Fanlobbus), 87, 90, 171, 244, 258, 266, 273, 320, 328n, 332, 334, 417, 488
Dunmore, 433
Durrow, 37, 43, 46
Durrus (Muintervara), 2, 80, 87, 259, 273, 320, 330, 331
Dysert O'Dea, battle of, 343

E

Edergole, *see* Etargabail
education, 371, 373, 374–7, 409, 486–91
Effyng, 422
Elizabeth Fort, 299
Elphin, dioc., 115, 360, 378, 445, 446
Emly (Imleach Ibair), dioc., xxxix, 68, 70, 79, 113, 115, 183, 313–15, 319, 324, 378, 384, 395, 397, 405, 452
——, monastery of, 49
Enachduan, *see* Annadown
Enach mid Brenin, *see* Kilbrennan
Ennis, 446, 487

Enniscorthy, 275
Enniskeane, 90, 254, 258, 273
Eoghanacht (Cinel Eoghan), xxx–xxxiv, 25, 52, 63
Errew, 78
Etargabail (Edergole), 197
Exeter, *see* St Nicholas's Abbey

F

faithche, see Cork
Fanlobbus, *see* Dunmanway
Farranmacteige, 160, 171
Farranvarrigane, 171
Fayd, manor of, 108, 158, 160, 169, 302, 312, 469
Fergus East, 14, 91, 257
Fergus West, 91
Fermoy (Cairn Thierna, Rathcormac), 61, 90, 107
—— *(de Castro Dei)*, 412, 465
Ferns, dioc., 17, 116, 183, 275, 312, 378, 422, 479
Ferrygowne, 443
Finure, 62, 88
Florence, 432
Foithrib Aedh, 16, 26
Foneragh *(Fonn Iartharach)*, deanery of, 1, 254, 259, 319, 320
Fonte Vivo, de, see Maur
Fore, 46
Fowey, 23
France, 168, 353
Franciscans (Friars Minor), 201, 203, 207, 208, 212, 216, 218, 298, 349, 372, 374, 429, 430, 432, 437–47, 448, 477–8, 487
——, Third Order, 211, 212, 393, 437–9, 447
Fratres Cruciferi, 197
Friars Minor, *see* Franciscans
Friars Preachers, *see* Dominicans

G

Gahannyh, friary of, 432, 440
Galbally, 446
Gallen, 46
Galveiston, *see* Killeenreendowney
Galway, 214, 446, 471, 487
Garranes Fort, *see* Raithleann
Garrivoe, 409
Gaul, xxxv
Gilbertines, 196
Gill Abbey *(de Antro*, Weyme), 17, 18, 24, 74–6, 93, 95–101, 174–5, 224–5, 261, 263–4, 266, 299, 319, 363, 364, 420, 439, 477–8, 489
Glanmire (Glenmaggyr, Glen-Maiur), 83, 237, 241, 255, 264, 272, 301, 303, 316, 333, 486

Glansalny (Glansalvy), deanery of, 254, 258, 319, 320
Glanworth, 204, 417, 432
Glendalough, 68
Glenmaggyr, Glen-Maiur, *see* Glanmire
Glenquin, 88, 106
Glounthane, 15, 17, 83, 89, 106, 237, 238, 355
Goleen, *see* Kilmoe
Gortnacrusha (Gortnegrosse), 272
Gougane Barra, 3, 5, 11, 13, 89, 91, 197, 306
Gowran Pass, 7
Graney (Grange), nunnery of, 266, 267
Grange, townland, 443
Granig, 144, 146
Great Island, *see* Clonmel
Greenmount *(Imaire an Aingil)*, 159
—— (Ross), 92
Greenville, 270
Grey Friary, *see* Shandon
Gurranebraher *(Teampull na mBráthar)*, 210, 220

H

Hammondeston, 138
heresies, *see* Albigenses; Hussites
Hildebrandine reform, 56
Holly Cross, 15, 91
Holy Trinity, *see* Christ Church
Hospitallers, 84, 131–3, 140, 173, 323, 477
hospitals:
    St John the Evangelist, 133, 301
    St Mary Magdalen, 301
    St Stephen, 300, 301, 303
Howth, 371
Hundred Court, *see* Cork, courts in
Hundred Years' War, 200, 343, 392
Hussites, 394

I

Ibathan (Ibawne), 106, 195–6
Ibrach (Iveragh), *see* Monasterium Ibracense
Ichtermurragh, 409
Idrone, bar., 8
Ifflanloe (Ui Floinn Lua), 61, 93
Imaire an Aingil, *see* Greenmount
Imleach Ibair, *see* Emly
Imokilly, bar., 107, 108
Inchidony, 86, 198
Inchigaggin, 160, 171
Inchigeela, 12, 61, 80, 133, 258, 262, 266, 270, 271, 273, 320, 330, 331, 334
Inchiquin, manor of, 162
Iniscathaigh, dioc., xxxix, 72, 79
Iniscuinge, 75, 87
Inis Doimhle, xlvi, xlvii

Inishkenny, xxxi, 84, 88, 170, 171, 233, 240, 256, 272, 312, 328n, 333, 334, 415, 423, 438, 492

Inislounaght, 182, 197

Inisluinge, 14, 82

Inis Pádraig, synod of, 77, 78

Inis Pich (Spike Island), xli, 83, 86, 91

Inniscarra, xxxiv, 14, 386

Innishannon, 86, 109, 142, 146, 150, 157, 163, 256, 265, 268, 269, 272, 274, 312, 317, 327, 331, 332, 334–6, 450, 483

Inshynashangane, 4

Insovenach, 109

Iona, 20, 37, 39, 40, 49

Ivagh (Ivagha), 1. *See also* Ui Eachach *(index of persons)*

Iveleary, 88, 91, 262

Iveragh (Ibrach), *see Monasterium Ibracense*

Iverni, xxx

Ivrea, 456–61

J

Jerpoint, abbey of, 187, 188, 197

Johnstown (Kileanna), 271

Johnstown (Co. Kilkenny), 11

K

Kahirultan, 414

Kells, synod of, xxxix, 7, 78–80, 81, 401, 493

Kenalethe (Kinalea) *citra*, deanery of, 158, 254–7

Kenalethe (Kinalea) *ultra*, deanery of, 158, 254, 257, 335

Kerry (Raith Maighe Deiscirt), *see* Ardfert

Kerrycurrihy, 83, 86, 92, 105, 106, 109, 158, 407

Kery (Kyrricurith), deanery of, 254, 255, 320

Kilbar, island, 23

Kilbarry, 22

Kilbarry (Warrenscourt), 3, 4, 5, 8, 89

Kilbonane, 257, 273, 319, 320, 331

Kilbree, 198

Kilbrennan (Enach mid Brenin, Strawhall), xxxviii

Kilbrittain, 90, 238, 242, 256, 264, 272, 274, 317, 331, 332, 334, 410, 423, 449, 450, 488

Kilbrogan, 84, 86, 133, 160, 161, 162, 163, 170, 171, 233, 238, 263, 272, 320, 330, 332, 397, 423

Kilbroney, 88

Kilcanway, 88

Kilcoe, 87, 198

Kilconnell, 442

Kilcrea castle; manor, 157, 442

Kilcrea friary, 91, 208, 432, 441, 442–5, 449, 450, 461

Kilcredan, 409

Kilcreevanty, 197

Kilcrohane, 2, 171, 259, 266, 273, 320, 330, 331, 482

Kilcullen, xxxvii

Kilcully, 85, 90, 91, 255, 266, 267, 271, 331, 332

Kilcummer, 270

Kildare, dioc., 60, 116, 183, 315, 378, 446, 479

Kildare, monastery of, 18, 37, 39, 46, 196

Kildarra, *see* Cloghan and Kildarra

Kileanna, *see* Johnstown

Kilelton, xli

Kilfenora, dioc., 72, 79, 113, 315, 319, 324, 353, 376, 384, 405

Kilgobban, xxxviii, 230, 241, 256, 264, 267, 272, 317, 331, 335, 363, 406, 486

Kilkenny, xxx, 6, 68, 144, 203, 212, 345–6, 348, 353, 372, 434, 446, 479

Killacloona, 15

Killacloyne, 15

Killala, dioc., 68, 275, 438

Killaloe, dioc., 54, 55, 68, 72, 79, 113, 115–17, 182, 183, 315, 319, 324, 357, 358, 360, 384, 389, 396, 416, 452, 480

Killanully, 83, 86, 239, 256, 272, 317, 330, 334, 418, 422, 423, 488

Killare, xxxvi

Killaspuglappan (Little Island), 85, 90, 93n, 255, 264, 272, 316, 331, 334, 368, 406, 482, 486

Killaspugmullane, 85, 238, 254, 255, 263, 264, 272, 316, 330, 332, 334, 414, 484

Killede, bar., 105, 107

Killeedy (Cill Íde), 25

Killeagh, 88, 162

Killeenbrenan, 437

Killeennagallive, 438

Killeenreendowney (Galveiston), 159, 205

Killeens, 81, 82, 264

Killoney (Killowen, Killowney, Kilroan), 164, 231, 243, 256, 268, 272, 317, 397

Killumney, 16, 170

Kilmacahill, 5, 7, 8

Kilmacdonagh, 409

Kilmacduagh, dioc., 115, 184, 358, 402

Kilmaclenine, 88, 161

Kilmainham, preceptory of, 133

Kilmallock, 344

Kilmeaton, 144

Kilmeedy (Kilmede), *see* Ballymartle

Kilmeen, 50

Kilmehalok (Kylmokeallog), 160, 184, 191, 427

Kilmichael, xxxix, 5, 12, 80, 149, 258, 262, 266, 270, 271, 273, 330, 331, 333, 442

Kilmocomoge, *see* Bantry
Kilmoe (Goleen), xxxvi, 87, 171, 259, 267, 273, 321, 333, 395, 440, 489
Kilmohanoc, *see* Kilmonoge
Kilmoney, 144, 331
Kilmonoge (Kilmohanoc), 106, 189, 192, 257, 273, 318, 330, 334
Kilmore, dioc., 275, 353, 416, 478
Kilmurry (Corco Airchind Droma, Dromorkan), xxxix, 3, 5, 90, 133, 150, 257, 262, 266, 273, 319, 331, 335, 442
Kilnaclona, 15
Kilnagleary (Kilnagleragh), 21, 86, 256, 272, 288, 380
Kilnaglory, xxxi, 16, 21, 239, 256, 264, 272, 317, 331, 335, 423
Kilnamartyra, 263
Kilnap, 26
Kilnarovanagh, 4, 270, 271
Kilpatrick, 257, 331, 333
Kilquane, 85, 90, 195, 255, 272, 316, 331
Kilroan, *see* Killoney
Kilshallow, 259
Kilshinahan, 86, 90, 239, 256, 272, 317, 335
Kilskohhanaght, 198
Kinalea, bar., xxxi, 11, 106, 141, 274
——, deanery of, *see* Kenalethe
Kinalmeaky, bar., xxxi, 1, 11, 106, 141, 163, 238, 274, 333
Kinneigh, xl, xli, 50, 71–72, 87, 90, 171, 228, 244, 254, 258, 266, 273, 321, 331, 332–4, 410, 417, 420
Kinsale, 82, 86, 109, 136, 139, 140, 157, 160, 163, 169, 170, 171, 256, 257, 266, 273, 301, 304, 312, 318, 328, 330, 331, 332, 334, 378, 384, 395, 403, 420, 427, 486, 487
Kinure (Kinnure), 144, 146, 150, 174, 181, 257, 273, 318, 331
Knockanewollin, *see* Ballinvollin
Knockavilly, 264, 272, 318, 330, 334, 335, 336
Knockburden, 170
Knockeygowgie, 443
Knocknamanagh (Ballinamanaghe, Cill Manach), 141, 150
Knockroe, 269, 449, 450
Kylmid, *see* Ballymartle
Kylmokeallog, *see* Kilmehalok
Kyltahan, *see* Donachmore
Kyrricurith, *see* Kery

L

Lackmalloe, 270
Lateran Council, fourth, 179–80, 200–201, 217, 230, 235, 291
——, fifth, 469, 474
Lazarists, 302

Leath Chuinn, 67
Leath Mogha, 63, 67
Lecceto, 431
Lee fisheries (Corincknopoge, Corringrahine, Macmaelpoill, Uadubgaill), 82
Leet Court, *see* Cork, courts in
Legan, 138, 139, 140, 319
Leighlin, dioc., 8, 68, 116, 183, 378, 469, 478, 479
Leighmoney, 146, 257, 273, 318, 331, 334, 423
Leinster, xxxvii, xlvii, xlviii, 6, 7, 8, 345, 401
lepers in Cork, 301, 302
Lerins, 35
Lileach, 2
Limerick, city, 5, 104, 154, 203, 205, 214, 216, 379, 408, 487
——, dioc., 65, 68, 69, 70, 79, 113, 183, 226, 231, 235, 313, 314, 315, 319, 324, 369, 376, 378, 384, 387, 405, 414, 437, 452
Liscleary, 157, 237, 256, 264, 268, 272, 294, 317, 331, 332, 334, 395, 482, 492
Liselton, xxxix
Lisheencoonlane, *see Raithin mac nAeda*
Liskillea, 170, 264
Lismore, dioc., 68, 69, 79, 116, 117, 183, 315, 319, 324, 358, 378. *See also* Waterford and Lismore
——, monastery, 40
Lisnacaheragh, 1, 2
Lissane, Upper and Lower, 276
Little Island, *see* Killaspuglappan
Lixnaw, 103
Loch Irce, 8–12
Longford, 437
Longum Vadum, 301. *See also* Cullen
Louvain, 445
Lusk, xliv
Lyons, Council of, 200
Lysuctdagh, 81

M

Macloneigh (Cluan Achad), 3, 84, 87, 91, 133, 230, 257, 270, 271, 273, 320, 330, 331, 333, 335, 423
Macmaelpoill, *see* Lee fisheries
Macroom, 3, 4, 85, 91, 262, 285, 386. *See also* Achad Durbcon
Magooly, 82
Mahon (Maghy), *see* Blackrock
Mahoonagh, 76
Maiden Bradley, priory of, 190
Maigue *(de Magio),* 142, 143, 175
Malbawne, 138
Mallow, 403
Mamucky, 271
manaig, 41 ff.

Mardyke, *see* Cloghan
Marmoutier, 35
Marmullane, *see* Passage West
Maur *(de Fonte Vivo)*, 449, 454, 458
Meath, dioc., xxxvii, 60, 69, 113, 115, 116, 183, 314, 315, 349, 364, 376, 378, 478
Meelick, 446
Mellifont, 77, 141, 197, 424, 477
Mendicant controversy, 221–3, 352, 476
—— movement, 200–202
Midleton *(de Choro Benedicti)*, 147, 148, 149, 292, 419, 478
Milan, 431, 436, 490
mills, 93, 136, 166, 210, 220, 308
mint, *see* Cork, mint in
Miros, 409
Mizen Head (Carn Ui Néid), xxx, xxxi, 1, 61, 70, 90, 254, 259
Moally, *see* Aglish
Mogeely, 108
Monaghan, 447
Monarea, 133, 308
Monasterium Ibracense (Ibrach, Iveragh), 74
Monasteroris, 447
monastic rules, 45
Moneycusker, 270
Monkstown (Ballinvannegh), 139, 140, 256, 266, 275, 306
Monteen Castle, 449
Mountmusic, 270
Mourne (Mora), preceptory, 133, 266
Moviddy, *see* Dundrinan
Moyne, 441
Muckross, friary of, 440
Muintervara, *see* Durrus
Mullingar, 275, 345
Multyfarnham, 442
Mungret, dioc., 79, 401
Munster, xxx, 52, 66, 72, 73, 102, 348, 401, 430
Murivechimelane, 105
Murragh (Newcestown), 71, 87, 90, 254, 258, 273, 320, 328, 330, 397, 483, 486
Murrisk, 434
Muscry-Donegan, cantred of, 62, 105, 106, 107, 108, 144
Muscrylyn (Musgrylin), deanery of, 3, 257
Muskerry, barony of, xxx, xxxvii, xxxix, xl, 11, 240, 262, 452
Muskerry Mittine, xl, xlvii, 2, 62, 106, 109
Mylane, 16

N

Nard, district of, 299
Nenagh, 214, 445, 446, 487
Newcestown, *see* Murragh
New Ross, 372, 446
Nohoval, 83, 86, 170, 171, 192, 232, 257,

263, 266, 273, 318, 330, 332
Norbonne, concordat of, 393
Normans in Cork, 89, 102, 103, 107–109, 156, 181, 406
Norsemen, 16, 20, 26, 46, 51
North Gate, 135, 288, 296
North Parish, *see* Saint Mary's
nuns in Cork, 194–9, 307

O

O'Bairre, sept, 259
Observant reform, 429–33, 477
Ocurblethan (Ucurp, Ui Cuirb Liathain), deanery of, 17, 105, 158, 254, 255
Offaly, 103
Oirnidhe, *see* Ballyvourney
Old Abbey, *see* Waterfall
Olethan, cantred of, 105, 106, 108, 194–5
Ossory, dioc., xxx, xxxvi, xxxvii, xliv, xlvi, 6, 8, 61, 116, 117, 181, 183, 350, 358, 378, 390, 394, 422, 479
Ostmen, cantred of, 104, 105, 153
Ovens (Athnowen), 15, 20, 83, 90, 133, 240, 257, 267, 273, 319, 331, 334, 442, 443
Oxford, council of, 104
——, university of, 375, 376, 384, 407, 487, 488, 490

P

papal provisions, 352, 354 ff., 483–6
parishes, classification of, 259 ff.
Passage West (Marmullane), 86, 244, 272, 320
Peñiscola, 392, 400
Peruvian parishes, 493
pilgrimages, 13
Pisa, council of, 385, 388, 389, 485
pluralism, 395, 421–3, 478
Portumna, 436
Poulnargid, 5
Praemunire, statute of, 356, 381, 482
prebends, election to, 236–42
procurations, *see* curial taxes
Provisors, statute of, 356, 381, 399, 482

Q

Quatuor personae, 173 ff., 325
Queen's Old Castle, 296
Quin, 439, 440, 441

R

Rafeen, 237
Rahan, 88
Raheen (Rathmyny), 205
Raithin mac nAeda (Lisheencoonlane), 17, 45, 276

Raithleann (Garranes Fort), xxx, xxxiv, 1, 54, 61
Raith Maighe Deiscirt, *see* Ardfert
Raphoe, dioc., 353, 360, 378, 479, 480
Rathanisky, 255
Rath Ard an Ghabhail, 5
Rathbreasail, synod of, 7, 54, 56, 59, 66 ff., 196, 257, 401, 493
Rathclarin, 256, 264, 272, 274, 317, 331, 335, 418, 450
Rathcooney, 238, 255, 264, 271, 331, 332, 335, 483
Rathcormac, *see* Fermoy
Rathdrought, 230, 256, 267, 272, 317, 331, 420
Rathmore (Parish of Tullagh), 196
Rathmyny, *see* Raheen
Ratisbon, 57, 71
Rearhinagh, 276
recluses, 306, 307
Red Abbey, 136, 218, 219, 221, 434, 435
Renowdran and Renrawre, 426
Resumption, act of, *see* Act of Resumption
revenues (clerical), 323, 330
—— (episcopal), 312–15, 320
Rimini, 431
Rincurran, 157, 257, 263, 264, 268, 273, 318, 330, 334, 335
Ringabella, 141, 256
Ringaskiddy (Rosbeg, Rossbeg, Temple-brackney), 86, 92, 170, 256, 265, 272, 312, 317
Ringmahon, 80, 329
Ringrone, 15, 157, 163, 230, 256, 266, 268, 272, 317, 324, 330, 332, 333, 334, 336, 397, 410, 423, 483, 486
Riverstick, *see* Cullen
Rochfordstown, *see* Ballymolmihill
Rocky Island, 92
Rome, 8, 24, 56, 58, 66, 79, 111, 118, 182, 201, 260, 275, 322, 356, 359, 364, 381, 382, 412, 420, 434, 451, 454, 456, 457, 463, 484
——, St Isidore's College, 445
Romerunners, 359, 370, 411
Rosbeg, *see* Ringaskiddy
Rosbrin, 444, 490
Roscrea, dioc., 72, 79, 447
Rosmunli, 395
Ross (Ros Ailithir, Rosscarbery), 49, 50, 106, 109
——, dioc., 62, 71, 72, 83, 86, 87, 89, 113, 115, 177, 185, 215, 226, 313, 314, 315, 319, 324, 360, 370, 378, 384, 395, 409, 448, 451, 455, 458, 462, 466, 480
Rossalough, 12
Rossbeg, *see* Ringaskiddy
Rossdaragh, 11
Ruskyn, 386

S

Saighir, *see* Ciaran of Saighir *(index of persons)*
St Anne, chapel of, 134, 290
St Brendan, church of, 299, 301
St Brigid, 84, 199, 230, 295, 298, 307, 326, 330
St Catherine (Cork), 165, 224, 255, 288, 292, 316, 331
St Catherine (Waterford), 137, 139, 266, 267, 375, 415, 481
St Finbarr, cathedral of, 23, 160, 164, 176, 245, 261, 289, 290, 300, 371
St Finbarr's South, 23, 133, 256, 276
St Finbarr's West, 276
St Fin Barre's Cathedral (C. of I.), 17, 20, 204, 244, 265, 290
St John of Jerusalem, 131–5
St John the Baptist, 134, 136, 194, 220, 296–7, 307
St John the Evangelist (Benedictines), 131, 135, 136–40, 182, 264, 272, 305, 317, 375, 378, 477
St Laurence, chapel of, 245, 296
St Mary's, Limerick, 183, 247
St Mary (North Parish), 22, 82, 211, 255
St Mary's Abbey, Dublin, 107, 141
St Mary of the Island, 183, 203, 204, 206, 207, 292, 364, 368, 432, 436, 437
St Mary Magdalen, 296
St Mary le Nard, 84, 166, 189, 243, 272, 299, 300
St Mary, Shandon, 17, 83, 157, 247, 289–92, 305, 375, 420
St Michael, 84
St Nessan, 84, 174, 226
St Nicholas, 119, 255, 272, 289, 299, 300, 301, 316
St Nicholas's Abbey, Exeter, 105, 106, 118, 119, 174, 175, 176, 189
St Patrick (Cork), 276
St Patrick (Dublin), 175, 226, 247, 374
St Peter (Bath), 84, 232, 245, 255, 267, 272, 289, 292, 305, 326, 330, 375, 378
St Peter (Cork), 135, 136, 139, 166, 266
St Philip, 297, 298, 375
St Sepulchre, 84, 118, 174
St Stephen, 295, 298, 375
St Thomas's Abbey, Dublin, 106, 118, 119, 133, 174, 175, 176, 181, 189, 224, 226, 234, 266, 292, 424
Salus Populi, *see* Pandarus *(index of persons)*
Sarsfield's Court, 157, 304
Sceilig Mhichíl, *see* pilgrimages
Schaffhausen, 392, 393
Schism (1378–1417), 381–5, 388–9, 391–4, 419, 429

Schull, 2, 84, 87, 90, 171, 259, 267, 273, 320, 328, 330
Scotland, 168, 192, 194, 214, 313, 324, 353
scribes, 37, 39, 40
Scurmore, 434
seals, episcopal, 246n, 469
Shanacashel, 271
Shanacloyne, 443
Shanbally, 236, 271, 316, 331, 334
Shandon, castle and manor of, 154, 157, 255, 263, 379, 407
——, Grey Friary of, 183, 208–11, 213, 216, 445, 446
——, parish of, 255, 263, 272, 316, 331, 334
Sherkin Island, 432, 441
Skehabeg, 205
Sletty, 12
Sleveens, *see* Coulcour and Sleveens
Slieve League, xxxviii
Soloheadbeg (Sulchuait), 52
South Gate, 135, 139, 221, 296
Sovereign Islands, 305
Spike Island, *see* Inis Pich
Srelane, 15, 20
Stoke, battle of, 424
Stowe Missal, 21, 22
Stradbally, 445
Strawhall, *see* Kilbrennan
Sulchuait, *see* Soloheadbeg
Synodus Hybernensis, 36, 41
Synssonerian, 301, 305

T

Tallaght, 46
taxations, papal, *see* curial taxes
Teampull na mBráthar, *see* Gurrane-braher
Templars, 134
Templebrackney, *see* Ringaskiddy
Templebreedy, 227, 256, 264, 272, 317, 330, 331, 333
Templebrian, 265, 312
Templemartin, 1, 84, 227, 272, 320, 330
Templemichael, 255, 256, 264, 272, 318, 331, 332, 492
Templetrine, 157, 256, 264, 267, 272, 317, 331, 334, 336, 397
Templeusque, 157, 238, 304, 331, 333
tenants, classification of, 161, 162, 166, 167, 169, 172
Terelton, xxxix, 270
Terryglass, 55, 78
Teutonic Knights, 394
Thomond (Tuadh Mumha), 69, 72, 74, 77, 104, 344, 440, 471, 472
Thurles, 275
Timoleague, 86, 216, 432, 442, 445, 449, 450, 453, 461

Tipperary, 5, 104, 218, 479
Tisaxon, 86, 257, 273, 318, 330, 491
tithes, 323, 328, 329, 335
Toames, xxxix-xl
Tobair Brenoke, 209
Tracton Abbey *(de Albo Tractu)*, 93, 131, 141 ff., 182, 205, 261, 266, 319, 394, 420
—— parish, 257, 263, 268, 477–8
trade, *see* Cork, trade of
Trim, 12, 50, 275, 345, 446
Tuadh Mumha, *see* Thomond
Tuam, archdioc., 68, 79, 113, 116, 194, 358, 360, 378, 383, 402, 422, 423, 438
Tuamgraney, 44
Tubrid, 141
Tullacondra, 62, 88
Tullow, 434
Turner's Cross, 80, 276, 302
Tyburn, 464

U

Uadubgaill, *see* Lee fisheries
Ucurp, *see* Ocurblethan
Uisneach, assembly of, 69
Umacciair, *see* Ui Mic Ciair *(index of persons)*
University College, Cork, 17
Urlar, 436
Utrecht, 399, 400

V

Vatican II, 202, 222, 429
vicars choral, 234, 242–4, 371
Vienne, council of, 134, 361
Villa Pontis, de, see Bridgetown

W

Wales, 168, 214, 313
Wallingstown, 195
Warrenscourt, *see* Kilbarry
Wars of the Roses, 333, 342, 408, 424, 425, 434, 452
Waterfall (Old Abbey), 438. *See also* Inishkenny
Waterford, 102, 103, 107, 112, 154, 181, 186, 194, 203, 205, 212, 377, 408,
——, dioc., 60, 65, 70, 79, 113, 116, 183, 313, 314, 315, 319, 324, 358, 369, 427, 446
Waterford and Lismore, 384, 396, 397, 402, 421, 463, 479
Watergrasshill, *see* Ardnageehy
Wexford, 68, 446
Weyme, *see* Gill Abbey
Whitechurch, 90
Winchester, 186, 190
Würzburg, 57

Y

York, 67
Youghal, 140, 162, 169, 204, 208, 408, 427
——, College of, 266, 267, 295, 408, 409,
    410, 414, 486, 491, 492
——, Dominicans of, 436
——, Franciscans of, 432, 442

DIOCESE OF CORK

SHOWING PARISHES

0   5   10 MILES

KERRY

C

Gougane Barra IVELEARY

BANTRY

DUNMANW

DRIMOLEAGUE

BANTRY BAY

CAHERAGH

CH.

MUNTERVARA

R O

SCHULL

GOLEEN